ASHLEY COURTENAY

ASHLEY COURTENAY RECOMMENDED HOTELS
Diamond Jubilee Edition

In Association with **The Daily Telegraph.**

The 60th edition of the Ashley Courtenay 'Let's Halt Awhile' series.

Front cover illustration:
Sharrow Bay Hotel, Ullswater, Cumbria.

Frontispiece:
Ashley Courtenay.

We are indebted to The National Trust for the loan of photographs, featuring their properties, which illustrate some of the introductions to the eight touring sections of this book.

Published by ASHLEY COURTENAY LIMITED

No part of this book may be reproduced in any form (except for reviews) without permission.

EDITOR: Peter Fuller.

CONTRIBUTORS: Peter Fuller; Robert Walker; Brian Sack; Peter Herbert; John Aust; Hugh Graham.

COMPILERS: Jill Thorne; Elizabeth Bathurst; Patsy Cotterill.

ASSESSORS: A & G Bezant; G & B Crompton; R & C Dean; R & R Farrimond; R & S Fontaine; R & J Fudge; A & D Horsfall; S & A Macpherson; J & A Maggs; P & T O'Neill; J & J Row; T Shepherd; J & P Steel; A & A Taylor; K & I Twemlow.

Whilst every care has been taken in the compiling of this guide, we cannot accept responsibility for any inaccuracies. It is important to note that the tariffs shown are only an indication of charges and, in many cases, the only ones available to us at the time of going to press. Similarly, the reported standards and facilities of the hotels reviewed are as known to us at the date of publication and we make no representation as to the continuance thereafter. Please write direct to the hotels respecting their 1993 tariffs.

The very first edition of the Ashley Courtenay guide was published in 1934 against the backdrop of the Great Depression. Sixty years later one could be forgiven for thinking that the World has advanced very little in those six decades, for this anniversary edition has been researched and compiled during a recession that has proved to be worse than anything most people have known since the dark days of the Thirties.

With package tour operators going down like nine-pins and reports of some hotels, particularly those relying heavily on the business sector and on an international clientele, practically giving their room nights away, no one can doubt that the tourist industry has been at the forefront of the economic turn down.

Yet, the hotels in this country are nothing if not resilient, especially the smaller, privately owned and personally managed variety, which, by their nature, are able to be flexible in management and quick to adapt to changing circumstances.

Indeed, our latest intensive study of the British hotel scene has shown once again that establishments which are dedicated to offering high standards and good value for money are continuing to fill their hotels with discerning guests. Although it may seem improbable in the present economic climate, our thirty hotel inspectors have continued to report instances this year where they have encountered 'no room at the inn' and have had to seek accommodation elsewhere.

So, do not be caught out when planning a visit to any of the hotels in this guide. Whilst you may be assured that each will be delighted to accommodate you, do not assume that they are all *desperate* to see you. The tried and trusted rule still applies: book in advance if you want to avoid possible disappointment.

SIXTY EDITIONS LATER ...

Regular users of this guide will know that in each new edition we usually include a special feature highlighting an important aspect of the hotel and catering scene. In recent years we have organised nation-wide competitions which have scrutinised subjects such as the quality and price (overpriced, perhaps) of hotel wines; the standards of personal service offered to home and overseas visitors; menus with healthy options, which are also imaginative and appetising; the care and pride hoteliers devote to their country house gardens; and the plight of tea drinkers faced with neglected hotel bedroom beverage-making facilities.

In this very special edition, however, we feel we can be forgiven if, just for once, we turn the spotlight onto ourselves. To be precise, onto Ashley Courtenay himself, who, before he died at the age of 98, lived long enough to oversee the production of fifty-three editions of his 'English Classic' and see them being distributed all over the world.

But the guide he created in 1934 is just part of the story of the remarkable life of an exceptional man. A writer, publisher, gourmet and connoisseur he certainly was. He was also an hotelier for many years, which gave him a deep insight into the hotel industry he loved so much.

Yet, perhaps his most impressive achievements derive from his ability to inspire others. A number of the country's most celebrated hoteliers have cause to thank Ashley Courtenay for the help and assistance he gave them in their early careers. Three of today's most distinguished hotel-keepers, therefore, together with a leading travel writer who knew Ashley Courtenay well, have contributed to our special Diamond Jubilee feature, *Life is Recommended*, which begins on page six of the preliminary section of this book.

OUR POLICY

Since its inception, this guide has tried to offer the type of guidance we would seek before we committed ourselves to staying at an hotel of which we had no prior knowledge. Of course, most guides present useful information, often by the use of symbols and a key. Our aim, however, is not simply to provide this kind of quantitative assessment, but also to give readers some insight into what an hotel is really like. Friendliness, the subtle qualities of service and the ambience of an hotel are subjects one is able to describe, but which are impossible to grade successfully.

We, therefore, do not attempt to differentiate by star, or otherwise, one type of hotel from another. We leave it to our readers' intelligence to gauge size and style from our descriptions. In every hotel we visit, however, there are certain underlying essentials that we look for, such as cleanliness, comfort, an intelligent appreciation of good catering, and the personal touch. These, to our minds, are the foundation stones of good hotel management.

BEAUTIFUL HOTEL GARDENS AND OUTSTANDING WINE LISTS.

Although we avoid the use of ubiquitous guide book symbols whenever we can, you will find our 'Flower' symbol and/or our 'Grapes' symbol included in some of the hotel entries. The former denotes that the particular hotel was successful in our *Grounds For Delight* competition and that its gardens are a major attraction to the visitor. The latter indicates that the hotel gained prominence in our *Cellar Search* competition last year and has a wine list which offers good vintages at value-for-money prices.

HOTEL TARIFFS

The tariffs included in each hotel entry of this edition may be approximate, for they are the only ones known to us at the time of going to press, and they are based on the hotels' minimum standard half-board (Dinner, Room and Breakfast) rates unless otherwise stated.

You will, of course, be required to pay more than the amount shown if you select a superior room, or stay at an hotel out of the low season. Very often, however, you will be able to take advantage of greatly reduced rates, based on, perhaps, Weekend, Mid-Week, or set-duration Breaks. Then, there are all manner of additional discounts available to you: late-booking bargains; hotel group and consortia reductions; Free-Stay promotions, where one is required to pay only for one's meals; and the ubiquitous 'Half-Price', or 'Two for One', offers which have been promoted by almost every national newspaper.

With the existence of such a variety of rates and offers, do the tariffs printed in this book have any validity at all? Well, of course they do, for they act as a pricing bench-mark when making a studied choice of our recommended hotels. By checking carefully the tariffs shown in this book and comparing, say, one against another, readers should be able quite quickly to determine an hotel's general pricing level. However, in all cases, we must stress the importance of contacting the hotels direct and obtaining their current tariffs.

We hope you find the 60th edition of our tried and trusted guide helpful according to your needs. For us it has been a labour of love, involving thousands of miles of travel, sleeping in thousands of beds, while as for meals and refreshment, liquid and solid, the thought appalls us.

If you have been using our guide for some years you will recognize the pattern of additions and deletions, which are a vital feature of each new edition. We are fully aware that a book of this nature can never be one hundred percent accurate, for the obvious reason that even before the final sheets have been run off the printing machine some hotels have changed hands; for better or worse. A chef has left here, a head waiter there. As in other spheres of life, there is a constant state of flux in the hotel world. 'When in doubt, leave out' is, and will remain, our firm policy. Yet, the omissions you will notice are not necessarily a silent indication that an hotel's standards have deteriorated, but in many cases are due to a change of ownership or management.

So, do make use of the *Ashley Courtenay Circle* if you want to know the very latest information we have about any hotel. The *Circle* is unique and is based on the simple premise that, if every member were to write and tell us of their personal impressions, favourable or otherwise, we should be in a much stronger position to answer the queries of other members. Also, in many cases, reports provided by members of the *Circle* lead to hotels being inspected by members of our team of assessors and being included eventually in the guide. You will find a Registration Card for the *Circle* in this book, and at the back is a supply of report forms. Please send all communications to:

**Ashley Courtenay Limited,
16 Little London,
Chichester,
West Sussex PO19 1PA.**

**Telephone: 0243 775521
Fax: 0243 531331**

CONTENTS

Foreword	II
DIAMOND JUBILEE 1933 - 1993	VI
AT A DISADVANTAGE	XV
Chapter 1-**THE SOUTH-WEST**	1
Avon, Cornwall, Isles of Scilly, Devon, Dorset, Somerset, Wiltshire	
Chapter 2-**THE SOUTH-EAST**	130
Berkshire, Hampshire, Isle of Wight, Kent, Surrey, East and West Sussex	
Chapter 3-**LONDON**	178
Chapter 4-**MID-ENGLAND**	186
Buckinghamshire, Cambridgeshire, Cheshire, Derbyshire, Essex, Gloucestershire, Hereford and Worcester, Hertfordshire, Lincolnshire, Norfolk, Northamptonshire, Oxfordshire, Shropshire, Staffordshire, Suffolk, Warwickshire, West Midlands	
Chapter 5-**NORTHERN ENGLAND**	250
Cleveland, Cumbria, Co Durham, Greater Manchester, Humberside, Isle of Man, Lancashire, Merseyside, Northumberland, North, South and West Yorkshire	
Chapter 6-**CHANNEL ISLANDS**	312
Alderney, Guernsey, Herm, Jersey, Sark	
Chapter 7-**WALES**	339
Clwyd, Dyfed, Mid, South and West Glamorgan, Gwent, Gwynedd, Powys	
Chapter 8-**SCOTLAND**	380
Borders, Central, Dumfries and Galloway, Fife, Grampian, Highland, Lothian, Strathclyde, Tayside, Western Isles	
Chapter 9-**STOP PRESS**	431
Chapter 10-**ASHLEY COURTENAY CIRCLE**	432
Alphabetical Place Index	443
Road Maps	451

SPECIAL DIAMOND JUBILEE FEATURE

Life is Recommended!

by Hugh Graham

For 98 years Ashley Courtenay lived in the sort of style most of us thought had ended when the Germans unwillingly signed the Treaty of Versailles to end the great war in 1918. And if style was the adjective that best described the manner in which he lived, then elegant is the word that best described him personally - an elegance in no way effeminate, but similar to that affected by Maurice Chevalier, whom he resembled quite remarkably - even to the cane he carried, just in case, during his last few years.

I met Ashley for the first time in Bond Street's Westbury Hotel in the Autumn of 1984. He was then 94, looked a very well preserved 70, and was presiding over a gathering of those dedicated men and women who assess the establishments eventually recommended by his guide. He was outlining his latest five year plan, which he very clearly expected to implement. It was self evident he considered 94 years to be no great age. He was still looking forward, planning for the future, when he died four years later at the age of 98, two years short of the century.

He was the most remarkable son of a most remarkable family. The Courtenays originated from Devon, and included a Roman Emperor (what else!?) way back. He was educated at Haileybury and went on to take a degree in history at Emmanuel College, Cambridge. Apart from an aged

Archdeacon he was, when I knew him, the oldest of the Old Boys. He read the Times obituaries every morning to learn who was left.

"I was intended for the church myself" he once confided "but found inns more agreeable than churches, although I am very interested in both!" After a stint at teaching and as a trainee with the General Electric Company, he decided to carve a career in advertising for himself. He found the world of advertising vastly stimulating because it allowed him to exploit the Barnum and Bailey side of his personality.

The First World War interrupted his advertising activities and Ashley was one of the first to join up and finished with the lofty rank of captain. Since style was Ashley's watchword, it will surprise nobody that he became briefly a member of the Duke of Westminster's bizarre squadron of armoured Rolls Royces. Membership of this elite band appeared conditional upon an ability to reverse the Rolls at 20 mph away from the hornets' nest they inevitably stirred up when they had driven furiously to the front lines, sprayed their machine guns at the enemy trenches only to disappear as soon as the Germans returned their fire. "The unfortunate Tommies had to remain in their own lines," Ashley remembered, "so we were not at all popular!"

After the war he set up a new advertising agency in Manchester where he was concerned principally with extolling the virtues of an unusual product; hot tripe in the winter, cold tripe in the summer. He persuaded the Manchester Evening News to launch a competition for the best recipes. The Mancunian mothers responded with hundreds of imaginative recipes which Ashley and his team collated into a cookbook. 'Just Tripe!' sold thousands of copies.

It was possibly this cookbook that provided him with background knowledge for the idea that was to make him a household name and to establish this country's best known hotel guide.

By then Ashley was already a prolific writer, having begun writing travel articles for The Morning Post, now The Daily Telegraph, revolving his explorations around his guide's recommendations. His articles were enormously popular and by the time the Second World War commenced he was writing eight regular columns for various publications.

But to begin the story of the guide we must go back a few years earlier. One Sunday afternoon, during the long hot summer of 1926 he was driving between Brighton and Portsmouth when he spied a sign nailed to a tree - "real Sussex cream teas, 100 yards on left." He turned down Hedgers Hill, Walberton, near Arundel, and there, nearly hidden by a blanket of honeysuckle, was a low, thatched cottage called Beam Ends, being run as tea rooms, rather appropriately, by a Mrs Poor. Whilst he enjoyed hot

Beam Ends, a delightful 16th Century thatched cottage, which has changed very little since Ashley Courtenay chanced to call there on 27th July 1926 and conceived the idea of producing his guide.

buttered scones, clotted cream and home-made jam, Ashley mused that such places deserved to be better known. This simple thought prompted Ashley to found Britain's leading hotel guide.

He spent nearly six years combing the home counties for the tea rooms, inns and country hotels he was eventually to recommend to other travellers.

The first edition, a modest affair, cost just one shilling (five pence) and he printed 1,000 copies. The first printing was sold out within a fortnight. Such was the demand he produced four further editions that year, his readers forcing him to promise he would up-date the guide annually.

There was much to get away from in the Thirties. Great Britain was in the grip of the sort of recession that we are all experiencing just now. Hitler was sabre-rattling in Germany, the peace our nation had enjoyed since 1918 looked increasingly fragile and most folk felt the need to escape to beauty and tranquillity as often as possible.

The establishments Ashley recommended provided his readers with the opportunity of spending a little time in surroundings where the cares of the world could be ignored for a short while. Then, as now, the guide concentrated on establishments that offered excellent value for money - and that meant neither cheap, nor expensive. Ashley had searched out those hostelries which, whether the price range was high or low, offered a great deal more than the tariff demanded.

And this simple philosophy remains the rock upon which the success of the Ashley Courtenay guide continues to be based. Soon the very mention of his name was sufficient to galvanise lethargic hotel managers into frantic activity, that sounded like the crack of doom in the mind of the most careless of waiters, and spurred lackadaisical chefs into producing at short notice their most sacred dishes.

He ventured into hotel ownership because he thought that since he was providing a service to hoteliers as well as the general public, he ought to have first hand knowledge of the problems hoteliers faced. He first bought Bramley Grange Hotel near Guildford, then The Kings Arms at Tedburn St Mary near Exeter, and lastly The Node at Codicote near Welwyn, a twenty-three bedroomed mansion, set in one hundred acres of beautiful grounds.

But his guide remained his first and abiding love and I have not the slightest doubt he would have been proud of the Diamond Jubilee edition. Beautifully produced in full colour, this volume would not look out of place on the shelves of a gentleman's library. Moreover, it continues to be published under Ashley's name. A fitting tribute to the man who created a style of hotel guide, which has been emulated by others, but never bettered.

Sharrow Bay Hotel, the quintessential English country house on the shores of Lake Ullswater in Cumbria. Here, over the past forty years, Francis Coulson and Brian Sack have created one of the most celebrated hotels in Britain.

by Brian Sack

A chartered surveyor flying in Hertfordshire as a member of the R.A.F. reserve, may seem an unlikely candidate for a career - or, rather, a vocation - as an hotelier. This however, was precisely my position in 1951 when I first met Mrs Ashley Courtenay.

The meeting was one of chance - or perhaps was negotiated by fate. A fellow pilot, Tony Thompson by name, invited me to join him for dinner at a hotel called The Node at Codicote in Hertfordshire. The house was quite bewitching and, after a sumptuous dinner, we were greeted by a lady of great charm who invited us to have a look around the hotel. Instinctively I knew that, despite all the cushy-comforts of my former work, I wanted to enter this enchanting world of 'hotels'. I indicated that I would throw up my job to do so and then discovered that our hostess was none other than Mrs. Ashley Courtenay who offered to help if ever I "decided to make the break".

In due course I was asked to go back into uniform for three months jet flying experience as the world situation was unsettled and anxieties were looming. The 'break' was thus made and I never again returned to my office. Instead I accepted the kind invitation that had been proferred that evening at The Node and was taken on for the princely sum of five pounds a week!

Mr and Mrs Ashley Courtenay were extremely kind and I learned an enormous amount in a very short time. Fate, however, was still waiting in the wings and, at the Ashley Courtenays' Christmas house party, I met a Mrs Trapp and her daughter, Eileen. Over the mince pies and port, I told them of my ideals and they immediately said that they knew of a young man in the Lake District who had opened an hotel on the shores of Ullswater called Sharrow Bay. He had been coping for three years on his own but was in great need of support. I wrote to Francis Coulson who promptly contacted the Trapp family to inquire after this strange chap who had written out of the blue! They convinced him that a meeting should be arranged as they felt sure this would be mutually advantageous.

And so, one weekend in March, I arrived at Sharrow and, like many others, was destined never to leave. The area, the house and, most important, the way in which Francis Coulson was running Sharrow and had been since he started three years previously, captivated me and I offered my services to him for the coming summer season as I felt that our ideals were absolutely identical.

One of the most wonderful compliments that we have been paid was by a rather tough South African gentleman who, after he had paid his account, commented that "this was a remarkable place as everything seems to be done with love", and that is, in fact, our philosophy.

Fate seemed to decree that two very different personalities should meet and so the ultimate partnership was created and Sharrow Bay went from strength to strength, and we can honestly say that, if it had not been for Mr and Mrs Ashley Courtenay, this would never have been possible.

An actor and a surveyor have since been joined by a biologist, a journalist, a teacher, as well as all those who had earlier in their lives decided to devote themselves to the hotel world; intent on creating welcoming comfort, fine *food and gracious service. We are a mixed crowd, and, whatever brought us together, we only hope that the Sharrow Bay legend will be able to continue forever.*

The famous gardens of Gravetye Manor reflect the peace and quiet of this magnificent country house, set in the Sussex countryside near East Grinstead. For thirty years Peter Herbert has maintained his hotel's world-wide reputation for faultless comfort and impeccable service.

by Peter Herbert

In the early 50's I was blessed with the advice and encouragement of three great men in the world of Hotels and Restaurants; Rudolph Richards of the Connaught, André Simon of the Wine & Food Society and Ashley Courtenay, the doyen of hotel writers at that time. As a young manager I treasured their views and criticisms, and above all the friendships that developed.

"AC" as he was called, before familiarity became possible with the passing of time, was a man of impish humour, almost schoolboyish in its charm and simplicity, yet his style of writing showed him to be a sophisticated and shrewd observer, homing in on salient points, and conveying unfailingly the true feeling of a place. No doubt his experiences of running an hotel with his wife gave him a great depth of understanding and sympathy for our calling, for he was never malicious in his writings, and always appreciative and swift to acknowledge achievement.

I learnt from his secretary of many years, Denise Cadisch, that many celebrities valued his judgement, and such as Sir Adrian Boult and Sir Gordon Richards would call at his St. James' office to discuss travel plans. His enthusiasm was insatiable, and conversation and correspondence on Hotels and Travel his greatest joy. After the sad death of his son, Ashley went back into the saddle when in his nineties, working until the very end of his long life. We met at the Gore Hotel in 1952, and were priveleged to arrange his wedding reception in the Elizabethan room, a period Restaurant which appealed to his imagination and vitality. In the mid-fifties he moved offices to Chichester, fortuitously about the time we came to Gravetye Manor, so good fortune kept us in close touch.

We had the joy of hosting his 96th Birthday party here at Gravetye, when he was in cracking good humour, and still reading without the aid of glasses at that great age. We awaited his centenary with much excitement, but alas, he died in his 99th year. He would surely be proud that this year marks the 60th Edition of 'his' Guide; long may it continue, perhaps to achieve that century he so narrowly missed!

John Aust is currently the Vice President of the HCIMA and one of the Country's leading hotel consultants.

by John Aust

I first met Ashley Courtenay in the front hall of the Imperial Hotel, Hythe when I was 23 years of age, having just left the Army Catering Corps after 5 years' service and was in my new position of senior assistant manager of this well known 4-star establishment, which Ashley made reference to as an hotel "where the country meets the sea".

I had been summoned by reception as a gentleman wished to see me and when we met I was informed that he wished to inspect all the rooms before going into dinner so that he could spend the remainder of the evening writing about the hotel for the next edition of his guide, due to be published in

1958. I asked him for written authority for such an inspection at which point he seemed to become exasperated.

I quickly pointed out to him that I was in the middle of conversing with guests who were enjoying dinner and was sure he would appreciate that it was inappropriate for me as an hotelier to have seen some diners and not others and if he would excuse me I would return to complete that duty. In those days the Imperial was very much a holiday hotel and I had introduced a number of innovative ideas for events for guests to partake in, like visiting the Varne lightship, going out in a fishing trawler, flying from Lydd to Le Touquet, trips on the Romney, Hythe and Dymchurch Railway, and was interested to find out guests' reaction to these arrangements.

When I came out from the dining room, Ashley was sitting in a corner of the lounge writing up notes and I suggested that he join me for a late dinner and that we would go around the hotel together next morning. During the meal I told Ashley that he need not worry about the fracas we had had as next time he came there would be a new manager at the Imperial as I was trying to raise money to buy the Mermaid Hotel at Rye.

He scoffed at this idea and said "you know it is full of woodworm". I said "yes, and I know how to treat it. If it was not full of woodworm I wouldn't be getting it for £8,000." He replied "you won't last there a year" and when I asked why, he said "you are a big hotel man and will never be happy in a 12 bedroom hostelry".

The rest of the visit went smoothly enough and I thought it unlikely we would meet again. However, I came to the conclusion that he was right about one thing, the Mermaid was not for me and shortly afterwards the vacancy of resident manager became available at the Imperial which I applied for and was appointed on my 24th Birthday.

A year later Ashley returned to do his next inspection and he confided to me that the proprietor of the Imperial, the late JW Marston, had contacted him regarding appointing a new manager for which they had advertised and that Ashley had recommended me for the post, though he thought both he and JW Marston might accrue a few more grey hairs from the experience!

I was to stay at the Imperial another 8 years and all subsequent visits were inspiring; Ashley always encouraged me in my work to improve the hotel and indirectly to improve my own career.

In 1964 I moved to the George Hotel, Colchester, which had a reputation for serving the finest, traditional dishes, Welsh Lamb and Scottish Beef, which really did come from where they say, by train via Oswestry and Aberdeen. The hotel for many years had been famous for the slogan "You can always get a lobster at the George" and I remember my wife and I having to work extremely hard, indeed, with the support of a very fine brigade of chefs, to maintain this hotel's reputation which was acknowledged at the time to be one of the best 3 Red Star AA hotels in England.

Ashley visited us once and I did not think in all honesty that he was over impressed. At the time the local council was digging a large hole in the middle of the one and only lounge, excavating for Roman ruins. Maybe at the time he was put off by the fact that my wife and I had police protection due to having unmasked a gang who had been pilfering wines and spirits from local establishments. Following our discovery, a home-made bomb had been placed under our car, but fortunately my army training allowed me to discover it before it did any damage.

Our next meeting was after I had taken up the position of General Manager at the Selsdon Park Hotel. This is where he felt I really belonged and said so with much enthusiasm as we sat on the terrace one evening. Looking around him he said "Hey Presto, isn't it marvellous that there is not a house in sight though we are only 13 miles from Trafalgar Square".

My last meeting with Ashley was when I attended his 90th Birthday party which was held in Avisford Park, Sussex, and what a magnificent occasion that was. Over the years my wife, Jackie, and his wife, Nancy, had got to know each other very well and Ashley himself was in fine form.

He was a man of great presence, a resolute character, a person always ready to help aspiring hoteliers, for he truly knew that it is not the easiest trade to be in love with. In his early days he could be a somewhat assertive person, but he matured into one who showed great kindness, especially in other people's adversity. I, along with many other hoteliers and friends, miss him very much.

Two years ago Beam Ends was re-opened as a 'spacious Tea Garden and restaurant in a tranquil setting' by Coral Stroud and her partner, Rick Botteley. Pictured taking tea are Coral Stroud and Peter Fuller, managing director of Ashley Courtenay Limited.

At a Disadvantage?

It is not our usual policy to announce in advance the subject of our special survey for the following year, but during 1993 our thirty-six hotel inspectors will be paying special attention to the facilities hotels provide for disabled people and those with general disabilities.

Hoteliers who do not cater for disabled people are ignoring a potential market of some 6.5 million individuals in the U.K. alone! A survey published recently by the English Tourist Board, on behalf of the Holiday Care Service charity, reports that only 9% of disabled people travel alone, compared with 44% who travel with one person and 47% who travel with two or more people.

The report concludes rightly that 'Anybody who turns away somebody in a wheelchair is also turning away that person's partner, friends and colleagues'. It also stresses that awareness training about the needs of disabled people should be included in basic staff training by holiday operators.

By natural progression, all this leads one onto the subject of the employment of disadvantaged people within the hotel and catering industry, which does, in some areas of its operations, offer such people an ideal environment for rewarding occupations. Whilst it is not in our brief to address this point in our forthcoming survey, we hope other organisations, more appropriate than ourselves, tackle the subject without further delay.

For our part, we will begin our hotel inspection tours early in 1993. To assist us in this particular research, we should like to hear from disabled people and organisations devoted to the problems faced by disadvantaged people. We would like to know of any special difficulties that hotels and restaurants present you, not just relating to general facilities, but also in staff attitudes and the reaction to you from other guests. You may nominate establishments for special praise, or where you feel the standards provided for your special needs are particularly lamentable.

Overleaf you will find a list of questions you may find useful when writing to us about the hotels and restaurants you visit next year. Following this is our current directory of Ashley Courtenay recommendations that provide certain facilities for disabled people. Send us your reports and you will be helping other people as well as yourself. We look forward to hearing from you.

We should like to state straight away that the primary purpose of the following questions is not to find fault for fault's sake. We appreciate that certain hotels, because of their age, style, position and other factors, cannot be made as accessible to people with disabilities as their owners would wish. We do feel, however, that *most* hoteliers could do more to attract disabled guests and to make these people's lives more comfortable during their stays. And we are not referring simply to costly measures and major hotel alterations. There are innumerable relatively simple improvements one could make to any hotel, which would enhance the hotel experience of many disadvantaged guests.

You may photocopy this page as many times as you wish, or use the questions to form your own reports. Our inspectors will be visiting thousands of hotels during 1993, but we do need to learn of your experiences at hotels within the U.K. to complete our findings. We look forward to hearing from you.

REPORT

Name of Hotel..

Address..

....

Date of visit/s...

Please underline one description in each case.

1.	Parking:	*Very difficult*	*Problematical*	*Easy*
2.	Entrance:	*Very difficult*	*Problematical*	*Easy*
3.	Restaurant:	*Very difficult*	*Problematical*	*Easy*
4.	Public rooms:	*Very difficult*	*Problematical*	*Easy*
5.	Bedroom:	*Very difficult*	*Problematical*	*Easy*
6.	Bathroom:	*Very difficult*	*Problematical*	*Easy*
7.	Public Toilets:	*Very difficult*	*Problematical*	*Easy*
8.	Hospitality:	*Insensitive*	*Understanding*	*Very helpful*

9. Further comments on any aspect which you feel may be helpful.

....

....

....

....

....

....

Ashley Courtenay Recommended Hotels with Facilities for the DISABLED

Section 1 Hotels

GREEN LAWNS HOTEL,
WESTERN TERRACE, FALMOUTH,
CORNWALL, TR11 4QJ

PENMERE MANOR HOTEL,
MONGLEATH ROAD, FALMOUTH,
CORNWALL, TR11 4PN

HOLNE CHASE HOTEL,
TWO BRIDGES ROAD, NR ASHBURTON,
DEVON, TQ13 7NS

ODDICOMBE HOUSE HOTEL,
CHILLINGTON, KINGSBRIDGE,
DEVON, TQ7 2JD

COLESTOCKS HOUSE,
COLESTOCKS, NR HONITON,
DEVON, EX14 0JR

COTTAGE HOTEL,
HOPE COVE, KINGSBRIDGE,
DEVON, TQ7 3HJ

FAIRMOUNT HOUSE,
HERBERT ROAD, CHETSTON,
TORQUAY TQ2 6RW

HOTEL RIVIERA,
THE ESPLANADE, SIDMOUTH,
DEVON, EX10 8AY

SOAR MILL COVE HOTEL,
SOAR MILL COVE, SALCOMBE,
DEVON, TQ7 3DS

THE TIVERTON HOTEL,
BLUNDELL'S ROAD, TIVERTON,
DEVON, EX16 4DB

ANTELOPE HOTEL,
GREENHILL, SHERBORNE,
DORSET DT9 4EP

HADDON HOUSE HOTEL,
WEST BAY, BRIDPORT,
DORSET.

HOTEL BUENA VISTA,
POUND STREET, LYME REGIS,
DORSET, DT7 3HZ

MOONFLEET MANOR,
MOONFLEET, NR WEYMOUTH,
DORSET. DT3 4ED

KNOLL HOUSE HOTEL,
STUDLAND, SWANAGE,
DORSET, BH19 3AH

KEMPS COUNTRY HOUSE HOTEL AND RESTAURANT,
EAST STOKE, WAREHAM,
DORSET, BH20 6AL

NORTHFIELD HOTEL,
NORTHFIELD ROAD, MINEHEAD,
SOMERSET, TA24 5PU

THE WALNUT TREE INN,
NORTH PETHERTON, BRIDGWATER,
SOMERSET, TA6 6QA

THE GEORGE INN,
NUNNEY, NR FROME,
SOMERSET, BA11 1PW

BLUNSDON HOUSE HOTEL,
BLUNSDON, SWINDON,
WILTSHIRE, SN2 4AD

Section 2 Hotels

AURORA GARDEN HOTEL,
14 BOLTON AVENUE, WINDSOR,
BERKS, SL4 3JF

HOLLINGTON HOUSE,
CHURCH RD, WOOLTON HILL,
NEWBURY, BERKS RG15 9XR

NEWTOWN HOUSE HOTEL,
MANOR RD, HAYLING ISLAND,
HAMPSHIRE, PO11 0QR

SWAINSTON MANOR HOTEL,
CALBOURNE,
ISLE OF WIGHT, PO30 4HX

COUNTRY GARDEN HOTEL AND RESTAURANT,
CHURCH HILL, TOTLAND BAY,
ISLE OF WIGHT, PO39 0ET

SINGLEWELL MANOR,
HEVER COURT RD, SINGLEWELL,
GRAVESEND, KENT. DA12 5UQ

BLACK MILL HOUSE HOTEL,
PRINCESS AVENUE, ALDWICK,
WEST SUSSEX, PO21 2QU

SOUTHDOWNS HOTEL,
TROTTON, ROGATE, PETERSFIELD,
HAMPSHIRE, GU32 5JN

THE KINGSWAY HOTEL,
MARINE PARADE, WORTHING,
WEST SUSSEX, BN11 1TH

Section 3 Hotels
CRANLEY HOTEL,
LONDON, SW5 0LA

Section 4 Hotels
DOLPHIN HOTEL,
BRIDGE FOOT, LONDON RD,
ST IVES,
CAMBRIDGESHIRE, PE17 4EP

ROWTON HALL HOTEL,
WHITCHURCH RD, ROWTON,
CHESTER, CHESHIRE, CH3 6AD

ST. DAVID'S PARK HOTEL,
ST. DAVID'S PARK, EWLOE,
CLWYD. (NEAR CHESTER)

THE CROFT COUNTRY HOUSE
GREAT LONGSTONE, BAKEWELL,
DERBYSHIRE, DE4 1TF

THE SAFFRON HOTEL,
10/18 HIGH STREET,
SAFFRON WALDEN,
ESSEX, CB10 1AY

NOEL ARMS HOTEL,
HIGH STREET,
CHIPPING CAMPDEN,
GLOUCESTERSHIRE, GL55 6AT

THE HARE & HOUNDS HOTEL,
WESTONBIRT, TETBURY,
GLOUCESTERSHIRE, GL8 8QL

PRESTBURY HOUSE HOTEL,
THE BURGAGE, PRESTBURY,
CHELTENHAM,
GLOS, GL52 3DN

PENGETHLEY MANOR,
HAREWOOD END,
NR ROSS-ON-WYE,
HEREFORDSHIRE, HR9 6LL

ORLES BARN HOTEL,
WILTON, ROSS-ON-WYE,
HEREFORDSHIRE, HR9 6AE

MOOR LODGE HOTEL,
BRANSTON, LINCOLN,
LINCOLNSHIRE, LN4 1HU

THE BLAKENEY HOTEL,
BLAKENEY, HOLT,
NORFOLK, NR25 7NE

HOTEL NELSON,
PRINCE OF WALES RD,
NORWICH, NORFOLK, NR1 1DX

KNIGHT'S HILL HOTEL,
KNIGHT'S HILL VILLAGE,
S. WOOTTON, KING'S LYNN,
NORFOLK, PE30 3HQ

BELFRY HOTEL,
MILTON COMMON,
OXFORD, OX9 2JW

UPLANDS HOTEL,
VICTORIA ROAD, ALDEBURGH,
SUFFOLK, IP15 5DX

MARLBOROUGH HOTEL,
SEA FRONT, FELIXSTOWE,
SUFFOLK, IP11 8BJ

THE RIVERSIDE INN,
RIVERSIDE DRIVE, BRANSTON,
BURTON-UPON-TRENT, STAFFS, DE14 3EP

NAILCOTE HALL HOTEL,
BERKSWELL,
WARWICKSHIRE. CV7 7DE

WELCOMBE HOTEL AND GOLF
COURSE, WARWICK RD, STRATFORD-
UPON-AVON,
WARWICKSHIRE, CV37 0NR

Section 5 Hotels
LOWBYER MANOR,
ALSTON,
CUMBRIA, CA9 3JX

ROTHAY GARTH HOTEL,
ROTHAY RD, AMBLESIDE,
CUMBRIA, LA22 0EE

ROTHAY MANOR HOTEL,
ROTHAY BRIDGE, AMBLESIDE,
CUMBRIA, LA22 0EH

APPLEBY MANOR HOTEL,
ROMAN RD,
APPLEBY-IN-WESTMORLAND,
CUMBRIA, CA16 6JD

BURN HOW GARDEN HOUSE
BACK BELSFIELD RD, BOWNESS-ON-
WINDERMERE,
CUMBRIA, LA23 3HH

LINDETH FELL COUNTRY HOUSE HOTEL,
BOWNESS-ON-WINDERMERE,
CUMBRIA, LA23 3JP

SCALE HILL HOTEL,
LOWESWATER, NR COCKERMOUTH,
CUMBRIA, CA13 9UX

LAKESIDE HOTEL,
NEWBY BRIDGE, ULVERSTON,
CUMBRIA,

THE BLACK SWAN,
RAVENSTONEDALE, KIRKBY STEPHEN,
CUMBRIA, CA17 4NG

LOW WOOD HOTEL,
LOW WOOD, WINDERMERE,
CUMBRIA, LA23 1LP

THE BELL IN DRIFFIELD,
MARKET PLACE, GREAT DRIFFIELD,
HUMBERSIDE, YO25 7AP

GRAND ISLAND HOTEL,
RAMSEY,
ISLE OF MAN,

MYTTON FOLD FARM HOTEL,
LANGHO WHALLEY,
LANCS, BB6 8AB

CHADWICK HOTEL,
SOUTH PROMENADE,
LYTHAM ST ANNE'S,
LANCASHIRE, FY8 1NP

BLUE BELL HOTEL,
BELFORD,
NORTHUMBERLAND, NE70 7NE

RIVERDALE HALL HOTEL,
KIELDER ROAD, BELLINGHAM,
NORTHUMBERLAND, NE48 2JT

LINDEN HALL HOTEL,
LONGHORSLEY, MORPETH,
NORTHUMBERLAND, NE65 8XF

THE PERCY ARMS HOTEL,
OTTERBURN,
NORTHUMBERLAND, NE19 1NR

THE PHEASANT HOTEL,
HAROME, HELMSLEY,
NORTH YORKSHIRE, YO6 5JG

FEVERSHAM ARMS HOTEL,
1 HIGH STREET, HELMSLEY,
NORTH YORKSHIRE, YO6 5AG

JERVAULX HALL,
JERVAULX, NR MASHAM, RIPON, N YORKS, HG4 4PH

Section 6 Hotels

HOTEL HOUGUE DU POMMIER,
CASTEL, GUERNSEY,
CHANNEL ISLANDS,

ST MARGARET'S LODGE,
FOREST LODGE, ST MARTIN'S,
GUERNSEY, C. ISLANDS,

ST PIERRE PARK HOTEL,
ROHAIS, ST PETER PORT,
GUERNSEY, C. ISLANDS,

HOTEL DE LA PLAGE,
HAVRE DES PAS, ST HELIER,
JERSEY, CHANNEL ISLANDS,

Section 7 Hotels

GATEWAY TO WALES HOTEL,
SEALAND, DEESIDE,
CLWYD CH5 2HX

ST. DAVID'S PARK HOTEL,
ST. DAVID'S PARK,
EWLOE, CLWYD.

THE HAND HOTEL,
LLANARMON-DYFFRYN-CEIRIOG,
NR LLANGOLLEN, CLWYD.

GLEN-YR-AFON HOUSE,
PONTYPOOL ROAD, USK,
GWENT, NP5 1SY

CARREG BRAN,
CHURCH LANE, LLANFAIRPWLL,
ANGLESEY. LL61 5YH

HENLLYS HALL HOTEL,
BEAUMARIS,
ISLE OF ANGLESEY,
GWYNEDD, LL58 8HU

SYCHNANT PASS HOTEL,
SYCHNANT PASS RD, CONWY,
GWYNEDD, LL32 8BJ

TREFEDDIAN HOTEL,
ABERDOVEY,
GWYNEDD, LL35 0SB

COED-Y-MWSTWR,
COYCHURCH, BRIDGEND,
MID-GLAMORGAN, CF35 6AF

HERONSTON HOTEL,
EWENNY, BRIDGEND,
MID-GLAMORGAN, CF35 5AW

Section 8 Hotels

HETLAND HALL HOTEL,
CARRUTHERSTOWN,
DUMFRIES & GALLOWAY

CLONYARD HOUSE HOTEL,
COLVEND, DALBEATTIE, KIRKS,
DUMFRIES & GALLOWAY.

MOFFAT HOUSE,
HIGH STREET, MOFFAT,
DUMFRIES & GALLOWAY,

POWFOOT GOLF HOTEL,
LINKS AVENUE, POWFOOT, ANNAN,
DUMFRIES & GALLOWAY.

BIRSE LODGE HOTEL,
ABOYNE, ABERDEENSHIRE,
GRAMPIAN, AB3 5EL

CRAIGELLACHIE HOTEL,
CRAIGELLACHIE, ABERLOUR,
BANFFSHIRE, GRAMPIAN,

PANNANICH WELLS HOTEL,
BALLATER,
GRAMPIAN.

CASTLE ARMS HOTEL,
MEY, CAITHNESS,
KW14 8XH

COUL HOUSE HOTEL,
CONTIN, BY STRATHPEFFER,
ROSS-SHIRE, HIGHLAND.

THE LODGE ON THE LOCH,
CREAG DHU, ONICH,
NR FORT WILLIAM,
HIGHLAND, PH33 6RY

FALLS OF LORA HOTEL,
CONNEL FERRY, BY OBAN,
ARGYLL, STRATHCLYDE.

TAYCHREGGAN HOTEL,
KILCHRENAN, BY TAYNUILT, ARGYLL,
STRATHCLYDE.

STONEFIELD CASTLE HOTEL,
TARBERT, LOCH FYNE, ARGYLL,
STRATHCLYDE.

NIVINGSTON HOUSE,
CLEISH, KINROSS-SHIRE,
TAYSIDE, KY13 7LS

BURNSIDE HOTEL,
19 WEST MOULIN RD, PITLOCHRY,
PERTHSHIRE, TAYSIDE, PH16 5EA

PARKLANDS HOTEL,
ST. LEONARDS BANK,
PERTH. PH2 8EB

THE SOUTH-WEST

Lizard Peninsula, Cornwall

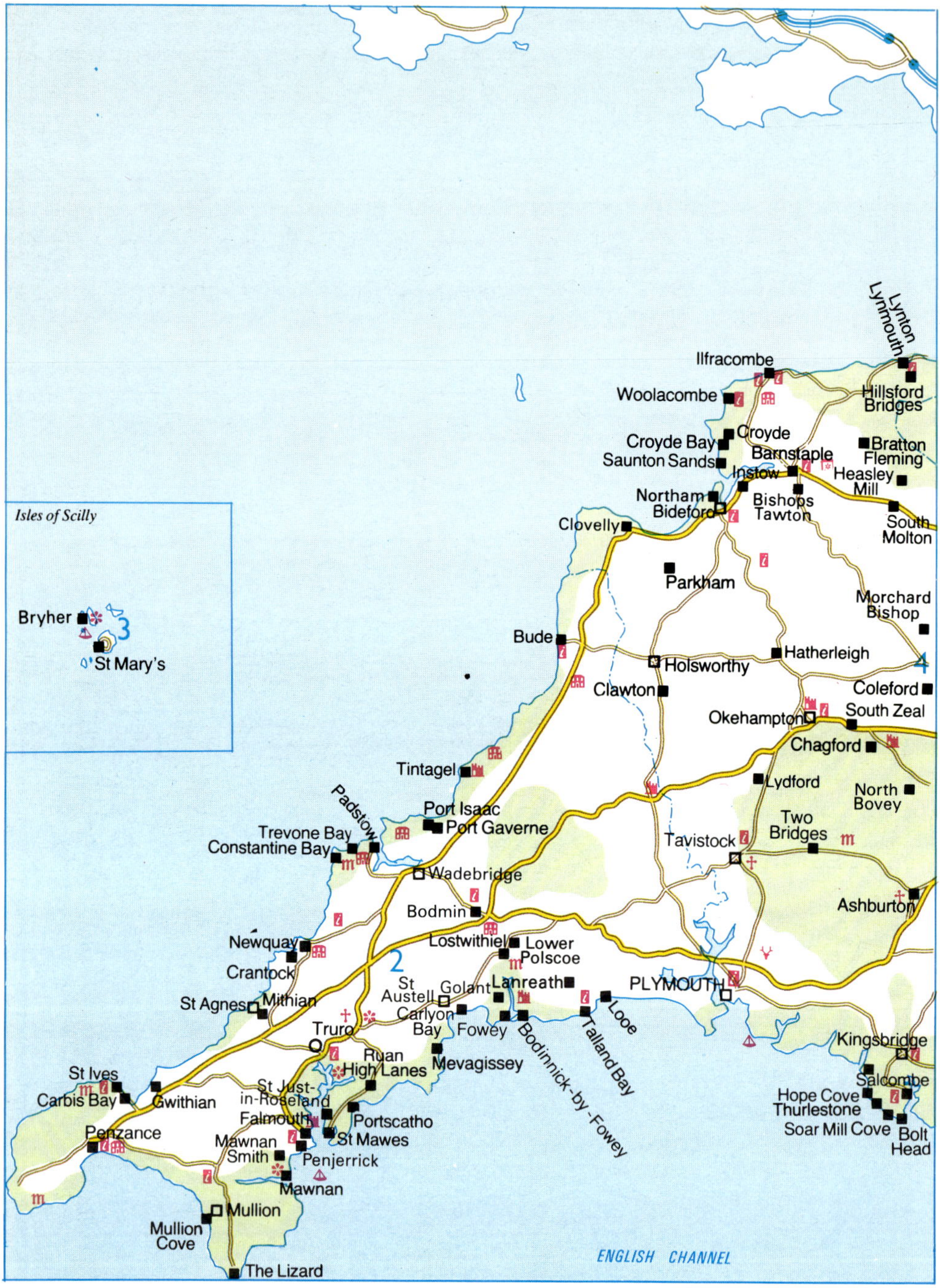

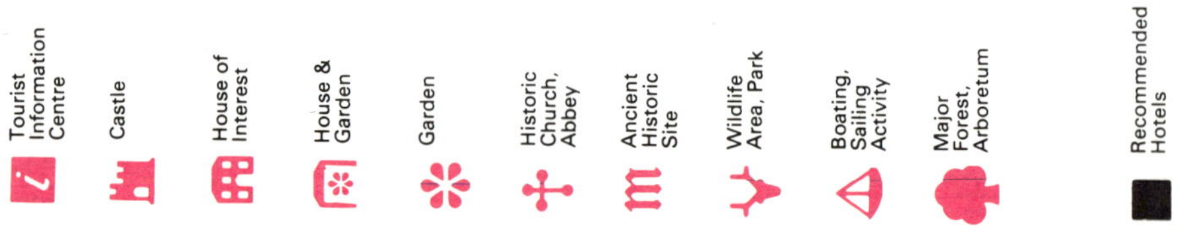

Tourist Information Centre	Castle	House of Interest	House & Garden	Garden	Historic Church, Abbey	Ancient Historic Site	Wildlife Area, Park	Boating, Sailing Activity	Major Forest, Arboretum	Recommended Hotels
										■

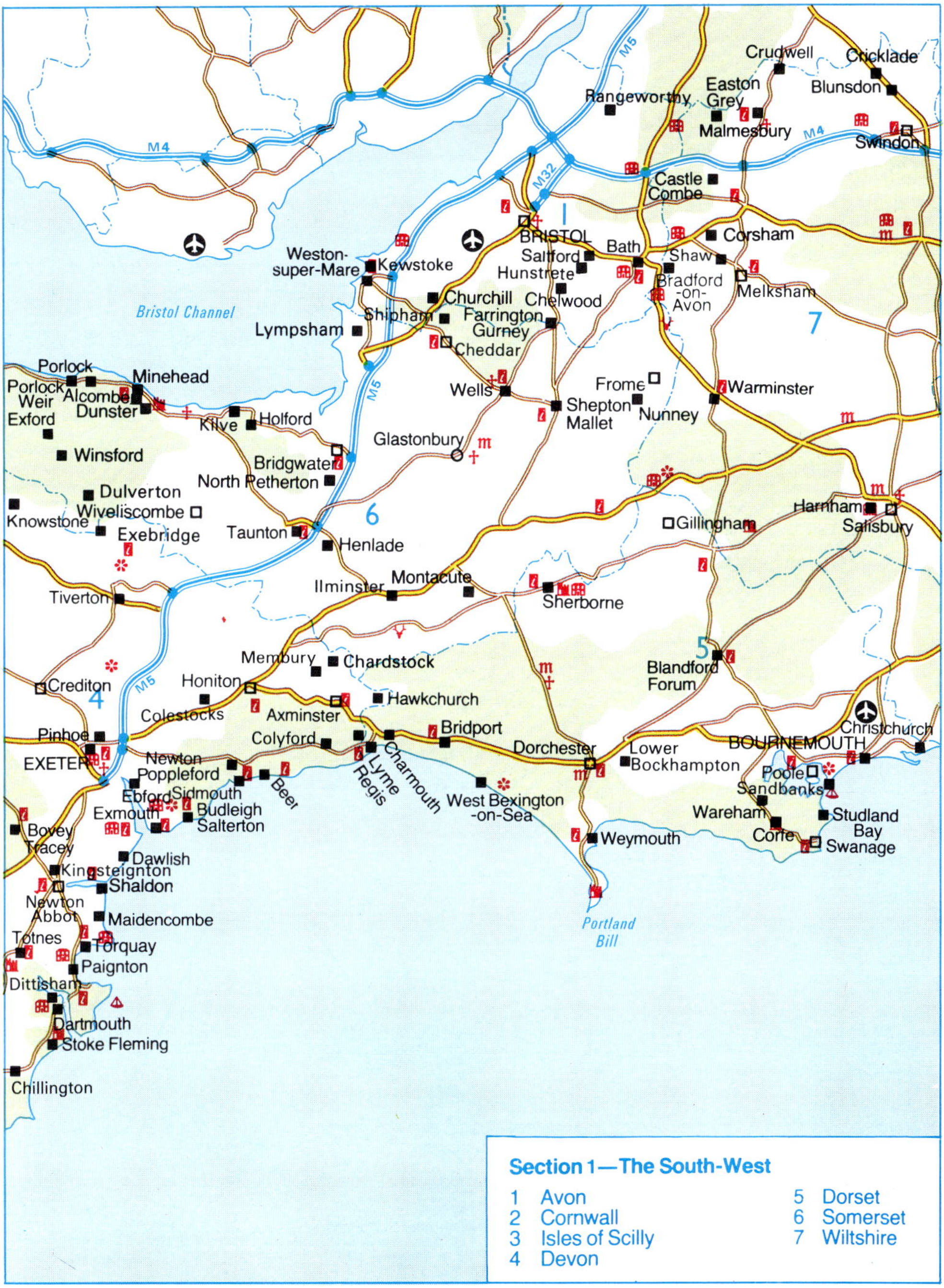

Section 1—The South-West
1 Avon
2 Cornwall
3 Isles of Scilly
4 Devon
5 Dorset
6 Somerset
7 Wiltshire
Bristol Channel
Portland Bill
M4
M5
M32
Crudwell
Cricklade
Blunsdon
Easton Grey
Rangeworthy
Malmesbury
Swindon
Castle Combe
BRISTOL
Corsham
Bath
Saltford
Shaw
Hunstrete
Bradford -on- Avon
Melksham
Weston-super-Mare
Kewstoke
Churchill
Chelwood
Shipham
Farrington Gurney
Lympsham
Cheddar
Porlock
Porlock Weir
Alcombe
Minehead
Dunster
Exford
Kilve
Holford
Wells
Frome
Warminster
Shepton Mallet
Nunney
Glastonbury
Winsford
Bridgwater
North Petherton
Dulverton
Knowstone
Wiveliscombe
Exebridge
Taunton
Henlade
Gillingham
Harnham
Salisbury
Tiverton
Ilminster
Montacute
Sherborne
Membury
Chardstock
Blandford Forum
Crediton
Honiton
Hawkchurch
Colestocks
Axminster
Pinhoe
Colyford
Bridport
Christchurch
EXETER
Newton Poppleford
Lyme Regis
Charmouth
Dorchester
Lower Bockhampton
BOURNEMOUTH
Ebford
Sidmouth
Beer
West Bexington -on-Sea
Poole
Sandbanks
Exmouth
Budleigh Salterton
Wareham
Studland Bay
Bovey Tracey
Corfe
Swanage
Weymouth
Dawlish
Kingsteignton
Shaldon
Newton Abbot
Maidencombe
Totnes
Torquay
Paignton
Dittisham
Dartmouth
Stoke Fleming
Chillington

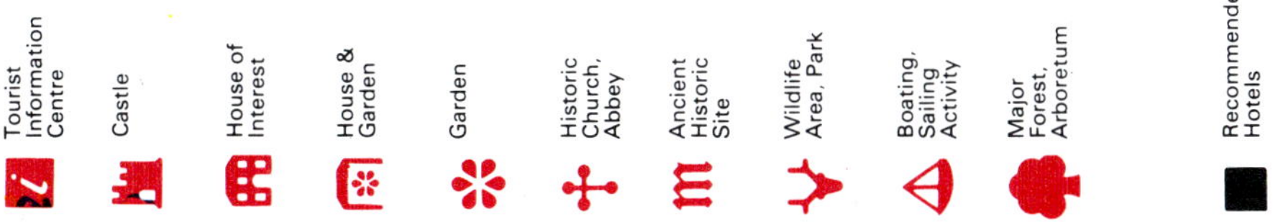

Tourist Information Centre
Castle
House of Interest
House & Garden
Garden
Historic Church, Abbey
Ancient Historic Site
Wildlife Area, Park
Boating, Sailing Activity
Major Forest, Arboretum
Recommended Hotels

Section 1 - The South-West

Avon, Cornwall, Isles of Scilly, Devon, Dorset, Somerset, Wiltshire

Avon

The seafaring city of Bristol lies at the heart of Avon, which is one of England's smallest counties. To the Saxons, the town was known as Bricgstoc, or 'the place by the bridge', and it was fitting, therefore, that, a thousand years later, Isambard Brunel chose this as the site of his famous Clifton suspension bridge, which spans the Avon Gorge. Another of Brunel's achievements is to be found in Bristol Docks, where his SS Great Britain, the world's first ocean-going ship to be built of iron, is open to the public. Do take time, too, to visit Bath, which has been a fashionable spa since Roman times because of its natural hot springs. Bath's exquisite Georgian architecture still remains, so that the city retains much of its eighteenth-century atmosphere.

Cornwall

Cornwall is a county of contrasts. There are the bleak moors of Bodmin and the sheltered waters of the Fal and Helford rivers. Cruel rocks lie cheek-by-jowl with smooth golden sands. On her northern coast, the surf roars almost ceaselessly; on her Riviera, blue-green waters lap lazily shorewards. Cornwall, with its mild climate, has achieved fame as a holiday county: in consequence, if you intend to go there during the height of the season, you are advised to book your accommodation well in advance. Most of our hotel recommendations are to be found beside, or close to, the sea. Most, too, are seasonal hotels, which close from, say, October to Easter, but there are, of course, exceptions and these are well worth seeking out.

Golden Cap Estate, Dorset

Isles of Scilly

So mild is the climate of the Isles of Scilly that exotic plants flourish there which grow nowhere else in the British Isles. This archipelago, consisting of well over 100 islands and islets, is, according to legend, the remnants of Lyonesse, a land ruled over by King Arthur, before it vanished beneath the Atlantic. Today, for birdlovers and botanists, for sea fishermen and those who thrill to the seclusion of small islands, the Isles of Scilly spell paradise. They lie about twenty-eight miles south west of Land's End and can be reached by both sea and air from Penzance.

Devon

Here is a county renowned for junket and cream, for fat ducks and tender chickens. Salmon swim up her rivers and lobster and crab queue up to take their turn in pots. South Devon is best explored in regions: between the Axe and the Exe, in and around Torbay and from Salcombe to Plymouth. The north Devon coastline, which runs between Bideford and Lynmouth, offers a wide array of attractions, for Devon has a hinterland which is full of interest: the scenic attractions of Dartmoor and mid-Devon must not be overlooked.

Dorset

Dorset's real charms are to be found in her magnificent, unspoilt coastline and her rural byways. Do visit, therefore, the sleepy villages, which lie in enfolding arable countryside, and coastal cu-de-sacs such as Worbarrow Bay. The county town is Dorchester, with its many mementos of Thomas Hardy, Dorset's greatest literary genius, who was born in the small hamlet of Higher Bockhampton and died at 'Max Gate', a house designed by himself, on the Wareham road.

Somerset

The name Somerset is Old English and means 'the land of the summer-farm dwellers'. It is known that cave-dwellers took shelter in the Mendip limestone over 12,000 years ago. Generations of Celts followed and they crowned almost every hill in this area with a 'camp'. Then came the Romans, who bisected the Somerset region with the Fosse Way, a military highway which ran from the Channel to the North Sea. It was not until the seventh century that the western extremity of Somerset, the kingdom of Dumnonia, became fully accessible to the 'English'. Here is a county steeped in history: visit the caves at Cheddar and Wookey, the cathedral city of Wells and the mysterious Glastonbury Tor, and you will begin to understand something of its spirit.

Wiltshire

Too many tourists pass through Wiltshire at speed: Amesbury, Marlborough and Stonehenge are but milestones on their journeys. We do urge you, however, to halt awhile at the recommendations in this chapter and to seek out some of the county's attractive villages, such as the Teffonts, Magna and Minor, the Wallops, Over, Middle and Nether, Castle Combe and Lacock. Linger, too, in Salisbury, the county's fascinating centre of religious, military and civic activities.

Section 1: Avon

Bath–Dukes' Hotel
Great Pulteney Street, Bath, Avon. BA2 4DN. Tel 0225 463512. Telex 449227

The splendour of Bath's architecture is exemplified in Great Pulteney Street, a classical Georgian parade without a single building dating from later than the eighteenth century. Dukes' Hotel lies here, zealously preserved both inside and out to offer the quietness and restfulness of a luxurious town house. Note the elegant entrance, the impressive staircase, the restful drawing room and the cosy bar... all appeal to the discerning guests and celebrities who stay here. Preserving our heritage is important, but an hotel, in order to maintain its standards, must ever keep abreast of the times. So, you will find modern notions of comfort at Dukes' Hotel. There is modernness behind the scenes, too, for the kitchens are pristine and the chefs daily prepare home-made soups, pâtés, bread, rolls etcetera, and light lunches and clotted cream teas are features of the daily fare. We have dined in the evening at Dukes' Hotel on terrine of chicken livers and asparagus, and breast of duck served on a bed of leeks. Delicious! Withal, the abiding memory of a visit to Dukes' Hotel is one of having been very well cared for. Resident proprietors, Tim and Rosalind Forester, provide the hotel with both an international and personal touch. As part of their tariff they offer *Daysaway* breaks, which include accomodation, breakfast and dinner for two nights at an excellent rate. And where better to treat yourself to a relaxing break than this lovely Georgian city? There is effectively free parking in the street around the hotel from 4.00pm to 10.00am.

Daily Terms from £80.00 (2 Nights DB&B)
Bed and Breakfast from £50.00
Single/£60.00 Twin/Double
Bar Lunch from £2.50
Dinner 2 course from £11.00, 4 course from £16.00. No Service Charge.

VAT inclusive. Credit Cards—Access, American Express, Visa. 4 Family Rooms. 10 Double, 4 Twin, 4 Single Bedrooms. 18 Private Bathrooms. 3 Private Shower Rooms. All Rooms with TV, Telephone, Radio, Baby-listening, Tea and

Coffee-making Facilities, Trouser Press, Hairdryer. Open all Year. Fully Licensed. Full Central Heating. Cocktail Bar. Conference Facilities. Children catered for. Dogs allowed. Street Parking Facilities. Nearby: Tennis, Croquet, Putting, Squash

Bath—Fountain House Hotel
9-11, Fountain Buildings, Lansdown Road, Bath. BA1 5DV. Tel 0225 338622. Fax 0225 445855

Service-suite accomodation offers more privacy and freedom than an ordinary hotel. It is not a new concept, but rarely have we seen it applied with such panache or so luxuriously as here in Bath. Fountain House stands on Lansdown Road, is a most elegant Georgian building dating from 1735 and a splendid example of the work of Wood the Younger. It has recently undergone a £1.25 million facelift, which has enhanced the original grandeur and added fourteen guest apartments. Each suite is quite outstanding in its comfort and appointments and is so complete you could not wish for better privacy. There are one, two and three bedroom apartments, all *en suite*, with kitchenettes displaying an impressive array of modern appliances and stocked with a gourmet basket of provisions, and exquisitely comfortable sitting-cum-dining rooms equipped with colour television and direct dial telephone. To this must be added five-star services, such as a chambermaid service, morning newspapers on request and a breakfast basket brought to your door just when you want it. The most friendly staff also provide a twenty-four hour valet service, a resident concierge, facsimile, and secretarial services and there is an in-house laundry for guest use, and a lift to all floors. As far as dining out is concerned, the reception will be happy to supply you with a list of all the best places in the city. At Fountain House you can entertain your friends freely in a luxurious apartment which becomes essentially your home. And the welcoming and caring staff are always on hand to pamper you with excellent service.

Bed and Breakfast from £42.00 per person in 2 Bedroom Suite and from £60.00 per person in a 1 Bedroom Suite.
Service Charge and VAT inclusive
Credit Cards—Access, American Express, Diners Club, Visa

8 Family Apartments, 6 Suites
All Suites with Private Bathrooms, TV, Telephone, Radio, Baby-Sitting service, Tea and Coffee-making Facilities, Hairdryer Open all Year. Residential Licence. Full Central Heating

Meeting Facilities. Lift.
Dogs allowed. Parking - lock up garages.
Night Porter
Nearby: Tennis, Croquet, Putting, Squash, Badminton, Swimming, Sauna, Solarium, Golf, Fishing, Riding, Shooting, Ballooning

Section 1: Avon

Bath—The Old Mill Hotel and Restaurant
Tollbridge Road, Bath, Avon. BA1 7DE. Tel 0225 858476

Perhaps more than any other of our historic cities, the fortunes of Bath have been linked with water. Her Roman Baths and Hot Mineral Sprays are unique, whilst the Avon just here is a river of perfection. This ancient Old Mill, now a superb hotel and restaurant, fits perfectly into the scene. It sits on the banks of the Avon, overlooking the mellow stone tollbridge and the weir at Batheaston. With rowing skiffs passing the end of its garden, and flowering trees as a backdrop, the surroundings are a revitalising tonic for the work-weary. Inside the hotel 'the water experience' is continued in the most original of ways. Turn with the wheel in the revolving *Water Wheel Restaurant*, rotating it twice every hour, thus giving guests varied views of the river! This, and the larger *Riverside* restaurant, the *Mill Bar* and lounge, and the intimate *Madeira Room*, provide a rich variety of menus, with many superb specialities. The Old Mill Hotel and Restaurant excels in wedding receptions and private parties for special occasions. There are charming bedrooms, most with river views, the special suites contain four-poster beds, and all the public rooms are spacious and delightfully furnished. Steps lead from the restaurant to the river, where boats pull in, and the hotel will be happy to arrange fishing rights and boating trips for you during you stay. The best compliment we can pay The Old Mill is that it is more than in keeping with the very high standards of Bath as a whole.

Bed and Breakfast from £35.00 (Single)
Bed and Breakfast from £48.00 (Double)
Special short break offers available - booking essential
Bar Lunch from £3.95
Lunch from £7.95 and A La Carte
Dinner from £7.95 and A La Carte

Gratuities at Guest's Discretion. VAT inclusive. Credit Cards—Access, American Express, Visa. 4 Family Rooms. 12 Double/Twin, 1 Single Bedrooms. 10 Private Bathrooms.
5 Private Shower Rooms.
All Rooms with TV, Telephone, Tea and

Coffee-making Facilities.
Open all Year. Fully Licensed.
Full Central Heating. Conference Facilities.
Children catered for. Dogs not allowed.
Parking Facilities. Fishing, Canal and Riverside Walks
Nearby: Boating, Golf

Bristol, Saltford–Brunel's Tunnel House Hotel
High Street, Saltford, Bristol, Avon. BS18 3BQ. Tel 0225 873873

Saltford, should be of interest to you, not because it contains a fine early Georgian Grade II listed building which was once the home of Isambard Kingdom Brunel, but primarily because this house now has become one of the best and most welcoming small hotels in the area. Several well-seasoned travellers who stayed here wrote to us in praise of Brunel's Tunnel House, so when we were next passing through Saltford we tried to engage one of the hotel's bedrooms. There are only seven bedrooms and, as we should have anticipated, they were all occupied. However, the proprietors, Mrs Muriel Mitchell and her daughter, Sarah, made us feel immediately at home and arranged for us to stay for dinner. Here one can enjoy fresh home-cooked food at its very best–traditional English and continental dishes, fresh ingredients, careful presentation and wines supplied by Harveys of Bristol. Even Brunel could not have put on a better repast for his privileged house guests. Nor could the ambiance have been more informal and relaxed than it is today. Before leaving we peeped into some of the bedrooms. They are all *en suite* and have the feminine touch: canopied beds; matching bedspreads and curtains; and welcoming items, such as baskets of fruit, mineral water and bowls of sugared almonds. The public rooms are notable for their antique furniture and accessories, whilst the garden has many shady places.

Special Weekend Rates on Request
Bed and Breakfast from £48.00(Double), £39.00(Single).
Silver Tray Supper from £5.50
Dinner from £14.00 Table D'Hôte
Service Charge and VAT inclusive
Credit Cards—Access, Visa, American Express.

6 Double, 1 Twin Bedrooms
1 Private Bathroom. 6 Private Shower Rooms. All Rooms with TV, Telephone, Radio, Tea and Coffee-making Facilities, Trouser Press, Hairdryer, Fruit Bowl, Sweet Dish, Mineral Water
Open all Year. Residential Licence.
Full Central Heating.

Cocktail Bar. Conference Facilities.
Children catered for.
Dogs allowed by Arrangement.
Parking Facilities
Nearby: Squash, Badminton, Swimming, Solarium, Sauna, Golf, Fishing

Section 1: Avon

Near Bath, Farrington Gurney—Country Ways
Marsh Lane, Farrington Gurney, Avon. BS18 5TT.
Telephone 0761 452449

Country Ways is such a marvellously apt name, we thought, for one of the most charming small hotels we have ever stayed at, for it encapsulates the essence of its attraction. If you occasionally get the feeling that you are personal friends, staying in the owners' private country cottage, it is probably because that is not very far from the truth. The 300 year old farmhouse has been transformed into an attractive and restful country house, which has been tastefully furnished throughout and has individually styled bedrooms. On arrival guests are attended to with the courtesy and care which would quickly erase the fatigue of a hazardous journey. The owners, Gareth and Janet Richards, have all the necessary enthusiasm and ability required to ensure that a stay at Country Ways is a truly relaxing experience. This expertise extends also to the kitchen as Janet is a competent chef, able to offer a wide range of superb dishes which is well supported by a well balanced wine list. All the bedrooms have private bathrooms and are typical of the style and comfort one expects from such a delightful hotel. Afternoon Tea can be enjoyed in the garden room or outside on the patio or lawns and there is also a well stocked bar. The surrounding countryside is surely some of the most beautiful in the county and ideal for those wishing to indulge in enchanting country walks. An excellent brochure is available and it would be wise to make an early booking at Country Ways as it is certain to be extremely popular.

Daily Terms from £85.00 (Double)
Bed and Breakfast from £60.00 (Double)
Dinner from £15.75 and A La Carte
Service Charge and VAT inclusive
Credit Cards—Access, Diners Club, Visa
1 Single, 1 Twin, 4 Double Bedrooms

5 Private Bathrooms
1 Private Shower Room
All Rooms with TV, Telephone, Radio, Tea and Coffee-making Facilities, Hairdryer
Open all Year
Residential and Restaurant Licence

Full Central Heating. Cocktail Bar
Children catered for.
Dogs not allowed
Parking Facilities
Nearby: Tennis, Squash, Swimming, Golf, Fishing

Section 1: Avon

Chelwood, Near Bath–Chelwood House
Chelwood, Avon. BS18 4NH. Tel 0761 490730. Fax 0761 490730 Ext. 504

Inland from the Bristol Channel and close to that scenic stretch of water, Chew Valley Lake, is a gem among small, de luxe hotels. Chelwood House dates from 1681 and, as it stands today, links us with the English renaissance of the arts and architecture. If history makes us wise, here it also makes one rejoice, for the comfort and elegance of this house are profound. Jill and Rudi Birk, their son Karl and their daughter Vanessa, have filled Chelwood House with antiques and excellent furniture and decorated every room in the most restrained manner and have introduced exquisite ornaments and paintings. One hardly needs to be told that above the impressive staircase the bedrooms are all individually styled and are the epitome of comfort. They all contain *en suite* bathrooms, colour television and telephones, and three rooms, styled with either a French, Victorian or Chinese theme, also have four-poster beds and are particularly eye-catching. The hotel has recently introduced a delightful "Restaurant in a Garden"– a conservatory-type dining room with a garden ambience. Chef-patron, Rudi, hails from Southern Bavaria and comes from a long line of experienced caterers. All this experience could not have been put to better effect than it is here. The *cuisine* is excellent cassoulet of seafood, smoked salmon, medallions of beef, fresh turbot in wine and herbs, and lots more, were offered whilst we were there and, of course, Bavarian dishes are a speciality. Highly acclaimed, too, are the home-made sweets, and Chelwood House's extensive breakfast menu, with some interesting and unusual choices.

Weekly Terms on Request
Bed and Breakfast from £75.00 (Double/Twin)
Lunch from £15.50 Table D'Hôte
Dinner from £17.50 and A La Carte
No Service Charge. VAT inclusive

Credit Cards—Access, Diners Club, Visa
1 Family Room. 4 Double, 2 Twin, 1 Single Bedrooms. 6 Private Bathrooms. 2 Private Shower Rooms. All Rooms with TV, Telephone, Tea and Coffee-making Facilities. 4 Rooms with Radio.

Hairdryer on request
Open all Year except Christmas
Residential and Restaurant Licence
Full Central Heating. Children over 10 years catered for. Parking Facilities.
Croquet. Nearby: Fishing, Riding, Sailing

Hunstrete—Hunstrete House
Near Chelwood, Hunstrete, Avon. Tel 0761 490490. Fax 0761 490732

This is truly a country house hotel of charm and elegance. Set in its own ninety-two acre estate this Georgian mansion is ideally situated for those wishing to explore the superb West Country and the historic city of Bath. Hunstrete House has long enjoyed an excellent reputation for both its standard of acommodation and its *cuisine*. Hunstrete House is well endowed with antique furniture, paintings and *objects d'art* and the dining room and library offer a feeling of warmth and wellbeing of the true country house hotel. The restaurant offers a comprehensive and varied menu, many ingredients of which are produced in Hunstrete's own gardens, and is well supported by an extensively stocked cellar. It is much favoured by non-residents as well as those who are fortunate enough to be enjoying a relaxing break. The service, as one would expect from a hotel of this calibre, is extremely efficient and we were left with the impression that the staff with their courteous approach genuinely cared that our all too brief stay was a success. The grounds, with grazing deer and Italian fountain as well as the scenic and tranquil countryside surrounding the estate, provide idyllic walks. There is a tennis court and a swimming pool at the hotel and a lake providing good fishing can be found nearby and golf and riding stables are also in the immediate area.

Bed and Breakfast from £95.00
Lunch from £16.00 and A La Carte
Afternoon Tea from £7.50
Dinner from £29.50 and A La Carte
Gratuities at Guest's Discretion
VAT Inclusive. Credit Cards—Access, Visa
1 Suite. 1 Single, 4 Double, 18 Twin Bedrooms

All Rooms with Private Bathrooms, TV, Telephone, Trouser Press, Hairdryer, Room Service
Open all Year. Fully Licensed
Full Central Heating. Cocktail Bar.
Library. Conference Facilities
Children over 10 years catered for
Guide Dogs only allowed

Parking Facilities
Hard Tennis Court,
Croquet Lawn,
Outdoor Heated Swimming Pool
Nearby: Golf, Fishing, Sailing, Riding, Shooting

Section 1: Avon

Churchill–Winston Manor Hotel
A38, Churchill, Avon. BS19 5NL. Tel 0934 852348

The slopes of the Mendip Hills on a sunny morning are a beautiful sight and, in the evening, the glow as the sun goes down over Blagdon Lake is equally memorable. Churchill village is at the foot of the Mendips and in its centre stands the former manor house, now Winston Manor Hotel. Only some ten minutes' drive from the M5 motorway (junction 21), and in reasonable proximity to good roads leading off in every direction, the hotel is an ideal base from which to explore the West Country. It is owned and personally managed by two ladies - Jill and Marion - whose many years' experience as professional hoteliers allows them to provide a friendly welcome in a relaxed manner. Imaginative menus based on freshly-prepared food make full use of local produce and traditional West Country fare. Sympathetic refurbishment, in keeping with the fine style of the attractive building, make this truly a 'home from home' where one can unwind in comfort. A unique feature, so far as we can recall, is an A-Z brochure detailing at least one location in the area, for every letter of the alphabet, worthy of a visit. Concrete evidence, if any were needed, of the multiple appeal of the Mendips and surrounding countryside. There's something for everyone: the nature-lover, photographer, historian, sportsman, equestrian, pot-holer, balloonist, rambler, steam enthusiast, engineer and craftsman. If you prefer simply to tour round, admiring the views and sampling the local refreshments, be sure to return in good time for the appetising and wholesome dinner at Winston Manor.

Special breaks from £75.00 per person 2 nights (DB&B). Bed and Breakfast from £59.00 (Twin/Double). Carvery Lunch from £9.50. Dinner from £13.95 Table D'Hôte Gratuities at Guest's discretion. VAT inclusive. Credit Cards—Access, American Express, Visa. 1 Family Room. 6 Double, 3 Twin, 5 Single Bedrooms. 7 Private Bathrooms. 7 Private Shower Rooms. All Rooms with TV, Telephone, Radio, Baby-listening, Tea and Coffee-making Facilities. Hairdryer available on request. Open all Year. Residential and Restaurant Licence. Full Central Heating. Cocktail Bar. Conference Facilities. Children catered for. Dogs allowed. Parking Facilities. Nearby: Golf, Fishing, Tennis, Squash, Badminton

Rangeworthy—Rangeworthy Court Hotel
Church Lane, Wotton Road, Rangeworthy, Avon. BS17 5ND. Tel 0454 228347. Fax 0454 228945

Rangeworthy is a small village just 12 miles north of Bristol, a few minutes drive from the M5, M4 and M32, on the B4058 towards Wotton-under-Edge. The seventeenth century former manor house lies off the main road, down Church Lane. Rangeworthy Court is an imposing "L" shaped building with three tall gables in each wing, and standing in 2 acres of well kept gardens. It was built for the family of Lord Chief Justice Sir Matthew Hale and completed in 1664. Many customers remark on the "welcoming" atmosphere of the building with its stone fireplaces, log fires and oak beams; and the relaxed feel of the public rooms, as well as the quiet of its country location. The hotel is family-run and has the facilities to make it as valuable to business visitors as it is relaxing to the holidaymaker. Tariffs for accommodation are at very modest levels for such distinguished surroundings, and the realistic pricing extends to the *table d' hôte* and *à la carte* menus in the 54-place dining-room. Conferences, wedding receptions and weekend/summer breaks are catered for. In addition to the numerous attractions of Bristol, guests at Rangeworthy can enjoy Berkeley Castle, Slimbridge Wildfowl Trust, Westonbirt Arboretum and the many honey-coloured homes in the picturesque Cotswold Hills.

Weekly Terms (DB&B) from £280.00
Daily Terms from £42.00
Bed and Breakfast from £70.00 (Double)
Bar Lunch from £4.00
Lunch from £9.95 Table D'Hôte
Dinner from £16.50 and A La Carte
Gratuities at Guest's Discretion.
VAT inclusive.

Credit Cards—Access, American Express, Diners Club, Visa
10 Double, 2 Twin, 2 Single Bedrooms
6 Private Bathrooms. 8 Private Shower Rooms. All Rooms with TV, Telephone, Tea and Coffee-making Facilities, Hairdryer
Open all Year. Residential and Restaurant Licence. Part Central Heating. Conference Facilities. Children catered for
Dogs allowed. Parking Facilities
Outdoor Heated Swimming Pool
Nearby: Tennis, Squash, Badminton, Swimming, Riding

Section 1: Avon

Weston-super-Mare—The Royal Pier Hotel
Birnbeck Road, Weston-super-Mare, Avon. BS23 2EJ.   Tel 0934 626644

Weston-super-Mare is one of the principal seaside resorts on the south-west coast and has wide, sandy beaches and an esplanade (Marine Parade) which extends for two miles. The Royal Pier Hotel is the only three-star, privately owned and managed establishment to stand at the water's edge and it is also conveniently situated only a short, pleasant walk from the town centre. The hotel's spacious restaurant, with extensive views over the sea, is widely acknowledged as a splendid venue for a special meal out. The decor, furnishing and ambience are most pleasing and there is a well-balanced choice of menus. One can commence one's meal with a pre-dinner *apéritif* in *Kennedy's*, the new cocktail bar. The talented chef chooses carefully from a wide range of traditional roasts and classical dishes, and diets and vegetarian meals can be catered for, if advance notice is given. The professional staff, some of whom have been here for years, give a highly personal service. The friendly *Prince Consort Bar* is a popular meeting place for a drink and here you can also enjoy home-cooked bar meals. The majority of the forty splendidly furnished bedrooms have *en suite* bathrooms and all rooms have colour television, radios, telephones and many have magnificent sea views. For families, there is a children's room. The comfortable public rooms make this a perfect choice, too, for private celebrations, for banquets or for top-level conferences.

Weekly Terms from £287.00
Daily Terms from £57.00
Bed and Breakfast from £46.00
Bar Meals from £2.00
Lunch from £8.25 and A La Carte
Dinner from £12.95 and A La Carte
Gratuities at Guest's Discretion. VAT inclusive. Credit Cards—Access, American Express, Diners Club, Visa. 4 Family Rooms. 2 Suites. 7 Double, 21 Twin, 6 Single Bedrooms. 33 Private Bathrooms. 5 Private Shower Rooms. All Rooms with TV, Telephone, Radio, Tea and Coffee-making Facilities, Trouser Press. Hairdryer and Baby-listening available on request. Open all Year. Fully Licensed. Lift. Cocktail Bar. TV Lounge. Conference Facilities. Children catered for. Dogs not allowed Parking Facilities. Night Porter. Nearby: Tennis, Putting, Squash, Badminton, Swimming, Solarium, Sauna, Golf, Fishing, Riding, Sailing, Windsurfing, Water Skiing, Shooting, Hang-gliding

Nr Weston-super-Mare, Kewstoke—The Commodore Hotel
Beach Road, Sand Bay, Weston-super-Mare, Avon. BS22 9UZ. Tel 0934 415778. Fax 0934 636438

Although only a few minutes' drive away from junction 21 of the M5 motorway, the Commodore nestles peacefully at the foot of Kewstoke Woods, by the beach of unspoilt Sand Bay. Guests feel thoroughly relaxed in this warmly-welcoming hotel, which has associations dating back to four fishermens's cottages in 1663. Original oak beams are sensitively blended into the spacious setting of the charming Commodore's Bar and Carvery. Some nineteen acres of grounds complete an away-from-it-all feeling, at the same time providing a children's play area, gardens, a meadow picnic area and ample parking facilities. Our Inspector describes the hotel as one of 'homely warmth, sensibly furnished, sumptuously victualled and competitively priced'. Most certainly the catering here is outstanding: in quality, choice and readiness to accommodate diners' individual requests. Not that many such requests will be necessary, because there is always available a good proportion of fat-free dishes, a hot vegetarian dish is on offer every day in the carvery and the chef is happy to use low-cholesterol products in grilling foods. Whole fruit sorbets and fresh fruit salad are offered at all times as alternatives to other dessert dishes. Especially commendable is the range and serving-times of light meals for children, coupled with baby-listening by Reception while parents dine. Efficient personal attention is given to individual guests and to business or social parties. Residents receive free toll passes for the scenic roads to Weston-super-Mare.

Weekly Terms from £245.00
Daily Terms from £43.50
Bed and Breakfast from £32.50
Bar Meals from £4.50
Lunch from £5.65 and A La Carte
Dinner from £11.00 and A La Carte VAT inclusive. All major credit cards accepted. 1 Family Room, 1 Suite. 12 Double, 2 Twin, 4 Single Bedrooms 11 Private Bathrooms. 5 Private Shower Rooms. All Rooms with TV, Telephone, Radio, Baby-listening, Tea and Coffee-making Facilities, Hairdryer Open all year. Fully Licensed. Cocktail Bar. TV Lounge. Conference Facilities Children catered for. Dogs not allowed. Parking Facilities. Putting, Golf Net, Children's Adventure Playground.

Section 1: Cornwall

Bude—Bude Haven Hotel
Flexbury Avenue, Bude, Cornwall. EX23 8NS. Tel 0288 352305

In a quiet avenue, with little traffic and no parking problems, this comfortable hotel - built around the turn of the century - overlooks a golf course and is within easy walking distance of the town and Crooklets Beach. Bude itself is an area of unspoilt natural beauty with many sporting diversions and, beside the wide sandy beaches, a large salt-water swimming-pool offering safe, free bathing all day. This part of the coast is renowned for superb surfing and for the miles of scenic cliff-top walks. Bude Haven is owned and run by a family partnership, comprising Roy and Pat Fraser with Gladys Piper (Pat's sister). Guests are assured of a genuine, relaxed welcome and of a new menu for each day's dinner, prepared by the ladies. We have witnessed some notable improvements in the amenities here under the direction of these enthusiastic proprietors. All thirteen bedrooms are fully *en suite* and the *décor* throughout the hotel is designed to complement the wood panelling and the stained glass windows of the hallway and staircase. Our considered assessment of Bude Haven is that, taking into account its location and the many nearby activities, it has an extremely competitive tariff.

Weekly Terms from £186.00
Daily Terms from £29.00
Bed and Breakfast from £21.00
Bar Snacks available
Gratuities at Guest's Discretion.
VAT inclusive.

Credit Cards—Access, American Express, Visa
1 Family Room. 6 Double, 1 Single, 4 Twin Bedrooms. 6 Private Bathrooms. 6 Private Shower Rooms. All Rooms with TV and Tea and Coffee-making Facilities

Hairdryer available on Request
Open all Year. Residential and Restaurant Licence. Full Central Heating. Cocktail Bar TV Lounge. Parking Facilities. Nearby: Tennis, Putting, Squash, Swimming, Golf, Fishing, Riding, Windsurfing

Bude—The Falcon Hotel
Falcon Bridge, Bude, Cornwall. EX23 8SD. Tel 0288 352005

You have a choice here between sixteen *en suite* bedrooms and ten self-catering apartments. Which style of accommodation you choose will be a matter of holiday preference, for all the rooms are exceptionally clean, comfortable and well equipped in their different ways. During this visit to The Falcon we had time only for a meal and sampled an excellent hot smoked trout with salad and *lasagne verdi* with a chopped mixed salad, at a most modest charge. This, too, was a bar lunch: more awaits you for dinner from three chefs. In fact, the *table d' hôte* and *à la carte* menus are also offered to non-residents attracting a good deal of patronage from the locals–always a recommendation. Resident owners Tim and Dorothy Browning have made a number of improvements to the fittings and décor, with the help of a local builder. Bedding, furniture and carpets are all very good quality and obviously chosen with care. For the health-conscious there are in-house sauna and solarium. Each of the self-catering apartments consists of a large lounge, bedroom, kitchen and bathroom. Bude itself, with its picture-book houses, beautiful beaches and eighteen-hole golf courses, has much of interest to encourage several visits. Then, for those who prefer a lazy, peaceful existence, there is much to be said for a comfortable chair in the lounge with a half-closed eye on life on the waters of the Bude canal.

All terms pertain to 1992
Daily Terms from £38.00 (Half Board)
Bed and Breakfast from £25.00
Bar Meals from £1.95
Sunday Lunch from £6.95 and A La Carte
Dinner from £15.00 and A La Carte
Gratuities at Guest's Discretion. VAT inclusive. Credit Cards—Access, American Express, Diners Club, Visa

3 Family Rooms. 7 Double, 4 Twin, 2 Single Bedrooms
11 Private Bathrooms.
5 Private Shower Rooms
All Rooms with TV, Baby-listening, Tea and Coffee-making Facilities, Telephone.
Hairdryer and Ironing Facilities available on Request. Open all Year.
Fully Licensed. Full Central Heating.

Cocktail Bar
Games Room. Conference Facilities
Children catered for. Dogs allowed.
Parking Facilities
Solarium, Sauna.
Nearby: Tennis, Putting, Squash, Swimming, Golf, Fishing, Riding, Sailing, Windsurfing, Water Skiing

Section 1: Cornwall

Bude–Hotel Penarvor   Crooklets Beach, Bude,
Cornwall. EX23 8NE. Tel 0288 352036. Fax 0288 355027

Despite providing all the essentials of a seaside town–firm golden sands, spectacular seas and magnificent coastal scenery–Bude has, to a great extent, avoided the mass inquisitiveness of tourists. Sir John Betjeman described it as the 'least rowdy' of British resorts and brushing, as it does, the kindly Gulf Stream, the unfriendly side of our climate is also minimised. However, the discerning know a thing or two, and many choose the Hotel Penarvor which adjoins Crooklets surfing beach and enjoys panoramic views of coastline and countryside. Leighton and Mair Davies are the owners here. Visitors will find ample parking space in front of the hotel and, within, they will discover spacious and luxuriously furnished public rooms. The bedrooms, all of which have a private bathroom, are also airy and well equipped. *The Crystal Room Restaurant* is eye-catching, with its crystal chandeliers and tasteful furnishings and décor. Here, prime Devon steaks and locally caught lobster feature on the interesting menus, and the wine list, too, has been thoughtfully compiled. The hotel offers the best of both worlds being only fifty yards from the beach and 150 yards from Bude and North Cornwall Golf course where the hotels' guests may enjoy a reduction on the green fees. Many memories will linger with you after a holiday with them, which will include the excellent and liberal catering, the hospitable atmosphere and the delightful grounds.

Weekly Terms from £195.00
Daily Terms from £30.00
Bed and Breakfast from £23.00
Bar Lunch from £1.00
Dinner from £12.50 and A La Carte
Gratuities at Guest's Discretion.
VAT inclusive.
Credit Cards—Access,

American Express, Visa.
2 Family Rooms. 9 Double, 5 Twin Bedrooms. 10 Private Bathrooms. 6 Private Shower Rooms. All Rooms with TV, Telephone, Radio, Baby-listening, Tea and Coffee-making Facilities
Open from March to end October.
Residential and Restaurant Licence

Full Central Heating. Cocktail Bar. Games Room. Conference Facilities. Children catered for. Dogs not allowed. Parking Facilities. Complimentary Mini-Gym, Solarium
Nearby: Tennis, Putting, Squash, Badminton, Swimming, Golf, Fishing, Riding, Sailing, Windsurfing

Carbis Bay–Boskerris Hotel   Boskerris Road, Carbis Bay,
Near St Ives, Cornwall. TR26 2NQ. Tel 0736 795295. Fax 0736 798632

Our overnight stay at this superbly positioned and friendly, family-run hotel was one of the highlights of a recent tour we made through Cornwall. Separated from St Ives by a pleasant cliff walk, the hotel occupies a magnificent position high on a hill, overlooking the bay. Our modernly appointed bedroom overlooking the well-kept garden, and the sea beyond, could not have been more comfortable. The residents' lounge is immaculately decorated, and it was here we enjoyed afternoon tea, before changing for dinner and meeting the owners, the Monk Family, in the welcoming cocktail lounge. Afterwards, we enjoyed a sumptuous dinner in the dining room. Mrs Monk supervises the cooking which is first class, and earned our highest praise, not only for the preparation but also for the efficient manner in which it was served. Open from Easter until early November, and open again at Christmas, you can be as quiet or as active at the Boskerris as your mood dictates. The secluded garden contains a heated swimming pool and riding, tennis, fishing, sailing, swimming and golf are all close at hand. In every way, we feel you will love this spick and span hotel as much as we did–we long to return.

Weekly Terms from £203.50
Daily Terms from £26.00
Bed and Breakfast from £21.00
Bar Lunch from £2.00
Dinner from £16.00
Gratuities at Guest's Discretion. VAT inclusive

Credit Cards–Access, Diners Club, Visa
3 Family Rooms. 7 Double, 6 Twin, 2 Single Bedrooms
16 Private Bathrooms
All Rooms with TV, Telephone, Radio, Baby-listening, Tea and Coffee-making Facilities.

Open from Easter to November, and Christmas
Residential Licence. Full Central Heating Cocktail Bar. TV Lounge. Games Room Children catered for. Dogs allowed Parking Facilities. Putting, Swimming Pool, Golf.

Section 1: Cornwall

Crantock–Crantock Bay Hotel
Crantock, Newquay, Cornwall. TR8 5SE. Tel 0637 830229

One mile beyond the picturesque village of Crantock is one of our most enduring recommendations, the Crantock Bay Hotel, a veritable haven of hospitality. Standing on West Pentire headland and surrounded by four acres of springy, flower-studded turf, the hotel enjoys breathtaking views across the golden sands of Crantock Bay. Guests can admire this sweep of natural beauty from the hotel's sunny terrace; they can continue to gaze on the ocean's ever-changing moods from within the hotel, too, for the majority of the bedrooms and all the public rooms face the bay. Brenda and David Eyles, the resident owners, make families with young children especially welcome and their needs have been thoughtfully foreseen with the provision of cots, high chairs, baby foods and laundering facilities. A recent major refurbishment has now provided an outstanding indoor pool, spa bath, toddlers pool, saunas and games room, and, in response to many visitors who were concerned about the increase in their waistlines, an exercise room. Meals in the bright and spacious restaurant are a high spot of each day, for they are skillfully prepared from only the freshest ingredients, using vegetables, fruit, eggs, and poultry produced on the hotel's land. One could so easily while away a weekend or several weeks at this lovely spot, exploring the unspoilt cliffs, coves and caves which extend east and west of the bay. Indeed, up to five generations of some families have been returning to this hotel for over forty years.

Daily Terms from £33.50
Bed and Breakfast from £23.50
Bar Lunch from £2.00
Dinner from £12.50 Table D'Hôte
Gratuities at Guest's Discretion.
VAT inclusive.
Credit Cards—Access, American Express, Diners Club, Visa

9 Double, 18 Twin, 8 Single Bedrooms
35 Private Bathrooms. All Rooms with TV, Radio, Baby-listening, Tea and Coffee-making Facilities. Hairdryer available on Request
Open from March to November.
Residential and Restaurant Licence
Full Central Heating. Cocktail Bar.

TV Lounge. Games Room. Conference Facilities. Children catered for. Dogs allowed.
Parking Facilities
Hard Tennis Court, Croquet, Putting, Indoor Swimming Pool, Sauna, Spa Bath, Toddlers Pool, Fishing, Windsurfing, Water Skiing

Falmouth–Carthion Hotel
Sea Front, Cliff Road, Falmouth, Cornwall. TR11 4AP. Tel 0326 313669

Falmouth has a dual personality. On one side is its land-locked harbour–considered to be one of the five most beautiful harbours in the world–where yachtsmen flock to the highways of the Fal and Helford rivers and the by-ways of innumerable creeks. Separated from this busy life by the rocky peninsula of Pendennis Point is the bay, which gives little hint of the activity of the town behind, and to all appearances might be many miles from such a commercial centre. The Shaw family has been here for some years, drawing a faithful clientele to the Carthion Hotel, which is situated on Cliff Road directly overlooking the sands and waters of the bay. We were so pleasantly received here and well served with lunch in a congenial lounge and dining-room, which provide picture-window views across the well-manicured sub-tropical garden out to the open sea. A complete tour of this welcoming and comfortable hotel was sufficient to explain why so many holidaymakers return year after year to the Carthion and how they must be loath to leave. Because of the hotel's position, it is a case of the higher one is, the better the view, and the south-facing bedrooms are, therefore, especially delightful. All the bedrooms have *en suite* bathrooms, central heating, radio/alarms, tea and coffee-making facilities and televisions. Where is the best place to stay in Falmouth? There are many best' places, but the Carthion has become the favourite hotel for many visitors to this popular resort.

Terms on Application
Gratuities at Guest's Discretion. VAT inclusive
Credit Cards—Access, American Express, Diners Club, Visa
10 Double, 6 Twin, 2 Single Bedrooms
All Rooms with Private Bath/Shower

Room, TV, Radio, Tea and Coffee-making Facilities
Open from March to October. Residential and Restaurant Licence
Full Central Heating. Cocktail Bar
Children over 10 years catered for. Dogs allowed by Arrangement

Parking Facilities.
Nearby: Tennis, Putting, Squash, Badminton, Swimming, Solarium, Sauna, Golf, Fishing, Riding, Sailing, Windsurfing, Water Skiing

Section 1: Cornwall

Falmouth–Green Lawns Hotel Western Terrace, Falmouth, Cornwall. TR11 4QJ. Tel 0326 312734. Fax 0326 211427

Whilst many Falmouth hotels crane their necks to obtain a view of the sea, Green Lawns, situated between the main beaches and the town, commands a fine vista of Falmouth Bay. The original house, which has Chateau-like spires, was once the home of Colonel Carne VC and *The Carnes Bar* displays momentos of that era. The name 'Green Lawns' is certainly appropriate! Our lunch here was excellent, the Garden Terrace was a cool, shady spot and the lawns, vivid flower beds and flowering shrubs were a magnificent sight. It was all so utterly restful, yet we did not have to look far for recreation. Within the hotel is the *Garras Leisure Club*-a large indoor heated swimming pool, a jacuzzi, a sauna, a solarium and a mini-gymnasium. Adjacent is the *Falmouth Club*, which provides tennis, squash and billiards. The Green Lawns employs eight chefs, who, between them, produce the numerous mouthwatering specialities which feature on the *table d'hôte* and *à la carte* menus. The *Garras Restaurant* which was extended in 1990, has been completely refurbished and the decor has been tastefully undertaken by an interior designer. The chefs are as adept at preparing a gourmet meal for one as they are at catering for 220 conference delegates and the *cuisine* is complemented by one of the finest wine lists in this part of Cornwall. The bedrooms reflect the high standards one sees throughout the hotel. New additions to the bedrooms are two new Honeymoon Suites with traditional four-poster beds and double jacuzzi spa-baths, as also is a new Executive Suite with jacuzzi spa-bath.

Weekly Terms (Half Board) from £300.00
Bed and Breakfast from £33.00
Bar Meal from £3.25
Lunch from £9.50 and A La Carte
Dinner from £17.00 and A La Carte
Credit Cards—Access, American Express,

Diners Club, Visa. 8 Family Rooms. 14 Double, 13 Twin, 5 Single Bedrooms 37 Private Bathrooms. 3 Private Shower Rooms. All Rooms with TV, Telephone, Radio, Baby-listening, Tea and Coffee-making Facilities, Hairdryer.

Trouser press available on request Open from 31st December to 24th December. Fully Licensed. Full Central Heating. 2 Cocktail Bars. Conference Facilities. Children catered for. Dogs allowed. Parking Facilities. Night Porter.

Falmouth—Penmere Manor Hotel Mongleath Road, Falmouth, Cornwall. TR11 4PN. Tel 0326 211411. Fax 0326 317588

When we are asked which qualities constitute an Ashley Courtenay recommended hotel we can do no better than quote Penmere Manor, for it seems to contain them all. Housed in an elegant Georgian country house and set in five acres of garden, woodland and palm trees, it reflects the personal pride of its owners, the Pope family. Since they acquired the hotel in 1969, each year has revealed further improvements. The Fountain Leisure Club (1987), one of the most luxurious we have seen, offers indoor pool, spa, sauna and mini-gym, also outside Giant Chess, croquet and a woodland fitness trail. The outdoor heated pool, open from May to September, is sited within the old walled garden, reputedly built by French prisoners of war. There is also an unusual cellar games room for the young, and the not so young, to play table tennis, darts and billiards. The bedrooms, whether in the original house or the modern wing, are certainly above average in their decor and appointment, and the Garden rooms offer superior size and facilities. We had nothing but praise for our dinner, chosen from a menu which has been carefully compiled. Because of Falmouth's exceptionally temperate climate and the hotel's position, overlooking Falmouth Bay and well sheltered by woodlands, Penmere Manor is especially suitable for early and late vacations.

Weekly Terms from £378.00
Daily Terms from £54.00
Bed and Breakfast from £40.00
Bar Lunch from £3.00
Dinner from £18.00 Table D'Hôte
No Service Charge. VAT inclusive
Credit Cards—Access, American Express, Diners Club, Visa
3 Family Rooms. 8 Double, 6 Twin,

10 Single Bedrooms. 12 Superior Double/Twin/Family Bedrooms 33 Private Bathrooms. 6 Private Shower Rooms. All Rooms with TV, Telephone, Radio, Baby-listening, Tea and Coffee-making Facilities, Hairdryer. 15 Rooms with Trouser Press Open all Year except Christmas

Fully Licensed. Full Central Heating. Cocktail Bar. Games Room. Conference Facilities. Children catered for. Dogs allowed. Parking Facilities. Croquet, Swimming Pool, Solarium, Sauna, Jacuzzi, Mini Gym. Nearby: Tennis, Putting, Squash, Golf, Fishing, Sailing, Windsurfing

Section 1: Cornwall

Falmouth–The Royal Duchy Hotel.
Cliff Road, Falmouth, Cornwall. TR11 4NX. Tel 0326 313042. Fax 0326 319420

There is a certain sameness about our leading seaside resorts, where the daily round centres upon the beaches, the promenades and the piers. Falmouth is an exception to this pattern, for, although its harbour and shopping centre are as busy as other towns in the height of the season, its uncrowded beaches, which lie beyond the rocky peninsula of Pendennis Point, are a joy to those who seek the unspoilt peace of sea and sand. It is hardly surprising, therefore, that most of Falmouth's premier hotels are to be found behind these south-facing sands and, of these, none is better sited than the long-established Royal Duchy Hotel. From the hotel's flower-decked terraces the views of one of Cornwall's loveliest bays are totally unrestricted, and the beaches lie just 100 yards from the doorstep. Brend Hotels, who own this and eight other leading West Country hotels, demand exacting standards in all their establishments and The Royal Duchy has recently been given a complete refit. Every bedroom now has *en suite* facilities and has been equipped in the modern manner. An indoor leisure complex has been added, which incorporates an impressive heated swimming pool, a sauna and solarium, a spa bath and a fitness area. Never before has the hotel enjoyed such a year-round appeal. The standards upon which The Royal Duchy has built its good reputation have never been more impressive than now. For the complete story, write to Mr D Reburn, the Manager.

Weekly Terms from £270.00 to £470.00 Bed and Breakfast from £43.00 Lunch from £9.00 and A La Carte Dinner from £15.00 and A La Carte Gratuities at Guest's Discretion. VAT inclusive. Credit Cards—Access, American Express, Diners Club, Visa

9 Family Rooms. 1 Suite. 18 Double, 20 Twin, 7 Single Bedrooms All Rooms with Private Bath/Shower Room, TV, Telephone, Radio, Baby-listening, Hairdryer. Open all year. Fully Licensed. Full Central Heating. Lift. 2 Cocktail Bars. TV Lounge.

Games Room. Conference Facilities. Dogs not allowed. Parking Facilities. Night Porter Putting, Indoor Swimming Pool, Solarium, Sauna, Spa Bath, Windsurfing Nearby: Tennis, Squash, Golf, Riding, Sailing, Water Skiing, Parascending, Jet Skiing, Water Bicycling, Canoeing

Falmouth–St Michael's & Falmouth Beach Hotels
Gyllyngvase Beach, Seafront, Falmouth. TR11 4NB. Tel 0326 312707/318084. Fax 0326 319147

What better place to unwind than the St Michael's & Falmouth Beach Hotels? There are 158 rooms, many of which have balconies with stunning views across the beautiful Cornish coast, and for those who prefer not to climb stairs, ground floor accommodation and lifts are available. All guests will find private bathrooms, colour television, radio, telephone and tea/coffee making facilities at their disposal. Suites and self-catering apartments, with full use of the hotels' services and amenities, are another option at these hotels. The brigades of chefs offer a wide spectrum of *cuisine* including vegetarian, on a daily basis. Special diets are no problem either, providing prior notice is given. For those who have come to pamper themselves, there is free membership of the 'Club St Michael's' and use of the aqua spas and sauna. For the more energetic, there is a gymnasium, reduced green fees at the local golf course, squash and watersports in this sailing and yachting haven. For those who enjoy the invigorating fresh air, there are beautiful walks in the area or in the hotels' three acre award winning gardens. One could not ask for a better location right on the beach and ten minutes' stroll from the heart of Falmouth. There are many delightful places to visit on excursions away from the town. An ideal location then for all the family, with baby-listening service and special childrens' activities organised during the high season..

Weekly Terms from £360.00 (DB&B) Daily Terms from £60.00 (DB&B) Bed and Breakfast from £47.00 Bar Lunch from £2.95 Lunch £6.90 Table D'Hôte Afternoon Tea from £2.25 Dinner from £16.00 Table D'Hôte No Service Charge. VAT inclusive Credit Cards—Access, American Express,

Diners Club, Visa 35 Family Rooms/Suites. 4 Self-catering Apartments. 89 Double/Twin, 36 Single Bedrooms All Rooms with Private Bathroom, TV with Video Channel, Telephone, Radio, Tea and Coffee-making Facilities, Baby-listening, Hairdryer, Trouser Press. Open all Year. Fully Licensed.

Full Central Heating. Cocktail Bar. Games Room. Conference Facilities. Children catered for. Dogs allowed. Parking Facilities. Night Manager Indoor Swimming Pool, Solarium, Sauna, Jacuzzi, Gymnasium, Beauty Salon, Windsurfing, Water Skiing Nearby: Tennis, Squash, Golf, Fishing, Riding, Sailing

Section 1: Cornwall

Near Falmouth, Mawnan Smith–Meudon Hotel
Mawnan Smith, Near Falmouth, Cornwall TR11 5HT
Tel 0326 250541. Fax 250543

For many years this showpiece hotel has been one of our first loves in Cornwall. Meudon lies between the estuaries of the Fal and Helford rivers in thickly wooded countryside. Along the stretch of Falmouth Bay known as Bream Cove nature has fashioned a secluded beach, which opens out from the foot of Meudon's show gardens. In the seventeenth century two coastguard's cottages were built at the head of this valley and, later, these were to be incorporated within the structure of Meudon Hotel–Cornwall's highest rated country house hotel. As a finishing touch, Meudon's eight and a half acres of grounds were landscaped in the eighteenth century by 'Capability' Brown. The setting for this luxury hotel is, therefore, unusually beautiful: rare flowering shrubs, giant rhododendrons and azaleas, eucalyptus, magnolia, camellia, banana and flame trees sweep down to the private beach. Meudon was still a private mansion when Mr and Mrs Harry Pilgrim began developing it into an hotel. With the help of their family they have transformed Meudon into a unique and most superior establishment. All bedrooms are en suite and individually furnished to a very high standard. The cuisine is described as 'English at its best'. It is certainly never less than sublime, with most produce being purchased from local farms and fishermen. Guests can try their own angling skills or swim and sail undisturbed. Meudon Hotel is open from February to November for those who like to feast on superb comfort, food, service and seclusion.

All Terms pertaining to 1992
Special 3 Day Breaks in spring and autumn
Weekly Terms from £415.00. Daily Terms from £60.00
Bed and Breakfast from £45.00
Lunch from £8.00 and A La Carte
Table D'Hôte Dinner £18.00 and A La Carte
Gratuities at Guest's Discretion.
All Terms are VAT inclusive

Credit Cards—Access, Diners Club, Visa
2 Balcony Suites, 2 Single Suites. 26 Double/Twin Bedrooms
All Rooms with Private Bath/Shower Room, TV, Telephone, Radio, Hairdryer, Trouser Press.
Tea and Coffee-making Facilities available on Request
Open from February to November

Residential and Restaurant Licence
Full Central Heating. Cocktail Bar. Children over 5 years are welcome. Dogs are welcome by arrangement. Parking Facilities. Golf (Complimentary), Fishing, Riding, Sailing, Windsurfing, Snorkelling Nearby: Tennis, Putting, Squash, Badminton, Swimming, Solarium, Sauna, Sailing, Windsurfing, Water Skiing

Section 1: Cornwall

Near Falmouth, Mawnan Smith—Trelawne Hotel
Mawnan Smith, Cornwall. TR11 5HS. Tel 0326 250226. Fax 0326 250909

Although the Trelawne is part of the Hospitality Hotels of Cornwall group, it has been owned and personally managed by the Gibbons family since 1972. Obviously there have been considerable changes over these years, but in the last eighteen months alone the improvements are substantial. All the bedrooms are now *en suite* and, together with the restaurant, lounges, bar and dining-room, they have been completely upgraded and re-decorated. Standing in two acres of open grounds, the hotel makes good use of its location by providing picture windows in the lounges and dining-room: most of the bedrooms have seaward views. Grant Mather, chef at the Trelawne, was trained at the Dorchester Hotel in London and for the past two years has won top honours at the Expo West Salon Culinaire. Guests can choose from comprehensive English and Continental menus and be assured of varied, wholesome and appetising fare. Within the hotel there is a heated swimming-pool and a games room with billiards, table-tennis and darts available. Mawnan Smith is only three miles from the manifold attractions of Falmouth, which include Pendennis Castle, and there is the charm of a seal sanctuary close to the Helford River estuary, a little beyond the notorious Frenchman's Creek. The Trelawne is actively involved in, and ideally situated for, Cornwall's annual Spring Gardens Festival which has become a major event in the county over the past two years.

Weekly Terms from £280.00
Bed and Breakfast from £42.00
Bar Lunch from £2.50
Afternoon Tea from £1.80
Dinner from £17.50 and A la Carte
Gratuities at Guest's Discretion.
VAT inclusive.
Credit Cards—Access, American Express,

Diners Club, Visa
1 Family Room. 6 Double, 1 Single, 6 Twin Bedrooms. All Rooms with Private Bath/Shower Room, TV, Telephone, Radio, Baby-listening, Tea and Coffee-making Facilities, Hairdryer. 8 Rooms with Trouser Press.
Open from March to end of December.

Residential and Restaurant Licence. Full Central Heating. Cocktail Bar
Games Room. Children catered for. Dogs allowed. Parking Facilities
Putting, Indoor Swimming Pool
Nearby: Golf, Fishing, Riding, Sailing, Windsurfing, Water Skiing

Nr Falmouth, Penjerrick—'The Home' Country House Hotel
Penjerrick, Nr Falmouth, Cornwall. TR11 5EE. Tel 0326 250427/250143

If you are looking for a home from home for your holiday at most reasonable prices, may we introduce you to the actual home of Mr and Mrs A Tremayne. Since 1962, the Tremaynes have been welcoming guests to their doors and the name of their house is no modern-day gimmick as it was called 'The Home' when it was first built in 1872. Today, it offers you and your family a friendly stay with comfortable bedrooms and a large lounge with colour television and a friendly dining-room. Leading off the dining-room is a large sun lounge, and the whole is furnished and carpeted to a high standard. In fact, after our last visit, the thought foremost in our minds was that The Home was one of the most welcoming and delightful places we had visited. Mrs Tremayne personally supervises the full English breakfasts and the table d'hôte dinners that offer good country fare at its best. Outside, there is a large sheltered garden and, for those who do not drive, a daily bus service stops right outside the gate from where you can easily reach the Helford River 'villages' and Falmouth itself, which is but two and a half miles away. The Home is set in unspoilt countryside and within eighteen minutes' walk is Maenporth, one of the most beautiful and safe bathing beaches in Cornwall. Here is a perfect spot for early and late holidays and we suggest you write for the brochure and complete list of directions. The visitors' book is a testimonial in itself of the many satisfied guests.

Weekly Terms from £130.00 per person
Daily Terms from £25.00 (Half Board)
Bed and Breakfast from £17.50
Packed Lunch available on Request
Dinner from £10.00 Table D'Hôte
Gratuities at Guest's Discretion.

VAT inclusive. 2 Family Rooms. 9 Suites. 4 Double, 2 Twin, 2 Single Bedrooms
5 Private Bathrooms. 5 Private Shower Rooms. All Rooms with Tea and Coffee-making Facilities
Open from March to October

Residential Licence. Part Central Heating TV Lounge. Children over 6 years catered for. Dogs allowed by Arrangement. Parking Facilities. Nearby: Tennis, Putting, Squash, Swimming, Solarium, Sauna, Golf, Fishing, Riding, Sailing, Windsurfing, Water Skiing

Section 1: Cornwall

Fowey—Carnethic House
Fowey, Cornwall. PL23 1HQ. Tel 0726 83 3336

An informal and friendly atmosphere here seems wholly appropriate for the peaceful, rural setting. David and Trisha Hogg's completely modernised large Georgian Estate House stands in beautifully maintained gardens, bordered by mature trees and shrubs. Tranquil surroundings in which to sit and relax, play a game of bowls, badminton, putting or croquet on the lawns. Freshen-up with a swim in the heated outdoor pool and take a short walk through the gardens to a winding leafy lane down to the beach. Enjoy the bustling quay-side activity or explore the coastal paths extending east and west. This is an area abounding with scenic and historic places to be visited on foot or by car and, at Carnethic House, the proprietors are always delighted to advise on routes to suit your personal preferences. Sporting attractions naturally include sailing, surfing, windsurfing, fishing and golf. A number of museums and gardens can be visited and there is a Woolley Monkey Sanctuary east of Looe, the Paul Corin Musical Collection at St Keyne and slate caverns at Ley. The informal atmosphere is most appealing; we thoroughly enjoyed an excellent *table d' hôte* dinner and found everywhere to be spotlessly clean. Most bedrooms have *en suite* bath or shower and all have television and tea and coffee-making facilities. There is ample parking space for cars and boats. Considering the charm of Fowey itself and the magnificent waterfront, Carnethic House has a tariff offering quite exceptional value for money.

Weekly Terms (Half Board) from £210.00
Daily Terms from £32.00
Bed and Breakfast from £20.00
Bar Lunch from £1.00
Dinner from £12.50 Table D'Hôte
Service Charge and VAT inclusive
Credit Cards—Access, American Express.

Diners Club, Visa. 2 Family Rooms. 4 Double, 1 Twin, 1 Single Bedroom.
7 Private Shower Rooms
All Rooms with TV, Radio, Tea and Coffee-making Facilities, Hairdryer.
Baby-listening available on Request
Open from February to November inclusive
Residential Licence. Full Central Heating

Cocktail Bar. Children catered for. Dogs allowed by Arrangement. Parking Facilities. Grass Tennis Court., Croquet, Putting. Badminton. Outdoor Swimming Pool.
Nearby: Squash, Sauna, Golf, Fishing Riding, Sailing, Windsurfing, Water Skiing, Shooting, Walking

Fowey–Marina Hotel
Esplanade, Fowey, Cornwall. PL23 1HY. Tel 0726 833315

Fowey is a unique place, with its natural harbour, sheltered position and deep waters which can still allow ocean-going ships to mingle with the ever-present sailing craft. The town is a web of narrow streets and quaint old buildings. The Marina Hotel was originally built for the Bishops of Truro and, because of its lovely position, we wager they dubbed it 'a little slice of heaven'! From the hotel the views of the estuary and the small craft bobbing at anchor are quite exceptional. Whenever we dine here we try, if possible, to obtain a window seat, for such a vista enhances any meal. We were greatly impressed with the welcome we received from the resident owners, David and Sheila Johns, and were delighted with the dinner prepared by their talented Chef Simon Trethewey. Their *table d' hôte* and *à la carte* dishes attract many non-residents and, we suspect, a fair number of guests from other hotels. If your holiday objective is to exchange a steering wheel for a tiller, you will be interested to learn that at the hotel an outside stairway leads to a secluded walled garden and moorings are available for the use of guests. The hotel has been completely refurbished and all the bedrooms have *en suite* facilities. Each room is attractively decorated and the soft furnishings include many of the delightful spring collections. In one of the rooms four marble pillars were discovered having been 'walled up' for over half a century. These now adorn the bedroom in which they were found.

Special rates for two or more nights (DB&B)
Weekly Terms from £285.00
Daily Terms from £42.00
Bed and Breakfast from £25.00
Bar Lunch from £2.00
Dinner from £15.50 and A La Carte
Gratuities at Guest's Discretion. VAT inclusive. Credit Cards—Access, American

Express, Diners Club, Visa
6 Double, 5 Twin Bedrooms
9 Private Bathrooms. 2 Private Shower Rooms. All Rooms with TV, Telephone, Radio, Baby-listening, Tea and Coffee-making Facilities. Hairdryer and Iron available on Request.
Open from March to November

Residential and Restaurant Licence. Full Central Heating. Cocktail Bar.
Conference Facilities
Children catered for. Dogs allowed.
Night Porter. Fishing, Sailing, Windsurfing
Nearby: Tennis, Swimming, Golf, Fishing, Riding, Sailing, Windsurfing, Water Skiing

Section 1: Cornwall

Fowey, Bodinnick-by-Fowey–The Old Ferry Inn
Bodinnick-by-Fowey, Cornwall. PL23 1LX. Tel 0726 870237

For 400 years, The Old Ferry Inn has stood at the edge of Fowey estuary in the picturesque hamlet of Bodinnick, extending a warm welcome to hungry and weary travellers. For the past twenty years, this comfortable inn has been a family-run concern, in the capable hands of Simon and Christine Farr. On entering the bar, we discovered a veritable treasure-house of antiques of a nautical kind–cutlasses, paintings, prints, ships' wheels, anchors, ancient navigating instruments and even some stuffed sea trout, which are enclosed in glass cases! We dined superbly in the elegant dining-room, where locally caught seafood is a speciality. The *table d'hôte* menu is changed daily and includes such choices as baked prawns, smoked mackerel pancakes or trout sautéd with orange and lemon juice. There is also a small *à la carte* menu containing scallops poached in white wine and fish sauce and other fresh fish delicacies, as available. There are five bedrooms in the original building and a further seven in a modern extension and all of them are very comfortable and spotlessly clean. Also in the new extension is a pleasant lounge with a patio terrace, and from here guests can enjoy lovely views across the Fowey estuary and out to sea. Noted especially for its friendly service and beautiful setting, The Old Ferry Inn is a truly delightful place in which to sojourn.

Weekly Terms from £305.00
Daily Terms from £46.00
Bed and Breakfast from £33.00
Bar Meal from £1.20
Afternoon Tea from £1.50
Dinner from £17.00 and A La Carte
Gratuities at Guest's Discretion.
VAT inclusive

Credit Cards—Visa, Access
1 Family Room. 4 Double, 6 Twin Bedrooms (Doubles can be let as Singles)
8 Private Bathrooms.
1 Private Shower Room
11 Rooms with TV
Open from March to October (Plus February and November B&B only)

Fully Licensed. Cocktail Bar
TV Lounge. Night Storage Heating and Convectors
Children catered for. Dogs allowed
Parking Facilities
Nearby: Golf, Fishing, Riding, Sailing, Windsurfing, Water Skiing,
Mooring can be arranged

Golant by Fowey–The Cormorant Hotel and Riverside Restaurant
Golant by Fowey, Cornwall PL23 1LL. Tel 0726 833426. Fax 0726 833426

Golant by Fowey is an unspoilt village with an accent on fishing, and with several outdoor sports available locally. Within a short drive there are many lovely secluded beaches and sandy coves, and the Cornish Coastal Path offering breathtaking walks. Situated high above the very beautiful Fowey Estuary, but close to it, the Cormorant Hotel affords magnificent views over the river from every bedroom, from the lounge and from the splendid swimming pool. Situated even higher than the hotel, the pool is heated all the year round, has full depth windows, a surrounding sun terrace, and a motor-driven sliding roof for hot summer days. This is an independent hotel, where resident proprietors Geoffrey Buckle and Sharon Thompson work closely with their French chef, Gilles Gaucher, to provide excellent *cuisine* with an emphasis on fresh produce especially sea fish and homecooked fare including bread, pasta, ice-cream, and marmalade. Complementing the food, served in a charming candle-lit dining room, is a wine list of quite exceptional distinction and variety, including one complete page devoted to half bottles and another to first growth and other top quality wines for connoisseurs. One's enjoyment here is completed by the relaxed atmosphere and the tranquil setting: a central location from which to explore the manifold charms of Cornwall. From each excursion, take renewed pleasure in returing to the Cormorant, with comprehensive amenities in every *en suite* bedroom.

Weekly Terms from £315.00 per person
Daily Terms from £50.00 per person
Bed and Breakfast from £36.00 (Sharing), £51.00 (Single)
Bar Lunch from £3.50
Light Luncheon A La Carte available
Dinner from £21.50 and A La Carte
Gratuities at Guest's Discretion. VAT inclusive. Credit Cards-Access, Visa

7 Double, 4 Twin Bedrooms
All Rooms with Private Bathroom, TV, Telephone, Radio, Baby-listening, Tea and Coffee-making Facilities, Hairdryer Trouser Press on request. Full Room Service. Open all year
Residential and Restaurant Licence

Full Central Heating. Cocktail Bar
Small Conference Facilities
Children over 12 years catered for. Dogs allowed. Parking Facilities
Indoor Swimming Pool, Fishing, Scenic Walks. Riding, Sailing and Windsurfing by special arrangement. Nearby: Tennis, Squash, Badminton, Golf, Water Skiing

Section 1: Cornwall

The Lizard, Housel Bay–Housel Bay Hotel
Housel Cove, The Lizard, Cornwall. TR12 7PG. Tel 0326 290417

It is always a delight to travel through the 'heel' of Cornwall, that high plateau of countryside south of the Helford River which meets the sea abruptly in a series of rocky headlands and sandy coves. The whole area is generally known as The Lizard, although the village of the name and the famous Lizard Point lie in the region's southernmost tip. Here you will find the Housel Bay Hotel, which has the distinction of being the most southerly two-star hotel in Britain. It has an elevated position, with well-kept gardens stretching to cliff land, which in turn gives access to a safe, sheltered, sandy beach. The hotel looks most attractive, for the owners, Freda and Derek Oswald, have recently completed a great deal of decorating and refurnishing of the restaurant, the lounges and the bedrooms. Recent additions are the installation of a lift and satellite television is now broadcast to all rooms. They have also engaged two very good chefs and offer *à la carte* as well as *table d'hôte* meals, with the accent on freshly prepared food. A paved terrace overlooking the ocean has recently been added on which teas and lunches may be served. To us, Housel Bay seems an excellent choice for a carefree, relaxing holiday. If you feel the need to unwind, a few days at Housel Bay Hotel, spent taking in the spectacular views and watching the coasters and ocean liners rounding Lizard Point, would be just the panacea you seek. An added bonus is the *Cornish Coastal Path*, which runs through the hotel's grounds. All the hotel's bedrooms have *en suite* facilities and are most comfortably furnished and, if you can turn your eyes away from the breathtaking views, you will note the attention to detail throughout the hotel.

Weekly Terms from £250.00
Daily Terms from £41.00
Bed & Breakfast from £25.00.
Bar Lunch from £5.00. Lunch from £8.00 and A La Carte. Bar Supper from £5.00

Dinner from £16.00 and A La Carte
Gratuities at Guest's Discretion. VAT inclusive. Credit Cards—Access, Visa
2 Four-poster Rooms, 11 Double, 8 Twin, 4 Single Bedrooms. 19 Private Bathrooms. 4

Private Shower Rooms. All Rooms with TV, Telephone, Radio, Tea and Coffee-making Facilities, Baby-listening. 14 Rooms with Hairdryer. Open from 12th Feb to 31st Dec Fully Licensed. 2 Cocktail Bars. TV Lounge

Looe—Fieldhead Hotel
Portuan Road, Hannafore, Cornwall. PL13 2DR. Tel 0503 262689. Fax 0503 264114

Should you elect to visit Looe, you must determine whether it is to be East or West Looe, for the two are separated by the river, which motorists can only cross by means of the Victorian seven-arched bridge lying well to the rear of the town. East Looe, by reason of its sandy bay and banjo-shaped pier, attracts the day visitors. If you want to stay in Looe, however, most of the good hotels are on the west bank and rise above the sea on Hannafore Point. One of the very best is the Fieldhead. With its foundations carved out of the rocky hillside, there is a pleasing solidity about this hotel. Yet, there is certainly nothing oppressively heavy. Inside it is light, bright and beautifully furnished. It was built at the turn of the century as a large family home and the original owners certainly knew how to pick their position. The views are quite outstanding from here, but, such is the terrain that the house and sloping grounds are on the same level. Around the heated swimming pool or in the well-stocked gardens, you will find invariably a sunny spot which is sheltered too. The views within are equally inviting. A pleasant bar, an elegant and comfortable lounge, a candlelit restaurant–each has individual appeal, yet they all share that marvellous eye-catching outlook over Looe Bay. It is clear that the hotel has recently undergone an enormous amount of refurbishment and that the owners, Pat and Bryan Norman, have been satisfied with only the highest standards. The bedrooms have either a private bathroom or shower. The food is first class and the friendliness is profound.

Weekly Terms from £160.00 (B&B)/£260.00 (DB&B). Daily Terms from £38.00
Bed and Breakfast from £25.00
Bar Lunch from £2.50
Dinner £12.95 from an A La Carte selection
Gratuities at Guest's Discretion. VAT

inclusive. Credit Cards—Access, American Express, Visa. 2 Family Rooms. 8 Double, 3 Twin, 1 Single Bedrooms. 12 Private Bathrooms. 2 Private Shower Rooms. All Rooms with Telephone, TV, Radio, Baby-listening, Tea and Coffee-making

Facilities. Open from February to December (incl Christmas). Residential and Restaurant Licence. Cocktail Bar. Games Room. Children over 5 years catered for. Dogs not allowed. Parking Facilities. Outdoor Swimming Pool

Section 1: Cornwall

Near Looe, Lanreath–The Punch Bowl Inn
Lanreath, Near Looe, Cornwall. PL13 2NX. Tel 0503 220218

Fowey, Looe and Polperro are all within hail of what can be described as a perfect inn–The Punch Bowl at Lanreath. Dubbed by one enthusiast as, 'a friendly old-world hostelry in a picturebook village', The Punch Bowl has a history of hospitality which stretches from 1620, the year in which it was first licensed. To the best of our knowledge, this is the only inn in Great Britain where the bars and the kitchens are licensed, resulting in such names as *The Farmers' Kitchen* (the snug), *The Men's Kitchen* (the bar) and *The Visitors' Kitchen* (the lounge) among others. You will also discover *The Lovers' Nook* and *The Priests' Hideout*. The Inn is now open all the year round. We are delighted to hear it, for the inn's huge fireplaces, central heating and cheerful old-world atmosphere will make it especially inviting on cold days. Bountiful fare, which was always connected with the hostelries of yester-year, is also one of The Punch Bowl's strong suits. Home-produced food and Cornish delicacies have made the dining room a popular venue with local communities and Real Ales are available in the Bars. Like the rest of the hotel, the bedrooms are full of character and some have four-poster beds. The Inn is conveniently situated close to the sea and course fishing and within thirty minutes drive of St Mellion and four other golf courses. Special three and seven day breaks are available.

Weekly Terms from £112.00	3 Holiday Cottages to let. 3 Family Rooms.	Open all year
Daily Terms from £18.50	6 Double, 2 Twin, 3 Single Bedrooms	Fully Licensed. Full Central Heating
Bar Lunch from £2.00	12 Private Bathrooms.	TV Lounge. Children catered for.
Dinner from £9.95 and A La Carte	2 Private Shower Rooms	Dogs allowed
Gratuities at Guest's Discretion.	All Rooms with TV, Tea and Coffee-making	Parking Facilities
VAT inclusive	Facilities. Radio and Hairdryer available on	Nearby: Tennis, Golf, Fishing
Credit Cards—Access, Visa	Request	

Near Looe, Talland Bay–Talland Bay Hotel
Talland Bay, Near Looe, Cornwall. PL13 2JB. Tel 0503 72667

So deliciously removed is this Cornish country house by the sea from the main stream of life that it can be difficult to find. Steep, narrow lanes run down from the A387 road between Looe and Polperro. One of these–actually quite clearly marked 'Talland Bay Hotel'–leads one to the hotel and, just beyond, to a tranquil beach flanked by headlands which rise to more than 300 feet. The house, parts of which date from the sixteenth century, seems perfectly designed for its holiday purpose. Blue-green Cornish sea and bracken-covered slopes complete the picture. Here, in short, is to be found restfulness, a high level of comfort and safe sea bathing. Given these assets as a starting point, Ian and Polly Mayman have, over the years, superimposed all the qualities which give Talland Bay Hotel its unique character–a delightful, oak-panelled dining-room, renowned for English and French dishes and shellfish specialities, a carefully assembled selection of wines to complement the *cuisine*, modernly equipped bedrooms and impeccable furnishings in every room. Without leaving the hotel and its grounds, guests may swim in the forty-foot pool, have a sauna and play croquet, putting, snooker, table tennis or darts. Nearby there is riding, sailing, water skiing, golf, tennis and sea and reservoir fishing. One of the main attractions of this hotel, however, is that one need do nothing at all! There are no promenades or piers here and the hotel has almost exclusive claim to this unspoilt, lovely spot.

Bed and Breakfast from £43.00	Bedrooms	Dogs allowed by
Bar Lunch from £3.50	All rooms with Private Bathroom, TV,	Arrangement. Parking Facilities. Putting,
Sunday Lunch from £8.75 Table D'Hôte	Telephone, Radio, Hairdryer, Trouser Press	Outdoor Heated Swimming Pool
Dinner from £19.50 and A La Carte	Open from mid-February to December	Solarium, Sauna
Gratuities at Guest's Discretion	Residential and Restaurant Licence	Nearby: Tennis, Squash, Golf, Fishing,
VAT inclusive. Credit Cards—Access,	Full Central Heating. Cocktail Bar	Riding, Sailing, Windsurfing, Water Skiing,
American Express, Diners Club, Visa	Games Room. Conference Facilities	Shooting, Hang-gliding
1 Suite. 19 Double/Twin, 4 Single	Children catered for.	

Section 1: Cornwall

Lostwithiel—Lostwithiel Golf and Country Club Hotel Lower Polscoe, Lostwithiel, Cornwall. PL22 0HQ. Tel 0208 873550. Fax 0208 873479

Our Inspectors loved everything about this hotel, summarising the atmosphere as one of friendliness and flexibility. 'Charming owners and staff teamed together with smiling precision to produce unrivalled hospitality'. Mellow stone barns have been converted into eighteen attractive *en suite* bedrooms featuring pastel coloured walls, beams, country pine furniture and colour co-ordinated furnishings. For the golfing enthusiasts, the beautiful new parkland course (18 holes, par 72) is supplemented by a practice area, a driving range, golf shop and tuition facilities. However, this Country Club was built with much more than golf in mind. There are excellent all-weather tennis courts, a heated indoor swimming-pool, snooker table and arrangements for squash or badminton to be played locally. Easy access to Cornwall's north and south coasts adds the interest of historic harbours, fishing villages, cliff walks, beaches, sailing and surfing. Meals for hotel guests are served in the clubhouse restaurant, *The Black Prince*, in which several of the adventurous dishes are of award-winning distinction. As you wine and dine you have views of the course and the Fowey valley. Alternatively, you can visit the upstairs bar, which serves buffet meals and light snacks. Little wonder that the two conference suites are in great demand for business seminars and private parties. All guests will be delighted with the solicitous service and perfect peacefulness of this unique country hotel.

Terms on application
Daily Terms from £43.00
Bed and Breakfast from £35.00
Bar Meals from £5.00. Dinner from £17.95
Table D'Hôte. Gratuities at Guest's Discretion. VAT inclusive.

Credit Cards–Access, Visa
4 Double, 12 Twin, 2 Single Bedrooms (some rooms on ground floor). 16 Private Bathrooms. 2 Private Shower Rooms. All Rooms with TV, Telephone, Baby-listening, Tea and Coffee-making Facilities,

Hairdryer. Open all year. Residential & Restaurant Licence. Restaurant Bar. Members Bar. TV Lounge. Conference Facilities. Children catered for. Dogs allowed. Parking Facilities. Tennis, Indoor Swimming Pool, Golf, Fishing

Mevagissey—The Spa Hotel
Polkirt, Mevagissey, Cornwall. PL26 6UY. Tel 0726 842244

Back in the eighteenth century, Mevagissey flourished by exporting pilchards, largely to Italy and, in common with many Cornish coastal villages, was involved in smuggling. Although relatively unspoilt, the tiny fishermen's cottages and fish cellars of the past are the shops and restaurants of today. The twelve-bedroom hotel enjoys a high proportion of returning guests and others responding to private recommendations. For personal reasons we had cause to make two visits here within ten days, an occurrence which gave us first-hand experience of the kind and considerate attention freely given by the resident proprietors Sheron and Al Snell. With its grassy banks, sun terrace, surrounding trees and expansive sea views, the Spa Hotel offers peace and privacy. An informal atmosphere is pleasantly complemented by the bright decor of the public rooms and the *en suite* bedrooms. Fishing trips can be arranged by the Spa Hotel, which include the provision of a well-equipped boat and an experienced skipper. In Mevagissey itself there is a folk museum, a model railway and all the interest of a working harbour. An outstanding scene awaits anyone taking the Cornwall coastal path to Dodman Point: in spring or late summer the yellow gorse on the 370-foot headland is seen set against the blue sea. It can be breathtaking.

All Terms pertaining to 1992
Weekly Terms from £182.50
Daily Terms from £30.50
Bed and Breakfast from £21.50
Bar Meal from £1.50
Dinner from £12.00 Table D'Hôte
Service Charge and VAT inclusive
Credit Cards—Access, Visa

1 Family Room. 2 Suites
6 Double, 2 Twin, 1 Single Bedrooms
All Rooms with Private Bathroom, TV, Tea and Coffee-making Facilities
Iron and Hairdryer available on Request
Open all Year
Residential and Restaurant Licence
Full Central Heating.

Bar. TV Lounge.
Vegetarians and Children catered for at no extra cost.
Parking Facilities.
Putting, Pool Table
Nearby: Tennis, Squash, Badminton, Swimming, Golf, Fishing, Sailing, Riding, Windsurfing, Water Skiing

Section 1: Cornwall

Mevagissey–Trevalsa Court Hotel
Polstreath Hill, Mevagissey, Cornwall. PL26 6TH. Tel 0726 842468

Built in the early 1930's for a retired tea planter, Trevalsa Court is today a most attractive hotel, personally run by the owner, Mrs S Allen. At the time of our visit, how we wished our stay could have been for a week or longer, as we were immediately impressed with the immaculate furnishings and the cleanliness which prevailed throughout the hotel. Note, as we did, the eye-catching oak-panelled hall, the tastefully decorated, relaxing lounge and the inviting dining-room, with its mullioned windows. Bedrooms, too, are well furnished and equipped with bath or shower rooms *en suite*, television and tea-making facilities. Mrs Allen is a most knowledgeable cook, who provides good English fare and goes to a lot of trouble to obtain the best produce. She is more than happy to cater, on request, for guests who need special or vegetarian diets. A *table d'hôte* dinner menu is available for residents between 6pm and 8pm, and, from 8pm onwards, an *à la carte* menu is offered to non-residents. The hotel is superbly situated, facing due south, overlooking many miles of coast and headlands. Below the hotel is Polstreath beach, accessible through the attractive gardens. Bathing and fishing from the rocks is, therefore, most popular with the many guests, who return year after year.

Weekly Terms (Half Board) from £252.00
Daily Terms from £36.00
Bed and Breakfast from £25.00
Bar Meal from £4.00
Afternoon Tea from £2.00
Dinner from £12.00 and A La Carte
Gratuities at Guest's Discretion
VAT inclusive

Credit Cards—Access, Visa
9 Double, 2 Single, 4 Twin Bedrooms
13 Private Bathrooms. 2 Private Shower Rooms. All Rooms with Colour TV, Tea and Coffee-making Facilities.
Hairdryer and Trouser Press available on Request. Open from February to November
Residential and Restaurant Licence

Full Central Heating. Cocktail Bar
Conference Facilities
Children catered for. Dogs allowed
Parking Facilities
Nearby: Tennis, Croquet, Putting, Squash, Badminton, Swimming, Solarium, Sauna, Golf, Fishing, Riding, Sailing, Water Skiing, Shooting

Mullion Cove–Henscath House Mullion Cove,
Near Helston, Cornwall. TR12 7EP. Tel 0326 240537

We take a special delight in seeking out quiet places of good quality. Near Mullion we have one such discovery. It is small, unpretentious and does not carry the appellation 'hotel', yet, if you rejoice in warm hospitality, good catering and homely comforts, Henscath House is one of the most delightful out-of-the-way places you could find. You must thread your way through National Trust land above the tiny harbour at Mullion Cove. Here, overlooking the sea and Mullion Island, is Henscath, a house of great individuality. The atmosphere reflects the beauty of its situation and the remarkable views this provides. There are only five letting rooms: all but one are fully *en suite* and there is central heating throughout. The public rooms are equally comfortable and the spacious drawing-room, lounge bar and dining-room all enjoy wonderful views. Frank and Daphne Crouch, with their son and daughter, Stephen and Sally, have created a very happy home for their guests. The location is away from the main routes and those in the know go there time and again. Swimming, surfing, riding and tennis are all close at hand and, for serious walking or for gentle pottering, the immediate countryside and cliff-tops offer many possibilities. Golfers are especially welcome, the *Mullion Golf Club* is a few minutes' drive away and a further eight courses are within easy reach.

All Terms pertain to 1992
Weekly Terms from £176.00 (Half Board)
Daily Terms from £26.00 (Half Board)
Dinner Table D'Hôte
No Service or VAT Charge
1 Family Room

2 Double, 2 Twin Bedrooms
2 Private Bathrooms
2 Private Shower Rooms
All Rooms with Tea and Coffee-making Facilities, Hot Towel Rails
Open early Spring to late Autumn

Residential Licence
Full Central Heating. Cocktail Bar
Drawing room with colour TV
Dogs not allowed. Parking Facilities
Nearby: Tennis, Golf, Fishing, Riding, Sailing, Windsurfing

Section 1: Cornwall

Newquay—Atlantic Hotel
Dane Road, Newquay, Cornwall. TR7 1EN. Tel 0637 872244. Fax 0637 874108

To spend a holiday at the Atlantic is as good as being at sea, but without any risk of discomfort. It is one of those few hotels where one can obtain a sea view from almost every window, for, from a spectacular cliff-top position, it looks from three sides upon the ever rolling, never ceasing Atlantic, and, since its nearest neighbour due west is America, the sunsets here can be simply dazzling. There are sands and surfing below; a swimming pool, spa bath, tennis courts and children's play area in the grounds; and inside a further swimming pool, spa bath, squash court, snooker and billiards, gymnasium and solarium. A golf course is just a chip shot away, and, whilst men may play, the ladies may be thankful for the hairdressing and beauty salons and the indoor shopping arcade. In fact, if we said the Atlantic Hotel was complete we may be overlooking one or two finer points. Allied to all this is the owners' determination to provide their guests with only the very best. In the past few years the hotel has been completely refurbished and the Cobley family has ensured that there have been no short cuts and that only the best materials and furnishings have been used. If you can drag your eyes away from the sea view, for every bedroom has one, you will note that your room is beautifully equipped and has its own bathroom, that the public rooms are stylish and designed for comfort, and the food served in both the spacious restaurant and the coffee shop is of a very high standard. Indeed, before this book goes to press we expect the Atlantic to have gained a four-star status and be one of only two such hotels in Cornwall.

Weekly Terms from £182.00	Dinner from £15.30 Table D'Hôte	Tea and Coffee-making Facilities, Trouser
Daily Terms from £54.00	VAT inclusive. Credit Cards—Access, Visa	Press, Hairdryer. Open all year. Fully
Bed and Breakfast from £42.00	21 Family Rooms, 2 Suites, 30 Double,	Licensed. Cocktail Bars. TV Lounge.
Bar Lunch from £2.00	11 Twin, 14 Single Bedrooms. All Rooms	Games Room. Conference Facilities.
Lunch from £8.90 Table D'Hôte	with Private Bath/Shower Room, TV,	Children catered for. Dogs allowed
Bar Supper from £4.00	Telephone, Radio, Baby-Listening,	Parking Facilities. Night Porter

Newquay–Hotel Riviera
1, Lusty Glaze Road, Newquay, Cornwall. TR7 3AA. Tel 0637 874251/877132. Fax 0637 850 823

When approaching Newquay from the west one reaches a high grassy headland, where the road turns sharply to the left and then runs down the hill towards the town's pretty harbour. At this point, however, to one's right, something else catches the eye–colourful flags, striped canopies and an attractive building sitting in a solus position above Lusty Glaze Beach. Such is one's first, tantalising glimpse of the Hotel Riviera. Further investigation reveals that here is an hotel which is styled for comfort and run with great flair. Head Chef, Mr John Brightling, and his team daily prepare an impressive selection of hot and cold dishes for the hotel's lunches and also an inviting array of English and Continental dishes for *La Corniche Restaurant*. If, by day, *La Piazza* appears to be particularly elegant for a coffee shop, this is explained after 8pm, when it is transformed into a very chic and intimate night-spot. In the hotel's grounds are sunny lawns and shady corners, a children's play garden, the ever-popular heated swimming pool and a paddling pool for children. Competitive spirits are catered for with the galleried squash court, the full-size snooker table and the provision of table tennis, electronic games and a children's indoor play area. There is a sauna, a launderette, the *Curlies* hairdressing salon and a medley of well-appointed bedrooms with colour and satellite television. There is, however, something more important at the Hotel Riviera than its amenities: there is something Continental about this hotel which more than justifies the name Riviera.

Weekly Terms (Half Board) from £195.00	VAT inclusive. Credit Cards–Access, Visa,	Hairdryer available on Request. Open all
Bed and Breakfast from £35.00	American Express	Year. Fully Licensed. Full CH. Lift. Cocktail
Bar Lunch from £3.50	9 Family Rooms. 23 Double, 8 Twin, 10	Bar. TV Lounge. Games Room
Lunch from £8.50 and A La Carte	Single Bedrooms. 36 Private Bathrooms	Conference Facilities. Children catered for
Dinner from £14.00 and A La Carte	14 Private Shower Rooms. All Rooms with	Dogs allowed by Arrangement
Gratuities at Guest's Discretion	TV, Telephone, Radio, Baby-listening.	Parking Facilities. Night Porter

Section 1: Cornwall

Newquay—The Kilbirnie
Narrowcliff, Newquay Cornwall. TR2 2RS. Tel 0637 875155

Cornwall's biggest resort and Britain's foremost surfing centre began with the building of a 'new quay' in the fifteenth century. It is in an area, however, which today seems purposely designed for holiday pleasure. High cliffs thrust out into the sea, thereby creating a series of sandy beaches. Because of the town's importance, in holiday terms, our hotel recommendations are numerous, but if you seek an hotel which is run on very personal and proficient lines, The Kilbirnie is an excellent choice. It is now owned by the Cobley family, who are well known in Newquay's hotel circles. The Kilbirnie occupies an ideal situation directly facing the sea and has all the modern amenities which one could wish to find, together with pleasing touches, such as plenty of floral displays, and also a log-burning fireplace in the entrance hall, despite Newquay's mild climate and the hotel's more than ample central heating. There is a good-size indoor heated swimming pool and also a sauna bath, which help to make the hotel an ideal place for those seeking an out-of-season holiday or just a short winter break. We, ourselves, have been returning to The Kilbirnie since 1948 and cannot recall ever having felt disappointed with the food, the comfort or the service. There is certainly nothing formal about the service here, and after many enjoyable days it has meant a lot to us to know that we were coming back to personalities who interested themselves in us and our movements.

Weekly Terms from £175.00
Daily Terms from £31.00
Bed and Breakfast from £26.00
Bar Lunch from £1.70
Dinner from £10.50 and A La Carte
Gratuities at Guest's Discretion. VAT inclusive. Credit Cards—Access, Visa

18 Family Rooms. 29 Double, 18 Twin, 10 Single Bedrooms
All Rooms with Private Bathroom, TV, Telephone, Radio, Baby-listening, Tea and Coffee-making Facilities, Hairdryer
Open all Year. Fully Licensed
Full Central Heating. Lift. Cocktail Bar.

Games Room. Children catered for. Dogs allowed by Arrangement. Parking Facilities. Night Porter. Indoor and Outdoor Swimming Pools, Solarium, Sauna
Nearby: Tennis, Croquet, Putting, Squash, Badminton, Golf, Fishing, Riding, Sailing, Windsurfing, Water Skiing, Hang-gliding

Newquay—Whipsiderry Hotel
Porth, Newquay, Cornwall. TR7 3LY. Tel 0637 874777

Whipsiderry Beach is one of the ten stretches of firm golden sands which Newquay claims as her own. The Whipsiderry Hotel lies closer, in fact, to Porth Beach, yet who could deny the hotel such an attractive name, particularly since it is such a warm and friendly establishment. When Ann and Dick Drackford took over the hotel in the early 1970's, it was little more than a seaside boarding house. What a remarkable transformation they have effected! They have extended and refashioned the hotel both within and without. The dining room can seat sixty people in comfort and there is a fine bar lounge, a television room, two further lounges (with excellent sea views) and a balcony terrace. Each bedroom is replete with a bathroom *en suite*, colour television, radio and an intercom system. Ann Drackford is a *Cordon Bleu* chef, although nowadays she primarily uses her talents to buy the freshest and the best produce she can for the hotel, which is generally assisted by her son Nicholas. The kitchens are presided over by Ann Roberts and another qualified full-time chef and between them they produce a good, varied menu. There is also an extensive and reasonably priced wine list of approximately eighteen bins. The hotel arranges fishing trips every week in the summer and sometimes has as many as four boats at a time leaving Newquay harbour for mackerel fishing. At the end of the day the fresh catch is cooked for all concerned. Badger watching has become a special feature after sunset from the hotel. It is hardly surprising to learn that seventy per cent of Whipsiderry's guests return year after year.

Weekly Terms from £125.50
Daily Terms from £24.50
Bed and Breakfast from £17.00
Bar Lunch from £3.00. Bar Supper from £2.00. Dinner from £7.75 Table D'Hôte
Gratuities at Guest's Discretion. VAT inclusive.

6 Family Rooms. 14 Double, 1 Twin Bedrooms. 6 Private Bathrooms. 18 Private Shower Rooms
18 Rooms with TV. All Rooms with Radio, Baby-listening, Tea and Coffee-making Facilities. Open from Easter to October, plus Christmas.

Residential and Restaurant Licence with live entertainments Cocktail Bar. TV Lounge. Games Room. Laundrette. Children catered for. Dogs allowed. Parking Facilities. Putting, Outdoor Heated Swimming Pool, Sauna

Section 1: Cornwall

Newquay–Trebarwith Hotel
Island Estate, Newquay, Cornwall. TR7 1BZ.
Tel 0637 872288

A visit to the Trebarwith Hotel is a truly impressive experience. Upon arrival one is always immediately affected by the beauty of the Trebarwith's superb location. From the beautiful sub-tropical gardens, terraced lawns and landscaped sun patio's, a breathtaking panorama across 20 miles of Cornwall's most spectacular coastline unfolds. Family owned and managed, by resident directors David and Gill Tarrant with son and daughter-in-law, Nigel and Jane. For over 30 years, now in their third generation, this family hotel is a credit to their dedication. This is exemplified by their attention to each and every detail, in particular to the well being of their guests and to the high quality of staff, service and comfort reminiscent of a bygone era. There is direct access onto the beach via a private staircase, the hotel is centrally situated, away from all traffic noise but just a minutes walk to the shops and town. Within the hotel, which is for residents only, there is a large indoor heated swimming pool, a solarium, sauna cabin and a Hydro spa bath. There is also a well equipped indoor games centre with full size snooker table, pool table, table tennis and amusement games. Alternatively, for complete quiet and comfort one can relax in the spacious sea-view lounges. To further enhance your enjoyment there is a delightful Cocktail Bar where you can order one of the famous cocktails before taking dinner in the surroundings of the elegant *Wedgwood Restaurant* with sea views from every table. The *cuisine* is mainly English with some international flavours. Evening entertainment is provided most evenings and there is even a forty seater mini cinema within the hotel for a 'night at the movies'. The bedrooms are furnished and equipped to a high standard and most enjoy superb sea views. For the full story, we recommend you telephone for the Tarrant's brochure depicting the Trebarwith in full colour as it truly is.

Bargain Breaks from £15.00 per day (DB&B). Weekly Terms from £140.00 (DB&B). Daily Terms from £20.00 (DB&B) Bar Lunch from £2.00 Dinner from £12.00 Table D'Hôte Gratuities at Guest's Discretion VAT inclusive. Credit Cards—Access, Visa

5 Family Rooms. 23 Double, 12 Twin, 2 Single Bedrooms. All Rooms with Private Bathroom Suite, TV, Telephone, Radio, Baby-listening, Tea-making Facilities, Hairdryer Open from Easter to November Residential and Restaurant Licence Full Central Heating. Cocktail Bar.

TV Lounge. Games Room. Children catered for. Dogs not allowed. Parking Facilities. Night Porter. Indoor Swimming Pool, Solarium, Sauna, Spa Bath, Fishing Nearby: Tennis, Putting, Squash, Badminton, Golf, Riding, Sailing, Windsurfing, Water Skiing

Section 1: Cornwall

Near Padstow, Constantine Bay–Treglos Hotel Constantine Bay,
Near Padstow, Cornwall. PL28 8JH. Tel 0841 520727. Fax 0841 521163

Numerous bays in the region of the Treglos Hotel offer surfing, water-skiing and wind-surfing, although further north-eastwards along the coast the boisterous Atlantic asserts itself quite strongly until one reaches Bude. Superb swimming is possible from the beaches of Porthcothan, Treyarnon, Constantine, Boobys and Harlyn, with rock pools exposed at low tide. At nearby Padstow, places of particular interest include a zoo, bird gardens and an aquarium, whilst extensive sands line the sea inlet from Padstow Bay to Little Petherick and towards Wadebridge. Within easy reach of the Hotel lies the National Trust coastal footpath - popular with ornithologists - offering miles of glorious rugged scenery. Cornwall is rich in National Trust and Heritage properties: so much so that the Treglos staff have produced a small book describing local routes. At the hotel, with its indoor swimming-pool, snooker table and no less than five elegantly-furnished lounges, the courteous service is maintained at a level which, today, is something of a rarity. In the restaurant, where gentlemen are requested to wear a jacket and tie at dinner, guests have a choice of six-course *table d'hôte* or extensive *à la carte* menus. Featured here are local fresh seafoods and meats, vegetables from their own kitchen gardens and home-made desserts with Cornish cream. With twenty-four-hour room service, and evening chambermaid service, nightly shoe-cleaning and a laundry service, one is here guaranteed a thoroughly relaxing holiday.

All prices pertain to 1992
Weekly Terms from £294.00
Daily Terms from £52.00
Bar Lunch from £2.50
Sunday Lunches from £10.95
Dinner from £18.00 and A La Carte
Gratuities at Guest's Discretion
VAT inclusive. Credit Cards—Access, Visa

3 Family Rooms. 3 Suites
3 Double, 28 Twin, 7 Single Bedrooms
All Rooms with Private Bath/Shower
Room, TV, Telephone, Radio,
Baby-listening
Open from 10th March to 6th November
Residential and Restaurant Licence
Full Central Heating. Lift. Cocktail Bar

Conference Facilities. Children catered for
Dogs allowed by Arrangement
Parking Facilities. Night Porter
Croquet, Indoor Swimming Pool, Surfing
Nearby: Tennis, Putting, Swimming,
Golf, Fishing, Riding, Sailing,
Windsurfing, Water Skiing, Shooting

Near Padstow, Trevone Bay–Green Waves Hotel
Trevone Bay, Near Padstow, Cornwall. PL28 8RD. Tel 0841 520114

The name 'Green Waves' is something of a misnomer for whenever we have visited this stretch of Cornish coast the sea has been as blue as turquoise, even when at its most spectacular. From the Newquay to Padstow road the approach to Trevose Head and Trevone Bay is via a maze of lanes and paths which affords the area a certain degree of seclusion. If your holiday requires unspoilt coastline, sandy coves and a lack of promenades then the Green Waves Hotel is a grand place, without being in any way grandiose. Brian and Margaret Chellew obviously love the place. They have been attracting guests there for over twenty-five years, with their high standards of cleanliness and comfort which are immediately obvious. There is a completeness about the comfortable bedrooms in the main house and the ground floor bedrooms, whilst the lounges, dining-rooms and newly completed bar are pleasant places in which to contemplate and reflect upon the really excellent food which the Chellews provide. The public rooms, however, usually come into focus in the evenings because by day guests pursue a variety of interests– deep-sea and shark fishing, water-skiing, golf on two first-class courses, sailing and enjoying the innumerable beaches. There are many places of interest within easy reach of the hotel; the picturesque port of Padstow, the market town of Wadebridge and several National Trust properties including Trerice House and St Michael's Mount.

Weekly Terms from £141.00
Daily Terms from £26.00
Bed and Breakfast from £18.00
Dinner from £9.00 Table D'Hôte
Gratuities at Guest's Discretion
VAT inclusive. 3 Family Rooms

8 Double, 6 Twin Bedrooms
3 Single Bedrooms
17 Private Shower Rooms
All Rooms with TV, Tea and Coffee-making
Facilities. Open from Easter to October
Residential Licence

Full Central Heating
Cocktail Bar. Snooker Room
Children over 4 years catered for
Parking Facilities
Nearby: Tennis, Golf, Fishing, Riding,
Sailing, Windsurfing

Section 1: Cornwall

Penzance–Mount Prospect Hotel
Britons Hill, Penzance, Cornwall. TR18 3AE. Tel 0736 63117. Fax 0736 50970

For a holiday, conference, business meeting or a longer stay, Penzance has much in its favour–a mild climate, a southern aspect and scenic charm. It is a wonderful centre for the tourist who wishes to visit the many interesting harbours and picturesque coves, as it lies in the centre of the area. The Mount Prospect Hotel fits perfectly into the scene. The owners are Mr and Mrs A Blakeley, and we continue to receive good reports about this family-managed hotel which overlooks the eastern end of Penzance Bay towards St Michael's Mount. Having undertaken a considerable amount of redevelopment work very recently here one encounters comfortable modern furnishings, restful lounges and a convivial cocktail bar. The dining room aspect provides spectacular views towards St Michael's Mount and across Mount's Bay, and it is here that we have dined well both at lunch and dinner, and have been further refreshed from the thoughtful collation of wines. Being a family hotel, bedrooms are spacious enough to take additional cots and beds and concessionary rates are available for youngsters sharing their parents' room. A whole wing of the hotel is now reserved for non-smokers. A full range of services is provided including a laundry service, valeting and travel arrangements to the Isles of Scilly and other districts can be made. The hotel boasts the only hotel swimming pool in Penzance. The businessman will find this an ideal venue for his sorties into the West Country, communications are good and the hotel service is excellent. If this should appeal, be tempted and write to the Blakeleys for their latest brochure and tariff details.

Weekly Terms from £295.00. Daily Terms from £49.00. Bed and Breakfast from £35.00. Bar Meals from £5.80 Dinner from £14.00 and A La Carte Gratuities at Guest's Discretion VAT inclusive. Credit Cards—Access, American Express, Diners Club, Visa 2 Family Rooms. 10 Double, 7 Twin, 5 Single Bedrooms. 21 Private Bathrooms. 3 Private Shower Rooms. All Rooms with TV, Telephone, Radio, Baby-listening, Tea and Coffee-making Facilities, Daily Fresh Fruit. Hairdryer available. Open all year. Residential and Restaurant Licence. Cocktail Bar. TV Lounge. Games Room. Conference Facilities. Children catered for. Dogs allowed. Hotel Parking. Night Porter. Outdoor Swimming Pool

Penzance–The Queen's Hotel
The Promenade, Penzance, Cornwall. TR18 4HG. Tel 0736 62371

First impressions count, and we were instantly attracted to the Queen's Hotel because of the pleasantness of its foyer. Revolving entrance doors, deep carpeting, tasteful furniture, interesting pictures and a graceful winding staircase all combined to create an atmosphere of unostentatious comfort. These impressions were confirmed as we continued our visit and took in pleasantly furnished and well-equipped bedrooms (all have *en suite* facilities, colour television and radio), attractive, spacious lounges and bar. A lunchtime buffet is served in the *Tudor Bar* each day and as well as an interesting menu there are plenty of local fish dishes and light snacks. A feature of the Queen's Hotel is its superb, south-facing location: the views from the lounges and the restaurant are quite breathtaking, taking in the sweep of Mount's Bay, St Michael's Mount and The Lizard. The service here cannot be faulted in any respect: we found all members of staff to be most courteous and attentive, and the Manager, Anthony Lishman, ensures that all departments run smoothly. All guests may enjoy the Hotel's sauna and jacuzzi. Penzance is a fine centre for touring the Land's End and Lizard peninsulas, and places of interest nearby include the Minack Theatre, the Maritime Museum and, of course, St Michael's Mount itself.

Weekly Terms from £294.00 Bed and Breakfast from £42.00 Bar Lunch from £3.25 Afternoon Tea from £2.05 Dinner from £15.00 Gratuities at Guest's Discretion VAT inclusive Credit Cards—Access, American Express, Diners Club, Visa 9 Family Rooms 20 Double, 27 Twin, 15 Single Bedrooms All Rooms with Private Bathroom, TV, Telephone, Radio, Baby-listening, Tea and Coffee-making Facilities Open all Year. Fully Licensed. Full Central Heating. Lift Conference Facilities. Children catered for Dogs allowed. Parking Facilities Night Porter. Solarium, Sauna, Health Club Nearby: Tennis, Putting, Squash, Badminton, Swimming, Golf, Fishing, Riding, Sailing, Windsurfing, Water Skiing, Shooting, Hang-gliding

Section 1: Cornwall

Port Isaac–The Castle Rock Hotel
Port Isaac, Cornwall. PL29 3SB. Tel 0208 880300

Our visits to Port Isaac have, over the years, taken on a comfortable pattern. We are normally so immersed in our mission of hotel-watching, that there is little time for anything else. At this delightful fishing village on the Atlantic coast, however, ten miles to the north of Wadebridge, we always find time to wander down to its little harbour, view the white-washed and slate-hung cottages tiered behind it, watch the stream which runs through the village, admire the scenic harbour and, if the time is right, see what the fishermen have brought forth from the sea. It is a beautiful place. Then we make a visit to an old friend–The Castle Rock Hotel–which is situated overlooking Port Isaac Bay with magnificent panoramic views of the north Cornish coastline. A most impressive programme of improvements has recently been completed; bedrooms refurnished and redecorated, restaurant re-styled and colour co-ordinated along with a new and refurbished bar, front office and reception area. The resident owners are a retired army major Geoffrey Wells and his wife Christine, who, with her sister Barbara and husband Steve provide every comfort. In addition to the traditional *table d'hôte* English menu, a lively *à la carte* is offered, featuring Port Isaac lobster and the complete range of locally caught sea food and speciality dishes, many of which are cooked at the table. Vegetarian and special diets can also be catered for. This hotel offers a delightful 'home from home' for all those who love the Cornish coastline–whether their interests lie in water sports, fishing, riding, or simply strolling along the magnificent cliff paths.

Budget Breaks available spring and autumn Christmas and NY programme available. Weekly Terms from £215.00. Daily Terms from £36.00. Bed and Breakfast from £25.00. Bar Food (Bar Bites) and Cream

Teas available. Dinner from £12.00 and A La Carte. Gratuities at Guest's Discretion. VAT inclusive. Credit Cards—Access, Visa. 1 Anniversary Suite. 1 Family Room. 1 Family Suite. 8 Double, 4 Twin, 2 Single Bedrooms. 11 Private Bathrooms. 3 Private

Shower Rooms. All Rooms with TV, Telephone, Radio, Baby-listening, Tea and Coffee-making Facilities. Open all Year. Fully licensed. Cocktail Bar. Sun Lounge. Full CH. Children catered for. Dogs allowed by Arrangement. Parking Facilities

Near Port Isaac–Port Gaverne Hotel
Near Port Isaac, Cornwall. PL29 3SQ. Tel 0208 880244. Fax 0208 880151

There is something special about old inns which engenders affection in man's heart. They promise snugness in the winter and informal friendliness at all times. This seventeenth-century specimen has the added advantage of lying within 100 yards of one of the most sheltered coves on the north Cornish coast. The little cove of Port Gaverne is separated from Port Isaac by a rocky headland. The candlelit dining room and the lounge bar, with their attractive timber beams, the cosy residents' lounge, and, above stairs, the nineteen *en suite* bedrooms put one on friendly terms with oneself, and after a night or a meal, one silently vows 'Here one day I will return'. And return its guests do, from all over the world! Such has been the success of Fred and Midge Ross's hotel that the premises across the lane have been converted to provide additional accommodation. This long, low building was originally a fish store and later a rope walk and sail loft. Known as The Green Door Cottages, these may be let as either self-catering accommodation or hotel suites, according to the guests' requirements. If you cannot stay at the hotel, however, do try to eat there. A fine *à la carte* menu is augmented daily by Chef's dishes and catches of the day. Dishes are based on fresh garden produce, locally grown meat and locally landed fish, with local lobster and crab available in season. A good selection of hot and cold specialities is also served in the bar. Above all, of course, as befits an ages-old inn, friendliness and personal service are so pronounced.

Weekly Terms from £315.00
Bed and Breakfast from £36.00
Buffet Lunch or Bar Meals from £3.50
Dinner from £16.50 A La Carte
VAT inclusive. Credit Cards—Access, American Express, Diners Club, Visa

9 Double, 7 Twin, 3 Single Bedrooms. 7 Self-catering Cottages
All Rooms with Private Bathroom, TV, Radio, Tea and Coffee-making Facilities, Telephone, Baby-listening, Hairdryer
Open all Year. Fully Licensed

Full Central Heating. Residents Lounge and TV Lounge
Children catered for. Dogs allowed Parking Facilities. Night Porter
Nearby: Squash, Golf, Fishing, Riding, Sailing, Windsurfing, Water Skiing

Section 1: Cornwall

Portloe—The Lugger Hotel
Portloe, Truro, Cornwall. TR2 5RD. Tel 0872 501322. Fax 0872 501691

The Powell family has been here since 1950, but then, if you lived in a slice of heaven would you wish to leave? One of the joys of visiting the Lugger Hotel is driving towards it through winding, narrow, high-banked lanes. Already you will feel the pace of life slowing. Then, suddenly, a steep descent brings one to a small cluster of houses and down to a series of seventeenth-century white-washed cottages clinging to the side of a narrow break in the cliffs. These cottages now form the Lugger Hotel. Fishermen haul their boats up the tiny beach almost to the hotel's door and the only hustle and bustle one is likely to see is the men mending their nets, or painting their boats. There are reminders of the hotel's origins in the cocktail bar, formerly the original parlour and once used by fishermen and smugglers. The lounge has an oak-beamed ceiling and a large stone fireplace. In many other respects, however, the Lugger Hotel is surprisingly modern. You will also find sauna and solarium rooms situated in the *Godolphin* bedroom wing. One of the hotel's best views of the cove is from the restaurant, so there is much here to delight the eye and the palate. The chefs prepare both English and continental dishes and their food is far removed from the ordinary. There is nowhere else quite like Portloe and the Lugger Hotel, which, incidentally, has been awarded the British Tourist Authority *'Commendation Award'* for sixteen consecutive years. Your host, Mr Steve Powell, is a member of the third generation of this famed Cornish hotel family.

Weekly Terms from £280.00
Daily Terms from £55.00 (DB&B)
Bar Lunch from £3.00
Sunday Lunch from £10.00 Table D'Hôte
Dinner from £17.50 and A La Carte
Gratuities at Guest's Discretion

VAT inclusive. Credit Cards—Access, American Express, Diners Club, Visa
2 Suites. 7 Double, 7 Twin, 4 Single Bedrooms. 14 Private Bathrooms
6 Private Shower Rooms
All Rooms with TV, Telephone, Radio,

Tea and Coffee-making Facilities, Hairdryer, mini safe, Bar.
Open from early February to early December. Residential and Restaurant Licence. Cocktail Bar. Children over 12 years catered for. Dogs not allowed

Portscatho—Gerrans Bay Hotel Tregassick Road, Gerrans,
Portscatho, Truro, Cornwall. TR2 5ED. Tel 0872 580338

Sometimes hoteliers, like estate agents, tend to be flamboyant in their announcements and brochures have to be taken with the proverbial 'pinch of salt'. Not so Mr and Mrs Brian Greaves who allow the picture to tell the tale in their colourful brochure of this delightful hotel. The Victorian house has been carefully enlarged and it speaks volumes about their philosophy of hotel living. Of course, nature has also been kind giving it a near perfect situation in the heart of the Roseland Peninsula less than half a mile from the sea. Reader reports tend to confirm our own observations that the Gerrans Bay is a small family hotel, run on very personal lines and which, upon every visit, appears to be spick and span and newly decorated. There is a well-stocked and pleasantly appointed bar, separate lounge with colour television and comfortably inviting bedrooms, some of which are on the ground floor, and all provide a private bathroom. The food is plentiful, appetising and wholesome; we are pleased to note that the restaurant is now open to non-residents for bar snacks, cream teas and evening meals. Resident visitors may take advantage of complimentary golf facilities at Truro and bowls at Veryan. Within easy reach of the hotel are wonderful beaches and coves including Carne, Portscatho and St Anthony Head. Here is, in fact, an hotel which cannot fail to please either the sportsman or the tourist looking for relaxing pastimes.

Weekly Terms from £240.00
Daily Terms from £38.50
Bed and Breakfast from £27.00
Bar Lunch from £3.00
Afternoon Tea from £2.00
Dinner from £16.50
Service Charge and VAT inclusive

Credit Cards—Access, American Express, Visa
2 Family Rooms. 4 Double, 6 Twin, 2 Single Bedrooms. 14 Private Bathrooms
All Rooms with Tea and Coffee-making Facilities. Open from April to October and at Christmas

Residential and Restaurant Licence
Full Electric Heating
Cocktail Bar. TV Lounge
Children catered for
Dogs allowed. Parking Facilities
Nearby: Tennis, Squash, Swimming, Golf, Fishing, Riding, Sailing, Windsurfing

Section 1: Cornwall

Portscatho—Rosevine Hotel Porthcurnick Beach,
Portscatho, Truro, Cornwall. TR2 5EW. Tel 0872 580 206/230

The name 'Rosevine' applies to both the Country House Hotel and to the sheltered hamlet across the bay from Portscatho, on the beautiful Roseland Peninsula. This is an area of intrinsic natural charm. Coastal paths run westwards and eastwards, several National Trust country houses and gardens are within easy reach, and the legendary Poldark Mine, St Michael's Mount and the Cornish Seal Sanctuary are just three examples of numerous local attractions. When the Georgian architects decided to fashion the manor house, which later became the Rosevine Hotel, they chose one of the area's choicest spots overlooking the sea and only yards from a safe sandy beach. Today, it retains three-and-a-half acres of gardens boasting many sub-tropical trees, shrubs and plants, and the whole gardens are floodlit at night. A delightful south-facing sun lounge and many of the bedrooms overlook these gardens and the sea. If there is eye appeal without, one could hardly be more comfortable within. The owners, Mr and Mrs Hearnden, have made the Rosevine warm, comfortable and very hospitable. All bedrooms have a bathroom or shower *en suite* and are equipped with colour television, telephone, tea and coffee-making and baby-listening facilities. As to matters of food, the hotels' top class chefs offer a wide variety of appetising menus utilising the freshly caught fish and other local produce which abounds in the Roseland peninsula. In addition, a vegetarian menu is always available.

Weekly Terms from £270.00 (Half Board)
Daily Terms from £40.00
Bed and Breakfast from £26.00
Bar Lunch from £5.25
Dinner from £16.00 Table D'Hôte
Gratuities at Guest's Discretion
VAT inclusive. Credit Card-Access, Visa

2 Family Rooms. 4 Double, 1 Single, 8 Twin Bedrooms. 1 Ground Floor Twin bedroom with private bathroom in Annexe. 14 Private Bathrooms. 1 Private Shower Room. All rooms with TV, Telephone, Radio, Baby-listening, Tea and Coffee-making Facilities. Hairdryer,

Laundry and Shoe Cleaning Service available on request. Open from April to October. Fully Licensed. Full CH. TV Lounge. Conference Facilities. Children catered for. Dogs allowed. Parking Facilities. Nearby: Tennis, Squash, Golf (com to Guests), Fishing

Ruan High Lanes–The Hundred House Hotel
Ruan Highlanes, Near Truro, Cornwall. TR2 5JR. Tel 0872 501336

Once an old Cornish country house, dating from 1790, the Hundred House is now a small hotel of charm and quality owned and personally run by Mike and Kitty Eccles. It is set in three acres of garden in the centre of the beautiful Roseland Peninsula, six miles from St Mawes, twelve miles from Truro and only one and a half miles from Pendower Beach. As soon as you step inside the wide hall with its handsome Edwardian handcarved staircase and antique furniture, there is a feeling of comfort and elegance. All ten bedrooms have full *en suite* bath/shower rooms, colour television and tea and coffee-making facilities. They are individually decorated to a high standard and have views over the garden and surrounding countryside. There are two charming single rooms and one of the twin rooms is on the ground floor. The four-course dinner menu changes daily and is prepared by Kitty Eccles, who provides delicious imaginative English cooking using the freshest of Cornish produce. The dining room is spacious and there is a comfortable bar overlooking the garden. On chilly evenings a log fire blazes in the sitting room where there are books of local interest. We received a most friendly welcome from Mr and Mrs Eccles who have created a hotel with a relaxed and friendly atmosphere. Visitors are treated more as family guests and return again to enjoy their hospitality.

Weekly Terms (Half Board) from £245.00
Daily Terms from £39.00
Bed and Breakfast from £29.00
Bar Lunch from £2.50
Dinner £17.50 Table D'Hôte
Gratuities at Guest's Discretion
VAT inclusive

Credit Cards—Access, Visa
4 Double, 4 Twin, 2 Single Bedrooms
6 Private Bathrooms
4 Private Shower Rooms
All Rooms with TV,
Tea and Coffee-making Facilities
Open from March to October

Residential and Restaurant Licence
Full Central Heating
Children over 6 years catered for
Dogs allowed
Parking Facilities
Nearby: Swimming, Golf,
Fishing, Riding, Sailing, Windsurfing

Section 1: Cornwall

St Agnes, Mithian—Rose-in-Vale Country House Hotel
Mithian, St Agnes, Cornwall. TR5 0QD. Tel 087 255 2202

Originally built as the winter residence of a local mine-captain, this medium-sized genuine Georgian country house dates from the mid-eighteenth century and also has close historical associations with the Cornish portrait painter, John Opie. The house nestles in a lovely quiet and secluded wooded valley just outside the tiny picturesque village of Mithian, between St Agnes and Perranporth on the magnificent North Cornish coast. Rose-in-Vale stands amidst its own 11 acres of beautifully kept lawns and flower beds, woods and meadows, with a trout stream running through. There are sun terraces and heated swimming pool, croquet and badminton in the gardens, and cosy log fires to cheer the cooler months of the year. Proprietors Tony and Vanda Arthur have last year carried out an extensive refurbishment programme to provide accommodation of high quality. The bedrooms, all *en suite*, have been beautifully and elegantly refurbished, and the emphasis at Rose-in-Vale is on personal yet unobtrusive service and a peaceful relaxing ambience. There are three pleasant and comfortable lounges. The *Trellis Room Restaurant* looks out over lawns to the woods beyond, and here you can sample thoughtfully prepared menus, created by an imaginative chef, using local produce, a variety of Cornish seafood and fresh vegetables from the Arthur family farm, complemented by a fine wine list. As well as the obvious attractions of the lovely beaches and coves in the locality, there are some very pretty walks designed to begin and end at the hotel, and the area is rich in National Trust houses and gardens and golf courses.

All terms pertaining to 1992
Weekly Terms (Half Board) from £236.25
Daily Terms from £40.00
Bed and Breakfast from £30.25
Dinner Table D'Hôte and A La Carte
Gratuities at Guest's Discretion

VAT inclusive. Credit Cards—Access, Visa
1 Four Poster Suite. 7 Double, 7 Twin, 2 Single Bedrooms. All Rooms with Private Bathroom, TV, Telephone, Baby-Listening, Tea and Coffee-making Facilities, Radio, Hairdryer.

Iron and Shoe Polish available on request.
Open from March to October inclusive.
Residential and Restaurant Licence.
Cocktail Bar. TV Lounge. Games Room.
Conference Facilities. Children catered for.
Dogs allowed. Parking Facilities

St Austell—Carlyon Bay Hotel
Carlyon Bay, Near St Austell, Cornwall. PL25 3RD. Tel 072681 2304. Fax 072681 4938

This is Cornwall's only four star hotel, and it provides the highest standards for its international clientele. A golf course (6,505 yards in length) stretches from the hotel, along its grounds and to the cliffs beyond. In all, the hotel owns 250 acres of coastal scenery, much of it given over to carefully tended sub-tropical gardens, although it also includes an outdoor heated swimming pool, hard tennis courts, putting and croquet greens and, of course, the spectacular links with their extensive clubhouse facilities, professional's shop and practice grounds. Within the grounds there is now a 9-hole approach course. Also a Childrens Adventure Paddock with Pets Corner. This sporting theme continues within the hotel, for here one will find another magnificent heated swimming pool, a solarium and sauna, a mini gym and a spa bath, two full size snooker tables and table tennis facilities. As befits an hotel in this category, the standards of comfort and service are also impressive. The public rooms exude good taste and all the bedrooms have bathrooms *en suite*. The dining room has recently been refurbished to create the delightful *"Bay View Restaurant"* which serves *haute cuisine* from both *table d'hôte* and *à la carte* menus and there is even a special *à la carte* menu available for children's meals. The dining room has recently been refurbished to create "The Bay View Restaurant". The beautiful *Churchill Suite* is an ideal venue for conferences, wedding receptions and other special functions. The Carlyon Bay is a Brend Hotel and thus a sister to other splendid establishments, such as the Victoria Hotel at Sidmouth, the Saunton Sands Hotel at Saunton and the Royal Duchy at Falmouth.

Weekly Terms from £350.00 to £620.00
Bed and Breakfast from £62.00
Lunch from £11.00 and A La Carte
Dinner from £18.50 and A La Carte

VAT inclusive. Credit Cards—Access, American Express, Diners Club, Visa
13 Family Rooms. 12 Double, 31 Twin, 18 Single Bedrooms. All Rooms with Private

Bath/Shower Room, TV, Telephone, Radio, Baby-listening, Hairdryer. Open all Year.
Fully Licensed. Full CH. Lift. 3 Cocktail Bars. Games Room. Snooker Room.

Section 1: Cornwall

Near St Austell, Carlyon Bay—Cliff Head Hotel
Sea Road, Carlyon Bay, St Austell, Cornwall. PL25 3RB. Tel 072 681 2345. Fax 072 681 5511

On a private road overlooking the sea, set in more than two acres of multi-coloured hydrangeas, this bright and modern hotel must appeal to all who are young at heart. A heated swimming pool in the gardens has a removable covering roof, allowing instant indoor-outdoor conversion according to weather conditions. Also a new Sauna, Solarium and Fitness Room has recently been added. Carlyon Bay is renowned for its vast expanse of beaches and coves. There are many attractive fishing villages within easy reach, and the excellent local facilities include riding, sea and river fishing, sailing, water skiing, golf, squash, badminton, tennis and a multigym. Those exploring the surrounding countryside via the clifftop paths will enjoy the tropical plants whose growth is encouraged by the exceptional climate of the Cornish Riviera. Guests attending the in-house entertainments, eating in the dining room with its sea view or relaxing in the cocktail bar or lounge, have the reassurance of a baby-listening service available in the *en suite* bedrooms. Family bedrooms and a family suite are also offered. Cliff Head Hotel has the facilities for weddings, parties and conferences; its entertainments lounge has its own bar and dance floor. A separate lounge is provided for that quiet read or friendly chat. In terms of courtesy, cleanliness, comfort and *cuisine* we were most impressed. Add to this a setting conducive to relaxation, with so many activities near at hand, and you have something to suit every taste.

Weekly Terms from £229.71
Daily Terms from £37.37
Bed and Breakfast from £28.17
Bar Lunch from £2.95
Dinner from £9.95 Table D'Hôte
Gratuities at Guest's Discretion

VAT inclusive. Credit Cards—Access, American Express, Diners Club, Visa
9 Family Rooms. 2 Suites
14 Double, 13 Twin, 14 Single Bedrooms
All Rooms with Private Bath/Shower Room, TV, Radio, Baby-listening, Tea and

Coffee-making Facilities
45 Rooms with Telephone
Open all Year. Fully Licensed. Full Central Heating. Conference Facilities. Children catered for. Dogs allowed. Parking Facilities. Night Porter. Swimming Pool

St Ives–The Garrack Hotel
Burthallan Lane, St Ives, Cornwall. TR26 3AA. Tel 0736 796199. Fax 0326 798955

Life flows easily and unobtrusively at The Garrack Hotel, which has recently celebrated twenty-six years of continuous ownership by the Kilby family: John, Frances, Michael and Stephen. Michael was trained at Claridges and in his capacity as hotel manager ably upholds the standards for food, pleasant service and conscientious attention to the comfort and welfare of their guests. Tucked away near to Clodgy Point, the hotel offers lovely views over green fields and low stone walls to the open sea and, from another side, over the picturesque Old Town (ten minutes' walk away) to St Ives Bay and Godrevy Lighthouse. A number of additions, extensions and improvements have been made during the Kilby's long period of ownership. Immediately adjacent to the hotel is a leisure complex consisting of a hydro spa, a heated indoor swimming-pool, a sauna and solarium, changing rooms, a bar and coffee shop serving light meals throughout the day. All this is contained within two acres of grounds, including lawns, flowerbeds and rock gardens, which are lit at night. A walled vegetable garden provides, in season, a plentiful supply of fresh produce for the table. They have good wines at exceedingly reasonable prices. Their charming restaurant is open to non-residents and, because of its established reputation and all the facilities of the recreation complex, they have recently been awarded an AA rosette, it is now open all the year round. The family deserves the international praise it receives, also the high commendations (ETB 4 Crown Commended) from tourist and motoring organisations. A jovial welcome awaits you.

Weekly Terms from £316.00
Bed and Breakfast from £34.00
Bar Lunch from £3.75
Dinner from £16.00 and A La Carte
Gratuities at Guest's Discretion
VAT inclusive. Credit Cards—Access,

American Express, Diners Club, Visa
18 Bedrooms.
All Rooms with Private Bath and/or Shower, Telephone, Radio, Baby-listening. TV and Hairdryer available on Request. Open all Year

Residential and Restaurant Licence
Full CH. Cocktail Bar. TV Lounge. Children catered for. Dogs allowed by arrangement Parking Facilities. Indoor Swimming Pool, Solarium, Sauna, Tennis, Putting, Squash, Golf, Fishing, Riding, Sailing.

Section 1: Cornwall

St Just-in-Roseland—Rose-da-Mar Hotel
St Just-in-Roseland, Near Truro, Cornwall. TR2 5JB. Tel 0326 270450

The family-run Rose-da-Mar is a charming, small luxury hotel set in an area of outstanding natural beauty on the lovely Roseland Peninsula. All its bedrooms have superb views over the broad sailing waters of the Carrick Roads, a sea inlet between Falmouth and St Mawes, extending inland to Truro. It is ideally placed for guests wishing to tour the region or for those who prefer a quiet, restful holiday in picturesque surroundings. Nearby are numerous enchanting coves and beaches and, for the sporting enthusiast, there are many varied facilities in the area. Resident owners David and Marilyn Brown maintain a very high degree of comfort, cleanliness and *cuisine*, ensuring that everyone can relax completely in this idyllic setting. A favourite spot is the sheltered sun terrace, overlooking a pleasant garden. For a scenic stroll, the tranquil St Just Pool is a popular choice. Some three miles north of the hotel is the King Harry Ferry which, to the west, takes one to the Trelissick Gardens and the network of country roads for which western Cornwall is famous. Here may be found small villages with quaint names, some relics of the tin-mining times, historic houses, the expansive Stithian's Reservoir and, at Gweek, a seal sanctuary. Without taking the ferry, motorists will find much of interest on the east bank, especially by driving northwards to the region of Probus. Also, the banks of the river Fal present a green and peaceful resting-place, a change from the coastal bays.

Terms on Application
Gratuities at Guest's Discretion
VAT inclusive
1 Family Room
3 Double, 4 Twin, 2 Single Bedrooms
4 Private Bathrooms

1 Private Shower Room
All Rooms with Tea and Coffee-making Facilities
Hairdryer available on Request
Open from March to October
Residential and Restaurant Licence

Full Central Heating
Cocktail Bar
Small dogs allowed
Parking Facilities
Nearby: Golf, Fishing, Riding, Sailing, Windsurfing

St Mawes—The St Mawes Hotel
The Seafront, St Mawes, Cornwall. TR2 5DW. Tel 0326 270266

If you feel like taking life quietly and comfortably; perhaps relaxing in your room, or on a private balcony, and watching the sun dance on sheltered waters, drop a line to this hotel, which is set right on the sea front at St Mawes. We returned to St Mawes recently on a bright sunny day when the tide was high and the sea was calm. In conditions such as these this distinctive hotel of seventeenth-century vintage looks especially inviting. The St Mawes Hotel and restaurant is renowned for its seafood; specialities include oysters, lobster, crab and mussels, as well as the many finned varieties. Do try, however, if you can, to stay at the hotel, for it has been most carefully modernized over the last ten years by the resident owners, Juliet and Clifford Burrows. It is clearly the aim of Mr and Mrs Burrows to please and the size of their hotel ensures that each guest enjoys the highest standard of comfort, plus the special personal attention which will turn his or her visit into a very memorable holiday. Every bedroom has its own bathroom and shower, self-dial telephone, colour television, a hairdryer and tea and coffee-making facilities. On the first floor, facing the sea, are two especially spacious rooms which can be considered as small suites. It is fortunate that this estuary town has such a jewel of a small hotel as the St Mawes (it has only seven bedrooms), for, thanks to its setting and the way it is conducted, we get as much pleasure in recommending it to our readers as in going there ourselves.

Weekly Terms from £260.00
Daily Terms from £41.00
Bar Lunch from £4.50
Lunch from £9.50 and A La Carte
Dinner from £16.00
Service charge and VAT inclusive

Credit Cards—Access, Visa
4 Double, 3 Twin Bedrooms
All rooms with private bathroom and shower, self-dial telephone, colour TV, Radio, Tea and Coffee-making Facilities, Hairdryers

Open from February to November
Fully Licensed. Part CH and Electric Fires. Cocktail Bar. Children over 5 years catered for. Dogs allowed. Parking Facilities nearby
Nearby: Golf, Sea Fishing, Sailing, Windsurfing, Water Skiing

Section 1: Cornwall

St Mawes-Idle Rocks Hotel
St Mawes, Cornwall. TR2 5AN.
Tel 0326 270771. Phone Free 0800 243 020. Fax 0326 270 062

'Water lapping lazily on the hotel's rocky foot-stool, casement windows wide open. Colourful curtains flapping in the gentle breeze. Idle Rocks, and idle luxury!' We penned these words recently whilst staying at the Idle Rocks, one of the most photographed hotels in Cornwall. There is no doubting its picturesqueness, for it rests its elbows on the window sill of Falmouth Bay. Consequently, you could enjoy sheltered seascapes throughout your stay from your bedroom, the restaurant and, of course, the promenade deck with its sea wall. However, the attractions of the Idle Rocks are more than skin deep. They now boast 4 Crowns Highly Recommended from the ETB. You will notice how many discerning local folk frequent the hotel's comfortable bar and attractive restaurant. How people go out of their way to enjoy morning coffee, bar lunches and mouthwatering afternoon teas with clotted cream here. The ambiance is so relaxed and friendly, and, of course, there is always the view. The owners, Mr and Mrs E K Richardson, have refurnished and re-equipped all the hotel bedrooms. This work has included installing direct dial telephones, remote control televisions, hairdryers, radio alarm clocks, new curtains, carpets and beds. The restaurant, bar and kitchens have been completely refurbished and are now under the direction of chef, Alan Vickops. The menus offer English and continental cuisine, with fresh local crab and other seafoods a speciality. Dine here and you are ever aware that Cornwall, with the seas around it, is a land of plenty. And finally, there is Phil Salter, the manager, who ensures that life at the Idle Rocks flows as smoothly as do the waters in and out of the estuary. As we say, idle luxury.

Terms on Application
Credit Cards—Access, American Express, Diners Club, Visa
5 Family Rooms
12 Double, 3 Twin, 2 Single Bedrooms
All Rooms with Private Bath/Shower

Room, TV, Telephone, Radio, Hairdryer, Tea and Coffee-making Facilities,
Baby-listening
Open all Year
Full Licence.
Full Central Heating

Cocktail Bar.
Children catered for
Dogs allowed by Arrangement
Parking Facilities
Nearby: Tennis, Golf, Fishing, Sailing, Windsurfing, Water Skiing

Section 1: Cornwall

Tintagel–Bossiney House Hotel
Tintagel, Cornwall. PL34 0AX. Tel 0840 770240

The north Cornish coastline, particularly around Boscastle and Tintagel, has always had an appeal to all appreciative of wild cliff scenery, romance and that type of contentment which can never be found in towns. For such, this country house, perched about half a mile from Tintagel, on the cliffs overlooking Bossiney Cove, will surely delight. Here the emphasis is on good English cooking with excellent choices and variation throughout all the menus, and really personal attention by the resident proprietors and their family. They give excellent value for money, and they and their staff work as a dedicated team to make your stay most comfortable. All the tastefully furnished bedrooms have sea or country views; seventeen, including the family suite, have either a private bathroom or shower room. Nine bedrooms are on the ground floor, which is ideal for those wishing to avoid stairs. There are three lounges, including a separate colour television lounge, and the *Drake Room Cocktail Bar*, a reminder that Sir Francis Drake represented Bossiney at Westminster. There are two and a half acres of attractive gardens and lawns, an interesting putting course and ample free car parking for all guests. The latest addition, in a continuing programme of improvement, is the *Log Cabin Leisure Complex*, which provides a heated indoor swimming pool, a sauna, a solarium and exercising equipment. The hotel is only a few minutes' walk from sandy beaches and magnificent cliff walks and is ideally situated for exploring an area full of interest and beauty.

Weekly Terms from £255.00	American Express, Diners Club	Residential and Restaurant Licence
Daily Terms from £37.00	1 Family Room. 12 Double, 6 Twin	Cocktail Bar. TV Lounge. Children catered
Bed and Breakfast from £28.00	Bedrooms. 11 Private Bathrooms	for. Dogs allowed by Arrangement
Dinner from £12.00 and A La Carte	6 Private Shower Rooms	Parking Facilities. Putting, Indoor Heated
Gratuities at Guest's Discretion	All Rooms with Tea and Coffee-making	Swimming Pool, Solarium, Sauna.
VAT inclusive. Credit Cards—Access,	Facilities. Open from Easter to late October	

Nr Wadebridge, St Kew Highway–Hendra Country Guest House
St Kew Highway, Nr Wadebridge, Bodmin, Cornwall, PL30 3EQ. Tel 0208 84343

If what you seek is a friendly family atmosphere in a totally unspoilt area of Cornwall, you are unlikely to do better than to book in here. Irene and Eddie Jones have spent some five years improving the comfort and facilities in this Grade II Listed Building, with its wealth of slate floors and two impressive slate fireplaces. Log fires supplement the central heating in the colder weather, ensuring a relaxed setting for the enjoyment of a drink, a quiet game of billiards or the exchange of information and experiences concerning the many local attractions. Your four-course dinner will be something out of the ordinary, all the food being home-made, with most of the vegetables home-grown, and will be enhanced by a good selection of wines stored in the cellar. The Jones make a point of offering to meet individual requirements, ranging from special dietary needs to provision for the cleaning and drying of sports equipment and clothing. In this area, golf, fishing, walking and horse-riding are within easy reach, as are various theme parks, gardens and museums. On Bodmin Moor, with its many natural features, stands Brown Willy, at 1375 feet the highest point in Cornwall. In the fishing village of Port Isaac, slate-hung houses have charming shell-decked gardens, and one narrow lane is aptly named 'Squeeze Belly Alley'. Whether you are travelling alone or as a family group, you can be assured of a warm welcome at Hendra and a good choice of nearby places of interest.

Weekly Terms from £192.00 pp	Visa. 1 Family Room. 1 Single, 1 Twin, 2	Residential Licence
Daily Terms from £29.50 pp	Double Bedrooms	Full CH. TV Lounge. Games Room
Bed and Breakfast from £17.50 per person	1 Private Bathroom. 4 Private Shower	Children catered for. Dogs allowed
per night/£108.00 per person per week	Rooms. All Rooms with TV, Radio, Tea	Parking Facilities. Croquet
Dinner from £12.00 Table D'Hôte	and Coffee-making Facilities	Nearby: Tennis, Squash, Badminton,
Gratuities at Guest's Discretion	Open from February to December	Swimming, Solarium, Golf, Fishing,
VAT not applicable. Credit Cards-Access,		Riding, Sailing, Windsurfing

Section 1: Isles of Scilly

Bryher—Hell Bay Hotel
Bryher, Isles of Scilly, Cornwall. TR23 0PR. Tel 0720 22947

If you long to get away from it all–really away–but with all the creature comforts of delightful accommodation and excellent food, look no further. Hell Bay Hotel is the only hotel on the beautiful unspoilt island of Bryher. It is an extensive conversion from an old Scillonian farmhouse and is family-owned and personally supervised by Sorrel Atkinson who pays particular attention to welcoming her guests, and making them feel at home. The two first-class chefs employed in the restaurant are well supplied with local produce and fresh locally caught fish, lobsters, crabs and oysters. There are ten "Garden Suites" all opening on to the hotel's attractive gardens. Each suite has a comfortable sitting room. The suites are individually decorated using island flowers as the theme. There are also family suites - again with sitting room and private facilities - which prove very popular, as the children are accommodated at reduced rates even though they have their own separate bedroom. Surrounding them are delightful gardens with lawns for children to play on, secluded areas for sunbathing and beautiful beaches with clear blue waters. There is also a pitch and putt course and a new croquet lawn. Unspoilt scenery, sub-tropical plants and wildlife are all around you. The hotel will organise your travel from Penzance, Lands End or Exeter - with a choice of ferry, helicopter or fixed wing aircraft. The hotel sends out a comprehensive information pack which includes colour brochure and details of travel, upon request.

Weekly Terms from £280.00	VAT inclusive. Credit Cards–Access, Visa	Open from mid-March to early October
Daily Terms from £40.00	2 Family Suites. 8 Suites	Fully Licensed. Full Central Heating
Bar Lunch from £2.25	4 Twin Bedroom. 3 Private Bathrooms	Cocktail Bar. Children catered for
Afternoon Tea from £2.00	7 Private Shower Rooms	Dogs not allowed. Putting, Fishing, Sailing,
Dinner from £17.00	All Rooms with TV, Tea and Coffee-making	Windsurfing, Croquet
Gratuities at Guest's Discretion	Facilities, Hairdryer	Nearby: Boat Trips, Birdwatching

St Mary's—Carnwethers
Pelistry Bay, St Mary's, Isles of Scilly, Cornwall. TR21 0NX. Tel 0720 22415

Situated above the beautiful bay of Pelistry on the opposite side of the main Isle of St Mary's to that of the main centre of Hugh Town this former farmhouse has built up a reputation as a high class guest house. Carnwethers stands in an acre of grounds close to the beach and amenities include an outdoor heated swimming pool, croquet lawn, games room and sauna. Nearby facilities for golf, diving, horse riding, cycling, sailing, windsurfing and subaqua can also be enjoyed. The service offered by resident proprietors Mr and Mrs Graham is both charming and welcoming and the peaceful and tranquil atmosphere of Pelistry ensures a comfortable and relaxing stay. The original farmhouse has been tastefully modernised and extended, at present there are ten bedrooms, all of which are pleasantly furnished and each equipped with bathroom or shower *en suite* and tea and coffee-making facilities. Mrs Graham offers a homely and enjoyable *table d'hôte* menu that is served straight from the oven and includes fresh local produce and daily catches from the sea to form the basis for every meal. There is an extensive variety of wines to accompany your meal from a very well stocked bar. During your stay do not miss the opportunity to sample the revelation of the famous Scillonian marmalade made on the premises from an ancient recipe.

Daily Terms from £32.00 (DB&B)	All Rooms with TV, Radio, Tea and	Children over 7 years catered for
Gratuities at Guest's Discretion	Coffee-making Facilities, Hairdryer	Dogs not allowed. Parking Facilities
VAT inclusive	Open from 1st April to 23rd October	Croquet, Putting, Outdoor Swimming Pool,
2 Family Rooms	Residential Licence	Sauna
4 Double, 1 Single, 3 Twin Bedrooms	Full Central Heating	Nearby: Squash, Golf, Fishing, Riding,
9 Private Bathrooms	Cocktail Bar	Sailing, Windsurfing, Nature Safaris,
1 Private Shower Room	TV Lounge. Games Room. Library	Cycling, Birdwatching, Sub Aqua

Section 1: Isles of Scilly and Devon

St Mary's—Tregarthen's Hotel
St Mary's, Isles of Scilly, Cornwall. TR21 0PP. Tel 0720 22540. Fax 0720 22089

Tegarthen's has a long-standing reputation for friendly hospitality and comfort and is still considered the premier hotel of the Island. Alfred Lord Tennyson braved the journey from Penzance to be one of the hotel's earliest visitors–he wrote his 'Enoch Arden' in its gardens. Today, the crossing is made by helicopter or comfortable modern steamer. Once there, however, the Island's charms seem little changed in 150 years. Life is uncluttered and uncomplicated, daffodils bloom in December, winter is almost non-existent and the many sub-tropical plants are a testimony to the mildness of the climate. Being quietly situated above the harbour, Tregarthen's offers its visitors grandstand views of all these attractions. Indeed, stay there and you will find yourself spending a good part of your holiday in the public rooms and on the sun terrace reflecting on the beauty of it all! If you can tear yourself away from the views, however, you will appreciate all the more the detailed thought that has gone into making Tregarthen's so homely and relaxing and one of the most welcoming places we have ever come across. The hotel has recently been refurbished to very good effect and we especially enjoyed the ambience of the spacious open plan public areas and the comfort of our well-equipped bedroom. Withal, Richard Chantrey has gathered around him an excellent team. In our experience, nothing is too much trouble for the young staff, whilst the chef's imaginative *cuisine* makes anticipation of dinner a day-long event. If you would enjoy the island life, simple and un-hurried, and have this allied to very high standards of comfort and service, you will find Tregarthen's a bolt-hole like no other.

Terms on Application. Bar Lunch from £2.50 Dinner from £19.00 Table D'Hôte Gratuities at Guest's Discretion. VAT inclusive. Credit Cards—Access, American Express, Diners Club, Visa 1 Suite. 5 Family Rooms. 8 Double, 12 Twin, 7 Single Bedrooms All Rooms with Private Bathroom, TV, Telephone, Radio, Tea and Coffee-making Facilities. Open from mid-March to mid-October. Fully Licensed. Part CH. Cocktail Bar. Dogs not allowed

Ashburton—Holne Chase Hotel
Two Bridges Road, Near Ashburton, Devon. TQ13 7NS. Tel 03643 471/2

This delightful country house is open all year round and is ideal for a winter or spring break, a long weekend or a relaxing holiday. Situated three miles north west of Ashburton on the Dartmeet/Two Bridges road, Holne Chase sits in twenty-five acres of its own grounds between the road and the River Dart, half a mile after crossing Holne Bridge, and is in one of the most sheltered positions within the Dartmoor National Park. You have the opportunity of eating like a gourmet in the hotel restaurant and choosing from a list of over 100 wines. The restaurant is open to non-residents, should you be touring this picturesque part of the country. Those fortunate enough to be staying at the Holne Chase Hotel will find much to amuse them. Balloons are occasionally launched from the grounds, the hotel has a salmon and sea-trout beat for guests and trout fishing is also available and there is Croquet and putting during the summer months. There is a delightful Victorian Pleasure Garden which is continually being improved and added to. The proprietors have recently completed a small library with a varied collection of books including a selection of 1st and 2nd World War Memoirs. Walking is another popular pastime, and golf, swimming and sailing are all within twenty miles from the hotel. In season there is also hunting and pony trekking. A number of special-interest weekends (some active, some less so) are offered during the winter and 5-day National Trust Breaks are also offered during April and October. All enquiries should be directed to the resident proprietors, Kenneth Bromage or Hugh Bromage.

All Terms pertaining to 1992 Summer and Winter Breaks on application Daily Terms from £57.50. Bed and Breakfast from £41.00. Bar Lunch from £4.00. Lunch from £13.75 Dinner from £18.50. Gratuities at Guest's Discretion. VAT inclusive Credit Cards—Access, American Express, Diners Club, Visa. 2 Suites. 1 Single, 4 Double, 7 Twin Bedrooms. 12 Private Bathrooms. 2 Private Shower Rooms. All Rooms with TV, Telephone, Radio, Tea and Coffee-making Facilities Most Rooms with Baby-listening, Hairdryer Open all Year. Residential and Restaurant Licence. Full CH. Conference Facilities Children catered for. Dogs allowed Parking Facilities. Croquet, Putting, Fishing

Section 1: Devon

Near Axminster, Chardstock—Tytherleigh Cot Hotel Chardstock, Axminster, Devon. EX13 7BN. Tel 0460 21170. Fax 0460 21291

When we first stayed at Tytherleigh Cot Hotel we marked our report 'best in its class'. Having been there again we updated this to 'in a class of its own'. Pat and Frank Grudgings have done wonders in the past few years with this thatched Grade II listed building. It is the oldest house in Chardstock, having been built in the fourteenth century, and was at one time the village cider house. The *Conservatory Restaurant* has an enormous following for its fine food and wines and has received the AA Rosette and RAC Restaurant Awards. The old barns within the grounds have been extensively renovated to provide luxury *en suite* bedrooms. In addition to the attractive bathroom, these suites contain all modern notions of comfort. There are extra touches, however, refrigerators with French champagne and colour television with video and film library. In addition to the above, the owners have now completed six special suites with a four-poster or half-tester bed and two with inglenook fireplaces and *double* jacuzzi baths. We have seen these rooms and summed them up in one word-fabulous! Yet, for all the modernness within, and the heated swimming pool in the grounds, Tytherleigh Cot still has a lovely olde-worlde ambiance about it. You will find it in an area which is deliciously rural and full of interest. The village of Tytherleigh lies in the rich green valley of the Axe beside the A358 Chard to Axminster road. Tytherleigh Cot Hotel will be found a mile or so to the west in the hamlet of Chardstock.

Weekly Terms from £349.90. Daily Terms from £58.55. Special rates available for 2 or more nights stay. Bed and Breakfast from £45.80. Bar Meal from £5.50. Lunch from £8.50 and A La Carte. Dinner from £16.95 and A La Carte. Gratuities at Guest's Discretion. VAT inclusive. Credit Cards—Access, Visa.

Gourmet and Champagne Breaks available. 4 Four Poster Suites with Jacuzzi Bath. 2 Half Tester Suites with Jacuzzi Bath. 6 Double, 4 Twin, 2 Single Bedrooms. All Rooms with Private Bathroom, TV, Telephone, Radio, Baby-listening, Tea and Coffee-making

Facilities, Trouser Press, Hairdryer, Video and Mini-bar. Open all Year. Full CH. Residential and Restaurant Licence. Conference Facilities. Children over 12 years catered for. Dogs allowed. Parking Facilities. Outdoor Heated Swimming. Pool, Solarium, Sauna, Shooting.

Barnstaple–The Royal & Fortescue Hotel Boutport Street, Barnstaple, Devon EX31 1HG. Tel 0271 42289. Fax 0271 78558

This splendid building has undergone a complete transformation since our last visit. Extensive re-modelling and total refurbishment has been accompanied by renewed enthusiasm and attentiveness by the staff, clearly and justifiably proud of their reborn hotel. Early mention must be made of the exceptional food here. There is everything available from a quick snack to an inexpensive bar meal, from a packed lunch to a gourmet dinner, all at most realistic prices. With its fifty *en suite* bedrooms, main function suite, seminar and conference rooms, the Royal & Fortescue Hotel has ample accommodation and facilities to ensure outstandingly successful business events and memorable social occasions. Here, too, we must commend a moderate tariff. On the edge of the town is the Barnstaple Hotel, also one of the Brend Group, and the vast range of health and leisure activities here are freely available to guests at the Royal & Fortescue. Spaciousness, comfort and a relaxing *décor* are evident in all parts of the hotel. It earned its present title following patronage by the late King Edward VII, then Prince of Wales, and still retains the character and charm from its days as a Coaching Inn. Barnstaple, the ancient 'capital' of North Devon, includes the seventeenth-century colonnaded arcade of Queen Anne's Walk and, in Farm Park, rare breeds of cattle, sheep, deer, poultry and water fowl. Not only is the town a popular shopping centre, it is a supremely central spot from which to tour the famous coastline and countryside of North Devon.

Weekly Terms from £250.00
Daily Terms from £30.00 per person (weekends)/£40.00 per person (Weekdays)
Bar Lunch from £2.50. Lunch from £6.75 and A La Carte. Bar Supper from £5.50 Dinner from £10.75 and A La Carte

Gratuities at Guest's Discretion. VAT inclusive. Credit Cards-Access, American Express, Diners Club, Visa
4 Family Rooms. 22 Double, 20 Twin, 4 Single Bedrooms. All Rooms with Private Bathroom, TV, Telephone, Radio,

Baby-listening, Tea and Coffee-making Facilities. Open all year. Fully Licensed Full CH. Lift. Cocktail Bar. Conference Facilities. Children catered for. Dogs allowed. Parking Facilities. Night Porter Swimming, Solarium, Sauna available

Section 1: Devon

Beer—Bovey House Hotel
Beer, Seaton, Devon. EX12 3AD. Tel 029 780 241

Bovey House is an Elizabethan country house brimming with character and atmosphere. It has a long and fascinating history, and is reputed to have been presented to Catherine Parr, in 1542, by King Henry VIII. Nowadays, the house is a thriving hotel and lacks nothing in the way of modern facilities: the rooms are light and airy and the house is centrally heated throughout. Nevertheless, its past is everywhere apparent, from the *Charles Room*, with its beautiful coffered ceiling, to the fine oak-panelled dining-room, where guests may wine and dine by candlelight. In the elegant panelled drawing-room you can relax and quietly soak up the peaceful ambience. The eleven bedrooms are all spacious, well furnished and well equipped. For honeymoon couples there is a delightful four-poster bedroom. You can be certain of an hospitable welcome from the resident proprietors, Mr and Mrs Cole, and their daughter and son-in-law, Mr and Mrs Gosden. They pride themselves on the personal service and attention they provide, ensuring that nothing is lacking to make each guest's stay really memorable. We were not surprised to learn that the excellent *cuisine* here is attracting much local attention. Our meal in the *Bovey Grill*, chosen from the *à la carte* menu, was superb in every respect. Bovey House Hotel is set between the picturesque villages of Beer and Branscombe–do come and sample some of its unique charms for yourself.

Weekly Terms from £240.00 (DB&B)
Bed and Breakfast from £23.00
Lunch from £10.50 Table D'Hôte
Dinner from £16.00 Table D'Hôte
Gratuities at Guest's Discretion
VAT inclusive. Credit Cards—Access, Visa
2 Family Rooms. 5 Double, 4 Twin Bedrooms. 5 Private Bathrooms.

3 Private Shower Rooms.
All Rooms with TV, Telephone, Radio, Baby-listening, Tea and Coffee-making Facilities
Hairdryer available on Request
Open from 8th Feb to 3rd Jan, except Christmas.
Residential and Restaurant Licence.

Part Central Heating. Cocktail Bar
Conference Facilities. Children catered for
Dogs allowed. Parking Facilities.
Nearby: Tennis, Croquet, Putting, Squash
Badminton, Swimming, Solarium, Sauna,
Golf, Fishing, Riding, Sailing, Windsurfing,
Water Skiing, Shooting, Hang-gliding

Near Bideford, Northam—Yeoldon Country House Hotel & Restaurant
Durrant Lane, Northam, Devon. EX39 2RL. Tel 0237 474400. Fax 0237 476618

For many years Bideford was north Devon's principal port, and, two miles away to the north, the estuary town of Appledore was famed for its ship building. These sheltered waters were busy with shipping during the last century, when many prosperous merchants and sea captains built homes for themselves along the banks of the River Torridge. Many of these country houses have become good hotels, and one of the best is Yeoldon House Hotel and Restaurant. Here Vivienne and Neil Turner have created an hotel which is ideal for both peaceful and purposeful holidays. The house has all the charm of a Victorian gentleman's residence and the setting could hardly be more tranquil: neat lawns sweep down to mature trees and, beyond these, the river flows gently to the sea. For those who wish to follow more earnest pursuits, however, the hotel offers a number of speciality holidays, with themes as diverse as 'Romance Renewed', 'Tarka the Otter', 'Wine Tasting', 'Shooting' and even 'Glass Blowing'. To accompany these activities there are individually characterised menus. Responsible for these is a chef with twenty years' professional experience in leading hotels, who joined the Yeoldon early in 1990. Whilst the hotel prospers and progresses, we are delighted to observe that its distinctive character remains unchanged. It is warm and hospitable, the service is willing and informal, and the furnishings have been chosen with great care. Mr and Mrs Turner also have the right approach to catering, with the English and continental dishes relying heavily on fresh local fish, meat and vegetables.

Daily Terms from £49.75
Bed and Breakfast from £47.50
Bar Lunch from £6.00. Lunch from £13.50
Dinner from £24.75. Gratuities at Guest's Discretion. VAT inclusive
Credit Cards—Access, Visa

2 Family Rooms. 1 Suite. 4 Double, 3 Twin Bedrooms. All Rooms with Private Bathroom, TV, Telephone, Radio, Baby-listening, Tea and Coffee-making Facilities. Open all year. Fully Licensed
Full Central Heating. Cocktail Bar. TV

Lounge. Conference Facilities.
Parking Facilities. Croquet, Putting, Sauna
Nearby: Tennis, Squash, Badminton,
Swimming, Solarium, Golf, Fishing, Riding,
Sailing, Windsurfing, Water Skiing,
Shooting, Hang-gliding

Section 1: Devon

Near Bideford, Parkham—Penhaven Country House
Parkham, Near Bideford, Devon. EX39 5PL. Tel 0237 451388/711. Fax 0237 451878

In wooded countryside behind Bideford Bay Alan and Maxine Wade have created this lovely country-house hotel from a former Victorian rectory. It is so ideally suited to its present role, and is so splendidly situated, that their endeavours brought them almost immediate recognition. Penhaven is a little piece of rural heaven. Nine acres of woodlands, traversed by a brook and a stream, contain a wealth of flora, fauna and footpaths and ensure utter seclusion. There are a further two acres of formal gardens into which they have constructed a Victorian 'Orangery' restaurant giving magnificent views across the valley. We were given a most friendly welcome upon arrival and were very quickly regretting that our itinerary allowed for only one night in such a delectable spot. The meals at Penhaven benefit enormously form the fresh local produce. Another feature which makes Penhaven Country House such an interesting venture is the five attractive serviced cottage suites complete with fitted kitchens, colour television and video facilities. Guests occupying these enjoy the full facilities of the hotel itself but with the added opportunity for relaxation in the seclusion of their own cottage. We imagine that a holiday here would be both restful and fun.

Weekly Terms from £360.00	2 Suites. 1 Ground Floor Suite	Conference Facilities
Daily Terms from £49.00	7 Double, 4 Twin Bedrooms	Children not catered for
Afternoon Tea from £2.00	12 Private Bathrooms	Dogs allowed. Parking Facilities
Dinner from £13.50 and A La Carte	12 Rooms with TV and Video Channel,	Nearby: Tennis, Croquet, Putting, Squash,
Gratuities at Guest's Discretion	Telephone, Radio, Tea and Coffee-making	Badminton, Swimming Pool, Golf, Fishing,
VAT inclusive	Facilities	Riding, Sailing, Windsurfing, Water Skiing,
Credit Cards—Access, American Express,	Open all Year.	Walking
Diners Club, Visa	Fully Licensed. Full Central Heating	

Bishops Tawton—Downrew House Hotel
Bishops Tawton, Near Barnstaple, Devon. EX32 0DY. Tel 0271 42497/46673. Fax 0271 23947

And now for Downrew House. One day, about fifteen minutes after we had been held up in the holiday traffic in Barnstaple, we turned left off the A377 road at Codden Hill Cross, about half a mile on the Exeter side of Bishops Tawton village. The signpost indicates 'Chittlehampton and Cobbaton', and very soon we were again held up...but this time by a drake, his spouse and their family, marching in single file across the road. Our destination lay a further mile along this country road. Downrew House was built in 1640, enlarged during the reign of Queen Anne and stands 500 feet up in twelve acres of gardens and meadowland. Country house hotels of this standard are at a premium. The atmosphere is relaxed and friendly, and the food is quite outstanding, with many of the vegetables, fruit and herbs required in the kitchen coming from the hotel's gardens. Here, too, lie some of Downrew's surprises. A secluded, palm-fringed outdoor swimming pool which is kept at a constant 80 degrees from Easter to October each year. An all weather tennis court, a croquet lawn and a private fifteen-hole approach and putt golf course, with holes of between sixty and 210 yards. Within the house there are also a billiards room, card room, games room and a solarium with Sontegra sunbed. The Johnson family limit the amount of guests to twenty-eight at any one time, and this means one is given the most personal service, in a quiet and friendly way. Downrew House makes a marvellous base from which to tour, but be warned, you may be tempted never to leave the house and the grounds.

Weekly Terms from £240.00 (Half Board)	Bedrooms. All Rooms with Private	Conference Facilities
Daily Terms from £48.00 (Half Board)	Bathroom, TV, Telephone, Radio, Tea and	Children over 7 years catered for
Dinner £16.50 and A La Carte	Coffee-making Facilities, Hairdryer, Ironing	Dogs and Cats welcome. Parking
VAT inclusive. Gratuities at Guest's	Facilities. Open all year	Facilities. Hard Tennis Court, Croquet,
Discretion. Credit Cards—Access, Visa	Residential and Restaurant Licence	Outdoor Heated Swimming Pool, Solarium,
2 Family Rooms. 4 Double, 6 Twin	Full Central Heating. Games Room	15-hole Golf Course

Section 1: Devon

Bovey Tracey—Coombe Cross Hotel
Bovey Tracey, Near Newton Abbot, Devon. TQ13 9EY
Telephone 0626 832476

Bovey Tracey is one of Dartmoor's Gateway Towns and from it one steps directly onto the Moor. The poet Gerard Manley Hopkins stayed here and was never able to forget the impression made on him by the 'steep dark lanes', the 'liquidness of the trees' and the colours of the ploughed fields. Just to the south of the town, only a few miles from the roar of civilisation, is the deliciously rural Coombe Cross Hotel. In the foreground is a most beautiful garden, filled with magnificent shrubs and plants. Behind the garden the surrounding countryside unfolds to give magnificent views of Dartmoor National Park. Malcolm and Veronica Day, the resident proprietors for many years, ensure that every need of their guests is catered for. The hotel which is well known for its excellent English cuisine, prepared personally by Mrs Day, has guests returning time and time again. There is a good wine list at modest prices to complement the freshly prepared dishes of the day. In the attractive restaurant, which has stunning views of the Moors beyond, we found service both attentive and friendly. The vast unspoilt 'last wilderness' is on one's doorstep here and within easy driving distance of the lovely South Devon coastline with the historic cities of Exeter and Plymouth nearby. Excellent value two or more day breaks are available all year round and for the additional enjoyment of guests, Coombe Cross now features a new leisure complex with indoor pool, sauna, solarium, spa pool and fitness suite. Whether for a summer or winter break, Coombe Cross offers excellent value all year round.

Weekly Terms (Half Board) from £260.00
Daily Terms from £41.50
Bed and Breakfast from £27.50
Lunch from £6.95. Dinner from £17.95
Gratuities at Guest's Discretion
VAT inclusive. Credit Cards—Access, American Express, Diners Club, Visa
2 Family Rooms
9 Double, 9 Twin, 4 Single Bedrooms

23 Private Bathrooms. 1 Private Shower Room. All Rooms with TV, Telephone, Radio, Baby-listening, Tea and Coffee-making Facilities, Trouser Press
Hairdryer available on Request
Drying Racks in Bathrooms.
Open all Year
Residential and Restaurant Licence. Full Central Heating. TV Lounge. Games Room

Dogs allowed by arrangement.
Conference Facilities. Parking Facilities.
Night Porter. Croquet, Indoor Swimming Pool, Sauna, Solarium, Fitness Suite
Nearby: Tennis, Putting, Squash, Badminton, Swimming, Solarium, Sauna, Golf, Fishing, Riding, Sailing, Windsurfing, Water Skiing, Shooting, Hang-gliding, Walking, Birdwatching

Section 1: Devon

Bratton Fleming—Bracken House Country Hotel
Bratton Fleming, Barnstaple, North Devon. EX31 4TG. Tel 0598 710320

This is great rambling and bird watching country. To the east of Bratton Fleming lies the protected natural beauty of Exmoor and, to the north and west, the magnificent North Devon coast; together they provide a wealth of differing panoramic views and fascinating small communities. We came here and sought out the highly regarded Bracken House Country Hotel. This former early Victorian rectory has been turned into a most charming hotel which stands in eight acres of gardens, woodland and pastures with superb views over countryside to the sea and Hartland Point. Lovers of the great outdoors will want to enjoy a protracted stay and, with a tariff offering accommodation and evening meal at really moderate rates, they will doubtless plan to re-visit at different times of the year. Our stay here endorsed all we had heard of Bracken House. Substantial breakfasts and three course dinners, freshly cooked using local produce wherever possible, are the basis of the catering. The latter is a set menu but one may at breakfast time choose an alternative for the evening meal: with prior notice vegetarian, special diets, likes and dislikes are catered for. We were delighted to accept the set menu and thoroughly enjoyed our meal. After dinner we relaxed in the library and drawing room with the cosiness of log fires, although here and in the attractive, comfortable *en suite* bedrooms full central heating keeps the hotel warm and inviting. The genial welcome, friendly and attentive service given by Jeremy Price provides true country hospitality.

Weekly Terms from £139.00
Daily Terms from £38.00
Bed and Breakfast from £28.00
Dinner from £10.00 Table D'Hôte
Gratuities at Guest's Discretion
VAT inclusive. Credit Cards-Access, Visa

4 Double, 4 Twin Bedrooms
6 Private Bathrooms. 2 Private Shower Rooms. All rooms with TV, Tea and Coffee-making Facilities
Hairdryer available on request
Open all year

Residential Licence. Full Central Heating.
Cocktail Bar. TV Lounge
Children over 12 years catered for. Dogs allowed. Parking Facilities
Croquet. Nearby:Swimming, Golf, Fishing, Riding, Sailing, Windsurfing

Budleigh Salterton—The Long Range Hotel
5 Vales Road, Budleigh Salterton, Devon. EX9 6HS. Tel 03954 3321

On the headland between Exeter and Sidmouth there is a concentration of historic and scenic places of interest inland, and many sporting activities along the coast. The Long Range hotel is close to the sea, with views of the Otter river valley, and the aim of the resident proprietors, Sue and Paul Griffin, is to offer their guests a relaxing holiday in the quiet atmosphere of a country hotel. In this, they continue to succeed most admirably, with prices maintained at very reasonable levels in these days of rising costs. All the food is home cooked and there is always a choice of main course or a cold dish and salad. As well as the residents' lounge there is a pleasant sun room and we found the whole of the hotel to be extremely well furnished and decorated. Standing in well-kept grounds, the Long Range is within easy reach of the many sporting and holiday amenities. Sailing is popular on this part of the coast and, a few miles west, windsurfing and water-skiing are widespread. In and around Budleigh Salterton there are museums, golf courses, gardens, castles, a steam railway, mill, Bicton Park and Aylesbeare Common, together with some notable view points. The resort itself is an attractive spot and essentially unspoilt, with a main bus route to Sidmouth and Exmouth only a hundred yards from the hotel. To find this gem, follow the sign on East Budleigh Road and turn down Raleigh Road into Vales Road.

Weekly Terms £200.00
Daily Terms £30.00
Bed and Breakfast £20.00
Packed Lunch £3.50
Dinner £10.00 Table D'Hôte
No Service Charge. VAT inclusive

6 Double/Twin, 1 Single Bedroom
All Rooms with Private Bath/Shower Room, TV, Tea and Coffee-making Facilities
Open all Year. Restaurant Licence
Full Central Heating. TV Lounge

50% reduction for children sharing room with parents
Dogs not allowed. Parking Facilities
Nearby: Tennis, Croquet, Putting, Squash, Swimming, Golf, Fishing, Riding, Sailing, Windsurfing

Section 1: Devon

Chagford—Easton Court Hotel
Easton Cross, Chagford, Devon. TQ13 8JL. Tel 0647 433469

Best known of several books written in this lovely old thatched Tudor house must be Evelyn Waugh's 'Brideshead Revisited'. A Grade II listed building, in the restoration process great care has been taken to preserve the original charming features, including the thatched roof, granite walls, oak beams and an inglenook fireplace complete with bread oven. The most recent change of ownership has, by far, been the happiest for this most peaceful hotel in its tranquil setting. Here one is away from the crowds yet ideally placed to explore all the fascinating backroads of the Dartmoor National Park. Castle Drogo, the garden at Finch Foundry, and Yarner Wood are just three of the many interesting places to visit. Dartmoor has the mystery and grandeur to provide an endless variety of delightful walks and breathtaking moorland scenery, with its high tors and fast-flowing rivers. Golf, riding, tennis, swimming and fishing are all available in the locality. If these activities generate healthy appetites, one is well catered for at Easton Court. A resident chef freshly prepares a five-course sumptuous meal each evening, served in the candle-lit high-ceilinged dining-room. There is a cosy library with a superb collection of old books and, in the lounge, a large open log fire. The seven double bedrooms have cottage-style low windows, giving lovely views of the garden and adjoining fields. In the capable hands of Mr and Mrs Graham Kidson, Easton Court has become a sheer delight. Only one warning: beware the sloping floors and low beams!

Seasonal Special Break Terms available
Weekly Terms from £294.00 per person
Daily Terms from £52.00 per person
Bed and Breakfast from £36.00 per person
Dinner from £19.50 Table D'Hôte
Gratuities at Guest's Discretion.

VAT inclusive
5 Double, 2 Twin Bedrooms
3 Private Bathrooms. 4 Private Shower Rooms. All Rooms with TV, Telephone, Radio, Tea and Coffee-making Facilities.
Open from February to December

Residential and Restaurant Licence
Full Gas/Radiators Heating
Cocktail Bar. TV Lounge.
Dogs allowed. Parking Facilities
Nearby: Tennis, Swimming, Golf, Fishing, Riding, Sailing, Water Skiing

Chagford—Mill End Hotel
Sandy Park, Chagford, Devon. TQ13 8JN. Tel 0647 432282. Fax 0647 433106

We have known this country hotel for many years and have always admired its tranquil setting on the banks of the River Teign in the Dartmoor National Park, 500 feet above sea level at the head of Fingle Gorge. Guests will enjoy the charming old water mill which today rotates just as smoothly as it probably did in bygone days. Despite the postal address, Mill End is *not* in the town of Chagford: visitors should stay on the main A382 road until it reaches the River Teign. From some viewpoints it is difficult to spot the road, so lush are the surrounding trees and hedgerows. Mill End, once a flour mill, was first converted to an hotel in about 1929. It is an ideal base from which to explore the greenest parts of Devon and is close to excellent fishing, golf and numerous walks beginning from the gates of the hotel. Drogo Castle overlooks Mill End's gardens, and many other interesting National Trust properties are within easy driving distance. All of the comfortable bedrooms at the hotel have a private bathroom and, after one has explored Dartmoor either by car or on horseback, a good night's sleep is assured after doing justice to the first-class menu. The food, in fact, deserves high praise and is a blend of simple and classic dishes. Fresh, quality ingredients are newly prepared each day; the wine list extends to over one hundred names; home-made desserts are praised by Mill End regulars and there is an award-winning selection of cheeses. Hazel and Nicholas Craddock run their hotel on very personal lines, achieving the atmosphere of a comfortable private house, with lots of little nooks and corners.

Weekly Terms from £375.00
Room Rate from £35.00
Light Lunch from £5.00. Lunch from £20.00 and A La Carte. Dinner from £20.00 Table D'Hôte Gratuities at Guest's Discretion
VAT inclusive. Credit Cards—Access,

American Express, Diners Club, Visa
2 Family Rooms
7 Double, 6 Twin, 2 Single Bedrooms
All Rooms with Private Bathroom, TV, Telephone, Radio, Baby-listening, Hairdryer, Tea and Coffee-making Facilities

Open all Year. Residential and Restaurant Licence. Full Central Heating. Cocktail Bar. TV Lounge. Children catered for. Dogs allowed. Parking Facilities. Fishing and Shooting in Season. Nearby: Tennis, Croquet, Squash, Swimming, Golf, Fishing

Section 1: Devon

Chagford—The Great Tree Hotel
Sandy Park, Chagford, Newton Abbot, Devon. TQ13 8JS.
Tel 0647 432491

An unusual name: an inviting drive; a delightful welcoming interior; and a southward view over Dartmoor which will be stamped indelibly on your memory. Such is the Great Tree, that country house hotel whose entrance gates are to be found about two miles from Chagford on the A382 road. There is no 'great tree' as such - but trees there are plenty, for the hotel stands in eighteen acres of grounds, much of which has been designated by the Nature Conservancy Council as being of special interest. Originally a hunting lodge, the house has been extensively modernised and refurbished over the years to provide an hotel of comfort and character. The owners, Beverley and Nigel Eaton-Gray are committed to retaining the relaxing, quiet and comfortable atmosphere for which the hotel has always been renowned. The emphasis is on quality and service, from the individually furnished bedrooms, each with private bathroom and telephone, to the elegant lounge and attractive dining room where imaginative table d'hôte meals are served. Fresh produce is used whenever possible, much of it being grown in the hotel's kitchen garden. A carefully selected wine list containing several château-bottled wines adds to the pleasure of dining here. If you seek an hotel which is run on a minimum of formality, where every room is in tune with an all-round suggestion of restfulness, you will relish a stay at The Great Tree Hotel during any time of the year. The hotel has been awarded the BTA country-house hotel/restaurant commendation.

Weekly Terms from £340.00 (DB&B)
Bed and Breakfast from £39.50
Bar Lunch from £1.50
Lunch from £9.95 Table D'Hôte
Dinner from £19.50 Table D'Hôte
Gratuities at Guest's Discretion
VAT inclusive. Credit Cards—Access,

American Express, Diners Club, Visa
7 Double, 4 Twin, 1 Single Bedroom
All Rooms with Private Bathroom, TV,
Telephone, Radio, Baby-listening, Tea and Coffee-making Facilities
Hairdryer available on Request
Open all Year. Fully Licensed

Full Central Heating. Cocktail Bar.
Dogs with valid vaccination certificate allowed.
Parking Facilities. Solarium.
Nearby: Swimming, Golf, Fishing, Riding, Shooting, Offshore Sailing

Section 1: Devon

Clovelly, Nr Bideford–Foxdown Manor
Hornscross, Bideford, Devon. EX39 5PJ
Tel 0237 451325. Fax 0237 451525

Nestling in sixteen acres of lush woodlands, Foxdown Manor was originally a very large and graceful Victorian House, and its associated stables and workshops have been beautifully converted to provide self-contained family accommodation. Not only is this a truly idyllic setting: it is an ideal location for exploring the varied charms and scenery of North Devon. A few minutes' drive westwards brings you to the car park at the top of Clovelly: on your walk down the cobbled narrow streets to the harbour, the steepness of the descent means you have only donkeys and sledges as company. A similar distance to the east lies the busy quay at Bideford, with twenty-four arches to its medieval bridge across the Torridge. This whole area has a wealth of interesting places: museums and mills, parks and potteries, forests and farms and, of course, a maze of country roads to be explored and long coastal footpaths for walkers. Outdoor sporting activities, on land or sea, also offer a wide choice. For the less energetic, a leisurely stroll through the hotel grounds, over ancient stone bridges crossing the river Yeo and past badger setts, fox dens or rabbit warrens, is an enchanting and refreshing experience. Foxdown Manor has an outdoor heated swimming pool, indoor hot spa pool, hard tennis court, croquet lawn, putting green and an indoor games room. From these diversions, enjoy the wide choice of delicious healthy food in the candle-lit dining room, relax by a blazing log fire in either of the two large lounges or retire early to your spacious ens bedroom with superb views of the North Devon countryside.

All Terms pertaining to 1992
Weekly Terms from £350.00 (Low Season from £280.00)
Daily Terms from £60.00 (Low Season from £50.00)
Bed and Breakfast from £35.00
Bar Lunch from £3.00.
Lunch from £10.00
Dinner from £16.50
Service Charge not applicable.

VAT inclusive. Credit Cards-Access, Visa
1 Family Room. 1 Suite. 4 Double, 1 Single, 2 Twin Bedrooms
6 Private Bathrooms.
2 Private Shower Rooms
All Rooms with TV, Telephone, Radio, Baby-listening, Tea and Coffee-making Facilities. Hairdryer available on request.
Open all year. Residential and Restaurant Licence. Full Central Heating.

Cocktail Bar.
TV Lounge. Games Room.
Conference Facilities
Children catered for. Dogs allowed.
Parking Facilities.
Hard Tennis Court, Croquet, Putting, Outdoor Heated Swimming Pool, Sauna.
Nearby: Squash, Badminton, Golf, Fishing, Riding, Sailing, Windsurfing, Water Skiing, Clay and Game Shooting

Section 1: Devon

Coleford, Near Crediton—Coombe House Country Hotel
Coleford, Near Crediton, Devon. EX17 5BY. Tel 0363 84487

Although Georgian in character, with all the grace and charm of that era, the cellars of Coombe House Hotel are even older (circa 13th Century) and are today a most intriguing bar. It is here that some of Cromwell's men are believed to have hidden, during the Civil War, before escaping through a secret tunnel to Crediton, some three miles away. Built originally as the Manor House of a large country estate, with space to accommodate a big family, servants and visitors, the original character has largely been preserved in the conversion to a distinctive country hotel. Now listed as a protected building of historic interest, it offers modern comforts in the fascinating public rooms and in the commodious *en suite* bedrooms. Hunters Restaurant, in former times the ballroom and, during the fifties, used for storing corn, provides a relaxing setting in which to enjoy the *à la carte* menu produced by chef David Lightfoot, who is London trained and is a *Confrère de la Chaîne des Rôtisseurs*. An elegant lounge overlooks the five acres of parkland surrounding the house, in which lie a sheltered, heated and floodlit swimming-pool, a hard tennis court and a putting course. The location is amidst some of Devon's loveliest undulating countryside, with an intricate network of narrow winding country lanes to places bearing such names as Woolfardisworthy, Cheriton Fitzpaine or Stockleigh Pomeroy. Major roads give easy access to the many charms of Exeter and the rugged appeal of Dartmoor.

Double from £53.00 per night inclusive
Single from £30.00 per night inclusive
Bar Meals from £1.65
A La Carte approx. £15.00
Credit Cards–Access, Visa
3 Family Rooms.

3 Double, 2 Single, 3 Twin Bedrooms
All rooms with colour TV, Radio, Coffee and Tea-making Facilities
Open all year.
Fully licensed.
Full Central Heating

Cocktail Bar. Residents Lounge.
Conference Facilities
Children catered for.
Dogs allowed.
Parking facilities.
Nearby: Squash, Golf, Fishing, Riding

Colyford—Swallows Eaves Hotel
Colyford, Colyton, Devon. EX13 6QJ. Tel 0297 53184

With Dartmoor uppermost in the minds of many holiday-makers, that delectable corner of Devon between the Axe and the Exe remains, to a large extent, unknown and so ... unspoilt. You may descend into it from Somerset, approach it from Exeter, or arrive from where Dorset meets Devon. We were pottering around this region, when Swallow Eaves Hotel caught our attention. It nestles at the centre of Colyford and about one-and-a-half miles from the sea. If the name intrigues, no less does the country setting, nor the friendliness which permeates the whole house. We had a look-see, and a month later took the opportunity to stay there. It was formerly a 'gentleman's residence' and there remains a profound suggestion of restfulness throughout Swallow Eaves. It is difficult not to feel at home here and, even if one does arrive fraught and travel weary, Jon and Jane Beck, the owners, will put you at your ease straight away. There was a complimentary pot of tea and biscuits laid for us in the garden. In our *en suite* bedroom were all the usual signs of modern comfort, plus fresh flowers and fruit, and even a torch just in case the power supply should fail! The meals are varied and excellent and cooked by Jane Beck, whilst Jon provides a good selection of wines. Little wonder we slept so soundly, and in the morning when the curtains were drawn a picture of a perfect English morning presented itself. This small hotel is run so efficiently and in such a friendly way we could not help signing off in the Visitors' Book, 'See you next year'.

Weekly Terms from £235.00
Daily Terms from £35.00
Bed and Breakfast from £25.00
Lunch by arrangement
Dinner from £14.50 Table d'Hôte
Service and VAT inclusive

Credit Cards–American Express
4 Double, 4 Twin Bedrooms
6 Private Bathrooms. 2 Private Shower Rooms. All Rooms with TV, Radio, Tea and Coffee-making Facilities, Hairdryer, Fruit
Open all Year

Residential and Restaurant Licence. Full CH
Children not catered for. Dogs not allowed
Parking Facilities
Nearby: Tennis, Swimming, Solarium, Sauna, Golf, Fishing, Sailing, Windsurfing

Section 1: Devon

Nr Crediton, Morchard Bishop—Wigham
Morchard Bishop, Near Crediton, Devon. EX17 6RJ.
Tel 036 37 350

It was in 1986 that this sixteenth-century Devon Longhouse was converted into an enchanting five-bedroom hotel, complete with a heated outdoor swimming-pool. Associated with the hotel is the thirty-acre farm in which it stands, providing the kitchens with fresh fruit, vegetables and dairy produce. This is a treasure-house for devotees of the country life and genuine home cooking. Quite specifically it is not for casual callers, smokers or small children. Nor, because of well-behaved resident dogs, can pets be accepted. This said, it provides the most hospitable, warm and comfortable surroundings one could wish for. Outside, the thatched roof and the garden are a real picture, while the beamed rooms and huge log-fires set the mood for the homely life within. There is a snooker room, two sitting-rooms and, in the combined dining-room and bar, guests help themselves to (and sign for) pre-dinner drinks. Meals are taken 'en famille' most evenings, usually with a set starter and main course, although specific requests in advance are happily met. All this contributes to the feeling that one is a member of a select house party. The personal quality of life at Wigham is reflected in their unusual brochure. With illustrations by John Crane it portrays a 'cut-away' view of the hotel rooms which is as informative as it is appealing, together with a painting of the rolling landscape around the hotel. Bookings are essential, and normally accepted for not less than two nights. Morchard Bishop lies some six miles north-west of Crediton, about two miles off the A377 road.

Daily Terms from £40.00 (DB&B per person)
VAT inclusive.
Credit Cards–Access, Visa (subject to 3% surcharge)
1 Family Room. 3 Double, 2 Twin Bedrooms

All Rooms with Private Bathroom, TV with video channel,
Tea and Coffee-making Facilities.
Hairdryer available on request.
Open all year.
Residential Licence

Full Central Heating.
Games Room
Dogs not allowed
Outdoor Heated Swimming Pool

Section 1: Devon

Croyde—Kittiwell House Hotel and Restaurant
Croyde, Devon. EX33 1PG.
Tel 0271 890247. Fax 0271 890469

Croyde is an almost perfect example of a pretty Devon village, famous for its multitude of thatched cottages. Pride of place amongst its buildings must be given to the sixteenth-century longhouse which, with a beautifully blended extension, has become Kittiwell House Hotel. Be sure to pay a call here if you are charmed by low, beamed ceilings, wood-panelled walls, blazing log fires and hospitality which is as warm and traditional as the surroundings. The proprietors are Jim and Yvonne Lang and their motto is 'care, comfort and cuisine'. Care you will find in abundance, for Jim and Yvonne have already taken great pains with the refurnishing and redecoration of their hotel. The result spells comfort, indeed, of the highest order, with cosy lounges and a bar waiting to receive you and well-equipped, centrally heated bedrooms providing the setting for a sound night's sleep. For romantics, a number of rooms Under the Thatch have four-poster beds and all the bedrooms have private bathrooms. As for the final word in their motto, 'cuisine', we can but recommend it to you wholeheartedly. Our table d'hôte meal was superb value for money: the food was very well prepared and presented and we must admit that we have eaten in more pretentious establishments and been offered less choice and charged far more! There is a comprehensive list of wines, too. Sixteenth-century atmosphere and twentieth-century luxury combine here in an irresistible way.

Weekly Terms (Half Board) from £315.00
Daily Terms from £50.00
Bed and Breakfast from £35.00
Sunday Lunch from £9.40 Table D'Hôte
Dinner from £15.70 and A La Carte
Gratuities at Guest's Discretion
VAT inclusive. Credit Cards—Access, American Express, Visa

2 Family Rooms. 8 Double, 2 Twin
Bedrooms. All Rooms with Private Bathroom, TV, Telephone, Radio, Baby-listening, Tea and Coffee-making Facilities. Hairdryer available on Request
3 Rooms with Four Poster Bed
Open from mid February to mid January
Residential and Restaurant Licence

Full Central Heating.
Cocktail Bar
Children catered for. Dogs allowed
Parking Facilities
Nearby: Tennis, Swimming,
*Golf, Fishing, *Riding, Sailing, Windsurfing, *Clay-Shooting, Nature Walking (* Special concessions)

Section 1: Devon

Croyde Bay, Braunton—Croyde Bay House Hotel
Moor Lane, Croyde, North Devon. EX33 1PA. Tel 0271 890270

If, however, you want to live within sight and sound of the sea at Croyde, somewhere informal and carefree, there is a marvellous little place tucked under the southern flank of the Baggy Point peninsula. It is one of those hotels which always come as a pleasant surprise when you first discover them. From the outside there is nothing much to distinguish Croyde Bay House from many Devon two-star hotels, except, of course, its superb position: looking along the whole expanse of Croyde Beach and with the sea nigh lapping at its foundations. Yet, step inside Croyde Bay House to be greeted by an atmosphere of welcome and friendliness. The lounge bar, in the original part of the house, is a favourite gathering point for guests, and so too is the spacious lounge, with its ample supply of comfortable chairs, good reading matter and games for all ages. The dining room is not a place for slimmers, for Mrs Penny does the cooking and she looks after her guests very well indeed. The helpings are generous to say the least and the dishes are wholesome and most appetizing. You will probably feel the need to either sleep-off or work-off such daily repasts. Well, the bedrooms are clean, comfortable and well equipped, and one has its own balcony. You will also discover a further lounge, which is a real suntrap, and a summer house in a corner of the walled garden. If you decide on the 'active' option, then Baggy Point offers outstanding walks and the countryside beyond is mostly unspoilt National Trust property.

Weekly Terms from £265.00
Daily Terms from £39.75
Bed and Breakfast from £30.00
Bar Lunch from £2.00
Dinner from £17.00
Gratuities at Guest's discretion

VAT inclusive. Credit Cards–Mastercard, Visa. 2 Family Rooms, 3 Double, 2 Twin Bedrooms. 5 Private Bathrooms. 2 Private Shower Rooms. All rooms with TV, Tea and Coffee-making facilities
Hairdryer available on request

Open from 1st March to Mid November
Restaurant and Residential Licence
Full Central Heating. Children catered for.
Dogs allowed. Parking Facilities
Croquet. Nearby: Tennis, Swimming, Golf, Fishing, Riding, Windsurfing

Near Dartmouth, Dittisham—Fingals Hotel and Restaurant
Old Coombe Farm, Dittisham, Near Dartmouth, Devon. TQ6 0JA. Tel 080422 398. Fax 080422 401

Fingals, at Old Coombe Manor Farm, is right off the beaten track, up the narrow high-banked lanes that are characteristic of the area. Consistent with its idyllic setting-a short distance back from the River Dart, amongst grazing fields-there is a relaxed and informal atmosphere engendered by Richard Johnston, your attentive host. It pervades the cosy library, the small television room and the snooker room with its three quarter size Victorian table. With just nine double bedrooms, all with bath or shower, the hotel lends itself to group bookings. There are two dining rooms: the restaurant with its original pine panelling and an oak-panelled residents' dining room, adjoining the bar, which has a warm inglenook fireplace at one end. A fixed price menu, changed nightly, betrays the host's experience in running a successful London restaurant for ten years. We enjoyed a most excellent meal, which made use of herbs freshly picked from their garden. This pretty area includes a grass tennis court, a croquet lawn, summerhouse and a beautiful mosaic designed swimming pool with an adjoining sauna and jacuzzi room beside a gentle flowing stream. To reach this delightful place, as you approach Totnes on A385 from the north-west, take a right turn towards Kingsbridge and one mile up the hill take a road to the left, signposted Cornworthy and Ashprington. Turn right after one and a half miles for Tuckenhay, drive through the village and two miles beyond turn right at the ruin towards Dittisham and East Cornworthy. Continue for one and a half miles down a steep hill and 100 yards after a small bridge, turn right. Bon voyage!

All Terms pertaining to 1992
Weekly Terms from £450.00 (Double)
Daily Terms from £65.00 (Double)
Bar Lunch from £1.50
Dinner from £25.00 Table D'Hôte
Gratuities at Guest's Discretion

VAT inclusive. 9 Double Bedrooms, 1 Self catering barn
All Rooms with Private Bathroom, Telephone, Radio, Tea and Coffee-making Facilities. Open from April to 3rd January
Residential and Restaurant Licence

Full Central Heating. Cocktail Bar. TV Lounge. Games Room. Conference Facilities. Children catered for.
Dogs allowed. Parking Facilities
Tennis, Croquet, Swimming Pool, Jacuzzi, Windsurfing

Section 1: Devon

Dartmouth—Royal Castle Hotel
The Quay, Dartmouth, Devon. TQ9 9PS
Tel 0803 833033

There are a number of historic buildings in the ancient land-locked port of Dartmouth and one of the most notable is this seventeenth-century coaching inn, which stands on the quayside. It is reputed that wreckage from the Armada was used as timber in its construction. It is certainly a recorded fact that seven reigning monarchs have slept under its roof since it was built in 1639! Currently, the holidaymaker and the passing traveller can make their headquarters here with confidence, for Mr and Mrs Nigel Way have refurbished it wisely and carried out improvements with full regard for the hotel's old-fashioned charm. They have already successfully upgraded the facilities to a three-star level. The hotel's many interesting features are too numerous to catalogue, although mention should be made of the Adam ceiling in the dining room and the original ships' timbers and the rare Lidstone iron cooking range in the Galleon Bar used for spit roasting during the cooler months. There is an entrance to a priest hole in one of the bedrooms and, for those who crave a four-poster bed, there is a choice of six. The dining room, with its bow windows overlooking the Dart, serves traditional English dishes which are almost entirely based on fresh Devonshire produce and the hotel has been awarded a Best of British Breakfast Award. Dartmouth itself is a place no visitor to south Devon should miss. Craft of almost every kind ply across its tidal waters–yachts, naval vessels, sailing boats and ferries–making a constantly changing scene.

Weekly Terms from £276.00
Daily Terms from £44.00
Bed and Breakfast from £36.00
Bar Lunch from £2.50
Sunday Lunch £8.95
Afternoon Tea from £2.50
Bar Supper from £2.25
Dinner from £13.50 and A La Carte

Gratuities at Guest's Discretion
VAT inclusive. Credit Cards—Access, Visa
20 Double/Twin, 4 Single Bedrooms
(Including 6 Family Rooms)
20 Private Bathrooms. 4 Private Shower Rooms. 25 Rooms with TV, Telephone, Radio, Baby-listening, Tea and Coffee-making Facilities

All Rooms with Hairdryers
Open all Year. Fully Licensed
Full Central Heating. 2 Cocktail Bars
Conference Facilities
Children catered for. Dogs allowed
Parking Facilities. Night Porter
Nearby: Tennis, Putting, Swimming, Solarium, Golf, Fishing, Riding, Sailing, Windsurfing, Water Skiing, Shooting

Section 1: Devon

Nr Dartmouth—Stoke Lodge Hotel and Restaurant
Stoke Fleming, Near Dartmouth, Devon. TQ6 0RA.
Tel 0803 770523

The A379 road climbs steeply from Dartmouth and, after about two miles, approaches the lovely unspoilt beach of Blackpool Sands and the peaceful village of Stoke Fleming, with its conspicuous church. This is the beginning of Start Bay, but we suggest you stop here, as we did recently, at the warm and welcoming Stoke Lodge Hotel. This seventeenth-century house has been much modernised and is now run on very personal lines by the Mayer family. We had found Stoke Lodge by chance the previous summer and had noticed how attractive the flower-bedecked gardens appeared, with their swimming pool and patio area. When we called in winter, the elements were beating against the windows, but we were warm and comfortable by a blazing log fire and enjoyed pleasant company and the memory of a really excellent dinner. The hotel is open all year and offers bargain-break packages from October to May, as well as special breaks for the Christmas and New Year periods. These are especially appealing now that the hotel has an indoor swimming pool, plus solarium, jacuzzi and sauna. There is also an all-weather tennis court. Stoke Lodge Hotel and Restaurant was, for us, a most happy find in this area of South Hams, which is noted for its natural beauty. In addition, they now also run the Scarlet Geranium Tearooms in Dartmouth, which are proving to be extremely popular. The quiet villages of Dartmoor, the entertainments of Torbay and the marvellous opportunities for sailing at Dartmouth and Salcombe are all within easy reach.

Weekly Terms from £252.50
Daily Terms from £42.00
Bed and Breakfast from £31.00
Bar Lunch from £4.95
Lunch from £8.50 and A La Carte
Bar Supper from £6.50
Dinner from £15.50 and A La Carte

Gratuities at Guest's Discretion
VAT inclusive. 5 Family Rooms
8 Double, 8 Twin, 3 Single Bedrooms
23 Private Bathrooms, 1 Private Shower Room. All Rooms with TV, Telephone, Radio, Tea and Coffee-making Facilities
Trouser Press and Hairdryer available on Request.

Open all Year. Residential and Restaurant Licence. Games Room. Conference Facilities. Children catered for. Dogs allowed. Parking Facilities
Swimming Pools, Solarium, Sauna, Tennis Court
Nearby: Fishing, Sailing, Windsurfing

Section 1: Devon

Dawlish Warren–Langstone Cliff Hotel
Dawlish Warren, Dawlish, Devon. EX7 0NA. Tel 0626 865155. Fax 0626 867166

Even on a day when the sky was the colour of gun-metal, Langstone Cliff Hotel was warm and inviting. We recall a pleasant bar, a good dinner, a comfortable room and the kind of ample hotel breakfast which sustains one for most of the day. It is only as the season progresses, however, that one can fully appreciate what a marvellous holiday centre this hotel is. There is, in fact, no need for guests to leave the hotel and its well-kept grounds, for they will find recreation and entertainment for the whole family already on hand. There are two heated swimming pools (one indoors and one outdoors), a Nordic solarium, two games rooms with table-tennis, a hard tennis court and swings and slides. The nineteen acres of lawns and woodland offer plenty of room for parents to sun themselves and for children to expend their energies in complete safety. A footpath leads directly from the grounds to the sands of Dawlish Warren and onto the adjoining eighteen-hole Warren Golf Club. Dawlish is probably the most ideally sited town in Devon from which to explore the West Country; just ten miles from Exeter and Torbay. The beauty of Dartmoor, with the Exe and Dart Estuaries are within a thirty minute drive.

Weekly Terms from £280.00
Daily Terms from £37.00
Bed and Breakfast from £29.00
Bar Lunch from £2.50
Lunch from £9.50 Table D'Hôte
Dinner from £13.50 Table D'Hôte
No Service Charge. VAT inclusive
Credit Cards—Access, American Express, Diners Club, Visa

47 Family Rooms. 4 Suites 10 Double, 7 Single Bedrooms
All Rooms with Private Bathroom, Satellite TV, Telephone, Radio, Baby-listening, Tea and Coffee-making Facilities. Hairdryer, Trouser Press.
Open all Year. Fully Licensed.
Full Central Heating
Lift. Cocktail Bar. TV Lounge

Games Room. Conference Facilities
Children catered for. Dogs allowed
Parking Facilities. Night Porter
Hard Tennis Court, Indoor and Outdoor Swimming Pools, Solarium, Snooker, Table Tennis.
Nearby: Putting, Squash, Golf, Fishing, Sailing, Windsurfing, Water Skiing

Exeter—Royal Clarence Hotel
Cathedral Yard, Exeter, Devon. EX1 1HD. Tel 0392 58464. Fax 0392 439423

Although Exeter is an important cathedral city, it is neatly bypassed by major roads. It is not our main purpose to tell you of Exeter, its cathedral, its guild-hall, its old houses, Roman walls and subterranean passages, but we would like to direct you to a central base for your excursions, be they of Exeter or of Devon as a whole. First then, we will lead you out of Exeter's narrow streets into the Cathedral Close where, in the north-east corner, stands the Royal Clarence, an English hostelry rich in history. We know the Royal Clarence very well, having dined and attended several functions there over the years. It was with personal pleasure, therefore, that we noted how attractive the hotel has become and how its facilities have been so greatly improved after a major refurbishment programme which took over twelve months to complete. Within this Georgian building there are fifty-six bedrooms and suites, each equipped for comfort with a private bathroom and shower, remote-control colour television, complimentary in-house videos, telephone, trouser press, hairdryer and beverage-making facilities. The luxurious *Bishops Bar*, the informal *Well House Tavern*, and the splendid *Raleigh Restaurant* are all popular rendezvous. There are also three superb rooms for functions for conferences and special occasions. There is limited parking for guests of the Royal Clarence, which has a prime site within this walled city.

Terms on Application
Gratuities at Guest's Discretion
VAT inclusive
Credit Cards—Access, American Express, Diners Club, Visa
3 Suites, 2 Four Poster Rooms

15 Double, 18 Twin Bedrooms, 18 Single Bedrooms
All Rooms with Private Bathrooms, TV, Telephone, Trouser Press, Hairdryer, Tea and Coffee-making Facilities
Open all Year

Fully Licensed. Full Central Heating
Lift. Cocktail Bar. Conference Facilities
Children catered for. Dogs not allowed
Limited Parking Facilities
Night Porter. Nearby: Squash, Badminton, Swimming Pool, Solarium, Sauna, Golf

Section 1: Devon

Near Exeter, Ebford—Ebford House Hotel
Exmouth Road, Ebford, Devon. EX3 0QH. Tel 0392 877658. Fax 0392 874424

Ebford House is a lovely Georgian country house, stylish and elegant, set in beautiful gardens, overlooking Woodbury Common, a National Trust area. Horseriding, hacking and walking can be enjoyed only 500 yards from the hotel and excellent shooting can be arranged in season. The beaches of Exmouth, Sidmouth and Budleigh Salterton are close by together with several coastal paths on which to enjoy the beautiful Devon coastline. For the golfing enthusiast, there are eight golf courses within a 30 minute drive and all of these pursuits can be organised by the helpful and friendly staff. Don and Samantha Horton have created a homely atmosphere, enhanced by personal attention. Don is justly proud of Horton's Restaurant which has acquired an AA red rosette and has a reputation for first class *cuisine*, with dishes imaginatively cooked and well presented, and menus individually created by the 'chef patron' himself. The personally selected wine list is very comprehensive and also covers the popular *Frisco's Wine Bar* in Ebford Cellars. Here the blackboard menu is full of speciality dishes and you can eat on the patio *'al fresco'* and enjoy the South West sunshine. All bedrooms are well appointed and, as with the reception rooms, very comfortable, and tastefully furnished. The hotel has its own leisure area including a sauna, solarium, jacuzzi/spa bath.

Bed and Breakfast from £62.00(Double)	10 Double, 4 Twin, 4 Single Bedrooms	Children catered for. Dogs not allowed
Bed and Breakfast from £48.00 (Single)	All Rooms with Private Bathroom, TV,	Parking Facilities.
Bar Meal from £2.00	Telephone, Radio, Baby-listening,	Solarium, Sauna. Jacuzzi
Lunch from £13.00	Tea and Coffee-making Facilities, Hairdryer	Nearby: Tennis, Putting, Squash,
Dinner from £19.75	Open all Year. Fully Licensed	Badminton, Swimming, Golf,
Gratuities at Guest's Discretion.	Full Central Heating. *Frisco's* Wine Bar.	Fishing, Riding, Sailing, Windsurfing,
VAT inclusive	*Horton's* Restaurant	Water Skiing, Shooting, Hang Gliding
Credit Cards—Access, Visa	Conference Facilitiesd.	

Near Exeter, Pinhoe—Gipsy Hill Country House Hotel
Gipsy Hill Lane, Pinhoe, Exeter, Devon. EX1 3RN. Tel 0392 65252. Fax 0392 64302

The location of Gipsy Hill Country House Hotel is superb, for it is close to the main holiday routes to south Devon and Cornwall (the M5 motorway and the main A30 road skirt by) and the centre of Exeter is just three miles away. From the windows of this nineteenth-century country house, however, and within the three acres of quiet grounds, one is predominantly aware of the panoramic views, which take in the Haldon range of hills as they sweep down to the estuary of the River Exe and, beyond, to the sea. The garden has a typically English charm and is decked out with herbaceous borders, stately trees, evergreen flowering shrubs and a pretty lily pond. Equally favourable is the impression created within the house, for the bedrooms and public rooms are most attractively appointed in a mélange of original and new styles, which blend most harmoniously. Since this is one of the principal hotels in the Exeter area and is close to the airport, it is also well equipped for business functions and special occasions. Such events are expertly organised and accommodated in three separate meeting rooms, the largest of which can hold parties of up to 200 people. We, however, visited Gipsy Hill as tourists looking for respite and good food. We are delighted to say that we also found a most friendly atmosphere and professionalism engendered in all departments by the resident owners, Geoff and Eileen Stockman. If you are using the M5 motorway, you are advised to turn off at Junction 30 to reach the hotel.

Bed and Breakfast from £33.25 per person	American Express, Diners Club, Visa	Hairdryer. Open all Year. Fully Licensed
Bar Meal from £1.00	4 Family Rooms, 2 Four Poster Bedrooms	Full CH. Cocktail Bar. TV Lounge.
Lunch from £8.50 and A La Carte	11 Double, 11 Twin, 9 Single Bedrooms	Conference Facilities
Dinner from £13.50 and A La Carte	All Rooms with Private Bathroom, TV,	Children catered for. Dogs allowed
Gratuities at Guest's Discretion	Telephone, Radio, Baby-listening, Tea and	Parking Facilities. Nearby: Tennis, Putting,
VAT inclusive. Credit Cards—Access,	Coffee-making Facilities, Trouser Press,	Squash, Badminton, Swimming, Solarium

Section 1: Devon

Exmouth—Balcombe House Hotel
Stevenstone Road, Exmouth, Devon. EX8 2EP. Tel 0395 266349

Balcombe House Hotel was a substantial private house until Philip and Sheila Haycox converted it, nineteen years ago, into a charming and well-run hotel. Mr and Mrs Haycox offer the visitor very good value for money and pride themselves on their good service, adhering always to the policy that their guests come first. The hotel itself reflects this policy, too, for it is fully modernised and comfortably furnished throughout. The twelve bedrooms are all spacious and well appointed, with private bathrooms, colour televisions (with in-house video), radio/clock alarms, tea-making facilities and hairdryers. In addition, there are three ground-floor rooms to assist guests who are unable to negotiate stairs and the front entrance has been thoughtfully provided with an entry ramp. The large, sunny lounge looks out over pretty gardens, and guests may watch television or choose a book from the large selection available. The well-stocked bar has a friendly atmosphere and is open to guests outside normal licensing hours. Sheila is in charge of the *cuisine*, which is of a high standard: traditional English fare is served and we found it well cooked and attractively presented. The secluded situation of Balcombe House, set in its own half acre of lawns and shrubberies, offers visitors a very peaceful atmosphere, although Exmouth's town centre is close at hand, as are two miles of golden sands and a wealth of leisure activities.

Weekly Terms (Half Board) from £207.00
Daily Terms from £33.50
Bed and Breakfast from £23.30
Bar Lunch from £6.00
Dinner from £10.00 Table D'Hôte
Gratuities at Guest's Discretion
VAT inclusive
1 Family Room

1 Single, 5 Double, 5 Twin Bedrooms
All Rooms with Private Shower Room, TV, Radio, Tea and Coffee-making Facilities, Hairdryer
Open from April to October
Residential Licence
Full Central Heating
Children over 10 years catered for

Dogs not allowed.
Parking Facilities
Nearby: Tennis, Putting, Squash, Badminton, Swimming Pool, Solarium, Sauna, Golf, Fishing, Riding, Sailing, Windsurfing, Water Skiing, Shooting, Hang-gliding

Exmouth—The Barn Hotel
Foxholes Hill, Exmouth, Devon. EX8 2DF. Tel 0395 224411

Do not be misled by the name, for The Barn Hotel is small and comfortable and so personally run by David and Diana Palfreman. The house is late Victorian and stone built and was designed by the architect Edward Prior in a most unusual 'butterfly' pattern, which ensures that most of the rooms overlook the estuary of the River Exe, Berry Head and the rising Haldon Hills. In the foreground is a lovely two-acre garden with a swimming pool, nine-hole putting green and a croquet lawn. We visited the hotel in March and the gardens were already in parts a colourful picture. Spring comes early indeed to this corner of Devon! Beyond the Hotel's grounds, just two minutes' walk away, is Exmouth's famed two miles of golden sands, whilst the town's centre is reached within fifteen minutes through the Madeira Walk and the Plantation. Though when you reach The Barn Hotel you may have little inclination to go further. For here is surely one of the most attractive home-from-homes in Devon. A sun trap. A floral paradise. Attractive bedrooms, elegant and comfortable, all centrally heated and with the majority having *en suite* facilities. A house of good food and contentment, where the days must pass all too quickly. In the vicinity there is fishing, riding, shooting, golf at 'Tivvy' (Tiverton), or one may prefer just to relax and watch the ships and yachts make their ways to and from the small harbour nearby. Personal recommendation has brought a high reputation to The Barn Hotel and we are happy to add our appreciation, too.

Weekly Terms from £246.00 (DB&B)
Daily Terms from £41.00
Bed and Breakfast from £29.00
Bar Lunch from £1.50
Lunch from £7.50 Table D'Hôte
Dinner from £12.00 Table D'Hôte
Gratuities at Guest's Discretion
VAT inclusive. Credit Cards—Access, Visa

4 Family Rooms. 1 Twin, 4 Double, 2 Single Bedrooms
All Rooms with Private Bathroom, TV with Video, Telephone, Tea and Coffee-making Facilities
Trouser Press and Hairdryer available on Request. Most Bedrooms have Sea Views
Open all Year. Residential and Restaurant

Licence. Full CH. Cocktail Bar. Conference Facilities. Children catered for Dogs not allowed. Parking Facilities
9-Hole Putting Green, Croquet, Outdoor Swimming Pool. Nearby: Tennis, Croquet, Putting, Squash, Badminton, Swimming, Golf, Fishing, Riding, Sailing, Windsurfing, Water Skiing

Section 1: Devon

Exmouth—Royal Beacon Hotel
The Beacon, Exmouth, Devon. EX8 2AF.
Tel 0395 264886/265269. Fax 0395 268890

Exmouth is a town one travels to, rather than through, so when one arrives, whether by road, train, or across the Exe by way of the Starcross ferry, you will have the feeling that here is an excellent 'journey's end' indeed. This is Devon's oldest resort and, as such, has a fair share of places claiming to be 'Exmouth's leading hotel'. Yet, there is one establishment which stands, literally, head and shoulders above the rest, with a real holiday setting, which puts you right with the world from the moment you open your eyes in the morning. Standing atop a grassy hillside overlooking the esplanade and golden sands, the Royal Beacon enjoys a truly superb position: fortunate guests look out across the blue waters of the Exe estuary. Beyond, there are panoramic views of the beautiful coastline of Torbay. Another feature of the hotel we especially like is the owner's aim of providing comfort with style and friendly hospitality. Perhaps the hotel's pièce de résistance, however, is Fennels Restaurant, with its emphasis on superb food and wine. Head Chef, Colin Day, ensures that the service is impeccable and the food is of a gourmet standard, making Fennels 'the' place to eat in the Exmouth area. Wise visitors, of course, ask Denis Larke, the Proprietor, to book them a room, thus securing a table for every mealtime throughout their stay! For many reasons we like life at the Royal Beacon. The house itself rejoices in Victorian spaciousness and elegance, whilst the appointments, both above and below stairs, are all one could need or desire. And after the sun sets one may play Bridge, enjoy a game of snooker, or, perhaps, just relax and ... be thankful.

Weekly Terms from £375.00 (Single)
Weekly Terms from £641.00 (Double)
Bed and Breakfast from £46.00.
Special Golfing Breaks at Woodbury Park Championship Course. Unlimited Golf any two days £105.00 incl VAT
Lunch from £6.95 and A La Carte
Afternoon Tea from £2.95
Dinner from £15.00 and A La Carte

Credit Cards–Access, American Express, Diners Club, Visa
4 Family Rooms. 1 Suite
6 Double, 11 Twin, 8 Single Bedrooms
All Rooms with Private Bath/Shower Room, TV with Video, Telephone, Radio, Baby-listening, Tea and Coffee-making Facilities, Trouser Press and Hairdryer
Open all Year

Fully Licensed. Lift. Full Central Heating
Cocktail Bar. Games Room
Children catered for
Dogs allowed. Conference Facilities
Parking Facilities
Nearby: Tennis, Croquet, Putting, Squash, Badminton, Swimming, Solarium, Sauna, Golf, Fishing, Riding, Sailing, Windsurfing, Water Skiing, Shooting, Hang-gliding

Section 1: Devon

Hatherleigh—The George Hotel
Market Street, Hatherleigh, Devon. EX20 3JN. Tel 0837 810454

Over 500 years old, with a thatched roof, blackened beams, open fireplaces and a cobbled courtyard, The George was originally a monks' retreat house, then, later, a coaching inn. It is now a Devon market-town hotel, which we are proud to recommend–especially to our overseas readers. It represents all that is best in our British heritage–age, homeliness, warmth and comfort. We have known The George personally for some thirty years. Its repute is deservedly high and we recommend it not only for the pleasure of its table, but for the comfort of its bedrooms and public rooms. The food is very good and interestingly presented and you will be able to choose excellent wines to complement your meals. The à la carte menu features superb North Devon and Cornish fish, prime local beef and fresh garden vegetables. If you eat from the bar menu you will find traditional dishes like Steak and Kidney Pie alongside vegetarian feasts. With its excellent location for touring the whole of Devon and much of Cornwall, it is not surprising that Hatherleigh is on motoring organisations' holiday routes to north and west Cornwall and is within three miles of the holiday route to central and southern Cornwall. Motorists on the A30 should especially note that The George is but a seven-mile diversion from Okehampton.

Bed and Breakfast from £30.00
Bar Meal from £3.75
Lunch from £12.00 (bookings only)
Afternoon Tea from £2.85
Dinner from £13.00 and A La Carte
Gratuities at Guest's Discretion
VAT inclusive. Credit Cards—Access, Visa
6 Double, 4 Twin, 1 Single Bedrooms

(3 Rooms with Four Poster Bed)
9 Rooms En Suite
All Rooms with TV, Telephone,
Baby-listening, Room Service
Hairdryer available on Request
Open all Year. Fully Licensed
Full Central Heating
Cocktail Bar. Games Room

Conference Facilities
Children catered for. Dogs allowed
Parking Facilities. Night Porter
Outdoor Heated Swimming Pool
Nearby: Tennis, Putting, Squash, Solarium,
Sauna, Golf, Fishing, Riding, Sailing,
Windsurfing, Water Skiing, Shooting,
Hang-Gliding

Hawkchurch—Fairwater Head Country House Hotel
Hawkchurch, Near Axminster, Devon. EX13 5TX. Tel 0297 678349

The village of Hawkchurch, with its flower filled lanes, sits high above the Axe valley, just five miles from the coast at Lyme Regis and virtually on the boundaries of Devon, Dorset and Somerset. Here lies Fairwater Head, an Edwardian country house set in an Ashley Courtenay award-winning garden, with magnificent views across the surrounding countryside. Nothing is allowed to disturb the peace and tranquillity. There are no conferences, wedding receptions or taped background music to intrude upon your holiday. From the moment you arrive you can be assured of a warm welcome and an invitation to take tea in the garden lounge or on the patio. The immaculate bedrooms are fully *en suite*, have comfortable easy chairs, fresh flowers, central heating and views of the gardens. Four ground floor rooms are ideal for those less agile. Each evening the award-winning chefs prepare a selection of starters, soups, main courses, and a sweet trolley that has become a feature of Fairwater Head. If you need special diets just mention this upon arrival. There is full silver service and candlelit dinners, with a grand piano played softly. For nine years Fairwater Head has been owned and cared for by Rita and Harry Austin, and daughter and son-in-law Judith and John Lowe, together with a team of twenty-two staff, all of whom take great pride in providing true hospitality and comfort. Not surprising that guests return year after year.

Weekly Terms from £350.00
Daily Terms from £51.00
Bar Lunch from £2.50
Lunch from £8.75 and A La Carte
Dinner from £18.50 and A La Carte
Gratuities at Guest's Discretion
VAT inclusive. Credit Cards—Access,

American Express, Diners Club, Visa
5 Double, 15 Twin, 1 Single Bedroom
All Rooms with Private Bathroom, TV,
Telephone, Radio, Tea and Coffee-making
Facilities. 14 Rooms with Baby-listening
Hairdryers available on Request
Open from March to December

Fully Licensed. Full Central Heating and
Log Fires. Cocktail Bar. Billiards Room
Children catered for. Dogs allowed by
Arrangement. Parking Facilities
Nearby: Croquet, Squash, Swimming, Golf,
Fishing, Riding, Sailing, Windsurfing,
Shooting

Section 1: Devon

Near Holsworthy—Court Barn Country House Hotel
Clawton, Holsworthy, Devon. EX22 6PS.
Tel 040927 219

Quietly situated hotels in the West Country, which lie away from the coastal resorts and outside the popular moors, are relatively few and far between. That is why country retreats like the Court Barn are such satisfying discoveries. This award-winning hotel is set in five acres of park-like gardens amid lovely countryside on the Devon/Cornwall border. We have stayed at the hotel and have sensed that we were a million miles from the holiday crowds and yet from here country lanes lead one to Holsworthy, within three miles, and to Bude, within seven miles and is a perfect touring centre. Court Barn was built in 1853 with Georgian influence and spaciousness in mind and has now been refurbished with many antiques and William Morris prints and fabrics. Log fires, ornaments, pictures and flowers give a homely atmosphere to this delightful house. Guests can enjoy eight charming bedrooms en suite, three Lounges, Bar, Games Room, Breakfast Room and candlelit Restaurant where five course dinners are the highlight of the day. Meals here are sure to be a delight, for Sue is a wonderful cook and uses fresh ingredients, such as Cornish fish, Devon beef, locally grown vegetables, cheese and cream from nearby farms to produce her mouthwatering dishes, all complemented by Robert's award winning wines. The hotel has many awards for Teas, Hospitality; BTA commended for "outstanding cuisine and relaxed atmosphere", Mercier Wine Awards 89/90/91/92, and is a Devon Hotel of Distinction. Do try and call here; Robert and Sue take pleasure in ensuring their guests' comfort and well-being.

Weekly Terms from £275.00 to £330.00
Daily Terms from £50.00 to £61.00
Bed and Breakfast from £35.00 to £43.00
Activity & Bargain Breaks (including champagne) from £48.00 (Daily)
Lunch from £10.50 and A La Carte
Bar Snacks from £2.00
Dinner from £16.00 to £19.00 (3 Course).
Gratuities at Guest's Discretion.

VAT inclusive. Credit Cards—Access, American Express, Visa. 1 Family Room. 1 Single Bedroom. 3 Double, 3 Twin Bedrooms. 4 Private Bathrooms. 4 Private Shower Rooms. All Rooms with Telephone, Radio, Baby-listening, Tea and Coffee-making Facilities, Trouser Press, Hairdryer, TV. Open all Year. Residential and Restaurant Licence. Cocktail Bar.

TV Lounge.
Games Room
Conference Facilities. Children catered for.
Dogs allowed by Arrangement.
Parking Facilities.
Lawn Tennis Court, Croquet, Badminton, Solarium, Small Chip and Putt Golf Course, Swimming, Golf, Fishing, Riding, Sailing, Windsurfing, Shooting, Archery

Section 1: Devon

Near Honiton, Colestocks—Colestocks House
Colestocks, Near Honiton, Devon. EX14 0JR. Tel 0404 850633

It is not often, in our experience, that hoteliers are given to fulsome praise of other similar establishments, but it was just such a recommendation which led us to Colestocks House. We had little difficulty in locating the hotel, for it lies, as we had been told, in lovely countryside about two miles north of the A30 road, between the villages of Feniton and Payhembury. Upon arrival at Colestocks guests must sigh with contentment when they behold such a peaceful scene. This sixteenth-century Grade II listed house stands pink-washed beneath an immaculate thatch and the two acres of delightful gardens are surrounded by a high cob wall. The town-dweller might imagine that in a house so old one should be prepared for a Spartan existence. This is far from the case here. There are two antique half tester bedrooms, one four poster and one room with a canopied brass bed. All of the bedrooms have bathrooms *en suite* and modern facilities. The hotel has been awarded a special commendation by one of the American Travel Organisations. The public rooms are most attractively furnished, and what could be more civilised than relaxing in the comfortable sitting room with French windows opening out onto the gardens? Henri and Jacqueline Yot have lived for many years in France and this has strongly influenced the *cuisine* at Colestocks. One may enjoy home-made pâtés, French regional dishes, a number of speciality dishes and mouthwatering sweets. All the meals are freshly prepared and we were most impressed with every dish we were proffered.

Weekly Terms from £220.00	8 Private Bathrooms. 1 Private Shower Room. All Rooms with TV, Radio, Tea and Coffee-making Facilities	Full Central Heating and Log Fires
Bed and Breakfast from £24.50		Cocktail Bar. Children over 10 years catered for. Dogs not allowed
Dinner from £14.75 Table D'Hôte		
Gratuities at Guest's Discretion	Open from 1st February to 21st November and Christmas	Parking Facilities. Croquet, Putting
VAT inclusive. Credit Cards—Access, Visa		Nearby: Tennis, Squash, Golf, Fishing, Riding, Hang-gliding
6 Double, 3 Twin Bedrooms	Residential and Restaurant Licence	

Hope Cove—Cottage Hotel
Hope Cove, Kingsbridge, Devon. TQ7 3HJ. Tel 0548 561555

John and Janet Ireland have but one purpose in life, to provide holidays of complete contentment. Set in two acres of grounds, with the most wonderful views of sea and coastline, the Cottage Hotel enjoys a magnificent position in this pretty and secluded Devon fishing village. Still unspoiled, yet tastefully developed from the original cottage of 1890, the hotel provides a relaxing atmosphere for all. The gardens descend to the beach making it convenient to bathe in safety from the hotel. You will find comfortable lounges, glorious views from the sun terraces and a style of service you thought had disappeared for ever. The hotel has an excellent reputation for food and wine, very well appointed accommodation and parking for fifty cars. The same high standard of traditional hospitality has been offered since 1973. Your children and dogs are very welcome. Choose from a selection of accommodation which includes *de luxe* balcony, double/balcony, family and single rooms. Bedrooms are attractively furnished with central or individual heating, radio and intercom. Most have sea views, direct dial telephone and colour TV. *De luxe* balcony rooms also include video and hairdryer. There are three lounges; one set aside for non-smokers, two with old brick fireplaces, wood panelling and oak beams and a small television lounge and a games room. The restaurant overlooks the harbour and has extensive views of the open sea. We were there one year early in May and sunbathed on the hotel terrace.

Daily Terms from £32.50	8 Double, 6 Twin, 9 Single Bedrooms	Conference Facilities. Children catered for
Bed and Breakfast from £21.00	17 Private Bathrooms. 2 Private Shower Rooms. Most Rooms with TV, Telephone, Radio, Baby-listening, Hairdryer	Dogs allowed. Parking Facilities
Bar Lunch from £1.60		Nearby: Tennis, Squash, Badminton, Swimming Pool, Solarium, Sauna, Golf, Fishing, Riding, Sailing, Windsurfing, Water Skiing
Sunday Lunch from £8.25 Table D'Hôte		
Dinner from £15.60 and A La Carte	Open from 31st January to 2nd January	
Service Charge and VAT inclusive	Fully Licensed. Part Central Heating	
12 Family Rooms	Cocktail Bar. TV Lounge. Games Room	

Section 1: Devon

Hope Cove–Hope Cove Hotel
Hope Cove, Nr Kingsbridge, Devon TQ7 3HH. Tel 0548 561233

Whether you are lying back in bed, sitting at table in the dining room, enjoying a drink in the bar or relaxing in the lounge, here you will have magnificent panoramic sea views through the double glazed picture windows. Virtually on your doorstep are safe, sandy beaches and dramatic cliff-top walks. Although Leo and Emily Clarke accquired the hotel only recently (it was previously known as Greystone), they are experienced hoteliers and no newcomers to this area. In a very short while, they have effectively transformed the place. Dogs are not now permitted, nor are there telephones in bedrooms to disturb the tranquillity of this open, green area of South Devon. Everything is bright and clean, the white cloths, cutlery and glass seem to sparkle in the dining room and each of the seven *en suite* bedrooms has comprehensive facilities. Orders for the three-course dinner are taken in the bar from a menu which is changed daily, giving you a freshly prepared meal without undue delay at your table. Service is efficient and cheerful, completing a welcoming hospitality which has promptly brought return bookings. At the time of our visit, railings were due to be erected to bring into use a large sun terrace. South of Hope Cove is Bolberry Down, an expanse of turf, gorse and bracken standing 400 feet above the sea with superb coastal and channel views. It is separated from the hotel by the headland of Bolt Tail, fortified during the Iron Age and the scene of many shipwrecks. Hope Cove itself is a crab and lobster fishing village with picturesque cottages. Golf, horse riding, fishing and sailing are available in the area.

Weekly Terms on application	VAT inclusive. Credit Cards-Access, Visa	Open from February to end December
Daily Terms from £32.50 (Half Board)	5 Double, 2 Twin Bedrooms	Restaurant and Residential Licence
Bed and Breakfast from £20.00	All Rooms with Private Bathroom, TV,	Full Central Heating. Cocktail Bar.
Bar Lunch from £4.75	Radio, Tea and Coffee-making Facilities,	Children over 7 years catered for. Dogs not
Dinner from £12.50 Table D'Hôte	Hairdryer. Pay 'phone available	allowed. Parking Facilities

Hope Cove—Tanfield Hotel
Hope Cove, Near Kingsbridge, Devon. TQ7 3HF. Tel 0548 561268

You certainly will not get lost on your way to the Tanfield Hotel, as John and Pauline Ward include with their brochure a very useful step-by-step explanation of how to navigate your way through the maze of south Devon lanes. Having arrived safely, we were certainly highly impressed by the changes wrought by the Wards' since they have been in possession of this small hotel. All the bedrooms now have television, tea and coffee-making facilities and hairdryers, as well as a private bath or shower room. The hotel is situated on a hill, overlooking the fishing village of Hope Cove, so the views from the windows are quite magnificent. The Tanfield now benefits from Mrs Ward's expertise in the kitchen and she takes a great delight in offering a fine variety of interesting food. Indeed, the thought of the six-course evening meal (which is included in the very reasonable tariff) is something to keep you going as you explore this beautiful area. Why not try the walk from Bolt Head to Bolt Tail–a favourite of all ramblers who know this spot. Hope Cove is surrounded by National Trust land and it is impossible not to be enraptured by the beauty of the cliffs, inlets and bays. There is a golf course at Thurlestone and opportunities for sailing and fishing abound. The Tanfield Hotel has been recommended by us for some time now, but under the Wards' ownership, we are even more enthusiastic about it.

Bargain Breaks Term available on Request	Credit Cards—Access, Visa	Full Central Heating
Weekly Terms (Half Board) on application	7 Double, 2 Twin Bedrooms	Cocktail Bar
Daily Terms from £30.00	2 Single Bedrooms	Children over 8 years catered for
Bed and Breakfast from £21.00	2 Private Bathrooms.	Dogs allowed
Bar Lunch from £2.00	9 Private Shower Rooms	Parking Facilities
Afternoon Tea from £0.65	All Rooms with TV, Tea and Coffee-making	Nearby: Tennis, Squash, Badminton,
Dinner from £11.00 Table D'Hôte	Facilities, Hairdryer	Swimming, Golf, Fishing, Riding,
Gratuities at Guest's Discretion	Open from March to November	Sailing, Windsurfing, Water Skiing
VAT inclusive	Residential and Restaurant Licence	

Section 1: Devon

Ilfracombe, Torrs Park—Elmfield Hotel
Torrs Park, Ilfracombe, Devon. EX34 8AZ. Tel 0271 863377

Since acquiring Elmfield as a guest house twelve years ago, Derek and Ann Doody have worked wonders transforming it into an exceptionally pleasant hotel, with fourteen bedrooms, all of which have *en suite* facilities. There is even a sauna, solarium, spa bath, small gym and a covered indoor swimming pool in the grounds, which is heated throughout the year! Elmfield was built in 1880 as a gentleman's residence and enjoys a really superb location on the side of a valley, not far from the famous Torrs Walk. The site was chosen especially for its delightfully secluded position and, today, the Wilder stream still bubbles its way through the beautiful terraced gardens, which are planted with an abundance of shrubs and flowers. During our last stay at the Elmfield our evening meal offered a choice of several main dishes, and the food was well cooked and presented and the portions were very generous. The bedrooms all have tea and coffee-making facilities, but instead of the usual small milk cartons, a container with fresh milk is left outside each bedroom in the morning. It is thoughtful touches such as this that make a stay at Elmfield Hotel such an enjoyable experience. Indeed, for anyone looking for somewhere to spend a pleasant and moderately priced holiday or short break, this personally-run two-star hotel should fill the bill in every respect. You will find the Elmfield, approached by a private drive, off Torrs Park Road and within easy walking distance of the sea and town centre.

Weekly Terms from £225.00
Daily Terms from £35.00
Bed and Breakfast from £38.00
Bar Lunch from £7.00
Dinner from £10.00 and A La Carte
Gratuities at Guest's Discretion

VAT inclusive. Credit Cards—Access, Visa
12 Double, 2 Twin Bedrooms
All Rooms with Private Bath/Shower Room, TV, Tea and Coffee-making Facilities, Clock Radio, Hairdryer
Open from April to November

Residential and Restaurant Licence
Cocktail Bar. Games Room. Dogs not allowed. Parking Facilities. Indoor Heated Swimming Pool, Sauna, Solarium, Spa Bath, Gym. Nearby: Tennis, Putting, Golf, Fishing, Riding, Sailing

Instow—The Commodore Hotel
Marine Parade, Instow, Devon. EX39 4IN. Tel 0271 860347. Fax 0271 861233

It is much debated whether the broad sweep of land between Croyde and Hartland Point is Barnstaple Bay or Bideford Bay. The two towns in question actually lie well back from the sea–Barnstaple on the River Taw and Bideford on the River Torridge. It is where these rivers converge, just before they flow into the bay, that you will find Instow and the delightful Commodore Hotel. The Commodore Hotel could hardly be better named for it commands breathtaking views across wide sands, an estuary, which is busy with sailing craft, and the blue sea beyond. The hotel is owned and personally managed by Mr and Mrs Bruce Woolaway, and the active involvement of two generations of the Woolaway family has ensured consistently high standards and a happy, friendly atmosphere here. We called early in the year, a relatively quiet period in the hotel's annual activity, but still found the standards of service, food and comfort to be commendably high. The hotel has been extended with great flair and imagination and, consequently, the bedrooms are all spacious and contain a private bathroom, colour television, central heating, beverage-making facilities, a radio and a baby-listening service. The quiet marine village of Instow is a sensible choice for a holiday at any time of the year. The hotel is easy to find as it is only minutes from the North Devon link road. The ebb and flow of the tide and the pleasures of water sports dictate the pace of life here.

Weekly Terms from £580.00
Daily Terms from £90.00
Bed and Breakfast from £79.00
Bar Meals from £4.80
Lunch from £10.50 and A La Carte
Dinner from £18.00 and A La Carte
Gratuities at Guest's Discretion

VAT inclusive. Credit Cards—Access, American Express, Visa
3 Family Rooms. 1 Single, 8 Double, 8 Twin Bedrooms. All Rooms with Private Bath Room, TV, Telephone, Radio, Baby-listening, Trouser Press, Hairdryer, Tea and Coffee-making Facilities

Open all Year. Fully Licensed
2 Cocktail Bars. Children catered for. Dogs not allowed. Parking Facilities.
Nearby: Tennis, Putting, Squash Badminton, Swimming, Golf, Fishing, Riding, Sailing, Windsurfing, Water Skiing

Section 1: Devon

Kingsteignton, Newton Abbot—Passage House Hotel
Hackney Lane, Kingsteignton, Newton Abbot, Devon. TQ12 3QH. Tel 0626 55515. Fax 0626 63336

Standing on a fourteen-acre riverside site overlooking the Teign estuary, this forty-bedroom luxury hotel-the first purpose-built one in this area for over half a century-was developed by the proprietor of the historic Passage House Inn, next door. His family has been in the catering business locally for thirty years, while the Manager at the new hotel worked for eleven years in an hotel long acclaimed in 'Let's Halt Awhile'. Such exceptional pedigrees are wholly appropriate to an hotel of such outstanding qualities as this impressive Passage House. Comprehensive facilities in all the executive and penthouse bedrooms include twenty-four hour satellite television, mini bars and original watercolour paintings of beautiful estuary scenes. No less than three separate suites and rooms are available for conferences and banquets catering for up to 120 people. The spacious *Lighterman's Restaurant* and the bar, which have views over the Estuary equalled only by the outlook from those bedrooms having balconies, provide a wide selection of superb dishes and fine wines. Hotel guests have use of the *Leisure Club* in the hotel, featuring a heated pool with underwater music and lighting, hydro-spa, steam room, sauna, solarium and gymnasium. Weekend and Special Interest Breaks provide opportunities to sample all the sporting, social, scenic and seaside attractions, which this modern hotel offers, in the glorious Devon surroundings. A separate entrance completes the privacy for business seminars or presentations.

Accommodation Terms on Application
Bar Lunch from £4.00
Lunch from £8.50 and A La Carte
Dinner from £14.75 and A La Carte
Gratuities at Guests Discretion
VAT inclusive. Credit Cards—Access,

American Express, Diners Club, Visa
1 Suite. 39 Single/Double/Twin Bedrooms
All Rooms with Private Bath/Shower Room, TV, Telephone, Radio, Tea and Coffee-making Facilities, Trouser Press, Hairdryer, Mini Bar

Open all Year. Residential and Restaurant Licence. Full Central Heating. Lift. Cocktail Bar. Conference Facilities
Children catered for. Dogs allowed by Arrangement. Parking Facilities. Night Porter. Indoor Swimming Pool, Fishing

Near Kingsbridge, Chillington—Oddicombe House Hotel
Chillington, Kingsbridge, Devon. TQ7 2JD. Tel 0548 531234

Oddicombe House has been in the hands of the friendly and competent owners Mr and Mrs R E Yapp for over twelve years now and each time we visit, we are most favourably impressed by the warm atmosphere and tasteful comfort of this hotel. We are grateful to a well travelled friend who, some years ago, recommended this delightful two-star country-house hotel to us. The hotel has not only sustained, but progressively improved its standards. During our last visit, we were most impressed with the ten well-furnished bedrooms and the comfortable public lounge, but most of all with the licensed restaurant for which the hotel has gained an excellent reputation with both residents and local people. If the dinner menus we saw are typical of the dishes served throughout the year, guests are in for a treat every evening! The attractive twin-gable fronted house, parts of which date back to 1762, is set in over two and a half acres of grounds with a beautiful outlook over the nearby hills to the south. For a relaxing summer holiday or a short break, Oddicombe House is an admirable choice. Within easy reach there are miles of coastal path with beautiful scenery and many birds to observe. Recreational pursuits include golf, swimming, sailing, fishing, windsurfing and riding. Finally we thought their tariff to be realistic and we suggest, therefore, that you write or telephone for a colour brochure including complete travel instructions.

Weekly Terms from £245.00
Daily Terms from £40.50
Bed and Breakfast from £28.50
Dinner from £14.00 Table D'Hôte
Gratuities at Guest's Discretion
VAT inclusive

2 Family Rooms.
3 Double, 5 Twin, 2 Single Bedrooms
7 Private Bathrooms
All Rooms with Tea and Coffee-making Facilities
Open from Easter to end October

Fully Licensed. Full Central Heating
Cocktail Bar
Children catered for
Dogs allowed
Parking Facilities
Outdoor Swimming Pool

Section 1: Devon

Near Kingsbridge, Chillington– The White House
Kingsbridge, Devon, TQ7 2JX
0548 580580

When bookings here are confirmed, prospective guests are invited to express a preference for duvets or sheets and blankets. This is simply one instance of the personal care which Michael Roberts and David Alford lavish on their patrons. We entered the attractively bright dining room to find hand written guests' names placed on each table. An adequate choice of dish for each course offers home-made food, delicious and courteously presented, with a fine selection of wines. A pre-dinner drink can be taken in the Normandy Bar Lounge, a cosy room, with exposed stonework, in the oldest part of the house. After dinner, browse through the wide selection of books in the drawing room, with its marble fireplace and Adam-style ceiling. In cooler weather, both these rooms have cheering log fires burning. Each of the seven individually furnished bedrooms has private facilities and, in the particularly spacious Master Suite, which is south-facing, there is a comfortable sitting area. Colour schemes and furniture throughout The White House breathe an air of quality and taste, with everything beautifully kept. It is a lovely Georgian house standing serenely at the end of a fine lawn with rose beds, shrubs, and a huge copper-beech dominating the scene. Located midway between Salcombe and Dartmouth, the hotel is centrally placed for exploring the whole South Hams coastline with its sandy beaches, rugged cliffs and quiet coves. The wild expanses of Dartmoor are within easy reach.

Weekly Terms from £260.75
Daily Terms from £42.50
Bed and Breakfast from £31.00
Dinner from £12.95
Gratuities at Guest's Discretion.
VAT inclusive
Credit Cards-Access, Mastercard, Visa

1 Family Room. 3 Double, 3 Twin Bedrooms
4 Private Bathrooms.
3 Private Shower Rooms
All Rooms with TV, Telephone, Radio, Tea and Coffee-making Facilities, Hairdryer
Open from Easter to After Christmas
Residential and Restaurant Licence

Full Central Heating. Cocktail Bar.
TV Lounge.
Children catered for. Dogs allowed.
Parking Facilities for 8 cars.
Croquet, Badminton
Nearby: Golf, Fishing, Riding, Sailing, Windsurfing, Water Skiing

Section 1: Devon

Lydford—Lydford House Hotel
Lydford, Okehampton, Devon. EX20 4AU. Tel 082 282 347. Fax 082 282 442

Lydford House Hotel is set in over eight acres of garden and pastureland and situated within the bounds of the Dartmoor National Park. William Widgery built the house in 1880 for use as his private home, and several of his original watercolour paintings of Dartmoor scenes are a feature of the residents' lounge. The proprietors, Ron and Ann Boulter, together with their son, Simon, ensure that 'home' is still the operative word for the Lydford House because, in addition to being family run, it specialises in excellent home cooking, with fresh local produce used wherever possible. Full English breakfast starts the day right and there is no such thing as 'self-service' at Lydford House, whilst the excellent and reasonably priced *table d'hôte* dinner menu, which changes each day, provides a wide choice for each course. All the individually styled bedrooms have private bathrooms and there are two ground-floor rooms, also with *en suite* facilities, which are very helpful to visitors who have difficulty climbing stairs. There is also a luxurious four poster room where you will feel extra-special for that honeymoon, anniversary or other special occasion. As a foretaste to a full holiday at Lydford House, many take advantage of the hotel's 'Take a Break' off-season terms. There is a riding stable in the grounds of the hotel, and this is under the personal supervision of the Boulter's daughter, Claire Knight, BHSII. Inclusive riding holidays are available or visitors can arrange casual riding whilst they are at the hotel. Beginners are welcome and expert instruction is available.

Weekly Terms (Half Board) from £250.00
Daily Terms from £42.50
Bed and Breakfast from £30.00
Lunch from £9.00 Table d'Hôte
Dinner from £13.00 Table d'Hôte
Gratuities at Guest's Discretion

VAT inclusive. Credit Cards—Access, American Express, Visa
2 Family Rooms. 4 Double, 4 Twin, 3 Single Bedrooms. 12 Private Bathrooms
1 Private Shower Room. All Rooms with TV, Telephone, Radio, Tea and

Coffee-making Facilities, Hairdryer, Laundry Facilities. Open all Year
Fully Licensed. Full Central Heating
Cocktail Bar. Children over 5 years catered for. Dogs allowed in Bedrooms only
Parking Facilities. Riding

Lynmouth—Bath Hotel
Lynmouth, Devon. EX35 6EL. Tel 0598 52238

Lynmouth... where Exmoor meets the coast in a most spectacular fashion and where the East and West Lyn meet before flowing into the sea. Whenever the conversation turns to this attractive resort two hotels spring to mind. They are the best in the area and enjoy the same owners. The Bath Hotel, overlooking picturesque Lynmouth Harbour, has been in the same family ownership since 1951. The hotel's popularity hinges on the policies laid down by Mr and Mrs A G Braunton, namely a warm welcome, good food and value for money. These triple attractions are now assiduously maintained by their daughters and sons-in-law. Consequently, visitors return year after year, attracted by appetising menus, which feature many speciality dishes, such as, in season, salmon from the hotel's own weir, and lobster from Lynmouth Bay. Comfortable bedrooms, a carefully selected staff, watchful supervision and boundlesss energy have also gone into the development of the Bath Hotel. The result is a compact, satisfying and well-run unit. Behind the hotel rise thickly-wooded cliffs, and beyond these is Exmoor, with its peaceful valleys, tumbling streams and famous beauty spots-the Valley of the Rocks and Lorna Doone Country. Lynmouth and these surrounding areas have inspired Wordsworth, Coleridge and Shelley, as well as Blackmore. The sister hotel of the Bath is The Tors Hotel, which will especially appeal to those who prefer a hill-side setting.

Weekly Terms from £230.00
Daily Terms from £38.50
Bed and Breakfast from £26.00
Lunch from £8.00 and A La Carte
Dinner from £14.00 and A La Carte
Service Charge and VAT inclusive.
Credit Cards—Access, American Express,

Diners Club, Visa.
14 Double, 1 Single, 9 Twin Bedrooms
(Larger Rooms can be let as Family Rooms). 23 Private Bathrooms
1 Private Shower Room
All Rooms with TV, Radio, Tea and Coffee-making Facilities, Telephone,

Baby-listening. Open from March to October inclusive. Fully Licensed. Cocktail Bar. Games Room. Children catered for. Dogs allowed. Parking facilities
Nearby: Tennis, Putting, Swimming (at associate hotel), Fishing, Riding

Section 1: Devon

Lynmouth—The Tors Hotel
Lynmouth, Devon. EX35 6NA. Tel 0598 53236

The north Devon coastline is surely the most spectacular in a country richly endowed with scenic charm, and this hotel stands in five acres of terraced wooded grounds on the slopes of Countisbury Hill. Under the ownership of Mr and Mrs A G Braunton, The Tors Hotel enjoys a magnificent site with public rooms, cocktail bar, terrace bar, and all but a few of the well-furnished bedrooms having a grandstand view of the Lyn Valley, sea and coastline. When not enjoying the scenic beauty of Lynmouth and Lynton from the cocktail bar or terrace one can enjoy the culinary pleasure of a good table, and a menu which often includes local salmon and lobster in season. The Tors makes an ideal honeymoon choice, as well as a holiday touring centre. The sea offers opportunities for bathing, boating and fishing. Inland, the National Park of Exmoor is perfect for hacking, hunting, hiking and motoring picnics, while the heated swimming pool and sunbathing terrace are an invitation to 'stay put'. The Tors opens on 1st March and remains open until the first week in January, with attractive discount terms for spring and autumn patrons. The early and late seasons are becoming increasingly popular as a time to enjoy the Exmoor countryside rather than during the traditional holiday periods.

All Terms pertaining to 1992
Christmas and New Year 3 day House Parties
Weekly Terms from £273.00
Daily Terms from £45.00
Bed and Breakfast from £35.00
Lunch from £10.00 and A La Carte
Afternoon Tea from £3.50
Dinner from £16.00 and A La Carte
Service Charge and VAT inclusive

Credit Cards—Access, American Express, Diners Club, Visa
5 Family Rooms
16 Double, 14 Twin Bedrooms.
All Rooms with Private Bathroom, TV, Telephone, Radio, Baby-listening, Tea and Coffee-making Facilities
2 adjoining rooms with communicating door
16 Rooms with Hairdryer
Open from 1st March to 3rd January

Fully Licensed. Full Central Heating Lift. Cocktail Bar. Terrace Bar.
TV Lounge. Games Room. Conference Facilities. Children catered for. Dogs allowed. Parking Facilities
Outdoor Heated Swimming Pool
Nearby: Tennis, Putting, Squash, Badminton, Golf, Fishing, Riding, Sailing, Windsurfing, Water Skiing, Shooting

Lynton—Chough's Nest Hotel
North Walk, Lynton, Devon EX35 6HJ. Tel 0598 53315

Architect-designed one hundred and thirty years ago for a Dutch millionaire, this splendid stone structure enjoys a superbly commanding position overlooking Lynmouth Bay at the end of a quiet cul-de-sac which culminates in a magnificent cliffside walk. We were delighted to have Chough's Nest brought to our attention: it is a real find and the majority of guests here confirm their satisfaction by making return visits. Tastefully furnished and beautifully maintained, the hotel's popularity owes much to the warm and friendly hospitality shown to everyone by Sylvia and Bob Harrop, the resident proprietors. Daytime snacks can be taken on the sun terrace with its panoramic views of Countisbury Headland and the Welsh Coast, the choice of excellent dishes served in the bright dining room always includes a vegetarian meal and, in the comfortable lounge, there is plenty of reading material. Your hosts make a point of being available to guests to answer questions or offer advice on the many interesting features of this picturesque area. They hold weekly slide shows detailing local beauty spots and, also weekly, the staff don period costume to serve a Lorna Doone dinner. Fishing trips and pony trekking are arranged by them for guests, and guidance given on local tennis, putting, golf, swimming and other amenities. Many walks begin here and, only a few minutes away, there are the village shops, the bus station and the cliff railway to Lynmouth. North Walk is one of the most spectacular coastal paths in Britain. Smoking is not permitted in this hotel and, in any event, you should be sound in body and mind to enjoy such dramatic terrain to the full where usually the only sound to be heard is the sea some four hundred feet below.

Weekly Terms from £200.00. Daily Terms from £30.00. Bed and Breakfast from £22.00. Dinner from £10.00. VAT not included. No Credit Cards accepted. 2 Family Rooms. 7 Double, 1 Twin, 2 Single Bedrooms. 7 Private Bathrooms. 5 Private Shower Rooms. All Rooms with TV, Tea and Coffee-making Facilities, Hairdryer. Open from Easter to mid-October. Restaurant Licence. Full CH. Children over 2 years catered for. Dogs not allowed. Parking Facilities

Section 1: Devon

Lynton—The Crown Hotel
Sinai Hill, Lynton, Devon. EX35 6AG. Tel 0598 52253

Formerly a Trust House, this eighteenth-century country coaching inn is today a delightful and comfortable hotel. Standing in a secluded position 500 feet above sea level, in one of Devon's prettiest villages, which overlooks the north Devon cliffs and the Bristol Channel, The Crown is an ideal place in which to relax for a night, a few days or longer. Under the personal ownership of Alan and Thelma Westgarth, we were impressed with the bedrooms upstairs, where there is a choice of twin, double or suite accommodation. The tariff is very competitive and there are reductions for children, whether or not they share their parents' room. We noted too the colour television, tea and coffee-making facilities and private bathroom in each attractively equipped bedroom. Downstairs is the old-world *Free House Bar* with its sturdy oak beams and an open fire during colder weather. From the kitchen come such treats as fresh Exmoor trout and locally caught lobsters. He also always makes use of fresh vegetables. For the energetic, there are miles of spectacular walks through coastal woodland and moorland scenery together with some first-class sea and river fishing. The Crown is a member of Wayfarer Inns (Consort) and special bargain breaks are offered throughout the year.

Weekly Terms (Half Board) from £200.00
Daily Terms from £32.50
Bed and Breakfast from £26.50
Bar Lunch from £2.00
Dinner from £14.00 Table D'Hôte
No Service Charge and VAT inclusive
Credit Cards—Access, Visa
3 Family Rooms. 3 Suites

8 Double, 2 Twin Bedrooms
15 Private Bathrooms
1 Private Shower Room
All Rooms with TV, Telephone, Radio, Baby-listening, Tea and Coffee-making Facilities
5 Rooms with Four Poster Beds
Open all Year except January

Fully Licensed. Full Central Heating
Children catered for. Dogs allowed
Parking Facilities
Nearby: Tennis, Putting, Squash, Swimming, Solarium, Sauna, Golf, Fishing, Riding, Sailing, Windsurfing, Water Skiing, Shooting, Hang-gliding

Lynton—Southcliffe Hotel
Lee Road, Lynton, Devon. EX35 6BS. Tel 0598 53328

On each occasion we visit Southcliffe Hotel, we invariably find that Adrian and June Kamp have been busy improving the standard of their welcoming hotel. All bedrooms have private bathrooms, colour television and beverage-making facilities, and hairdryers. Two of the rooms have special features with balconies, which prove very popular with regular guests. There is still, however, nothing pretentious about Southcliffe, which, happily, remains a warm, comfortable and very friendly place, where the food is always most appetising–the hotel is licensed, so you can enjoy a glass or two of wine with your meals. The house was built in the late nineteenth century and has many attractive features, including doors and a staircase made of pitch pine. Many elements combine to make this a relaxing hotel–the pleasing architecture, the attractive colour schemes, central heating–yet most of the credit must go to the owners who work so hard to ensure that their guests are made to feel at home. In addition to preparing home-cooked breakfasts and dinners, Mrs Kamp is happy to provide packed lunches on request. Lynton itself, beloved by poets such as Wordsworth, Coleridge and Shelley, is an unspoilt holiday resort, which, with its twin town, Lynmouth, sits on Devon's north coast. Here the East and West Lyn meet before they flow out to the sea. Inland is Exmoor which supports the last of England's wild red deer. If you would like a dress-circle position on the north Devon coastline and are looking for comfortable accommodation at a very reasonable price, you will find Southcliffe Hotel an excellent choice.

Weekly Terms from £210.00
Daily Terms from £32.00
Bed and Breakfast from £21.00
No Service Charge. VAT inclusive
Credit Cards—Access, Visa
6 Double, 2 Twin Bedrooms

2 Private Bathroom.
6 Private Shower Rooms
All Rooms with TV, Tea and Coffee-making Facilities, Hairdryer
Open from March to October
Residential Licence

Full Central Heating
Children over 5 years catered for
Dogs allowed by Arrangement
Private Parking for 10 cars
Nearby: Tennis, Putting, Fishing, Riding, Bowls, Walking

Section 1: Devon

Lynton—Hewitt's Hotel and Restaurant
North Walk, Lynton, Devon. EX35 6HJ
Tel 0598 52293. Fax 0598 52459

Few men are lucky enough to fall in love with a woman and a view at the same time and to be able to build a house to please one and capture the other from that very same spot. No wonder Thomas Hewitt's happy house which he called the The Hoe, but which is now Hewitt's Hotel has a delightful feel about it, taking us back to that leisurely golden age when Victoria was Queen and all was well with the English countryside. If Sir Thomas Hewitt returned to the hotel he would find very few changes. It is still a happy house. Lynton and Lynmouth are joined by a famous water operated funicular railway, which was the first to be built in this country. It was conceived and planned in the house now known as Hewitt's Hotel and Sir Thomas was one of its founders. Hewitt's is set in twenty-seven acres of secluded woodland, on the North Devon and Cornwall Coastal path-yet the lovely town of Lynton is only a short walk away. There are spectacular views over Lynmouth Bay from the 150-foot sun terrace. Within there is a magnificent sweeping staircase and oak-pannelled lounges with fine stained-glass windows and comfortable antique furnishings which add to the air of tranquility and luxury. The bedrooms are large and airy and most have sea views. The owners of the hotel live in situ. Accordingly they are inviting you into their own home where the informal atmosphere with a friendly welcome and cheerful service relaxes the most tired traveller. The cuisine at Hewitt's is excellent and the Restaurant is reputed to be one of the best in the area. Chef, Robert Schyns, uses only fresh ingredients, and creates dishes of originality and flair with a continental touch.

Weekly Terms from £322.00
Daily Terms from £58.00
Bed and Breakfast from £39.00
Bar Lunch from £1.85
Lunch from £13.50 Table D'Hôte
Afternoon Tea from £2.50
Dinner from £19.50 and A La Carte
VAT inclusive

Credit Cards—Access, Visa.
1 Family Room. 5 Double, 1 Single,
3 Twin Bedrooms
9 Private Bathrooms
All Rooms with TV, Telephone, Radio,
Baby-listening, Hairdryer
Open all year except 3 weeks in January
Fully Licensed. Full Central Heating

Cocktail Bar. Conference Facilities
Children catered for.
Dogs not allowed.
Parking Facilities
Nearby: Tennis, Putting,
Swimming, Golf,
Fishing, Riding, Sailing,
Windsurfing, Water Skiing

Section 1: Devon

Near Lynton, Hillsford Bridges—Combe Park Hotel
Hillsford Bridges, Lynton, Devon. EX35 6LE. Tel 0598 52356

Tracing Somerset's western county boundary upwards from where it follows Dane's Brook, one might expect to find that it embraced the twin towns of Lynton and Lynmouth. However, just north of Pinkworthy Pond it veers east into Exmoor Forest and thence along the line of Bridgworthy Water to the sea. This places Hillsford Bridges securely in North Devon and it is here, in five acres of grounds and surrounded by deciduous woodland in an unspoilt valley, that the beautiful and well-run Combe Park Hotel stands. Formerly a seventeenth-century hunting lodge, it has benefited from an extended programme of improvements under the direction of proprietors Shirley and David Barnes and John Walley. It now maintains first class standards in both service and *décor*. The food is well planned and prepared and, whilst the policy is to have a set evening meal, guests are always at liberty to request other dishes earlier in the day. Fresh vegetables are always on the menu, according to season. There are nine comfortable bedrooms, all with private bathrooms, and the Hoar Oak Water lulls one into a blissful sleep as it tumbles along in front of the house. Log fires supplement the central heating, with two lounges and a residents' bar affording opportunities for relaxing and socialising. Facilities for riding and for salmon and trout fishing are nearby and, with Exmoor National Park's vast open spaces beside one, it is a walker's paradise. Dogs are welcomed and packed lunches are available.

Weekly Terms from £230.00
Daily Terms from £40.00
Bed and Breakfast from £28.00
Dinner from £15.75 Table D'Hôte
Gratuities at Guest's Discretion. VAT inclusive

3 Family Rooms. 4 Double, 2 Twin Bedrooms. 7 Private Bathrooms. 2 Private Shower Rooms. All Rooms with Tea and Coffee-making Facilities
Open from mid March to end October and Christmas

Residential and Restaurant Licence
Full Central Heating. TV Lounge
Children over 12 years catered for
Dogs allowed. Parking Facilities
Nearby: Tennis, Putting, Golf, Fishing, Riding, Sailing, Birdwatching

Membury—Lea Hill Hotel and Restaurant
Membury, Near Axminster, East Devon. EX13 7AQ. Tel 040 488 388

What a delightful place this is and what an unspoilt location with its tranquil views across glorious countryside. As you climb the hill to Lea Hill, along its winding, tree-lined drive you are greeted by a picturesque scene of thatched roofs, stone walls and flower-filled terraces. Here life flows with a rural gentleness. The interior of the property also retains the same unique character with original flagstones, inglenook fireplaces and age-worn oak beams. The new resident proprietors, David and Sonia Banks, who have owned country house restaurants in the past, do all they can to make their guests feel at home. All guests are treated to a Devon cream tea on arrival and have a daily newspaper, all included in the tariff. The dining room is situated in the oldest part of the hotel and its historic charm and ambiance is complemented with candlelight, together with crisp linen, sparkling glassware and cutlery. The menus are changed daily and all the food is prepared and cooked to order from locally produced ingredients. Adjacent to the main building are two stone barns which have been carefully restored and renovated to provide additional bedrooms furnished with antique pine. The hotel is situated on the East Devon/Somerset/Dorset borders close to the pretty village of Membury. Part of its charm is that it is more than a little off the beaten track but the Banks will provide you with a map to find them! Lea Hill is so utterly peaceful, unspoilt and friendly we are somewhat loath to tell anyone else about it, lest it be spoilt.

Bed and Breakfast from £80.00 (Double)
Bed and Breakfast from £60.00 (Single)
Luncheon from £17.50
Dinner from £23.50
Gratuities at Guest's discretion
VAT inclusive. Credit Cards-Access,

Eurocard, Visa
1 Suite. 7 Double, 4 Twin, 2 Single Bedrooms
All Rooms with Private Bathroom, TV, Telephone, Radio, hospitality tray, Hairdryer
Open from March to 3rd January

Fully Licensed. Children over 10 years welcome. Dogs permitted
Parking Facilities.
Nearby: Squash, Badminton, Swimming, Golf, Fishing, Riding, Sailing, Windsurfing, Water Skiing

Section 1: Devon

Newton Poppleford, Near Sidmouth—Southern Cross
Newton Poppleford, Near Sidmouth, Devon. EX10 0DU. Tel 0395 68439

Ten miles east of Exeter, and only four miles from Sidmouth, you'll find Newton Poppleford on the A3052 road. Here you are well placed for exploring the many byways of Devon and, in fact, the concentration of castles, country parks and gardens, viewpoints, nature reserves, galleries and golf courses, picnic sites, a mill and a steam railway, all in the locality, singles out Southern Cross as an admirable base. There is an atmosphere which brings holiday guests back, year after year, while the warm Irish charm of the owner, Miss Eileen McKenna, lifts this establishment well above the normal guest-house standard. Southern Cross comprises an old-world cottage blended into a new wing, reflecting the personality of Miss McKenna. Healthy home cooking is presented in a luxury manner. The cream teas offered have, in fact, gained a very high reputation and they are held in such high regard that the council officials from around the area make a point of bringing their overseas visitors to Southern Cross, to partake of a true Devonshire cream tea. Amongst the particular areas to visit we would name Bicton Park, Aylesbeare Common, Fernwood and, of course, the cathedral city of Exeter. A great deal of wind-surfing and sailing is popular on the nearby coast at Budleigh Salterton and Exmouth. Some ten miles to the east one can make an interesting call on the Seaton and District Electric Tramway Company. Only a few miles further and one is in the historic port of Lyme Regis.

Terms on Application
Gratuities at Guest's Discretion
VAT extra

1 Single, 4 Double, 3 Twin Bedrooms
Open all Year
Unlicensed

Storage and Electric Heaters in Bedrooms
Dogs allowed
Parking Facilities

North Bovey—Blackaller Hotel and Restaurant
North Bovey, Devon TQ13 8QY. Tel 0647 40322

Blackaller - the West Country name for the Black Alder tree - was once a seventeenth-century woollen mill and lies on the banks of the Bovey river. North Bovey is one of the loveliest of the many villages scattered throughout Dartmoor, sometimes referred to as 'The Last Remaining Wilderness'. These isolated small communities have an unspoilt charm contrasting sharply with the open moor, which has one of the largest concentrations of Iron Age and Prehistoric sites in Northern Europe. The hotel has just five bedrooms, all with *en suite* facilities and each one carrying the name of a bird: we stayed in 'Nuthatch'. Your hosts in this comfortable sanctuary are Hazel Phillips and Peter Hunt, whose warm welcome and delicious home-made food bring them fine compliments in their guest book, endorsed by a high proportion of visitors making return reservations. Homely touches here include dried flower arrangements, a selection of books in your room, a tall grandfather clock, your bed turned down for you, floral prints and hanging bedheads, pretty bathrooms, and scrumptious sweets served in lovely china. Not to mention Pip, their well-behaved terrier. Breakfasts here are a delight, as is all the catering, making the best possible use of appetising local produce. Here is the healthiest of eating, coupled with comfort and attentive service, everything representing excellent value for money. This is an area to captivate lovers of the great outdoors, historians and walkers. The charming small market towns of Chagford and Moretonhampstead are only a few minutes' drive away.

Bed and Breakfast from £25.00
Bar Lunch from £5.00
Afternoon Tea from £3.00
Dinner from £15.00
Gratuities at Guest's Discretion.
VAT inclusive

No Credit Cards accepted.
2 Double, 1 Single, 2 Twin Bedrooms
All Rooms with Private Bathroom, TV, Tea and Coffee-making Facilities, Hairdryer
Open from February to end December
Residential and Supper Licence

Oil Heating. Bar.
Small Conference Facilities.
Children catered for. Dogs allowed
Parking Facilities.
Fishing, Riding, Birdwatching, Walking
Nearby: Tennis, Golf

Section 1: Devon

Near Okehampton, South Zeal—The Oxenham Arms
South Zeal, Okehampton, Devon. EX20 2JT. Tel 0837 840244

Scheduled as an Ancient Monument, The Oxenham Arms nestles at the base of Dartmoor's celebrated Cawsand Beacon. The inn is believed to have been built in the latter part of the twelfth century by lay monks and, in later times, it has been featured in the novels 'The Beacon', 'John Herring' and 'Westward Ho!'. In addition to the romantic associations, there is much of historic and architectural interest and, in the immediate vicinity, several magnificent walks. A monolith set in the wall of a small lounge behind the bar is thought to have been shaped by man 5000 years ago and, despite deep digging, its foundations have never been reached. It is simply one of many features that lovers of old beams, large open fireplaces, stone mullioned Tudor windows, pewter, copper and the like, will find fascinating here. Also, guests can experience Anglo-American hospitality, since James H Henry hails from Louisiana, whilst his wife is English. One consequence of this is that the catering is pleasantly out of the ordinary and, in the fine old dining-room with a granite pillar supporting the beam, one can enjoy the breakfasts, luncheons and dinners that are available all the year round. Throughout the hotel, the introduction of modern comforts has not been allowed to detract from the picturesque and time-worn features. Travelling westwards on the A30, look out for the village of South Zeal a few miles beyond Whiddon Down. The Oxenham Arms is in the village centre: a veritable refuge, especially on a winter's night.

Bed and Breakfast from £25.00
Bar Lunch from £3.50
Lunch from £8.50 A La Carte
Bar Supper from £3.50
Dinner from £15.50 Table D'Hôte
Gratuities at Guest's Discretion

VAT inclusive. Credit Cards—Access, American Express, Diners Club, Visa
4 Family Rooms. 6 Suites
5 Double, 5 Twin Bedrooms
10 Private Bathrooms. 3 Private Shower Rooms. 8 Rooms with TV, Telephone,

Tea and Coffee-making Facilities
Open all Year. Fully Licensed. Electric Heating. TV Lounge. Conference Facilities
Children catered for. Dogs allowed
Parking Facilities. Nearby: Tennis, Squash, Badminton, Swimming, Golf, Fishing

Paignton—Redcliffe Hotel
Marine Drive, Paignton, Devon. TQ3 2NL. Tel 0803 526397. Fax 0803 528030

Paignton, Brixham and Torquay each have a snug little harbour packed with pleasure craft, a reminder that Torbay was once one of the country's foremost fishing areas. Today, its miles of reddish sands, backed in places by red sandstone cliffs, are a holidaymaker's playground, allowing the area to be styled, the 'English Riviera'. The appropriately named Redcliffe has been one of Torbay's principal hotels for many years. We suspect that almost every hotel here lays claim to a view of the sea. The Redcliffe, however, goes one better than most of the others. It stands on a small promontory, with the sea practically washing its foundations, and so close are all its public rooms to the high-water mark that, at times, staying there is almost like being at sea, but without any of its discomforts. This resemblance to a liner continues within, for there is a ballroom, games room, cocktail bars and lounges, hairdressing salon, plus a restaurant offering catering and cellar of distinction. For deck sports one can substitute putting and a heated swimming pool. All the bedrooms either look out onto the sea or the gardens, with their spacious lawns and terraces. There is a medley of accommodation available, from spacious family rooms to singles, and every room has a television, telephone and radio, and all have either a private bathroom or shower. You could not wish for a better headquarters, and when touring has palled, within walking distance one will find that every conceivable holiday pursuit has been anticipated.

Weekly Terms from £273.00
Daily Terms from £47.00
Bed and Breakfast from £39.00
Bar Lunch from £1.25
Sunday Lunch from £7.95 Table D'Hôte
Dinner from £13.75 and A La Carte
Gratuities at Guest's Discretion
VAT inclusive. Credit Cards—Access, Visa

3 Family Rooms. 18 Double, 26 Twin, 12 Single Bedrooms. 52 Private Bathrooms
7 Private Shower Rooms. All Rooms with TV, Telephone, Radio, Tea and Coffee-making Facilities, Baby-listening
Open all Year. Fully Licensed
Full Central Heating. Lift. Cocktail Bar
TV Lounge. Games Room. Ballroom

Hairdressing Salon.
Conference Facilities
Children catered for. Dogs not allowed
Parking Facilities. Night Porter
Putting, Outdoor Swimming Pool, Fishing.
Nearby: Tennis, Squash, Badminton, Solarium, Sauna, Golf, Riding, Sailing, Windsurfing, Water Skiing

Section 1: Devon

Paignton—Sunhill Hotel   Alta Vista Road, Paignton, Devon. TQ4 6DA. Tel 0803 557532. Fax 0803 663850

In a fine elevated position-the road is called Alta Vista-this delightful hotel overlooks the park, with boating lake, and these, with the beach, are easily accessible directly from the hotel. The public rooms and most bedrooms have excellent views over Goodrington beach and Tor Bay, with Brixham in the distance. A major programme of refurbishment and extension has recently been completed, the hotel now offering twenty-eight guest rooms ranging from single to family accommodation, a lift to four of the five floors, a sizeable conference room, a sauna and a full size snooker table. Resident Proprietors Mr and Mrs Bewick, with their young and enthusiastic staff, gave us friendly and attentive service and we rate Sunhill as giving excellent value for money. Three chefs produce very appetising meals which are served in the spacious dining room overlooking the sea. Special diets are catered for, on request. A great many local attractions are available to guests here, including a model village, aircraft and motor museums, Paignton Zoo, Buckfast Abbey, craft and leisure centres, Kent's Cavern, Dart Valley Steam Railway and the National Shire Horse Centre. Torquay, with its many beaches and theatres, is only a short ride away, as is Brixham with its quaint shops and museum, and where time has stood still in some places. Sporting activities include fishing, golf, windsurfing, waterskiing, sailing and horseriding. Two and four day Mini Breaks are arranged for horse-racing enthusiasts.

Weekly Terms from £246.00 (Half Board)
Daily Terms from £40.00 (Half Board)
Bed and Breakfast from £29.00
Bar Lunch from £1.50
Dinner from £11.00 Table D'Hôte
Gratuities at Guest's discretion.
VAT inclusive. Credit Cards-Access,
American Express, Visa
4 Family Rooms, 14 Double, 4 Twin, 6 Single Bedrooms. 19 Private Bathrooms
9 Private Shower Rooms
All rooms with colour TV, Telephone, Radio, Tea and Coffee-making facilities, Baby-listening. Hairdryer available on request. Open all year
Residential and Restaurant Licence
Lift. Cocktail Bar. Snooker Room.
Conference Facilities. Children catered for.
Dogs allowed by arrangement
Parking Facilities. Sauna. Nearby: Putting, Squash, Badminton, Swimming, Golf

Salcombe—Grafton Towers
Moult Hill, Salcombe, Devon. Tel 054884 2882

Salcombe and its surrounding beautiful countryside has become a prime location for many Television and Film productions. After the Poirot episode 'Peril at End House' filmed in Salcombe in 1989, the telephones rang at L.W.T. for five days commenting on the beauty of the locations and enquiring where the film was made. Capturing the wonderful mixture of rolling countryside, woodland and sea, Grafton Towers nestles in the side of the hill and is entirely sheltered from the prevailing winds. The house faces south overlooking Prawle Point, the English Channel and the time-warp landscape of Limebury Point. The bedrooms have lovely country and sea aspects. But rarely will you be in your room; there is too much to do outside. A garden with outstanding views. A sandy bathing beach just below. Spectacular coastal walks around Bolt Head and Sharpitor Gardens, a refreshing ferry boat trip to the town, or, when the mood dictates golfing, sea fishing, or a sail. The original Victorian dining room, a favourite venue for discerning locals, has an attractive Adam fireplace and offers an excellent range of food and wines. That important alliterative, *cuisine*, comfort and care, appears to be the practised motto of Grafton Towers. A good choice of 'Refined English Cooking' is always available using the best fresh local produce. All sweets are home made and a favourite is *Normandy Pear Tart* with Devon clotted cream. The Chef uses the famous Salcombe crab for his *Crab Pancakes Mornay*. There are sufficient attractions in this corner of Devon to fill a score or more of varied holidays at Grafton Towers.

Terms on application
Dinner from £13.50 and A La Carte
Gratuities at Guest's Discretion
VAT Inclusive. Credit Cards—Access, Visa
1 Family Room. 1 Single, 6 Double, 6 Twin Bedrooms. 9 Private Bathrooms
2 Private Shower Rooms
Most Rooms with TV, Radio, Baby-listening, Tea and Coffee-making Facilities, Hairdryers
Open from Easter to Mid October
Residential and Restaurant Licence
Part Central Heating. Cocktail Bar
Children catered for. Dogs allowed
Parking Facilities. Nearby; Tennis, Squash, Swimming, Solarium, Sauna, Golf, Fishing, Riding, Sailing, Windsurfing, Water Skiing, Magnificent Coastal Walking

Section 1: Devon

Salcombe—Tides Reach Hotel
South Sands, Salcombe, Devon. TQ8 8LJ
Telephone 054 884 3466. Fax 054 884 3954

It is difficult to remain objective when writing about an old friend, and that is just what the Tides Reach Hotel is ... one of our most enduring recommendations. Fortunately, the Edwards family has, over the years, amassed a whole army of enthusiasts who will confirm that this is one of the best hotels on the south Devon coast. It is also a fact that because of the hotel's continual development and improvement, this is a story that can be written and rewritten over and over again. When we first recommended the Tides Reach, (what an apt name that is) we judged it to be a pleasant holiday hotel in a favoured position, overlooking the sandy cove of South Sands. Now, many years later, after it has been acclaimed by food experts and has had praise heaped upon it by organisations throughout the world, one is hard pressed to find another hotel which can compete with its all-embracing facilities. A heated indoor swimming pool, a jacuzzi pool, a Finnish sauna, steam bath, squash and windsurfing (tuition and hire) are just some of the amenities here. There are many more. During a recent visit, we met Mr and Mrs Roy Edwards' son, who represents the family's fifth generation of hoteliers. We were able to see the newest developments at the hotel, which include more de luxe bedrooms with en suite facilities, a function suite and a well equipped games room. You will find the Tides Reach Hotel on the western flank of the Salcombe estuary between the Inner Harbour and Bolt Head.

Terms on application
Bar Lunch from £3.25
Afternoon Tea from £3.50
Dinner from £23.50 and A La Carte
Gratuities at Guest's Discretion
VAT inclusive
Credit Cards—Access, American Express, Diners Club, Visa
3 Family Suites

18 Double, 18 Twin Bedrooms
All Rooms with Private Bathroom, TV, Telephone, Radio, Tea and Coffee-making Facilities available
Open from March to November
Fully Licensed. Full Central Heating
Lift. Cocktail Bar
Games Room, Snooker Room
Children over 8 years catered for

Dogs allowed. Parking Facilities
Night Porter.
Squash, Indoor Heated Swimming Pool, Solarium, Sauna, Multi-gym,
Beach Boat House
Nearby: Tennis, Golf, Fishing, Riding, Sailing, Windsurfing, Water Skiing, Shooting

Section 1: Devon

Salcombe—The Sunny Cliff Hotel
Cliff Road, Salcombe, Devon. TQ8 8JX. Tel 054 884 2207

The Sunny Cliff Hotel is situated on the Salcombe hillside on the very edge of the estuary and is less than five minutes' walk from the centre of the town. The views across the water to East Portlemouth and Mill Bay are quite breathtaking, and visitors can spend many pleasant hours watching the movements of sailing dinghies, racing cruisers and the Salcombe crab fishermen as they return with their catch. Mr and Mrs John Ireland, with their resident managers and assisted by well-educated and efficient girls, have created a friendly and informal atmosphere here. It is an ideal hotel for families, as children are genuinely welcomed and thoughtfully catered for with the provision of high chairs, cots and children's suppers. There are nineteen bedrooms, all of which are most attractively furnished; nine rooms are *en suite* and have tea and coffee-making facilities. The spacious and pleasant dining room overlooks the estuary and guests can enjoy good, English food, complemented by a well chosen wine list, whilst enjoying superb, panoramic views. For entertainment, there is a television in all rooms and, set against the sea wall below the hotel, a swimming pool, surrounded by a paved terrace for sunbathing. The hotel even has its own moorings, so enthusiastic sailors can bring their own dinghies and spend their days navigating the beautiful Salcombe estuary. Even landlubbers will find that there is a wealth of tempting activities awaiting them in this, the most southerly part of Devon–from perambulation of quaint South Hams villages to exploration of beautiful cliff paths.

Weekly Terms from £225.00	5 Family Rooms	Residential and Restaurant Licence
Daily Terms from £35.00	1 Single, 8 Double, 5 Twin Bedrooms	Part Central Heating. Cocktail Bar. TV
Bed and Breakfast from £26.00	Bedrooms. 9 Private Bathrooms. 2 Private	Lounge. Children catered for
Bar Lunch from £1.50	Shower Rooms.	Dogs allowed. Parking Facilities.
Dinner from £11.50 Table D'Hôte	All rooms have TV and Tea making	Outdoor Swimming Pool, Fishing, Sailing,
VAT inclusive. Credit Cards—Access, Visa	Facilities. Open all Year	Windsurfing

Near Salcombe, Thurlestone—Heron House Hotel
Thurlestone Sands, Near Salcombe, S. Devon. TQ7 3JY. Tel 0548 561308

In a region renowned for natural, uncommercialised beauty, this hotel stands a mere fifty yards from a large sandy beach, in a National Trust protected area. Surrounded by unspoilt countryside, with spectacular coastline views across to Plymouth Sound, Heron House is on a coastal path leading to remote coves and bays. It has been owned and managed by the same family since 1983, during which time it has been improved up to its present high standard, now offering a country house atmosphere with a private *en suite* bathroom or shower room for every bedroom. A spacious outdoor swimming pool, surrounded by a large patio area, is heated from May through to September, with a waitress service for those seated or sunbathing at the poolside. Indoors, guests can visit the solarium, relax in the uncrowded bar lounge or retreat to a reading lounge, overlooking the swimming pool. We must make special mention of the five-course dinners. An adequate choice is offered at each stage of one's meal, every dish having that special quality to raise it to the level of something truly memorable. The owners are rightly proud of their chef, Liz Lee. From Heron House there are many activities to be enjoyed, most of them quite close by. Rambling along cliff-top paths or in river valleys, temporary membership of golf Clubs, riding, boating, fishing and swimming. Short drives will take you to the historic towns of Totnes, Buckfastleigh, Brixham and Torquay. Don't miss exploring Dartmoor National Park and be sure to return in time for that exceptional dinner!

Weekly Terms from £255.00	3 Family Rooms, 11 Double, 4 Twin	call. Open from 6th February to 31st
Daily Terms from £41.00	Bedrooms. 9 Private Bathrooms	December. Fully Licensed. Full Central
Bed and Breakfast from £35.00	9 Private Shower Rooms	Heating. Cocktail Bar. Games Room.
Bar Lunch from £2.50. Dinner from £15.00	All rooms with TV, Telephone, Radio,	Conference Facilities. Children catered for.
Gratuities at Guest's discretion	Baby-listening, Tea and Coffee-making	Dogs allowed. Parking Facilities
VAT inclusive. Credit Cards–Access, Visa	facilities, Hairdryer, Early morning alarm	Outdoor Swimming Pool, Solarium

Section 1: Devon

Near Salcombe, Bolt Head—Bolt Head Hotel
Bolt Head, Salcombe, Devon. TQ8 8LL.
Tel 0548 843751. Fax 0548 843060

With its 'Tail' up and its 'Head' down, the western flank of the Kingsbridge peninsula is a part of more than 1,000 acres of National Trust land. At Bolt Head, with but a short path dividing it from the lapping waves, this friendly hotel might well describe its attractions with the alliterative–sand, scenery and sunshine. There is a small beach, so peaceful and personal that children can be left to their own devices whilst parents relax. The hotel relishes its position and from bedroom, dining room and lounge one's constant panoramic view is blue water, green hills and coloured sails. On our recent visit we found everything was to the highest standards and we are sure that this splendid hotel will go from strength to strength. The hotel is comfortable and well appointed and the fine cuisine and well-stocked cellar are both highly regarded. Upstairs is everything which pertains to modern bedroom comfort; private bathrooms and showers, radio and intercom, central heating and tea and coffee-making facilities. This area is a natural haven for all those seeking the outdoor life. The hotel has an open-air heated swimming pool, and golf, fishing, riding and sailing are all on your doorstep. What about sunshine? Bolt Head is the most southerly point in Devon. There is no need to enlarge on that.

Terms on Application
Gratuities at Guest's Discretion
VAT inclusive
Credit Cards—Access, American Express, Diners Club, Visa
8 Family Rooms, 1 Family Suite
2 Double, 15 Twin, 4 Single Bedrooms

All rooms with Private Bath/Shower
Rooms, TV, Telephone, Radio, Baby-listening, Tea and Coffee-making Facilities, Hairdryer
Open from 29th March to 10th November
Fully Licensed
Full Central Heating

Cocktail Bar. Games Room
Children catered for
Dogs allowed
Parking Facilities
Outdoor Heated Swimming Pool
Nearby: Golf, Fishing, Riding, Sailing, Windsurfing, Water Skiing

Section 1: Devon

Saunton Sands—The Saunton Sands Hotel   Saunton Sands
Near Braunton, Devon. EX33 1LQ. Tel 0271 890212. Fax 0271 890145

The most obvious reason for The Saunton Sands Hotel's continuing popularity is its superb position. The hotel, family owned and managed, faces due south directly overlooking five miles of glorious surfing beaches and is sheltered by the rolling north Devon countryside around. All bedrooms have a private bathroom and, like all the public rooms, are spacious and very comfortably furnished. Much of the hotel has in fact been redecorated recently to a luxurious standard. The lounges, ballroom and restaurant all command magnificent views over the sands and broad sweep of Barnstaple Bay. Food is invariably first class with a choice of over 130 fine wines. Every conceivable facility for a really enjoyable family holiday or off-season break is close at hand–including a heated indoor swimming pool and a newly built heated outdoor swimming pool, sauna, solarium, squash and tennis courts, billiard room, putting green, mini-gym, games room, television lounges, nursery, boutique and hairdressing salon. Luxury self-contained apartment suites within the grounds are also available. For golfers there is the challenge of the championship Saunton course right next door, whilst for nature lovers there is Exmoor and the Braunton Burrows Reserve close by. Throughout the year there is a full entertainment programme including film shows, dinner-dances, live groups and discotheques. To find the hotel, take the A361 out of Barnstaple, turn left at Braunton traffic lights and drive for about three miles on the road towards Croyde.

Weekly Terms from £280.00 to £560.00
Bed and Breakfast from £58.00
Lunch from £11.50 and A La Carte
Dinner from £18.50 and A La Carte
VAT inclusive. Credit Cards—Access, American Express, Diners Club, Visa

20 Family Rooms. 25 Double, 41 Twin, 6 Single Bedrooms. All Rooms with Private Bathroom, Satellite colour TV, Telephone, Radio, Baby-listening, Hairdryer
Open all Year. Fully Licensed
Full Central Heating. Lift. 2 Cocktail Bars.

TV Lounge. Games Room. Snooker Room Conference Facilities. Dogs allowed by Arrangement. Parking Facilities. Night Porter. Hard Tennis Court, Putting, Squash, Indoor and Outdoor Heated Swimming Pools, Solarium, Sauna, Spa Bath

Shaldon—Glenside Hotel
Ringmore Road, Shaldon, Devon. TQ14 0EP. Tel 0626 872448

Attractive colour-washed houses clothe the steep and wooded hills which rise above the southern bank of the Teign estuary. Close to the red sands, and almost at the water's edge, is Glenside Hotel, looking most inviting behind attractive gardens. Built originally as a private residence in about 1820, the house has been extended over the years and served as a school before being carefully converted into a restful and homely hotel. There is little of the ordinary hotel atmosphere at the Glenside. There is a definite personal touch which you will appreciate the more when you have met Derek and Ann Newbold, who own and manage it. It was a surprise and a pleasure for us to meet Mr and Mrs Newbold here, for they have been caring hoteliers for over twenty-five years and we knew them very well whilst they were at their previous hotel, The Dainton at Paignton. They are now running the Glenside with the same care and enthusiasm as then. The Glenside's bedrooms are comfortable and well equipped and the hotel's catering, whilst being traditional, is of a very high standard. One of our fellow guests here was full of praise for the vegetarian dishes she had been offered. From the hotel's vantage point there is nearly always 'life' to be seen on the water, with Teignmouth across the way. Here at the Glenside is a holiday spot which can be restful or restless, as one wishes-golf, sea and river fishing, boat trips, sailing, windsurfing and birdwatching are all at hand. From Shaldon to Torquay the road ascends abruptly, and from the heights above one gets some fine views of sea and coastline.

Weekly Terms from £160.00 (DB&B)
Daily Terms from £25.50 (DB&B)
Bed and Breakfast from £17.00
Dinner from £9.50 Table D'Hôte
Gratuities at Guest's Discretion
VAT inclusive. 1 Family Room

4 Double, 3 Twin, 2 Single Bedrooms
1 Private Bathroom
6 Private Shower Rooms
All Rooms with TV, Tea and Coffee-making facilities. Open all Year
Residential and Restaurant Licence

Full Central Heating. Cocktail Bar
Children catered for. Dogs allowed
Parking Facilities. Nearby: Tennis, Putting, Squash, Swimming, Solarium, Sauna, Golf, Fishing, Riding, Sailing, Windsurfing, Water Skiing, Bowling

Section 1: Devon

Sidmouth—The Belmont Hotel   The Esplanade, Sidmouth,
Devon. EX10 8RX. Tel 0395 512555. Telex 42551 EXONIA G REF BREND 9

Two of the largest and undoubtedly best hotels in Sidmouth, The Victoria and The Belmont, both in the four-star category, are under the same direction, the Brend family, and it is just a matter of personal choice which one prefers. There is something restful about The Belmont Hotel. Guests may make use of the luxurious indoor and outdoor heated swimming pools, sauna, solarium, spa bath, snooker and other recreational facilities of the Victoria Hotel next door. Yet, the full appreciation of The Belmont is to be found in its relaxing surroundings and warming service. It is somewhere where all the best features of comfort, good food and good friends, are preached, practised, and ... perfected. The gardens are a picture and a pleasure, and the outlook, from a slight eminence on the seafront, is superb. Within, The Belmont has been extensively rejuvenated of late and the results are really first class. Every bedroom now offers *en suite* facilities and all are most comfortably appointed. Downstairs, the restaurant and lounges have never looked more luxurious, or inviting. It takes no time to drop into a gentle pattern of life at The Belmont: an inviting armchair to ease one's muscles; a pre-lunch drink on the terrace, perhaps; and later a gentle round of putting on the front lawn. And that spectacular unrestricted sea view is one's constant companion. It is all as idyllic as it sounds.

Weekly Terms from £255.00 to £550.00
Bed and Breakfast from £55.00
Lunch from £10.50 and A La Carte
Dinner from £16.50 and A La Carte
Gratuities at Guest's Discretion. VAT inclusive. Credit Cards—Access, American Express, Diners Club, Visa
6 Family Rooms, 2 Suites. 10 Double,

27 Twin, 8 Single Bedrooms
All rooms with Private Bathroom, TV, Telephone, Radio, Tea and Coffee-making Facilities, Hairdryer
Baby-listening and Trouser Press available on request. Open all year. Fully Licensed.
Full Central Heating
Lift. Cocktail Bar. Conference Facilities.

Children catered for.
Dogs allowed by arrangement
Parking Facilities. Night Porter. Putting Nearby: Tennis, Croquet, Squash, Badminton, Swimming, Solarium, Sauna, Golf, Fishing, Riding, Sailing, Windsurfing, Shooting

Sidmouth—The Littlecourt Hotel

Seafield Road, Sidmouth, Devon. EX10 8HF. Tel 0395 515279

Sidmouth used to be just a tiny fishing village, encircled to the north by protective hills and situated between fine reddish cliffs though which the River Sid flows and trickles into the sea. In the nineteenth century, it was 'discovered' and very quickly blossomed into a smart Regency resort. Many noted people came to live here, including the Duke and Duchess of St Albans, who had this fine house (now The Littlecourt Hotel) built in Seafield Road. It is a gracious and elegant place in which to stay and provides a country house environment in a town situation. One recalls the keen and personal interest which the resident owner, Mr J S Reeder, takes in his guests' welfare, the solidness of the woodwork in the well-proportioned rooms, the attractive swimming pool in the garden and the food–full of fresh Devon produce and very satisfying. Many a diet must have come to grief on the extensive sweet trolley! Our bedroom, with bathroom *en suite*, was quite spacious enough for daytime comfort and although there are three family rooms, Mr Reeder tries not to have too many children in the hotel at the same time, so that the restful atmosphere is not unduly disturbed. The hotel duly deserves its AA and RAC two star awards and the three crowns commended by the West Country Tourist Board. We enjoyed our stay at The Littlecourt, the stroll down to the Esplanade a few minutes' walk away and the fragrance of the hotel's garden. There can be only one disturbing thought at The Littlecourt Hotel ... the thought of leaving.

Weekly Terms from £169.00
Daily Terms from £31.00
Bed and Breakfast from £25.00
Bar Lunch from £2.00
Lunch from £5.95 Table D'Hôte
Dinner from £11.50 and A La Carte

Gratuities at Guest's Discretion.
VAT inclusive. Credit Cards—Access, Visa
3 Family Rooms. 5 Double, 9 Twin, 4 Single Bedrooms. 12 Private Bathrooms. 6 Private Shower Rooms. All Rooms with TV, Radio, Baby-listening, Tea and

Coffee-making Facilities. Hairdryer available on Request
Open 12th March to November
Residential and Restaurant Licence
TV Lounge. Conference facilities
Children catered for. Dogs allowed

Section 1: Devon

Sidmouth—Hotel Riviera
The Esplanade, Sidmouth, Devon. EX10 8AY
Telephone 0395 515201. Fax 0395 577775

Leaving the A3052 coast road behind, you will be rather thrilled to drive down into Sidmouth, a town that is deliberately 'shy' of trippers, promenades and piers, but has more first-class hotels in proportion to its population than any town we know. So, we will begin with one of the very best hotels and the one which holds the most prominent position on the Esplanade-The Hotel Riviera. It is a most handsome building, which blends well with the Regency town houses and Victorian cottages of this dignified resort. The real charm of the Hotel Riviera, however, lies within, for it has recently been refurbished, and this has enhanced the comfort throughout without detracting in any way from the charm and elegance, for which the Hotel Riviera is renowned. To all this is allied the highest standards of personal attention. You would expect this at one of Sidmouth's leading hotels, but at the Riviera they also pride themselves on a quality of service that belongs to a more gracious age. It is reflected in the welcome you receive as you pass through the foyer and in the friendly attention of the staff who have been proud to work there for many years. It is a warm, family atmosphere appropriate to a fine hotel. You will certainly look forward to a meal in the comfort of the elegant dining room with its splendid sea views, where every dish is a delight, expertly served and complemented by a wide selection of wines and there is no better place to end the day than in the Regency Bar, with its atmosphere of relaxed luxury. The Riviera is a luxurious sanctuary in any season, it offers specially reduced terms during Autumn, Winter and Spring, as well as for weekends, and there is a comprehensive programme for the Christmas and New Year period.

Weekly Terms (Half Board) from £350.00
Daily Terms (Half Board) from £50.00
Room and English Breakfast from £43.00
Luncheon from £11.50 and A La Carte
Devonshire Tea from £3.50
Dinner from £18.50 and A La Carte
Gratuities at Guest's Discretion
VAT inclusive. Credit Cards—Access, American Express, Diners Club, Visa

5 Double, 17 Twin, 9 Single Bedrooms. (Family Rooms and Suites available).
All Rooms with Private bathroom, TV and video link, Telephone, Radio.
Baby-listening, Hairdryer, Trouser Press, 24 hour Room Service,
Complimentary toiletries, bathrobes, fresh fruit, flowers.

Open all Year.
Fully Licensed. Full Central Heating.
Lift. Cocktail Bar. Piano Bar.
Conference Facilities. Night Porter.
Nearby: Tennis, Croquet, Putting, Squash, Badminton, Swimming, Solarium, Sauna, Golf, Fishing, Riding, Sailing, Windsurfing, Game Shooting

Section 1: Devon

Sidmouth—Royal Glen
Glen Road, Sidmouth, Devon. EX10 8RW. Tel 0395 513221/578124/578125

Once the residence of the late Duke and Duchess of Kent and their infant daughter Princess Victoria, afterwards to become Queen of England and Empress of India, the historic aspect has been preserved whilst modern standards of comfort now obtain. Known earlier as Woolbrook Cottage, the Royal Glen of today, under the proprietorship of Mr O G Crane, is faithfully furnished in true Victorian character. Nowhere is the graceful charm more evident than in the uniquely oval-shaped drawing room and dining room. Air-conditioning in the restaurant ensures maximum comfort for diners sampling the excellent *cuisine* and, in the lounge bar, the impressive *décor* is enhanced by views of the gardens and sea through arched glass doors. Guests may find their overnight accommodation arranged in the *Duchess of Kent's Boudoir*, the *Duke of Kent's Bedroom* or the *Princess Victoria's Nursery*, each distinctively furnished. The elegance of the surroundings even extends to the heated indoor swimming pool. However, it was the picturesque setting of this thirty-four bedroom hotel that first commanded our attention. At the foot of a sheltered dell, within sight of the sea, the Royal Glen's immaculate castellated lines and neatly trimmed greenery proclaims the devoted care extended to both premises and patrons. Guests are within easy reach of the coast from Exmouth to Lyme Regis. Those looking for a very special Christmas occasion can do no better than stay a week or longer at the Royal Glen.

Weekly Terms from £200.00 (DB&B)
Daily Terms from £35.00
Bed and Breakfast from £25.50
Lunch from £6.50 and A La Carte
Dinner Table D'Hôte and A La Carte
Gratuities at Guest's Discretion.

VAT inclusive. Credit Cards—Access, American Express, Visa
4 Family Rooms. 4 Double, 17 Twin, 9 Single Bedrooms. 22 Private Bathrooms.
10 Private Shower Rooms
All Rooms with TV, Telephone. Some

Rooms with Hairdryer. Open from Feb to Dec.. Residential and Restaurant Licence. Full CH. Cocktail Bar. TV Lounge. Dogs allowed but not in Public Rooms. Children over 8 years catered for.
Parking Facilities. Putting

Sidmouth—Royal York and Faulkner Hotel
The Esplanade, Sidmouth, Devon. EX10 8AZ. Tel 0395 513043/513184. Fax 0395 577472

The Royal York & Faulkner Hotel, a fine example of Regency architecture, is situated in an unrivalled position at the centre of the esplanade, directly overlooking the sea and adjacent to the picturesque shopping centre. The hotel offers excellent facilities, with emphasis on comfort, *cuisine* and friendly efficient service, under the personal supervision of the resident proprietors, Mr and Mrs Peter Hook, whose family has run the hotel for over fifty years. The amenities include three comfortably furnished lounges, the tastefully refurbished *Faulkner Lounge Bar* overlooking the sea, and intimate *York Bar*. Two intercommunicating sea facing dining rooms offer excellent *cuisine* with a varied choice of menu and the *York Tapp Buttery Restaurant* serves a selection of light or full lunches daily. The fully modernised, well appointed bedrooms all have *en suite* facilities and a large number enjoy sea views. Situated on the lower ground floor and serviced directly by the lift is the award winning, luxuriously appointed Leisure Complex which comprises a large Jacuzzi/Spa Pool, Sauna, Solarium and range of exercise equipment. More recent additions to the now extensive range of indoor activities include a superb purpose built Indoor Short Mat Bowls Rink and Full Sized Snooker Table. Attractions to enjoy during your visit include the many delightful walks in and around Sidmouth that offer spectacular coastal scenery, gardens and floral decorations. As a touring centre the town is well situated for visiting the whole of glorious Devon and remains one of the most unspoilt of resorts in the area.

Weekly Terms from £187.50. Daily Terms from £27.50 (Half Board)
Bed and Breakfast from £22.00
Luncheon from £6.00 (3 course A La Carte). Dinner from £13.00 Table D'Hôte (5 course). Gratuities at Guest's Discretion.

VAT inclusive. Credit Cards—Access, Visa
8 Family Rooms. 9 Double, 29 Twin, 22 Single Bedrooms (all with Private Facilities)
34 Bathrooms. 34 Shower Rooms
All Rooms with TV and Video link, Telephone, Radio, Tea and Coffee-making

Facilities. Open all Year. Closed January Fully Licensed. Full CH. 2 Lifts. 3 Bars. 2 Lounges. Buttery Restaurant. Conference Facilities. Children catered for. Dogs allowed. Baby Listening. Special diets by arrangement. Parking Facilities

Section 1: Devon

Sidmouth—Salcombe Hill House Hotel
Beatlands Road, Sidmouth, Devon. EX10 8JQ. Tel 0395 514697/514398/578570

A good-looking house of the Georgian era, this hotel stands in rolling grounds of about two and a half acres, just below Salcombe Hill. A reader from Bristol wrote to us explaining that she had been returning here for many years and, in view of the high standards which she said never faltered, warranted an extra spot of the limelight. Having visited the hotel ourselves, we are delighted to give it just that. It is a house of ample proportions and has a roominess which allows the choice of mingling or solitude, depending on one's mood. We gave one of the lounges the prefix 'sun', for its floor-to-ceiling windows allow sun and light in, and also give a lovely southern aspect across the the grounds. We enjoyed a well cooked and particularly well presented lunch and later, whilst we wandered around the hotel, enjoying the lovely public rooms, we found that we agreed with everything our Bristol reader had said. Full Board terms are available here and include afternoon tea with home-made cakes! For those on Half Board Terms there is a good choice of sandwiches and bar snacks available. The beaches and amenities of Sidmouth are a short walk away, but many will find the scope of the hotel's gardens to be ample. There is a grass tennis court and a very attractive heated swimming pool and there are many sunny corners in which to set up one's garden chair. At Salcombe Hill House, Grahame, Brenda and Neil Hook provide everything one would seek for a traditional seaside holiday.

Mini Break and other Terms on Application
Bar Lunches available at varying prices
Lunch from £8.50 and A La Carte
Dinner from £12.50 and A La Carte
Gratuities at Guest's Discretion
VAT inclusive. Credit Cards—Access, Diners Club, Visa. 5 Family Rooms
5 Double, 15 Twin Bedrooms, 6 Single

Bedrooms. All Rooms have private facilities, TV, Telephone, Radio, Tea and Coffee-making Facilities
Hairdryer available on request
Open from 1st March to 31st October
Fully Licensed. Full CH. Lift. Cocktail Bar.
Games Room.
Children over 3 years catered for.

Dogs allowed (except in Public Rooms).
Parking Facilities. Night Porter
Grass Tennis Court, Putting,
Outdoor Heated Swimming Pool
Nearby: Croquet, Squash, Golf (reduced green fees for Residents), Fishing, Riding, Sailing, Windsurfing

Sidmouth—Victoria Hotel
The Esplanade, Sidmouth, Devon. EX10 8RY. Tel 0395 512651. Fax 0395 579154

For many years this celebrated four-star hotel has offered the highest standards of personal attention and, whatever one's age or tastes, every effort will be made to pamper you. It was opened in the last year of Queen Victoria's reign and immediately became a favoured retreat of the aristocracy and the well-to-do. The grand origins of the hotel are still displayed in the elegant proportions of its rooms, and the furnishings and décor are chosen to suit. The hotel has never been guilty of falling behind the times, however, and it now offers every modern amenity one could wish for. Inside there is a beautifully styled swimming pool, a spa bath, sauna and solarium, a mini-gym and table-tennis, snooker and pool tables. There is also a laundry, and a first-class hairdressing service is available. Within the five acres of grounds you will find the *Pavillion* swimming pool, hard tennis courts, an eighteen-hole putting green and a private beach terrace. If you are looking for a quiet spot in which to relax, then the comfortable lounges and private balconies offer many tranquil corners and splendid elevated views. At meal times a team of chefs produces *haute cuisine* of a type which befits a premier hotel, although, here again, the guest's personal preferences are always catered for. Finally, a few words about the bedrooms and apartments–each has *en suite* facilities, plus a colour television with video link, a radio and a telephone. The great majority are also south facing, many have balconies and all have room service available twenty-four hours a day.

Weekly Terms from £290.00 to £539.00
Bed and Breakfast from £64.00
Lunch from £11.00 and A La Carte
Dinner from £18.50 and A La Carte
Gratuities at Guest's Discretion. VAT inclusive. Credit Cards—Access, American Express, Diners Club, Visa
5 Family Rooms. 3 Suites. 18 Double, 22

Twin, 13 Single Bedrooms
All Rooms with Private Bathroom, TV, Video, Telephone, Radio, Hairdryer
Trouser Press available on Request
Open all Year. Fully Licensed
Full CH. Lift
Cocktail Bar. Games Room. Snooker Room
Conference Facilities. Dogs not allowed

Parking Facilities. Night Porter
Hard Tennis Court, Putting, Indoor and Outdoor Swimming Pools, Solarium, Sauna, Spa Bath.
Nearby: Tennis, Croquet, Squash, Badminton, Golf, Fishing, Riding, Sailing, Windsurfing, Water Skiing, Shooting, Hang-gliding

Section 1: Devon

Sidmouth—Westcliff Hotel
Manor Road, Sidmouth, Devon. EX10 8RU. Tel 0395 513252

We have happily recommended this delightful hotel for many years under the co-proprietorship of Mrs Harding, her daughter and Son-in-law, Mr & Mrs Malloch Brown. Westcliff truly has the most enviable position, situated on the Western end of the seafront. Many of the bedrooms facing South and East, not only overlook the beautifully kept award winning hotel gardens and swimming pool, but also enjoy fabulous coastal views stretching along the whole of the esplanade and cliffs beyond. The rooms on the Western side overlook the magnificent Connaught Gardens, Peak Hill and the cliffs above Western beach, the main bathing beach. The unique peaceful location means that 35 of the 40 comfortable and well equipped bedrooms have sea views. All have integral bath or shower room and toilet, remote colour TV, radio, baby listening, direct dial telephones, hairdryers and hospitality tray. The recently refurbished lounges, cocktail bar and restaurant all enjoy spectacular coastal views. A good selection of English, Continental and Vegetarian dishes appear on the *table d'hôte* menu, supplemented by *á la carte*. The bar lunches are locally renowned. Leisure facilities include a jacuzzi, sunbed, games room, fitness room and putting green. Westcliff is the nearest hotel to Sidmouth Golf Course and is one of the few frontal hotels in Sidmouth providing extensive parking within the grounds.

Weekly Terms from £301.00
Daily Terms from £45.00
Bed and Breakfast from £36.00
Sunday Lunch from £9.00 Table D'Hôte
Dinner from £18.25 and A La Carte
Gratuities at Guest's Discretion
VAT inclusive. Credit Cards—Access, Visa

8 Family Rooms. 7 Double, 25 Twin, 8 Single Bedrooms
35 Private Bathrooms. 5 Private Shower Rooms. All Rooms with TV, Telephone, Radio, Baby-listening, Hairdryer
20 Rooms with Trouser Press
Open from Mid March to end of October

Fully Licensed. Lift. Cocktail Bar. Games Room, TV Lounge. Children catered for.
Dogs not allowed. Parking Facilities. Croquet, Putting, Indoor and Outdoor Swimming Pools, Solarium, Mini Tennis, Table Tennis, Fitness Room. Nearby: Tennis, Croquet, Putting, Squash

Soar Mill Cove, Near Salcombe—Soar Mill Cove Hotel
Soar Mill Cove, Salcombe, Devon. TQ7 3DS. Tel 0548 561566

We make no secret of the fact that Soar Mill Cove has been one of our favourite hotels for some years, and we always look forward to our visits here. One of several noteworthy features is the variety in the *cuisine* and the freshness of the produce used, which is *sans pareil*. Whether we lunch or dine here, the occasion is always outstandingly enjoyable, particularly the fish freshly arrived from the Barbican market in Plymouth. We continue to receive complimentary comments from our readers about the food. Little wonder, when the *table d'hôte* menus include such specialities as brill with wild mushrooms, fresh mussels glazed with a cream sauce, and fillet of young local lamb served with a minted shallot and red wine sauce, all accompanied by tender, seasonable vegetables. It is evident that Keith and Norma Makepeace continue the resounding success they have made of their hotel which, as they state unashamedly in their brochure, they love and care deeply about. The service they provide is caring, too, and you will find at Soar Mill Cove Hotel, all the little extra touches which make you feel welcomed as a family guest. Every room is immaculately appointed and the bedrooms are beautifully equipped. All rooms have patio doors to their own private terraces which open on to the gardens. Within the five acres of grounds are a pretty, landscaped outdoor swimming-pool as well as an indoor pool, always kept at 88 degrees, a grass tennis court and a putting green. They guarantee no conferences when other guests are at the hotel to ensure peace and quiet. The hotel's brochure will whet your appetite and you will find, as we did, that the reality is even better than its description.

Weekly Terms from £380.00. Daily Terms from £60.00. Lunch from £12.00 and A La Carte. Dinner from £28.50 and A La Carte
Gratuities at Guest's Discretion

VAT inclusive. Credit Cards—Access, Visa
2 Family Rooms. 1 Suite. 5 Double, 5 Twin Bedrooms, 2 Single Bedrooms. All Rooms with Private Bathroom, TV, Telephone,

Radio, Baby-listening, Tea and Coffee-making Facilities, Trouser Press, Hairdryer. Open from 12th Feb to 29th Dec
Residential and Restaurant Licence

Section 1: Devon

Southerton, Near Budleigh Salterton—The Coach House Hotel and Restaurant
Southerton, Near Budleigh Salterton, Devon. EX11 1SE. Tel 0395 68577

In the wooded countryside betwixt the Axe and the Exe, where Devon shades into Dorset, we have discovered a small hotel and restaurant, which is so deliciously tucked away it seems to guard jealously its seclusion. Actually, we cannot claim to have 'discovered' the Coach House at Southerton, for many discerning people have visited it and some of them have written to us in praise of what they have found there. Built in 1905 to accommodate coaches belonging to the old Southerton House, the hotel is a mixture of architecturial styles. There is a delightful landscaped garden, extending to two and a half acres, with a stream and rustic bridge in its 'secluded' corner. The rooms are airy and light, in true country house fashion, with windows looking out on the lawns and flower beds. The bedrooms, two of which are four-poster rooms, have bathrooms equipped with unusual touches, such as enormous bath towels and freshly laundered bath robes. Over all this Dave and Vera Alcock, the owners, reign with skill and charm... as well they may. The Coach House is very quiet, very serene and not a little dignified. A perfect place for a relaxing break, or for a quiet holiday in the lovely valley of the Otter... fishing, golfing, swimming and hunting are all at hand. We loved our *en suite* bedroom, *Barouche*, and we also peeped into the equally attractive *Cabriolet* and *Clarence* rooms on the ground floor. Clearly, Mr and Mrs Alcock have refurbished their hotel with an eye for taste.

Weekly Terms from £200.00
Daily Terms from £34.00
Bed and Breakfast from £25.00
Dinner from £13.50 and A La Carte
Gratuities at Guest's Discretion
VAT inclusive. Credit Cards—Access, Visa

5 Double, 1 Twin Bedrooms
5 Private Bathrooms. 1 Private Shower Room. All Rooms with TV, Telephone, Radio, Tea and Coffee-making Facilities, Hairdryer. Open all year
Residential and Restaurant Licence

Full Central Heating. Cocktail Bar. Lounge.
Children not catered for
Dogs not allowed. Parking Facilities
Nearby: Croquet, Putting, Swimming, Golf, Fishing, Riding, Sailing, Windsurfing, Water Skiing, Shooting

South Molton—Marsh Hall Country House Hotel & Restaurant
South Molton, Devon. EX36 3HQ. Tel 0769 572666

Situated on the Southern slopes of the foothills to Exmoor National Park this lovely Victorian country house, set in three acres of lawns and woodland, enjoys superb views over the Mole River valley towards South Molton. Reputedly built by the local Squire for his mistress, Marsh Hall has a welcoming atmosphere to those seeking peace and quiet and the appeal of a bygone era. Stained glass windows, chandeliers and tesselated tiled floors combine to cheer the weary traveller while the spacious lounge and licensed bar rejoice to the crackle and pop of log fires in winter, making this a truly worthwhile place to stay throughout the year. The generously proportioned bedrooms, with colour TV, hairdryer, direct dial telephone, clock/radio and refreshment facilities each have *en suite* facilities. The Squire's Room features an elegant four-poster, curved bathroom and raised seating area with extensive views over the grounds. The lovely pink and green restaurant serves a four course silver service dinner with mouth watering dishes devised from local fare including Exmoor Venison, Brown Trout and Guinea Fowl, while the sweet trolley is designed to add inches to the waistline. The gardens have some fine mature specimen trees including the Chinese and standard tulip, while the rhodedendrons and wild flowers are a delight in late spring. Royal Horticultural Society members find Marsh Hall the ideal base to stay while visiting Rosemoor and other notable botanic gardens in the area.

All Terms pertaining to 1992
Weekly Terms from £336.00
Daily Terms from £49.50
Bed and Breakfast from £38.00
Dinner from £18.50 Table D'Hôte
VAT inclusive

Credit Cards—Access, American Express, Visa
4 Double, 1 Single, 2 Twin Bedrooms
5 Private Bathrooms. 2 Private Shower Rooms. All Rooms with TV, Telephone, Tea and Coffee-making Facilities, Hairdryer

Open all Year. Residential and Restaurant Licence. Full Central Heating
Cocktail Bar. Lounge. Conference Facilities
Dogs allowed. Ample Parking
Nearby: Tennis, Squash, Golf, Fishing, Riding

Section 1: Devon

South Molton—Park House Country House Hotel
South Molton, Devon. EX36 3ED.
Tel 0769 572610

On the southern fringe of Exmoor, approached from the road running between the town of South Molton and the village of North Molton, just 200 yards south of the A361, is a gem amongst small country hotels. Here, all who prefer the personally run period country house will rejoice. On arrival, the unique ambience of this lovely place is immediately apparent outside, in the ideal setting of house and gardens within a horseshoe of ancient beech, chestnut and oak trees and inside, amidst the antique furnishings and warm atmosphere. From the inner hall a beautiful curved Regency staircase leads to a galleried landing of fine stone arches supported by pillars of red Devon marble. The rooms are impeccably furnished and everywhere fresh flowers, books, magazines and personal bric-a-brac full of interest. Anne Gornall is a Constance Spry trained *Cordon Bleu* cook and each meal is freshly prepared using only the best possible local produce. The fixed price three course dinner menu offers several choices for each course. Seventy fine wines are listed (Cellar Search Award) which are a perfect complement. Above stairs are eight spacious double *en suite* bedrooms, each individually furnished and decorated. A truly lovely garden of colour (Grounds for Delight Award) surrounds this stone built manor house with sweeping lawns and it includes a secluded walled garden which is a haven of tranquility. A winding driveway lined with poplars and limes leads one from the impressive wrought iron gates through park-like grounds to reach the house. Whilst at Park House one is apt to forget the proximity of South Molton. It is a fifteen minute stroll to this attractive Georgian market town, with its numerous antique shops, art galleries and interesting museum. Of Park House? The whole hotel is a testimony to the skills of Anne and Michael Gornall. It is one of the most charming country hotels on our list and, if you appreciate true quality, you will agree.

All Terms pertaining to 1992
Weekly Terms from £350.00
Bed and Breakfast from £35.00
Bar Lunch from £5.00. Sunday Lunch from £12.00. Dinner from £15.00 for fixed price A La Carte. Gratuities at Guest's Discretion.

VAT inclusive
1 Family Room. 4 Double, 3 Twin Bedrooms. 5 Private Bathrooms, 3 Private Shower Rooms. All Rooms with CTV, Tea and Coffee-making Facilities, Hairdryer, Radio/Alarm clock

Open all Year. Residential and Restaurant Licence. Full Central Heating
Cocktail Bar/Lounge. TV Lounge.
Conference Facilities. Dogs allowed by Arrangement. Parking facilities
Croquet, Fishing, Shooting, Riding

Section 1: Devon

Near South Molton, Heasley Mill—Heasley House Hotel
Heasley Mill, Near South Molton, Devon. EX36 3LE. Tel 059 84 213

Actually, words fail us over Heasley House. It is so rural and peaceful that all we can really say is 'Visit Heasley House for yourself'. South Molton is part of the postal address, but really it is neither here nor there, for apart from reaching it from South Molton (five miles southwards) it is also accessible from all the gateway towns which open onto the southern part of Exmoor. We have always felt most attracted to the house and have found the owners, Mr and Mrs Trevor Tate, so amiable. So much thought goes into the running of the hotel, and always towards the comfort and enjoyment of their guests ... and the garden is really delightful. Heasley House was built in the middle of the eighteenth century, when it housed the captain of a former copper mine, which has long since disappeared. Today, since there are only eight bedrooms, and the emphasis is on comfort and personal service, Heasley House is nearly always full, but what friendliness and welcome we can promise those who are fortunate to find a vacant room there one day! The bedrooms are equipped in country style, with hand basins and the *most* comfortable beds, and the majority have either a private bathroom or shower room. Of course, this patch is a land of plenty, so only the best from land and sea goes into the hotel's kitchens. If you would live within the boundaries of the Exmoor National Park, where rural Devon merges with unspoilt Somerset, do seek out Heasley House, where simplicity and sophistication blend equally well.

Weekly Terms from £225.00
Daily Terms from £32.50
Bed and Breakfast from £18.50
Dinner from £10.95 Table D'Hôte
Gratuities at Guest's Discretion

VAT inclusive. 3 Double, 5 Twin Bedrooms
2 Private Bathrooms. 3 Private Shower Rooms. Open from February to November
Residential and Restaurant Licence
Full Central Heating

TV Lounge.
Children catered for. Dogs allowed
Parking Facilities
Nearby: Tennis, Swimming, Golf, Fishing, Riding

Nr South Molton—Knowstone Court Country House Hotel
Knowstone, South Molton, Devon. EX36 4RW. Tel 03984 457/511. Fax 03984 457

Maybe you would prefer to stay somewhere small and *de luxe*, very rural and with plenty of history behind it. Look up Knowstone Court, which lies in that beautiful stretch of countryside between Tiverton and South Molton, from where Exmoor is but a stepping stone away. Knowstone Court has sheltered the clergy of Knowstone and Molland for centuries, and is a house which has seen the very best of life, and not a little eccentricity, in its time. Note the hook at the top of the stairs, used by one incumbent to haul himself up by pulley when he had wined and dined too well! During our stay we saw no such excesses, but, clearly, one still enjoys the best of comfortable country-house living at Knowstone Court, for the present owners, Janice and Peter Cozens, would not wish for anything less. They run their hotel almost as if it were their private home. It is elegant throughout, beautifully kept and full of antiques, including an 18th century sedan chair with painted panel on the landing. The informality and relaxing atmosphere of Knowstone Court are quite profound. In the case of the Knowstone Court's *cuisine*, the food is simply superb, in both quality and variety, and the wines are a fitting complement. The Bridal Suite has a crowned bed and luxurious bathroom. The rivers Exe, Mole and Taw are famous for salmon and trout; hunting, shooting, riding or Golf could have been arranged for us; and close by the moors and scenic coastline offer every inducement for walking. They have recently been justly awarded 3 Crowns Highly Commended by the ETB.

Daily Terms from £45.00
Bed and Breakfast from £32.00
Bar Lunch from £5.00
Lunch from £12.00 Table D'Hôte
Dinner from £18.00 Table D'Hôte
Gratuities at Guest's discretion

VAT inclusive. Credit Cards–Access, American Express, Visa
7 Double and 2 Twin Bedrooms.
5 Private Bathrooms. 4 Private Shower Rooms. All rooms with TV, Telephone, Tea and Coffee-making facilities, Baby-listening

Hairdryers available on request.
Open all year. Fully Licensed.
Cocktail Bar. Conference Facilities
Children catered for. Dogs welcome.
Nearby: Indoor Swimming, Golf, Fishing, Riding, Sailing, Windsurfing, Shooting

Section 1: Devon

Tiverton—The Tiverton Hotel Blundell's Road, Tiverton, Devon. EX16 4DB. Tel 0884 256120. Fax 0884 258101

The Tiverton Hotel displays all the virtues of a modern hotel. It is purpose built and lies in convenient proximity to the main routes into Devon–Junction 27 of the M5 motorway is just six miles away. The standards of personal service we received here were as attentive as one could wish for and the quality of the food we enjoyed was exceptionally good. With so many local places of interest to visit, the Tiverton Hotel is ideal for both short breaks and longer traditional holidays. The situation is, of course, ideal. The old market and lace making town of Tiverton lies in the beautiful valley of the Exe between the two national parks of Exmoor and Dartmoor and, from its central position, both the north and south coasts of Devon are within a twenty mile delightful drive. The hotel itself affords a great deal of comfort in rooms which are notable for their spaciousness and equipment. A private bathroom, remote-control colour television with radio, beverage-making facilities, direct-dial telephone, hairdryer, trouser press and iron, are standard amenities in every bedroom. There is an attractive restaurant and bar lounge. Many visitors to Devon will need little inducement to move inland during the summer months to avoid the holiday throng, but The Tiverton Hotel also provides a number of speciality weekend and weekly breaks with such activities as picnic rides, fishing and golf to keep one occupied. Vouchers for reduced entry to many mid-Devon attractions, National Trust and historic houses and gardens are available free to Tiverton Hotel guests.

Terms on Application.
Bargain Breaks available all Year
No Service Charge. VAT inclusive
Credit Cards—Access, American Express, Diners Club, Visa
75 spacious Bedrooms

All Rooms with Private Bath/Shower, TV, Telephone, Radio, Tea and Coffee-making Facilities, Hairdryer, Baby-listening, Trouser Press and Iron, Sitting area.
Open all Year. Fully Licensed.
Central Heating in all Bedrooms

Cocktail Bar. Conference Facilities
Children catered for. Dogs allowed
Parking facilities. Night Porter.
Nearby: Tennis, Squash, Swimming, Golf, Fishing, Riding, Sailing, Windsurfing, Water Skiing, Hang-gliding

Torquay, Chelston–Fairmount House Hotel Herbert Road, Chelston, Torquay, Devon TQ2 6RW. Tel 0803 605446

Because Chelston is not shown on every atlas, make a note that Fairmount - a veritable gem of a small hotel - is set above picturesque Cockington Valley. Built in 1900 as a five bedroom family house, complete with servants' quarters and cellars, it stands in mature gardens overlooking the quiet, residential valley of Chelston. In their fifteen years of ownership, Noel and Maggie Tolkien have restored the original charm of the building and established a loyal clientele whose numerous return visits testify to the excellence of the accommodation. All eight bedrooms have *en suite* bathrooms or shower and toilet, and each one has a name taken from 'Lord of the Rings'. With their high ceilings, individual matching colour schemes, attractive furniture and thoughtful additions to the usual range of amenities, they achieve a homely and comfortable atmosphere. Two of the bedrooms are on the lower ground floor, with their own private doors opening directly onto the garden. South-facing over the secluded garden is the Victorian Conservatory Bar, with French doors to the sheltered sun-trap of the patio. All our fellow guests were as delighted with the food and wine as we were, with personal service from Maggie and Noel, respectively. They accept well behaved dogs here and have three of their own: wire-haired dachsunds Rosie, Merry and Pippin. Torquay is renowned for its mild climate and long hours of sunshine; Cockington Village is a famous beauty spot, and places of historic interest and scenic charm lie on every side inland to unspoilt Dartmoor.

Weekly Terms from £232.00
Daily Terms from £35.00
Bed and Breakfast from £24.50
Bar Lunch from £4.00
Sunday Lunch available in summer
Dinner from £10.50 (unavailable on

Sundays in summer). Gratuities at Guest's Discretion. VAT inclusive. Credit Cards-Access, American Express, Eurocard, Visa. 3 Family Rooms (Also used as Twin Bedrooms). 3 Double, 2 Single Bedrooms. 2 Private Bathrooms.

6 Private Shower Rooms. All Rooms with TV, Radio, Tea and Coffee-making Facilities, toiletries. Open from early March to early Nov. Residential Licence. Part CH (All rooms heated). Cocktail Bar. TV Lounge. Children catered for. Dogs allowed.

Section 1: Devon

Torquay—Orestone Manor Hotel
Rockhouse Lane, Maidencombe, Torquay, Devon. TQ1 4SX.
Tel 0803 328098. Fax 0803 328336

The only official Country House Hotel in Torbay, yet Orestone Manor is only 3 miles from the centre of Torquay. Set in over 2 acres of magnificent gardens, offering peace and tranquility with superb views across Lyme Bay, Orestone Manor was built in the early 1800's as a private residence and has over the past thirty years been tastefully extended to an hotel. In early 1991 the Restaurant (strictly non-smoking) was extended to provide a spacious elegant restaurant, with wonderful views and ambiance, in which to dine. The resident proprietors, Mike and Gill Staples and family, have created an excellent reputation for the food they serve. It is the only hotel in Torbay to have received a prestigious Rosette for its fine cuisine. They call it 'The Menu with a Tasteful Difference', and it is truly not only different, but also very tasteful. The menu is changed daily and there is always a vegetarian dish available. The wine list complements the food. The high standards in the kitchen are complemented throughout the hotel. The bedrooms are very well appointed; all have en suite facilities, colour television, direct-dial telephone and tea and coffee-making facilities. There is an outdoor swimming pool, (open and heated from June to September). Orestone Manor is a British Tourist Authority commended hotel and AA 3 Star, with a rate of 70 percent, one of the highest in Torquay.

Weekly Terms from £245.00
Daily Terms from £40.00
Weekly Bed and Breakfast from £203.00
Daily Bed and Breakfast from £35.00
Bar Meal from £6.50
Sunday Lunch from £9.50
Dinner from £22.50 and A La Carte
Gratuities at Guest's Discretion.

VAT inclusive
Credit Cards—Access, Visa
3 Family Rooms. 8 Double, 7 Twin Bedrooms.
All Rooms with Private Bathrooms, TV, Telephone, Radio, Tea and Coffee-making Facilities.
Hairdryer and Iron available on Request

Open all Year except January.
Residential and Restaurant Licence.
Full Central Heating. Cocktail Bar
Conference Facilities. Parking within own grounds. Outdoor Heated Swimming Pool (June-September)
Nearby: Tennis, Squash, 5 Golf Courses, Fishing, Riding, Sailing, Windsurfing

Section 1: Devon

Torquay–The Osborne Hotel
Hesketh Crescent, Meadfoot, Near Torquay, Devon TQ1 2LL.
Tel 0803 213311. Fax 0803 296788.

Set in the centre of Torquay's most elegant Regency landmark, Hesketh Crescent (referred to by Lady Angela Burdett-Coutts as 'Bath by the sea'), is the renowned Osborne Hotel. In five-and-a-half acres of palm-fringed gardens, which sweep down to secluded Meadfoot Beach, The Osborne boasts facilities usually associated with much larger hotels. Outdoors there is tennis, putting and a heated pool, whilst the Leisure Centre offers an indoor heated pool, sun beds, gym, full-size snooker table and games room. The Osborne, however, is a small, privately-owned hotel, with just twenty-three bedrooms, and has the character and atmosphere of a country-house hotel. Consequently, it is 'known' for personal service and as a place where attention to detail is paramount. Indeed, there is much that makes The Osborne Hotel somewhere special at which to stay. Every bedroom is individually designed, as befits this historic building, whilst the Luxury Apartments, which can be rented weekly through the hotel, could not be more replete in their comfort and facilities. The acclaimed Langtry's à la carte Restaurant is also a major attraction, and, within the Crescent is Raffles, the hotel's second restaurant, a relaxed Bar-Brasserie, which is open all day and offers a wide selection of dishes, plus garden barbeques on the terrace throughout the summer. And allied to this impressive array of amenities is the hotel's location–situated just minutes from the harbour, and with uninterrupted views across the Bay, The Osborne epitomises everything that is best on the English Riviera.

Seven nights for the price of six
Daily Terms from £59.00
Bed and Breakfast from £45.00
English Breakfast from £9.75
Continental Breakfast from £5.25
Bar Lunch from £3.00
Afternoon Tea from £2.80
Bar Supper from £5.00
Dinner from £19.50
Service Charge and VAT inclusive

Credit Cards-Access, Switch, Visa
2 Family Rooms. 6 Suites. 7 Double, 1 Single, 7 Twin Bedrooms
9 Private Shower Rooms. All rooms with Private Bathroom, TV, Telephone, Radio, Baby-listening, Tea and Coffee-making Facilities, Hairdryer.
Trouser Press available on request.
4 Rooms with balconies
Open all year. Fully Licensed

Full Central Heating. Lift. 2 Cocktail Bars.
Games Room. Conference Facilities
Children catered for. Dogs not allowed.
Parking Facilities. Night Porter
Tennis, Putting, Swimming, Solarium, Sauna.
Nearby: Croquet, Squash, Badminton, Golf, Fishing, Riding, Sailing, Windsurfing, Water Skiing, Shooting, Hang-gliding, Ballooning

Section 1: Devon

Totnes—Royal Seven Stars Hotel The Plains, Totnes, Devon. TQ9 5DD.
Tel 0803 862125/863241. Fax 0803 867925

Totnes tends to hide her light, not under the biblical bushel, but in the shadow of her prosperous neighbours, Paignton and Torquay. Yet, this is one of England's most ancient boroughs where, according to legend, Brutus, grandson of the Trojan Aeneas, sailed up the river Dart and founded the British race. The river still affords the most scenic approach to Totnes and we would urge you to join one of the regular steamers if you want to enjoy riverine beauty which is denied to motorists. Totnes is 6 miles from Torbay and the coast and about 30 minutes drive from the Dartmoor National Park. And when visiting the town you must stay at the Royal Seven Stars Hotel, appropriately owned by Olde Worlde Inns Limited. It was built in 1660, the year when the monarchy was restored in England, and has been a part of the town's social life ever since. As one passes under the huge porch and into its attractive and interesting entrance hall, the historical associations of the hotel are easy to appreciate. Patrons of the past, however, would be very surprised to discover the array of modern facilities which now await the visitor. Most of the bedrooms have been equipped with *en suite* bathrooms and all modern facilities. There are four-poster rooms with *en suite* facilities available at a supplementary charge. We also noted that a great deal of refurbishment and redecoration had taken place since our previous visit, especially in the bar, the entrance hall and the corridors. Lovers of good hotels and historic houses owe a debt of gratitude to the likes of Mr K G A Stone, the hotel's manager, who has run this hostelry since 1963.

Weekly Terms (Half Board) from £225.00
Daily Terms from £40.00
Bar Meal from £3.95. Lunch from £8.00
Dinner from £16.00 Table D'Hôte
Gratuities at Guest's Discretion
VAT inclusive. Credit Cards—Access,

Diners Club, Visa. 2 Family Rooms
12 Double, 3 Twin, 1 Single Bedroom
12 Private Bathrooms plus Showers
All Rooms with TV, Telephone, Radio,
Tea and Coffee-making Facilities and
Hairdryer available on Request

Open all Year. Fully Licensed.
Full Central Heating. Cocktail Bar.
Conference Facilities
Children catered for. Dogs allowed
Parking Facilities. Nearby: Tennis,
Swimming, Fishing, Riding, Sailing

Two Bridges—Prince Hall Hotel Two Bridges, Yelverton,
Devon. PL20 6SA. Tel 082 289 403. Fax 082 289 676

'Luxury in the wilds' would aptly describe this hotel. Set in the heart of the Moor, Prince Hall, a place where all stress is relieved, occupies a beautiful and secluded position with views across the West Dart to open moorland. A majestic tree-lined drive leads to the house which was built in 1787 on the site of Prynshall which dates back to 1411. It is now run as a comfortable hotel by Mr and Mrs J C Denat. There are eight bedrooms, all beautifully furnished and prettily decorated. Both the upstairs and downstairs rooms impressed us very much; gourmet cooking is done by French owner-chef with fresh local produce used whenever possible. Apart from being considered as a prime halting place on a Devon-Cornwall tour, Prince Hall Hotel must be noted for a holiday proper. Being in the centre of Dartmoor it is practically in the centre of Devonshire! One day you can visit the North Devon coast, another the South Devon seaboard... they are both an easy drive from the hotel. And if you intend to give your car a holiday too, where better for walking, fishing or riding. Views from the dining room, from the residents' lounge, the bar, and from most of the windows, are of open moorland. The peace of this lovely place may be disturbed only by the occasional canter of wild ponies, or the call of a curlew. And how one enjoys a good meal and a quiet night's sleep when at an altitude of 1,100 feet! To locate the hotel take the A38 from Exeter to Ashburton (or if coming from Plymouth take the A386 to Yelverton) and follow signs for Princetown and Two Bridges. The Hotel is situated just off the B3357.

Daily Terms from £42.50 (DB&B)
Bed and Breakfast from £32.50
Bar Lunch for residents only
Dinner £18.50 Table D'Hôte (4 course)
Gratuities at Guest's Discretion
VAT inclusive. Credit Cards—Access,

American Express, Diners Club, Visa
4 Double, 1 Single, 3 Twin Bedrooms
5 Private Bathrooms. 3 Private Shower
Rooms. All Rooms with TV, Telephone, Tea
and Coffee-making Facilities
Hairdryer available on request

Closed over Christmas and New Year
Residential and Restaurant Licence
Full Central Heating. Cocktail Bar
Children catered for. Dogs welcomed
Parking Facilities. Nearby: Fishing, Riding,
Shooting, Croquet, Putting, Swimming, Golf

Section 1: Devon

Woolacombe—Devon Beach Hotel The Esplanade, Woolacombe, Devon. EX34 7DJ. Tel 0271 870449

The headlands of Morte Point and Baggy Point embrace the three-mile golden strip which is Woolacombe's beach. Preserved by the National Trust it affords unlimited recreation, fascinating rock pools, sand, cowrie shells and a sunny climate. Above the famous Barricane Beach where, at high tide, rock formations fashion a natural swimming pool, the Devon Beach Hotel offers magnificent views and unimpeded access to the whole panorama. Still owned by the same family who have done so much to promote its image, the active management is in the experienced hands of Mr and Mrs H B Morrall. Its solid, white faced exterior gives little hint of the endeavour which has added private bathrooms, central heating, entertainment, video film shows, a solarium and a heated indoor swimming pool to the amenities. Most inviting, we thought, are the penthouse rooms with, of course, bathroom and toilet *en suite*. Although essentially a family hotel, where the needs of all ages are cared for, the hotel aims at high standards of comfort and *cuisine* and their chef appreciates that he has to care for grown-ups equally as well as for their offspring. Fishing trips can be arranged from Lee and Ilfracombe and steamer excursions to Lundy Island. For those with a car there are many interesting places within easy reach and there are two golf courses at nearby Saunton (one championship) and one at Ilfracombe.

Weekly Terms from £190.00 Daily Terms from £30.00 Bed and Breakfast from £25.00 Bar Lunch from £2.75 Dinner from £12.50 and A La Carte No Service Charge. VAT inclusive Credit Cards—Access, Visa 24 Family Rooms. 3 Suites	17 Double, 7 Twin, 9 Single Bedrooms 26 Private Bathrooms Self-catering unit which sleeps up to 6 people. All Rooms with TV and In-House Video, Radio/Intercom, Baby-listening, Tea and Coffee-making Facilities Open from Easter to early October Residential and Restaurant Licence	Part CH.. Cocktail Bar. Games Room Children catered for. Dogs allowed in Bedrooms only. Parking Facilities. Indoor Heated Swimming Pool, Solarium. Nearby: Tennis, Putting, Squash, Badminton, Swimming, Solarium, Sauna, Golf, Fishing, Riding, Sailing, 9 Hole Golf Course, Windsurfing, Water Skiing, Hang-gliding

Woolacombe—Little Beach Hotel The Esplanade, Woolacombe, Devon. EX34 7DJ. Tel 0271 870398

You may question why an hotel which sits adjacent to the finest sand and surf beach in this part of Devon, and fully three miles of it, should be known as 'Little Beach'. We have yet to discover the answer, but guests of Little Beach need only concern themselves with the fact that this is a small, personally run hotel offering very high standards. The house was built for a wealthy Edwardian gentleman, who had the foresight and the influence to pick one of the finest sites along the coastal track for his new home. Little Beach became an hotel during the twenties and was gradually adapted for that purpose. In recent years, however, whilst its modernisation has continued, great steps have been taken to restore the original atmosphere, to recreate, as far as possible, an Edwardian gentleman's country house by the sea. Fortunately, the resident proprietors, Brian and Nola Welling, have a keen interest in antiques, and Brian, in particular, has put his hobby to very good effect within the hotel where he has now opened a small antique shop. There are ten comfortable bedrooms, eight of which have either a private bath or shower, and some of the rooms open on to a large balcony, where guests may relax whilst enjoying the view over the bay. Nola is in charge of the hotel's *cuisine*. Her home made dishes and freshly prepared food were certainly one of the highlights of our stay here. The hotels in this area tend to be on the large side, so if you seek somewhere that is smaller and more personal, you should consider Little Beach.

Weekly Terms from £210.00 Daily Terms from £31.00 Bed and Breakfast from £23.50 Dinner from £12.50 Table D'Hôte No Service Charge. VAT inclusive Credit Cards—Access, Visa	7 Double, 1 Twin, 2 Single Bedrooms 4 Private Bathrooms. 4 Private Shower Rooms. All Rooms with TV, Radio, Telephone. Hairdryer available on request Open from March to November Residential and Restaurant Licence	Full Central Heating. Cocktail Bar Children over 7 years catered for Dogs allowed. Parking Facilities Nearby: Putting, Squash, Swimming, Golf, Fishing, Riding, Windsurfing, Shooting, Hang-gliding

Section 1: Devon

Woolacombe—Watersmeet Hotel
Mortehoe, Woolacombe, North Devon. EX34 7EB
Telephone 0271 870333. Fax 0271 870890

A uniquely picturesque location, first-class amenities and devoted resident owners: once again this splendid hotel earns our whole-hearted commendation (and further accolades from the motoring organisations). In our 1992 Guide we wrote "We are constantly impressed with the practical way in which Mr and Mrs J B Wheeldon are raising the standard of their hotel and improving the facilities it provides". This observation is even more relevant today. Quality furniture and furnishings in the bedrooms and the public rooms, attentive service from a loyal team of senior staff and, in the octagonal Pavilion Restaurant, award-winning cuisine. In fact, the bill of fare - with its emphasis on seafood specialities - receives so much praise from visitors and local patrons that a book of recipes has been compiled and a four-day residential course held for budding chefs. Other outstanding features of this enterprising hotel include Bridge holidays and a painting week. From the Watersmeet, private steps lead to the south-facing beach below, a paradise for sunbathers with the firm, clean sands. In 1991 and 1992, the Woolacombe beach was awarded a European blue flag for cleanliness. Within the hotel grounds there is lawn tennis, a heated swimming-pool and croquet, with many other sporting activities available locally. If any further evidence of excellence be needed, we can record that the majority of guests book return visits.

Weekly Terms from £300.00
Daily Terms from £45.00
Dinner from £24.50 and A La Carte
Gratuities at Guest's Discretion
VAT inclusive
Credit Cards—Access, American Express, Diners Club, Visa

12 Double, 9 Twin, 4 Single Bedrooms
All Rooms with Private Bathroom, TV
Open from Mid February to December
Fully Licensed. Full Central Heating
Cocktail Bar. Games Room
Conference Facilities
Children catered for.

Dogs allowed by arrangement
Parking Facilities
Grass Tennis Court, Croquet, Outdoor Swimming Pool
Nearby: Putting, Squash, Golf, Fishing, Riding, Sailing, Windsurfing, Shooting, Surfing, Walking

Section 1: Devon

Woolacombe—Woolacombe Bay Hotel
Woolacombe, Devon. EX34 7BN. Tel 0271 870388

The Woolacombe Bay Hotel was built in an era which knew gracious living, and this is reflected in the high standards one sees here today. From the elegant chandelier-hung restaurant to the comfortably appointed bedrooms, each fully equipped with an *en suite* bathroom, one could hardly seek a more attractive holiday location. Indeed, if ever there was an antidote to city life and modern pressures, it is to be found in the all-embracing facilities of Woolacombe Bay Hotel. There are two large heated swimming pools—one inside and another in the magnificent, six-acre grounds. In other parts of the gardens are two tennis courts (these are floodlit at night), a nine-hole pitch and putt course, croquet and swing-ball! Inside, the recreational facilities continue. There are three squash courts (one glass-backed), a fitness room, a games room, a billiard room, a sauna, a solarium, a spa bath and short mat bowling. Every year the amenities of the hotel are either enhanced or extended. The *Victorian Mews* include a carvery, bistro, hairdressers and an elegant parade of shops. *Bertie's Bar* is another feature. There is also a wing of self-contained apartments, which offer spacious accommodation for the discerning holidaymaker. After a day's activities, it is a delight to savour drinks on the terraces, to view the gardens and the adjoining beach and sea (the sunsets are magnificent) and to anticipate the chef's skill to come. For anyone seeking luxurious surroundings, unobtrusive service and a congenial atmosphere, Woolacombe Bay Hotel is a fine choice.

All Terms pertaining to 1992
Weekly Terms from £200.00
Daily Terms from £50.00. Bar Meal from £5.00. Sunday Lunch from £8.00 and A La Carte. Dinner from £17.00
Gratuities at Guest's Discretion
VAT extra. Credit Cards—Access, American Express, Diners Club, Visa

11 Family Rooms. 13 Suites
1 Single, 10 Double, 24 Twin Bedrooms
All Rooms with Private Bathroom with Shower, TV, Telephone, Radio, Baby-listening, Tea and Coffee-making Facilities, Hairdryer. Open from February to December. Fully Licensed. Lift. Cocktail Bar. TV Lounge. Games Room.

Conference Facilities. Children catered for.
Dogs not allowed. Parking Facilities.
Night Porter.
Hard Tennis Court, Croquet, Putting, Squash, Indoor and Outdoor Swimming Pools, Solarium, Sauna. Nearby: Golf, Fishing, Riding, Sailing, Windsurfing, Water Skiing, Shooting, Hang Gliding

---

Have you returned your membership form?
By simply completing and returning to us the registration card inserted in this book you will automatically become a 1993 member of the Ashley Courtenay Circle, an invaluable link between author and reader. For members, we compile and revise each year special listings of hotels which offer particular amenities, such as a sauna, swimming pool, golf course (or adjacent), four-poster beds, facilities for the disabled, special Christmas programmes, vegetarian dishes, non-smoking areas and self-catering facilities. We can even direct you to hotels which are especially pleased to receive young children and dogs. These lists are free of charge. Just send a stamped addressed envelope.

Section 1: Dorset

Blandford Forum—La Belle Alliance   Whitecliff Mill Street, Blandford Forum, Dorset. DT11 7BN. Tel 0258 452842

This excellent establishment can best be described as a 'licensed restaurant with rooms'. First emphasis on the catering may well be appropriate–the resident proprietors Philip and Lauren Davison already have a splendid reputation for their food of which more anon–but in no way should this description imply any criticism of the rooms. There are six *en suite* bedrooms (including a ground floor room), recently re-decorated, the usual facilities added to by such thoughtful items as a sewing kit, bottled mineral water and plenty of reading matter. Our extensive tour of the premises gave us the opportunity to admire the freshness of the redecoration throughout, the dining room in particular looking most attractive. The French-style *cuisine* is a treat not to be missed. Full advantage is taken of the location being in the heart of farmland: the best of fresh produce is used with modern flair applied to country heartiness. A menu which is changed every few weeks with the seasons will tempt the most demanding gourmet and the supporting wine list is exceptionally wide ranging. We must commend to readers the 'Short Gourmet Breaks' available here at attractive all-in rates. Blandford Forum has been described as having one of the most satisfying Georgian ensembles anywhere in England. Certainly it is a natural centre for exploring the lovely Dorset countryside. La Belle Alliance–the name has strong associations with the Battle of Waterloo–is a spacious Victorian house a short walk from the centre of Blandford on the road to Shaftesbury.

2 day Breaks from £89.00 per Person Bed and Breakfast from £45.00 (Single)/£58.00 (Double/Twin) Dinner from £21.00 Gratuities at Guest's Discretion VAT inclusive. Credit Cards—Access,	American Express, Visa 1 Family Room. 3 Double, 2 Twin Bedrooms. 6 Rooms with Private Bathroom, TV, Telephone, Tea and Coffee-making Facilities, Hairdryer, Trouser Press. Open all Year except first	three weeks in January. Residential and Restaurant Licence. Full Central Heating Cocktail Lounge. Children welcome. Dogs allowed in Bedrooms only. Parking Facilities. Nearby: Swimming, Solarium, Sauna, Golf, Fishing, Riding

Bournemouth—Burley Court Hotel
Bath Road, Bournemouth, Dorset. BH1 2NP. Tel 0202 552824

The courteous and helpful attitude of the porter on our arrival at Burley Court Hotel set the pattern for the rest of our visit. During our stay we were impressed above all with the admirable combination of friendliness and efficiency with which the hotel is run. This has been a family business for over thirty years and Mr and Mrs Hasker, the charming owners, are constantly aiming to set ever higher standards of cuisine, service and cleanliness. The bedrooms are all very pleasantly furnished and are equipped with private bathrooms, colour television, radios and telephones. There is also a quite exquisite Honeymoon Suite. All the public rooms are both comfortable and elegant and there is a good view of the attractive outdoor swimming pool and patio from the lounge. Burley Court enjoys an excellent location in Bath Road, close to the beautiful beaches of Bournemouth. The cliff lift and the pier are also nearby. There is a large car park at the hotel and, for those who prefer not to drive, buses into the town centre stop frequently outside the hotel. Good organisation is the key to Burley Court's success, ensuring its guests a relaxing and enjoyable stay at prices which are very good value for money. We would especially recommend the excellent short break packages, including the 'Getaway Weekend' and the 'Easter and Christmas Package' breaks.

Weekly Terms from £195.00 Daily Terms from £35.00 Bed and Breakfast from £29.50 Bar Lunch from £2.00 Dinner from £9.70 Gratuities at Guest's Discretion VAT inclusive Credit Cards—Access, Visa	5 Family Rooms, 2 Family Suites 11 Double, 12 Twin, 6 Single Bedrooms 36 Rooms with Private facilities En Suite All Rooms with TV, Telephone, Radio, Baby-listening, Tea and Coffee-making Facilities Hairdryer available on Request Open from January to December	Residential and Restaurant Licence Full Central Heating. Lift. Cocktail Bar TV Lounge. Games Room Children catered for. Dogs allowed Parking Facilities. Night Porter Outdoor Swimming Pool, Solarium Nearby: Tennis, Putting, Squash, Golf, Fishing, Riding, Sailing, Windsurfing, Water Skiing

Section 1: Dorset

Bournemouth—The Carlton Hotel
East Overcliff, Bournemouth, Dorset. BH1 3DN. Tel 0202 552011

One of Bournemouth's best, by a mile, and the last remaining privately owned five-star hotel in Britain. The Carlton Hotel is, therefore, unique and well lives up to its classification. From the moment you step into the plush reception hall that subtle thing called 'atmosphere' takes charge. The smile of welcome is given for the sake of gladness rather than gratuity and can never be duplicated by a forced greeting. How we enjoy returning each year to The Carlton and how our readers mete out consistent praise for the standards they find there. In the recent past the hotel has been almost totally refurbished, yet one can live here luxuriously without feeling awed by ostentation. Never will you want to go out for a meal. The kitchen has been restructured to the most exacting standards and *Carlton Restaurant* prides itself on providing the finest wines and international *cuisine*. There is a Health Club (one almost says 'of course') with a mini-gym, spa bath, sauna, steam cabinets, solarium and beauty treatments. There seems to be very little that this luxury hotel cannot offer by way of comfort and activity for all tastes and all age groups. It stands in a most enviable position on the top of East Cliff, yet is a mere five minutes' walk from the centre of Bournemouth. There are endless opportunities for relaxing by the swimming pool or enjoying the hotel's lovely gardens. Most of the hotel rooms face south, giving one glorious views from the Isle of Wight to the Purbeck Hills. There is much we have not mentioned-the historical associations, unique decor, lovely rooms, enormously wide beds and spacious bathrooms. Let us say simply we can find no fault with The Carlton.

Bed and Breakfast from £98.00 (Single), £150.00 (Double)
Dinner, Bed and Breakfast from £79.00 (minimum of 2 nights)
Lunch from £17.50. Dinner from £23.50

VAT inclusive. All major credit cards accepted. Open all Year. Fully Licensed Full Central Heating. Lift. Cocktail Bar Games Room. Conference Facilities Children catered for. Dogs not allowed

Parking Facilities. Night Porter Outdoor Heated Swimming Pool, Solarium, Sauna, Mini-Gym, Snooker. Nearby: Tennis, Squash, Croquet, Putting, Badminton, Golf, Fishing, Riding, Sailing

Bournemouth—Cliffeside Hotel
East Overcliff Drive, Bournemouth, Dorset. BH1 3AQ. Tel 0202 555724. Fax 0202 294810

One of the quartet of well sited hotels in Bournemouth operated by the Arthur Young group, and of the family hotels in the town run on professional and proficient lines, Cliffeside has a wide following. It stands on East Cliff, so sea views are one's constant companion, and the shops and theatres are just a ten minutes' walk away. To ensure that parents, as well as their offspring, enjoy carefree holidays the hotel provides many thoughtful extras. Children's supper trays are served in the bedrooms during the early evening, so that mother and father can enjoy a quiet dinner later on. A baby-listening service is offered and, of course, the sheltered heated swimming pool and the games room are centres of constant activity. Guests will also be able to use the amenities offered at the new leisure complex at the Queens Hotel due for completion at the end of 1992. The Cliffeside's decor and fitments reflect the needs of families, but you will be impressed with the high standard of cleanliness throughout and the pleasant service. Every bedroom comes with a colour television, radio and telephone, and have either a bathroom or shower *en suite*. A front facing room also has the inestimable advantage of dress-circle views of the sea, and the higher one is the better the outlook! The Cliffeside is open throughout the year and during the winter months it takes on a more restful disposition, with short break holidays and functions coming more to the fore. What does not change, however, is the hotel's desire to offer value for money.

Weekly Terms from £270.00
Daily Terms from £40.00
Bed and Breakfast from £35.00
Bar Lunch from £2.00. Lunch from £8.25
Table D'Hôte. Bar Supper from £3.50
Dinner from £15.95

Gratuities at Guest's discretion
VAT inclusive. Credit Cards–Access, Visa
4 Family Rooms. 21 Double, 29 Twin, 8 Single Bedrooms. 50 Private Bathrooms
12 Private Shower Rooms
All rooms with TV, Telephone, Radio.

Baby-listening, Tea and Coffee-making facilities, Hairdryer. Open all year
Fully Licensed. Full Central Heating
Children catered for. Dogs allowed
Outdoor Swimming Pool, Solarium, Sauna, Table Tennis, Pool

Section 1: Dorset

Bournemouth–The Cumberland Hotel East Overcliff Drive, Bournemouth, Dorset. BH1 3AF. Tel 0202 290722. Fax 0202 311394

The attractive Cumberland Hotel stands in a prominent position on East Overcliff and delights its visitors with superb sea views over Poole Bay. The interior of the hotel is as pleasing as the exterior. The Young Family, whom we have known for several years as the owners of another of our recommended hotels, acquired The Cumberland recently and they and their staff have worked tirelessly to bring about many improvements here. They have succeeded admirably and the hotel is already acquiring a reputation for its excellent facilities and the high standard of comfort which it offers. The oak-panelled dining room, for example, which seats 300 people, has recently been redecorated and beautifully fitted out. The food served here is delicious and special diets can be catered for on request. Outside, a splendid swimming pool, a children's pool and a sun terrace ensure that warm days can be spent in total relaxation. Guests will also have use of the amenities offered at the new leisure complex at the Queens Hotel due for completion at the end of 1992. A regular programme of evening entertainments is offered. The Cumberland is truly an hotel which offers something for everyone. Children are welcomed and special reductions are available if they share a room with their parents. For businessmen, there are excellent conference facilities, including overnight accommodation for up to 190 delegates. We have no hesitation in recommending this splendid hotel: the Young Family and their friendly, pleasant staff will, we know, give you a warm welcome and we ourselves eagerly await our next visit.

Terms on Application
Bar Lunch from £2.30
Lunch from £8.25 Table D'Hôte
Bar Supper from £2.30
Dinner from £16.95 Table D'Hôte
Gratuities at Guest's Discretion

VAT inclusive. Credit Cards—Access, Visa
6 Family Rooms. 1 Suite
32 Double, 51 Twin, 12 Single Bedrooms
All Rooms with Private Bath/Shower
Room, TV, Telephone, Radio,
Baby-listening, Tea and Coffee-making

Facilities, Hairdryer. Trouser Press
available on request. Open all Year
Residential and Restaurant Licence
Full Central Heating. 2 Lifts.
Cocktail Bar. TV Lounge.
Games Room. Conference Facilities.

Bournemouth—East Anglia Hotel Poole Road, Bournemouth, Dorset. BH2 5QX. Tel 0202 765163. Fax 0202 752949

Bournemouth's main industry must be hotels, and the town has so many we are always diffident about picking out this and that. Yet, we found such a good and friendly feeling at the East Anglia that we warmed to it immediately. It is not surprising that it has a pronounced personal touch, for it has been run by the same family for nearly forty years. They have continually upgraded and refurbished the hotel and this has resulted in very high standards. The hotel has much to offer in the way of comfort, whether it be in the various lounge areas, with their restful decor, or bedrooms, so tastefully furnished and beautifully kept. We found the dining room a joy to behold, with its carefully chosen colour scheme, and, of course, the hotel enjoys the renowned expertise of Jacques Fischer, the French Head Chef, who married into the family, and prepares fine English-style *cuisine* for your delight. The town centre, beach and Bournemouth International Centre are just minutes away, and a wide range of leisure activities is provided at the hotel, including a luxury outdoor heated swimming pool (seasonal), sauna, jacuzzi, solarium, mini-gym and games room. During the summer months there is evening entertainment and dancing, also Easter, Christmas and New Year programmes are organised. Separate from the main hotel is a conference and banqueting suite with a most impressive ballroom. As a postscript we would add that the East Anglia is one of those rare hotels where reality outshines the hotel's brochure. And, of course, it is one of the friendliest places on earth.

Special Break Terms available
All Terms pertaining to 1992
Weekly Terms from £274.05 (DB&B)
Daily Terms from £45.50 (DB&B)
Bed and Breakfast from £32.50
Sunday Lunch from £7.75 Table D'Hôte

Bar Lunch from £1.75. Dinner from £14.00
Table D'Hôte. VAT inclusive. Credit
Cards–Access, American Express, Diners
Club, Visa. 10 Family Rooms
23 Double, 23 Twin, 17 Single Bedrooms
59 Private Bathrooms. 14 Private Shower

Rooms. All Rooms with TV, Telephone,
Radio, Baby-listening, Tea and
Coffee-making Facilities. Hairdryer
available on request. Open all Year. Fully
Licensed. Full CH. Lift. Cocktail Bar.
Games Room. Conference Facilities.

Section 1: Dorset

Bournemouth—Hinton Firs Hotel Manor Road, East Cliff, Bournemouth, Dorset. BH1 3HB. Tel 0202 555409

Set back from the cliff top, in the heart of the tree-lined East Cliff and set among pines and rhododendrons, Hinton Firs is renowned for its warm and friendly atmosphere. The addition of a leisure complex has proved popular with people of all ages. The indoor pool, complete with underwater jetstream, spa pool and sauna, overlooks the sheltered gardens, sun terrace and existing outdoor pool. Children are most welcome at all times and for those under five, special evening meals are served between 5.30 and 6.00 pm. Parents can then relax in the friendly cocktail bar before enjoying a delicious dinner in the recently refurbished dining room, where high standards of food, service and decor are constantly maintained. At midday, a choice of hot and cold snacks is offered. The bedrooms are bright and cheerful, and all of them, including a number of single rooms, have their own bath or shower, and are equipped with colour television, direct dial telephone, radio, baby-listening and tea-making facilities. From many of the rooms you may enjoy the view of the pool and garden. Bournemouth's mild climate, sandy beaches and fine coastal views ensures that it remains a thriving resort. Under the personal supervision of Roger and Mary Waters for over 20 years, Hinton Firs continues to be a favourite to which many guests frequently return, year in year out.

Weekly Terms from £280.00 (DB&B)
Daily Terms from £40.00 (DB&B)
Bed and Breakfast from £35.00
Bar Lunch from £4.00
Afternoon Tea from £0.75
Dinner from £12.25 Table d'Hôte (A La Carte available)
No Service Charge. VAT inclusive
Credit Cards—Access, Visa

12 Family Rooms
14 Double, 14 Twin, 12 Single Bedrooms
48 Private Bathrooms,
4 Private Shower Rooms
All Rooms with TV, Telephone, Radio, Baby-listening, Tea and Coffee-making Facilities
Open all Year
Residential and Restaurant Licence

Full Central Heating. Lift.
Cocktail Bar. TV Lounge.
Games Room. Conference Facilities.
Children catered for. Dogs not allowed
Parking Facilities. Night Porter
Indoor and Outdoor Heated. Swimming Pool, Sauna. Nearby: Tennis, Croquet, Putting, Squash, Golf, Fishing, Riding, Sailing, Windsurfing, Water Skiing

Bournemouth—Langtry Manor Hotel Derby Road, Bournemouth, Dorset. BH1 3QB. Tel 0202 553887. Fax 0202 290115

When Mrs Pamela Hamilton Howard bought this distinctive manor house, which was built in 1877 by King Edward VII for his true love, Lillie Langtry, she had no idea that within a few months the story would be televised in one of the most acclaimed series, and that the house would become universally known. Originally called the 'Red House' it is, today, furnished with much of the original period pieces including the King's chair. Mrs Hamilton Howard has also restored the building, as near as possible, to its Victorian state, revealing original fireplaces and much evidence of Lillie's personality. Throughout, she has created a feeling of peace and contentment where good food and wine combine to make you feel at one with an age that has largely disappeared. All the bedrooms are delightfully appointed and the addition of modern amenities has in no way detracted from their period theme. There are also four beautiful luxury suites with four-poster beds, including Lillie's and Edward's own rooms. By chance, we timed our visit to coincide with the hotel's Saturday Edwardian Dinner Party. All six courses are displayed for your choice by staff in Edwardian dress - a truly impressive example of the chef's art. A short "son et lumiere" gives a flavour of the history of this lovely house and its famous occupants. "Welcome" and "Celebration" weekends include this special treat. Seek out Langtry Manor - it is an experience to be savoured and creates a desire to return.

Weekly Terms from £275.00
Bed and Breakfast from £44.50
Dinner from £19.75 and A La Carte
Gratuities at Guest's Discretion
VAT inclusive
Credit Cards—Access, American Express, Diners Club, Visa
3 Four Poster Suites, 3 Suites

4 Double, 4 Twin Bedrooms
13 Private Bathrooms, 1 Private Shower Room
All Rooms with TV, Telephone, Radio, Tea and Coffee-making Facilities, Hairdryer
Open all Year.
Full Central Heating. Residential and Restaurant Licence

Cocktail Bar. Conference Facilities
Dogs allowed by Arrangement
Parking Facilities
Nearby: Tennis, Putting, Squash, Badminton, Swimming, Solarium, Sauna, Golf, Fishing, Riding, Sailing, Windsurfing, Water Skiing, Shooting, Hang-gliding, Flying

Section 1: Dorset

Bournemouth—The New Durley Dean Hotel Westcliff Road, Bournemouth, Dorset. BH2 5HE. Tel 0202 557711. Fax 0202 292815

Following extensive alterations and refurbishment, this hotel comes very close to being 'all things to all people'; this it achieves with no trace of compromise. For the businessman and the holidaymaker there are the features and facilities to match the many facets of the Bournemouth area. The sheer spaciousness of the hotel, enhanced by an airy decor, results in such diverse activities as conferences and club functions, live music and quiet conversation, swimming in the indoor pool, toning-up in the Trymnasium or enjoying a relaxed meal-all of these and more-flourishing happily together under one roof. The Sports and Leisure Centre of Durley Dean offers table tennis, billiards, Turkish steam room, sauna, solarium and exercise apparatus for rowing or cycling. From the catering in *The Green Room* restaurant to the wide range of fully equipped bedrooms, guests have a choice that will meet all reasonable requirements. Despite this impressive variety, the atmosphere is one of relaxation and comfort. Clearly a great deal of skill has been applied to the introduction of modern amenities without losing the charm of the Victorian era. From the hotel, guests have immediate access to Bournemouth's outstanding selection of stores, theatres, boutiques and restaurants, to Thomas Hardy country and to the seaside. Nearby is the ancient town of Poole, with one of the largest natural harbours in the world. Sportsmen will find tennis, golf, cricket, fishing and football all close at hand. Pony trekking and water sports, the motor museum at Beaulieu.... the list continues.

Weekly Terms from £209.50
Daily Terms from £34.50
Bed and Breakfast from £32.50
Room Rate from £28.50. Bar Lunch from £2.95. Lunch from £4.50 and A La Carte
Bar Supper from £1.95

Dinner from £13.50 and A La Carte
Gratuities at Guest's discretion
VAT inclusive. Credit Cards—Access, American Express, Visa
32 Family Rooms. 4 Suites
26 Double, 25 Twin, 25 Single Bedrooms

All Rooms with Private Bath and Shower Room, TV, Telephone, Radio, Baby-listening, Tea and Coffee-making Facilities, Trouser Press, Hairdryer. Open all Year. Fully Licensed. Lift. 2 Cocktail Bars. Games Room. Conference Facilities

Bournemouth—The Queens Hotel Meyrick Road, Bournemouth, Dorset. BH1 3DL. Tel 0202 554415. Fax 0202 294810

We have heard it said that Bournemouth has some one thousand hotels and guesthouses. Doubtless there are many good places other than those we mention. Yet, the three-star Queens Hotel certainly merits your attention; it is good to behold and pleasant to dwell in. The Queens is one of a trio of excellent, family run hotels run by Arthur Young (the others being the Cumberland Hotel and the Cliffeside Hotel), which also claim some of the best sites on the East Cliff. If the Queens looks well groomed from the outside, step inside, and one quickly detects detailed comfort in every room. There are 115 bedrooms, all *en suite*. Some of these rooms have balconies and some are classified as 'luxury bedrooms'. For daytime comfort there is an elegant and light lounge. For warmth throughout the year there is central heating. For toddlers and those with tired limbs, a lift. And for recreation, a well equipped games room. Development of a new leisure complex to include indoor swimming pool, gymnasium, sauna and steam room and jacuzzi is due for completion at the end of 1992. Behind the scenes is a chef who clearly takes pride in the food which he and his team produce in the kitchens. There are *table d'hôte* menus for both luncheon and dinner and the hotel is proud to claim that these offer a choice of forty-five different dishes. The Queens also justifies its tag, 'the all year round hotel', for it offers mini-breaks and special programmes for Christmas, New Year and Easter. If you like an hotel which is informal, very friendly and is run on popular and proficient lines, you will like it here.

Weekly Terms from £270.00
Daily Terms from £38.00
Bed and Breakfast from £35.00
Lunch from £8.50 Table D'Hôte
Bar Supper from £3.75
Dinner from £15.95 and A La Carte

Service Charge and VAT inclusive
Credit Cards—Access, Visa
7 Family Rooms. 5 Suites
32 Double, 55 Twin, 16 Single Bedrooms
All Rooms with Private Bathroom, TV, Telephone, Radio, Baby-listening, Tea and

Coffee-making Facilities, Hairdryer
10 Rooms with Trouser Press
Open all Year. Fully Licensed. Lift. Cocktail Bar. TV Lounge. Games Room. Conference Facilities. Children catered for. Dogs allowed. Parking Facilities.

Section 1: Dorset

Bournemouth—Trouville Hotel Priory Road, West Cliff, Bournemouth, Dorset. BH2 5DH. Tel 0202 552262. Fax 0202 293324

The three star Trouville sits squarely in the mainstream of Bournemouth's hotels. Yet, it has many distinctions and, consequently, has gained a sizable army of enthusiasts. The Trouville was acquired recently by the Arthur Young Group, who already own a trio of excellent hotels in Bournemouth, and for some years it has been our pleasure to visit the Queens, The Cumberland and the Cliffside hotels and to pass on letters of praise we have received about them from our readers. So, we are more than convinced that the Trouville will now enjoy a welcome impetus from its new owners. Indeed, the hotel has recently completed a major refurbishment programme and knowing this group as well as we do, we are certain you will find the improvements to the highest standard. Of course, the Trouville already has major attractions. An excellent location near the lovely West Cliff area and adjacent to both the Winter Gardens and the International Conference Centre. A restaurant which is greatly prized in the town for its varied menus and moderately priced wines. Eighty bedrooms containing all those modern niceties one has come to expect, including private bath or shower room. The hotel also provides entertainment during the high season, whilst a solarium, sauna, jacuzzi and trimnasium are available to guests throughout the year. Guests will also have the use of amenities at the new leisure complex at the Queens Hotel due for completion in 1992. The future for this hotel looks good and our inspectors have already dubbed it 'true bliss'.

Weekly Terms from £238.00
Daily Terms from £35.00
Bed and Breakfast from £31.00
Bar Lunch from £3.00
Dinner from £14.95 Table D'Hôte
Gratuities at Guest's Discretion. VAT inclusive. Credit Cards—Access, Visa
14 Family Rooms. 1 Suite. 24 Double, 27 Twin, 8 Single Bedrooms
All Rooms with Private Bath/Shower Room, TV, Telephone, Radio, Baby-listening, Tea and Coffee-making Facilities, Hairdryer. Open all year.
Residential and Restaurant Licence. Full CH. Lift. Cocktail Bar. Conference Facilities
Dogs allowed. Parking Facilities. Night Porter. Solarium, Sauna, Jacuzzi, Trimnasium

Bournemouth—Woodcroft Tower Hotel Gervis Road, East Cliff, Bournemouth, Dorset. BH1 3DE. Tel 0202 558202. Fax 0202 551807

A paved patio and more than an acre of lawns and gardens sheltered by pine trees-and yet you are only a few minutes' walk from the ZigZag and cliff lift leading down to the beach and promenade. All of Bournemouth's cinemas, theatres and shops are within easy reach and its renowned International Centre is only a short walk away. Proprietors Valerie and Michael Kemp are not new to us at Ashley Courtenay. For 25 years Mr Kemp has been a chef/proprietor and, while running a hotel in Wareham, established an excellent reputation. Today he still retains full control of the cooking assisted by a dedicated team of chefs creating imaginative menus using fresh local produce. Mrs Kemp and her brother Martin look after the 'front of house' together with a loyal and caring staff. Woodcroft Tower is a large hotel with a spacious feel about it combined with a welcoming decor. An impressive ballroom offers dancing in the season. The hotel also caters for wedding receptions, conventions and social functions. Our inspection of the hotel confirmed what we expected: everything in immaculate order, guests making their second or third visits and a tariff showing most reasonable prices. In a location with all the seaside attractions of Poole Bay, the Solent and the Isle of Wight, the countryside of the New Forest and the history surrounding Wimborne Minster, this hotel on Bournemouth's famous East Cliff is a valuable base for a wide range of activities.

Weekly Terms from £210.00
Daily Terms from £35.00
Bed and Breakfast from £25.00
Bargain Breaks available-terms on application
Bar Lunch from £2.00
Dinner from £12.00
Gratuities at Guest's Discretion
VAT inclusive. Credit Cards—Access, Visa
4 Family Rooms
17 Double, 1 Single, 16 Twin Bedrooms
21 Private Bathrooms
17 Private Shower Rooms
All Rooms with remote control colour TV, Telephone, Radio, Baby-listening, Tea and Coffee-making Facilities
Open all Year
Residential and Restaurant Licence
Full Central Heating
Lift. Quiet Lounge. Cocktail Bar. Conference Facilities
Children catered for. Dogs not allowed
Parking Facilities. Night Porter. Putting Nearby: Tennis, Squash, Swimming

Section 1: Dorset

Bournemouth—Wychcote Hotel   2 Somerville Road, West Cliff, Bournemouth, Dorset. BH2 5LH. Tel 0202 557898

And now for our other discovery in Bournemouth. We were put on its track when calling at a first-class New Forest Hotel, where Tessa Parham had held a high managerial position for some time. 'Now', we were told, 'she is achieving her ambition of owning her own hotel....and she is doing splendidly!' So, a stay at Wychcote became a 'must' for us. The hotel is situated in a quiet road, and yet is within easy distance of the town centre and Durley Cliff and beach. We stayed there on a very warm night, and so had our window fully open, but were not disturbed by any noise. Our introduction to Wychcote Hotel, however, was complimentary tea and homemade cakes—a greeting reserved for all arriving guests. Inside, the original Victorian house has been most carefully restored and furnished with appropriate pieces. Tessa said that she and her husband, Steve, now had everything in good order, but we had no idea that the hotel would be utterly immaculate....*everywhere*. As one would expect from the hotel's most reasonable tariff, the five-course dinner menu is not extensive, but Tessa's food is excellent in every way and the wines are most reasonably priced. There was a consensus among our fellow guests that you could not want for better fare, nor for more pleasant and caring service, than one is treated to here. If you feel jaded and want a 'breather', make a note of Wychcote Hotel, with its comforts and generous owners it is a 'home of new life'.

Weekly Terms from £160.00 per person
Daily Terms from £25.00 per person
Bed and Breakfast from £20.00 per person
English Breakfast £5.00
Afternoon Tea from £1.50
Dinner from £6.00 Table D'Hôte
Gratuities at Guest's Discretion
VAT inclusive

Credit Cards–Access, Visa
1 Family Room, 6 Double, 1 Single, 4 Twin Bedrooms
2 Private Bathrooms
8 Private Shower Rooms
All rooms with Radio, Tea and Coffee-making facilities, TV. Hairdryer available on request

Open from 1st February to 10th January
Residential Licence. Full Central Heating
TV Lounge. Children over 5 years catered for. Dogs not allowed. Parking facilities
Nearby: Tennis, Putting, Squash, Badminton, Swimming, Golf, Fishing, Sailing, Windsurfing, Water Skiing, Theatre and Arts Centre.

Bridport—Haddon House Hotel
West Bay, Bridport, Dorset. Tel 0308 23626/25323

While we were enjoying our lunch at this delightful Regency style country hotel, we chanced to meet a couple who were staying there for the fourth time. This, we felt, was proof enough that Wing Commander and Mrs W W J Loud must be doing an excellent job in looking after their many guests. The hotel is situated within 200 yards of the picturesque harbour and coast of West Bay, and it overlooks beautiful countryside ideally located for touring Dorset, Devon and Somerset. Golfers will be keen to know that right opposite the hotel is a well-maintained eighteen-hole golf course which offers special reduced green fees for hotel guests. Boating and deep-sea fishing can be arranged. Other amenities in the area include a swimming pool, riding, tennis and bowling and many interesting fossils can be found on the cliffs nearby. West Dorset is approximately 400 square miles of unspoilt countryside. The scenery is fantastic with a marvellous variety of sandy beaches, towering cliffs and shingle banks which include the famous Chesil Beach. We are not surprised that our friends were returning for the fourth time! All of the bedrooms at Haddon House are attractively furnished and provide a private bathroom and shower and all the modern facilities you require. There is full central heating and plenty of space for parking your car. The menus offered in the dining room are varied, and include a generous selection of home cooked dishes and fresh fish, with a good selection of well chosen wines to complement your meal. The hotel is open throughout the year and offers bargain breaks and special weekend terms with every possible care taken to ensure your personal comfort and enjoyment.

Terms on application. Bar Meal from £1.25
Lunch from £9.50 and A La Carte
Dinner from £14.50 and A La Carte
Gratuities at Guest's Discretion

VAT inclusive. Credit Cards—Access, American Express, Diners Club, Visa
2 Family Rooms. 4 Double, 4 Twin, 2 Single Bedrooms. All Rooms with Private

Bath/Shower, TV, Telephone, Radio, Baby-listening, Tea and Coffee-making Facilities, Trouser Press, Hairdryer, Toiletries. Open All Year. Fully Licensed.

Section 1: Dorset

Bridport—Roundham House Hotel Roundham Gardens, West Bay Road, Bridport, Dorset. DT6 4BD. Tel 0308 22753/25779. Fax 0308 421145

As its name implies, this historic town has a port, although this lies one-and-a-half miles to the south at West Bay a place of unspoilt charm in spite of its popularity. Yet, West Bay has more attraction than simply its vertical sandstone cliffs, small harbour and commercial fishing fleet, for nearby is a lovely country residence with an outstanding position, overlooking the sea and the Dorset countryside. Pat and David Moody have transformed Roundham House into a little hotel 'gem' since they took it over in 1988. The refurbishment has been total, the styling and decor are truly delightful, and, in recognition of the new high standards which now prevail, the hotel's status and grading have reached new heights; they are now the proud possessors of one red rosette from the AA. Visualise a habitation which is imbued with the personal touch of its owners, where one's comfort seems to be pre-eminent and the enjoyment of good food a way of life. The extensive *table d'hôte* menus are quite outstanding and Mr and Mrs Moody take a great pride in them. There is a wide choice of accommodation available for such a small hotel, and all the rooms are equipped to a very high standard. But the outstanding sense of spaciousness one feels when staying there is due to the position of the hotel. The grounds encompass about one acre of terraced gardens, in which guests may stroll and relax. We hardly need to expound on the almost endless holiday opportunities which Wessex provides. Roundham House spells friendliness, cosy nights and excellent fare a little house of contentment.

Bed and Breakfast from £32.50 (Single)
Bed and Breakfast from £45.00 (Double)
Dinner from £12.50 Table D'Hôte
(Menu Changed Daily)
Gratuities at Guest's Discretion
VAT inclusive. Credit Cards—Access,

American Express, Diners Club, Visa
2 Family Rooms. 1 Single, 3 Double, 2 Twin, Bedrooms. All Rooms with Private Bath/Shower Room, TV, Telephone, Hospitality Tray, Electric Blankets Baby-listening, Hairdryer and

Ironing Facilities available on Request
Open from 1st February to Mid November - Please check. Residential and Restaurant Licence. Full CH. Cocktail Bar
Children catered for by Arrangement
Dogs not allowed. Parking Facilities

Charmouth—The Queen's Armes Hotel
The Street, Charmouth, Bridport, Dorset. DT6 6QF. Tel 0297 60339

When defeated by Cromwell in 1651 at the Battle of Worcester, Charles II took refuge for a time at this famous fifteenth-century hotel. With the help of a local boatman, the king planned to escape to France, but his presence was betrayed and he was forced to flee the town on horseback instead. There are, of course, dozens of inns which lay claim to being 'probably the oldest in England', but, in our choice of favourite hostelries, age is not as important as the mellow atmosphere and good food, good wine and genuine hospitality. All these The Queen's Armes Hotel in Charmouth can offer in abundance. One need not, therefore, be a lover of antiquity to derive great satisfaction from visiting this hotel. It is warm and extremely comfortable, all but one of the bedrooms are *en suite*, the catering and the cellar are highly regarded and we defy almost any guest to leave the hotel without first having become friends of the owners, Peter and Jenny Miles. They are in constant attendance and we cannot over-emphasise the friendly nature of the service they provide. There is a three-quarter acre garden at the rear of the hotel and adequate parking space behind that. Charmouth's beaches are only five minutes' walk away. At low tide one may walk below the rocky headland, along West Beach to Lyme Regis. From East Beach, above the cliffs, a coastal path climbs Stonebarrow Hill, eventually reaching Golden Cap (617 feet), the highest point on the south coast.

Terms on Application
Dinner from £10.50 and A La Carte
Gratuities at Guest's discretion
VAT inclusive
Credit Cards—Access, Visa
5 Double, 3 Twin, 3 Single Bedrooms

6 Private Bathrooms
5 Private Shower Rooms
All Rooms with TV, Tea and Coffee-making Facilities, Toiletries
Hairdryer available on Request
Open from 3rd week in February

to end October. Full Central Heating
Residential and Restaurant Licence
Cocktail Bar. TV Lounge. Dogs allowed
Children over 5 years catered for
Parking Facilities. Nearby: Tennis, Putting, Golf, Riding, Sailing, Windsurfing

Section 1: Dorset

Christchurch–The Waterford Lodge Hotel
87 Bure Lane, Friars Cliff, Christchurch, Dorset BH23 4DN.
Tel 0425 278801. Fax 0425 279130

East of Christchurch, extending to little-known Keyhaven, is a twelve-mile stretch of coastline which will repay investigation by anyone seeking holidays and Breaks away from the cut-and-dried amenities of popular resorts. The Solent breezes mingle with pure New Forest air just here, and the pace of life . . . just slows. This is not to suggest that one cannot engage in activities, such as sailing from Lymington, riding from nearby stables, enjoying superb cliff walks, or taking ferry trips to the Isle of Wight, it is just that life seems unhurried hereabouts and one comes away feeling fully refreshed. The choice of where to stay in the area has been made easier with the Waterford Lodge Hotel's emergence as one of the best three-star hotels in the Christchurch and Bournemouth district. It has the convenience of a town house, yet the ambience of a country house–look out onto the lovely garden and you will see what we mean. Pundits sing its praises and anyone who stays at the hotel for any length of time clearly develops a great affection for it. There is no secret–the Badley family are the heart, soul and working partners of Waterford Lodge and are ideal hosts besides. Their hospitality is always genuine and never mannered. The facilities are modern, yet Waterford Lodge has a very 'homely' atmosphere which puts one immediately at one's ease. There are two lounges and a residents' bar, so you can be as convivial or separate as the mood dictates, and the bedrooms could not be more comfortable. When we visited the hotel it was fully booked, but we enjoyed a superb dinner, which was so imaginative and well-presented we were constrained to pass our compliments to the chef. Those staying at the hotel are able to enjoy free swimming at the nearby Two Rivermeet Leisure Centre, plus a twenty-five percent discount on squash, badminton, golf and table tennis at the centre. If you prefer gentle perambulations, the award-winning Friars Cliff Beach is a few hundred yards away from the hotel, whilst picturesque Mudeford Harbour is close by.

Weekly Terms from £329.00 pp sharing double/twin. Daily Terms from £47.00 pp sharing (DB&B) minimum of 2 nights Bed and Breakfast from £43.00 per person sharing. Bar Lunch from £2.50 Lunch from £10.50 Table D'Hôte

Dinner from £18.50. Gratuities at Guest's Discretion VAT inclusive. Credit Cards-Access, American Express, Diners Club, Visa 2 Family Rooms. 2 Suites. 18 Double, 18 Twin Bedrooms. All Rooms with Private

Bathroom, TV, Telephone, Radio, Baby-listening, Tea and Coffee-making Facilities, Hairdryer. Open all year Residential and Restaurant Licence. Full CH. Cocktail Bar. Games Room. Conference Facilities.

Section 1: Dorset

Bridport—Roundham House Hotel Roundham Gardens, West Bay Road, Bridport, Dorset. DT6 4BD. Tel 0308 22753/25779. Fax 0308 421145

As its name implies, this historic town has a port, although this lies one-and-a-half miles to the south at West Bay a place of unspoilt charm in spite of its popularity. Yet, West Bay has more attraction than simply its vertical sandstone cliffs, small harbour and commercial fishing fleet, for nearby is a lovely country residence with an outstanding position, overlooking the sea and the Dorset countryside. Pat and David Moody have transformed Roundham House into a little hotel 'gem' since they took it over in 1988. The refurbishment has been total, the styling and decor are truly delightful, and, in recognition of the new high standards which now prevail, the hotel's status and grading have reached new heights; they are now the proud possessors of one red rosette from the AA. Visualise a habitation which is imbued with the personal touch of its owners, where one's comfort seems to be pre-eminent and the enjoyment of good food a way of life. The extensive *table d'hôte* menus are quite outstanding and Mr and Mrs Moody take a great pride in them. There is a wide choice of accommodation available for such a small hotel, and all the rooms are equipped to a very high standard. But the outstanding sense of spaciousness one feels when staying there is due to the position of the hotel. The grounds encompass about one acre of terraced gardens, in which guests may stroll and relax. We hardly need to expound on the almost endless holiday opportunities which Wessex provides. Roundham House spells friendliness, cosy nights and excellent fare a little house of contentment.

Bed and Breakfast from £32.50 (Single)	American Express, Diners Club, Visa	Ironing Facilities available on Request
Bed and Breakfast from £45.00 (Double)	2 Family Rooms. 1 Single, 3 Double, 2	Open from 1st February to Mid November -
Dinner from £12.50 Table D'Hôte	Twin, Bedrooms. All Rooms with Private	Please check. Residential and Restaurant
(Menu Changed Daily)	Bath/Shower Room, TV, Telephone,	Licence. Full CH. Cocktail Bar
Gratuities at Guest's Discretion	Hospitality Tray, Electric Blankets	Children catered for by Arrangement
VAT inclusive. Credit Cards—Access,	Baby-listening, Hairdryer and	Dogs not allowed. Parking Facilities

Charmouth—The Queen's Armes Hotel
The Street, Charmouth, Bridport, Dorset. DT6 6QF. Tel 0297 60339

When defeated by Cromwell in 1651 at the Battle of Worcester, Charles II took refuge for a time at this famous fifteenth-century hotel. With the help of a local boatman, the king planned to escape to France, but his presence was betrayed and he was forced to flee the town on horseback instead. There are, of course, dozens of inns which lay claim to being 'probably the oldest in England', but, in our choice of favourite hostelries, age is not as important as the mellow atmosphere and good food, good wine and genuine hospitality. All these The Queen's Armes Hotel in Charmouth can offer in abundance. One need not, therefore, be a lover of antiquity to derive great satisfaction from visiting this hotel. It is warm and extremely comfortable, all but one of the bedrooms are *en suite*, the catering and the cellar are highly regarded and we defy almost any guest to leave the hotel without first having become friends of the owners, Peter and Jenny Miles. They are in constant attendance and we cannot over-emphasise the friendly nature of the service they provide. There is a three-quarter acre garden at the rear of the hotel and adequate parking space behind that. Charmouth's beaches are only five minutes' walk away. At low tide one may walk below the rocky headland, along West Beach to Lyme Regis. From East Beach, above the cliffs, a coastal path climbs Stonebarrow Hill, eventually reaching Golden Cap (617 feet), the highest point on the south coast.

Terms on Application	6 Private Bathrooms	to end October. Full Central Heating
Dinner from £10.50 and A La Carte	5 Private Shower Rooms	Residential and Restaurant Licence
Gratuities at Guest's discretion	All Rooms with TV, Tea and Coffee-	Cocktail Bar. TV Lounge. Dogs allowed
VAT inclusive	making Facilities, Toiletries	Children over 5 years catered for
Credit Cards—Access, Visa	Hairdryer available on Request	Parking Facilities. Nearby: Tennis, Putting,
5 Double, 3 Twin, 3 Single Bedrooms	Open from 3rd week in February	Golf, Riding, Sailing, Windsurfing

Section 1: Dorset

Christchurch–The Waterford Lodge Hotel
87 Bure Lane, Friars Cliff, Christchurch, Dorset BH23 4DN.
Tel 0425 278801. Fax 0425 279130

East of Christchurch, extending to little-known Keyhaven, is a twelve-mile stretch of coastline which will repay investigation by anyone seeking holidays and Breaks away from the cut-and-dried amenities of popular resorts. The Solent breezes mingle with pure New Forest air just here, and the pace of life . . . just slows. This is not to suggest that one cannot engage in activities, such as sailing from Lymington, riding from nearby stables, enjoying superb cliff walks, or taking ferry trips to the Isle of Wight, it is just that life seems unhurried hereabouts and one comes away feeling fully refreshed. The choice of where to stay in the area has been made easier with the Waterford Lodge Hotel's emergence as one of the best three-star hotels in the Christchurch and Bournemouth district. It has the convenience of a town house, yet the ambience of a country house–look out onto the lovely garden and you will see what we mean. Pundits sing its praises and anyone who stays at the hotel for any length of time clearly develops a great affection for it. There is no secret–the Badley family are the heart, soul and working partners of Waterford Lodge and are ideal hosts besides. Their hospitality is always genuine and never mannered. The facilities are modern, yet Waterford Lodge has a very 'homely' atmosphere which puts one immediately at one's ease. There are two lounges and a residents' bar, so you can be as convivial or separate as the mood dictates, and the bedrooms could not be more comfortable. When we visited the hotel it was fully booked, but we enjoyed a superb dinner, which was so imaginative and well-presented we were constrained to pass our compliments to the chef. Those staying at the hotel are able to enjoy free swimming at the nearby Two Rivermeet Leisure Centre, plus a twenty-five percent discount on squash, badminton, golf and table tennis at the centre. If you prefer gentle perambulations, the award-winning Friars Cliff Beach is a few hundred yards away from the hotel, whilst picturesque Mudeford Harbour is close by.

Weekly Terms from £329.00 pp sharing double/twin. Daily Terms from £47.00 pp sharing (DB&B) minimum of 2 nights Bed and Breakfast from £43.00 per person sharing. Bar Lunch from £2.50 Lunch from £10.50 Table D'Hôte

Dinner from £18.25 Gratuities at Guest's Discretion VAT inclusive. Credit Cards-Access, American Express, Diners Club, Visa 2 Family Rooms. 2 Suites. 18 Double, 18 Twin Bedrooms. All Rooms with Private

Bathroom, TV, Telephone, Radio, Baby-listening, Tea and Coffee-making Facilities, Hairdryer. Open all year Residential and Restaurant Licence. Full CH. Cocktail Bar. Games Room. Conference Facilities.

Section 1: Dorset

Corfe—Mortons House Hotel
Corfe Castle, Dorset. BH20 5EE. Tel 0929 480988

But do you really know Corfe? For the visitor, Corfe has something of more importance than her tenth century castle set steeply above the picturesque village, where the walls of the houses, and even the roofing slates, dormers and tall chimneys, are fashioned from Purbeck stone. We have in mind this hotel showpiece in one of the village's privileged peaceful spots. This truly wonderful old building has just celebrated its four-hundredth anniversary and was constructed originally in the shape of an 'E' to honour Queen Elizabeth I. It came as a pleasant surprise to 'discover' Mortons House, and a marvellous treat to stay there, and whilst the stone fireplaces, oak-panelled drawing room with some fine carvings, original hall, and *Elizabethan* guest room with a four-poster bed and dressing room, were to be expected, we were astonished to find also seventeen bedrooms, full of character but very modernly equipped, and two boasting spa baths. Under the very personal care of Mr and Mrs David Langford, Mortons is receiving every possible attention to detail in its transformation into a *de luxe* hotel and the end results are clearly in keeping with the very high standards of Corfe as a whole. The food presented to us at breakfast and dinner was outstanding, and afternoon cream teas in the delightful walled gardens could hardly be a more relaxing experience. Already we are longing to return to Mortons to be separated from the tourist throng, but not isolated from the history and beauty of the village.

Terms pertain to 1992	Credit Cards–Access, Visa	Children catered for.
Bed and Breakfast from £37.50	2 Suites, 12 Double, 3 Twin Bedrooms	Well behaved dogs allowed.
Bar Lunch from £5.00	17 Private Bathrooms	Parking Facilities
Lunch £15.00 Table D'Hôte	All rooms with TV, Telephone, Radio,	Croquet.
Afternoon Tea £3.50	Baby-listening, Tea and Coffee-making	Nearby: Putting, Squash, Badminton,
Dinner £22.50 Table D'Hôte	facilities. Open all year	Swimming, Solarium, Golf, Fishing, Riding,
Gratuities at Guest's discretion	Fully Licensed. Full Central Heating	Sailing, Windsurfing, Water Skiing
VAT inclusive	Conference Facilities	

Nr Dorchester—Yalbury Cottage Country House Hotel & Restaurant
Lower Bockhampton, Dorset. DT2 8PZ. Tel 0305 262382

Set in pastoral farmland on the fringe of Thomas Hardy's hamlet Mellstock, this lovely old cottage-long, low and beautifully thatched-is one of those impressive period pieces for which Dorset is renowned. You may now spend a night here in real comfort; but if you are a wise traveller you will, however long or short your visit, see to it that you arrive in time for a meal, for it is by the food as much as anything else that you will remember Yalbury Cottage. Proprietors Rolf and Pauline Voss transformed their home firstly into a restaurant and comparatively recently into an exquisite small hotel. (Guests return again and again.) Having stayed here ourselves we can understand why. Pauline has designed the interior of the hotel with great flair. The *en suite* bedrooms (there are only eight) have been equipped to suit the hour and one's mood; a hairdryer, bathrobes and facecloths, clothes brush and expensive toiletries are standard niceties. We even found that a long mirror in the bedroom concealed an ingeniously placed ironing board and iron! The Gourmet Dinner was everything we hoped it would or could be; there are five courses from which to choose and the preparation and presentation of each dish is first class. Rolf Voss has direct connections with wine growers both in Germany and France, visiting and staying with them, and takes great pride in choosing vintages. From this quiet little backwater the whole of Wessex lies at one's feet, yet it is so nice to return to this beamed and inglenooked retreat with its kindly owners.

Short Breaks available	Gratuities at Guest's Discretion.	Hairdryer, Bathrobes, Toiletries
Bed and Full English Breakfast from £84.00 (Double)	VAT inclusive. Credit Cards—Access, Visa	Open from January to December
	6 Double, 2 Twin Bedrooms	Restaurant Licence. Full Central Heating
Supper menu from £14.00 for 3 courses A La Carte)	All Rooms with Private Bathroom, TV, Telephone, Radio/Alarm, Tea and	Dogs not allowed. Parking Facilities Nearby: Golf, Fishing, Riding, Shooting
Gourmet menu by arrangement	Coffee-making Facilities, Ironing Facilities,	

Section 1: Dorset

Near Dorchester—The Manor Hotel
West Bexington-on-Sea, Dorset. DT2 9DF
Tel 0308 897616

Just a few yards from Chesil Beach and only a stone's throw from the rope-making town of Bridport, is The Manor Hotel—a beautiful and ancient place, weathered by centuries of sun and wind. It was once the manor house for the village of Bexington (formerly known as 'Bessington'), but now, as an hotel, it dispenses country house hospitality to all who are fortunate enough to find their way to it. Within easy reach are the great sandy stretches of Weymouth, Charmouth and Lyme Regis and nearby West Bay offers offers boating and sea fishing. Richard and Jayne Childs are the proprietors of The Manor Hotel and they do everything they can to ensure that each of their guests is made thoroughly at home. The stone lined cellar has now been made into a charming bar, The Cellar, and a most imaginative range of bar meals is offered here. In the restaurant, which now seats up to sixty people, superb table d'hôte meals are offered, with choices such as West Bay Scallops, cooked with ginger and parsley in filo pastry and Noisettes of Lamb, grilled pink, served with onion and mint sauce guaranteed to stimulate even the most blasé tastebuds! Guests can relax after their meal in the residents' lounge, which overlooks the pretty, flower filled garden. There are thirteen bedrooms, each of which comes equipped with direct-dial telephone, television, radio, baby-listening and tea and coffee-making facilities. Do try to engage one of them soon: you will find that a booking at the Manor Hotel is the beginning of a relaxing and memorable holiday.

Weekly Terms from £325.00
Daily Terms from £54.00
Bed and Breakfast from £35.50
Bar Meal from £4.25
Lunch from £12.50 (2 course)/£14.95 (3 course)
Dinner £18.95 (4 course)
3 course Supper menu £14.95
Gratuities at Guest's Discretion

VAT inclusive
Credit Cards—Access,
American Express, Visa, Diners Club
1 Family Room. 12 Double Bedrooms
9 Private Bathrooms
4 Private Shower Rooms
All Rooms with Telephone, TV, Radio, Baby-listening, Tea and Coffee-making Facilities, Hairdryer

Open all Year
Fully Licensed. Full Central Heating
Conference Facilities
Children catered for. Dogs not allowed
Parking Facilities
Nearby: Tennis, Squash, Golf, Riding, Sailing, Windsurfing, Water Skiing, Shooting

Section 1: Dorset

Lyme Regis—The Alexandra Hotel
Pound Street, Lyme Regis, Dorset. DT7 3HZ. Tel 0297 442010. Fax 0297 443229

The Alexandra stands as high up in our estimation as it does in reality. The former has ensured that it is one of our most enduring Dorset recommendations, whilst the latter has bestowed upon it one of the finest seaward views on the south coast. Set in its own magnificent grounds, The Alexandra dates from 1735, when the original house was the dower house of the Dowager Countess Poulett, and was later owned by the Duc du Stacpoole. However, no hotel can hope to exist in these competitive days on the halo of tradition. Individually or collectively, one always fares well at The Alexandra. Meals here are a joy and always an inducement for a bottle or glass of wine. Menus, without being elaborate, offer a good variety of choice and the portions are always plentiful and well cooked. After dining, one can relax in a most delightful conservatory, which overlooks the lawns and Lyme Bay. Bedrooms, too, are praiseworthy and all have private bathrooms. There are many delightful walks along the cliffs towards Seaton and Charmouth, where the scenery is beautiful and fishing, sailing, windsurfing and golf are all available nearby. Under the expert direction of Mr and Mrs David Haskins, The Alexandra fits any occasion, be it social or seasonal, and fully justifies its high reputation. Having stayed, dined and wined here on many occasions, we should know.

Weekly Terms from £270.00
Daily Terms from £50.00
Bed and Breakfast from £40.00
Bar Lunch from £4.40
Lunch from £10.50 and A La Carte
Dinner from £17.50 and A La Carte
Gratuities at Guest's Discretion
VAT inclusive

Credit Cards—Access, Visa
6 Family Rooms
9 Double, 7 Twin, 2 Single Bedrooms
23 Private Bathrooms
1 Private Shower Room. All Rooms with TV, Telephone, Radio, Baby-listening, Tea and Coffee-making Facilities, Hairdryer
Open from February to December

Fully Licensed. Full Central Heating.
Cocktail Bar.
Children catered for
Dogs allowed. Parking Facilities.
Nearby: Tennis, Putting, Squash, Badminton, Solarium, Golf, Fishing, Riding, Sailing, Windsurfing, Water Skiing

Lyme Regis—Hotel Buena Vista
Pound Street, Lyme Regis, Dorset. DT7 3HZ. Tel 0297 442494

Lyme sits on a beautiful stretch of coastline at the point where Devon meets Dorset. The suffix, 'Regis', dates from as far back as 1284, when Edward I granted the town a charter and used the port as a base from which to attack the French. Since Victorian times, however, it has taken on the rôle of an elegant and select holiday resort. In an area with such a remarkable sea-board, the position of Hotel Buena Vista is a marvellous asset for any hotel. It is set back, off the main road, on the west side of the town, and looks straight down onto the Cobb and harbour. A quiet and peaceful garden lies in front of this charming Regency house. In many respects the hotel has retained a country house ambience, even though the town and beaches lie within five minutes' walk. Guests have a choice of relaxing in one of the two lounges or in the sun lounge which faces the south. All the bedrooms, which have recently been refurbished are *en suite* and are equipped with colour television, direct-dial telephones, radios and tea and coffee-making facilities. Also available is a self-contained second floor unit, the *Tivoli Room*, an extra luxurious double room with lounge area and *en suite* bathroom enjoying panoramic views of Lyme Bay on three sides. (This room is approached by a winding staircase and would not really be suitable for elderley or disabled guests.) The Buena Vista is under the capable direction of the resident proprietors, Gordon and Gill Forsyth and Frank and Shirley Meadows, who are continuing the hotel's policy of offering guests comfort, personal service and good English food. Their menus are varied and are changed every day.

Weekly Terms from £234.00
Daily Terms from £39.00
Bed and Breakfast from £30.00
Dinner from £12.50
Gratuities at Guest's Discretion
VAT inclusive. Credit Cards—Access,

American Express, Diners Club, Visa
1 Family Room. 1 Suite
8 Double, 4 Twin, 4 Single Bedrooms
18 Private Bathrooms. All Rooms with colour TV, Telephone, Radio, Baby-listening, Tea and Coffee-making

Facilities. Hairdryer available on Request
Open all Year. Residential and Restaurant Licence. Full CH. Cocktail Bar
Conference Facilities. Children catered for.
Dogs allowed. Parking Facilities.
Nearby: Tennis, Putting, Squash, Golf

Section 1: Dorset

Lyme Regis—The Kersbrook Hotel
Pound Road, Lyme Regis, Dorset. DT7 3HX. Tel 02974 42596/42576

Built in 1790 as a holiday retreat for landed gentry, Kersbrook is a thatched, listed hotel set high above Lyme Bay in its own acre of picturesque gardens. In their ten years' ownership, Mr & Mrs Stephenson, helped by John Fowles, author of *The French Lieutenant's Woman*, have researched the intriguing history of the property and its Royal associations. Careful modernisation and an extension to the dining areas to meet increasing patronage by non-residents have fully preserved the warm and comfortable ambience. International Chef Norman Arnold services the *à la carte* and *table d'hôte* menus, and his background includes cheffing for Presidents of the USA and for our Royal Family. His culinary artistry is a major feature of the Kersbrook experience. We have included this hotel in our guide for several years now and are, if anything, more impressed than ever with the standards achieved on all counts. Added to this are the pleasures of gardens restored to their glorious eighteenth-century layout and the superb views of the Dorset coast. Only a few miles to the west lie further scenic and historic sites in the county of Devon. Returning from these visits to the attractively-panelled lounges of the hotel, its *Blue Quiet Room* and fascinating antiques is rewarding and memorable.

Weekly Terms from £190.00 (B&B).
£300.00 (DB&B)
Bed and Breakfast from £30.00
Bar Lunch from £6.50
Steak & Fish Bar Menu from £7.50
Dinner from £16.50 and A La Carte
Gratuities added at 10%
VAT inclusive. Credit Cards-Access, Visa
1 Single, 6 Double, 3 Twin Bedrooms

5 Private Bathrooms.
5 Private Shower Rooms.
All Rooms with TV, Tea, Coffee and Chocolate-making Facilities, Iron, Hairdryer, Fruit Baskets, Books, Gift Packs
3 Rooms with Telephone.
4 Rooms with Trouser Press.
Open all Year (except three weeks at Christmas).

Residential and Restaurant Licence.
Cocktail Bar. Lounge
Dogs allowed. Parking Facilities.
Nearby: Tennis, Putting, Squash, Badminton, Swimming Pool, Solarium, Golf, Fishing, Riding, Sailing, Windsurfing, Water Skiing, Shooting, Walking, Climbing

Near Poole, Sandbanks—Harbour Heights Hotel
73 Havens Road, Sandbanks, Dorset. BH13 7LW. Tel 0202 707272. Fax 0202 708594

The name describes it perfectly and there is no question that the view, regarded as one of the best in the south of England, is one good reason for choosing the Harbour Heights as a holiday base. From the terrace and sea-facing windows, the immediate prospect is a beautiful terraced garden, which stretches away from the hotel to a curtain of trees. Beyond the view of the trees is Poole Harbour, the second largest natural harbour in the world, with Brownsea Island sitting in the centre. If you can drag yourself away from the view, you will find that the Harbour Heights is a very well run hotel. It attracts a great deal of local patronage, as well as an all year round holiday clientèle. Our bedroom contained a colour television, tea-making facilities, an *en suite* bathroom and, in the bay window, a table and two easy chairs, where a cup of tea and the view were a splendid way to begin our stay here. The public rooms are spacious and well furnished and the dining room always looked attractive with flowers and candles on the tables. The Shee and Burden families have worked very hard since coming here and their guests are benefiting enormously from it. You will find the hotel on the outskirts of Bournemouth in the Sandbanks district, which means that it is well placed for most recreational pursuits.

Weekly Terms from £330.00
Bed and Breakfast from £46.00
Bar Lunch from £4.50
Afternoon Tea from £2.00
Bar Supper from £7.00
Dinner from £16.00 and A La Carte
No Service Charge. VAT inclusive
Credit Cards–Access, American Express, Diners Club, Visa

5 Family Rooms. 1 Suite
24 Double, 6 Twin, 13 Single Bedrooms
40 Private Bathrooms.
9 Private Shower Rooms
All Rooms with TV, Telephone, Radio, Baby-listening, Tea and Coffee-making Facilities, Trouser Press.
Hairdryers available on Request.
Open all Year

Fully Licensed. Full Central Heating
Lift. 2 Cocktail Bars.
Conference Facilities
Children catered for. Dogs allowed
Parking Facilities. Night Porter.
Nearby: Tennis, Putting, Squash, Badminton, Swimming, Solarium, Sauna, Golf, Fishing, Riding, Sailing, Windsurfing, Water Skiing

Section 1: Dorset

Sherborne—The Antelope Hotel
Greenhill, Sherborne, Dorset DT9 4EP. Tel 0935 812077. Fax 0935 816473

Our visit to this listed eighteenth-century hotel in 1992 was only five months after it had been newly acquired by David Daniels. However, the twenty-two years of experience that Mr Daniels has, in major London hotels and in Paris, was already clearly evident. We can well understand why - in one of his previous appointments - he was presented with the 'Hotelier of the Year' award. The high standard of the Continental and English cuisine prompted our Inspectors to observe that 'the food is far better than the menu suggests!' No problem here. Comprehensive amenities, comfortable furnishings and the friendly, efficient service make The Antelope as valuable to the business traveller as it is attractive to the touring holidaymaker. Conferences, banquets and receptions for up to eighty people are well served by the Thomas Hardy room. It has natural daylight but is readily adapted to presentations, with audio-visual equipment available for hire. Only four miles from the busy industrial and commercial centre of Yeovil, and with good roads radiating in every direction, the hotel offers executives a most convenient base. Equally, the location is ideal for exploring the many interesting sites in Somerset and Dorset. Sherborne's 'New' Castle was built by Sir Walter Raleigh in 1594 and has a lake and gardens by Capability Brown. For centuries, gloves have been made in Yeovil and, at Yeovilton, the Fleet Air Arm Museum and Concorde exhibition must be visited.

Weekly Terms from £315.00
Daily Terms from £45.00
Bed and Breakfast from £39.95
Bar Meals from £3.00
Lunch from £5.00. Dinner from £4.95
Service Charge and VAT inclusive
Credit Cards-Access, American Express,

Diners Club, Visa
2 Family Rooms. 2 Suites.
7 Double, 3 Twin, 5 Single Bedrooms
All Rooms with Private Bath and Shower Room, TV, Telephone, Radio,
Baby-listening, Tea and Coffee-making Facilities, Trouser Press, Hairdryer

Open all year. Fully Licensed
Individual heating in each Room
Cocktail Bar. Games Room in Bar.
Conference Facilities.
Children catered for. Dogs allowed.
Parking Facilities. Night Porter.
Nearby: Tennis, Croquet, Putting, Squash

Sherborne—The Eastbury Hotel
Long Street, Sherborne, Dorset. DT9 3BY. Tel 0935 813131. Fax 0935 817296

Nestling quietly behind this eighteenth-century town house is a walled garden of one acre with shrubs, formal planting, listed cedar and walnut trees, and a fragrant rose garden. An unusual and most attractive feature is a garden dining room, massive areas of glass tastefully softened by quality drapes. Our dinner was excellent and the table d'hôte offered a good choice of courses with the additional selection of an à la carte menu also available. Much has changed here over the last two years and, in all respects, it is for the better. Special mention must be made of the bedrooms. Each is individually named after an English garden flower and decorated by the Laura Ashley design consultancy. Because the hotel is much patronised by the parents of boys at Sherborne School, we would advise advance booking during term-time. A prime objective of the staff here is to ensure that the same personal service is given to the relaxing holidaymaker, the busy executive (for whom telex is available) and to all guests at receptions and other functions. Sherborne has the greatest wealth of medieval buildings in Dorset and it provides a striking contrast with the bustle of Yeovil, a short distance away and just across the border with Somerset. Between the two, visitors have numerous opportunities to visit both ancient and modern buildings: Sherborne Abbey with nearby almshouses and a museum devoted to local history, Yeovil with an intriguing mixture of traditional and contemporary industries.

Bed and Breakfast from £72.50 (Single)
Bed and Breakfast from £49.00 (Twin) pp
Lunch from £12.00 and A La Carte
Afternoon Tea from £4.50
Dinner from £20.00 and A La Carte
Gratuities at Guest's Discretion

VAT inclusive. Credit Cards—Access, Visa
5 Double, 4 Twin, 6 Single Bedrooms
All Rooms with Private Bathroom, TV, Telephone, Radio, Baby-listening, Tea and Coffee-making Facilities, Trouser Press, Hairdryer. Open all Year

Fully Licensed. Full Central Heating
Cocktail Bar. Conference Facilities
Children catered for. Dogs not allowed
Parking Facilities. Nearby: Tennis, Putting, Squash, Badminton, Swimming, Solarium, Sauna, Golf, Fishing, Riding

Section 1: Dorset

Studland Bay—Knoll House Hotel Studland, Swanage, Dorset. BH19 3AH.
Tel 092944 251. Fax 092944 423

For over thirty years the Ferguson family have run this fine independent country house hotel. It enjoys a unique position on the Dorset Heritage coast and, as development elsewhere along our coast line increases from year to year, the long sandy beach and unspoilt open hinterland of the Isle of Purbeck become more and more attractive. Here, with National Trust land on all sides, you will find in Knoll House an oasis for rest, recreation, civilized comfort and, above all, a relaxed, friendly atmosphere with plenty of open space. Indoors, a Health Spa with plunge pool, jacuzzi, sauna, Turkish steam room, solarium and gym. Outdoors, a large heated pool, two hard tennis courts, a nine-acre private golf course, delightful gardens with direct access to Studland's famous three mile beach, one of the cleanest and safest in Britain. Every generation will find holiday fulfilment; many grandparents return with their extended families. The menus are always in tune with the seasons in their variety; the food and wine list at Knoll House are remarkably good. Important amenities for families with young children are the separate children's dining room with its own kitchen, menus and helpful staff, a superb adventure playground with its famous pirates' ship, games rooms and nursery, self-service laundry and airing room. The extensive grounds spell freedom and safety for youngsters; there is sufficient space for all ages to co-exist happily together. It is hardly surprising that Knoll House is one of the best known hotels in Britain, loved by young and old alike.

Weekly Terms from £470.00 Full Board	20 Twin, 30 Single Bedrooms. Many ground floor rooms.	Open from Easter to end of October
Daily Terms from £67.00 Half Board		Residential and Restaurant Licence
Bed and Breakfast from £59.00	30 Family Suites. 56 Private Bathrooms	Part CH. Cocktail Bar. TV Lounge. 3
Lunch £15.00 Table D'Hôte	All Rooms with Telephone	Games Rooms. Children's Dining Room.
Dinner £17.00 Table D'Hôte	Hairdryer available on Request	Baby-listening by evening staff. Fashion
No Service Charge. VAT inclusive	TV for Hire. Radio on loan	Boutique. Dogs welcome. Parking Facilities

Studland Bay—The Manor House Beach Road, Studland, Near Swanage
Dorset. BH19 3AU. Tel 092944 288

Since 1950, this charming and romantic old Gothic manor house has been the home of the Rose family. The oldest part of the present building dates from *circa* 1750 and in the early 1800s many additions and embellishments were made to the original structure. While providing all the amenities of a first-class hotel, it is the Roses' aim to maintain the comforts and atmosphere of a country house of bygone days. How well they have succeeded! Nestling in the heart of the unspoilt village of Studland, The Manor, with its sixteen acres of secluded gardens and grounds, overlooks a magnificent seascape across the bay to Bournemouth and the Isle of Wight. The beach and safe sea-bathing are but a few minutes' walk from the house and three miles away is Poole Harbour with a wealth of opportunity for the boating and sailing enthusiast. Inside The Manor, the Roses have preserved the character and charm through tasteful furnishings while adding such modern amenities as central heating and private bathrooms in most of the charming bedrooms. In the dining room, with its interesting medieval carvings and Elizabethan capitals, we enjoyed first-class *cuisine* and cellar. Fresh local seafood is always featured on the menu. Like the dining room the main lounge looks out over the lawns to the sea and the oak-panelled residents' bar with its Victorian prints of Dorset scenes is a popular meeting place before and after meals.

Weekly Terms from £270.00	6 Family Rooms. 2 Suites	Residential and Restaurant Licence
Daily Terms from £46.00	4 Double, 6 Twin Bedrooms	Full Central Heating. Cocktail Bar
Bed and Breakfast from £28.50	13 Private Bathrooms	Children over 5 years catered for
Bar Lunch from £3.50	5 Private Shower Rooms	Dogs allowed but not in Public Rooms
Afternoon Tea from £1.50	All Rooms with colour TV, Radio, Tea and Coffee-making Facilities, direct dial telephone, Hairdryer	Parking Facilities. 2 Hard Tennis Courts, Croquet. Nearby: Putting, Golf, Riding, Sailing, Windsurfing, Water Skiing, Coastal Walks, Nature Reserves
Dinner from £18.50 Table d'Hôte		
Service included. VAT inclusive		
Credit Cards—Access, Visa	Open 31st January to 17th December	

Section 1: Dorset

Wareham—Kemps Country House Hotel and Restaurant
East Stoke, Dorset. BH20 6AL. Tel 0929 462563. Fax 0929 405287

Originally built as a Victorian rectory, Kemps is situated in open countryside rising from the valley of the Frome, with lovely views over the Purbeck Hills. We received a most warm and courteous reception from the owner, Paul Warren, whose wife directs her skills mainly towards the restaurant. This is an area of the hotel enjoying the highest reputation, based on imaginative use of fresh local produce and reflected in a large number of regular visitors. There is no doubt that the Warren family is doing more than maintaining the excellent standards of décor, service and comfort for which Kemps is justly famous: a new extension has been completed during 1989 providing luxurious bedrooms and a function room with its own kitchen and bar, which were most impressive. The interior of the hotel is pristine, with Sanderson wallpapers and matching curtains, and the Victorian atmosphere carefully preserved in the fittings and furnishings of the public rooms. In particular, the colour scheme and quality tableware in the restaurant evidences the superior standards achieved. Too numerous to itemise are the small touches of thoughtful consideration that can make so large a contribution to a guest's overall relaxation and enjoyment. Beside the Country House is a separate coach house, converted to include four *en suite* rooms. Close by are picturesque Dorset villages, superb beaches at Studland, National Trust coastal walks and a wide range of sports facilities. Three beautiful golf courses are only a few minutes' drive away.

Weekly Terms from £227.50
Daily Terms from £45.00
Bed and Breakfast from £27.50
Lunch from £7.95 and A La Carte
Dinner from £16.95 and A La Carte
Gratuities at Guest's Discretion
VAT inclusive. Credit Cards—Access, American Express, Diners Club, Visa

4 Family Rooms. 9 Double, 2 Twin Bedrooms. 11 Private Bathrooms
3 Private Shower Rooms
(1 Four-Poster and 1 Half Tester with Whirlpool Baths)
All Rooms with TV, Telephone, Tea and Coffee-making Facilities, Baby-listening
Open all Year

Residential and Restaurant Licence
Full Central Heating. Cocktail Bar
Conference Facilities.
Dogs not allowed
Children catered for. Parking Facilities
Nearby: Tennis, Squash, Swimming, Golf, Fishing, Riding, Sailing, Windsurfing, Water Skiing

Near Weymouth, Moonfleet—Moonfleet Manor Moonfleet, Near Weymouth, Dorset. DT3 4ED. Tel 0305 786948

The name 'Moonfleet' immediately conjures up the eponymous tale of smuggling and adventure set on the Dorset coast. Moonfleet Manor was featured in the story and the summer house referred to in the book can still be found in the grounds. The manor house offers its present day visitors scope to exercise not only their imaginations, but also their physical skills, for it is now run as a superb hotel, where the emphasis is on fun and fitness for all age groups. Jan and Bruce Hemingway, the proprietors for the past twenty years, have developed a wide choice of facilities, including an indoor swimming pool and children's learning pool, a sauna, a gymnasium, a games room, two squash courts, two tennis courts, two full-sized snooker tables and a large sandpit. A four rink, indoor bowls hall, with an adjoining lounge bar which overlooks the playing area, is a recent addition to this impressive list of amenities, as is the two lane nine pin automatic skittles imported from Germany. Everything for holiday enjoyment has been thought of here: the public rooms are very spacious and well furnished and include the Cellar Bar with its discreet discotheque. The magnificent view from our balcony window over Chesil Bank was a reminder that the beautiful coastline and lush countryside of Dorset was awaiting discovery the following day. The 18th century Coach House, to the west of the main house, has been fully restored and converted to three 'cottages', each with 2 bedrooms and open-plan lounge/kitchenette, to be used as either hotel or self-catering accommodation.

Weekly Terms from £250.00
Daily Terms from £39.00
Bed and Breakfast from £35.00
Bar Lunch from £2.50. Lunch from £7.50
Dinner from £11.50 and A La Carte
Gratuities at Guest's Discretion

Credit Cards—Access, American Express, Visa. 9 Family Rooms. 16 Double, 6 Twin, 6 Single Bedrooms. 37 Private Bathrooms
All Rooms with TV, Telephone, Radio, Baby-listening, Tea and Coffee-making Facilities. 2 Rooms with Hairdryer, Trouser

Press. 2 Ground Floor Rooms, suitable for disabled Guests. 1 Four Poster Room.
Open all Year. Fully Licensed
Cocktail Bar. Lift. Games Room.
Conference Facilities. Children catered for.
Dogs not allowed. Parking Facilities

Section 1: Somerset

Alcombe, Near Minehead—Alcombe House Hotel
Alcombe, near Minehead, Somerset. TA24 6BG. Tel 064370 5130

Right on the edge of Exmoor, just one mile from the medieval village of Dunster with its magnificent castle and yarn market, lies Alcombe House Hotel. Set on the A39, the hotel is in the centre of the delightful little village of Alcombe which has a history dating back to the 14th Century, and many of its cottages housed the Castle's servants in bygone days. Alcombe House is a Grade II listed Georgian building and its interior has been refurbished to provide 20th Century comfort whilst retaining its Georgian appeal. There is an air of calm and restfulness throughout the hotel and because the maximum number of guests taken at any time is just twelve, all residents are assured of personal and attentive service. Lyn Stevens, the friendly owner, endeavours to make her visitors feel as though they are staying in a gracious private house and old fashioned courtesy and friendliness are assured. This homely, companionable retreat with a restful sitting room, a cosy well-stocked bar, a good spread of periodicals, offers excellent cuisine in the ultimate candle-lit Dining Room, where we enjoyed delicious home-made soup, breast of duck with mulberry and port sauce and exquisite gingersnap baskets filled with strawberries and cream. The six *en suite* bedrooms, ranging in style from the spacious and elegant to the old world charm of chintz, oak beams and sloping ceilings, are all well appointed. Having travelled extensively throughout the world Lyn Stevens has an awareness of the high standards of comfort and attention to detail today's traveller expects. She makes her guest feel truly at home and is happy to advise on scenic excursions.

All terms pertaining to 1992
Weekly Terms from £215.00
Daily Terms from £35.00
Room and Breakfast from £23.00
Dinner from £16.50 Table d'Hôte
Gratuities at Guest's discretion

VAT inclusive. No Credit Cards
4 Double, 2 Twin Bedrooms
5 Private Bathrooms. 1 Private Shower Room. All Rooms with TV, Tea and Coffee-making Facilities, Hairdryer
Open from March to 1st January

Residential and Restaurant Licence
Part Central Heating
Dogs allowed by arrangement
Parking Facilities
Nearby: Solarium, Sauna, Golf, Fishing, Riding

Near Bridgwater, North Petherton—The Walnut Tree Inn
North Petherton, Somerset. TA6 6QA. Tel 0278 662255. Fax 0278 663946

Coaching inns have long played an important part in the national life, for they have, for centuries, provided shelter for weary travellers, as well as a meeting place for the local community. Many still function in these ways today, and we found a perfect example in the little Somerset village of North Petherton. The Walnut Tree Inn started life in the nineteenth century, but rarely in its history, we think, can it have offered such attractive accommodation, mouth watering food and welcoming hospitality as it does now. Richard and Hilary Goulden are exceedingly amiable hosts and one is made to feel immediately at home in the pleasant reception lounge, the bar and the *Cottage* grill room, which are warmed by log fires in winter and decorated with flowers and green plants in summer. The bedrooms, suite and four-poster room are spacious and individually furnished in country style–each fully equipped with a private bathroom, colour television, beverage-making facilities and even electric blankets and a writing-desk. In the air conditioned *Sedgemoor* restaurant, soft lighting and a warm colour scheme create a relaxed atmosphere in which to enjoy superb dishes created from Somerset produce, including duck, salmon, trout and locally grown vegetables. Upstairs, the *Quantock Suite* provides facilities for conferences and wedding receptions for up to seventy people. You will find this delightful haven of hospitality on the A38 Taunton to Bristol road: it is easily accessible, being only one mile from Exit 24 of the M5 motorway.

Bed and Breakfast from £70.00
(Twin/Double)
£48.00 (Single)
Bar Meal from £3.50
Lunch from £6.50 and A La Carte
Afternoon Tea from £2.50
Dinner from £12.00 and A La Carte
Gratuities at Guest's Discretion

VAT inclusive.
Credit Cards—Access, American Express, Diners Club, Visa
1 Suite. 20 Double, 5 Twin, 2 Single Bedrooms
All Rooms with Private Bath/Shower Room, TV, Telephone, Radio, Baby-listening, Hairdryer, Tea and

Coffee-making Facilities
21 Rooms with Trouser Press
Open all Year. Fully Licensed.
Full Central Heating. Conference Facilities
Children catered for. Dogs by request only.
Parking Facilities.
Night Porter. Solarium.
Nearby: Health Club, Golf, Fishing, Riding

Section 1: Somerset

Nr Cheddar—Daneswood House Hotel and Restaurant
Shipham, Near Cheddar, Somerset.
Tel 0934 84 3145. Fax 0934 84 3824

When the Domesday Book was compiled the village was known as 'Cipeham', meaning 'Sheep Village', reflecting the main occupation of the area 900 years ago. Visitors to Shipham must still love the rural charms of this broad band of the Mendip Hills. The thirty-six mile stretch of the Mendip Way, from Weston-super-Mare to Wells and beyond, passes through this tranquil village. Do halt here, though, for Daneswood House has a glorious position and a husband and wife team who are making quite a name for themselves for the high standards they have set. Having called here, ourselves, for an excellent dinner and a look around, we would stress that Daneswood is certainly not only a place in which to dine and move on. Essentially she must be lived in. Inspect the bedrooms yourself—they are so restful and complete for comfort and you will wish to stay for at least a day or two. The honeymoon suite has a king-size bed, sunken bath, Victorian love seat and many delightful accessories. All the rooms have private facilities and a wide range of modern etceteras, including satellite television. Meals at Daneswood House are taken in three rooms which adjoin each other—the restaurant, the charming breakfast room and the air-conditioned conservatory. There is also an attractive lounge/bar. When the weather permits there is a barbecue, with tables and chairs, for meals in the alfresco style. It is all so pleasantly relaxed. You will find five golf courses in the area, plus fishing, tennis, yachting and plenty to do on horseback, in car, or afoot. Daneswood House is very, very English: in its character, in its fare, as well as in the welcome one receives from David and Elise Hodges.

Terms on Application
Special Breaks available
Dinner A La Carte or Table D'Hôte
Restaurant open to Non Residents
(Monday to Saturday, and Sunday Lunch)

Credit Cards— Access, American Express, Diners Club, Visa
All Rooms with Private Bathroom, TV, Telephone, Tea and Coffee-making Facilities, Hairdryer, Trouser Press
Full Central Heating

Special rates by arrangement for children sharing parent's room
Dogs by special arrangement
Conference Facilities
Parking Facilities

Section 1: Somerset

Dulverton–Ashwick House Hotel
Dulverton, Somerset TA22 9QD. Tel 0398 23868

Built at the turn of the century for a wealthy Bristol business man, Ashwick House offers spacious and comfortable accommodation in an atmosphere of peace and quiet. This charming Edwardian Country estate with six acres of beautiful ground is situated over 1,000 foot up on the hills of Exmoor overlooking the wooded Barle Valley. Inside there is a baronial hall, with its long broad gallery and log fire which is highlighted by an original William Morris wallpaper over ninety years old. Many of the bedrooms enjoy breathtaking views and are generously equipped with many thoughtful touches. As Ashwick House is a small hotel, private parties, weddings and business functions are usually given the exclusive use of the hotel. Friendly and attentive service and the high standards of food and wine, make this lovely old house as distinctive for company use as it is attractive for the holidaymaker. It stands within this national park close to the Somerset/Devon county boarder, ideally located for scenic walks and many drives off the busy highways.

Daily Terms from £49.50 per person (DB&B)
Bed and Breakfast from £37.00 per person
Lunch from £12.75 Table D'Hôte
Afternoon Tea from £1.75
Dinner from £19.75 Table D'Hôte
Gratuities at Guest's Discretion.
VAT inclusive

No Credit Cards accepted
4 Double, 2 Twin Bedrooms
All Rooms with Private Bathroom, TV, Telephone, Radio, Trouser-Press, Hairdryer, Fresh Fruit, Cassette Recorder, Fresh Flowers, Talking Scales
Open all year
Residential Licence

Full Central Heating
Cocktail Bar.
Conference Facilities
Children over 8 years catered for.
Dogs not allowed.
Parking Facilities
Solarium
Nearby: Riding

Dulverton—The Lion Hotel Bank Square, Dulverton, Somerset. TA22 9BU.
Tel 0398 23444

The character of Dulverton has been fashioned from the charming Barle valley in which it sits, the fishing this provides, and the fact this is an important stepping-off point for the Exmoor National Park and the Lorna Doone country. Her narrow streets and passageways are a great attraction, yet it is with her surroundings that one quite falls in love, for at Dulverton there are countless opportunities for exploration: Tarr Steps, Winsford, Hele, Barle and Bury Bridges, are all within walking range. The only hotel in this small, cosy town is a real 'find' for anyone seeking high standards of food and comfort and authentic old-world atmosphere. The Lion Hotel has stood in Bank Square for nearly 500 years and has played host to both the high and the humble in its history. The Duke of Wellington is known to have stayed there. For the antiquarian, especially, here, then, is the genuine article. The tone of the hotel today is spot on, for the modern comforts in no way detract from the traditional rural charm of The Lion. The *en suite* bedrooms may be superior in their equipment, but there is nothing fancifully modern about this hotel. And whilst the hotel has much to exhibit of the past, there is evidence always of Dulverton's present. For here the talk is of recreational fly fishing, rough shooting, clay pidgeon shooting, bird watching and walking; of Moorland Rover Tours; even of hot air balloon flights, all of which are arranged by the hotel for its guests.

Daily Terms from £34.50
Bed and Breakfast from £19.50
Bar Meals from £1.50
Daily Lunch Specials available
Dinner from £16.50
Gratuities at Guest's Discretion

1 Family Room. 4 Double, 4 Twin, 3 Single Bedrooms. All Rooms with Bath and Shower Room, TV, Telephone, Tea and Coffee-making Facilities.
Open all year including Christmas and New Year

Residential and Restaurant Licence
Full Central Heating. TV Lounge
Children catered for. Dogs allowed
Parking Facilities
Nearby: Tennis, Squash, Swimming, Golf, Fishing, Riding, Sailing, Shooting

Section 1: Somerset

Dunster—Exmoor House Hotel
West Street, Dunster, Somerset. TA24 6SN. Tel 0643 821268

To the sportsman Exmoor spells paradise, with its fishing, trekking and rough shooting. In feudal Dunster we stayed in a marvellous little place, Exmoor House Hotel, which is not only ideally suited as a base for these pursuits, but also for touring the beauties of Somerset and North Devon. The owners have created a 'home from home' atmosphere which is greatly appreciated by all who stay at Exmoor House. One couple told us, 'We've been here for one week and haven't used our car once. There are so many wonderful walks starting from the front door.' It is quite evident that this Grade II Georgian building is a great attraction in this area. Comfortable, spacious rooms, which are light and airy in summer and warmed by central heating in winter, offer homely comfort. There are seven double (or twin) bedrooms, all with *en suite* facilities. In addition, you will find a residents' Drawing Room, a Garden lounge, an attractive walled garden and a delightful candlelit Dining Room. The latter is the scene of happy evenings with friendly company. Phyl and Brendan Lally, the enthusiastic and caring hosts, ensure that guests have every attention, excellent food served in a relaxed atmosphere with a wide repertoire of wholesome country fare. Imaginative specialities using fresh West Country produce from first class suppliers are complemented by an extensive wine list. With courtesy and understanding Brendan Lally makes each guest feel particularly welcome. The enthusiastic couple give of their utmost skill and dedication to make your stay a pleasant and memorable experience.

Weekly Terms (Half Board) from £231.00	Diners Club, Visa. Non-smokers only	Open from February to November
Daily Terms from £34.00 (Bargain Break)	4 Double, 3 Twin Bedrooms	(also Dunster Candlelight Weekend (early
Bed and Breakfast from £23.00	All rooms with Private Bath/Shower Rooms	December). Residential/Restaurant
Dinner from £14.50 Table D'Hôte	1 Bathroom/Shower Room (General use)	Licence. Drawing Room with TV. Dogs
Service Charge and VAT inclusive	All Rooms with TV and Radio	allowed by prior Arrangement. Street
Credit Cards—Access, American Express,	Hairdryer available on Request	Parking. Nearby: Tennis, Golf, Fishing

Exebridge—Anchor Inn Hotel
Exebridge, Dulverton, Somerset. TA22 9AZ. Tel 0398 23433

Exmoor is a very private, very beautiful place. Bordered by tiny, neatly hedged fields and meadows, the land is gently creased by deeply wooded valleys and criss-crossed by sparkling rivers and streams. An unforgettable stay at the Anchor Inn at Exebridge will help you unlock its secret beauty. The Anchor is a 17th Century Coaching Inn nestling on the banks of the River Exe, which rises high on Exmoor. Mentioned in R D Blackmore's 'Lorna Doone', this old Inn has been expertly modernised to provide the very best of comfort and excellent *cuisine*, yet retains all its old world charm and atmosphere. Stopping for an excellent lunch, the welcome we received from John and Judy Phripp, the owners, could not have been more warm and friendly, and the Inn's beautiful setting with its riverbank gardens is outstanding. Their Stable Restaurant provides a delicious array of home-cooked fare, with local specialities including venison and trout, accompanied by fresh vegetables from local suppliers. For lighter meals, the comprehensive bar menu offers an unusually wide selection and choice. Whether you wish to spend your time exploring the Moor, following the magnificent North Devon Coast, fishing, riding, shooting or visiting one of the many National Trust properties close at hand, or just relaxing, the Anchor Inn at Exebridge can be your stepping stone to all these pursuits and many, many more. This is one of the best ways we know to find the true Exmoor; secret valleys, whispering streams, narrow paths which unfold over old stone bridges. John and Judy will be delighted to share their beautiful countryside and surroundings with you.

Weekly Terms from £250.00 (£265.00	Gratuities at Guest's Discretion	Radio, Tea and Coffee-making Facilities.
Superior). Bed and Breakfast from £32.00	VAT inclusive. Credit Card—Access, Visa,	Open all Year. Fully Licensed. Full CH. TV
Bar Lunch from £2.00	3 Double, 3 Twin Bedrooms	Lounge. Games Room. Conference
Lunch from £9.50 and A La Carte	2 Private Bathrooms. 4 Private Shower	Facilities. Children catered for. Dogs
Dinner from £15.95 and A La Carte	Rooms. All Rooms with TV, Telephone,	allowed. Parking Facilities. Fishing

Section 1: Somerset

Exford—The Crown Hotel.
Exford, Near Minehead, Somerset. TA24 7PP. Tel 064 383 554. Fax 064 383 628

The all-season appeal of Exford–it is practically in the centre of the moor–is for country life lovers, and with hunting, hacking, fishing, rough shooting and walking available at the front door, it is all a question of tearing oneself away from the warmth and hospitality of The Crown. Many will find that exceedingly difficult. Suffice it to say that the furnishings and décor never slip below excellence and the bedrooms, each with bathroom *en suite*, colour television, tea and coffee-making facilities, radio, telephone, hairdryer and trouser press. The *cuisine* here is excellent: a gourmet standard, three-course menu, which is changed daily, is offered and the produce used is always very fresh. Rural pursuits are very much to the fore here. Guests are welcome to bring their dogs and even their horses (the hotel offers stabling). The Crown also has an international reputation as a centre for hunting and holiday packages are arranged for those who like to participate in this sport. If you would appreciate living in a beautifully maintained seventeenth-century coaching inn and enjoying country life, then you should not overlook this delightful hotel.

Bargain Breaks all year
Bed and Breakfast from £30.70
Bar Meal from £1.50
Afternoon Tea from £0.70
Dinner from £12.95 and A La Carte
Gratuities at Guest's Discretion.
VAT inclusive

Credit Cards—Access, Visa
2 Family Rooms. 8 Doubles, 1 Single, 5 Twin Bedrooms
All Rooms with Private Bathroom, TV, Telephone, Radio, Tea and Coffee-making Facilities, Hairdryer, Trouser Press
Open all Year. Fully Licensed.

Full Central Heating. Cocktail Bar.
Dogs allowed.
Parking Facilities
Nearby: Tennis, Putting, Squash, Badminton, Swimming, Solarium, Sauna, Golf, Fishing, Sailing, Windsurfing, Water Skiing, Shooting, Hunting

Near Frome, Nunney—The George at Nunney
Church Street, Nunney, Near Frome, Somerset. BA11 4LW. Tel 0373 836458/836565

On the eastern fringe of the Mendip hills is situated the picturesque village of Nunney, one of England's oldest hamlets. It is a place steeped in history–the Saxons and the Romans left their marks and, later, Cromwell's soldiers laid siege here. Nevertheless, the fourteenth-century moated castle still stands in all its ruined splendour, probably the most impressive example of its kind in Somerset. There is a profusion of old houses and the village has now been declared a conservation area, thus preserving it for posterity. It was in this quiet backwater that we made a real find, The George at Nunney, and became acquainted with David and Marjorie Page, the charming and efficient hosts. The inn dates back to the fourteenth century, but it has been modernised with the utmost taste, retaining all the original charm and character and yet ensuring that guests will lack no comfort. The ten bedrooms have been decorated in a distinctive style, each with either private or *en suite* bath or shower room. Colour televisions, in-house movies, telephones and tea-making facilities are standard in all rooms and, for a little extra, you can enjoy the luxury of a four-poster bed. The dining room is delightful, with a wide ranging menu to suit every taste. There is also a large selection of meals in the Bars for those wishing to be less formal. Do enquire about the very modestly priced bargain breaks (including Christmas) which you can enjoy here and treat yourself to a few days away from it all.

Terms on Application
Bargain Breaks from £15.00 per person per night
Gratuities at Guest's Discretion. VAT inclusive.
Credit Cards—Access, Visa

3 Family Rooms, 3 Double, 4 Twin Bedrooms. 6 Private Bathrooms.
4 Private Shower Rooms
All Rooms with TV, Telephone, Tea and Coffee-making Facilities, Baby-listening, Hairdryer. (1 Room with 4-poster Bed)

Open all Year. Fully Licensed
Regular dinner dances
Full Central Heating. Cocktail Bars
Dogs allowed by arrangement.
Parking Facilities
Nearby: Golf, Riding, Fishing, Shooting

Section 1: Somerset

Holford—Combe House Hotel
Holford, Bridgwater, Somerset. TA5 1RZ.
Telephone 027 874 382

At the foot of the Quantock Hills, famed for their pathways, ponies and red deer, and only three miles from Bridgwater Bay, lies a seventeenth-century house, once a Tannery. Still retaining its huge water-wheel (the third largest in the country), this is Combe House, set amidst the romantic and beautiful open countryside of Butterfly Combe. For over ten years this long and low country-house hotel has received sympathetic decoration and refurbishment, in the cottage style, by the resident Danish proprietor family of the Bjergfelt's. Although in a sheltered spot, Combe House is 500 feet above sea level, affording easy ascent to Danesboro' Triscombe Stone and Willsneck, the highest points in the Quantock Hills with distant sea views of the Welsh coast. Within the hotel's five acres of gardens and grounds, the mill stream still flows between fine lawns, under the shade of a giant monkey-puzzle tree and an ancient yew. Inside the beamed building, with its charming collection of pictures, porcelain and period furniture, guests can enjoy a heated indoor swimming-pool, with sauna and solarium, as alternative leisure to riding, croquet or tennis on the hard court. There is a relaxed and comfortable atmosphere permeating the bedrooms and all the public rooms. In the well-appointed dining-room one can rely on sound country fare, based on fresh garden vegetables, the courtesy of old-fashioned service and, yes, genuine Somerset cream.

Weekly Terms from £248.00
Daily Terms from £35.00
Bed and Breakfast from £28.00
Bar Meal from £3.00
Afternoon Tea from £3.00
Dinner from £14.50 Table D'Hôte
Gratuities at Guest's Discretion.
VAT inclusive
Credit Cards—Access, American Express, Visa

2 Family Rooms
5 Double, 8 Twin, 5 Single Bedrooms
17 Rooms with Private Bathrooms
TV, Telephone, Tea and Coffee-making facilities in all rooms
Radio, Baby-listening, Trouser Press and Hairdryer available on Request
Open from Mid March to November
Residential and Restaurant Licence
Full Central Heating. Cocktail Bar

Small Conference Facilities
Dogs allowed in some bedrooms, not in Public Room except Bar
Parking Facilities
Hard Tennis Court, Croquet, Indoor Heated Swimming Pool, Solarium, Sauna.
Nearby: Squash, Badminton, Golf, Fishing, Riding, Sailing, Windsurfing, Water Skiing, Shooting

Section 1: Somerset

Kilve—Meadow House
Sea Lane, Kilve, Bridgwater, Somerset. TA5 1EG.
Tel 027874 546 Fax 027874 663

This veritable haven of tranquillity offers a warm, personal welcome of a quality to match the unspoilt charm of the surrounding countryside and coastline with its beautiful cliffside walks. Visitors will immediately be captivated by this former Georgian Rectory, by the eight acres of grounds including private stream side walks, the scenic views and the dramatic beach. This is famous for its fossils and has even had a poem written about it by Wordsworth. Guests receive every consideration from the friendly resident hosts, Howard and Judith Wyer-Roberts, with fresh flowers, mineral water, home-made biscuits, hair dryers, filter and decaffeinated coffees supplementing the usual television and telephone. Meals are English traditional and include a number of Victorian and earlier specialities. Extensive use is made of local produce and many fruits and vegetables are provided from the kitchen garden. Their cellar houses many fine wines with Rhones and Clarets particularly well represented and amongst its many accolades was the recent 'West Country Best Cellar of the Year' Award. Within the luxuriously furnished house there is a splendid library, drawing room, both with log fires, and the candlelit dining room. Breakfast and Dinner may be served in the conservatory, overlooking a rockery, with French windows leading to the terrace, croquet lawn and gardens. Meadow House is the perfect base for exploring the surrounding district with many National Trust properties, the beautiful village of Dunster and the 265 square miles of Exmoor, home of red deer, grouse, ponies and sheep.

Special 'Off Season' Terms available
Weekly Terms from £650.00 (Double)
Daily Terms from £116.00 (Double)
Bed and Breakfast from £78.00 (Double)/£55.00 (Single)
Dinner £19.00 Table D'Hôte (open to non residents).
Service and VAT inclusive

Credit Cards—Access, American Express, Visa.
4 Suites. 5 Double Bedrooms
(Twin Bedrooms available on Request)
8 En Suite Bathrooms
1 Bedroom with Private Bathroom
All Rooms with TV, Radio, Tea and Coffee-making Facilities, Hairdryer, Flowers, Mineral Water

8 Rooms with Telephone. Open all year
Residential and Restaurant Licence
Conference Facilities. Children and Dogs by arrangement. Ample Parking. Croquet, Extensive gardens, pond, nature walks by stream within the property
Nearby: Golf, Fishing, Riding, Clay pigeon shooting, Windsurfing, Shooting, Walking

Section 1: Somerset

Ilminster—The Shrubbery Hotel
Ilminster, Somerset. TA19 9AR. Tel 0460 52108. Fax 0460 53660

Although The Shrubbery is the venue for most of the local organisations and groups, in their thirty years here Mr and Mrs Stuart Shepherd have achieved a perfect balance between public function and the special needs of individual guests. Conveniently situated at the half-way stage between London and Lands End, and with a high reputation for comfort and conviviality, it is little wonder that the hotel is an ever-popular rendezvous with UK tourists and overseas visitors. Guests making repeated return bookings are testimony to, amongst other things, the superb *cuisine* at value-for-money prices. Succulently-served fish, meat and fowl are accompanied by the finest ingredients in season, vegetarians are not forgotten, and all dishes are synonymous with healthy eating. The Shrubbery's cellar includes wines from all around the world and anyone requiring a light lunch can obtain this at a competitive price in the spacious lounge bar. Business seminars are catered for and a magnificent ballroom can accommodate 200 guests. Within the delightful Victorian Country House there are fourteen charming *en suite* bedrooms, most with commanding views of the fine Somerset countryside, and six of them garden bedrooms (three on the ground floor). Outside the hotel there is the tranquillity of terraced sun-trap lawns, into which is set a 25-metre heated open-air swimming-pool. This whole area enjoys a moderate climate and, within a five-mile radius, guests have the sixteenth century Barrington Court and curiously-named Cricket St Thomas Wildlife Park to visit in the locality.

Weekly Terms from £280.00	6 Double, 1 Single, 7 Twin (including 2 Family) Bedrooms	Open all year. Fully Licensed. Full Central Heating. Cocktail Bar. TV Lounge
Daily Terms from £45.00	All Rooms have private Bath and Shower Room, TV, Telephone, Radio, Baby-listening, Tea and Coffee-making Facilities. Hairdryer available on request. Mini Bars in Executive Rooms	Conference Facilities. Children catered for. Dogs allowed. Parking Facilities. Outdoor heated Swimming Pool, Fishing from Hotel Boat at Lyme Regis. Nearby: Tennis, Squash, Solarium, Sauna, Golf, Riding
Bed and Breakfast from £35.00		
Bar Lunch from £3.50. Lunch from £10.00		
Bar Supper from £5.00. Dinner from £15.00		
Gratuities at Guest's Discretion. VAT inclusive. All major credit cards accepted		

Minehead—The Beacon Country House Hotel
Beacon Road, Minehead, Somerset. TA24 5SD. Tel 0643 703476

At the beginning of this century, the Beacon was regarded by the natives of Minehead as one of the best built and most beautifully furnished houses in the town. Its original owner, one of the country's leading whisky distillers, insisted on what, in favoured Edwardian houses, was known as the 'quality'. Today, this lovely house retains its quality and characteristics. Around it are twenty acres of attractive lawns and landscaped gardens with a swimming pool. There is a resident badger colony here, foxes call at night, and stables and a livery service are adjacent to the hotel. If this were not enough, the views across a valley one way and of Minehead another are a magnificent 'extra', for which there is no added charge! Within, there are eight luxury bedrooms, all *en suite*, and with direct-dial telephone, television and the last word in comfort. And withal, the family owners have a special formula in that everyone should feel totally at home and receive the most personal attention. Few hotels in our experience, have such an all year round appeal. Exmoor as one's background and the sea as one's footstool—we could hibernate happily, knowing that we should always be warm, comfortable and welcome. Yet there is, perhaps, an even bigger attraction. The food draws discerning diners from far and wide. Traditional French specialities and regional dishes appear on the menu and every dish is cooked individually and with great care. Furthermore, if you have a special preference, or dietary needs, just mention this to the owners and they will see that you are well catered for, too.

Weekly Terms from £315.00	VAT inclusive	Hairdryer available on Request
Bed and Breakfast from £40.00 per room (2 persons)	Credit Cards—Access, Visa	Open all Year. Residential and Restaurant Licence. Full Central Heating. Cocktail Bar
Bar Meal from £1.50. Lunch from £12.95	6 Double, 2 Twin Bedrooms	Children by arrangement. Dogs allowed by Arrangement. Parking Facilities
Dinner from £20.00 A La Carte	6 Private Bathrooms. 2 Private Shower Rooms. All Rooms with TV, Telephone, Radio, Tea and Coffee-making Facilities	Outdoor Swimming Pool, Riding
Gratuities at Guest's Discretion.		

Section 1: Somerset

Minehead—Beaconwood Hotel
Church Road, North Hill, Minehead, Somerset. TA24 5SB. Tel 0643 702032

Even without its two acres of landscaped gardens, grass tennis court and outdoor heated swimming pool, we would be impressed. A most attractive hotel in a location offering absolutely superb views of the Exmoor countryside and the sea in Bridgwater Bay. Nor do the enthusiastic owners rely on these priceless assets to obtain year-round patronage. Good taste is reflected in the colourful yet restful decor, comfortable furnishings and spotless cleanliness. A convivial atmosphere extends from the popular bar, which is just like an old country inn, to the delightful sunlounge with a good supply of contemporary glossy magazines. Chef is Mrs Alison Roberts, of the resident owning couple, who carefully selects fresh produce from the hotel vegetable garden to incorporate into the wholesome and imaginative dishes, complemented by a variety of starters and home made soups, and an attractive sweet trolley, served in the spacious dining room, with its panoramic scenes through elegant wide arches. Of the sixteen bedrooms, all have television, direct-dial telephones, intercom and beverage-making facilities, most have *en suite* bathrooms and several have private south-facing balconies. Four communal rooms, well placed garden furniture and picture windows all enhance the atmosphere of good company and attentive service. Only 100 yards away is the start of the Somerset and North Devon Coastal Path. Beaconwood Hotel has a most competitive tariff and, on the back of the list, they detail no less than thirty local places of interest. The list of sporting and recreational activities is also impressively long.

Weekly Terms from £193.00
Bed and Breakfast from £29.50
Bar Lunch from £2.50
Dinner from £13.50 Table D'Hôte
Service Charge and VAT inclusive
Credit Cards—Access, Visa
2 Family Rooms. 1 Single, 5 Double,

8 Twin Bedrooms. 4 Private Bathrooms
3 Private Shower Rooms
10 Private Bath and Shower Rooms. All Rooms with TV, Tea and Coffee-making Facilities, Telephones, Clock radios, Baby listening. Hairdryers and ironing facilities available on request

Open all Year. Residential Licence.
Cocktail Bar. Conference Facilities.
Children catered for Dogs allowed. Parking Facilities. Grass Tennis Court, Outdoor Heated Swimming Pool
Nearby: Putting, Solarium, Golf, Fishing, Riding, Windsurfing

Minehead—Benares Hotel
Northfield Road, Minehead, Somerset. TA24 5PT. Tel 0643 704911

The Benares Hotel is not an hotel to visit if you wish to swim or play tennis, use a jacuzzi or lift weights, these facilities just do not exist. What does exist, however, is a sublimely comfortable hotel where it is possible to achieve that most difficult goal...relaxation. Peter Maskrey and Ray Thomas have concentrated all their efforts on creating an atmosphere of friendliness, comfort and well-being. During their seven years as proprietors of the Benares Hotel, it has undergone a complete programme of refurbishment and the outcome demonstrates Peter's mastery of his former occupation of many years, that of interior designer. Ray's domain is the kitchen, and from there he produces, daily, a five course dinner with interesting choices to suit both plain and more exotic tastes. The sweet table regularly features up to fourteen different home made puddings. What better way to end a day exploring Exmoor than to return to the Benares Hotel and anticipate the glories of a well cooked dinner followed by a stroll along the promenade before retiring to your bedroom where you are offered the choice of blankets or a duvet. If you are lucky enough to have booked a room with a balcony, now is the time to gaze across the moonlit bay to the Quantock Hills beyond. This, then, certainly is the hotel to choose if you wish to unwind, relax and enjoy calm, efficient, yet unobtrusive service.

Weekly Terms from £305.00
Daily Terms from £46.00
Bed and Breakfast from £35.00
Bar Lunch from £3.00
Afternoon Tea from £1.20
Dinner from £17.00 and A La Carte
Gratuities at Guest's Discretion
VAT inclusive

Credit Cards–Access, American Express, Diners Club, Visa
3 Family Rooms
6 Doubles, 6 Twins, 4 Single Bedrooms
18 Private Bathrooms
1 Private Shower Room
All Rooms with TV, Radio, Telephone, Baby-listening, Tea and Coffee-making Facilities

1 Room with Trouser Press and Hairdryer
Open from 22nd March to 5th November
Residential and Restaurant Licence
Full Central Heating. Cocktail Bar
Dogs allowed. Parking Facilities
Nearby: Tennis, Putting, Swimming, Golf, Fishing, Riding, Sailing, Windsurfing, Shooting

Section 1: Somerset

Minehead—Channel House Hotel
Church Path, Off Northfield Road, Minehead. TA24 5QG.
Tel 0643 703229

It's always a great pleasure for us to report on our stay at Channel House as it offers its guests exceptionally high standards of quality and comfort. The hotel is situated on the lower slopes of Minehead's picturesque North Hill and peacefully stands in two acres of secluded and beautifully maintained gardens from which you can enjoy lovely views of both Exmoor and the sea. On arrival at the hotel you will receive, as we did, a genuinely warm welcome from the resident proprietors, Brian and Jackie Jackman, who will show you to one of their eight delightful bedrooms, all of which have superb *en suite* facilities and lovely views. Each room is individually decorated with delicate pastel shades and furnished to the very highest standards. One easily settles into the relaxed and friendly atmosphere of this hotel. You can unwind in the comfort of the sitting room, or the tastefully furnished cocktail bar, or as we did by strolling around the secluded gardens and enjoying the views. What makes this hotel such a joy to visit is the careful attention Jackie has given to every detail of the impeccable decor, the quality of which is always a topic of conversation amongst fellow guests. Brian and Jackie have in their eight years at Channel House created a country house hotel of the finest quality and have firmly established themselves on the gastronomic map. Brian has a great love and flair for cooking and shops personally each day for fresh local produce from which he creates dishes of rare excellence. Jackie, as well as being a charming hostess produces the most delicious sweets. The menus offer something for everyone incuding vegetarian. Everything is made on the premises, even the bread, which is another of Jackie's talents. In the attractive dining room, Jackie is assisted by one of their three smiling daughters, who together help create the warm and intimate atmosphere that is such a pleasure to experience. We can highly recommend a stay at this really excellent hotel, not only for the superb food and total comfort but also for its excellent position which is perfect for exploring Exmoor and North Hill by car or by foot.

Weekly Terms from £290.00. Daily Terms from £52.50. Bed and Breakfast from £47.50 Daily/£255.00 Weekly Dinner from £16.00 Table d'Hôte Gratuities at Guest's Discretion

VAT inclusive. Credit Cards—Access, Diners Club, Visa.
1 Suite. 2 Double, 5 Twin Bedrooms. All Rooms with Private Bathroom with bath and shower, TV, Telephone, Radio, Tea and Coffee-making Facilities, Hairdryer, personal Ironing centres. Open from March to November and Christmas. Residential Licence. Full CH. Cocktail Bar. Dogs not allowed. Private car park. Night Porter

Section 1: Somerset

Montacute—The King's Arms Inn
Montacute, Somerset. TA15 6UU
Tel 0935 822513

Montacute House is one of the most important country houses in the West Country: it is an example of Tudor domestic architecture at its best and visitors can view a wealth of tapestries, English furniture, heraldic glass, plasterwork and panelling, as well as a trim early Jacobean garden. In the nearby village of Montacute, we have now discovered another gem and we would urge our readers not to miss it, if they enjoy the traditionally warm welcome of an English inn, with first-class cuisine and comfort. The King's Arms Inn is a handsome sixteenth-century building, constructed, like many of the local houses, in Ham stone, which has mellowed beautifully over the centuries. It offers eleven charming bedrooms, each of which has a private bathroom, colour television, a radio/alarm, tea and coffee-making facilities, a refrigerated mini bar and a telephone. Each room has been elegantly decorated with its own individual colour scheme. There are two honeymoon rooms (one of which has a four-poster bed), which have co-ordinated drapes and de luxe facilities. Downstairs, The Windsor Room is a relaxing lounge area in which guests can enjoy pre-dinner drinks and take coffee after their meal. Our dinner was served in the very elegant Abbey Room and we relished every bite. We were particularly impressed, too, with the kindness and courtesy of the staff: the welcome here is truly warm and this speaks volumes about the dedication of the owners. Do try to spend a few days with them: Montacute is an ideal centre for touring the surrounding area, which abounds with country houses, gardens and National Trust properties, and the Dorset coast is a comfortable drive away.

Weekly Terms from £260.00
Daily Terms from £46.00
Bar Meal from £3.95
Afternoon Tea from £2.20
Dinner from £16.00 A La Carte
Gratuities at Guest's Discretion.
VAT inclusive

Credit Cards—Access, American Express, Diners Club, Visa
8 Double, 3 Twin Bedrooms
All Rooms with Private Bathroom, TV, Telephone, Radio, Tea and Coffee-making Facilities, Baby-listening, Mini-bar Hairdryer available on Request
Open all Year.

Residential Licence
Cocktail Bar.
Full Central Heating
Children catered for.
Dogs not allowed
Parking Facilities
Nearby: Squash, Badminton, Shooting

Section 1: Somerset

Minehead—Northfield Hotel Northfield Road, Minehead, Somerset, TA24 5PU. Tel 0643 705155. Fax 0643 707715

We are delighted to observe the current prosperity of this handsome hotel, which is situated in a quiet road from which it takes its name. With Exmoor as one's background and the sea as one's footstool, it is not surprising that so many contented guests have stayed, played and hibernated here over the years. Today, the Northfield ranks in the top echelon of the West Country's hotels. In their search to move standards onwards and upwards, the proprietors have greatly strengthened the Northfield's all-year-round appeal with the addition to the hotel's facilities of the impressive *Dolphin Club*. Within this fine complex is an indoor heated swimming pool, a spa bath, a steam room and a mini-gymnasium and exercise room. There is also the separate *Willow Suite* with bar and dance floor for special celebrations, dinners or weddings, an increased capacity cocktail bar, and large car park within the grounds. To complement the facilities within, there is a lovely two-acre landscaped garden without. The sea, which laps clean, flat sands, lies a mere 100 yards away. A short walk into the town allows one to play tennis and squash, go on fishing and boating trips or hire a horse (this is a splendid area for riding because Exmoor lies so close to the sea). With hearty appetites to cater for, it is not surprising that the chef at Northfield takes his task seriously and is proud of the interesting selection of dishes he provides. Special diets can be catered for by arrangement. This hotel is ideally designed for family holidays, be they long summer vacations or shorter winter breaks.

Weekly Terms from £364.00
Daily Terms from £47.00 (minimum 2 days)
Lunch from £4.00 A La Carte (Monday to Saturdays). Sunday Lunch from £9.75 Table D'Hôte
Dinner from £14.95 Table D'Hôte
Gratuities at Guest's Discretion

Credit Cards—Access, American Express, Diners Club, Visa.
7 Family Rooms. 6 Doubles, 8 Twins, 3 Single Bedrooms. 23 Private Bathrooms. 1 Private Shower Room. All Rooms with TV, In-house Video, Telephone, Radio, Baby-listening, Tea and Coffee-making

Facilities, Hairdryer. Room Service available. Some Rooms with Trouser Press. Open all Year. Fully Licensed. Lift. Full Central Heating. Cocktail Bar. Dogs allowed. Parking Facilities. Putting, Indoor Swimming Pool, Spa Bath, Steam Room, Mini Gymnasium, Sunbed, Solarium

Porlock—The Oaks Hotel
Porlock, Somerset. TA24 8ES. Tel 0643 862265

There are three Porlocks, Porlock itself which nestles at the foot of its famous hill, Porlock Weir and West Porlock, which lies midway between the two and is so small one is apt to pass through it without noticing its existence. We can think of no more charming excuse to stay in Porlock itself than The Oaks Hotel. This beautifully refurbished Edwardian country house stands in a superbly elevated position, surrounded by wide lawns and the majestic trees from which it takes its name. From here, one views the pretty thatched cottages of the village below, the rich Somerset countryside and, beyond, the glistening waters of Porlock Bay. The Oaks is clearly Tim and Anne Riley's love, for the house is filled with quality period furniture, contains every modern necessity and gleams with the care lavished upon it. Log fires flicker a warming welcome, every room is so utterly comfortable, and the bedrooms are as complete in their fitments as one could wish for. Anne's *cuisine* is predominately English, with fish dishes, seasonal game, venison and local Gressingham duckling being specialities. The sweets, too, are mouthwatering and you will find Anne very happy to pander to particular dietary needs. Tim, meanwhile, keeps a cellar of over seventy bins, with wines to suit every taste. And how will you spend your days here? With a hearty English breakfast; a woodland walk on Exmoor, where buzzards soar and wild ponies abound; and return to The Oaks for, perhaps, a drink in anticipation of the dinner to come. You will soon feel on top of the world, but, of course, at The Oaks you very nearly are!

Daily Terms from £50.00
Bed and Breakfast from £37.50
Afternoon Tea from £1.00
Dinner from £19.00
VAT inclusive. 2 Family Rooms
5 Double, 3 Twin Bedrooms

10 Private Bathrooms
10 Private Shower Rooms
All Rooms with TV, Radio, Telephone, Tea and Coffee-making Facilities, Hairdryer
Open all Year
Residential and Restaurant Licence

Full Central Heating. Cocktail Bar
Dogs allowed by Arrangement
Parking Facilities
Nearby: Tennis, Putting, Swimming Pool, Golf, Fishing, Riding, Sailing, Shooting, Hang-gliding

Section 1: Somerset

Porlock Weir—The Anchor Hotel and The Ship Inn
Porlock Weir, Exmoor, Somerset. TA24 8PB.
Tel 0643 862636

Porlock Weir is a small natural harbour with wooded cliffs which overlook Porlock Bay. It is a picturesque spot and ideally situated for those wishing to enjoy the magnificent countryside of Exmoor National Park. The sixteenth-century Ship Inn and the comfortable, nineteenth-century Anchor Hotel are now combined under the ownership of Donald Wade and Pandy Sechiari. The result is a relaxing hostelry, providing friendly hospitality, excellent food and attractive accommodation. The Harbour Restaurant, as its name suggests, overlooks the harbour and provides a cosy setting for candlelit evening meals. It is particularly renowned for its succulent steak and fresh fish dishes. During the high season, the Ship Restaurant is open and, with its beamed ceiling and cottage-style décor, offers an old-world atmosphere in which to enjoy good English fare. In addition, there is a choice of three bars, ranging from the elegance of the Anchor Bar to the traditional friendliness of The Ship's public bar. Comfortable lounge areas and twenty-five well equipped bedrooms (most of the latter have en suite facilities and sea views) complete the accommodation in the hotel. We were most impressed with everything we found here, from the courteous welcome we received when we arrived to our well prepared and expertly served meal in the restaurant. We were able to meet and chat to several fellow guests and discovered that they were all as delighted with the hotel as we were: do seek it out soon.

Weekly Terms from £335.00
Daily Terms from £52.00
Bed and Breakfast from £38.00
Bar Lunch from £3.50
Afternoon Tea from £3.00
Bar Supper from £4.25
Dinner from £17.50 and A La Carte
Service Charge and VAT inclusive

Credit Cards—Access, Visa
3 Family Rooms. 11 Double, 9 Twin, 3 Single Bedrooms.
20 Private Bathrooms.
8 Private Shower Rooms
All Rooms with TV, Telephone, Radio, Baby-listening, Tea and Coffee-making Facilities. 8 Rooms with Hairdryer

Open all Year
Fully Licensed. Full Central Heating
Cocktail Bar. Conference Facilities.
Dogs allowed. Parking Facilities
Nearby: Tennis, Putting, Swimming, Golf, Fishing, Riding, Sailing, Windsurfing, Water Skiing, Shooting, Hang-gliding

Section 1: Somerset

Shepton Mallet—Charlton House Hotel
Charlton Road, Shepton Mallet, Somerset. BA4 4PR. Tel 0749 342008

Take a charming country manor house, built in 1671, and surround it with six acres of well-kept grounds secluded with numerous trees including a 200 year old copper beach, including immaculate lawns, rose gardens, a small lake stocked with trout and a waterfall. Locate it in the Mendip Hills and place it in the capable hands of dynamic hoteliers. The result is a first-class establishment and the sort of hotel we take great pride in recommending–in this instance for a number of consecutive years. The dusty pink *décor* of the restaurant–with a conservatory extension overlooking the gardens–makes a tasteful setting for the silver and crystal, crisp white napery and fresh flowers. We have noted the use of fresh produce on the well-balanced and interesting menu and, in particular, found the choice of sweets as original and mouthwatering as we have seen anywhere. All the bedrooms have *en suite* facilities and each one is furnished in a distinctive style, ranging from light and airy, through four-poster suites to quaint beamed ceilings. The original Manor House itself is listed as being of architectural and historical interest. Not so is their swimming-pool complex, which is built in the Swedish style with adjoining sauna, showers and changing-rooms. Only six miles away is the historic city of Wells, whilst Wookey Hole, Cheddar Gorge, Longleat, East Somerset Steam Railway and the Georgian City of Bath are within easy driving reach.

Daily Terms from £115.00 (Double) (minimum 2 days)
Bed and Breakfast from £90.00 (Double)
Lunch from £14.00 and A La Carte
Dinner from £19.00 and A La Carte
Gratuities at Guest's Discretion
VAT inclusive.
Credit Cards—Access, American Express,

Diners Club, Visa
2 Family Rooms.
2 Single, 10 Double, 3 Twin Bedrooms
All Rooms with Private Bathroom (1 with Shower), TV, Telephone, Radio, Tea and Coffee-making Facilities, Baby-listening, Hairdryer. Open all Year
Residential and Restaurant Licence

Central Heating. Lounge Bar
Conference Facilities.
Dogs allowed by Arrangement.
Parking Facilities
Hard Tennis Court,
Indoor Swimming Pool, Sauna
Nearby: Squash, Golf, Fishing, Riding, Shooting

Taunton—Rumwell Manor Hotel
Rumwell, Taunton, Somerset. TA4 1EZ. Tel 0823 461902. Fax 0823 254861

Rumwell Manor, the former lovely home of the Cadbury family built in 1804 as part of their 200-acre estate, retains its delightful architectural features and charm as an intimate Country House Hotel. Within its five acres of informal wooded lawns one can soak up the tranquillity of the lush surroundings or take a bracing swim in the open-air pool. From the hotel, the view over the Vale of Taunton Deane towards the Blackdowns is a panorama of rolling green fields punctuated by clusters of broad trees. Somerset is a county of contrasts, from heather-covered moors to sea-level marshes, from thatched cottages to stately homes, from the lofty Wellington obelisk commemorating the victor of Waterloo to the deep enchantment of the caves in Cheddar Gorge. At Rumwell Manor, on the A38 road not far from junction 26 of the M5 motorway, one is ideally located for visits to numerous sites of scenic or historic interest. Although the hotel is not marked on our atlas, the location bears the words 'Sheppy's Farmhouse Cider'. This is not a beverage we sampled, but we can commend the splendid choice of forty-two wines, including an award-winning Somerset white wine, available from the cocktail bar. Two candle-lit restaurants offer wholesome English fare from *table d'hôte* and *à la carte* menus, featuring high quality local produce, a selection of nutritious vegetarian dishes, and home-made desserts. Something to be savoured after a day out walking, riding, fishing, canal boating, playing golf or ambling round Taunton's prestigious covered shopping area.

Weekly Terms from £280.00
Daily Terms from £54.50 (Single), £84.00 (Double). Bed and Breakfast from £40.00 (Single), £55.00 (Double)
Bar Lunch from £4.50. Lunch from £8.95
Bar Supper from £5.50. Dinner from £14.50

Gratuities at Guest's Discretion. VAT inclusive. Credit Cards–Access, American Express, Visa
3 Family Rooms. 11 Double, 6 Twin Bedrooms. All Rooms with Private Bathroom, TV, Telephone, Radio,

Baby-listening, Tea and Coffee-making facilities. Open all year. Residential and Restaurant Licence. Cocktail Bar. TV Lounge. Conference Facilities
Children catered for. Dogs allowed
Parking Facilities. Outdoor Swimming Pool

Section 1: Somerset

Near Taunton, Henlade—The Falcon Hotel
Henlade, Taunton, Somerset. TA3 5DH. Tel 0823 442502. Fax 0823 442670

Efficient and considerate management is evident throughout this exceptionally comfortable hotel. Our first mention must be of the restaurant, open to non-residents, where the diversity of succulent dishes for every course makes return visits irresistible, particularly as prices are most reasonable. There is an accent on healthy eating but the appeal of the menu tempts one to over-indulge, especially with the carefully-chosen wine list to complement the meal. Thoughtful attention has obviously been paid in the equipping of the bedrooms - each with its own bath or shower, with toilet - where the fullest facilities include the provision of mineral water, trouser-press and hairdryer, individual thermostats for the central heating and the availability of baby-listening. Non-smokers will appreciate the special consideration given them in the allocation of bedrooms and of seating in the dining-room. A spacious meeting room, that can be arranged to serve a variety of functions from a lecture theatre seating thirty to buffet luncheons for up to fifty people, is available for such occasions as wedding receptions or business conferences. Henlade is supremely accessible, being only a mile or so from junction 25 of the M5 motorway, on the A358 road to Ilminster. Close to the fine market town of Taunton, the Falcon Hotel is also a comfortable base from which to visit the Quantock Hills to the north and the Blackdown Hills to the south. The whole of this region abounds with places of historic, scenic and natural interest.

Weekly Terms and Breaks on Application
Daily Terms from £56.00
Bed and Breakfast from £45.00
Lunch from £7.00 and A La Carte
Dinner from £12.50 and A La Carte
Gratuities at Guest's Discretion. VAT inclusive. Credit Cards–Access, American Express, Visa.

2 Family Rooms. 4 Double, 4 Twin, 3 Single Bedrooms.
11 Private Bathrooms.
2 Private Shower Rooms.
All Rooms with TV, Telephone, Radio, Tea and Coffee-making Facilities,
Baby-listening, Hairdryer and Trouser Press, Mineral Water, Washing Powder and Shoe Cleaning Kits
Open All Year except Christmas Day and Boxing Day. Residential and Restaurant Licence. Full Central Heating and log fires. Cocktail Bar. Conference Facilities. Children catered for. Parking Facilities. Gardens. Nearby: Tennis, Putting, Squash, Badminton, Indoor Swimming Pool

Wells—The Ancient Gate House Hotel and Restaurant
Sadler Street, Wells, Somerset. BA5 2RR. Tel 0749 672029

The exterior of The Ancient Gate House Hotel and Restaurant is quite unpretentious, but, once you step inside, we are sure you will be completely charmed. It is certainly tiny, with low ceilings, narrow corridors and a winding stone staircase, but one must bear in mind that it was built in the days when the average height of an Englishman was only a little over five feet! It has a unique situation, too, for it faces the thirteenth-century west front of Wells Cathedral and is positioned within the cathedral precincts. There is a *table d'hôte* menu at lunchtime and dinner in the evenings may be taken *à la carte*. The modern appointments in the bedrooms are in contrast to the ancient fabric of the building, although four of the rooms are furnished with four-poster beds. It is a further surprise to find an excellent Italian restaurant within The Ancient Gate House, and a wealth of fresh produce from the Somerset countryside forms the basis of traditional Italian dishes and an English *table d'hôte* selection. This hotel also has a long frontage onto the cathedral green, where tea can be taken under the lime trees on warm afternoons. Mr F and Mrs H L Rossi are the proprietors of the hotel and their team can be congratulated on making one's stay in this small and historic city a most pleasant experience.

Weekly Terms from £280.00
Daily Terms from £40.00
Bed and Breakfast from £35.00
Bar Meal from £1.95
Lunch from £5.80 and A La Carte
Dinner from £11.75 and A La Carte

Credit Cards—Access, American Express, Diners Club, Visa
1 Family Rooms. 6 Doubles (6 with en suite facilities), 2 Twin Bedrooms, 1 Single Bedroom
All Rooms with TV, Telephone,

Tea and Coffee-making Facilities
Open all Year. Fully Licensed.
Full Central Heating
Dogs allowed. Parking Facilities
Nearby: Tennis, Squash, Swimming, Sauna, Golf, Fishing, Riding

Section 1: Somerset

Near Weston-Super-Mare, Lympsham—Batch Farm Country Hotel
Lympsham, Somerset. BS24 0EX. Tel 0934 750371

Set amidst over fifty acres of their own farmland, Mr and Mrs Brown's charming hotel is a peaceful haven, close to three miles of sea and sand. It has been in their family for three generations but only relatively recently has it been enlarged and modernised. Situated midway between the resorts of Weston-super-Mare and Burnham-on-Sea, all of the Batch Farm's ten *en suite* bedrooms have panoramic views of either the Mendip Hills or the Quantock Hills and the surrounding countryside. In the spacious dining room with its exposed beams, guests can choose traditional English-style dishes from *table d'hôte* or *à la carte* menus, where the emphasis is on fresh local produce. Sweets, too, are home made and, between courses, diners can admire the wide green lawns overlooked by the dining room. The three comfortable lounges, one with television, also have a similar outlook. Visitors have the freedom to walk over the surrounding farmland and to fish in the River Axe which flows through the grounds. Horse riding, swimming, tennis, golf and several other sporting activities are available locally. Easily accessible from Lympsham are the historic city of Bristol, the gorge and caves at Cheddar, the Georgian spa city of Bath and, one of the smallest and loveliest of England's cathedral cities, Wells, situated at the foot of the Mendip Hills. To reach the hotel, leave the M5 motorway at junction 22, taking the A38 towards Bristol. In about one mile, take the A370 from the roundabout, signposted Weston-super-Mare. After some two miles further, turn left for Lympsham village.

Weekly Terms from £226.00 (DB&B)
Daily Terms from £38.00 (DB&B)
Bed and Breakfast from £27.00
Bar Meal from £5.00. Dinner from £11.00 and A La Carte. Gratuities at Guest's Discretion. VAT inclusive.

Credit Cards—Access, American Express, Diners Club, Visa
2 Family Rooms. 2 Suites. 2 Double, 2 Twin Bedrooms. All Rooms with Private Bathroom, TV, Tea and Coffee-making Facilities. Baby-listening, Trouser Press and Hairdryer on Request
Open all Year except Christmas
Residential and Restaurant Licence.
Cocktail Bar. TV Lounge. Conference Facilities. Children catered for. Dogs not allowed. Parking Facilities. Croquet, Fishing

Winsford, Exmoor National Park—The Royal Oak Inn
Winsford, Somerset. TA24 7JE. Tel 064 385 455/6/7/8. Telex 46529 ROAK G

The American naturalist and novelist, William Hudson, wrote of Winsford that it was 'fragrant, cool, grey-green immemorial peace—second to no English village in beauty, running waters, stone thatched cottages, hoary church-tower'. The village is fortunate, too, in having this twelfth-century inn, which looks immaculate beneath a toupée of thatch. The Royal Oak is an excellent example of the best type of country inn, where sporting opportunities abound. Here there is hunting, fishing, walking, riding, golf and birdwatching. And, allied to all this, you will find a very personal aspect and the highest standards of comfort and care. There is nothing fancifully modern about the Royal Oak Inn, that would not be in keeping with its open fireplaces and oak beams, but each of the individually-styled bedrooms in the main house is well equipped and has a private bathroom. There are additional *en suite* bedrooms within the courtyard of the inn. Furthermore, the Royal Oak Inn is well known to one and all as an ideal lunching and dining *rendezvous* in its neighbourhood. The food is very good indeed the menus are changed daily to give the widest selection, and the wines are interesting and reasonably priced. The Royal Oak is very, very English in its character, predominantly in its fare, all local or home grown, as well as in the welcome one receives from the owners, Sheila and Charles Steven. We have found here warmth in winter, an airy lounge in summer and always a cosy bar where the leading locals forgather. If Exmoor National Park beckons you, do stay here... it is too good to miss!

Terms on Application
Bar Meal from £2.50
Lunch from £12.50
Afternoon Tea from £1.70
Dinner from £20.00 Table d'Hôte
Gratuities at Guest's Discretion

VAT inclusive
Credit Cards—Access, American Express, Diners Club, Visa
1 Family Room. 1 Suite, 10 Double, 2 Twin Bedrooms
All Rooms with Private Bathroom, TV,

Telephone, Radio, Hairdryer
Open all Year. Fully Licensed
Full Central Heating. Children catered for
Dogs-cleaning charge £3.50 per night if in room or kennel provided free of charge
Parking Facilities. Fishing, Riding, Shooting

Section 1: Wiltshire

Bradford-on-Avon—Leigh Park Hotel Leigh Road West, Bradford-on-Avon, Wiltshire. BA15 1AR. Tel 02216 4885. Fax 02216 2315

Presented by Queen Elizabeth I to the Earl of Leicester in 1574, this charming Georgian mansion stands on high ground in five acres of landscaped gardens. On a clear day, the historical White Horse of Westbury Downs, ten miles away, is visible over the Wiltshire countryside. Within a unique, walled kitchen garden, vegetables, herbs, greengages, cherries, peaches and figs are grown for the restaurant and, from the hotel vineyard with its 570 Reichensteiner vines, some 600 litres of German white grapes will be produced in 1992. On the south side of the hotel is the celebrated *Wiltshire Restaurant,* where the favourites are Rosette of smoked salmon with dill mayonnaise, Wellington style fillet of beef with Madeira Sauce and breast of Barbary Duck wrapped in pastry with truffle sauce. Neil Davies, the chef, will gladly produce special dishes to meet individual requests and, to complement the outstanding *cuisine*, there is a wine list exceeding sixty first-class bottles and many exceptional clarets. Large and small functions - whether social or business - are comprehensively provided for, if necessary quite isolated from the rest of the hotel. Extensive personal facilities can be found in the twenty-one tastefully decorated *en suite* bedrooms, all furnished to meet the highest standards of comfort. Additionally, there are four family rooms and an executive suite. A quite excellent hotel, near to Longleat Safari Park, Cheddar Caves and the Royal Crescent Bath.

(The following terms apply per couple twin/double.)
Weekly Terms from £343.00
Daily Terms from £69.50
Bed and Breakfast from £76.00
Bar Lunch from £8.50. Lunch from £15.30.
Bar Supper from £10.00
Dinner from £18.95. VAT inclusive.

Credit Card—Access, American Express, Diners Club, Visa. 5 Family Rooms, 1 Suite 8 Double, 3 Twin, 5 Single Bedrooms All Rooms with Private Bath/Shower Room, TV, Telephone, Radio, Baby-listening, Tea and Coffee-making Facilities. 13 Rooms with Trouser Press and Hairdryer. Open all year

Fully Licensed. Full Central Heating Cocktail Bar. TV Lounge. Games Room Conference Facilities. Children catered for. Dogs allowed. Parking Facilities. Tennis, Croquet, Vineyard. Nearby: Putting, Squash, Badminton, Swimming, Solarium, Sauna, Golf, Fishing, Riding, Sailing, Shooting, Hang-gliding

Castle Combe—The Manor House Castle Combe, Near Chippenham, Wiltshire. SN14 7HR. Tel 0249 782206. Fax 0249 782159

The outstanding Cotswold village of Castle Combe has something of greater importance than its picturesque rough hewn stone cottages, its pack-bridge over the Bybrook and its ancient market cross. Castle Combe's prize is the Manor House. The present Manor was started in the fourteenth century and added to by the Jacobeans in 1664. In the past forty years the Manor has been a country club, and then an hotel, but it has never been a finer country house than it is today. The owners have employed the most skilful designers and craftsmen to refurbish the house within, whilst a dedicated team of gardeners has ensured that the Manor enjoys the most perfect situation twenty-six acres of formal English and Italian gardens, with spacious lawns running down to the Bybrook, and there are lovely views across the tree-shaded valley beyond. The bedrooms in the house have really spacious and luxurious bathrooms, which are fitted in period style. Four-poster and half-tester beds add to the ambiance of some of the rooms. Close by are the *Mews Cottages*, which have also been refurbished to the highest standards of luxury. Whether you are fortunate enough to stay at the Manor, or have reserved a table in the delightful restaurant, you will sense a strong personal touch. The *Cuisine Moderne* and *Traditional English* dishes are all cooked to order and the wine list is extensive. The refurbishment has also created two executive meeting rooms and a restaurant for functions. Under the personal supervision of Mr Martin Clubbe, the Manor House is an outstanding hotel in 'Britain's most beautiful village'.

Room Rate from £100.00. Bar Lunch from £6.50. Lunch from £16.95 Table D'Hôte
Dinner from £32.00 Table D'Hôte
Credit Cards—Access, American Express, Diners Club, Visa
3 Suites, 33 Double/Twin Bedrooms.

All Rooms with Private Bathroom, TV, Telephone, Radio, Hairdryer. Open all Year. Fully Licensed. Full Central Heating. Cocktail Bar. Conference Facilities. Dogs allowed by Arrangement. Parking Facilities. Night Porter. Hard Tennis Court, Croquet,

Outdoor Heated Swimming Pool, Fishing, Mountain bikes, Archery. Nearby: Putting, Squash, Badminton, Solarium, Sauna, Golf, Riding, Shooting, Saloon car racing, Clay Pigeon shooting, Skid pan trials, Go-kart racing, Hot Air Ballooning

Section 1: Wiltshire

Corsham—Rudloe Park Hotel Leafy Lane, Corsham, Wiltshire. SN13 0PA. Tel 0225 810555. Fax 0225 811412

The contrast between Wiltshire's rolling chalk uplands and its fertile lowlands, renowned for their dairy produce, gave rise to the saying 'as different as chalk from cheese'. Rudloe Park is not so much an hotel, but more a graceful way of life. Within its four acres of beautifully maintained gardens and lawns, with ornamental shrubs, a magnificent vine and 20,000 bulbs which burst into bloom in the spring, it breathes an air of maturity and grace. The views from here, across unspoilt countryside, reach as far as the city of Bath. There is an extensive and frequently varied *à la carte* menu, offering the most delectable food, which caters for all tastes, and even for vegetarians. The restaurant is open every day for lunches which range from snacks to complete feasts. In order to savour the excellent roast beef served on Sundays, it is wise to book three weeks ahead. This popular hotel has won awards for the best cheese trolley in the country, best wine list, best German wine list and the good value for money, food and service award. The remarkable cellar, which carries a fine selection of several hundred wines from many countries, was overall national winner of the Gilbey Wine List Award. Each of the eleven bedrooms (three of which have a four-poster bed) has *en suite* facilities and contains those small thoughtful touches which mean so much: a bowl of fruit, sherry, mineral water, biscuits, toiletries and a newspaper. During one's stay here, home-made afternoon teas can be enjoyed in the lovely gardens.

'Great Breaks' available for 2 or more days
Bed and Breakfast from £80.00 (Double)
Bed and Breakfast from £55.00 (Single)
Lunch from £14.50 and A La Carte
Dinner from £17.00 and A La Carte
VAT and service inclusive
Credit Cards—Access, American Express, Diners Club, Visa.

1 Family Room. 8 Double, 2 Twin Bedrooms. (All Rooms may be let as Singles).
All Rooms with Private Bathroom, TV, Telephone, Radio, Baby-listening, Tea and Coffee-making Facilities, Hairdryer. Open from January to December. Fully Licensed.

Full Central Heating. Lounge Bar.
Conference Facilities
Children over 10 years catered for
Dogs allowed by Arrangement
Parking Facilities. Croquet
Nearby: Tennis, Putting, Squash, Badminton, Swimming, Solarium, Sauna, Golf, Fishing, Riding, Shooting

Harnham—The Rose & Crown Hotel Harnham Road, Salisbury. Wiltshire. SP2 8JQ. Tel 0722 327908. Fax 0722 339816

Five rivers meet in the thirteenth-century city of Salisbury, which is within easy walking distance of Harnham, and whose cathedral has the highest spire in England (123 metres). On the banks of the River Avon and within its own three-quarters of an acre of beautifully landscaped rose gardens, the hotel has shrubs planted to form an impressive crown. These are prominent in the views from the Rose & Crown, across the river and on to the cathedral. To dine in the conservatory is to have the unusual opportunity to cook your own meal. On request, a tray will be brought to your table carrying a solid granite stone pre-heated to over 300 degrees Celsius-and it remains exceedingly hot for up to forty minutes. Also on the tray are your strips of sirloin beef or king prawns, previously steeped in the hotel's own secret marinade, and with seasoning alongside. Whether you elect for this experience, or prefer to be served with ready-to-eat food, there is an excellent choice of fresh produce, ranging from wild mushrooms to Avon trout. Several venues within the hotel cater for different sizes of social or conference activities, with a full range of menus to suit every occasion. Some of the bedrooms have original beams and four-poster beds, some are modern, spacious family rooms and three are arranged to suit disabled guests. With fresh flowers, personal toiletries and the attentive service, this is a memorable base from which to visit historic Salisbury and the beautiful West Country.

Bed and Breakfast from £70.50
Bar Lunch from £4.50
Lunch from £9.25 and A La Carte
Bar Supper from £3.75
Dinner from £13.50 Table D'Hôte
Credit Cards–Access, American Express, Diners Club, Visa

6 Family Rooms, 2 Suites
8 Double, 12 Twin Bedrooms
All rooms with private Bathroom, TV, Telephone, Radio, Baby-listening Tea and Coffee-making Facilities, Trouser Press, Hairdryer. Open all year
Fully Licensed. Full Central Heating

Cocktail Bars. Conference Facilities
Children catered for. Dogs by arrangement only. Parking Facilities. Night Porter
Nearby:Tennis, Croquet, Putting, Squash, Badminton, Swimming, Solarium, Sauna, Golf, Fishing, Riding, Sailing, Windsurfing, Water Skiing, Hang-gliding, Shooting

Section 1: Wiltshire

Malmesbury—The Old Bell Abbey Row, Malmesbury, Wiltshire. SN16 0BW. Tel 0666 822344. Fax 0666 825145

A magnificent wisteria covers the exterior walls of this delightful hotel and thus conceals from all but the most observant eyes the original thirteenth-century structure, which has been much enlarged over the years. The hotel stands in the shadow of the abbey and guests must often be reminded of those medieval days when The Old Bell was an abbot's hostelry. In keeping with this tradition of hospitality, there is a reputation here for superb food and faultless service. The menu ranges from *nouvelle cuisine* to rib of beef, roasted to your order. There is also a very extensive wine list. Visitors, particularly those from overseas, love to come and live within the ancient walls of the house and laze in the peaceful garden, where time seems to have stood still. They are rarely surprised to learn that there is a haunted room! Comfort at The Old Bell is, however, very much up to date, for all the bedrooms are centrally heated and have a private bathroom. One room has a four-poster bed. Malmesbury itself, the oldest borough in England, is a Cotswold hill town moated by the River Avon and has a history which goes back well over 1,200 years. The walk beside the River Avon is particularly beautiful: geese were once driven over the Goosebridge to the water meadows and kingfishers may still be seen darting across the river's sparkling waters.

Bed and Breakfast from £72.50 (Single)
Bed and Breakfast from £49.00 (Twin, per person)
Lunch from £12.00 and A La Carte
Afternoon Tea from £4.50
Dinner from £20.00 and A La Carte
Gratuities at Guest's Discretion.
VAT inclusive

Credit Cards—Access, Visa
1 Suite. 22 Double, 5 Twin,
9 Single Bedrooms
All Rooms with Private Bathroom, TV, Telephone, Radio, Baby-listening, Tea and Coffee-making Facilities, Trouser Press, Hairdryer
Open all Year

Fully Licensed.
Full Central Heating
Cocktail Bar
Conference Facilities
Dogs not allowed
Parking Facilities. Night Porter
Nearby: Tennis, Swimming, Solarium, Sauna, Golf, Fishing, Riding, Shooting

Nr Malmesbury, Crudwell—Mayfield House Hotel Crudwell, Malmesbury, Wilts. SN16 9EW. Tel 0666 577409/577198 Fax 0666 577977

Originally mentioned in the Domesday Book, Crudwell is a picturesque village on the southern fringe of the beautiful Cotswold Hills, not far from the source of the River Thames. It lies between Malmesbury, with its ancient Abbey, and Cirencester, an old Roman town with an authentic Roman Villa and a museum which houses a fine collection of Roman antiquities. This whole area is steeped in history and rich in natural beauty. King Edward II was murdered in Berkeley Castle and, also on the banks of the Severn estuary, Peter Scott founded the Slimbridge Wildfowl Trust. Stately homes, gardens and parks are to be found in almost every direction, often reached through enchanting villages where time seems to have stood still. Not to be missed are the Rhododendron Gardens at Bowood House or the natural beauty of Westonbirt Arboretum with its blaze of autumn colours. What could be a more appropriate location for discovering all the antique shops, craft markets and museums than a transformed Victorian house with extensions offering twenty charming *en suite* bedrooms, a sixty-cover restaurant and a beautiful walled garden? Traditional English *cuisine*, lightly cooked using the best produce available, has the effect of 'topping up the human batteries' according to our Inspectors. With so many attractive walks and other outdoor activities on hand, a good appetite is assured. Ponies and hunters, to be seen in the fields around the golden Cotswold cottages, provide steady work for the Crudwell blacksmith.

Terms on Application
Bar Meal from £3.00
Lunch from £3.00 and A La Carte
Dinner from £12.00 and A La Carte
VAT and Service inclusive
Credit Cards–Access, American Express, Visa.

2 Family Rooms
8 Double, 8 Twin, 4 Single bedrooms
All Rooms with Private Bathroom, TV, Telephone, Baby-listening, Tea and Coffee-making Facilities
Open all Year. Residential and Restaurant Licence. Full Central Heating. Cocktail Bar

Meeting Facilities. Children catered for
Dogs allowed. Parking Facilities
Croquet.
Nearby: Tennis, Squash, Badminton, Swimming, Solarium, Sauna, Golf, Fishing, Riding, Sailing, Windsurfing, Water Skiing, Shooting

Section 1: Wiltshire

Nr Malmesbury—Crudwell Court Hotel & Restaurant
Crudwell, Near Malmesbury, Wiltshire. SN16 9EP. Tel 0666 577194/577355. Fax 0666 577853

From Cirencester take the road for Malmesbury (A429) and you will find the village of Crudwell after about five miles, though we are not sure that we ought to tell you about Crudwell Court there, for it will rob you of the surprise we had, when we first came upon it. There is a three-acre walled garden, which is laid out in a rather formal way with lily ponds and a heated swimming pool and the magnolias are simply glorious. The house is lovely, too. It is 300 years old, a Cotswold stone vicarage with an attractive flagstoned entrance hall, spacious rooms with elegant windows, log fires, and, outside, a garden gate which leads to the Saxon village church. We loved the reception lounge with its soft lighting and ample supply of books; the drawing room with deep chairs and sofas and log fire; and the panelled restaurant, where Chris Amor, the talented chef, presents his repertoire of mouth-watering dishes. The hotel has every right to claim that it has an ideal situation, with so much in compass and London just seventy minutes away by train. Yet, we would choose to follow a self-contained life here, with a comfortable chair, a log fire and plenty of books and newspapers to read.

Weekly Terms on Application
Bed and English Breakfast from: £47.00
Single, £88.00 Double
Bar Lunch from £3.50. Lunch from £14.50
Table D'Hôte
Dinner from £19.50 Table D'Hôte
Gratuities at Guest's Discretion.
VAT inclusive.

Credit Cards—Access, American Express, Diners Club, Visa
3 Family Rooms. 11 Double/Twin (incl. 2 Deluxe Rooms and 2 Superior Rooms),
All Rooms with Private Bathroom, TV, Telephone, Radio, Tea and Coffee-making Facilities, Room Service. Open all Year.
Residential and Restaurant Licence.

Full Central Heating. Conference Facilities
Children catered for. Dogs allowed
Parking Facilities. Croquet, Outdoor Heated Swimming Pool
Nearby; Tennis, Putting, Squash, Badminton, Solarium, Sauna, Golf, Fishing, Riding, Water Skiing, Shooting, Cotswold Water Park, Polo

Near Malmesbury, Easton Grey—Whatley Manor
Easton Grey, Wiltshire. SN16 0RB. Tel 0666 822888. Fax 0666 826120

This corner of Wiltshire, with its Cotswold-stone buildings and intriguing place names has a very mellow atmosphere. Whatley Manor, stone-roofed and creeper-clad, fits perfectly into these surroundings. We derive enormous personal pleasure from renewing our recommendation of this lovely hotel and encouraging our readers to stay here. There are 18 charming bedrooms in the Manor House, three of which, in the Terrace Wing, were added in 1990. Across the courtyard there are a further 10 bedrooms and one large suite in the *Court House*. Surrounding the house are ten acres of grounds which extend to a peaceful stretch of the River Avon. Here one can stroll in the hotel's formal gardens, play tennis on the new, all-weather court, play croquet on the lawn, swim in the attractive heated pool or possibly do a little trout fishing on the Avon. There is a relaxed, timeless quality within the hotel, too. Elegance abounds in the richly panelled reception rooms and beautifully appointed bedrooms. We found it a treat to stay in such delightful surroundings, to be served so assiduously and to dine like lords. When some well-known friends of ours want to get away from the media and disappear from the public eye, they can very often be found at Whatley Manor. Indeed, for anybody wishing to escape city life and the daily domestic round, this superb hotel is a luxurious retreat. It is not too far from Bath: turn off the M4 at Junction 17 and then take the B4040 road towards Easton Grey.

Bed and Breakfast from £110.00 (Double/Twin)
Bar Lunch from £4.00
Lunch from £15.00
Dinner from £27.00
Gratuities at Guest's Discretion.
VAT inclusive.
Credit Cards—Access, American Express,

Diners Club, Visa
3 Family Rooms, 18 Double, 8 Twin Bedrooms. All Rooms with Private Bathroom, TV, Telephone, Baby-listening, Hairdryer. Open all Year
Full Central Heating . Residential and Restaurant Licence.
Cocktail Bar. Games Room.

Conference Facilities
Dogs allowed.
Parking Facilities.
Night Porter.
Hard Tennis Court, Croquet, Putting, Outdoor Swimming Pool, Snooker Table
Tennis, Solarium, Sauna, Fishing, Jacuzzi.
Nearby: Squash, Golf, Riding, Sailing

Section 1: Wiltshire

Near Melksham, Shaw—The Shaw Country Hotel
Bath Road, Shaw, Near Melksham, Wiltshire. SN12 8EF. Tel 0225 702836/790321. Fax 0225 790275

Believed to have been built in the late sixteenth century, this elegant country hotel today has every modern amenity whilst retaining a relaxed atmosphere. The *Mulberry Restaurant* which takes its name from the tree-reputed to be as old as the house itself-whose shadow falls across the lawns in front of the restaurant, enjoys an excellent reputation among locals and visitors. Here the emphasis is on fresh produce embodied in classical and innovative English and French *cuisine*. A full lunch is served every day with, on weekdays, the alternatives of a bar snack or a competitively priced business lunch. In the evenings, *table d'hôte* and *à la carte* menus are available, with a wide selection of wines including bottles of red and white French wines bearing the Mulberry's own label. All twelve *en suite* bedrooms have breath-taking views across open countryside, much of which is designated as 'of outstanding natural beauty'. Guests may well appreciate the guidance offered by John, Gabrielle and their staff concerning local events and places to visit, since the choice is very wide indeed. Longleat is probably the best known of the Stately Homes, because of its wildlife park, and there are museums, golf courses, riding schools and theatres. The National Trust village of Lacock lies only a few miles away while a wealth of interest awaits the visitor to the Roman City of Bath. At the hotel, granted two-star rating and awarded four crowns and a 'Commendation' by the West Country Tourist Board, guests can relax in the attractive gardens. An ideal location for the holidaymaker, tourist or business visitor.

Bed and Breakfast from £40.00 (Single), £59.00 (Double). Bar Lunch from £2.50
Lunch from £7.50 and A La Carte
Bar Supper from £5.00
Dinner from £10.50 and A La Carte
Gratuities at Guest's Discretion. VAT
inclusive. Credit Cards—Access, American Express, Visa
7 Double, 3 Twin, 3 Single Bedrooms
All Rooms with Private Bath/Shower Room, TV, Telephone, Radio, Baby-listening, Tea and Coffee-making Facilities, Biscuits, Fruit
3 Four Poster Bedrooms, one with Jacuzzi Bath. Open all Year
Fully Licensed. Full Central Heating
Lounge. Conference Facilities
Dogs not allowed. Parking Facilities

Near Swindon, Blunsdon—Blunsdon House Hotel
Blunsdon, Swindon, Wiltshire. SN2 4AD. Tel 0793 721701. Fax 0793 721056

Should you be travelling north of Swindon on the A419, look out for the sign to Blunsdon. Here, in a perfect rural setting, what was once a large Victorian country house has been transformed and extended to provide luxury accommodation and a truly magnificent leisure club. This comprises a swimming-pool, spa pool, solaria, a beauty department, squash courts, a supervised gymnasium, steam rooms, saunas, skittle alley, snooker room, darts, *petanque piste*, 'artificial grass' tennis court, children's games room, computer games rooms, a mile of woodland jogging track and a *crèche*. The enterprising owners, Mr and Mrs Peter Clifford, are currently constructing their own nine-hole par 3 golf course. Complementing all these facilities, the sumptuously-furnished bedrooms cater for business people and holidaymakers; also, there are three executive suites and a room suitable for guests in wheelchairs. For honeymooners, two suites offer the luxury of double-size baths and four-poster beds. Conference and syndicate rooms provide seclusion for meetings, discussions or presentations. The attractive Ridge Restaurant, with its friendly staff, is a perfect setting for the enjoyment of imaginative *cuisine* from both fixed price *à la carte* and *table d'hôte* menus. A valuable alternative is Carrie's Carverie, an informal venue offering an excellent choice of dishes at very reasonable prices. Blunsdon House has a ballroom, exhibition space, on-site parking and even boasts a helipad. With so much on offer, advance bookings are most advisable, especially for two and three-night Getaway Weekend Breaks.

Weekly Terms on Application
Bed and Breakfast from: £92.50 Double/Twin, £69.50 Single
Lunch from £11.75 and A La Carte
Dinner from £11.75 (Carverie). Dinner from £17.00 (Restaurant)
Gratuities at Guest's Discretion. VAT inclusive. Credit Cards—Access, American Express, Diners Club, Visa
15 Family Rooms. 1 Suite. 20 Prestige Rooms with Spa Bath
25 Double, 20 Twin, 5 Single Bedrooms
All Rooms with Private Bath and Shower Room, TV, Telephone, Radio, Baby-listening, Tea and Coffee-making Facilities, Trouser Press, Hairdryer. Most Rooms with Wall Safe. Open all Year. Fully Licensed. Lift. Cocktail Bar. Games Room.

Section 1: Wiltshire

Near Swindon, Cricklade—Cricklade Hotel and Country Club
Common Hill, Cricklade, Wiltshire. SN6 6HA. Tel 0793 750751. Fax 0793 751767

Thirty acres of peaceful grounds surround Cricklade Hotel, a beautiful and dignified house built at the turn of the century by a German gentleman, who admired traditional English architecture. The house is, once again, privately owned and has recently been refurbished to the highest possible standards. The result is the creation of one of the most relaxing and comfortable establishments we know in this area. Here the businessman or holidaymaker can unwind completely in his or her superbly equipped bedroom or in the luxurious lounge. The food in the *à la carte* restaurant is mouthwatering to say the least, prepared from fresh local ingredients and presented with the utmost care and attention to detail. Facilities for sports enthusiasts are much to the fore here and include an indoor swimming pool, Turkish steam room, spa bath, solarium, fitness centre, snooker tables and a tennis court. In addition, fully equipped Conference areas offer an ideal venue for business meetings (for those who work to a tight schedule, there is even a helipad). We came away from Cricklade most impressed with all that was on offer there, but even more impressed with the high calibre of the staff. Mrs Kearney, Manageress, has the rare ability to create a warm and friendly rapport between all her staff and the result is kind, efficient service for every guest.

Weekly Terms on Application
Daily Terms from £88.00
Bed and Breakfast from £70.00
Lunch from £12.00 and A La Carte
Afternoon Tea from £2.00
Dinner from £18.00 and A La Carte
Gratuities at Guest's Discretion
VAT inclusive. Credit Cards—Access, American Express, Visa

2 Suites. 32 Double, 4 Twin, 9 Single Bedrooms
All Rooms with Private Bath/Shower Room, TV, Telephone, Radio, Tea and Coffee-making Facilities, Hairdryer, Trouser Press
Open from January to December
Fully Licensed. Full Central Heating.
Games Room. Cocktail Bar. Dogs not allowed. Parking Facilities
Children over 14 catered for
Conference Facilities. Night Porter. Hard Tennis Court, Indoor Swimming Pool, Solarium, Sauna, Spa Bath, 9-hole Golf Course, Snooker Room, Gymnasium
Nearby: Squash, Badminton, Riding, Sailing, Windsurfing, Water Skiing, Shooting, Hang-gliding

Warminster—The Old Bell Hotel
Market Place, Warminster, Wiltshire. BA12 9AN. Tel 0985 216611

Much of Warminster's past is retained in its wealth of houses, shops and inns which were built during the eighteenth and nineteenth centuries. The Old Bell Hotel is the best surviving example of the old inns dating from the sixteenth century. It is centrally situated in the market place and has been most skilfully converted, so that it caters for modern-day travellers and yet preserves its historic atmosphere. There are twenty individually styled bedrooms in the hotel, ten *en suite*, plus four exquisitely appointed *en suite* bedrooms in the *Bell House* with period furniture and soft grey woodwork overlooking a charming garden. This-and the ample parking space-are unusual benefits in the centre of a busy thoroughfare. Excellent catering ranges from lunchtime snacks in the lounge bar or fresh salads and home-made dishes in the Chimes Bar, through candlelit dinners in the exposed beam restaurant to special celebrations for ninety diners in the Party Room. Mervyn Parrish is the driving force here, his experience and enthusiasm ensuring that each guest receives efficient and friendly service. The staff at The Old Bell are particularly helpful and courteous and we would recommend this hotel for its warm hospitality and the good value offered by special holiday breaks, some including riding, or fishing on a three mile stretch of the river.

Bed and Breakfast from £39.00 (Single), £58.00 (Double)
Lunch and Dinner available
Gratuities at Guest's Discretion.
VAT inclusive
Credit Cards–Access, American Express, Visa

2 Family Rooms. 7 Double, 6 Twin, 5 Single Bedrooms
Most Rooms have Private Bath/Shower Room.
All Rooms with TV, Telephone, Radio, Tea and Coffee-making Facilities. Hairdryer available on request

Open all year. Fully Licensed.
Full Central Heating.
Lounge. Conference Facilities
Dogs allowed by arrangement.
Parking Facilities
Nearby: Tennis, Putting, Squash, Swimming, Solarium, Sauna, Golf, Fishing, Riding, Sailing

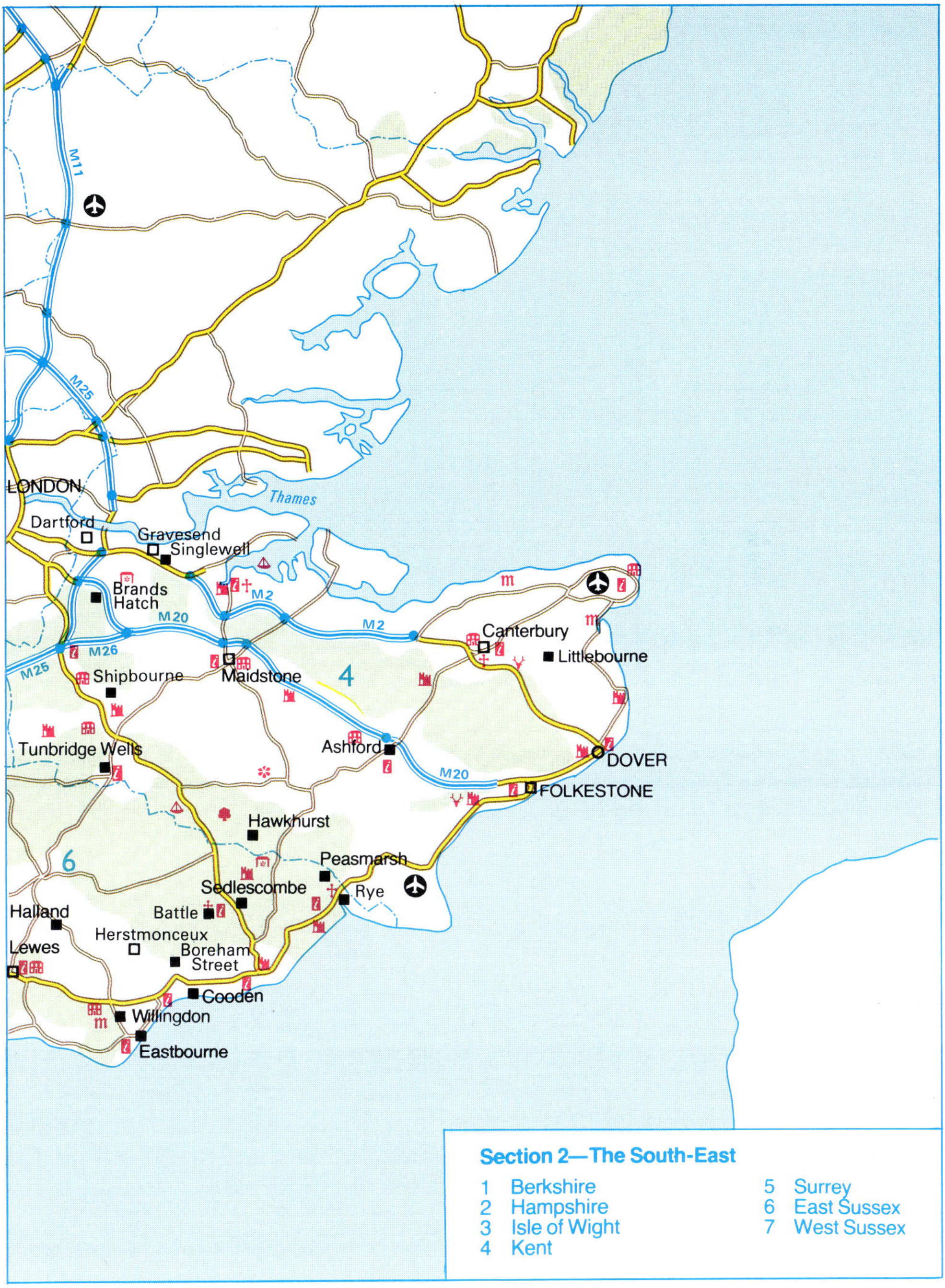

Section 2—The South-East

1. Berkshire
2. Hampshire
3. Isle of Wight
4. Kent
5. Surrey
6. East Sussex
7. West Sussex

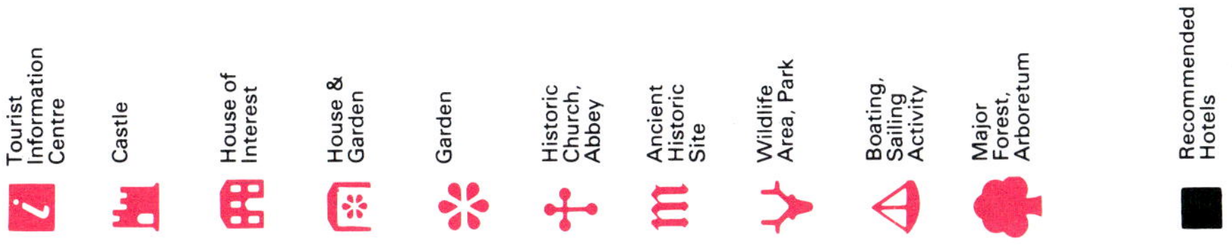

Tourist Information Centre	Castle	House of Interest	House & Garden	Garden	Historic Church, Abbey	Ancient Historic Site	Wildlife Area, Park	Boating, Sailing Activity	Major Forest, Arboretum	Recommended Hotels
									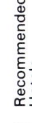	

THE SOUTH-EAST

Scotney Castle, Kent

Section 2 - The South-East

Berkshire, Hampshire, Isle of Wight, Kent, Surrey, East and West Sussex

Berkshire

The Thames forms the northern boundary of Berkshire and the county's riverside towns, with their attractive bridges, are a good starting point for anyone wishing to explore this area. Although east Berkshire is increasingly being swallowed by London for dormitory purposes, it does contain the county's most outstanding attraction: Windsor Castle remains one of Britain's greatest historic legacies. It was started by William the Conqueror and has been the residence of the sovereigns of England for over 800 years. West and north-west Berkshire remain wonderfully unspoilt. The Vale of the White Horse and the downs contain quiet villages, amongst which Farringdon can be counted the showpiece.

Hampshire

'Of Hant-shire' wrote John Speed in 1672, 'the soile is rich for Corne and Cattel, pleasant for pasturage, and plenteous for woods; in a word, in all commodities, either for Sea or Land, blessed and happy.' The New Forest was then no terrain for tourists, Southampton had age to its credit but no size, and Bournemouth, barely 100 years old, was almost non-existent. All are marvellous attractions today. Little changed, however, are the villages of the Itchen and Test valleys, where Easton, Avington, Ovington, Wherwell and Longparish still possess much of their original charm. Few English cities repay unhurried study as much as Winchester, which was formerly the capital of Wessex.

Bodiam Castle, East Sussex

Isle of Wight

Just twenty-three miles long by thirteen miles wide, the Isle of Wight has a dolls' house quality which charms the thousands of visitors who spend their holidays there every year. The island is also remarkable in the variety of scenery within its small area. In the course of a single day, it is possible, if one so wishes, to play beside the sea on a fine sandy beach, to stroll beside peaceful estuaries, investigate the island's rural hinterland and still find time to stride across breezy cliff tops. There are three regular ports of entry to the island: Cowes, Ryde and Yarmouth, which are approached from Southampton, Portsmouth and Lymington respectively. If you seek tranquility, go there out of the high season. The island is rarely cold during winter, for there are places where one is sheltered from the north and east.

Kent

'Everybody knows Kent'. So said Jingle in The Pickwick Papers. How many people, however, really know this, one of England's most historic counties? Kent was the first of the English kingdoms--an historic map, painted in tempera, in the Medici Palace in Florence, shows Kent as being part of England. The county received some of our island's earliest visitors and tens of thousands now pass through it each year as they travel to and from the Continent. Few of our hotel recommendations, however, are designed solely for transitory visitors: stay at any one of them and you will find much of interest, both historically and scenically, nearby.

Surrey

Surrey is a county of infinite charm, despite the fact that London has infiltrated into her outskirts. Travel some twenty miles into Surrey and it is possible, within a matter of minutes, to be out of sight and sound of populated areas. Turn off the Hog's Back to discover Compton and Puttenham. Between Guildford and Horsham is beautiful countryside, where you will find delightful villages such as Chiddingfold and Dunsfold. The Tillingbourne Valley is picturesque, but, for a myriad of byways and scenic beauty of the first order, turn off to Pitch Hill and Friday Street. The North Downs reach their highest points at Leith Hill and Box Hill (the latter has associations with George Meredith, John Keats and Dickens' 'Markis O'Granby'). All this is just forty miles from the heart of London--little wonder it is a rural playground for countless townsfolk.

East and West Sussex

The words 'pastoral' and 'prosperous' are fitting descriptions of Sussex, a county divided into east and west sectors. The county was the setting for many events which helped shape England's destiny: Norman supremacy took hold at Senlac Hill in 1066; the defeat of Henry III at Lewes, in 1264, laid the foundation of Britain's parliamentary system; and, in this century, another would-be invader was driven off in the skies above Sussex and Kent. Today, thousands of people flock to Sussex to enjoy her seaboard and to ramble on the South Downs. In mid-Sussex you will find silent hammer ponds, reminders of those days when the surrounding woods rang with the sounds of iron being smelted. Many overseas visitors know about the stone villages of the Cotswolds, but how many have heard of the equally attractive half-timbered houses constructed of hard Sussex oak? This beautiful county is worth getting to know.

Section 2: Berkshire

Bray-on-Thames—Monkey Island Hotel Bray-on-Thames, Maidenhead, Berkshire. SL6 2EE. Tel 0628 23400. Fax 0628 784732

One mile downstream from Maidenhead lies Monkey Island; sweeping lawns, ancient walnut trees, an abundance of roses and other flowering shrubs and amidst all this stands the Monkey Island Hotel, an impressive Georgian style building. Totally restored during 1987, it now provides guests with outstanding facilities. Originally built as a fishing lodge, later additions were built, such as a temple, now the *Wedgwood Room*, with its beautiful high relief plasterwork or the *Monkey Room*, with its domed ceiling painted by the eighteenth century French artist Andie de Clermont, famous for depicting this style of art; monkeys fishing, shooting, boating–all dressed in the fashion of the day; and it is said that the name of the hotel originated here. As an hotel, it provides every comfort to its guests; each of the twenty-seven bedrooms is furnished and equipped to the highest standard and has river or garden views. The restful setting makes this the perfect venue for conferences, banqueting and smaller private functions. The individual guest is well looked after too, with the *Terrace Bar* for a cocktail and a delicious light bar meal. Or there is the regency style *Pavilion Room Restaurant* offering superb international *cuisine* in most elegant surroundings. For larger functions there are the *River Room*, the *Temple Room*, the *Boardroom* or octagonal panelled *Wedgewood Room*. Close by is a variety of places to visit. Apart from picturesque Bray itself, Henley, Marlow and Ascot are all but a short drive away, as is Windsor.

Daily Terms from £84.00
Breakfast from £5.50
Bar Meals available daily
Lunch from £12.00 and A La Carte
Dinner from £17.00 and A La Carte.
Gratuities at Guest's discretion.
VAT inclusive.
Credit Cards—Access, American Express,

Diners Club, Visa
2 Suites. 8 Double, 13 Twin, 2 Single Bedrooms. All Rooms with Private Bathroom, TV, Telephone, Radio, Tea and Coffee-making Facilities, Hairdryer. 2 Rooms with Trouser Press. Open All Year except 26th December to 10th January inclusive. Fully Licensed.

Full Central Heating.
Cocktail Bar
Conference Facilities. Children catered for.
Dogs not allowed. Parking Facilities.
Porter. Nearby: Tennis, Croquet, Putting, Squash, Badminton, Swimming, Solarium Sauna, Golf, Riding, Sailing, Windsurfing, Water Skiing, Shooting

Nr Maidenhead–The Norfolk House Restaurant & Hotel Bath Road, Taplow, Maidenhead , Berks. SL6 0AP. Tel 0628 784031. Fax 0628 23687

Maidenhead and contiguous Taplow stand on opposing sides of the River Thames and in different counties–the former is in Berkshire and the latter is in Buckinghamshire. Together, these towns form an attractive riverside resort, where grassy slopes lead down to the river's edge, yachts tug at their moorings and fishing is a popular pastime. One of the best small hotels currently available on the Thames, set in an oasis of tranquility, is the Norfolk House Hotel. Built in the early eighteen-hundreds it was at one time the local Manor House. Combining outstanding service with a luxurious atmosphere, the restaurant offers superb *cuisine* and has an excellent wine cellar. Both the restaurant and the drawing room overlook the terraced gardens, the swimming pool and woodlands. The restful library and conservatory provide the perfect setting for before and after dinner drinks. Private suites are also available for dining, executive meetings and conferences and can accommodate up to eighty guests. Norfolk House would satisfy anyone seeking high standards, good value and an excellent location within easy reach of Windsor, Eton, Ascot and Henley and London is only twenty five miles away.

Prices pertaining to 1992
Weekly Terms from £285.00 (B&B)
Bed and Breakfast from £40.00
Lunch from £12.50 and A La Carte
Light Lunches are available
Dinner from £15.95 and A La Carte
Credit Cards–Access, American Express, Diners Club, Visa

5 Double, 4 Twin, 2 Single Bedrooms
All Rooms with Private Bath/Shower Room, TV, Telephone, Radio, Baby-listening, Tea and Coffee-making Facilities, Trouser Press, Hairdryer
Open all Year. Fully Licensed. Full Central Heating.
Cocktail Bar. TV Lounge

Conference Facilities.
Children catered for. Dogs allowed by arrangement. Parking Facilities.
Croquet, Outdoor Swimming Pool.
Nearby: Tennis, Putting, Squash, Badminton, Solarium, Sauna, Golf, Fishing, Riding, Sailing, Windsurfing, Water Skiing, Shooting, Hang-gliding

Section 2: Berkshire

Near Newbury, Thatcham—Regency Park Hotel
Bowling Green Road, Thatcham, Newbury, Berkshire. RG13 3RP
Tel 0635 871555. Fax 0635 871571

The M4 motorway passes within a seven minutes' drive of Thatcham, but it might just as well be 70 miles! Long may the fast lanes direct all but the leisurely traveller to London, Wales and the West Country and leave the quiet village of Thatcham to its own devices. Having said that, we should stress that the Regency Park Hotel is almost completely new—it was opened in August 1988 and the facilities are as modern as one could wish for. It was a tremendous pleasure for us to visit this hotel and experience the friendly, courteous manner of all the staff. Built around the core of a substantial family home, but with a brand new extension, and situated in five acres of countryside, the Regency Park is gaining a well deserved reputation for its comfort, care and remarkable cuisine. The bedrooms are among the most spacious we have seen for an hotel of this size and all are furnished to an extremely high standard, with pleasing decor. They also incorporate almost every notion of modern comfort and convenience. The restaurant is appropriately called Terraces, and adjoining this is Fountains Bar. There is also an excellent Business Centre, with a wide range of facilities, which can accommodate up to sixty people. You will even find an hotel shop selling gifts, newspapers and cigarettes. With Newbury, Ascot and Windsor all nearby, the Regency Park Hotel is ideally placed for anyone who follows racing.

Room Rate from £75.00
Special Weekend break rates available: £45.00 per person per night (DB&B). VAT and service inclusive (Minimum 2 nights stay, one to be a Saturday)
Breakfast English: £8.95. Breakfast Continental: £5.95
Bar Lunch from £3.50
Lunch from £13.95 and A La Carte
Afternoon Tea from £4.50

Dinner from £18.50 and A La Carte
Service Charge and VAT inclusive
Credit Cards—Access, American Express, Diners Club, Visa
1 Suite. 30 Double, 15 Twin, 4 Single Bedrooms.
All Rooms with Private Bathroom, TV, Telephone, Radio, Baby-listening, Tea and Coffee-making Facilities, Trouser Press, Hairdryer, Fresh Fruit.

Open all Year. Fully Licensed.
Full Central Heating. Lift.
Cocktail Bar.
Conference Facilities.
Children catered for.
Dogs allowed. Parking Facilities.
Night Porter
Nearby: Tennis, Squash, Badminton, Swimming, Golf, Fishing, Riding, Sailing, Windsurfing, Water Skiing, Shooting

Section 2: Berkshire

Near Newbury, Woolton Hill–Hollington House
Church Road, Woolton Hill, Nr Newbury, Berkshire RG15 9XR
Tel 0635 255100. Fax 0635 255075

Quite exceptional on all counts, this grand country house has very recently been opened as a luxury hotel by an enterprising and talented couple who, during more than thirty years in Melbourne, Australia, had purchased and run three restaurants and a prestigious hotel. On returning to the UK, it took them almost two years to locate a property meeting their exacting specification, followed by a period of structural change, immaculate decoration and the introduction of superb furnishings. We have only the very highest praise for what they have achieved. With John and Penny Guy came a most outstanding head chef - Richard Lovett - whose cuisine, in our considered view, will impress even the most learned gourmets. Accompanying the fine menus is a wine list representing the ultimate in careful selection. Hollington House stands in fourteen acres of established woodland gardens, and was built originally in 1904 as a private residence. The grandeur of the grounds fully complements the elegance of the décor and the quality of the amenities within the hotel. All of the twenty large bedrooms benefit from the special attention paid to bathrooms. They are spacious, well lit, and most contain double whirlpool baths and shower cabinets, some with two large, powered shower heads. These exemplify the policy behind every innovation here: only the best will serve. The pattern is set once you enter the oak-panelled galleried hall, step out onto the terrace or relax in one of several plush sitting rooms. For anyone who appreciates the refinements and splendours of a private hotel run by professionals, Hollington House will fulfil every promise.

Bed and Breakfast from £80.00 (Single), £110.00 (Double), £150.00 (Junior Suite)
Lunch from £16.00
Afternoon Tea from £6.00
Dinner from £25.00
Gratuities at Guest's Discretion. VAT inclusive. Credit Cards-Access, American Express, Visa

20 Double Bedrooms (12 Twin on request)
All Rooms with Private Bath and Shower Room, TV, Telephone, Radio, Tea and Coffee-making Facilities, Trouser Press, Hairdryer, Dressing Gowns.
Open all year.
Residential and Restaurant Licence.
Full Central Heating. Lift

Conference Facilities.
Children over 7 years catered for.
Dogs not allowed.
Parking Facilities.
Hard Tennis Court, Croquet, Putting, Outdoor Swimming Pool
Nearby: Golf, Fishing, Riding, Shooting

Section 2: Berkshire

Nr Reading, Silchester–Romans Hotel & Restaurant
Little London Rd, Silchester, Berks. RG7 2PN. Tel 0734 700421. Fax 0734 700691

It was known as *Calleva Atrebatum* by the Romans, but long before they had arrived Silchester was an important site. There was a great Celtic earthworks here and later a large town grew up, which served as the capital of the *Atrebates* tribe. Silchester's greatest legacies are Roman, however, and this hotel, in its name, is a reminder of these. Romans Hotel and Restaurant is reached from Little London Road, but is set well back in grounds which are spacious enough to contain terraces and gardens, an outdoor heated swimming pool, two hard tennis courts and a kitchen garden. Within this beautiful Lutyens designed house one can feel really cosseted. The furnishings are most elegant and comfortable, and the bedrooms, all *en suite*, are sufficiently large to be called suites. We have known the owners, Michael and Kay Riley, for many years and their friendly caring service is another important feature of Romans. We know you will be pampered and rested here and the food will be second to none. If you have a particular interest in Roman antiquities you will need no second bidding to visit Silchester. For the best views of the Roman walls, still rising to fifteen feet in places, drive a mile further on to St Mary's Church and then follow the footpaths to the centre of the site. Breezes blow off the Hampshire Down and through ancient forests where King John hunted. It is a marvellous place for a weekend break, and one which is so convenient to London.

Bed and Breakfast from £60.00
Lunch from £15.00 Table D'Hôte
Dinner from £18.50 Table D'Hôte
Service Charge and VAT inclusive. Credit Cards–Access, American Express, Visa.
1 Family Room. 5 Double, 4 Twin, 14 Single Bedrooms

23 Private Bathrooms. 1 Private Shower Room. All Rooms with TV, Telephone, Radio, Tea and Coffee-making Facilities, Trouser Press, Hairdryer
Open all Year except at Christmas and New Year. Fully Licensed.
Full Central Heating. Cocktail Bar.

Conference Facilities
Children catered for.
Dogs allowed
Parking Facilities. Night Porter
Tennis, Outdoor Heated Swimming Pool
Nearby: Golf, Fishing, Riding, Sailing, Windsurfing

Near Reading, Twyford–The Bird in Hand Hotel
Bath Road, Knowl Hill, Twyford, Berks. RG10 9UP. Tel 0628 826622/822781

It has stood beside the old London to Bath road for around 600 years; a veteran among inns which has played host to kings and commoners, hunting parties and, no doubt, highwaymen. Legend has it that, because of the hospitality he received at this tavern, George III evoked a Royal Charter giving the proprietor the right to serve wine and beer by day and night! Alas, this licence no longer exists. For the past thirty years Jack and Maura Shone have been the custodians of the Bird in Hand and running it as a very popular country inn and restaurant. Recently, however, they have added a new bedroom wing, and the inn has become known as an hotel. Jack Shone remarked to us that he hoped this extension will, like the original building, be admired for many years to come. So carefully has the new wing been planned and designed, we have little doubt that it will. Within, the bedrooms are delightful (the decor is entirely of the owners' choosing) with one room especially adapted for the needs of the disabled. The Bird in Hand has a new dining room, too, in which the hotel can display its high reputation for good food, service and presentation. The menus are varied to suit all tastes and there is a most reasonably-priced wine list. Mrs Shone is a dab-hand at soda bread and what a welcome change this is from the usual bread rolls! Withal, this is a very comfortable hotel, the atmosphere is friendly and relaxed, and all the staff seem to want to give of their best. London is quickly reached from here, by using the M4 motorway, whilst there are many local attractions... Windsor, Henley, Marlow and the Thames Valley.

All Terms pertaining to 1992
Weekend Breaks from £90.00
Bed and Breakfast from £70.00
Lunch from £9.75 and A La Carte
Cold Buffet from £5.95
Dinner from £11.75 and A La Carte

VAT inclusive. Credit Cards–Access, American Express, Diners Club, Visa. 1 Family Room. 2 Double, 11 Twin, 1 Single Bedroom. 12 Private Bathrooms. 3 Private Shower Rooms. All Rooms with TV, Telephone, Tea and Coffee-making

Facilities, Trouser Press, Hairdryer. 1 Bedroom suitable for Disabled Guests.
Open all Year. Fully Licensed. Full Central Heating. Cocktail Bar. Conference Facilities. Children catered for.
Dogs not allowed. Parking Facilities

Section 2: Berkshire

Streatley-on-Thames – The Swan Diplomat
Streatley on Thames, Berks. RG8 9HR. Tel 0491 873737

There are a number of Thames-side hotels of merit, yet we cannot help thinking that the river laps with affection the garden frontage of The Swan Diplomat, for there an inn has stood for generations. Each successive owner has contributed something towards its betterment, so the facilities have always been desirable. Today, however, after a great deal of rebuilding and considerable refurbishment, it is difficult not to feel that the hotel and its situation present an image of English rural perfection. One can live here luxuriously without feeling awed by ostentation. The furnishings and fittings throughout strike a high note of quality and the colour schemes could not be more harmonious. The bedrooms are spacious and modernly equipped, all have delightful bathrooms and either enjoy views into the Streatley hills or have balconies overlooking the Thames. To emphasise The Swan's riverside position, an early 1900's Oxford college barge was obtained and, following a year's painstaking refurbishment, it makes a splendid venue for small meetings and cocktail parties. Guests may also take advantage of the hotel's own health and fitness club, whilst conference delegates have excellent facilities available in six superb suites, but the most popular feature of The Swan is undoubtedly its food. Gourmets and gourmands from far and wide prize the classical and imaginative *cuisine* which is served in the *Riverside Restaurant*. In the summer here is an hotel which reflects the holiday spirit, whilst out of season it is a restful haven.

Weekly Terms from £450.00
Bed and Breakfast from £95.00
Light Lunch from £8.50. Lunch from £21.50 Table D'Hôte. Dinner from £25.00 Table D'Hôte. Gratuities at Guest's discretion. VAT inclusive. Credit Cards–Access, American Express, Diners Club, Visa

1 Suite. 21 Double, 12 Twin, 10 Single Bedrooms. 2 Double Rooms with Facilities for disabled Guests. All Rooms with Private Bathroom, TV and Satellite, Telephone, Radio, Baby-listening, Hairdryer, Tea and Coffee-making Facilities, Mini bar.
Open all Year. Fully Licensed. Full CH.

1 Cocktail Bar. TV Lounge. Conference Facilities. Room service
Children catered for. Dogs allowed at Management's discretion. Parking Facilities. Night Porter.
Croquet, Badminton, Bicycle Hire, Row Boat Hire, Indoor Fitness Pool, Solarium

Windsor – Aurora Garden Hotel
14, Bolton Avenue, Windsor, Berkshire. SL4 3JF. Tel 0753 868686. Fax 0753 831394

One of the greatest needs in towns of major historical importance such as Windsor is for an hotel which can offer quietude and accessibility. In both respects, Aurora Garden Hotel makes an admirable choice. Situated in the peacefully residential Bolton Avenue, this carefully converted family house is a very welcome 'new face' on the hotel scene of this ancient town. Officially opened in the spring of 1986 by the Duke of Marlborough, the hotel is well equipped in the modern manner and each bedroom has a shower room, colour television, direct-dial telephone and beverage-making facilities. We should stress, however, that there is nothing functional or austere about the hotel, for it is beautifully furnished and is decorated in most restful shades. The welcome one receives could not be more traditional either and we detect here all the virtues of a privately owned and personally managed establishment. We enjoyed a superb meal at the Aurora Garden. There are several menus including a vegetarian menu, with all dishes freshly prepared and attractively presented. As one would expect, the garden is a special feature of the hotel. It contains waterfalls, pools and underwater lighting which give the whole scene a delightful 'aurora' at night. In 1990 the new Garden Restaurant was added, beautifully decorated with a clematis theme and a panoramic view of the interesting garden. This has given the scope needed for gaining a reputation locally for good food and enabled them to win the local 1991 European Cuisine Award. In 1992, the hotel was awarded the prestigious AA Rosette for its good food.

Weekend Breaks (min. 2 Nights) DB&B from £49.00 per person per night
Bed and English Breakfast from £60.00 Lunch from £13.95 and A La Carte
Dinner from £17.50 and A La Carte
Gratuities at Guest's Discretion. VAT

inclusive. Credit Cards–Access, American Express, Diners Club, Visa
1 Family Room. 8 Double, 2 Twin, 3 Single Bedrooms. 3 Private Bathrooms. 13 Private Shower Rooms. All Rooms with TV, Telephone, Radio, Tea and Coffee-making

Facilities. Baby-listening and Hairdryer on request. Open all Year. Residential and Restaurant Licence. Full CH.
Cocktail Bar. Conference Facilities. Children catered for. Dogs allowed. Parking Facilities

Section 2: Hampshire

Brockenhurst–Cloud Hotel
Meerut Road, Brockenhurst, Hampshire. SO42 7TA. Tel 0590 22165/22254

Of the many delightful places in the New Forest, none surpasses this peaceful backwater for sheer rurality. The views from every angle are the embodiment of rural life: forest ponies, a lone donkey not yet awake, flora and fauna blending with century-old trees, and perhaps some riders coming in from a pre-breakfast canter from a nearby riding stables. Such is the pace of life here if you want to follow it. Yet, although you are out of the mainstream, you are not isolated, for the centre of Brockenhurst, the Forest's most attractive and amiable village, is less than ten minutes' stroll away. You should expect no grand trappings at the Cloud Hotel, they would not be in keeping, but Mrs Owton, the owner, has sought and perfected a homely, comfortable and cosy ambience which, frankly, is the most effective panacea for modern stress we have yet discovered. You will find modern notions of comfort at the Cloud, of course, such as televisions in the bedrooms, it is just that we wager you will be rather disinclined to turn yours on! There are four comfortable lounges, a bar, an attractive restaurant and a relaxing garden especially for guests, where full cream teas are served. The hotel's all-year-round appeal is underlined by full central heating and log fires. If you are a lover of synthetic entertainment the Cloud Hotel is not for you, but there is a legion of country pursuits to be followed in the area, whilst Mrs Owton arranges painting, nature walks, golfing, horse riding and gourmet dinner weekends throughout the year. Altogether the Cloud combines friendliness, comfort, informality, recreation and location in a manner which would be difficult to surpass.

Weekly Terms from £235.00
Daily Terms from £47.00
Bed and Breakfast from £33.00
Bar Meal from £6.00. Sunday Lunch from £12.00. Dinner from £15.00 Table D'Hôte
Gratuities at Guest's Discretion. VAT inclusive. 5 Family Rooms. 6 Double, 8 Single, 5 Twin Bedrooms
All Rooms with TV, Radio, Tea and Coffee-making facilities
Some rooms en-suite
Open from 1st February to 30th November

Residential and Restaurant Licence
Full CH. TV Lounge. Children catered for.
Dogs allowed at £3.50 per Day. Parking Facilities. Nearby: Tennis, Swimming, Golf, Riding, Sailing, Windsurfing, Water Skiing, Shooting

Brockenhurst—The Watersplash Hotel
The Rise, Brockenhurst, Hampshire. SO42 7ZP. Tel 0590 22344

Brockenhurst may have derived its name from words meaning 'badger's wood' and, with almost 100,000 acres of New Forest on one's northern doorstep, there is a considerable variety of beautiful scenery with much to interest the naturalist. To the east there is the appeal of the National Motor Museum, also an abbey and the interior of Palace House at Beaulieu to be visited. On the west and east banks, respectively, of the estuary, there are a Maritime Museum and the colourful Exbury Gardens. Easily accessible is the south coast from Bournemouth round to Southampton water and, from the nearest point, Lymington provides a ferry service to the Isle of Wight. All New Forest hotels have an advantage, for, although they may be sited in villages, they can still provide the benefits and atmosphere of a country house. Indeed, Robin and Judy Foster's hotel is, to our minds, a model of all that a family-run hotel should be. There will be a personal welcome from your hosts when you arrive and all your needs will be efficiently and kindly catered for. In the bar lounge, one may select from an unusually large number of malt whiskies and, with an excellent choice of freshly-made dishes available at every meal-time, sample English home cooking at its best. Most of the house has been recently refurbished to a high standard. It is a house of character standing within two acres of sheltered gardens in which is situated one of the area's most attractive heated swimming-pools. By arrangement, children's high teas are served and a baby patrol provided. There is a games room in the hotel and, nearby, a whole range of aquatic activities, court games, health sports and hang-gliding.

Weekly Terms from £260.00
Daily Terms from £48.00
Bed and Breakfast from £38.00
Lunch from £9.95 and A La Carte
Dinner from £18.00 Table D'Hôte

Gratuities at Guest's Discretion
VAT inclusive. Credit Cards—Access, Visa
5 Family Rooms. 8 Double, 3 Single, 7 Twin Bedrooms. 20 Private Bathrooms. 3 Private Shower Rooms. All Rooms with TV,

Radio, Telephone, Tea and Coffee-making Facilities, Baby-listening. Baby Patrol and Hairdryer available on Request. Open all Year. Residential Licence. Full CH. Cocktail Bar. TV Lounge. Games Room.

Section 2: Hampshire

Brockenhurst—Whitley Ridge Country House Hotel
Beaulieu Road, Brockenhurst, Hants. SO42 7QL. Tel 0590 22354

Set deep in the heart of the New Forest lies this lovely small secluded Country House hotel, once a Royal Hunting Lodge and former home of the Bowes-Lyon family. It has recently undergone major refurbishment to enhance the original Georgian features and create the atmosphere of an elegant country house. We have known Mr & Mrs Law for some years and know they are never satisfied unless they are offering their guests the highest standards; they are ETB 4 Crowns Highly Commended. They have in Whitley Ridge a charming hotel in a beautiful setting seemingly so remote yet close to many well known places of interest. The eleven bedrooms, including a four-poster and Georgian room, are individually decorated with great attention to detail chintz curtains frame the long windows and in the bathrooms the use of mahogany, marble and gold fittings reflect a bygone era. Downstairs the *décor* is of the same high quality. The sitting room, cocktail bar and dining room look out to the green fields where Forest ponies graze peacefully, and log fires burn in winter. In the adjoining Wyllie Room, so named after the artists William and Harold Wyllie, you step back into an age of graciousness this room is particularly suitable for business meetings, seminars and private dinner parties. Whitley Ridge prides itself on the high standard of food served in its restaurant and this is reflected both in the excellent *à la carte* and *table d'hôte* menus which change daily. Go up the drive to this lovely Georgian house as it will repay your investigation many times over.

Weekly Terms from £280.00
Half Board from £44.00 per night (min 2 nights). Single Half Board from £54.00 per night (min 2 nights)
Bed and Breakfast from £38.00
Lunch from £9.50 and A La Carte
Dinner from £16.50 and A La Carte

Gratuities at Guest's Discretion. VAT inclusive. Credit Cards—Access, American Express, Diners Club, Visa
1 Family Room. 8 Double, 3 Twin, 1 Single Bedrooms. 8 Private Bathrooms.
5 Private Shower Rooms. All Rooms with TV, Telephone, Radio, Tea and

Coffee-making Facilities. Hairdryer available on request. Open all Year.
Residential Licence. Full CH.
Cocktail Bar. TV Lounge. Conference Facilities. Children catered for. Dogs allowed. Parking Facilities. Hard Tennis Court. Nearby: Croquet, Putting

Burley—The Moorhill House Hotel
Burley, Near Ringwood, Hampshire. BH24 4AG. Tel 0425 403285. Fax 0703 283719

Moorhill House has been a hive of activity recently, for its owners, Care Hotels plc, have refurbished it from top to bottom. Now, once again, peace reigns supreme here, with only the occasional hoot of an owl or the dawn chorus to disturb the profound silence of the forest. A half-mile woodland drive separates the hotel from the rest of the world, and the splendid three-acre garden merely emphasises that here is perfect privacy. All this is not to imply a certain rusticity, for the house has beautiful Victorian country house proportions, which even before the recent changes were effected held the promise of a comfortable rural lifestyle. That is now, unquestionably, a reality. Naturally, you must be prepared to enjoy the country for all it offers. Clean air unpolluted by smoke, the best of produce and the best of food, a slower pace ... and freedom. For the rest, new decor, carpeting, soft furnishings and elegant furniture play their part, as does the newly styled indoor recreation area, with its heated swimming pool, spa bath and sauna. The bedrooms, too, are beautifully styled and eminently comfortable. You may play croquet, badminton and miniature golf in the grounds, or, perhaps, go and watch Burley's cricket eleven on the village green. On hand are all the recreations for which the New Forest is famous. But if you just need to drop out for a while choose Moorhill, where everything is done for you ... and you will preserve your sanity.

Weekly Terms on request
Bed and Breakfast from £36.50 per person
Bar Lunch from £2.50
Dinner from £11.75 and A la Carte
VAT inclusive.
Credit Cards—Access, American Express, Diners Club, Visa
5 Family Rooms. 1 Suite. 13 Double,

3 Twin, 2 Single Bedrooms
All Rooms with Private Bath/Shower Room, TV, Telephone, Radio, Baby-listening, Tea and Coffee-making Facilities, Hairdryer.
Open all Year.
Residential Licence. Full Central Heating. Cocktail Bar.

Conference Facilities.
Children catered for. Dogs allowed.
Parking Facilities. Croquet,
Putting, Badminton, Indoor Swimming Pool, Sauna
Nearby: Tennis, Squash, Solarium, Golf, Fishing, Riding, Windsurfing, Water Skiing, Shooting, Hang Gliding

Section 2: Hampshire

Cadnam—Bartley Lodge
Cadnam, New Forest, Hampshire SO4 2NR. Tel 0703 812248. Fax 0703 812075

The entrance gates abut the Cadnam-Lyndhurst road, barely half a mile from junction one of the M27. Drive in confidently, however, if you enjoy peace and privacy, for Bartley Lodge was built, planned and positioned so that its occupants could always be in touch with the country ways of the forest. The founder of the New Forest Hounds erected the house in 1759 as a hunting lodge. Yet, this huntsman clearly appreciated the finer points of gracious living. Step into the panelled hall, with its minstrel's gallery and large open fireplace, and you will experience his grand design. Bartley Lodge will surely strike you as not only graceful architecturally but generous in its spaciousness and appointments. We dined in a splendid dining room, the *Crystal Restaurant*, and later, through french windows, we stepped out onto a sunny terrace. In front were well-groomed lawns, beyond a covered heated swimming pool, two all weather hard surface tennis courts and a lake which abounds with wildlife. The *cuisine* at Bartley Lodge reflects the very best of the New English style of cooking and brought home to us the benefits of living in, and reaping produce from, the country. Stay here if you possibly can. The rooms are all *en suite*, restfully furnished and very well equipped with modern niceties. With its unusual *Hunters Bar*, and the small *Tudor Room* and the *Baronial Banqueting Suite* for special functions, Bartley Lodge follows the pattern of a first-class country house hotel.

Weekly Terms on request
Bed and Breakfast from £36.50 per person
Bar Lunch from £2.50
Dinner from £11.75 and A La Carte
VAT inclusive. Credit Cards—Access, American Express, Diners Club, Visa
1 Family Room. 2 Suites. 9 Double, 5 Twin, 2 Single Bedrooms

All Rooms with Private Bathroom, TV, Telephone, Radio, Baby-listening, Tea and Coffee-making Facilities, Hairdryer.
1 Room with Trouser Press
Open all Year. Fully Licensed.
Full Central Heating.
Cocktail Bar.
Conference Facilities

Children catered for. Dogs allowed.
Parking Facilities. Two all weather hard surface Tennis Courts, covered heated Swimming Pool
Nearby: Tennis, Croquet, Putting, Squash, Badminton, Solarium, Sauna, Golf, Fishing, Riding, Sailing, Windsurfing, Water Skiing, Shooting, Hang Gliding

Near Christchurch, Avon–Tyrrells Ford Hotel
Avon, Christchurch, Hampshire. BH23 7BH. Tel 0425 72646

This charming 3-star country house hotel, parts of which date back to the eighteenth century, stands in ten acres of beautiful grounds on the edge of the New Forest. Once again we are delighted to report wide-ranging improvements and extensions under the direction of the devoted resident proprietors, Anna and Ivan Caplan. Total refurbishment of the bedrooms and upgrading of all the bathrooms throughout the hotel means there is a tasteful freshness in all parts of the hotel. We were most impressed by the discreet way in which conference facilities have been introduced. These areas, which can serve also as function rooms, are skilfully arranged so as not to intrude on the privacy of the hotel guests. The hotel's panelled, candlelit *à la carte* restaurant has earned independent commendations as has the extensive bar menu: both dining room and bars provide views of the lawns and unspoilt countryside. An outstanding feature of the building is a majestic *Minstrel's Gallery* in the residents' lounge, shown to best advantage by thoughtful lighting and a restful décor. The Tyrrells Ford is reached down an attractive woodland drive off the B3347 Ringwood to Christchurch road, some four miles from each town. Within easy reach are the sheltered Poole Bay, the excellent shops of Bournemouth, historic Wimborne Minster, the harbour and beaches of Christchurch, and all the natural beauty of the New Forest, ideal for walks and picnics. In the cooler seasons, the hotel's full central heating is complemented by open log fires, and visitors are assured of an equally warm welcome.

Weekly Terms from £245.00
Bed and Breakfast from £35.00
Bar Lunch and Supper from £4.95
Lunch from £10.95 and A La Carte
Dinner from £16.95 and A La Carte
Gratuities at Guest's Discretion.

VAT inclusive.
Credit Cards—Access, Visa
6 Double, 5 Twin, 5 Single Bedrooms.
(Some Rooms can be let as Family Rooms)
12 Private Bathrooms. 4 Private Shower Rooms. All Rooms with TV, Telephone,

Radio, Tea and Coffee-making Facilities.
Hairdryer available on request
Dry Cleaning Service. Open all Year. Fully Licensed. Full Central Heating and Log Fires. Conference Facilities. Dogs not allowed. Parking Facilities

Section 2: Hampshire

Emsworth–Brookfield Hotel Havant Road, Emsworth, Hampshire. PO10 7LF. Tel 0243 373363. Fax 0243 376342

The new A27 road, which links Chichester and Havant, now carries all the passing traffic, so an air of sedateness has returned to the old, picturesque coast road. Here, amid the tidal creeks and the farmlands, the Brookfield, just to the west of Emsworth, is now able to enjoy an even quieter country-house environment. And, allied to this, you will find that the Brookfield is an excellent example of the very best proprietor-run hotel. Mr Drew Gibson must surely be everyone's idea of 'mine host' and he is justly proud of the hotel which he and his family have created. In 1987 its *Hermitage Restaurant* won the prestigious 'National Eating Out Week' award for the high standard of *cuisine* and the originality of the theme. This recently refurbished restaurant has now been given a more elegant and spacious feel to make any occasion even more memorable. We stayed at the Brookfield recently and we revelled in the warm, comfortable surroundings. The hotel offers executive bedrooms, and even has a honeymoon suite with a four poster. All the rooms, however, are *en suite* and are fully equipped with modern necessities. We also noted that the Brookfield has comprehensive function and conference facilities for up to 140 people. For many visitors, though, the attraction of the hotel will be its glorious position for holidays in an area which abounds with interest. We lived at the Brookfield in great comfort, and greatly appreciated the care we received from the Gibson family, who clearly live for their hotel.

Daily Terms from £68.00(Double) Lunch from £13.50 and A La Carte Afternoon Tea from £0.95 Dinner from £13.50 and A La Carte Gratuities at Guest's Discretion. VAT inclusive. Credit Cards—Access, American Express, Diners Club, Visa	20 Double, 14 Twin, 7 Single Bedrooms All Rooms with Private Bath/Shower Room, TV, Telephone, Radio, Tea and Coffee-making Facilities, Trouser Press, Hairdryer Open from 2nd January. Residential and Restaurant Licence. Full Central Heating.	Cocktail Bar. Conference Facilities Children catered for. Dogs not allowed Parking Facilities. Night Porter. Nearby: Tennis, Putting, Squash, Badminton Swimming, Sauna, Solarium, Golf, Fishing, Riding, Sailing, Windsurfing, Water Skiing, Hang-Gliding

Hayling Island—Cockle Warren Cottage Hotel
36 Seafront, Hayling Island, Hampshire. PO11 9HL. Tel 0705 464961/464838

Cockle Warren is a delightful cottage hotel set in a large garden on Hayling Island seafront. You could not wish for better comfort, or more attentive and personal service than you will find here. David Skelton carried our cases to our bedroom *(The Honeysuckle Room,* and just as pretty as its name implies) and invited us to take tea downstairs beside the log fire. Among the home-made fare was melt-in-the-mouth shortbread, our first taste of Diane Skelton's expertise in cooking. This was a fitting proem to what was to come: a dinner which was utterly delicious and expertly presented. An attractive conservatory adds light and space to the dining room and this overlooks the heated swimming pool. The outlook onto the subtly-lit pool at night is a memorable feature of one's dinner. Cockle Warren has five very pretty bedrooms, each equipped with the usual modern etceteras, and they look either onto the sea or the patio garden and pool. Two have four-poster suites, and they have all been designed for comfort, from a carafe of madeira right down to the miniature sewing basket and the discreetly tucked-away iron and board in the cupboard. We must admit, we were unsure what we were going to find at this small hotel, but we could not have been more impressed. This cottage hotel offers good food, wine and contentment, where only the best is good enough. Hayling Island is famous for racket sports as well as sailing and golf, you can also go swimming, riding and fishing or simply relax and take it easy at Cockle Warren and listen to the sound of the sea just a few yards away.

Bed and Breakfast from £56.00 (Double) Bed and Breakfast from £35.00 (Single) Bar Supper from £8.50. Dinner from £23.50 Credit Cards—Access, Visa 5 Double, 1 Twin Bedroom 1 Private Bathroom. 4 Private Shower	Rooms. All Rooms with TV, Telephone, Radio, Trouser Press, Hairdryer, Iron, Sewing Kits, Toiletries, Madeira Wine. Full Room Service and Laundry Service Open all year. Residential Licence. Full CH. Lounge with log fire	Children over 9 years catered for. Dogs allowed (not in bedrooms). Parking Facilities. Outdoor heated Swimming Pool Nearby: Tennis, Putting, Squash, Badminton, Golf, Fishing, Riding, Sailing Sailing, Windsurfing, Water Skiing

Section 2: Hampshire

Hayling Island—Newtown House Hotel Manor Road, Hayling Island, Hampshire. PO11 0QR. Tel 0705 466131. Fax 0705 461366

On one of England's tiniest and most sheltered islands (Hayling measures only four miles by two miles) is one of the cosiest and most friendly hotels we know...Newtown House. It is not in the least bit pretentious, but the owners have done a tremendous job of introducing modern facilities, to the extent of building an indoor leisure complex with heated swimming pool, gymnasium, jacuzzi and solarium, a hard tennis court and further recreational amenities indoors. Joy, the receptionist, has been at the hotel for ten years, and her kindness and helpfulness epitomise the welcome one receives from everyone associated with Newtown House. The hotel began life as a farm in the early part of the nineteenth century—the annex adjacent to the hotel is the original farmhouse—and is listed as being of exceptional historic interest. You will note the distinctive character in the *Oak Bar*, where old ships' beams, oak panelling, polished floors, rugs and comfortable armchairs promote the homely atmosphere. The bar overlooks the gardens and the leisure complex. During our stay we were allocated one of the hotel's older rooms, which was equipped to an equally high standard of comfort and utility. We slept well and dined well and thought the menu, especially, provided excellent value for money. The hotel is a good choice for a country-cum-seaside break. The island is surrounded by marvellous sailing waters and ringed with sandy beaches. Newtown House is very busy during weekdays, so contact Mr A Witkowski, the general manager, in advance of your visit.

Weekly Terms (Half Board) from £258.00 pp. Bed and Breakfast from £35.00 Bar Lunch from £4.50. Lunch from £8.15 Table D'Hôte. Bar Supper from £5.00 Dinner from 13.50 Table D'Hôte Gratuities at Guest's Discretion. VAT inclusive. Credit Cards—Access, American Express, Diners Club, Visa. 3 Family Rooms. 12 Double, 4 Twin, 9 Single Bedrooms. 17 Private Bathrooms. 9 Private Shower Rooms. All Rooms with TV, Telephone, Radio, Baby-listening, Tea and Coffee-making Facilities, Hairdryer. Open all Year. Fully Licensed. Full Central Heating. TV Lounge. Conference Facilities. Children catered for. Dogs allowed. Parking Facilities. Hard Tennis Court, Indoor Leisure Complex with Heated Pool, Sauna, Gym, Jacuzzi and Solarium. Nearby: Squash, Badminton, Golf, Riding, Sailing, Windsurfing, Water Skiing

Lymington—Stanwell House Hotel and Railings Restaurant High Street, Lymington, Hampshire. SO41 9AA. Tel 0590 677123. Fax 0590 677756

Even those who visit Lymington but briefly, on their way to catch the ferry to Yarmouth on the Isle of Wight, must be captivated by this pretty, Georgian town. In past centuries its harbour rivalled in importance with Southampton and Portsmouth, but today yachts and yachting dominate its daily life, with yacht brokers and ship's chandlers lining its cobbled Quay Street. In keeping with Lymington's nautical traditions, the town's principal hotel is owned by Clipper Hotels. However, step inside the Stanwell House Hotel and you will find yourself in quiet and elegant surroundings which will transport you far from quotidian bustle. There is a tradition of good hotelkeeping at Stanwell House which stretches as far back as the eighteenth century. Recently the hotel has been almost entirely refurbished, but none of its character and charm have been lost. All the bedrooms have private bathrooms and those in the *Mouton Wing* have delightful views of the courtyard and walled garden. As you may discern from the name of this wing, and the fact that each room is named after one of the famous Bordeaux châteaux, fine wine is very much a way of life at this hotel. The extensive wine list of the *Railings Restaurant* has an outstanding reputation, with prices ranging from around £7.00 to £300.00 a bottle! Although the menus are changed regularly, the high quality of the *cuisine* never varies. For the businessman, the hotel is equipped with facsimile facilities, and the *Garden Suite* is ideal for small executive meetings and functions.

Bed and Breakfast from £72.50 (Single)/£49.00 (Twin per person) Lunch from £12.00 and A La Carte Dinner from £20.00 and A La Carte Gratuities at Guest's Discretion VAT inclusive. Credit Cards—Access, Visa 1 Suite. 17 Double, 11 Twin, 6 Single Bedrooms. All Rooms with Private Bathroom, TV, Telephone, Radio, Baby-listening, Tea and Coffee-making Facilities, Trouser Press, Hairdryer Open all Year. Fully Licensed Full Central Heating. Cocktail Bar Conference Facilities. Children catered for. Dogs not allowed. Parking Facilities nearby Night Porter. Nearby: Tennis, Squash, Swimming, Golf, Fishing, Riding, Sailing Windsurfing, Water Skiing

Section 2: Hampshire

Near Lymington—Passford House Mount Pleasant Lane, Lymington, Hampshire. SO41 8LS. Tel 0590 682398. Fax 0590 683494

An outstanding country house hotel if there ever was one. Yet, you need not be a country lover to appreciate its clean air and sunshine unpolluted with smoke. Standing in ten acres of well-cared-for grounds, with the natural glades of the New Forest adding a sense of countryfied freedom to one's comings and goings, Passford is so likeable, and a great attraction to overseas visitors. The reason for this lies partially in its true English character. The long-fronted Georgian house is full of character, which is complemented by antique furniture, a panelled lounge, cocktail bar, and all convey an air of informality. The bedrooms are individually planned and several rooms are on the ground floor, many being ideal for families. Special features are the de-luxe bedrooms, including a superb four-poster, having recently been refurbished and are great value for that little extra. The restaurant is superb and the high standard of catering befits an elegant country house. And overall is the guiding hand of the proprietors, Mr and Mrs Heritage, who keep their hotel as fresh as spring and care for their visitors so well. Passford House has a nine-hole putting green, croquet lawn, hard tennis court, plus a newly built leisure complex consisting of a heated swimming pool, sauna, solarium, multi gym and a games room. Within walking distance is Lymington with its modern exclusive yachting facilities. For all seasons of the year, Passford House provides a lovely setting. Before reaching Lymington from Brockenhurst, look out for the Passford House sign at the turning on the right for Sway.

Bed and Breakfast from £53.50.
De Luxe Rooms Bed and Breakfast £60.00
Bar Lunch from £3.50
Lunch from £10.50 Table D'Hôte
Dinner from £19.50 Table D'Hôte
Gratuities at Guest's Discretion.

VAT inclusive. Credit Cards—Access, American Express, Visa
5 Family Rooms. 2 Suites. 13 Double, 29 Twin, 5 Single Bedrooms
All Rooms with Private Bathroom, TV, Telephone, Radio, Baby-listening, Tea and

Coffee-making Facilities, Trouser Press, Hairdryer. Open all Year. Fully Licensed Full CH. Cocktail Bar. TV Lounge.
Conference Facilities. Children catered for.
Dogs allowed. Parking Facilities. Night Porter. Hard Tennis Court, Croque, Putting

Lyndhurst—Forest Lodge Hotel Pikes Hill, Romsey Road, Lyndhurst, Hants. SO43 7AS. Tel 0703 283677. Fax 0703 283719

On our recent travels we were completely surprised at the changes which had taken place at the Forest Lodge Hotel. It is now part of Care Hotels plc, who also own Bartley Lodge at Cadnam, the Moorhill House Hotel at Burley and the Beaulieu Hotel near Lyndhurst. Situated at Pikes Hill, just off the Romsey Road, it is only five minutes' walk from the centre of Lyndhurst. Originally built as the dower house of the Notherwood Estate, this Georgian mansion stands in an acre and a half of lovely gardens and grounds. Inside the hotel a friendly welcome awaits you and this is when we realised that, although the same building, it has been totally refurbished and redecorated to provide ample and spacious accommodation. The *Forest Restaurant*, which overlooks the gardens, is an extremely pleasant venue for dinner, with quality napery and a pleasant, yet stylish atmosphere. There is a covered heated swimming pool within the well maintained grounds. Lyndhurst provides an ideal base for exploring the New Forest with all its attractions, yet is close to Winchester, Salisbury, Bournemouth and Beaulieu, to name but a few. Riding, fishing, cricket and polo are all within reach of Forest Lodge and with so much to offer, one almost takes for granted the care and comfort one receives at this ever welcoming hotel.

Weekly Terms on request
Bed and Breakfast from £36.50 per person
Bar Lunch from £2.50
Sunday Lunch from £10.00
Afternoon Tea from £2.50
Dinner from £11.75 and A La Carte
VAT inclusive. Credit Cards—Access, American Express, Diners Club, Visa

1 Family Room. 10 Double, 10 Twin, 2 Single Bedrooms
All Rooms with Private Bathroom, TV, Telephone, Radio, Baby-listening, Tea and Coffee-making Facilities, Hairdryer
Open all Year. Fully Licensed. Full Central Heating. Cocktail Bar.
Conference Facilities.

Children catered for.
Dogs allowed.
Parking Facilities
Covered heated Swimming Pool
Nearby: Tennis, Croquet, Putting, Squash, Badminton, Solarium, Sauna, Golf, Fishing, Riding, Sailing, Windsurfing, Water Skiing, Shooting, Hang Gliding

Section 2: Hampshire

Nr Lyndhurst, Beaulieu Road—The Beaulieu Hotel
Beaulieu Road, Lyndhurst, Hants. SO42 7YQ. Tel 0703 293344. Fax 0703 283719

Beaulieu Road Station is not sure whose child it is, for it lies in splendid isolation on the undulating B3056 road, being some five miles from anywhere of importance. There is a railway halt, a livestock yard and that well-known New Forest landmark, The Beaulieu Hotel. All three have been there to serve the famous auctions, which take place six times a year, when forest ponies are sold to the highest bidder. Until recently the hotel was happy to continue fulfilling this well-established role and to proffer refreshment to the passing motorist. The owners, however, Care Hotels plc, have four of the New Forest's nicest country-house hotels and they were determined to invest The Beaulieu Hotel with the same high standards found in their other establishments. How they have accomplished this transformation is something of a master-stroke. The large bars have all gone, to be replaced by a comfortable lounge, an intimate restaurant and a conservatory-style function room. Above stairs, all the bedrooms have been refurbished in most attractive country styles, using pretty prints and good-quality fabrics, and each is equipped to a very good level indeed. We have dined recently in the hotel's *Hungry Horse Restaurant* and can recommend it to you unreservedly.

(Only Bed and Breakfast rates are available from 1st March to 31st October 1993)
Weekly Terms on request
Bed and Breakfast from £36.50 per person
Bar Lunch from £2.50. Lunch from £10.00
Dinner from £11.75 and A La Carte
Gratuities at Guest's discretion. VAT inclusive. Credit Cards—Access, American Express, Diners Club, Visa
1 Suite, 1 Twin, 16 Double Bedrooms
All rooms with TV, Telephone, Radio, Baby-listening, Tea and Coffee-making Facilities, Hairdryer
Open all year. Fully Licensed. Full Central Heating. Cocktail Bar. TV Lounge.

Conference Facilities
Children catered for. Dogs allowed.
Parking Facilities. Simulated Clay Pigeon shooting, Riding can be arranged
Nearby: Tennis, Croquet, Putting, Squash, Badminton, Swimming, Solarium, Sauna, Golf, Fishing, Sailing, Windsurfing, Water Skiing

Milford-on-Sea—South Lawn Hotel
Lymington Road, Milford-on-Sea, Lymington, Hants. SO41 0RF. Tel 0590 643911. Fax 0590 644820

Externally and internally one could not wish for a brighter, cleaner or more colourful hotel. Potted plants and fresh flowers are featured in many places and, as the name implies, there is a lush green lawn surrounded by shrubs and mature trees. A short drive will take one to the National Motor Museum at Beaulieu or to the New Forest. The hotel is just half a mile from Milford village and only about one mile from the sea. It has been under the ownership of Ernst and Jennifer Barten since opening in 1971. They have constantly striven to make improvements and, recently, the bedrooms have been refurbished. The food is a major attraction at South Lawn, and the welcoming restaurant - which overlooks the surrounding gardens - is well patronised by local residents. To accompany the modestly-priced dinner, there is a sound wine list. This area of the coast, east from Christchurch, through Milford, little-known Keyhaven and on to Lymington, is one which will repay investigation by those who seek a holiday base away from the more crowded popular resorts. A comfortable and relaxing stay is assured here and we believe their off-season breaks present an ideal opportunity to unwind, with winter breaks available at special rates. There are two first-class golf courses in the locality and, of course, the usual seaside activities. Reference has already been made to the excellent catering and, to this, we should add that we were impressed with the clean and functional layout of the modern kitchen.

All Terms pertaining to 1992
Weekly Terms from £365.85
Daily Terms from £56.50
Bed and Breakfast from £42.00
Lunch from £9.75
Afternoon Tea from £1.75
Dinner from £14.50 and A La Carte
Gratuities at Guest's Discretion.

VAT inclusive
Credit Cards—Access, Visa
6 Double, 18 Twin Bedrooms
All Rooms with Private Bathroom, TV, Telephone, Radio, Trouser Press, Hairdryer
Open from 14th January.
Residential and Restaurant Licence
Full Central Heating.

Lounge Bar.
Children not catered for.
Dogs not allowed
Parking Facilities
Nearby: Tennis, Squash, Swimming, Golf, Fishing, Riding, Sailing, Windsurfing, Water Skiing, Shooting

Section 2: Hampshire

Milford-on-Sea—Westover Hall Hotel & Restaurant Park Lane, Milford-on-Sea, Hampshire. SO4 0PT. Tel 0590 643044. Fax 0590 644490

Three bands of colour dominate the coastline near Milford on Sea; the aquamarine of the Solent's waters, the white of the limestone cliffs, and the viridian of the cliff top turf. Just across the garden from the quiet beach is Westover Hall, an imposing mansion house, which dates from 1897. It has beautiful mullioned windows and tile-hung walls outside, and inside, delicate panelling and numerous fireplaces abound the rooms. The hotel is run on a very personal basis by Swiss couple Pierre and Edina Roth, who have a wealth of hotel experience behind them. This was clearly evident on our most recent visit, when we were so impressed with all we saw that we decided to stay the night and have dinner. The restaurant and intimate bar both have superb views across the Solent. We were served with good, traditional *cuisine* which was complemented by an extensive yet affordable wine list and excellent friendly service. Above stairs, all the bedrooms are spacious and luxuriously appointed with private bathrooms, colour televisions, tea and coffee-making facilities and telephones and some have the same excellent views across the gardens towards the sea. A limousine service is available to guests arriving at either Gatwick or Heathrow or, more locally, either Southampton's Eastleigh or Bournemouth's Hurn airports. With all the attractions of the New Forest close to hand this is an ideal place to stay and relax, and we certainly felt sad at having to leave but we look forward to visiting here again in the near future.

Weekly Terms from £297.50 and from £336.00
Daily Terms from £45.00 and from £50.00
Bed and Breakfast from £30.00 and from £40.00
Lunch from £12.25. Bar Supper from £2.75
Dinner from £14.45

VAT inclusive. Credit Cards—Access, American Express, Diners Club, Visa
2 Bed-sitting Rooms. 4 Double, 4 Twin, 2 Single Bedrooms. All Rooms with Private Bathroom, TV, Telephone, Tea and Coffee-making Facilities, Radio
Open all Year. Fully Licensed

Part Central Heating and Electric Radiators. Conference Facilities
Children catered for. Dogs allowed at Management's Discretion
Parking Facilities. Croquet
Nearby: Tennis, Swimming, Golf, Fishing, Riding, Sailing, Windsurfing, Water Skiing

New Milton–Chewton Glen New Milton, Hampshire, BH25 6QS. Tel 0425 275341. Fax 0425 272310

Everything that made fashionable country living the English ideal is to be found here, in a wooded valley between the New Forest and the sea. Martin Skan made Chewton Glen an outstanding hotel even before country houses of this type became the desirable place at which to stay, and the standards of quality which he has set here have become bench-marks of excellence throughout the hotel industry. The house is almost three hundred years old and came to prominence when Captain Marryat wrote his celebrated novel, 'The Children of the New Forest' here in 1846. Its claim to eminence as one of Britain's finest hotels, however, was not achieved instantly by means of a large infusion of money. On the contrary, it has taken Mr Skan twenty-five years of dedication, and no small measure of pioneering spirit, to achieve the high standards of good taste he sought. In this he has been aided by a loyal team who share his attention to detail. Thus, you will find an environment which is luxurious, but also completely relaxing; service which is naturally given and is never mannered; and cuisine which has made Chewton Glen's *Marryat Restaurant* one of the finest in the country. A magnificent indoor swimming pool, indoor tennis courts, spa, steam room and saunas, Life Fitness gym, skilled therapists and a unisex hairdressing salon are all available. There is also an outdoor pool and a nine-hole golf course in the hotel's seventy acres of gardens, parkland and woodlands. In 1991 the ETB voted Chewton Glen the 'Best Hotel in England' and Martin Skan has justly been voted 1991 Hotelier of the Year, although there is little doubt that his most enduring tribute is this Palladian-style mansion set amidst the English oaks of Hampshire.

Discounts available for weekly stays
Daily Terms from £255.00 (2 people)
Room Rate from £178.00. Lunch from £22.50 Table D'Hôte. Dinner from £39.00

Service and VAT included
Credit Cards–Access, American Express, Diners Club, Visa. 1 Family Room. 13 Suites. 44 Double/Twin Bedrooms. All

Rooms with Private Bath and Shower, TV, Telephone, Radio, Trouser Press, Hairdryer, Safe, Sherry Decanter. Open all year. Fully Licensed. Full Central Heating.

Section 2: Hampshire

Near Petersfield, Langrish–Langrish House Langrish, Petersfield, Hampshire. GU32 1RN. Tel 0730 266941. Fax 0730 260543

In more opulent times it was quite usual to own a London town house and a country estate. The Wilbraham Hotel, off Sloane Street, has all the elegance and charm of a quiet town house and we have used it as our London base on many occasions. Under the same ownership is this beautiful rural alternative set deep in the rolling countryside of Hampshire. When we visited it recently we detected the same zest for work and practical eye for detail which has become the hallmark of The Wilbraham and its director, Miss Monique von Kospoth. Built around the core of a sixteenth-century farmhouse and extended in 1600 using mellow malmstone, it is painstakingly preserved both inside and out. To this inveteracy has been sympathetically added every modern comfort. Thus you will find bedrooms (their matching colour schemes are a pure delight) each providing central heating, *en suite* bathroom and colour television among its country-house appointments. In view of its eminent parentage we had come to Langrish House with high expectations of its restaurant and we were not to be disappointed. The menu was limited but well chosen and our choices were beautifully prepared. In the cellars are two further intimate dining-rooms and a bar. To quote directly from our inspector's report, 'This was a peaceful, luxurious stay. It was lovely to be pampered and we were very sorry to move on.'

Bed and Continental Breakfast from £59.00(Double)
Afternoon Tea from £1.55
Dinner from £12.00 A La Carte
Gratuities at Guest's Discretion. VAT inclusive. Credit Cards—Access, American Express, Diners Club, Visa

6 Double, 6 Twin, 6 Single Bedrooms
All Rooms with Private Bathroom, TV, Telephone, Radio, Baby-listening. Tea and Coffee-making Facilities, Hairdryer and Iron and Ironing Board and Trouser Press available on Request
Closed from December 25th to January 1st
Residential and Restaurant Licence.

Full Central Heating/. Double insulation
2 Cocktail Bars. TV Lounge.
Conference/Banqueting Facilities. Children catered for. Dogs allowed by Arrangement
Parking Facilities
Nearby: Tennis, Squash, Badminton, Swimming, Golf, Riding

Portsmouth, Southsea—Queen's Hotel Clarence Parade, Southsea, Portsmouth, Hampshire. PO5 3LJ. Tel 0705 822466. Fax 0705 821901

For more than one hundred years the splendid Edwardian-style building of the Queen's has dominated the front at Southsea. Whilst introducing all of today's modern facilities and comforts, the character of yesteryear's gracious living has not been lost through its total refurbishment. Many original features such as ceiling mouldings, high skirtings and scrolled cornices have been retained along with enamel baths, and porcelain bathroom fittings with gold finishes throughout. Panelled walls and crystal chandeliers grace the luxurious *Princess Restaurant* which overlooks the garden terrace and the heated swimming pool. Throughout the hotel, windows are sumptuously pelmeted, in many locations framing breathtaking views of the sea. After disclosing the object of our unannounced visit, we were given a conducted tour of the hotel - which boasts one hundred bedrooms - by the General Manager. We were most impressed with the uniformly high standards of *décor* and cleanliness: only in the layouts and colour schemes were welcome variations and individual characterisations to be seen. All the facilities are here for holding prestigious conferences, grand social events or personal holidays to be remembered. The Queen's can, on request, make a helicopter landing port available, charter pleasure yachts and arrange car hire including vintage Bentleys. Close at hand is Fun Acres, the largest amusement complex on the south coast; three casinos, the world-famous Naval Heritage ships and an excellent shopping centre are a few of the many other attractions of this area.

Weekly Terms from £346.50
Bed and Breakfast from £55.00
Lunch from £7.75 Table D'Hôte
Dinner from £13.75 Table D'Hôte
VAT inclusive. Credit Cards–Access, American Express, Diners Club, Visa

6 Family Rooms. 1 Suite. 22 Double, 29 Twin, 12 Single Bedrooms
All Rooms with Private Bathroom, TV, Telephone, Radio.
Hairdryer available on request
Open all year. Fully Licensed. Full Central

Heating. 2 Lifts. Cocktail Bar. Conference Facilities. Children catered for.
Guide dogs only allowed. Parking Facilities. Night Porter. Outdoor Swimming Pool. Nearby: Tennis, Putting, Squash, Indoor Swimming, Solarium, Sauna, Golf

Section 2: Hampshire

Rotherwick, Near Hook–Tylney Hall
Rotherwick, Near Hook, Hants. RG27 9AJ.
Tel 0256 764881. Fax 0256 768141

The grandeur of this magnificent mansion is matched by the splendour of its setting and a standard of service which is second to none. Tylney Hall was built in the late nineteenth-century on the site of an earlier manor house and is set in sixty-six acres of beautiful Hampshire countryside. Despite the imposing surroundings, we were received in a friendly and courteous manner and cannot think of a single detail that could be bettered in respect of the excellent lunch. All the public rooms and the several bedrooms we saw have a stately elegance, a relaxing spaciousness that make one's visit truly memorable. Every modern amenity is provided to ensure that each guest, whether alone or in a party, can choose the degree of privacy or participation to suit his or her mood. The hotel has ninety-one bedrooms and two charming lakeside suites especially designed for honeymooners plus leisure facilities comprising an indoor heated swimming pool, jacuzzi, sauna and a work-out gym. Inside the mansion, admire the intricately carved oak ceiling of the Italianate Lounge, enjoy a pre-dinner drink in the wood-panelled library bar, dine in the glass-domed restaurant or play a game of snooker. Outside activities include an outdoor heated swimming pool, tennis and croquet in the grounds, and arrangements for visitors to participate in local golf, horse-riding, hot air ballooning or archery. For that special occasion, book a suite with a four-poster bed or jacuzzi bath. Here is the place to luxuriate in the grand old style with every modern facility.

Weekly Terms on Application
Bed and Breakfast from £92.00
Lunch (three courses) from £20.00
Dinner from £25.00 Table D'Hôte
Service Charge and VAT inclusive
Credit Cards–Access, American Express, Diners Club, Visa

25 Suites, 51 Double, 15 Twin Bedrooms
All Rooms with Private Bath/Shower Room, TV, Telephone, Radio, Baby-Listening, Trouser Press, Hairdryer.
Open all year. Fully Licensed.
Full Central Heating. Bar.
Snooker Room.

Conference Facilities.
Dogs not allowed. Parking Facilities.
Night Porter.
Hard Tennis Courts, Croquet, Indoor and Outdoor Heated Swimming Pools, Sauna, Multi-gym.
Nearby: Golf, Horseriding.

Section 2: Hampshire

Winchester—The Wykeham Arms 75 Kingsgate Street, Winchester Hampshire. SO23 9PE. Tel 0962 853834. Fax 0962 854411

Winchester, historic capital of the Saxon and Norman kings of England "reposes in her sweet green valley low down amidst the swelling hills that compass her about. No English city has a nobler record in the past, or a life more peaceful in our rushing, hasteful age" (Dean Kitchin's *Winchester*). Tucked away in the quiet and oldest part of the city, neatly sandwiched between the College and the Cathedral, is a hostelry in the truest and finest meanings of the word. As you step into the Wykeham Arms, a certain something takes over and 'all is well with the world'. We make no claim to discovering this excellent establishment: Graeme Jameson and his wife Anne have, in recent years, accumulated a most impressive collection of commendations and accolades for their outstanding quality as an hotel, a pub, a pub caterer and as a wine pub. What we can say is that we are able to endorse every word in their most attractively-designed brochure. During our visit, we spotted the artist Charles Sutton who lives locally and provided illustrations of the Wykeham Arms for the brochure. In one of the bars, antique Winchester College desks serve as tables. The choice of food and wine in this hostelry is quite exceptional, with every wine offered by the glass or by the bottle, and pleasant service available in The Bishop's Room or the Old Watchmaker's Shop. Gracing the unique *décor* throughout, there are over 600 paintings, prints, cards and memorabilia. On our next visit, we are determined to have an overnight stay.

Bed and Breakfast from £62.50 (Single)/£72.50 (Double)
Lunch from £5.00
Dinner from £10.00. (No food served on Sundays)
Gratuities at Guest's Discretion.
VAT inclusive.

Credit Cards-American Express, Master Card, Visa
4 Double, 3 Twin Bedrooms (All rooms can be let as single bedrooms)
All Rooms with Private Bath/Shower Room, TV, Telephone, Radio, Tea and Coffee-making Facilities, Hairdryer,

Mini Bar.
Open all year. Fully Licensed. Full Central Heating. Children over 14 years catered for. Dogs allowed.
Parking Facilities. Sauna.
Nearby: Tennis, Indoor Swimming, Golf, Fishing

Infallible?
The answer is no because even as these lines are being written, hotel ownership, management and staff are changing somewhere. Invaluable? Yes, because by joining the Ashley Courtenay Circle (no extra charge) you can check up with us at any time during the current season.

A reminder.
Some of the tariffs in this book are those quoted for 1992. As prices will probably have changed for 1993, please check before booking. Please also note that the weekly and daily hotel rates shown in this book are for half board only (dinner, room and breakfast) unless otherwise stated.

Section 2: Isle of Wight

Bonchurch–Bonchurch Manor Hotel Bonchurch Shute, Bonchurch, Isle of Wight. PO38 1NU. Tel 0983 852868

The unspoilt village of Bonchurch has several claims to fame: the little Norman church of St Boniface (from which the village derives its name) is said to be one of the smallest in the country; Landslip Walk draws many visitors to its steep but enchanting terrace gardens and the village has also had several celebrated residents, notably Swinburne, Dickens and Shaw. We are sure that even these fastidious literati would have delighted in the gracious comfort which we discovered recently at Bonchurch Manor Hotel, a mellow Victorian country house which is surrounded by verdant grounds. Every room of this spacious house is charmingly furnished: Victorian panelling, antique furniture and pretty chintz fabrics abound. We especially liked the lounge, which has a pale pink and blue colour scheme and settees which the friendly proprietors, Mandy and Bob Brister, cheerfully admit are 'overstuffed'! A coal fire was burning in one grate here when we arrived on a cool evening recently and we found many other guests already basking in its warmth–and enjoying the happy, relaxed atmosphere which prevails at this hotel. Our six-course *table d'hôte* dinner in the bright and well-managed dining-room was mouthwatering and, unsurprisingly, the restaurant has become a popular venue for non-resident diners. Resident guests do, however, have the advantage of being able to retire to their comfortable bedrooms. Here one can drift contentedly to sleep, enveloped in the peace which only country-dwellers can experience, knowing that, in the morning, such delights as Horseshoe Bay and Smugglers' Haven await discovery.

Daily Terms from £42.00 (winter)/£47.00 (summer) per person per night (DB&B) Special Weekly Terms from £266.00 (winter)/£306 (summer) for 7 nights Winter prices from 3rd October to 30th April Summer prices from 1st May to 3rd Oct

Lunch from £8.00 Table D'Hôte Dinner from £15.00 and A La Carte Service Charge at Guest's Discretion. VAT inclusive. Credit Cards–Visa (Deposits only) 5 Double, 5 Twin, 2 Single Bedrooms 8 Private Bathrooms. 4 Private Shower

Rooms. All Rooms with TV, Telephone, Radio, Tea and Coffee-making Facilities, Hairdryer. Open from February to December. Fully Licensed. Full CH and Log Fires. Cocktail Bar. Children over 7 years catered for. Dogs allowed.

Calbourne—Swainston Manor Hotel Calbourne, Isle of Wight. PO30 4HX. Tel 0983 521121. Fax 0983 521406

And now on to Calbourne, an excellent centre for holiday visitors of a quiet turn of mind. Yet, there is something quite outstanding there, in both a social and an historical sense, for Swainston Manor has a recorded history dating back to 735 and has lately been adapted to provide the highest standards of hotel hospitality. When King Edward I stayed at Swainston in 1285 he was so charmed with the place that he took it over for himself. Swainston Manor Hotel today reflects mainly the Georgian era and, with its adjoining eleventh-century chapel used for receptions and banquets, stands in thirty-two acres of lush countryside. In the house itself there is the rich feeling of being able to make free and full use of deep-carpeted rooms, which feature handsome panelling, immaculate marble fireplaces and classic columns. And upstairs a choice of three suites and fourteen *en suite* bedrooms, with their 'hand-built' mattresses and splendid views. We first visited the Manor one fine afternoon, and so the guests were all out and about. Yet, it seemed so obviously 'lived in', with its crackling log fires, reading matter and the polish on the furniture. It may seem a little hackneyed to say that the food is good, because the type of people who stay there would not otherwise return. But it is consistently good and warrants the excellent wines which are laid down in the Swainston cellars. You may not have use of the ballroom, or the inner dining room, but the indoor swimming pool will probably attract you and the split-level *Admirals' Bar* will form part of your nightly agenda.

Weekly Terms from £359.95 Daily Terms from £53.50 Bed and Breakfast from £38.00 Bar Lunch from £3.50. Lunch from £9.50 and A La Carte. Bar Supper from £4.25 Dinner from £15.95 and A La Carte

10% Service Charge. VAT inclusive Credit Cards—Access, American Express, Diners Club, Visa. 2 Family Rooms. 3 Suites. 9 Double, 3 Single Bedrooms. All Rooms with Private Bathroom, TV, Telephone, Radio, Baby-listening, Tea and

Coffee-making Facilities, Trouser Press, Hairdryer. Open all Year. Fully Licensed. Full Central Heating. Cocktail Bar. Conference Facilities. Children catered for. Dogs allowed. Parking Facilities. Indoor Swimming Pool.

Section 2: Isle of Wight

Chale—The Clarendon Hotel and Wight Mouse Inn
Chale, Isle of Wight. PO38 2HA. Tel 0983 730431

There must be many tourists who scurry along the 'Military Road' to and from Freshwater, and give cursory attention to the fine old church at Chale. They should take heed of the amusing sign which will direct them to the happy and carefree Clarendon Hotel. Until 11th October, 1836, it was known as The Wight Mouse Inn. It was then renamed The Clarendon Hotel after a ship which was wrecked on nearby Blackgang Chine, its timbers being used in the construction of many local houses. Today it carries both names: the hotel is placid and relaxed even in the height of summer and the adjoining inn is convivial and offers a variety of real ales and 365 whiskies, three excellent children's rooms and entertainment (which will not disturb your sleep) nightly. Your hosts are John and Jean Bradshaw, who have done wonders in the twelve and a half years they have been here. Not only do they offer good value but their country-style bedrooms are nicely appointed, the public rooms are comfortable and freshly decorated, and the whole hotel benefits from the interesting selection of prints and paintings which adorn its walls. Writing about interiors, it is appropriate to mention that Mrs Bradshaw is obviously proud of her kitchen from where she provides marvellous lunches for the inn and well-planned dinner menus to the hotel, as a result of which, the Inn has won the Egon Ronay's Guide 'Family Pub of the Year GB 1990'. If you are interested in walking, riding, or just want a restful holiday, then we suggest that The Clarendon will suit you well.

Weekly Terms from £185.00 (DB&B)
Daily Terms from £34.00 (DB&B)
Bed and Breakfast from £25.00
Bar Meal from £3.00
Lunch from £4.00 and A La Carte
Dinner from £9.00 and A La Carte

Gratuities at Guest's discretion. VAT extra
1 Family Suite. 6 Family Rooms. 1 Double,
5 Double/Twin Bedrooms
All Rooms (except Double/Twin Rooms)
with TV, Tea and Coffee-making Facilities,
Radio/Alarm. Hairdryer available in all

Bathrooms. Baby-listening always available Open all year. Fully Licensed.
Full Central Heating. TV Lounge.
Games Room. Children especially catered for. Dogs allowed. Parking Facilities.
Petanque, Fishing, Riding, Sailing

Freshwater Bay—Farringford Hotel
Bedbury Lane, Freshwater Bay, Isle of Wight. PO40 9PE. Tel 0983 752500/752700. Telex 477575

There cannot be a more gracious building on the island than this late Georgian house with its Gothic-style windows and castellated walls which nestles amidst 200 acres of lawns and woodland. The former home of Lord Tennyson, it is not surprising that its picturesqueness and tranquillity should have inspired such vivid prose. The Poet Laureate's bedroom, number three, is, like many in the main building, a gracious apartment. The ground floor lounges are designed for individual comfort and these lead to the impressive restaurant, built to cater for 100 people in uncrowded comfort. It is no wonder that Farringford food is renowned throughout the island, and many take advantage of the hotel's regular candlelit dinner-dances. We should emphasise that such is the layout of Farringford, all ages and tastes can be catered for. An unusual feature is its optional self-catering suites, which are ideal for families of up to six people. They are situated in the *Cottage Suites*, which form a delightful quadrangle of cottages, and in the *Tennyson Garden Suites* and recently converted stable flats. The latter, to our minds, raise the self-catering concept to new heights. The grounds accommodate a sports pavilion, a hard tennis court, croquet, a swimming pool and a nine-hole par-3 golf course. We cannot hope to tell you a tithe of the story here, so write to Mr and Mrs I F Cerise, who endeavour to make Farringford a haven at any time of the year.

Spring and Autumn Mini Break Terms on Request. Full Christmas Programme available. Weekly Terms from £204.00
Daily Terms from £34.00
Bed and Breakfast from £24.00
Lunch - Sundays only from £8.00

Dinner from £13.00 and A La Carte
Gratuities at Guest's discretion. VAT inclusive. Credit Cards—Access, American Express, Diners Club, Visa. 8 Family Rooms. 24 Suites. 1 Double, 8 Twin, 3 Single Bedrooms. All Rooms with Private

Bathroom, TV, Telephone, Radio, Baby-listening, Tea and Coffee-making Facilities. Hairdryer available on request. Open all Year. Fully Licensed. 2 Cocktail Bars. TV Lounge. Games Room. Conference Facilities. Dogs allowed.

Section 2: Isle of Wight

Ryde—Ryde Castle Hotel
Esplanade, Ryde, Isle of Wight. Tel 0983 63755

Island residents and visitors owe a great debt of thanks to Mr and Mrs Peter Dickins, for their enthusiasm for this historic house is unbounded. The centuries have created numerous historic features at Ryde Castle, from Tudor to the recent past. The Castle has tremendous character and much of the old has now been faithfully restored, such as the Tudor ceilings and the tower from where can be seen the point at which Henry VIII's flag ship, the Mary Rose, sank. The double rooms have a choice of four poster or half tester beds. Armour, swords and pikestaffs abound in the Castle. There is a gallery dedicated to Henry VIII's wife, Katherine Parr, with a unique personally commissioned painting of her on display. The Castle is said to have a resident and friendly ghost. In addition to having a keen interest in history, the Dickins and their staff believe in very high standards and the hotel is very comfortable. We called there to sample the hotel's *businessmen's* luncheon menu. All three courses were first class. Above stairs the bedrooms are superbly equipped with modern etceteras. Full secretarial office services are available to the businessman. There is a menu available until Midnight. So, do not overlook Ryde, which sits behind colourful gardens and enjoys spectacular views across the Solent. But wherever you stay on the island, and personally, we follow the maxim 'where I dines well I sleeps ', and how comfortable are the beds at Ryde Castle, do make a point of eating at this hotel, where you can also dance if you wish. There are more weekend breaks than we have seen before, with every interest served.

Weekly Terms from £299.00
Daily Terms from £55.00
Bed and Breakfast from £45.00
Bar Lunch from £1.25. Lunch from £3.00 and A La Carte. Dinner from £13.95 and A La Carte. Gratuities at Guest's discretion

VAT inclusive. Credit Cards–Access, Visa
2 Family Rooms. 9 Double, 3 Twin,
6 Single, 9 Executive Bedrooms
7 Rooms with Four Poster Beds
All Rooms with Shower and most with Bathroom. All Rooms with TV, Telephone,

Radio, Tea and Coffee-making Facilities,
Hairdryer, Trouser Press, Iron.
Baby-listening on Request. Open all year.
Fully Licensed. ConferenceFacilities
Children catered for.
Dogs allowed by Arrangement

St Lawrence, Nr Ventnor—The Lawyers Rest Hotel
Undercliff Drive, St Lawrence, Isle of Wight. PO38 1XF. Tel 0983 852610

And now, by taking a short detour from Ventnor, to enable you to sample the scenic beauty of the neighbourhood , we will introduce you to one of our 'finds' of the year. First, then, we will head for St Catherine's Point and after two miles encounter the village of St Lawrence. The road is bordered on the right by precipitous cliffs, but the Undercliff proper is below us. Between the two is an hotel with a most intriguing name...The Lawyers Rest. The house was built in 1840 by the Earl of Yarborough on one of the best sites on the island. It is in no way grandiose and has the atmosphere of a small country house. We were due to call here for lunch, yet so welcoming are the owners, Geoffrey Phillips (a former solicitor, hence the legal theme of the hotel) and Ann Dex, that we were compelled to stay for dinner, sleep like kings in a most comfortable bed and enjoy a delicious breakfast before leaving. If you can tear your eyes away from the outstanding view, you will see that the hotel has been restored and renovated with great taste, not only with decor in mind, but also very much for the comfort of guests, and in the elegant public rooms there are some splendid clocks and a collection of porcelain legal figures. For dinner we chose from a quite unusual menu, in that it contained not only traditional favourites, but also some with tempting eastern names. Our wine was from nearer home, a Vouvray, excellent and the colour of the sunshine which bathed us.

All terms pertaining to 1992
Weekly Terms (Half Board) from £245.00.
Daily Terms (Half Board) from £39.00
Bar Lunch from £7.50. Lunch from £7.50 A La Carte. Dinner available to Non-Residents by prior booking.

VAT inclusive. Gratuities at Guest's Discretion. Credit Cards—Access, American Express, Visa. 5 Double, 2 Twin, 1 Single Bedrooms
4 Private Bathrooms. 4 Private Shower Rooms. Hairdryer, Iron, Shoe Cleaning

available on Request
Open all Year except November and Mid-Week from December to February (inclusive). Fully Licensed. Cocktail Bar. Meeting Facilities. Children over 10 years catered for. Dogs allowed by arrangement.

Section 2: Isle of Wight

Sandown—Melville Hall Hotel Melville Street, Sandown, Isle of Wight. PO36 9DH. Tel 0983 406526

Melville Hall is very unpretentious, but if you like homeliness, very comfortable. The owners, Lyn and Ken Wells, continue to work hard to improve the facilities of this three star hotel and their efforts have already brought good results. All the bedrooms have *en suite* facilities and are fitted with telephone, colour television with three satellite channels, hairdryer, and beverage making facilities. The public rooms are spacious and nicely decorated. It has many facilities, yet will satisfy those who are inclined to follow quieter pursuits. Within the grounds of Melville Hall there is a nine hole putting green, an outdoor heated swimming pool with patio surround and numerous sunny and sheltered spots in which one can simply relax. Whatever your mood may dictate you should enjoy the sociable and informal atmosphere at Melville Hall and we know that Lyn and Ken will be working hard to ensure you have a happy stay. For the rest, you will not have to travel far. The twin resorts of Sandown and Shanklin are situated on sheltered Sandown Bay and both provide all the traditional seaside entertainments and are popular for family holidays. Melville Hall clearly fits into the scene, for there are seven large family rooms and four two bedroomed suites among the medley of accommodation. The hotel scores on good standards of food and care, value for money and an understanding of holiday requirements, but most of all on the dedication of its owners.

Weekly Terms (Half Board) from £240.00
Daily Terms from £39.00
Bed and Breakfast from £30.00
Bar Lunch from £1.50
Dinner from £9.00 and A La Carte
Gratuities at Guest's Discretion
VAT inclusive. Credit Cards–Access,

American Express, Diners Club, Visa
7 Family Rooms. 4 2-Bedroomed Suites
11 Double, 8 Twin, 3 Single Bedrooms
29 Private Bathrooms. 4 Private Shower Rooms. All Rooms with TV, Telephone, Radio, Hairdryer, Tea and Coffee-making Facilities. Open all Year. Fully Licensed

Full Central Heating. Conference Facilities.
Children catered for
Dogs not allowed. Parking Facilities
Putting, Outdoor Swimming Pool
Nearby: Tennis, Squash, Badminton, Swimming, Solarium, Sauna, Golf, Riding, Windsurfing, Water Skiing

Shanklin—Bourne Hall Country Hotel Luccombe Road, Shanklin, Isle of Wight. PO37 6RR. Tel 0983 862820. Fax 0983 865138

Hotels, like finger-prints, can look alike and yet they are all different. Our initial impressions of Bourne Hall were that here is another of those country-house hotels set in lovely surroundings, run by caring and dedicated owners. When one gets to know the hotel, however, one realises that it has its own unique characteristics. Here, for instance, you will find two swimming pools, one inside and another in the sheltered gardens. There are also sauna, solarium and jacuzzi facilities. Indeed, during our stay at Bourne Hall we were more than content to spend our spare moments within the lovely grounds. Expressly run as a family holiday hotel, Bourne Hall attracts a happy blending of youth and maturity. You have only to stay there to witness that Mr Shears and his two sons are continuously involved and so the details of good hotel management are not overlooked. Our bedroom was spacious and well furnished and had a private bathroom attached. We were further impressed with the service, menus and food provided in the dining-room. Having stayed there, we feel Bourne Hall is an asset to our guide and it speaks volumes for the consistency you will find when we tell you that we met guests who have been returning to the hotel for many years.

Weekly Terms from £185.00
Daily Terms from £39.00
Bed and Breakfast from £30.00
English Breakfast £6.20
Dinner from £14.00 Table D'Hôte
Gratuities at Guest's Discretion.
VAT inclusive
Credit Cards–Access, Diners Club, Visa
2 Family Rooms. 4 Suites 14 Double,

10 Twin Bedrooms
All Rooms with Private Bathroom, TV, Telephone, Radio, Baby-listening, Tea and Coffee-making facilities
Open from February to December.
Residential and Restaurant Licence
Full Central Heating.
Cocktail Bar. Games Room
Conference Facilities

Children catered for. Dogs not allowed.
Parking Facilities
Grass Tennis Court, Croquet, Badminton, Indoor and Outdoor Heated Swimming Pools,
Solarium, Sauna, Jacuzzi
Nearby: Squash, Golf, Fishing, Riding, Sailing, Windsurfing, Water Skiing, Hang Gliding

Section 2: Isle of Wight

Shanklin—The Hartland Hotel   Victoria Avenue, Shanklin, Isle of Wight. PO37 6LT. Tel 0983 863123

There are two Shanklins–the well-known summer resort which sits on high ground above its esplanade, pier and sandy beach and the 'Old Village' at the southern end, which consists of just a few thatched houses and an inn. The situation, however, in rich vegetation close to Shanklin Chine, has drawn flattering prose from both Longfellow and Keats. Nearby is one of the island's premier hotels, although The Hartland has built its reputation more on the provision of modern comforts and an extensive range of amenities. The house was built at the turn of the century as a country gentleman's residence and great care has been taken to furnish it in the style of the period. If you visit it today, however, you will find a superb indoor heated swimming pool, a spa bath, a sauna, a solarium and a fully equipped gymnasium. Your bedroom will certainly contain a colour television, telephone and beverage-making facilities, bath or shower room and may even provide a four-poster bed! Above all, however, the hotel is well known for its food. The *Victorian Restaurant* serves a variety of mouthwatering *à la carte* meals in the evening, complemented by a varied selection of wines. The table staff, dressed in the most attractive period costume, are especially helpful and efficient. The Hartland Hotel is located in a quiet, tree-lined avenue and is run on very personal lines by Stephen and Lesley Hall.

Weekly Terms from £218.00
Daily Terms from £36.00
Bed and Breakfast from £23.00
All Rooms with Private Bath/Shower Room, TV, Telephone, Tea and

Coffee-making Facilities
(Some Rooms with 4-poster Bed)
VAT inclusive
Credit Cards—Access, Visa
Open all Year

Parking Facilities
Indoor Heated Swimming Pool,
Solarium, Sauna, Spa Bath,
Gymnasium

Shanklin–The White House Hotel   Eastcliff Promenade, Shanklin, Isle of Wight. PO37 6AY. Tel 0983 862776

One Shanklin hotel we have stayed at recently is The White House, which stands back in an open position on the famous cliff walk and enjoys magnificent sea views. It is the type of hotel we choose when we do not want to be too dressy. The White House is not formal–there is a natural homely and personal atmosphere. One quickly senses the personal supervision of Bernard and Valerie Ward, who own it. Here one's visits to Shanklin are much less expensive than at the larger establishments, but are none the less very comfortable on that account. There is central heating throughout and the bedrooms, all with private bathrooms, have beverage trays, and some also boast balconies and sea views. The menu is limited to a few choices but there is something for every taste and the wines are reasonably priced. As we dined we could not help but gaze out to sea; there really are the most wonderful panoramic views to be had from The White House. Breakfast the following morning was, indeed, a feast. Our lasting impressions of The White House are that it is a very happy house, where the friendly service is exceptionally good, with Mr and Mrs Ward so eager to please all their guests. In fact, if we were asked to summarise why people return to The White House year after year, we should say it was the cleanliness, the cooking and the personal touch. Yes, those three, even above the excellent tariff. Being open most of the year, the hotel arranges a varied programme for those wishing to stay there over the Christmas period and will even assist guests with their ferry arrangements to and from the island.

Weekly Terms from £196.00
Daily Terms from £30.00
Bed and Breakfast from £23.00
Bar Lunch from £2.50
Dinner from £10.00 Table D'Hôte
Gratuities at Guest's Discretion. VAT

inclusive. Credit Cards—Access, American Express, Diners Club, Visa
1 Family Room. 2 Twin, 1 Single, 7 Double Bedrooms. 2 Private Bathrooms. 9 Private Shower Rooms
All Rooms with TV, Radio, Baby-listening,

Tea and Coffee-making Facilities,
Telephone, Hairdryer
Open from Feb to Oct, plus Christmas.
Residential Licence. Full Central Heating
TV Lounge. Children catered for. Dogs not allowed. Parking Facilities

Section 2: Isle of Wight

Totland Bay–Country Garden Hotel Church Hill, Totland Bay, Isle of Wight. PO39 0ET. Tel 0983 754521. Fax 0983 754521

West Wight, and Totland Bay in particular, has a quiet appeal. Behind Totland's gentle curve of golden sands, its little pier and the high grassy Turf Walk is a really superb hotel–the Country Garden Hotel. As its name suggests, the hotel is set in beautiful gardens, extending to two acres and with fine views of the Solent and the Dorset coastline. Within the house itself, which was once a Victorian country residence, are spacious and comfortable rooms, all beautifully decorated and maintained. There are sixteen bedrooms, which are fully equipped with private bathrooms, colour television, radios, telephones, fridge, hairdryer and tea and coffee-making facilities. In the restaurant, overlooking the garden, you may relish superb *cuisine*, with dishes prepared from the freshest of local produce. The owners of this lovely place seem determined to set ever higher standards. From this restful base, you can take some of the many short walks through unspoilt countryside, owned by the National Trust, to Alum Bay and The Needles. Country Garden Hotel is also an ideal base for exploring the rest of the island by car or, if you are not a motorist, by public transport, for buses stop close by the hotel.

Terms on Application
Lunch from £8.50 and A La Carte
Dinner from £14.00 and A La Carte
Gratuities at Guest's Discretion
VAT inclusive.
Credit Cards—Access, Visa
1 Suite. 4 Twin, 5 Double Bedrooms.

All Rooms with Private Bath and Shower,
Satellite TV, Telephone, Radio, Tea and
Coffee-making Facilities, Fridge, Hairdryer
Open all year
Residential and Restaurant Licence
Full Central Heating. Cocktail Bar
Small Conference Facilities
Children catered for.

Dogs allowed
Parking Facilities.
Night Porter
Nearby: Tennis, Putting, Squash,
Badminton, Swimming, Solarium, Sauna,
Golf, Fishing, Riding, Sailing, Windsurfing,
Water Skiing, Hang Gliding

Totland Bay—Sentry Mead Hotel Madeira Road, Totland Bay, Isle of Wight. PO39 0BJ. Tel 0983 753212

This commanding hotel has undergone a transformation since Mike and Julie Hodgson took over here. We were delighted by the warmth of welcome and impressed by the seemingly conflicting blend of intimacy and spaciousness. Possibly the soft harmony of colours achieves such a happy combination. West Wight is an ideal area for a relaxed break, away from crowds but with the most attractive stretches of beach and countryside close at hand. Formerly a Victorian residence, none of the original charm has been lost with the introduction of full central heating, with *en suite* facilities in every bedroom. There is distinct emphasis on personal attention here, with a first-class standard of food and wine at lunch-time and a comprehensive *table d'hôte* menu at dinner. All food is prepared by the proprietors using fresh local farm and fish produce whenever possible. Special diets are catered for. Adjoining the comfortable main lounge there is a sun lounge, affording views of the spectacular West Wight sunsets. Sentry Mead itself stands in spacious gardens, at the edge of Totland's renowned Turf Walk, with superb views of the Solent. The Hotel specialises in watercolour painting holidays run by the artist Muriel Owen, Vice-President of the Society of Women Artists. Choosing to live locally she understands the beauty of the area. Her courses here are spread over the year and her holidays have been featured in the Sunday Express. English Heritage own a permanent exhibition of her island work at Yarmouth Castle and she has recently made a teaching video entitled "Farmhouses in watercolour".

Weekly Terms from £195.00
Bed and Breakfast from £30.00
Bar Lunch from £1.50
Dinner from £9.00 Table D'Hôte
Gratuities at Guest's Discretion.
VAT inclusive. 4 Family Rooms

2 Single, 5 Double, 3 Twin Bedrooms
8 Private Bathrooms. 6 Private Shower
Rooms. All Rooms with TV, Radio,
Baby-listening, Tea and Coffee-making
Facilities. Open all year
Residential and Restaurant Licence

Full Central Heating. Children catered for
Dogs allowed by arrangement
Parking Facilities. Putting.
Nearby: Tennis, Squash, Indoor Swimming
Pool, Golf, Fishing, Riding, Sailing,
Windsurfing, Hang-gliding

Section 2: Isle of Wight

Ventnor—St Maur Hotel
Castle Road, Ventnor, Isle of Wight. PO38 1LG
Tel 0983 852570

Situated on a series of natural terraces above beautiful bathing beaches, Ventnor has an almost Mediterranean atmosphere. Indeed, its exceptionally mild climate has earned it the name of 'The English Riviera'. Steephill Cove, with its charming tea garden, the Undercliff, verdant Ventnor Park and the Botanical Gardens all combine to create an ideal holiday environment here. If you are looking for a congenial base from which to explore these attractions, do consider the St Maur Hotel. It is located only a few minutes' walk away from the beach and sits quietly behind immaculately tended lawns and flowerbeds. Within, you will find comfortably furnished and spacious rooms, including a bar lounge and a separate television lounge. We thoroughly enjoyed our evening meal at St Maur Hotel recently: all the dishes were well prepared and served in most generous portions. Even the heartiest appetites, whetted on outdoor pursuits and health-giving air, are certain to be more than satisfied. The owners are Mr and Mrs J Groocock, and their son, David, who manages the hotel, is a perfect host. The family's dedication to the needs of their guests is summed up neatly in the brochure, which states: 'Your pleasure is our business . . . and our business is our pleasure'. You will, we are sure, find that a stay here is, indeed, a pleasure–and this will not be spoiled when the time comes to pay the bill, for the tariffs are extremely reasonable.

Weekly Terms from £189.00
Daily Terms from £27.00
Bed and Breakfast from £21.00
Dinner from £8.50 Table D'Hôte
Gratuities at Guest's Discretion.
VAT inclusive
Credit Cards—Access, Visa

3 Family Rooms. 7 Double, 3 Twin,
3 Single Bedrooms
10 Private Bathrooms. 3 Private Shower Rooms
All Rooms with Tea and Coffee-making Facilities

Open from February to December
Residential Licence. Full Central Heating.
Cocktail Bar. TV Lounge
Children catered for. Dogs not allowed.
Parking Facilities
Nearby: Tennis, Putting, Golf, Fishing

Section 2: Isle of Wight and Kent

Ventnor—Burlington Hotel
Bellevue Road, Ventnor, Isle of Wight   PO38 1DB.   Tel 0983 852113

Young and old alike can enjoy the Isle of Wight and, of the many attractive centres, Ventnor must be rated as one of the best. South-facing on a coast with numerous places of interest, it has a mild climate thanks to the protection from cooler north winds provided by the scenic high cliffs. Immediately inland from the town is St Boniface Down, at almost 800 feet the highest point on the island, affording superb views over the south-east coast from St Catherine's Point to Culver Cliff. Westwards from Ventnor, in a very short distance, lie botanic gardens, a smuggling museum, a rare breeds park and tropical bird park. To the north, at Godshill, a model village, toy museum and natural history centre are only a few miles away. From the three-storey hotel, with its bay windows and balconies, you have only to step outside to the heated private swimming-pool. All of the tastefully-decorated bedrooms have private *en suite* facilities and many have uninterrupted views of the English Channel. Very competitive all-in-terms are offered for bed, breakfast and an excellent *table d'hôte* evening dinner, including a special four night mini break package including the ferry. Book the four poster bed suite for a week and a bottle of champagne will greet you on arrival.

Weekly Terms from £224.00 pp (DB&B)
Daily Terms from £32.00 pp
Bed and Breakfast from £26.00 pp
Dinner from £9.50 Table D'Hôte
Gratuities at Guest's Discretion.
VAT inclusive
Credit Cards - Access, Mastercard, Visa
8 Family Rooms. 4 Double, 6 Twin,
5 Single Bedrooms

20 Private Bathrooms.
3 Private Shower Rooms
All Rooms with TV, Telephone, Radio, Tea and Coffee-making Facilities, Hairdryer, Clock, Toiletries
Open from March to end of October
Fully Licensed. Full Central Heating.
Cocktail Bar
TV Lounge. Games Room

Children over 3 years catered for.
Dogs not allowed.
Parking Facilities.
Heated outdoor Swimming Pool
Nearby: Tennis, Putting, Squash, Golf, Fishing, Riding, Sailing, Windsurfing, Water Skiing

Ashford, Eastwell Park—Eastwell Manor
Eastwell Park, Boughton Lees, Nr Ashford, Kent. TN25 4HR. Tel 0233 635751. Fax 0233 635530

Eastwell Manor is one of that small band of hotels which appeals especially to the gourmet, the antiquarian and those who seek standards which are higher than the normal. It sits in beautiful countryside, close to Canterbury and the channel ports, but seemingly miles from anywhere in the privacy of its own sixty-acre park. The manor dates back to 1069 and it was here that Richard Plantagenet, natural son of Richard III, lived until his death in 1550. It is a large, elegant building, approached by a long drive lined with trees, which lends itself admirably to being a gracious and exclusive country-house hotel. Step inside and you will quickly appreciate that everything has been done to ensure that this has become a reality. The spacious rooms have been beautifully restored and sympathetically furnished, with virtually no expense spared, and reflect a harmonious blend of an opulent past and modern comforts. We stay here when we can and dine here as often as possible, and always enjoy the sense of occasion which is associated with each visit. The hotel's food is, as one would expect, exceptional. Traditional English cooking is combined with gourmet French dishes and the cellar is very well stocked with bottles–from *vin ordinaire* to specially bottled French wines and exclusive champagne. Tennis, croquet, squash and trout fishing are all possible pursuits for the hotel's guests. You will find Eastwell Manor off the A251 road halfway between Ashford and the village of Challock Leas, which is about half an hour's drive from Dover or Folkestone.

Bed and Breakfast from £95.00
Bar Lunch from £6.00
Lunch from £16.00 and A La Carte
Dinner from £27.50 and A La Carte
Gratuities at Guest's Discretion. VAT inclusive. Credit Cards—Access, American

Express, Diners Club, Visa
5 Suites. 13 Double, 5 Twin Bedrooms
All Rooms with Private Bathroom, TV, Telephone, Radio, Baby-listening, Trouser Press, Hairdryer, Mini Bar
Open all year. Fully Licensed

Full Central Heating. Lift. Cocktail Bar
Snooker Room. Conference Facilities
Children catered for. Dogs allowed.
Parking Facilities. Night Porter. Hard Tennis Court, Croquet, Pitch and Putt, Boules, Falconry, Archery, Shooting

Section 2: Kent

Brands Hatch, Dartford—Brands Hatch Thistle Hotel Brands Hatch, Dartford, Kent. DA3 8PE. Tel 0474 85 4900. Fax 0474 85 3220

Set in the 'garden of England' at the entrance to the famous Brands Hatch Motor Circuit, the Brands Hatch Thistle Hotel takes pride of place. Mr Tom Carr, the general manager, took us on an extended tour of this hotel. Once inside, an Italianate atmosphere pervades the air; highly polished floors, beautiful rugs and comfortable leather sofas. Beyond is the elegant restaurant with its stone columns and rich decor where dinner is served in style by friendly, yet efficient staff. On a less formal note, the *Brasserie Concorde*, provides guests with refreshments and light meals throughout the day and this French style ambience provides the ideal setting for meeting friends or enjoying a quiet cup of coffee. All of the 130 bedrooms have a private bathroom, colour television, radio, telephone, hairdryer, trouser press and twenty-four hour room service. Conference facilities at the Brands Hatch Thistle hotel are well provided for with the large *de Havilland Suite* and several smaller syndicate rooms to cater for every occasion. With all the facilities of the 500-acre parkland setting of the motor circuit at one's finger tips, many companies take advantage of this easily accessible location. A typical corporate day could include activities such as parascending, circuit racing, hovercraft flying, clay pigeon shooting, go karting, archery, racing car simulators or an Autotest and plans are in hand for a leisure centre to be added to the many facilities already available. We were most impressed with this hotel and we are certain you will feel the same.

Room Rate from £80.00
Lunch from £14.95 and A La Carte
Dinner from £18.95 and A La Carte
Gratuities at Guest's Discretion. VAT inclusive. Credit Cards—Access, American Express, Diners Club, Visa
4 Family Rooms. 2 Suites. 64 Double,

60 Twin Bedrooms.
All Rooms with Private Bath and Shower Room, TV, Telephone, Radio, Tea and Coffee-making Facilities, Trouser Press, Hairdryer, Room Safe.
Baby Listening available on Request
Open all Year. Fully Licensed.

Full Central Heating. Cocktail Bar.
Conference Facilities. Children catered for.
Dogs allowed at Management's Discretion.
Parking Facilities. Night Porter.
Nearby: Tennis, Squash, Badminton, Swimming, Solarium, Sauna, Golf, Riding, Shooting

Near Gravesend, Singlewell—Singlewell Manor Hotel Hever Court Road, Singlewell, Gravesend, Kent DA12 5UQ. Tel 0474 353100. Fax 0474 354978

We were most impressed that a hotel with forty-one bedrooms, extensive banqueting and business facilities, and a health suite, should achieve such a welcoming atmosphere and offer a personal, attentive service. On top of this, the *cuisine* here is excellent value for money and the location ideal for Euro-travellers or visitors to 'The Garden of England'. Manor Hotel is adjacent to the London-Dover A2/M2 Motorway, only four miles from junction 1 of the London Orbital Motorway, M25. Only minutes away, in Gravesend, is the River Thames with medieval maritime connections and, for long distance walkers, the meeting point of the Weald Way and Saxon Shore Way. Undeniably a valuable site for conferences and seminars, receptions and celebrations. Continental tourists will appreciate the cosmopolitan ambience and staff whose language skills include French, Portuguese, Spanish and Italian. A continental influence is in evidence also in the imaginative and varied *cuisine*, presented most professionally and at commendably moderate prices. Everything here is handled with an enthusiastic and flexible attitude, ensuring that a special social event, new product launch or a 'Continental Themed Night' runs smoothly and successfully. Major companies and prominent people have patronised Manor Hotel within the first few months of its opening and we have no doubt that its popularity will develop rapidly as the date for the opening of the Channel Tunnel draws nearer. All guests benefit from the availability of a swimming pool with jet stream, sauna and steamroom.

Weekly Terms available
Bed and Breakfast from £49.95 (Monday to Thursday), £40.00 (Friday to Sunday)
Bar Meals from £5.00
Lunch from £11.95 (Sunday, 3 courses)
Dinner from £9.75 and A La Carte

Gratuities at Guest's Discretion. VAT inclusive. Credit Cards-Access, American Express, Diners Club, Visa
3 Family Rooms. 2 Suites. 16 Double, 17 Twin Bedrooms. All Rooms with Private Bathroom, TV, Telephone, Baby-listening,

Tea and Coffee-making Facilities, Trouser Press, Hairdryer. Jacuzzi in suites.
Open all year. Fully Licensed
Full Central Heating. Cocktail Bar. TV Lounge. Conference Facilities
Children catered for. Guide Dogs only

Section 2: Kent

Hawkhurst—The Tudor Court Hotel
Rye Road, Hawkhurst, Cranbrook, Kent. TN18 5DA. Tel 0580 752312. Fax 0580 753966

Whilst journeying around southern England one encounters many towns and villages with the suffix 'hurst' (the word means a wood or glade), and in the area of Kent there is quite a concentration. Hawkhurst is of particular interest, not only for its associations with William Penn, Quaker and founder of Pennsylvania, USA, but also because of the notorious 'Hawkhurst Gang', a band of smugglers who were operating in Kent and Sussex in the eighteenth century. Legend has it that they used the inn, which is now The Tudor Court, as a meeting place to organise their nefarious activities. Needless to say, its present-day clientele are attracted by more reputable and rewarding inducements. Tony and Pat Climpson are understanding hosts who work very hard to ensure that The Tudor Court retains the charm, warmth and affability of a small country hotel. Our *table d'hôte* luncheon was a joy, with fresh local produce much in evidence. This hotel has been enhanced where necessary and thus one can enjoy bedrooms with all modern sophistications, including bathrooms *en suite*. Ideally situated amongst the hop gardens and orchards of the Weald of Kent, The Tudor Court has gained a considerable reputation for its outstanding gardens, *cuisine* and comfort. The Cinque Ports of Rye and Winchelsea are nearby, as are the castles of Bodiam, Herstmonceux and Scotney. For the children, the Camber Sands are a *must*.

Weekly Terms from £289.00 (DB&B)
Daily Terms from £48.00 (DB&B)
Bed and Breakfast from £40.00
Lunch from £11.50 and A La Carte
Dinner from £13.00 and A La Carte
Service Charge and VAT inclusive. Credit Cards—Access, American Express, Diners Club, Visa.

1 Family Room. 5 Double, 7 Twin, 5 Single Bedrooms. 2 Rooms with Four Poster Bed. All Rooms with Private Bath/Shower Room, TV, Telephone, Radio/Alarm, Tea and Coffee-making Facilities, Trouser Press, Hairdryer
Open all year. Fully Licensed.
Full Central Heating. Cocktail Bar.

V Lounge Conference Facilities. Children catered for. Dogs allowed at Management's discretion. Parking Facilities. Tennis, Croquet, Putting Children's Play Area.
Nearby: Squash, Golf, Fishing, Riding, Sailing, Drives in Horse-drawn Traps, Visits to local Vineyards, Ballooning

Littlebourne—The Bow Window Inn
High Street, Littlebourne, Canterbury, Kent. CT3 1ST. Tel 0227 721264

If you have a liking for old inns you will not want to pass by this little picturesque gateway into the past, which lies in the old village of Littlebourne, some three miles to the east of Canterbury. Do not expect the ultra-modern; it would not be in keeping with the wealth of exposed beams, the huge Kentish fireplace, the four-poster beds and other associations of bygone days. Yet, the essentials are now to be found there *en suite* bedrooms with colour television, radio/alarm, beverage-making facilities and central heating. The owners are at pains to ensure that personality and individuality permeate the Bow Window Inn of today. Step into the quiet cosy bar after night-fall and you will find a pint and a pipe and the company blend royally. This is also an ideal room in which to take morning coffee or the hotel's speciality afternoon teas. They apologised to us one Friday afternoon that the bedrooms were fully booked, so we settled for a very enjoyable meal, and stayed on and on, enjoying the traditional ambiance of this 300 year old country cottage. The catering here is English at its best just as it should be in an old English inn. You will like the friendly Bow Window Inn and the surrounding country. Canterbury can be fully explored, and the Channel Ports are close by, so, as part of one's holiday, a day can be spent in France. But do not overlook the exploration of the mellow towns and villages of this area of which St Nicholas at Wade and Fordwich are two examples.

Weekly Terms from £212.00
Bed and Breakfast from £58.00 (Double)
Bar Lunch from £2.95
Dinner from £10.95 and A La Carte
Gratuities at Guest's Discretion. VAT inclusive. Credit Cards—Access, American Express, Visa

2 Family Rooms. 4 Double, 3 Twin, 1 Single Bedrooms. All Rooms with Private Bath/Shower Room, TV, Radio, Tea and Coffee-making Facilities. 2 Rooms with Hairdryer. Open all year.
Residential and Restaurant Licence.
Full Central Heating.

Cocktail Bar. Conference Facilities Children catered for. Dogs not allowed Parking Facilities.
Nearby: Tennis, Putting, Squash, Badminton, Swimming, Solarium Sauna, Golf, Fishing, Riding, Sailing, Windsurfing, Water Skiing, Country Walks

Section 2: Kent

Shipbourne, Tonbridge–The Chaser Inn Stumble Hill, Shipbourne, Tonbridge, Kent TN11 9PE. Tel 0732 810360

We are delighted to up-grade the entry for this country inn to the main body of our Guide (from the Stop Press section last year). The professionalism of Michael and Vivien Nix was already well known to us from their success at another establishment, prior to this latest acquisition. Built in the 1880's, The Chaser Inn is a Colonial style building with an impressive porticoed front overlooking Shipbourne village green. In its thirty-eight seater restaurant, with a beamed vaulted ceiling and panelled walls, every course offers a choice from the creative set menu, complemented by an extensive wine list. There is also an imaginative range of food available every lunchtime and evening in the two bars. A conducted tour of the Inn confirmed our best expectations: comfortably furnished, clean and tidy and well equipped. Situated on the A227 road between the market towns of Tonbridge and Sevenoaks in the heart of the Garden of England, the hotel is a most valuable resting place mid-way between London and the south coast. With motorways M25, M20 and M26 only minutes away, it is perfectly placed to meet the needs of both business traveller and tourist. For receptions, as a base for sporting activities or visits to the historic villages, vineyards, open-air and indoor museums, gardens and hop farms that are gathered in this area, The Chaser Inn will serve you well. It has fifteen *en suite* bedrooms, keeps traditional ales, and has a most realistic tariff structure. They request that pipes and portable telephones are not taken into the restaurant!

Bed and Breakfast from £45.00	American Express, Visa	Open all year. Residential Licence
Bar Meals from £2.75	6 Double, 4 Twin, 5 Single Bedrooms	Full Central Heating.
Lunch from £12.50 Table D'Hôte	6 Private Bathrooms. 9 Private Shower	Conference Facilities
Dinner from £19.75	Rooms. All Rooms with TV, Telephone,	Children catered for. Dogs allowed.
Gratuities at Guest's Discretion	Radio, Baby-listening, Tea and	Parking Facilities. Nearby: Tennis,
VAT inclusive. Credit Cards-Access,	Coffee-making Facilities, Hairdryer	Swimming, Golf, Riding, Sailing

Tunbridge Wells–The Royal Wells Inn Mount Ephraim, Tunbridge Wells, Kent. TN4 8BE. Tel 0892 511188. Fax 0892 511908

Our atlas shows the town as 'Royal Tunbridge Wells' and the Inn owes its own regal title to Queen Victoria who, as a young princess, made frequent visits in the early nineteenth century. Today, the hotel still carries the royal coat of arms. It presents an imposing picture, the first two storeys of the frontage being almost entirely glass-clad. A major feature of the Inn is a magnificent conservatory restaurant which, with its intimate lounge bar, is a popular eating place open to non-residents and guests alike. Here the emphasis is on fresh produce, attractively presented and complemented by the delights of an extensive wine cellar. The Royal Wells has twenty-three bedrooms, all with period furniture and two with four-poster beds. They also contain modern luxuries such as satellite television. Although the hotel is family-run and of modest size, it offers comprehensive and flexible conference facilities, and delegates will appreciate the amenities of the two bars. The main lounge bar is spacious and comfortable, you can relax with afternoon tea or a pint of real ale. The *Wells Brasserie* is a fascinating place to take a snack or light meal, as you are surrounded by motoring memorabilia of the world's classic cars. Also, the hotel bus is a 1909 Commer once owned by the founder of the Automobile Association, Lord Lonsdale. The Royal Wells Inn overlooks the Common and is just a short walk from the town centre. It is an ideal base from which to explore the 'garden of England', with its historical and picturesque places of interest, including Chartwell, Hever Castle and the Bluebell Railway.

Bed and Breakfast from £50.00(Single), £70.00(Double/Twin). Bar Meals from £4.00 Lunch from £11.50 and A la Carte. Sunday Lunch from £13.50 and A La Carte. Dinner from £13.50 (Mon to Thursday) and A La Carte. Service Charge and VAT inclusive.	Credit Cards—Access, American Express, Diners Club, Visa 9 Double, 5 Twin, 7 Single Bedrooms. 2 Rooms with Four Poster Beds All Rooms with Private Bath/Shower Room, TV, Telephone, Radio, Tea and	Coffee-making Facilities Baby-listening, Hairdryer and Ironing equipment available on Request Open all Year except Christmas Day and Boxing Day. Fully Licensed. Lift. Conference Facilities. Children catered for.

Section 2: Kent and Surrey

Tunbridge Wells—The Spa Hotel Mount Ephraim, Tunbridge Wells, Kent. TN4 8XJ. Tel 0892 520331. Fax 0892 510575

When Mr George Goring was chosen 'Hotelier of the Year' in 1990 it was a fitting recognition of how much the famous Goring family have done over three generations to promote hotel excellence in Britain. For seventy-five years and more their hotel near Buckingham Palace has stood for traditionalism and excellence, and it comes as no surprise to discover that the family's other hotel, beautifully poised in the Royal Borough of Tunbridge Wells, relies on the same time-honoured virtues. We make our way gladly to the celebrated Spa Hotel. The name is a reminder of those days when 'taking the waters' was the fashion and The Spa Hotel had its own range of chalybeate baths and medical attendants, and guests could have their treatments without going out-of-doors! Whilst fashions change, the ambience of former years permeates still its lovely rooms and its beautiful outlook–across fifteen acres of landscaped gardens, containing two large lakes. The elegant bedrooms, all individually styled, are superbly equipped in every respect. The grand Regency restaurant is one of the best places at which to dine in Kent. Wander the rooms ... the *Equestrian Bar*, the lounge renowned for its sumptuous afternoon teas, the Grand Ballroom and function suites ... and you will find the feeling of well-being infectious. It is said that life goes in cycles. Well, taking to the waters has, once again, become a stylish pastime here, for the hotel's leisure facilities include a swimming pool and spa pool, one of the best hotel gymnasiums in England, tennis, saunas, sunbeds, beauty therapy, hairdressing and much more.

Bed and Breakfast from £82.00 Room Rate from £74.00 Weekend Breaks available Bar Lunch from £5.00. Lunch from £10.00 Bar Supper from £7.50 Dinner from £25.00 Table D'Hôte	10% Service Charge. VAT inclusive. All major Credit Cards accepted 2 Family Rooms, 4 Suites. 21 Double, 26 Twin, 23 Single Bedrooms. All rooms with Private Bathroom, TV, Telephone, Radio, Baby-listening, Radio, Tea and	Coffee-making Facilities, Hairdryer. Trouser Press in some rooms Open all year. Fully Licensed. Lift. Equestrian Bar. Games Room. Conference Facilities. Children catered for. Dogs not allowed. Parking Facilities. Night Porter

Bagshot—Pennyhill Park London Road, Bagshot, Surrey. GU19 5ET. Tel 0276 71774. Fax 0276 73217

One feels like writing Pennyhill Park in capital letters, for it is one of the loveliest small country manor houses in the land. This perfect specimen lies forty minutes by road from the heart of London, easily accessible from the M3 motorway and is a short drive from Royal Ascot race course and Windsor castle. Major golf courses such as Wentworth and Sunningdale, as well as polo at Smiths Lawn are favourite haunts of clients staying at the Pennyhill Park. Here leisured luxury has prevailed since early Victorian times and whether you take your ease in the exquisite rooms, or relax in sunny weather in equally famous gardens, or by the swimming pool, Pennyhill Park is not only pleasing but soothing. The *cuisine* is so much out of the ordinary that it is a delight to entertain and be entertained in such surroundings. Bagshot itself could hardly be more aptly named, for it was once part of the vast royal hunting grounds of Windsor Great Forest and the early Stuart kings kept a hunting lodge there. The Pennyhill Park Country Club reflects this tradition, with tennis courts and Roman style swimming pool, an executive golf course which spans down to the three acre lake, and horse riding and clay pigeon shooting facilities. There is professional tuition available for most of these sports. We have heard persistent reports about its high standards and excellent management and can confirm that it is all quite stunning–the 120 acres of legendary estate, the Edwardian ambience, the outstanding award winning *Latymer* restaurant and the house itself with interest at every turn.

Room Rate from £108.00 Lunch from £20.00 and A La Carte Dinner from £28.00 and A La Carte Gratuities at Guest's Discretion VAT inclusive. All major Credit Cards accepted	6 Suites. 59 Double, 11 Twin Bedrooms All Rooms with Private Bathroom, TV, Telephone, Radio, Baby-listening, Room Service, Valet Service, Hairdryer Open all Year. Fully Licensed. Full Central Heating. Cocktail Bar.	Meeting Facilities. Children catered for. Dogs not allowed. Parking Facilities. Night Porter. 3 Hard Tennis Courts, Putting Green, Outdoor Heated Swimming Pool, Solarium, Sauna, Golf, Fishing, Riding, Clay Shooting. Nearby: Squash, Badminton

Section 2: Surrey

Croydon, Sanderstead—Selsdon Park Hotel
Sanderstead, South Croydon, Surrey. CR2 8YA
Tel 081 657 8811. Fax 081 651 6171

The history of Selsdon Park spans over a thousand years. In the early Anglo-Saxon period, during the time of Alfred the Great, the area was named 'Selle Dun', which meant 'mansion on the hill'. We see today a splendid example of nineteenth-century, Gothic-style architecture. That building, however, is only a part of what is now Selsdon Park Hotel for, within ten years of being opened as an hotel by Allan Doble Sanderson in 1925, it had trebled in size and this magnificent Jacobean-style house now spans a total of 850 feet! Selsdon Park's latest addition is the elegant Cambridge Wing, containing twenty-one bedrooms and a 700 square foot conference room whose contemporary decor complements the ancient charm of the main building. The hotel's imaginative leisure complex, which comprises an exclusive tropical pool, two squash courts, a gymnasium plus a health suite, containing jacuzzi, sauna, steam bath and sun-beds provides a perfect environment for relaxation throughout the year. The hotel's conference suites and 170 bedrooms also undergo constant refurbishment. Despite these impressive new features, the hotel retains its strong links with golf. Within the 200-acre grounds, which are famous for magnificent rhododendrons and centuries-old Lebanon cedars, is a championship eighteen-hole golf course 6,402 yards in length. In other parts of the grounds are floodlit all-weather and grass tennis courts and an open-air swimming pool. It is sometimes very difficult to believe that Selsdon Park is only thirteen miles from the centre of London. Maitre de Cuisine, Freddie Jones, and his brigade, provide table d'hôte and à la carte dishes which befit the hotel's international reputation.

Weekly Terms from £623.00
Room rate from only £57.00
Lunch from £19.50 and A La Carte
Afternoon Tea from £6.00 (Residents only)
Dinner from £24.00 and A La Carte
Service Charge and VAT inclusive
Credit Cards—Access, American Express, Diners Club, Visa
1 Family Room. 7 Suites. 50 Double, 80 Twin, 40 Single Bedrooms

All Rooms with Private Bath/Shower
Room, TV, Telephone, Radio,
Baby-listening, Trouser Press,
Hairdryer,Tea and Coffee-making Facilities,
Room Bar. Open all Year.
Fully Licensed.
Full Central Heating.
3 Lifts. Cocktail Bar.
Snooker Room.
Conference Facilities

Children catered for.
Dogs allowed.
Parking Facilities.
Night Porter
2 Grass and 2 All-weather Floodlit Tennis Courts, Croquet, Putting, Squash, Indoor and Outdoor Heated Swimming Pools, Solarium, Sauna, 18-hole Golf Course Jacuzzi, Steam Bath, Gymnasium, Boules, Children's Play Area, Jogging Track

Section 2: Surrey and East Sussex

Haslemere—Lythe Hill Hotel Petworth Road, Haslemere, Surrey. GU27 3BQ. Tel 0428 651251. Fax 0428 644131

Haslemere lies only two miles south of the much-improved A3 road, in an area abounding with interesting and historic sites throughout the greenest part of West Sussex, between the North Downs and the South Downs. The Hotel's excellent brochure details these places, provides a clear map and illustrates the superior quality of the accommodation and the immediate surroundings. Lythe Hill is much more than an hotel! It really is a medieval farm hamlet which comprises the main hotel on one side and the old-world *Auberge de France* on the other. The former is a luxury hotel converted with great care from the main farm buildings. Here one can be as social or as private as the mood dictates. All the tastefully furnished bedrooms and suites have private bathrooms. There is an excellent English restaurant, a cocktail bar which adjoins the cleverly designed *Italian Garden Room* and a fully equipped, self-contained, air-conditioned conference centre which in no way interferes with the other residents. On the other side of the hamlet is the fourteenth-century *Auberge de France*, famous for its wine cellars and for the presentation of French *cuisine* at its very best, and, there are five luxuriously appointed rooms, one with a four-poster bed. Therefore, you have the choice of eating at one or both restaurants during your stay, and all the hamlet for your choice of bedroom. Standing in fourteen acres of beautiful countryside the Lythe Hill includes facilities for indoor games, as well as a croquet lawn and a tennis court on the premises.

Room Rate from £84.00
Lunch from £16.50 and A La Carte
Dinner from £16.50 and A La Carte
Gratuities at Guest's Discretion. VAT inclusive. Credit Cards—Access, American Express, Visa

13 Suites. 13 Double, 14 Twin Bedrooms.
All Rooms with Private Bathroom, TV, Telephone, Radio, Baby-listening, Trouser Press, Hairdryer, Bathrobes
Open all Year. Fully Licensed. Full Central Heating. 2 Cocktail Bars. Conference

Facilities Children catered for.
Dogs allowed. Parking Facilities. Night Porter. Hard Tennis Court, Croquet, Clay Pigeon Shooting by arrangement, Boules
Nearby: Squash, Swimming, Golf, Fishing, Riding

Battle—Powder Mills Hotel Powdermill Lane, Battle, East Sussex. TN33 0SP. Tel 04246 5511. Fax 04246 4540

In the heart of 1066 country, history alone could distinguish this Georgian country house hotel: it was the chief of the Battle gunpowder mills and was reputed to have made the finest gunpowder in Europe. Many artefacts from the mills still remain in the grounds. Yet again, the beautiful architecture and picturesque setting beside a seven-acre specimen carp fishing lake would be sufficient to make a visit truly memorable. However, in our book it is *The Orangery*-their restaurant-which is the major appeal of this exceptional hotel. Is it the young head chef, Paul Webbe, or the charming and efficient restaurant staff who achieve internationally appealing levels of *cuisine* and service? Clearly, proprietors Douglas and Julie Cowpland are as perceptive in their appointment of staff as they are in the selection of excellent wines listed. Private guests or conference delegates will find food and drink to suit every pocket and every palate, from a competitively priced three course set menu, or a full vegetarian menu to an *à la carte* selection to delight the gourmand. For the businessman there are photocopying and fax facilities and, by arrangement, secretarial services. For relaxation, 150 acres of walks, woodlands and lakes provide a lovely diversion, as scenic in the wintertime as it is in summer. Internally, some enhancements and improvements are very recent. We particularly admired the black and white marble tiled floor, cane furniture, enormous plants, statuary and delicate curtains in the *Orangery*. All bedrooms have *en suite* facilities and most are furnished with fine antiques.

Terms on Applicaton
Bar Lunch from £5.50
Lunch from £13.50 Table d'Hôte
Dinner from £15.00 and A La Carte
Gratuities at Guest's Discretion
VAT inclusive. Credit Cards–Access, Visa

1 Family Room, 1 Suite
7 Double, 6 Twin Bedrooms
All Rooms with Private Bathroom, TV, Telephone, Baby-listening, Trouser Press
Open all Year
Residential and Restaurant Licence

Full Central Heating. Cocktail Bar
Conference Facilities. Children catered for
Dogs allowed. Parking Facilities.
Tennis, Croquet, Outdoor Swimming Pool, Fishing
Nearby: Golf, Riding, Shooting

Section 2: East Sussex

Near Battle, Sedlescombe—Brickwall Hotel The Green, Sedlescombe, Near Battle, East Sussex. TN33 0QA. Tel 0424 870253

Built in 1597 with all the charm and character of the Tudor period, Brickwall had, from its conception, the framework for a small hotel of high standards. Guiseppe and Gail Pollio, the owners, are determined to retain its original atmosphere whilst appreciating the needs of the present day. During our long association with this hotel we have watched a series of progressive improvements, such as the replacement of the ground-floor wing with a unit of fifteen centrally heated bedrooms with bathrooms *en suite*. In fact, the whole hotel is now centrally heated and with twenty-three private bathrooms to twenty-three rooms, is attracting an all-the-year clientèle. Mr and Mrs Pollio have also had new kitchen equipment installed at the Brickwall. Catering standards are high. Fresh fish, meat, poultry, eggs and vegetables in season are used. Such a policy always pays off–the word gets around that here you find value for money. As Brickwall remains open all the year, great attention has been paid to internal comfort particularly when the weather is inclement. On the day of our visit there was a pleasant log fire going in the newly furnished lounge. There is period furniture, a plentiful supply of reading matter, a games store for younger visitors on half-term occasions and, of course, a separate reading lounge. For those who do not know this delectable corner, where Kent and Sussex converge, or those who are determined to visit again, should write to Brickwall for their tariff folder. Opportunities for recreation, rural rambles, golf in the golf course near the village and sightseeing abound.

Weekly Terms from £260.00
Daily Terms from £45.00
Bed and Breakfast from £29.00
Lunch from £10.00 Table D'Hôte
Dinner from £13.50 Table D'Hôte
Gratuities at Guest's Discretion. VAT inclusive. Credit Cards—Access, American Express, Diners Club, Visa
1 Family Room. 1 Suite. 7 Double, 11 Twin, 3 Single Bedrooms
All Rooms with Private Bathroom, TV, Telephone, Radio, Baby-listening, Tea and Coffee-making Facilities. Hairdryer available on request. Open all Year.
Residential Licence. Cocktail Bar.
Conference Facilities. Children catered for.
Dogs allowed. Parking Facilities.
Outdoor Heated Swimming Pool

Brighton—Adelaide Hotel 51, Regency Square, Brighton, East Sussex. BN1 2FF. Tel 0273 205286. Fax 0273 220904

Sooner or later most people find themselves on the seafront at Brighton, and if, as so many people do, you decide to remain here, you will have a bountiful supply of Hotel Babylons from which to choose. Yet, we have found a rather rare hotel in the town. And it is a perfectly-run hotel...very first class. You can stay on Brighton's front if you like, and pay front-of-stall prices, but we guarantee that you will not be any more comfortable than if you reside at the Adelaide Hotel. The sea is still no more than a minute's walk away and the outlook is onto grassy Regency Square and a neighbourhood of beautifully restored regency town houses. The Adelaide is a Grade II listed building, which has been tastefully adapted to provide twelve peaceful bedrooms, all *en suite* and equipped with modern et ceteras, a comfortable lounge and an attractive dining room. The catering comprises huge breakfasts, three-course *table d'hôte* dinners by arrangement and substantial snacks provided as room service at all reasonable times of the day. We could, of course, write about the excellence of the furnishings, appointments and colour schemes. But that would still not bring out the real quality of the Adelaide, which, to our minds, is the friendliness of the place. The owners, Mr and Mrs Buxton, will see to it that you go away in praise of the welcome, the food and the comfort...and you will be remarkably surprised at the moderation of the bill. Parking is never easy in Brighton, but there is an underground car park beneath Regency Square and the charges are quite reasonable.

2 Night Weekend/Midweek Break £88.00 to £120.00 Double (B&B)
Bed and Breakfast £55.00 to £75.00 (Double). Dinner from £12.50 Table D'Hôte
Service Charge and VAT inclusive
Credit Cards—Access, American Express, Diners Club, Visa
1 Family Room. 6 Double, 1 Twin, 3 Single Bedrooms, Four-Poster Room
3 Private Bathrooms.
9 Private Shower Rooms
All Rooms with TV, Telephone, Radio, Tea and Coffee-making Facilities, Trouser Press, Hairdryer. Closed at Christmas. Residential Licence. Full CH. Children catered for. Dogs not allowed. Nearby: Tennis, Squash, Swimming, Solarium, Sauna, Golf, Fishing, Riding, Sailing

Section 2: East Sussex

Nr Brighton, Hove—St Catherine's Lodge Hotel, Seafront,
Kingsway, Hove, East Sussex. BN3 2RZ. Tel 0273 778181. Fax 0273 774949

Brighton and Hove seem indivisible; only a monument on the front denotes the boundary. Of the two, however, the latter is noticeably quieter. With so many attractions at Brighton, day-trippers and sightseers are easily induced to stay within its confines and, in consequence, Hove can afford to adopt the relaxed pace of a dormitory town. Here you will find Regency terraces with bow fronts and tall pilasters, and well-manicured lawns dipping to the sea. Overlooking the Medina Lawn is St Catherine's Lodge Hotel which we found most impressive on our recent visit. It claims an extended stretch of the Kingsway facing full south so that many of the rooms enjoy a solus sea-facing position. The view of greensward is dominant, too, in the attractive dining-room where we lunched on ample *table d'hôte* choices (*à la carte* was also available) and concluded, upon paying our bill, that here really is excellent value for money. It is obvious that Mr John Houlton, the proprietor, has picked his team with care for those at the front of the house are personable, the housekeeper fastidious and the chef well-versed and experienced. Those who appreciate studied all-round comfort will like St Catherine's Lodge, so close to its boisterous seaside companion and yet so pleasingly remote.

Weekly Terms from £225.00	Diners Club, Visa	Games Room
Bed and Breakfast from £29.00	3 Family Rooms. 2 Four Poster Rooms. 23	Conference Facilities (24hr. Delegate Rate
Bar Lunch from £3.50	Double, 13 Twin, 12 Single Bedrooms	£60). Children catered for.
Lunch from £5.60 and A La Carte	40 Private Bathrooms	Dogs allowed
Afternoon Tea from £2.50	All Rooms with TV, Telephone,	Parking Facilities. Night Porter
Dinner from £13.50 and A La Carte	Baby-listening, Room Service.	Nearby: Theatres, Cinemas, Leisure
Service Charge and VAT inclusive.	Open all Year. Fully Licensed. Full Central	Centre, Tennis, Swimming, Golf, Fishing,
Credit Cards—Access, American Express,	Heating. Lift. Cocktail Bar. TV Lounge,	Sailing, Windsurfing, Water Skiing

Near Brighton, Hove—Whitehaven Hotel Wilbury Road,
Hove, East Sussex. BN3 3JP. Tel 0273 778355. Fax 0273 731177

This seventeen-bedroomed, privately owned hotel is, we feel, an admirable recommendation for all who prefer the personal touch of resident owners. The Townend Family have the happy knack of making all their guests feel at home. The word luxury is very often misused, but we have no hesitation in describing the bedroom appointments as luxurious, for each has a fully equipped bath/shower room and toilet *en suite*, colour television, radio, direct-dial telephone, trouser press, hairdryer and tea and coffee-making facilities. Indeed, an air of elegance and style prevails throughout the hotel, which includes a lounge for non-smokers and the *Rolling Clock Restaurant* which, under the direction of the Townend daughter Peta, offers a superb choice of individually created dishes and an extensive range of fine wines to complement them. We would certainly recommend the Whitehaven to our overseas readers, who may be glad of helpful advice on where to go and what to see. If you are a golfer, Mr Townend will be glad to advise you on the local Courses. The hotel is very well situated, being in a quiet street with easy free parking and the attractions of Regency Brighton and the South Downs are all close at hand. For anyone who dislikes being a unit in a large hotel, the Whitehaven would be an admirable choice. We are always on the lookout for similar hotels to the Whitehaven in other areas, so perhaps our readers can put us wise.

Weekly Terms from £210.00 per person	1 Family Room. 1 Four-Poster Suite. 4	Children over 8 years catered for.
Bed and Breakfast from £25.00 per person	Double, 5 Twin, 6 Single Bedrooms	Dogs not allowed.
Bar Lunch from £3.00	11 Private Bathrooms. All Rooms with	Parking Facilities. Solarium
Lunch from £13.00 and A La Carte	Private Shower Room, TV, Telephone,	Nearby: Tennis, Putting, Squash,
Dinner from £13.00 and A La Carte	Radio, Tea and Coffee-making Facilities,	Badminton, Swimming, Solarium,
Gratuities at Guest's Discretion. VAT	Trouser Press, Hairdryer. Open all Year.	Sauna, Golf, Fishing, Sailing,
inclusive. Credit Cards—Access, American	Residential and Restaurant Licence.	Windsurfing, Shooting, Hang-gliding
Express, Diners Club, Visa	Cocktail Bar. Conference Facilities.	

Section 2: East Sussex

Eastbourne–Downland Hotel 37 Lewes Road, Eastbourne, East Sussex. BN21 2BU. Tel 0323 32689

We have so often been asked for 'a good place to stay in Eastbourne...not expensive, conveniently located for the sea, but not one of its hotel Babylons on the front'. Well, we have found a truly excellent place and with a restaurant which has recently won an AA Rosette and RAC Award of Merit. The Downland Hotel sits placidly away from the mainstream of tourist activity, yet is just a few minutes away from the town centre and seafront. Since Patrick and Stephanie Faulkner took over the Downland as its owners they have stepped-up the facilities all round. The restaurant, with its attendant bar, has been replanned and completely refurbished. Clearly, there is now a greater emphasis on imaginative and extensive *cuisine*, with Mr Faulkner's great experience as a chef being put to very good use. This is not to imply that the bedrooms have been treated in any way *sotto voce*. Each contains an *en suite* bathroom or shower, a colour television, telephone, radio, baby-listening, central heating and beverage-making facilities. Guests have free membership of the nearby Ball Park, Eastbourne's outstanding Sports and Leisure Club and indoor tennis resort. It seems to us that, when staying at the Downland, you will not have to forego any of the comfort of more pretentious hotels; everything is of a high standard and represents excellent value for money. It is quite clear that the owners have the comfort and well-being of their guests at heart and are anxious to make them feel at home in this hotel. You can stay on Eastbourne's front if you like, but we guarantee that you will not be more comfortable.

Short Breaks from £75.00 (2 nights DB&B) Weekly Terms (Half Board) from £195.00 Bed and Breakfast from £27.50 Dinner from £17.50 and A La Carte Gratuities at Guest's Discretion. VAT inclusive. Credit Cards—Access, American Express, Diners Club, Visa. 3 Family Rooms, 1 Four Poster Bedroom. 7 Double, 1 Single, 2 Twin Bedrooms. 7 Private Bathrooms. 7 Private Shower Rooms. All Rooms with TV, Telephone, Radio, Baby-listening, Tea and Coffee-making Facilities. Hairdryer and Trouser Press available on request. Open all Year except January. Residential and Restaurant Licence. Conference Facilities. Children catered for. Dogs not allowed. Parking Facilities. Nearby: Tennis, Croquet, Putting

Eastbourne–Farrar's Hotel. 3-5, Wilmington Gardens, Eastbourne, East Sussex. BN21 4JN. Tel 0323 23737

For ourselves, visiting Farrar's is like calling on a good friend and we would say to anybody seeking a homely, friendly and personal hotel, pin your faith on Farrar's hotel. We arrived here recently for refreshment and appreciated anew how very comfortable an hotel it is with its own distinctive personality. The furnishings and antique and unusual ornaments which abound have something to do with its individuality. It is situated on Wilmington Gardens, only 300 yards from the sea, and opposite the Congress Theatre where first-class entertainment is the order of the day. Although the hotel is well established, every visit reveals something new to see. All bedrooms now have *en suite* facilities and all public rooms, including the bar have recently been extended and refurbished. The traditional seaside holiday, once derided, is now back in vogue and Farrar's Hotel displays all of its virtues: three excellent meals a day, tea to be taken in the comfortable lounge, a delightful garden with views to the South Downs, two lifts reaching to every floor and porters on duty day and night. Only minutes away from the hotel is Eastbourne's main shopping centre and there are many holiday and sporting attractions, including bowls and tennis, and golf on the Royal Eastbourne Course. If you travel to Eastbourne from London on the A22, the journey takes only a couple of hours.

Weekly Terms from £267.00 Daily Terms from £43.00 Bed and Breakfast from £33.00 Bar Lunch from £1.90 Lunch from £2.50 and A La Carte Dinner from £12.00 Table D'Hôte Gratuities at Guest's Discretion. VAT inclusive. Credit Cards—Access, American Express, Visa 3 Family Rooms. 8 Double, 20 Twin, 14 Single Bedrooms 35 Private Bathrooms. 10 Private Shower Rooms. All Rooms with TV, Telephone, Radio, Baby-listening, Tea and Coffee-making Facilities. Hairdryer available on request. Open all Year. Residential and Restaurant Licence. Full Central Heating. Lift. Cocktail Bar. TV Lounge. Conference Facilities. Children catered for. Dogs allowed. Parking Facilities. Night Porter. Nearby: Tennis, Croquet, Putting, Squash, Badminton, Swimming, Solarium Sauna, Golf, Fishing, Riding, Sailing, Windsurfing, Water Skiing, Hang-gliding

Section 2: East Sussex

Eastbourne—The Lansdowne Hotel King Edward's Parade, Eastbourne, East Sussex. BN21 4EE. Tel 0323 25174. Fax 0323 39721

Those of our readers who are looking for an hotel which still believes in providing the highest standards in service and comfort should plan on spending their next mini-break or holiday at the first-class three-star Lansdowne Hotel. There are not many places, today, where you can find an hotel which is so interested in the welfare of its guests, where there is not one but two rooms for snooker, and again not one but two separate rooms for television, to watch your favourite programme in colour on BBC1 or ITV. It is because of this thoughtfulness that so many return year after year to relax in the well-appointed lounges (one of which is set aside for non-smokers). There is also an attractive *Regency Bar*, the *Card Room* and two spacious restaurants. Light lunches are served daily throughout the year. The *cuisine* and cellar are well planned and we were further impressed with many of the 127 bedrooms we inspected, all of which have a private bathroom *en suite*. The hotel has full central heating and two lifts for easy access to all floors. The Lansdowne is privately owned and occupies an ideal sea-front position with glorious views of Beachy Head and is opposite the Western Lawns and flower-decked slopes to the Wish Tower. This seafront hotel is within three minutes' walk of the Congress and Devonshire Park theatres, the Winter Garden and shopping area. Special 'Bargain Break' terms are available during the autumn, winter and spring, as well as special-interest holidays including bridge weekends, golf, rambling and watercolour painting packages.

Weekly Terms from £266.00 (Jan/Feb only)
Bed and Breakfast from £38.50
Lunch from £5.00 A La Carte
Dinner from £14.75 and limited A La Carte
Service Charge and VAT inclusive
Credit Cards—Access, American Express,

Diners Club, JCB, Visa. 6 Family Rooms.
2 Suites, 2 Superior Singles. 19 Double, 60 Twin, 42 Single Bedrooms
113 Private Bathrooms. 14 Private Shower Rooms. All Rooms with TV, Telephone, Radio, Tea and Coffee-making Facilities,

Baby-listening, Hairdryer. Trouser Press available on request. Open from 10th January to 31st December. Fully Licensed. 2 Lifts. Cocktail Bar. 2 TV Lounges. Games Room 2 Snooker Rooms. Conference Facilities.

Near Eastbourne, Willingdon—Chalk Farm Hotel. Coopers Hill, Willingdon, Eastbourne, Sussex. BN20 9JD. Tel 0323 503800

And last, but by no means least, we shall lead you to one of Eastbourne's surprises. Little do those on the crowded promenade realise that just two-and-a-half miles away, nestling at the foot of the South Downs on Coopers Hill, are a number of people rejoicing in quiet seclusion, enjoying an extensive old-world garden, a well-stocked bar and outstanding fare at Chalk Farm Hotel ... perhaps some are staying there, for there are a number of delightful guest rooms, the Downs inviting one to walk or hike, golf courses all around (one just five minutes away), little hamlets with quaint pubs to discover, and simply lazing, of course. Here is a perfect example of a seventeenth-century Sussex farmhouse, full of character and facing south, which has been so flawlessly adapted for hotel purposes. Within the well-tended grounds is a kitchen garden providing fresh herbs, vegetables and fruit for the table. The hotel's reputation for excellent *cuisine* is already well established, with people travelling far and wide to eat there. The rest of the hotel is as pleasing as the restaurant. There is a comfortable lounge, a cocktail bar and bedrooms replete with colour television, beverage trays, telephones and central heating, and most have adjoining baths or showers. Every time we revisit Chalk Farm there is something new to admire: good-quality recarpeting, new furniture, or fresh decor in just the right hues. Chalk Farm is, indeed, a labour of love for the Coleman family and they could not make it more hospitable. And the crowds? They could be a million miles away.

Terms on Application
Gratuities at Guest's discretion. VAT inclusive. Credit Card–Access, Visa
1 Suite, 2 Family Rooms, 5 Double, 1 Single, 1 Twin Bedrooms

3 Private Bathrooms. 4 Private Shower Rooms. All Rooms with TV, Telephone, Tea and Coffee-making facilities
Open all Year. Residential and Restaurant Licence. Full Gas Central Heating.

Cocktail Bar. TV Lounge. Conference Facilities. Children catered for. Dogs allowed. Parking Facilities.
Nearby: Tennis, Putting, Squash, Badminton, Golf

Section 2: East Sussex

Near Herstmonceux, Boreham Street—White Friars Hotel
Boreham Street, Herstmonceux, East Sussex. BN27 4SE. Tel 0323 832355. Fax 0323 833882

Known originally as Montegue House, this Grade II listed building dates from 1721 when it formed part of the local Ashburnham Estate. Its long frontage of mellow brickwork, and the distinctive chimneys, have for many years made it a famous landmark to visitors and locals alike. Our impressions were favourable from the outset, as we studied the menu over a drink in the beamed bar lounge. Further praise to a hard-worked waitress who brought us warm rolls and chilled water, and efficient service for the competitively priced *table d'hôte* lunch. What a pleasure to have linen napkins! The dining-room is beautifully decorated and the menu offered a good choice for all three courses. On identifying ourselves, we were given a conducted tour of the twelve bedrooms in the hotel itself: there are a further eight in converted cottages nearby. We were also shown the spotless kitchens, where the chef was busily preparing *canapés* for a promotional press meeting scheduled for that afternoon. We had lunched in the *Ashburnham Restaurant* and an alternative location in small dining areas in the cellar, offering an *à la carte* menu. These are named *Monks, Friars, Novices, Curates* etc and, adjoining these, a *Naughty Corner*! Altogether a comfortable and relaxing establishment, set in beautiful, well kept grounds. White Friars can accommodate conferences for up to fifty delegates and social functions for up to ninety people. All guests will find the area interesting, attractive and easily accessible.

Weekly Terms from £250.00
Daily Terms from £56.00
Bed and Breakfast from £45.00
Bar Lunch from £3.50
Lunch from £9.50 and A La Carte
Dinner from £15.95 and A La Carte
Service and VAT inclusive
Credit Cards—Access, American Express,

Diners Club, Visa. 2 Family Rooms
9 Double, 6 Twin, 3 Single Bedrooms
18 Private Bathrooms.
2 Private Shower Rooms.
All Rooms with TV, Telephone, Radio, Baby-listening, Tea and Coffee-making Facilities, Hairdryer.
12 Rooms with Trouser Press.

Open all Year
Residential and Restaurant Licence
Cocktail Bar. TV Lounge. Conference Facilities. Children catered for. Dogs allowed. Parking Facilities
Croquet, Putting. Nearby: Tennis, Fishing, Riding, Sailing, Windsurfing, Water Skiing, Golf

Halland, Nr Lewes—Halland Forge Hotel & Restaurant
Halland, Nr Lewes, E. Sussex. BN8 6PW. Tel 0825 840456. Fax 0825 840773

This attractive three-star hotel, adjacent to several acres of garden and woodland, is an ideal touring centre for the south east and Sussex coast. The charming oak-beamed *Forge Restaurant*, which is built on the site of the original old forge, is fully licensed. There is an extensive choice offered on the *table d'hôte* and *à la carte* menus, complemented by fine wines and friendly service. The *Coffee Shop* offers a prestigious alternative to the *Forge Restaurant* and is open all day for light meals or snacks. The comfortable *Anvil Lounge Bar*, with a log fire in winter, is an ideal rendezvous for an *apéritif* before your meal or for relaxing afterwards. The hotel has facilities for functions, wedding receptions and conferences. Those who have experienced the high standards set by Mr and Mrs J M Howell, the proprietors, and travellers seeking a quality establishment will need little bidding to come here. The twenty tastefully furnished bedrooms, which are housed in a separate block, each have a private bathroom, television, radio, telephone and tea and coffee-making facilities. There is central heating throughout and a large car park. Short-break and holiday tariffs are available on request. Halland is a small hamlet situated on the cross of the A22/B2192, four miles south of Uckfield. Easily accessible from the hotel are Crawley and Tunbridge Wells, to the north, and an important stretch of the south coast from Brighton to Hastings and the port of Newhaven.

Weekly Terms (Half Board) from £248.00
Daily Terms from £40.00
Bed and Breakfast from £37.00 per person sharing double room
Coffee Shop Lunch from £5.65
Lunch from £8.95 and A La Carte
Dinner from £12.50 and A La Carte
Gratuities at Guest's Discretion.

VAT inclusive. Credit Cards—Access, American Express, Diners Club, Visa
2 Family Rooms. 11 Double, 7 Twin Bedrooms. 17 Private Bathrooms. 3 Private Shower Rooms. All Rooms with TV, Telephone, Radio, Tea and Coffee-making Facilities, Trouser Press.

Hairdryer. Open all Year. Fully Licensed.
Conference Facilities. Children over 5 years catered for. Dogs allowed at Management's Discretion.
Parking Facilities
Nearby: Woodland Walks, Gliding, Motor Sports

Section 2: East Sussex

Near Rye, Peasmarsh–Flackley Ash Hotel
Peasmarsh, Near Rye, East Sussex. TN31 6YH.
Tel 079 721 651. Fax 079 721 510

This is an impressive hotel and Clive and Jeanie Bennett, the proprietors, are a most hard-working couple. Building upon the inherent virtues of this attractive Georgian country house (dating from about 1770), with its five acres of grounds, the Bennetts have established quite a reputation for their cuisine. Having a close liason with the Rye Bay fishing fleet, their menus feature poisson dishes–fresh dabs, plaice, and sole. Best Scotch beef is also a speciality at Flackley Ash and a selection of fresh vegetables is always available. Mention should be made, too, of the superb bar snacks and lunches. Recent developments include new de luxe bedrooms and suites. The bedrooms are spotlessly clean and particularly well appointed, with private bathroom, beverage-making facilities and central heating. There are also three special rooms with four poster beds. The indoor swimming pool, saunas, spa-bath, solarium, mini-gym and floatation tank ensure an indoor activity during inclement weather. As the hotel is situated between the charming town of Rye and the Weald, there are many places of interest to visit; Bodiam Castle, Bateman's, Rye, Camber Sands and Winchelsea. Special weekend bargain breaks and midweek breaks are available. We had received good reports about Flackley Ash Hotel and we were delighted with what we found. It was even better than we had expected.

Weekly Terms from £300.00
Bed and Breakfast from £44.50 per person
Bar Lunch from £5.00
Lunch from £11.95 Table D'Hôte
Bar Supper from £7.95
Dinner from £16.50 and A La Carte
Gratuities at Guest's Discretion. VAT inclusive. Credit Cards—Access, American Express, Diners Club, Visa

2 Family Rooms. 2 Suites. 16 Double, 12 Twin Bedrooms. 30 Private Bathrooms. 2 Private Shower Rooms. All Rooms with TV, Telephone, Trouser Press, Radio, Tea and Coffee-making Facilities, Hairdryer. 10 Rooms with Wall Safe. Open all Year. Fully Licensed

Cocktail Bar. Lounge. Conference Facilities
Children catered for. Dogs allowed
Parking Facilities.
Croquet, Indoor Swimming Pool, Solarium, Sauna, Spa Bath, Mini Gym, Floatation Tank, Beautician and Massage
Nearby: Tennis, Squash, Golf, Fishing, Riding

Section 2: East Sussex
Rye–The Old Vicarage Hotel & Restaurant
15 East Street, Rye, East Sussex TN31 7JY. Tel 0797 225131

Rye is unique; it stands alone. The motorist can enter, but only just. Its streets are small and tortuous, so when you go there take our advice–park outside the city walls and then stroll if you want to appreciate Rye's quaintness, its cobbled streets, its magnificent view and dominating position over Walland Marsh. Then, if you feel the call of the past is in you at all, you will not be content until you have slept within Rye's ancient walls. So let us commend you to The Old Vicarage, a most amiable house with associations with Henry James, now an elegant family-run hotel with a very personal touch. It is also quite tiny in terms of its number of bedrooms, there being only four, yet each is spacious and furnished in period style. Some have complete Tester beds, whilst all boast *en suite* facilities and numerous modern notions of comfort. The house is . . . quite perfect, and, for all its smallness, The Old Vicarage was judged winner of the 1990 AA's best Newcomer Award for the South East of England. Quite an achievement! The food is clearly one of its main attractions, for Sarah Foster is a dedicated cook, who prepares an extensive *a la carte* selection and mouth watering and well priced *table d'hôte* dishes. The restaurant, with views over the River Rother estuary and Romney Marsh, adds to the delight of eating here. There is also an attractive cocktail bar. Both Mrs Foster and her husband could not be more welcoming to their guests and it is easy to see why their hotel, in its timeless location, should have become a bolt-hole for those seeking an escape from stressful lives. So, when you get there, please do not get 'fussed' about parking your car. It is possible to park outside the hotel overnight and there is even limited parking there during the day. But our suggestion is to give your car a break, too, for there is a small free car park not far away.

Weekly Terms from £280.00-£290.00 (Half Board). Daily Terms from £39.00-£51.00 (Half Board)
Bed and Breakfast from £28.00-£40.00
Dinner from £10.95 Table D'Hôte/£14.20-£19.80 A La Carte
Gratuities at Guest's Discretion

VAT inclusive. Credit Cards-American Express, Mastercard, Visa
2 Family Rooms. 2 Double Bedrooms
All rooms with Private Bathroom, Colour TV, Telephone, Radio, Tea and Coffee-making Facilities.
Hairdryer on request.

Open from the end of January to early January. Residential and Restaurant Licence. Full Gas Central Heating. Cocktail Bar. Children catered for. Dogs allowed Nearby: Tennis, Putting, Squash, Golf, Fishing, Riding, Sailing, Windsurfing

Have you returned your membership form?
By simply completing and returning to us the registration card inserted in this book you will automatically become a 1993 member of the Ashley Courtenay Circle , an invaluable link between author and reader. For members, we compile and revise each year special listings of hotels which offer particular amenities, such as a sauna, swimming pool, golf course (or adjacent), four-poster beds, facilities for the disabled, special Christmas programmes, vegetarian dishes, non-smoking areas and self-catering facilities. We can even direct you to hotels which are especially pleased to receive young children and dogs. These lists are free of charge. Just send a stamped addressed envelope.

Section 2: West Sussex

Near Arundel, Burpham—Burpham Country Hotel
Burpham, Arundel, West Sussex. BN18 9RJ. Tel 0903 882160

Yet, for those who prefer somewhere quiet and peaceful in a pleasant environment we warmly recommend the Burpham Country Hotel. Reputed to have been, in earlier times, a hunting lodge for the Duke of Norfolk, this charming hotel has superb views over the South Downs and is situated in one of the most peaceful and unspoilt villages in West Sussex. Mr and Mrs E Potter, the resident owners, have done much to provide all those big and little things which they consider essential to their guest's comfort. Perhaps, too, it is their dedication to this former rectory which means that they are constantly striving for ever higher standards. You will notice how freshly renovated and redecorated is the exterior. Inside the rooms are bright and beautifully kept. Although Arundel to Burpham is but just 'across the water', access to the hotel is a ten-minute drive along a pleasant winding country lane which eventually reaches an open space by an inn and a part-Norman church. Before then the hotel's sign is on your right. Rurality is assured along with comfort and the personal touch, whilst the hotel's *cuisine* is prepared from fresh local produce. Vegetarians are also catered for. This is a restful base from which to explore the many places of interest in the area.

Weekly Terms on Application
Daily Terms from £43.75
Bed and Breakfast from £30.50
Inclusive breaks (min 2 days) all year
Dinner from £13.25 Table D'Hôte
VAT inclusive. Credit Cards—Access, Visa
5 Double, 1 Single, 4 Twin Bedrooms

9 Private Bathrooms.
1 Private Shower Room
All Rooms with TV, Tea and Coffee-making Facilities. Hairdryer available
Open all Year.
Residential and Restaurant Licence
Full Central Heating. Cocktail Bar.

Conference Facilities
Children over 12 years catered for.
Dogs not allowed
Parking Facilities
Nearby: Tennis, Putting, Squash, Badminton, Swimming, Golf, Fishing, Riding, Windsurfing, Horse Racing

Bognor Regis, Aldwick—Black Mill House Hotel
Princess Avenue, Aldwick, West Sussex. PO21 2QU. Tel 0243 821945. Fax 0243 821316

For many years, Mr and Mrs Geoffrey Soothill, now assisted by their son and his wife, Mr and Mrs Gerard Soothill, have been welcoming their visitors into this friendly hotel, which lies to the west of Bognor Regis. Chichester is the home base of Ashley Courtenay Limited and so we know Mr and Mrs Soothill very well. We do, therefore, have a soft spot for their amiable hotel, but other hotel guides sing its praises, too, and there are many visitors who would stay nowhere else. All the bedrooms have colour television, direct-dial telephone, radio/intercom, listening service and tea and coffee-making facilities, although room service has been retained. The majority of the twenty-six rooms have private bathrooms. There is a most attractive cocktail bar, and the restaurant which serves a good selection of food and wines is always open to non-residents for lunch and dinner. Two comfortable lounges are available, one with colour television and the other for non-smokers, and also a games room with small snooker table, table tennis and darts. There is a large enclosed garden, well stocked with roses and herbaceous borders. Black Mill House is situated in a quiet avenue leading to Marine Gardens and the sea is just 300 yards away. A short-break tariff is offered throughout the year and the hotel is an ideal base for those visiting the Chichester Festival Theatre, Goodwood House, the Roman palace at Fishbourne, Arundel, the Wildfowl Trust or Parham House or for those wishing to go to the races. The hotel is a very comfortable retreat out of season and is open during Christmas.

2 Day Short Breaks from £68.00
Weekly Terms from £216.00 sharing double/twin. Bed and Breakfast from £27.00. Bar Lunch from £2.50
Lunch from £7.95 Table D'Hôte
Dinner from £10.45 Table D'Hôte

Gratuities at Guest's Discretion. VAT inclusive. Credit Cards—Access, American Express, Diners Club, Visa
6 Family Rooms. 5 Double, 6 Twin, 9 Single Bedrooms. 10 Private Bathrooms. 8 Private Shower Rooms. All Rooms with

TV, Telephone, Radio/Intercom, Baby-listening, Tea and Coffee-making Facilities. Hairdryer available on request. Open all Year. Fully Licensed. Full CH. Cocktail Bar. TV Lounge. Games Room. Small Conference Facilities. Lift

Section 2: West Sussex

Near Chichester, Charlton—Woodstock House Hotel Charlton, Near Chichester, West Sussex. PO18 0HU. Tel 0243 63 666

Nobody knows Sussex properly until they have explored its backbone, the Downs. Here is an area that must not be hurried over... you must be content to wander in and out of by-lanes, drive up steep roads and descend into picturesque valleys, and pause in hidden villages. And, yet, you will still not *know* the Downs unless you have stayed there. Within sight of Goodwood Racecourse, and sheltering below the heights of the forest which bears its name, is the hamlet of Charlton. It has two claims to fame. Formerly it was the base of one of the most famous Hunts in England. Today it is better known for Woodstock House Hotel. Here all who prefer the small country-house type hotel will rejoice. For most of the day the sun never lets Woodstock House out of sight and the inner courtyard garden, which is overlooked by a balcony, is a suntrap. To these inherent virtues the owners, Mr and Mrs McGovern, have added within every comfort. We loved the colour schemes and the furnishings. What could not be replaced appears to have been renovated. Note the attractive fireplaces in the dining room and the lounge. The bedrooms are equally pleasing. They offer the guest television and beverage-making facilities and one room has a four-poster bed. Mrs McGovern heads the kitchen team and is responsible for the interesting and varied menus. Woodstock House is now open to non-residents and is fully licensed. There is more to tell, but with all the improvements we see, Woodstock House remains essentially a peaceful, rural home. The hotel also offers special weekend breaks.

Getaway Breaks October to March
2 Days (DB&B) from £77.00 Per Person
Weekly Terms (Half Board) from £262.00
Daily Terms from £38.50
Bed and Breakfast from £27.50
Dinner from £15.50 A La Carte

Gratuities at Guest's Discretion. VAT inclusive. Credit Cards—Access, Euro Club, Mastercard, Visa
3 Double, 4 Twin, 4 Single Bedrooms. 4 Private Bathrooms. 5 Private Shower Rooms. All Rooms with TV, Tea and Coffee-making Facilities. Hairdryer available on request. Open all Year. Fully Licensed. Full Central Heating Open Fires. Cocktail Bar. Children catered for by arrangement. Dogs allowed by arrangement. Parking Facilities.

Nr Chichester, Nyetimber–The Inglenook Hotel & Restaurant 255 Pagham Road, Nyetimber, Bognor Regis, West Sussex. PO21 3QB. Tel 0243 262495. Fax 0243 262668

Before concluding your tour of the Sussex coast you will be quite delighted if you dip into the county's southern-most peninsula. Here is a little gem of a place if you seek friendliness allied to very high standards. We like the sixteenth-century Inglenook, where the Honour family has presided for over eighteen years. It is an eye-catcher on a quiet road, particularly when its window-boxes and flower beds are at their colourful best. For all its picturesqueness without, however, step inside and you are likely to blink in astonishment, for whilst its centuries-old features and cottage ambience are intact, the decor, comforts and accessories are of the highest order. Yet, the really grand feature of The Inglenook is the relaxed way of life there; you may come and go as you please, then eat and sleep royally, for Mrs Honour is a born hostess and she and the Chef, her son, are great cooks. The restaurant is open every day for luncheon and dinner, and, since the famous Selsey lobsters and crabs queue up off-shore to leap into the pots, it is not surprising one notes many seafood specialities. Elect to stay at The Inglenook and there are further surprises in store. Quaint but spacious bedrooms, each individually decorated. There is even an entrancing Bridal Suite complete with jacuzzi-whirlpool bath! Close by, the *Millstone Cottage* provides further accommodation in the form of six *en suite* rooms. Whilst at the hotel itself, a banqueting room, conference room and a restful garden complete the attractions of this marvellous 'find', just a stone's throw from so much interest, yet quiet enough to qualify as a peaceful hide-away.

Weekly Terms from £210.00 pp (DB&B)
Daily Terms from £45.00 pp
Bed and Breakfast from £47.00 (Single), £70.00 (Double). Bar Meals from £2.50
Lunch from £9.25 (3 course) Table D'Hôte
Dinner from £12.95 (3 course) Table D'Hôte

Gratuities at Guest's Discretion. VAT inclusive. Credit Cards-Access, American Express, Diners Club, Visa. 1 Family Room. 12 Double, 4 Twin, 2 Single Bedrooms. 15 Private Bathrooms. 3 Private Shower Rooms

All Rooms with TV, Telephone, Radio, Tea and Coffee-making Facilities, Trouser Press, Hairdryer. Baby-listening available on request. Open all year. Fully Licensed Full CH. Cocktail Bar. TV Lounge. Conference Facilities. Children catered for.

Section 2: West Sussex

Climping–Bailiffscourt Hotel   Climping, Littlehampton, West Sussex. BN17 5RW.
Tel 0903 723511. Fax 0903 723107

This rural parish, of which Bailiffscourt forms a major part, possesses the only unbuilt stretch of West Sussex coastline where pasture and plough flank sands and sea. Here in Norman times Benedictine monks farmed, supervised by the bailiff who lived in the court. After the dissolution of the monasteries, a succession of workers farmed the land and it was the late Lord Moyne who completely rebuilt Bailiffscourt on medieval lines. Some forty years ago it was opened as an hotel, and it is now operated by Bailiffscourt Ltd and managed by Tim Lamming. The unusual and attractive buildings have undergone thoughtful and imaginative changes. There are comfortable oak-panelled rooms with log fires and a particularly fine restaurant where you will find excellent food, wine and service. Coupled with this medieval background, all modern-day comforts have been provided. The bedrooms, some with four-poster beds, are all individually decorated, each having private bathroom, colour television, radio and telephone. The high standards practised above stairs are also apparent in the kitchen and cellars. Bailiffscourt is a classic in reproduction, for nothing has been faked. Stone, woodwork and massive wooden doors have been collected from many sources and are all authentic. In our opinion this hotel is unique historically, structurally and gastronomically.

Accommodation Terms on Application Lunch from £15.50 Table D'Hôte Afternoon Tea from £3.50 Dinner from £25.00 Table D'Hôte, Saturdays. Gourmet 5 course menu at £30.00 Gratuities at Guest's Discretion. VAT inclusive. Credit Cards—Access, American Express, Diners Club, Visa	3 Suites. 18 Doubles including 3 Suites, 2 Single Bedrooms All Rooms with Private Bathroom, TV, Telephone, Radio, Baby-listening, Hairdryer and Room Service. 9 Rooms with Four Poster Beds and Open Log Fires Open all Year. Fully Licensed. Full CH. Cocktail Bar. Conference Facilities Children over 8 years catered for. Dogs	allowed (Basket and Food Provided) Parking Facilities. Night Porter. 2 Hard Tennis Courts, Croquet, Outdoor Swimming Pool, Golf Practice Area, Riding available at next-door Stables, Clay Pigeon Shooting by Arrangement, Helicopter Landing Pad. Nearby: Squash, Badminton, Swimming, Solarium, Sauna, Golf, Fishing, Sailing, Windsurfing

East Grinstead—Woodbury House Hotel and Garden Room Restaurant   Lewes Road, East Grinstead, West Sussex. RH19 3UD. Tel 0342 313657. Fax 0342 314801

The boundaries between Kent, Surrey and East and West Sussex all meet close to the ancient town of East Grinstead. The town's name is derived from the Saxon 'Greenstede', a green clearing in the great Wealden forest which once dominated this area. Just half a mile south of East Grinstead on the A22 road is this very attractive gabled hotel. If you appreciate country pursuits, a rural outlook and friendly surroundings, Woodbury House, an hour's drive from both London and the South Coast, would be an ideal answer to the problem of where to stay. Fourteen bedrooms, each individually styled and furnished to a high standard with excellent *en suite* bath or shower facilities, ensure your comfort. Remote-control television, radio, direct-dial telephone and beverage-making facilities are standard amenities in all bedrooms. As an alternative to the impeccable *cuisine* served in the well appointed and elegant *Garden Room Restaurant*, the menu in the attractive *Conservatory Bistro* will equally appeal. Another addition is the *Buckmaster Room* which provides a perfect venue for private parties or meetings for up to sixteen people. The top class Chef's *table d'hôte* and *à la carte* luncheon and dinner menus are superb and the hotel's traditional Sunday Lunch is a great attraction. Here then, is a friendly hotel of character with an inviting atmosphere. Tastefully furnished and well maintained throughout it offers its guests first class comfort, *cuisine* and service. We are delighted to recommend it to you.

Weekly Terms from £458.00 Daily Terms from £52.50 Bed and Breakfast from £55.00 Bistro Lunch from £3.50 Lunch from £14.95 Table D'Hôte Afternoon Tea from £3.50 Dinner from £14.95 and A La Carte VAT inclusive	Credit Cards—Access, American Express, Diners Club, Visa 1 Family Room, 6 Double, 4 Twin, 2 Single Bedrooms 1 Room with Four Poster. 7 Private Bathrooms. 7 Private Shower Rooms All Rooms with TV, Telephone, Radio, Tea and Coffee-making Facilities	Open all Year except Boxing Day Fully Licensed Full Central Heating Cocktail Bar. Conference Facilities Children catered for. Dogs allowed Parking Facilities Nearby: Tennis, Squash, Swimming, Sauna, Golf, Riding

Section 2: West Sussex

Near Haywards Heath, Slaugham–The Chequers Inn
Slaugham Village, Nr Handcross, West Sussex, RH17 6AQ
Telephone 0444 400239

It was in 1990 that one of our readers commented in her helpful report on The Chequers: 'It must be one of the best-kept secrets in the Gatwick area'. If superb cuisine, first-class service, and every comfort in spacious rooms are anything to go by, the secret must now be out. With London (Gatwick) Airport only a quick drive away, and the diverse activities at nearby Horsham and Crawley, this efficiently run small hotel deserves to have all of its deluxe en suite bedrooms fully booked at all times. Personable proprietors Paul and Sue Graham maintain a warm and friendly ambience hand-in-hand with impeccable personal attention to the requirements of each guest. In the attractive restaurant, displaying on its walls some notices of well known theatrical performances, one soon realises that gourmet-like fare is the order of the day, with sea food a particular speciality. (One complete section of the menu - which includes humorous comments on every dish - is headed 'Le Fish'). In the summer months you can dine Al Fresco in the terraced garden and, indoors or out, the lure of an extensive wine list makes an overnight booking advisable, even without the added charms of a four-poster suite, a spa or a double bath. Here, then, is a delightful country atmosphere in one of the prettiest villages in Sussex, as appealing to holidaymakers as it is convenient and relaxing to the European businessman or local executive. The amenities are many, the furnishings luxurious and the tariff exceedingly reasonable.

Weekly Terms from £395.00
Daily Terms from £65.00
Bed and Breakfast from £49.00
Bar Lunch from £3.75
Lunch from £16.50 and A La Carte
Bar Supper from £6.50
Dinner from £17.50 and A La Carte

Service Charge at 10%. VAT inclusive
Credit Cards-Access, American Express, Visa
3 Suites. 6 Double Bedrooms
All Rooms with Private Bathrooms, TV, Telephone, Radio, Tea and Coffee-making Facilities, Trouser Press, Hairdryer

Open all year. Fully Licensed
Full Central Heating. Cocktail Bar
Children catered for. Parking Facilities
Nearby: Tennis, Squash, Swimming, Solarium, Sauna, Golf, Fishing, Riding, Sailing, Windsurfing, Shooting, Hang-gliding

Section 2: West Sussex

Pulborough–Chequers Hotel
Church Place, Pulborough, West Sussex. RH20 1AD. Tel 0798 872486. Fax 0798 872715

As one travels southwards along the Roman 'Stane Street' the Downs get closer till, at Pulborough, we are almost at their feet. Yet, Chequers enjoys a lofty position itself, being atop a sandstone rise. It started life as an old posting station, and has now established an enviable reputation for being one of the most comfortable and friendly family-owned hotels in the South. It is quite clear that guests love the elegant and homely touches of this Queen Anne Hotel, and record their appreciation of the happy times they have enjoyed here. Visitors are attracted to the rural Englishness of Chequers in increasing numbers, whilst many guests return regularly. The secrets of its success are continuity—the Searancke family have owned and run Chequers for more than 30 years—and the fact that the facilities here have always kept abreast of the times. Chequers remains small and intimate but recent refurbishment has increased the number of bedrooms and has highlighted the restaurant, with excellent furnishings and attractive decor. There is a garden Conservatory where you can just relax or enjoy coffee, light lunches or afternoon tea. The catering at Chequers is far removed from the ordinary and befits the smart surroundings in which it is served. Here are bedrooms so individual in character that guests will often amend their holiday plans to ensure that they can stay in the room of their choice. Being, as we are, professional hotel hunters we look at Chequers objectively. Yet, in many ways we also view it as a very dear friend. Whether it is a case of walking, motoring, or just losing oneself in the South Downs for a while, Chequers Hotel affords you a grand opportunity.

BARGAIN BREAKS AVAILABLE AND SPECIAL CHRISTMAS PROMOTION
Weekly Terms from £248.00
Daily Terms from £38.50
Bed and Breakfast from £32.50

VAT inclusive. Credit Cards—Access, American Express, Diners Club, Visa
3 Family Rooms. 1 Four-poster Room. 1 Single, 4 Double, 2 Twin Bedrooms (4 bedrooms on ground floor)

All Rooms with Private Bath/Shower Room, TV, Telephone, Tea and Coffee-making Facilities, Trouser Press, Hairdryer. Open all year. Full CH. Residential and Restaurant Licence

Trotton, Near Midhurst–Southdowns Hotel & Restaurant
Trotton, Rogate, Nr Midhurst, Hants. GU31 5JN. Tel 0730 821521

The pride of Sussex are her South Downs–whale-back shapes, grass-covered slopes and exhilarating air. Tucked away at the foot of these slopes is the aptly-named Southdowns Hotel, set in four acres of landscaped grounds and with a vista encompassing wide lawns, mature trees and, of course, the Downs themselves. On warm days these gardens are a tranquil setting for the enjoyment of drinks and snacks, but, come rain or shine, the accent in the air-conditioned *Country Restaurant* is on excellent *cuisine*. A variety of tempting menus is offered, all with apt, rural titles, such as the 'Poacher's Menu' and 'Squire's Menu'. Which ever you chose, there is excellent choice and the food is skilfully prepared and presented ... and represents very good value for money. When spending a day or two at Southdowns, in addition to being allocated a comfortable and very well-appointed bedroom, you will also receive complimentary membership of the *Kingfisher Club* leisure complex. But if this sounds too strenuous, and all you really want to do is drop out of the rat race and relax for a while, then you will find the attractive newly-added Conservatory very therapeutic. In any event, you are certain to be well cared for by your hosts, Richard Lion and Dominic Vedovato, for they have created at Southdowns Hotel and Restaurant a most welcoming atmosphere. Albeit tucked away, the hotel is not difficult to find: when approaching Trotton on the A272 road from Midhurst, take a left turn past The Keeper's Arms and you will see the hotel one mile along this road, on the right-hand side.

Weekly Terms on Application
Daily Terms from £37.50
Lunch from £8.50 and A La Carte
Dinner from £12.50 and A La Carte
Gratuities at Guest's Discretion. VAT inclusive. Credit Cards—Access, American

Express, Visa
2 Family Rooms. 8 Double, 11 Twin Bedrooms. All Rooms with Private Bath/Shower Room, TV with Teletext, Telephone, Radio, Baby-listening, Tea and Coffee-making Facilities, Trouser Press,

Hairdryer. Open all Year. Fully Licensed. Full CH. Cocktail Bar. Conference Facilities Children catered for. Dogs not allowed. Parking Facilities. Croquet, Indoor Heated Swimming.Pool, 2 Tennis Courts, Solarium, Sauna, Fishing.

Section 2: West Sussex

Worthing-Cavendish Hotel 115/116 Marine Parade, Worthing, West Sussex. BN11 3QG. Tel 0903 236767. Fax 0903 823840

In a prime sea-front location, close to the pier and pedestrianised shopping precinct, this four-storey building dates from the mid 1860's. Run by a couple with extensive experience as hoteliers, the modernisation and refurbishment of the Cavendish is a model of efficiency. It now offers comfortable accommodation based on a very modest tariff. There is nothing pretentious here: all things are done well. Meals are freshly prepared, the menu offering an adequate choice of appetising dishes. A friendly atmosphere pervades the building, which is attractively furnished, quiet and relaxing. The Proprietors are happy to cater for private business or social functions and, if required, can supply audio-visual equipment for conferences. Worthing, of course, has a great deal to offer the touring holidaymaker and the visiting business delegate. It has an outstandingly fine selection of shops, a wide choice of restaurants, a good range of entertainments and sports, and a long promenade with numerous beaches suitable for swimming and other seaside activities. Bus services and the main line rail stations are within walking distance of the hotel and, only a short drive inland, one has the charm of many historic villages and the open grandeur of the rolling South Downs. A little to the west lies Arundel, county town of West Sussex, with its Cathedral, Castle, Wildfowl Trust and, at nearby Amberley, the fascinating Chalk Pits Museum.

Daily Terms from £40.00
Bed and Breakfast from £25.00
Bar Meals from £2.95
Dinner from £9.95
Gratuities at Guest's Discretion. VAT inclusive
Credit Cards-Access, American Express, Diners Club, JCB, Visa

11 Double, 6 Single Bedrooms
14 Private Bathrooms
All rooms have TV, Telephone, Radio, Tea and Coffee-making Facilities. Some rooms have Hairdryer
Open from 2nd January to 24th December
Fully Licensed.
Full Central Heating

Cocktail Bar. Conference Facilities
Children catered for.
Dogs not allowed
Parking Facilities.
Night Porter
Nearby: Putting, Swimming, Sauna, Golf, Fishing, Riding, Sailing, Windsurfing, Water Skiing, Shooting

Worthing–The Kingsway Hotel Marine Parade, Worthing, West Sussex. BN11 3QQ. Tel 0903 237542/3. Fax 0903 204173

This three-star appointed hotel has been for many years under the personal supervision of the Howlett family who have owned it for over twenty years. It occupies a prime south-facing position on the five-mile-long seafront, close to the western end of the traffic-free shopping precinct and near many of the town's entertainments. Whatever the season, the Kingsway provides competitive and comfortable accommodation for holiday or business guests, with consistently high standards of catering and service. Its complement of twenty-eight *en suite* bedrooms, which includes thirteen singles, all have modern etceteras. They are double-glazed, have individually thermostatically controlled central heating and most have sea views. You will find in this hotel two tastefully furnished sea-facing lounges (one non-smoking), a companionable bar lounge with a comprehensive Buttery menu, a patio with summer-time service and a lift to all floors. In the elegant restaurant one has a choice of traditional service from an *à la carte* menu or the selection of roast joints, prepared dishes and fresh fish from the Carvery menu. Their Windsor room caters for private functions from intimate family parties to business seminars on a residential or daily basis. The Kingsway offers exceptionally good value in 'Mini-weekend' breaks, which are offered all year round. In addition to being in an ideal location for the enjoyment of Worthing's many local attractions, the hotel is well placed for visits to Arundel Castle, Chichester Cathedral, Fishbourne Roman Palace, Goodwood and Brighton.

Weekly Terms from £250.00
Daily Terms from £41.50
Bed and Breakfast from £27.50
Lunch from £6.75 and A La Carte
Bar Meals from £1.50
Dinner from £13.95 and A La Carte

No Service Charge. VAT inclusive
Credit Cards—Access, American Express, Visa. 1 Family Room. 6 Double, 8 Twin, 13 Single Bedrooms
20 Private Bathrooms. 8 Private Shower Rooms. All Rooms with TV, Telephone,

Radio, Baby-listening, Tea and Coffee-making Facilities, Hairdryer
Open all Year. Fully Licensed. Full Central Heating. Lift. Conference Facilities
Children catered for. Dogs allowed
Parking. Facilities. Night Porter

LONDON

Fenton House, Hampstead

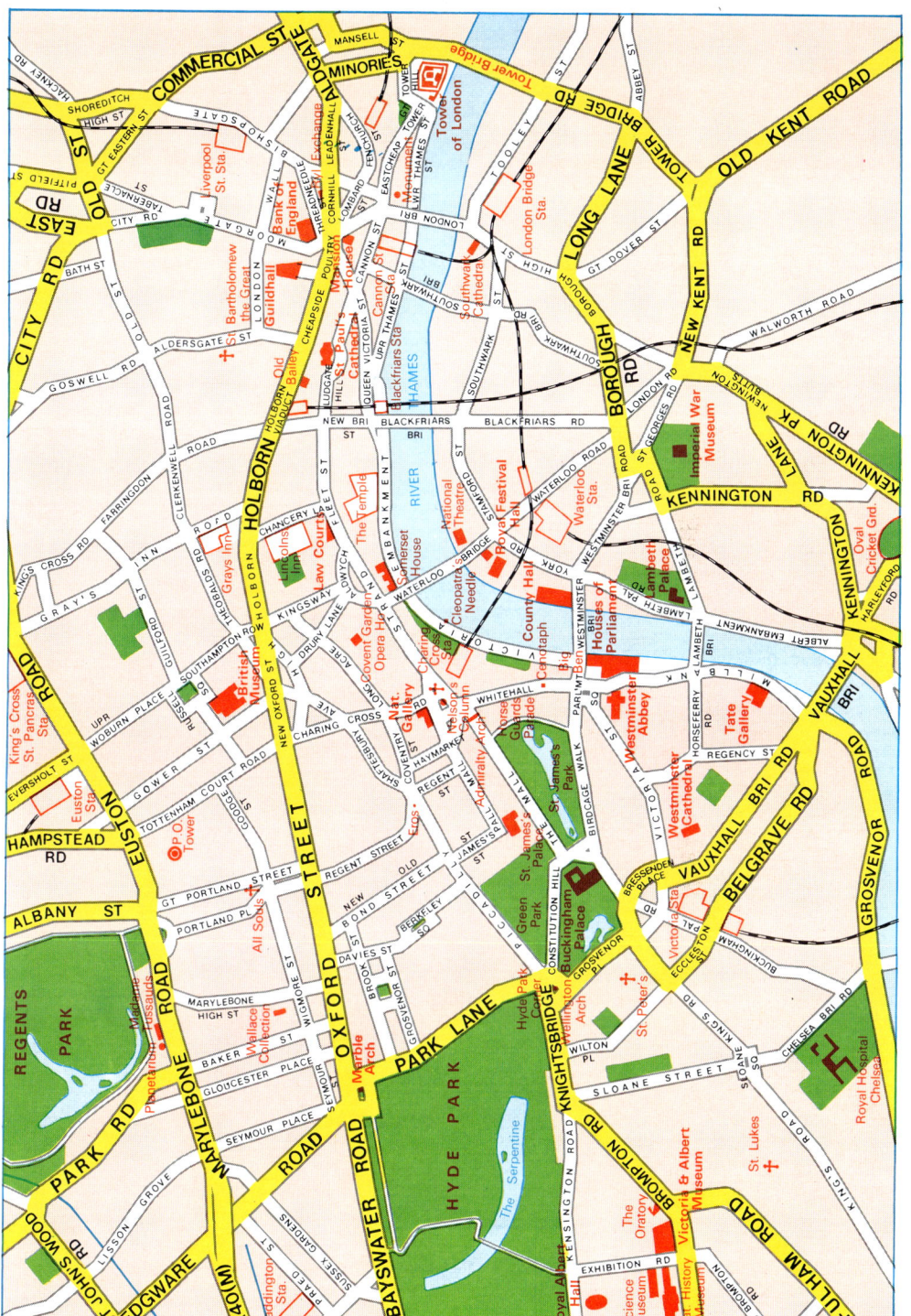

Section 3 - London

London and Greater London

London may be fairly described as one of the most fascinating three-dimensional history books in the world. It lies in a great clay saucer of land which has suffered neither obliterating floods, nor earthquakes, nor any major natural disaster for at least 1,000 years. In consequence, each successive generation has left some surviving tokens of its presence here. The Romans, Normans, Tudors, Georgians and Victorians have all left behind outstanding legacies of their times.

The city has always attracted the most talented, ambitious and influential individuals and their families. Here Shakespeare staged his plays, Samuel Pepys began his diary and Karl Marx wrote his irascible masterpiece. The character of London has always been liberal and diverse.

The hotels featured in this section of Let's Halt Awhile reflect our personal choices, for these are the places which we prefer to use when we visit London. They differ from each other in size and character, but we have found great satisfaction in the standards they provide and we therefore recommend them to you. For easy reference, these recommendations are listed in alphabetical order and appear in the index at the back of the book under the postal district in which they are located. In many ways, these districts hold the key to London's charm, for it is not a cliche to say that London is made up of clusters of villages. Seek out such districts as Bloomsbury, Whitehall and Chelsea and you will soon come to appreciate their individual characters.

Osterley Park, London

Section 3: London

The Abbey Court Hotel, W2
20, Pembridge Gardens, London. W2 4DU.
Tel 071 221 7518. Fax 071 792 0858

It is an absorbing subject tracking down luxury accommodation in London which can be had at a sensible price. Our postbag bulges with requests for advice on this subject, especially from overseas. Well, we have now found a superb place, which is furnished with impeccable taste and provides the visitor with a very elegant London headquarters. The Abbey Court lies off the Bayswater Road on the north side of Kensington Gardens. The house was built around 1830, so, as you would imagine, it has beautifully proportioned rooms. These inherent qualities are complemented with matching fabrics, lovely colour schemes, interesting prints, lampshades just placed where needed, comfortable chairs and many personal touches. We loved the Italian marble bathrooms with their whirlpool baths. And there are most carefully chosen antiques throughout the hotel. The service extends to ample breakfasts, including home-made muesli, warm brioches and croissants, and light snacks and drinks throughout the day. There is a charming conservatory where guests may relax and order snacks or drinks at any time. Here at the Abbey Court everything is provided without fuss or ostentation. Mr David Abbots, the general manager, greeted us most warmly and his staff could have hardly been more charming. If you seek a good address in London, where standards are extremely high, sleep in a brass or four poster bed and feel you are in luxurious home-from-home, then we recommend The Abbey Court to you.

Room Rate from £90.00 (Single)/£130.00 Double
Continental or English Breakfast £9.00
24Hr Room Service (Snacks and Drinks)
Corporate Rates available. Gratuities at Guest's Discretion.
VAT inclusive.

Credit Cards—Access, American Express, Diners Club, Visa
7 Double, 6 Twin, 6 Single Bedrooms. Four Poster Bedrooms. All Rooms with Private Bathroom, TV, Telephone, Radio, Trouser Press, Hairdryer, Bathrobes. Laundry and Valet Service available on Request.

Open all Year. Residential Licence.
Full Central Heating. Garden.
Children over 12 years catered for.
Dogs not allowed. Parking Facilities in NCP Car Park. Night Porter.
Nearby: Tennis, Swimming, Solarium, Sauna, Riding, Jogging

Section 3: London

Academy Hotel, WC1
17-21, Gower Street, London. WC1E 6HG. Tel 071 631 4115. Fax 071 636 3442

The recent completion of a second refurbishment programme, to include a brand new restaurant and reception, makes the Academy Hotel an ideal choice for both the businessman and the visitor to London. Meeting room facilities, secretarial help and good quality lunch and dinner are just some of the services on offer to the businessman, while close proximity to all the major theatres, sights of interest and shopping districts make it an ideal choice for the traveller. Originally built around 1770, the Hotel is three beautifully converted Georgian buildings. A superbly designed restaurant with occasional live music, offers lunch and dinner, and a cosy library leading onto a delightful patio garden where guests can enjoy a cocktail or afternoon tea on summer days. The Hotel has two new air-conditioned studio suites for added comfort on long stays. Most rooms have *en suite* showers/WC and all rooms have central heating, colour television, telephone, tea and coffee making facilities. Personal service by the friendly staff is standard in this comfortable hotel and they are very knowledgeable on theatre bookings and the best travel arrangements. Covent Garden Opera House, the British Museum and the Law Courts are but a few places to visit within minutes of this very conveniently located hotel.

Daily Terms from £65.00 plus VAT
Bar Meal from £6.50
Lunch from £12.50
Afternoon Tea from £6.50
Dinner from £17.50
Credit Cards-Access, American Express, Diners Club, Visa

1 Family Room. 14 Double, 7 Twin, 8 Single Bedrooms. 2 air-conditioned Studio Suites. 4 Private Bathrooms.
22 Private Shower Rooms
All Rooms with TV, Telephone, Radio, Baby-listening, Tea/Coffee-making Facilities.

Open all Year. (Christmas/New Year Special Breaks)
Full Central Heating. Children welcome.
Dogs not allowed.
NCP Car Parking Facilities.
Night Porter
Nearby: Swimming, Solarium, Sauna

The Cranley Hotel, SW5
10-12 Bina Gardens, South Kensington, London, SW5 0LA. Tel 071 373 0123. Fax 071 373 9497

Victorian splendour and the comforts of today's living are here combined in impeccably tasteful and luxurious rooms and suites designed exclusively for the discriminating visitor. Meticulous refurbishment included restoration of many original features, such as the large floor to ceiling bay windows and Victorian fireplaces, discreetly setting off the antiques and *objet d'art* which grace every room. Modern amenities are all provided, but their presence has not been allowed to be intrusive. Every one of the thirty-six units has a luxurious bathroom and a kitchenette equipped with refrigerator and microwave oven; The Cranley has Continental or full English breakfast available on request. Superb furnishings in bold colours, with a strong sense of style, provide a perfect setting for the elegant pictures, graceful drapes and remarkable examples of needlepoint. Everything here is in accord with the character of South Kensington which, since the great Victorian age, has been regarded as a select part of London. With Knightsbridge, Chelsea and West Brompton virtually on their doorstep, guests can take a leisurely stroll to some of the most famous museums and shopping streets in the world, to the river Thames or to the Royal Albert Hall. All of London's great theatres, fine restaurants and public parks are close by, and there is fast travel available to and from Heathrow Airport. Even so, at The Cranley you are in a very quiet area. Referring to Kensington in 1705, John Bowack in his 'Antiquities of Middlesex' wrote "... has ever been resorted by persons of quality.... is inhabited by gentry and persons of note".

Weekly Terms on request
Daily Terms from £104.00
Gratuities at Guest's Discretion. VAT inclusive. All major Credit Cards accepted
8 Suites. 12 Double, 12 Twin, 4 Single Bedrooms

All Rooms with Private Bath and Shower Room, TV, Telephone, Radio, Tea and Coffee-making Facilities, Trouser Press, Hairdryer.
Most Rooms have a small kitchenette
Open all year. Residential Licence

Full Central Heating. Lift. Cocktail Bar.
Children catered for. Small dogs allowed.
Night Porter
Nearby: Tennis, Croquet, Putting, Squash, Badminton, Swimming, Solarium, Sauna, Golf, Fishing, Riding, Shooting

Section 3: London

The Goring Hotel, SW1 15 Beeston Place, Grosvenor Gardens, London.SW1W 0JW. Tel 071 396 9000. Fax 071 834 4393

Here is an hotel which so many of our readers, especially those from overseas, seek out as their London base. The reasons for this are simple. To begin with it has such an excellent address, claiming, as it does, a good part of placid Beeston Place, in the heart of London, just behind Buckingham Palace and within easy reach of Victoria Station, the royal parks and Parliament Square. Its permanence and consistent high standards are bound up with the continuous involvement of the Goring family for three generations. That the hotel was purposely built in 1910 by Mr O R Goring, makes it all the more unique. The Goring Hotel is uncompromisingly traditional; you will find no plastic or stainless steel here, for the furnishings and décor emphasise the time-honoured virtues of service and hotelmanship, for which it is renowned. The public rooms are spacious and immaculately kept, as are the well-equipped bedrooms. The Goring family are particularly proud that the hotel was the first in the world to provide a private bathroom and central heating to every bedroom. We have dined here to satisfaction in the restaurant on a number of occasions, and can attest to the excellence of the *cuisine* and cellar, and the good value which they both provide. The long-serving staff, under the direction of Mr George Goring and Mr William Cowpe, are unfailingly helpful and do their utmost to make one's stay a happy one.

Room Rate from £115.00 (Single)
Room Rate from £165.00 (Double/Twin).
Room Rate from £200.00 (Suite)
Bar Lunch from £10.00
Lunch from £15.50 and A La Carte
Afternoon Tea from £9.50
Dinner from £24.00 and A La Carte
10% Service Charge.

VAT inclusive
Credit Cards–Access, American Express, Diners Club, Visa
5 Suites. 5 De Luxe Double, 19 Double, 20 Twin, 32 Single Bedrooms
All Rooms with Private Bath/Shower Room, TV, Telephone, Radio, Hairdryer
Valet Service available on Request

Open all Year. Fully Licensed.
Full Central Heating
Lift. Cocktail Bar. Conference Facilities
Dogs not allowed.
Children catered for. Parking Facilities.
Night Porter
Nearby: Tennis, Croquet, Squash, Badminton, Swimming, Solarium, Sauna

Kensington Manor Hotel, SW7, 8 Emperor's Gate, South Kensington, London. SW7 4HH. Tel 071 373 3163. Fax 071 373 3163

Whether you are a business executive with an exhibition stand at Olympia or Earl's Court, or a visitor taking-in the Science Museum, Natural History Museum or the Victoria and Albert Museum, this small but elegant hotel is ideally situated. It is a late Victorian building in an almost traffic free cul-de-sac, superbly located in elegant South Kensington, one of London's most fashionable and opulent areas. The Hotel is literally 4 minutes walk from **Gloucester Road Tube Station**, serving multiple lines and a direct link to Heathrow Airport and 5 minutes in the cab to Harrods. There is also a nearby underground car park. Kensington Manor Hotel has a twenty-four hour residential liquor licence and drinks are served in rooms, with ice buckets available on request. Some rooms have small refrigerators, there is night porterage and an unusually wide range of services. These include a same day laundry and valet service, travel arrangements, theatre tickets, car hire, telex, cheque and credit card facilities, free newspapers and early morning calls. A buffet breakfast, served every day, has the widest choice of fare we recall. Most guests will be out for the day and, in this area, there is no shortage of restaurants to suit virtually every taste and any pocket. All the bedrooms are very well equipped, tastefully furnished, and most have bathroom or shower *en suite*. While there is no TV Lounge at Kensington Manor Hotel, the Breakfast Room is converted to a comfortable and quiet lounge after breakfast hours.

All terms pertaining to 1992
Daily Terms (Bed and Breakfast) from £55.00-£65.00 (Single) £69.95-£86.00 (Double). Suite for 4 persons from £110.00 Gratuities at Guest's Discretion.
VAT inclusive. All major Credit Cards accepted. 1 Suite.

6 Double, 4 Twin, 3 Single Bedrooms
7 Private Bathrooms. 7 Private Shower Rooms. All rooms with TV, Telephone, Radio, Mini Bar, Tea and Coffee-making facilities, Hairdryer, Trouser Press
Open all Year. Residential Licence.
Full Central Heating.

Children catered for. Dogs not allowed.
Night Porter. Parking Meter Facilities and Underground Car Park.
Nearby:Tennis, Croquet, Squash, Badminton, Swimming, Solarium, Sauna, Kensington Gardens.

Section 3: London

The Langham Hilton, W1 1 Portland Place, Regent Street, London W1N 3AA.
Tel 071 636 1000. Telex 21113

When the Prince of Wales opened the Langham in 1865 it was the largest building in the capital, and one of the marvels of the age. In the first seventy-five years of its glorious history it was recognised as London's most fashionable gathering place. Dvorak and Toscanini were guests; so too were Oscar Wilde, Mark Twain and Arnold Bennett. This splendour was abruptly terminated in September 1940, when war damage meant that the Langham ceased to function as a hotel. Having acquired the property in 1986, Hilton International began the painstaking work of reconstruction in November 1987. This mammoth task was completed in 1991, with the very latest of modern technology expertly blended in with the re-creation of period authenticity. Any qualitative assessment of this uniquely magnificent hotel could all too easily become a series of superlatives, since we are quite unable to fault anything at all. An impressively grand external architecture encompasses 410 rooms distributed over the nine floors; a further twelve rooms with meeting facilities, and the ballroom, provide reception, banquet or theatre settings for numbers from a handful to several hundreds. From the marble floors and pillars of the lobby to the incomparable quality of the spacious private suites, the setting and the service recall a bygone age of the stately style of life. *Memories of the Empire* is the meticulously restored dining room, where the extensive menu includes the very best of traditional English food. Superb accommodation by any standards.

Daily Terms from £165.00
Bed and Breakfast from £178.00
Bar Lunch from £6.50. Lunch from £19.50
Afternoon Tea from £10.75
Dinner from £29.50. Service and VAT extra
Credit Cards–Access, American Express,

Diners Club, Visa. 28 Suites, 195 Double, 162 Twin Bedrooms. All Rooms with Private Bathroom, TV, Telephone, Radio, Trouser Press, Hairdryer, Mini Bar
Open all Year. Fully Licensed
Full Central Heating. Lift

2 Cocktail Bars. Conference Facilities
Children catered for. Dogs allowed
Parking Facilities. Night Porter. Nearby: Tennis, Squash, Badminton, Swimming Solarium, Sauna, Golf,
Driving Range, Riding

Wilbraham Hotel, SW1 1 Wilbraham Place, Sloane Street, London. SW1X 9AE.
Tel 071 730 8296. Fax 071 730 6815

To this day, Belgravia is still the most sought-after residential area of London, a centre of Victorian elegance and fashion. From here, it is only a short walk to the Royal Albert Hall, to a group of museums including the Victoria and Albert, to Kensington Gardens or to Buckingham Palace. In this locality are the world-famous Knightsbridge stores, the quaint charm of Chelsea and, of course, the River Thames. This, then, is the setting for the Wilbraham, just off Sloane Street and occupying three imposing Victorian houses. Just a few minutes' by taxi from the main-line rail or the coach stations of Victoria. An ideal base for the UK or Overseas visitor seeking the quiet charm of an elegant town-house from which to see London. The imaginative use of furnishings and *décor* - particularly in evidence in the bedrooms, where even the lampshades match the curtains and bedcovers - display the personal influence of the managing director, Miss Monique von Kospoth. A high percentage of the rooms have private bathrooms and all have television and telephones. Downstairs, there is the *Bar and Buttery*, which is open every day except Sunday for snack meals, as well as for more substantial lunches and dinners. Children are welcomed by the friendly staff and are catered for with the provision of cots and a baby-sitting service. After the glamour of the City's vast choice of theatres, restaurants and shops, guests will appreciate returning to the first-class service of a smaller, personally-run hotel.

Bed and Breakfast from £40.00
Bar Lunch from £4.00
Lunch from £5.00 and A La Carte
Afternoon Tea from £1.50
Bar Supper from £4.00
Dinner from £6.00 and A La Carte

Gratuities at Guest's discretion. VAT extra
10 Family Rooms. 4 De Luxe Rooms. 14 Double, 25 Twin, 11 Single Bedrooms
34 Private Bathrooms. 6 Private Shower Rooms. All Rooms with TV, Telephone, Room Service. Hairdryer.

Ironing Facilities and Baby-sitting available on Request. Open all year. Full Central Heating. Residential Licence. 2 Lifts.
Cocktail Bar. TV Lounge
Children catered for. Dogs not allowed
Parking nearby. Night Porter

Section 3: Greater London

Richmond on Thames—Richmond Gate Hotel
Richmond-upon-Thames, Surrey. TW10 6RP. Tel 081 940 0061. Fax 081 332 0354

It was in 1637 that Charles I enclosed Richmond Park as a private hunting preserve and, to this day, its 2500 acres are roamed by herds of deer. Undoubtedly the proximity of the River Thames is a major factor in the continuing appeal of this corner of outer London, in which also lie Hampton Court Palace (residence of Henry VIII in Tudor England) and the world-famous botanical gardens at Kew. Only a few yards from Richmond Park, and with superb views over it, stands Richmond Gate Hotel. Originally a collection of four private eighteenth-century buildings, it became an hotel some fifty years ago. For the tourist or the business executive it is an ideal location. Central London is a mere eight miles away, there is a variety of rooms at the hotel for conferences, receptions or private parties and, in the immediate vicinity, a wealth of interest in antique shops, riverside public houses, galleries and the Richmond Theatre. Local views are of such charm that they have been immortalised by such painters as Turner and Reynolds. Even in the walled garden of the hotel a peaceful venue for afternoon tea or drinks in the evening you could be in the heart of the country. Throughout the Richmond Gate, the dignified decor enhances the elegant and traditional surroundings, including luxury four poster rooms and leather button-backed chairs in the Club Lounge. Perhaps the heart of the hotel lies in the graceful dining room Gates, where the head chef continues a fine history of hospitality.

Weekly Terms from £455.00
Daily Terms from £90.00
Bar Meals from £7.50
Lunch from £15.50
Afternoon Tea from £5.00
Dinner from £17.50
Gratuities at Guest's Discretion.

VAT inclusive
3 Family Rooms. 1 Suite. 15 Double, 15 Twin, 20 Single Bedrooms
All Rooms with Private Bathroom, TV, Telephone, Radio,
Tea and Coffee-making Facilities,
Trouser Press, Hairdryer
Open all year. Fully Licensed.

Full Central Heating. Cocktail Bar.
Conference Facilities
Children catered for.
Dogs not allowed.
Parking Facilities.
Night Porter
Squash. Nearby: Tennis, Putting, Riding

Richmond on Thames–Richmond Hill Hotel 146-150, Richmond Hill,
Richmond-on-Thames, Surrey. TW10 6RW. Tel 081 940 2247. Fax 081 940 5424

The largest of London's royal parks is at Richmond. Its six square miles of woodland and great stretches of bracken, where the Queen's red deer wander, have become *Rus in Urbe* for many Londoners. Close to the northern perimeter of the park, where one can command a famous view down the wooded valley of the Thames to a long stretch of silver water, stands this appropriately named hotel, which has seen a great deal of restoration in recent years. We enjoy its informal and welcoming atmosphere and have always received efficient, pleasant and courteous service from the staff. It is a busy hotel, with over 120 well-equipped bedrooms and a flourishing restaurant. In 1987, however, the Richmond Hill Hotel was completely modernised, and standards throughout are very high. The hotel's situation is, of course, an ideal one for wining and dining–we eat there regularly ourselves. As a base for visitors to London, however, it must have an even greater appeal. Here on the summit of Richmond Hill, with an entrance to the park a minutes' walk away, one can have all the advantages of country pursuits, yet be able to reach Waterloo Station within fourteen minutes and be in the heart of the West End in half an hour. So, too, can one make excursions into the South of England and the Thames Valley quickly and easily. In every regard–location, atmosphere and service–the Richmond Hill Hotel exudes a sense of civilised leisure.

Bed and Breakfast from £79.00 (Single)
Bed and Breakfast from £90.00 (Double)
Lunch from £13.00 and A La Carte
Afternoon Tea from £5.00
Dinner from £17.50 and A La Carte
Service Charge and VAT inclusive
Credit Cards–Access, American Express,

Diners Club, Visa
4 Family Rooms. 38 Double, 32 Twin, 44 Single Bedrooms. 119 Private Bathrooms.
4 Private Shower Rooms
All Rooms with TV, Telephone, Radio, Tea and Coffee-making Facilities, Hairdryer, Trouser Press. Executive Rooms with Mini

Bar. Open all year. Fully Licensed.
Full Central Heating. Lift. Cocktail Bar.
Dogs allowed. Conference Facilities
Parking Facilities. Night Porter. Squash.
Nearby: Tennis, Badminton, Swimming, Solarium, Sauna, Golf, Riding

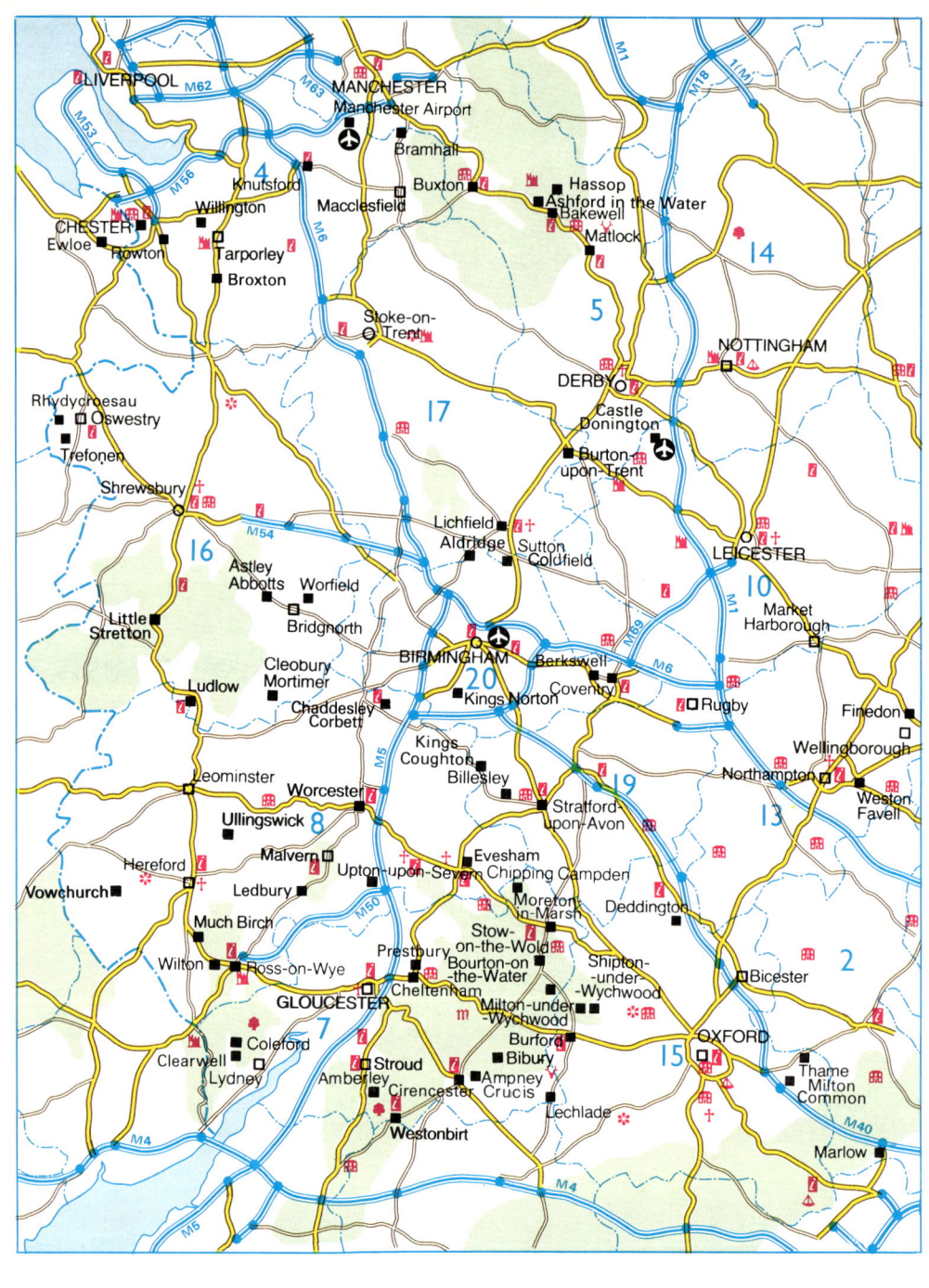

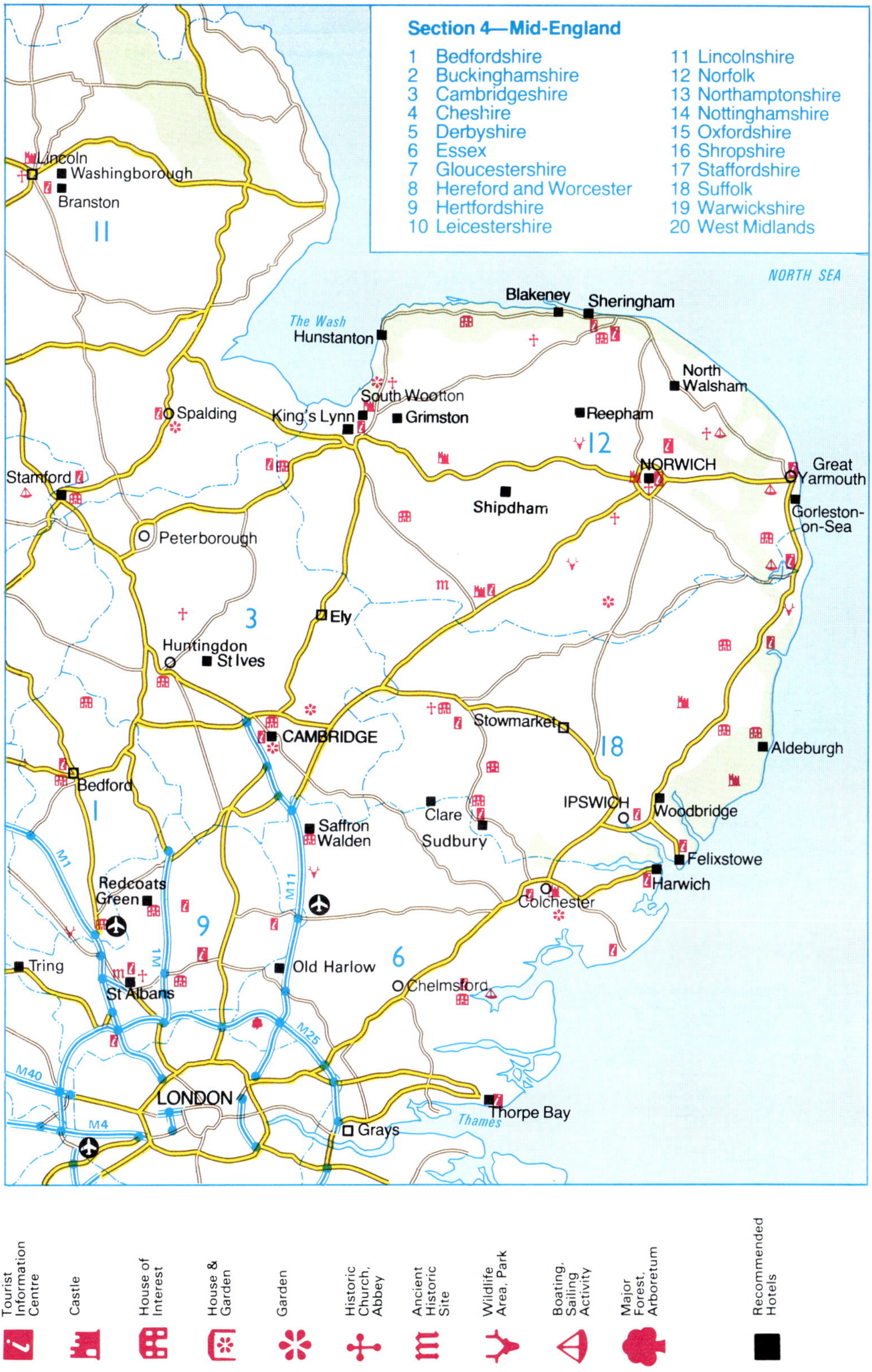
Section 4—Mid-England
1 Bedfordshire
2 Buckinghamshire
3 Cambridgeshire
4 Cheshire
5 Derbyshire
6 Essex
7 Gloucestershire
8 Hereford and Worcester
9 Hertfordshire
10 Leicestershire
11 Lincolnshire
12 Norfolk
13 Northamptonshire
14 Nottinghamshire
15 Oxfordshire
16 Shropshire
17 Staffordshire
18 Suffolk
19 Warwickshire
20 West Midlands
NORTH SEA
The Wash
Lincoln
Washingborough
Branston
11
Blakeney
Sheringham
Hunstanton
North Walsham
South Wootton
Spalding
King's Lynn
Grimston
Reepham
12
NORWICH
Great Yarmouth
Stamford
Shipdham
Gorleston-on-Sea
Peterborough
3
Ely
Huntingdon
St Ives
Stowmarket
CAMBRIDGE
18
Aldeburgh
Bedford
1
IPSWICH
Woodbridge
Clare
Saffron Walden
Sudbury
Felixstowe
M1
Redcoats Green
Harwich
M11
Colchester
9
Tring
Old Harlow
6
M1
Chelmsford
St Albans
M25
M40
LONDON
Thorpe Bay
M4
Thames
Grays
Tourist Information Centre
Castle
House of Interest
House & Garden
Garden
Historic Church, Abbey
Ancient Historic Site
Wildlife Area, Park
Boating, Sailing Activity
Major Forest, Arboretum
Recommended Hotels

MID-ENGLAND

Ickworth, Suffolk

General Introduction to Section 4

In terms of the area it covers and the number of counties it contains, this chapter is the largest in this book. For ease of reference, within this section the counties are featured alphabetically, and within each county the towns are similarly listed. However, since we are concerned here with several of the most important scenic regions of Britain, in the following introductory pages the counties are grouped in four main tourism areas: the Thames Valley and Chilterns; East Anglia; Cotswolds, Shakespeare Country and Wye Valley; and The Shires.

Section 4A - The Thames Valley and Chilterns

Buckinghamshire, Oxfordshire

Though The Thames starts its excursion to the sea in Gloucestershire and winds and wends its way through Berkshire, Buckinghamshire, Surrey, Middlesex, Kent and Essex, all claiming a share of its banks, The Thames Valley definition of this section confines itself to its most popular reaches. The Chilterns, too, cannot be strictly defined. With bewildering change one passes from Oxfordshire into Buckinghamshire, and even into Hertfordshire. The counties of Buckinghamshire and Oxfordshire, together with Berkshire, however, encompass the heart of these regions.

Buckinghamshire

This elongated county has its head in the 'shire' country and its feet on the banks of the Thames. Although Windsor is in Berkshire, Eton, on the opposite bank, is in Buckinghamshire. The main feature of the county is the Chiltern Hills. Visit too, Stoke Poges, Chenies, Chequers (the country home of incumbent Prime Ministers), Stowe and Burnham Beeches.

Cliveden, Buckinghamshire

Oxfordshire

The colleges of Oxford together form a most important part of Britain's heritage. Within a square mile of Carfax are no less than 653 buildings which are listed as being of historic or architectural merit. In contrast to Oxford's busy High Street, the colleges and cloisters have a calmness which inspires reflective thought. This county, too, has many quiet rural spots, if you but seek them out. Woodstock Park, the upper Thames at Clifton Hampden and Newbridge, Minster Lovell, Studley Priory and Weston-on-the-Green are such places. Oxfordshire is a county in which it is never too late to improve one's education.

Section 4B - East Anglia

Bedfordshire, Cambridgeshire, Essex, Hertfordshire, Lincolnshire, Norfolk and Suffolk

For centuries this area was isolated from the rest of England by the Fens, Lea Marshes and Epping Forest, whilst its long coastline, stretching from the Thames to the Humber, has no deep-water harbours. So, the pattern of life here, with its largely agricultural outlook, has remained unchanged until relatively recently. The unspoilt nature of East Anglia is easily found and that is why it is such a magnet for the tourist. One needs hardly be reminded, too, that East Anglia is Constable country; that Lavenham in Suffolk is one of Britain's most picturesque villages; that Bedford was the home of John Bunyan, and at Huntingdon Oliver Cromwell was born.

Bedfordshire

Too many travellers pass through the flat plains of Bedfordshire unaware of the interest which abounds there. The following are certainly worth visiting - Dunstable (to see gliding), Whipsnade Zoo, Luton Hoo (a vast mansion famed for its art collection) and Woburn Abbey.

Cambridgeshire

The university city of Cambridge is the major attraction. Be sure to walk along the famous 'Backs', see King's College chapel and, particularly if you come from the USA, visit Emmanuel College where John Harvard was educated. The other main attraction of the county is Ely Cathedral, which dominates the surrounding fen country.

Essex

From a tourism point of view, Essex is one of Britain's most underrated counties. It was in this gentle rolling countryside that the Romans sited their capital, Camulodunum, which today is Colchester. From the earliest times, therefore, it has had excellent roads. The best of Essex is to be found in her little clap-boarded villages and her select resorts, such as Frinton-on-Sea.

Hertfordshire

Agriculture is the dominant feature of this attractive county. Wheat and barley, in particular, have been grown in this region for many centuries. Here are some of the places we suggest you should discover: Chipperfield, Little Gaddesden, Ayot St Lawrence (former home of George Bernard Shaw), Waterend, St Albans Abbey and Hatfield House.

Lincolnshire

The flat landscape of Lincolnshire leaves one with the impression of huge skies and far horizons. The ground, however, is a rich mosaic, made up of large bulb fields and seas of waving corn. Visit Spalding in late spring and you will see the results of the tulip and daffodil industry at their most colourful. Boston is associated with the Pilgrim Fathers, but the county's greatest attraction is the Roman city of Lincoln, where the cathedral stands high above the surrounding fen land.

Norfolk

The largest and least populated county in the broad peninsula of East Anglia, Norfolk, because of its location, is rarely visited by those who are just passing through. Its visitors go there purposefully and flock to such places as Norwich, the Broads, the salt marshes around Blakeney and the varied coastline.

Suffolk

This is the most eastern county in England. Its prosperity derived from wool, but it is universally known for the pastoral scenes painted by John Constable. Note such lovely spots as Clare, Lavenham and Long Melford. Pargeting is a feature of many of the old houses in the region.

Section 4C - Cotswolds, Shakespeare Country and Wye Valley

Gloucestershire, Hereford and Worcester, Warwickshire

For gaining one's first knowledge of the Cotswolds and the Shakespeare country, one cannot do better than follow the varied course of the A46, which commences among the hot springs of Bath. From there, just missing Chipping Sodbury, it makes its way through the pleasant South Cotswolds - Nailsworth and its trout lakes, Stroud and its five valleys, and Painswick with its yew trees - to Cheltenham. Then via Winchcomb it pushes northwards to Stratford-upon-Avon and Warwick. And because Hereford and Worcester is such a close neighbour of Gloucestershire, we have included this county's attractions - Wye Valley and Malvern Hills - in this section.

Stowe Landscape Garden, Buckinghamshire

Gloucestershire

The mighty River Severn, the Forest of Dean (a fairy-tale forest in the Grimm tradition) and numerous beautiful Cotswold villages are a trio of attractions which make this county scenically outstanding. It is an area in which one should meander and never be in a hurry. Haste is waste in Gloucestershire.

Hereford and Worcester

This was formerly part of the ancient kingdom of Mercia, a region where the boundary swung to and fro between Wales and England. In the early 1970's the lines were redrawn again and these two separate counties were brought together as one. Hereford invites one to the Wye Valley, whilst Worcester's pride is the Malvern Hills. Visit Broadway, the city of Worcester, Evesham, Pershore and Bewdley.

Warwickshire

Stay a night at Meriden and you will have slept in the most central point in England. Warwickshire's position, and the fact that it contains Stratford-upon-Avon, ensure that it is one of the busiest tourist areas in Britain. Many come on Shakespearian pilgrimages, to see the bard's birthplace, his burial place and Anne Hathaway's cottage, and to visit the Royal Shakespeare Theatre. It would be a pity, however, to overlook Warwick or Royal Leamington Spa. Although it is a county with plenty of accommodation, sometimes the hotels cannot cope with the demand, so we do recommend that you make a reservation in advance.

Section 4D - Central England; The 'Shires'

Cheshire, Derbyshire, Leicestershire, Northamptonshire, Nottinghamshire, Shropshire, Staffordshire, West Midland

Something of a *pot-pourri* this section, comprising eight counties in the very heart of England, which we have grouped for convenience under the heading *The 'Shires'*. So this region of the book is the most varied, both scenically and historically. It encompasses the 'Peak District', the 'Shires', the major parts of the 'Welsh Marches' and the 'Black Country'. The majority of these counties are landlocked. Of Northamptonshire, Fuller points out 'bordereth upon more counties than any other in England, being nine in number'. So here is the very hub of England, with ancient churches galore, historic buildings, spectacular moors, pastoral meadows, celebrated hunts and folklore in abundance. Within these counties all aspects of England's rural and industrial heritage is to be found.

Cheshire

Who has not heard of Cheshire cheese, product of the dairy lands of this region? Cheshire is also famous for its many black and white or 'magpie' houses. Moreton Hall, near Congleton, is a classic example. The countryside is deliciously varied, for Cheshire shares the Pennines and the Peak District with its neighbours. The county's main glory, however, is the walled Roman city of Chester.

Derbyshire

Within this county lies the major part of the Peak District, with its famous dales, such as Miller's Dale, Monsal Dale and Dovedale. This is a remote and wild part of central England, where one may hear just the sound of the wind or, perhaps, the cry of a curlew. Buxton is a spa town, 1,000 feet above sea-level and Matlock is a good centre for touring.

Westbury Court Garden, Gloucestershire

Leicestershire

Leicestershire has a variety of scenery. Charnwood Forest is almost totally untamed and contrasts dramatically with most of the county's rolling countryside. Many people know only of Leicestershire's industrial areas, but it has attractive rural parts, too, and is famous for Stilton cheese.

Northamptonshire

The traveller will look in vain for imposing scenery hereabouts, but the lover of gentle countryside and history will find rich rewards in Northamptonshire. It is the county of 'spires and squires' because of its wealth of medieval churches and its manor houses. Americans, in particular, are attracted to Sulgrave, Little Brington, Adams Cottage at Floore and Trapston Church, all places with associations with George Washington.

Nottinghamshire

Inextricably linked with the legend of Robin Hood. The forest of Sherwood, which once covered a fifth of the county, is now nothing more than a modest remnant. Some delightful parts of the forest have survived in the 'Dunkeries', such as Welbeck, Clumber and Thoresby. Little has remained of Nottingham's original Norman castle, for it was demolished by the Parliamentary forces during the Civil War. Visitors should also include Southwell on their itineraries, for Southwell Minster is a fine example of a small English cathedral.

Shropshire

The border between England and Wales bows quite markedly to ensure that Shropshire remains English soil. However, the character of the county, both geographically and spiritually, has a great deal of Welshness about it. The River Severn divides Shropshire in two. The little lake district around Ellesmere in the north is flat but picturesque, although the best area for touring is the southern half of the county. Visits to Church Stretton and Ludlow are worthwhile preludes to travelling along the Wye Valley.

Staffordshire

Many tourists do not realise that although Staffordshire includes the potteries and the so-called Black Country, there are vast areas of the county which are renowned for their unspoilt scenic beauty. Staffordshire shares with Derbyshire the Beresford and Dovedale valleys. Take the Leek to Buxton road and you will see those curious rock formations, the Roaches and Hen Cloud. Lichfield Cathedral is associated with Dr Johnson, and Burton-upon-Trent is one of the major homes of the British brewing industry.

West Midlands

This region of England is popularly regarded as 'the Midlands', but the county name correctly locates it as 'West' Midlands. It is dominated by the industrial areas of Birmingham, Coventry and Wolverhampton, but do not be misled into thinking that commerce is its only attraction. No other area of Britain is better served by motorways and major roads, so it is an excellent base from which to visit some beautiful countryside. Also, because the area serves the needs of a large number of businessmen, its hotels are generally of a good modern standard.

Section 4: Buckinghamshire and Cambridgeshire

Marlow—Danesfield House
Medmenham, Marlow, Buckinghamshire. Tel 0628 891010. Telex 848078

This magnificent ninety-three bedroom house stands in a commanding position overlooking the River Thames, between Marlow and Henley. The first known house on this escarpment was built in 1664 and it was in the 1750's that the name 'Danesfield' was used for the first time, on the occasion of one of several cycles of demolition and rebuilding. Construction of the present house, originally, occupied 300 workmen for three years: a similar period was required to convert the property from offices into the superb and luxurious hotel opened in July 1991. Everything here is of the highest imaginable standard: the facilities, the comfort, the service, the *cuisine*, the outlook and the location. Private guests who expect nothing but the best will be more than satisfied. Business groups seeking prestigous premises for top level conferences will find every need fulfilled. From the helicopter landing area to the two excellent restaurants—*English* and *Italian*—every conceivable requirement is met supremely well. The quite exceptional interior decor and furnishings have been achieved with such a light and delicate touch that, despite the vast size, the whole hotel is charming and restful. For weddings and private functions one is assured of a truly memorable event. Guests can participate in fishing, golf, horseriding, gliding, sailing and shooting, they can view the Chiltern Hills from sixty-five acres of grounds and formal gardens, or visit nearby Windsor, Oxford, Eton, Disraeli's home, Milton's Cottage and the caves of West Wycombe.

Weekly Terms on request
Daily Terms from £162.50 Double
Bed and Breakfast from £87.50 (p.p. sharing). Bar Lunch from £15.00
Lunch from £21.50 Table d'Hôte
Afternoon Tea from £12.50

Dinner from £32.00 Table d'Hôte
Service and VAT inclusive
All major Credit Cards accepted
17 Suites, 8 Single, 68 Double Bedrooms
All Rooms with Private Bathroom,
TV,Telephone, Radio, Trouser Press,

Hairdryer..24 Hour Room Service
Open all Year. Fully Licensed
Full Central Heating. Lift. Cocktail Bar.
Conference Facilities. Children catered for
Dogs not allowed. Parking Facilities.
Night Porter. Tennis, Croquet, Outdoor pool

Cambridge—The Garden House Hotel
Granta Place, Mill Lane, Cambridge. CB2 1RT. Tel 0223 63421. Fax 0223 316605

It is difficult to say which of the sister universities is more pleasing architecturally, but the greenery of Cambridge's 'Backs' is unparalleled at Oxford. The Garden House Hotel is aptly named for it fronts the River Cam, and is designed to take full advantage of its lovely setting, affording guests a delightful riverain and rural environment within the city. Indeed most rooms have views over the gardens and river. There is a total of 118 luxury guest rooms and executive suites on three floors, an unusual and attractive reception area off Granta Place and a cocktail bar with a spacious lounge to one side and a magnificent restaurant on the other. The Garden House is one of the city's top-grade hotels and is a member of Queen's Moat Houses Hotels. In the beautifully kept gardens within the three-acre site guests can relax and enjoy watching the swans and waterfowl and the summer boaters. Conference organisers should also note that the hotel is able to cater for parties of up to 200 people. We cannot praise too highly the initiative of the management of The Garden House Hotel and the excellence of its food, service and facilities. You will find not only top-quality facilities here, but also that everything is presented with a great deal of flair, making it a comfortable centre from which to explore the many interesting features of this thriving university town.

All Prices pertain to 1992
Bed and Breakfast from £82.00 Single:
£115.00 Double/Twin
Breakfast £7.50 Supplement
Bar Lunch from £5.50
Lunch from £9.95 and A La Carte
Afternoon Tea from £5.45
Dinner from £18.95 and A La Carte
Gratuities at Guest's discretion

VAT inclusive. Credit Cards–Access,
American Express, Diners Club, Visa
7 Family Rooms. 6 Suites
28 Double, 83 Twin Bedrooms
All Rooms with Private Bath/Shower
Room, TV, Telephone, Radio,
Baby-listening, Tea and Coffee-making
Facilities, Hairdryer, Mini-bar, Trouser
Press

Open all Year. Fully Licensed
Full Central Heating
3 Lifts. Cocktail Bar
Conference Facilities. Parking Facilities
Guide Dogs only allowed. Night Porter
Fishing, Punting
Nearby: Tennis Courts, Squash,
Badminton, Swimming Pool, Sauna, Golf,
Riding

Section 4: Cambridgeshire and Cheshire

St Ives, Huntingdon—The Dolphin Hotel Bridge Foot, London Road, St. Ives, Cambridgeshire. PE17 4EP. Tel 0480 66966. Fax 0480 495597

Oliver Cromwell once had a farm near St. Ives and his statue stands in the town's market-place. In the Middle Ages a great Easter Fair was held here where the Kings of England bought robes for their servants, and merchants came from Europe to buy English cloth. For nearly eight hundred years now a market has filled the central street of the town every Monday. The Dolphin Hotel has a prime position on the banks of the Great Ouse, close to the fifteenth-century bridge which has a curious chapel built halfway across it. Visitors can take their drinks from a well-stocked bar on to the patio overlooking the river and old St. Ives or watch the craft from the bright and spacious *Waterside Restaurant*. There are forty-seven bedrooms, all with *en suite* bathrooms, the provision of writing desks and ample storage space making them ideal for both business guests and holiday visitors. For receptions, parties or conferences there is a self-contained *Meadow Suite* which combines total privacy with superb views of the river. The river journey from Huntingdon to St. Ives passes the twin villages of Hemingford Abbots with its attractive meres and Hemingford Grey with its thatch and mellow brick cottages. For a leisurely break in the Fenlands, the Dolphin Hotel is a delightful venue with first-class comfort and exceptional *cuisine*.

1992 Terms
Bed and Breakfast from £55.00
Bar Lunch from £3.00
Lunch from £12.95 and A La Carte
Dinner from £12.95 and A La Carte
Gratuities at Guest's Discretion
VAT inclusive
Credit Cards—Access, American Express,

Diners Club, Visa
2 Family Rooms. 9 Double, 32 Twin, 2 Single Bedrooms
2 Doubles suitable for disabled
(All Double/Twin Rooms let as Singles)
All Rooms with Private Bathroom, TV, Telephone, Radio, Tea and Coffee-making Facilities, Hairdryer

Open all year. Fully Licensed
Full Central Heating. Conference Facilities
Dogs allowed by arrangement
Parking Facilities. Night Porter. Fishing
Nearby: Tennis, Squash, Badminton, Swimming Pool, Golf, Fishing, Riding, Sailing, Windsurfing

Fuller's Moor, Near Chester, Broxton—Frogg Manor Fullers Moor, Nantwich Road, Broxton, Chester, CH3 9JH. Tel 0829 782629. Fax 0829 782238

High in the Broxton Hills, within eight acres of woodland and landscaped gardens, a recently refurbished grade II listed period house of Georgian origins offers casual comfort. It retains the atmosphere and grace of the Georgian era, with traditional decor and period furniture. Your friendly host, John Sykes, will immediately put you at your ease, make you welcome and demonstrate that here you are assured of personal attention in a pleasantly relaxed manner. Furnishings and colour schemes throughout, have obviously been chosen with great care and good taste: they are seen to best advantage because skilled consideration has been given to lighting location. Dimmer switches are adjusted to suit each course during dinner: even the garden, with its marble Aphrodite, is floodlit at night. Soft sofas, chandeliers, elegant drapes, soft background music and gleaming brass bedsteads, all add to the romantic setting. Why the name? There is a large pond populated by the creatures, although the proprietor admits to once having a friend called Frog. People continue to present him with large and small copies of the amphibians, in various materials. Nor are these the only interesting items on display. A wind-up gramophone with a brass horn, and a corner occupied by a chess set and board are only two of many *objets* of novel or antique appeal. Should you over-indulge in the tempting home-made steak and kidney pies and toffee puddings, you could switch to the vegetarian meals or the increasingly popular 'fat free' dishes.

Weekly Terms from £313.00
Daily Terms from £48.65
Bed and Breakfast from £27.65
Bar Lunch from £2.50. Lunch from £11.50 and A La Carte. Afternoon Tea from £3.50
Dinner from £21.00 and A La Carte

Service and VAT inclusive
All Major Credit Cards accepted
1 Suite, 6 Double Bedrooms
(Doubles can be let as Singles)
4 Private Bathrooms, 2 Private Shower Rooms. All Rooms with TV, Telephone,

Radio, Baby-listening, Tea and Coffee-making Facilities, Trouser Press, Hairdryer, Ironing Facilities. Open all Year. Residential and Restaurant Licence. Full Central Heating. Conference Facilities Children catered for. Dogs allowed

Section 4: Cheshire

Near Chester, Rowton—Rowton Hall Hotel Whitchurch Road, Rowton, Chester. CH3 6AD. Tel 0244 335262. Fax 0244 335464

Wherein lies its charm? *Langdale Restaurant*, with its olde-worlde elegance and restful blend of warm colours and mellow lighting, must take pride of place. Here the lover of good food is attracted to a restaurant with a reputation which is second to none. Chef Roger Price has great experience in international *cuisine*. Having gained experience for some years on the continent and in various top class hotels in the United Kingdom, he joined Rowton Hall twelve years ago. He is able to draw on the hotel's garden and greenhouses for the majority of the vegetables, fruit and herbs he needs, and all the desserts, some of the finest you will find, are home-made in the kitchen. Needless to say, the *à la carte* is well balanced and the *table d'hôte* changes from day to day. Rowton Hall was built as a private house in 1779 and was converted into an hotel only in 1955. Whilst it has been modernised where necessary, it has also been preserved almost entirely as it was built and boasts many delightful features. Note the superb staircase and elegant fireplaces, one of which is by Robert Adam. The bedrooms are also praiseworthy and all provide full facilities, whilst retaining the style and atmosphere of a country house. Rowton Hall is owned by Stuart and Diana Begbie and stands in some eight acres of grounds, with award-winning gardens and far reaching views across Chester to the Welsh hills. The Hotel also boasts a most attractive and well equipped leisure centre with excellent facilities. This is a delightful hotel, with a receptive ambiance. The Hall itself contributes much, but the owners and their team do the rest.

Bed and Breakfast from £72.00
Bar Lunch from £1.50
Lunch from £10.00 and A La Carte.
Afternoon Tea from £2.50
Dinner from £15.50 and A La Carte
Gratuities at Guest's discretion
VAT inclusive

Credit Cards–Access, American Express, Diners Club, Switch, Visa
3 Family Rooms. 3 Four Poster Rooms
21 Double, 1 Single, 14 Twin Bedrooms
All Rooms with Private Bath/Shower Room, TV, Telephone, Radio, Tea and Coffee-making Facilities, Trouser Press.

Open from 30th December to 24th December. Fully Licensed
Full Central Heating. Cocktail Bar
Conference Facilities. Dogs allowed
Parking Facilities. Night Porter
Croquet, Hamiltons Sport and Leisure Club with Swimming Pool
Nearby: Golf, Riding, Squash

Knutsford—Longview Hotel and Restaurant 51-55 Manchester Road, Knutsford, Cheshire. WA16 0LX. Tel 0565 632119. Fax 0565 652402

Visitors to this attractive Cheshire market town will find, overlooking the large common, this lovely, comfortable, friendly hotel of quality where Pauline and Stephen West who have enjoyed offering hospitality for the last fifteen years, extend a warm welcome to all their guests. The hotel is both larger and more attractive than it looks from the outside. Furnished with many antiques that reflect another age, the West family has been careful to retain the character and elegance of this Victorian building. All the twenty-three very comfortable bedrooms offer the modern amenities required by today's traveller, and are prettily decorated using cotton prints while little touches like the dried flowers and pin cushions give the rooms that cared for feeling, which is echoed throughout the hotel. As soon as one steps into the reception area, one is greeted by the warmth of an open log fire crackling away in the cottage black leaded range. The cosy cellar bar offers a wide range of beverages and old, deep-seated couches in which many an hour could be whiled away. The restaurant, which has gained a very good reputation, offers excellently prepared dishes served in a very pleasant, relaxed period setting where diners can look out over the common, once a Victorian racecourse. Vegetarians too, are well catered for and we have glowing reports from guests concerning the friendly welcome, personal attention and the quite outstanding quality of the meals for which the AA have awarded their rosette.

Bargain Breaks available
Weekday (B&B) from £46.00 Single, £65.00 Double. Weekend Special (B&B) from £32.00 Single, £55.00 Double
Bar Lunch from £11.50. Lunch from £11.50
Bar Supper from £5.00
Dinner from £13.25 Table d'Hôte
Gratuities at Guest's Discretion
VAT inclusive. Credit Cards–Access, American Express, Visa

1 Family Room
11 Double, 5 Twin, 6 Single Bedrooms
All Rooms with Private Bathroom, TV, Telephone, Radio, Baby-listening, Tea and Coffee-making Facilities, Trouser Press, Hairdryer. Open all Year except Christmas/New Year.
Residential and Restaurant Licence
Full Central Heating. Cocktail Bar

Children catered for
Dogs allowed in rooms only
Parking Facilities
Nearby: Tennis, Squash, Swimming, Golf, Riding, Windsurfing

Section 4: Cheshire

Near Chester, Ewloe–St David's Park Hotel
St David's Park, Ewloe, Clwyd. CH5 3YB
Telephone 0244 520800

At this splendid hotel, elegance is the keynote both outside and within. Several characteristics made an outstanding impression on us, not least of these the courtesy of all the staff, something which contributes so much to the pleasure of a visit. We lunched in their Fountains Restaurant, where tempting, imaginative à la carte, gourmet and carvery meals are available seven days a week. The food was quite delicious, the setting sparkling and spacious, the service attentive but unobtrusive and our enjoyment was enhanced by a background of light music on a grand piano. During our visit we overheard many complimentary comments. All the public rooms here are fully air conditioned, and every beautifully decorated bedroom has an en suite bathroom, and all modernities. In addition to a number of suites and studio rooms, the hotel has provided ladies executive rooms, no-smoking rooms and rooms especially designed for the disabled–nothing has been forgotten. Externally, the hotel has an attractive Georgian style facade, which is designed around an inner courtyard and set in landscaped gardens. This theme extends to the Leisure Club with its excellent facilities. For the businessman or for those wishing to explore the beauties of North Wales, Chester and the many other places of interest in this area, St. David's Park makes a superb base.

Room Rate from £72.00 (Single Occupancy)
Breakfast: English £7.95
Breakfast: Continental £5.95
Bar Meal from £3.75
Lunch from £10.95 Table d'Hôte
Afternoon Tea from £4.00
Dinner from £14.95 Table d'Hôte
Service Charge and VAT inclusive

Credit Cards–Access, American Express, Diners Club, JCB, Visa
13 Family Rooms. 7 Suites
50 Double, 50 Twin Bedrooms
All Rooms with Private Bathroom, TV, Telephone, Radio, Tea and Coffee-making Facilities, Trouser Press, Hairdryer, Mini-Bar
Open all Year

Fully Licensed. Full Central Heating
2 Lifts. Cocktail Bar
Conference Facilities
Children catered for
Dogs allowed in public areas
Parking Facilities. Night Porter
Indoor Swimming Pool, Solarium, Sauna, Beautician, Snooker Room
Nearby: Golf, Fishing, Riding, Shooting, Hang-gliding

Section 4: Cheshire and Derbyshire

Near Tarporley, Willington—Willington Hall Hotel
Willington, Near Tarporley, Cheshire. CW6 0NB. Tel 0829 52321

Willington Hall was built by Col Tomkinson, who made his fortune during the Peninsular War. Fifteen years ago, one of his descendants, Richard Tomkinson, decided to go into partnership and convert this lovely house into an hotel. His partner, Ross Pigot, is responsible for managing the hotel. There are just ten beautifully furnished bedrooms, all with a bathroom *en suite*, colour television, radio, tea and coffee-making facilities and a telephone. *A la carte* lunches and dinners are served in the restaurant every day and tasty bar meals are available. Willington Hall, set in parkland overlooking verdant Cheshire countryside, is a most attractive setting for private parties. It is best approached from the A51 Tarporley to Chester road, turn right at the Bulls Head at Clotton and Willington Hall will be found a mile along on the left. It is a convenient base for those who wish to explore the fascinating city of Chester but who prefer the tranquillity of a country-house hotel. A short drive brings one to Delamere Forest, where one can enjoy numerous gentle walks, mainly through pine woods. A few miles to the south the Peckforton Hills rise above the Cheshire plain. Beeston Castle, built by the Earl of Chester in 1220 and dismantled in 1646, stands on a precipitous outcrop of sandstone just to the north of these hills. It has magnificent views over the surrounding countryside and of the Welsh mountains.

Bed and Breakfast from £55.00 Single
Room Rate from £49.00 Single
Bar Meal from £6.00
Lunch A La Carte
Dinner from £14.50 A La Carte
Gratuities at Guest's discretion

VAT inclusive
Credit Cards–Access, Diners Club, Visa
3 Double, 5 Twin, 2 Single Bedrooms
All Rooms with Private Bathroom, TV, Telephone, Radio, Tea and Coffee-making Facilities

Open all Year except Christmas Day
Fully Licensed. Full Central Heating
Cocktail Bar. Small Conference Facilities
Dogs allowed. Parking Facilities
Hard Tennis Court
Nearby: Golf, Riding

Ashford-in-the-Water–Riverside Country House Hotel Fennel Street,
Ashford-in-the Water, Derbys. DE4 1QF. Tel 0629 814275. Fax 0629 812873

Ashford-in-the-Water! What a quaint sounding Derbyshire name, and how appropriate for a village which grew around a busy ford over the river Wye. It lies a mile or so to the west of Bakewell, where three old bridges arch gracefully over the river. Apposite, too, is the name of this superior country house, which sits in an acre of attractive gardens bordered on one side by the Wye. The Riverside Country House Hotel has fifteen *en suite* bedrooms and advance booking is advisable, but it really is a superb place in which to stay and dine. Roger and Sue Taylor have furnished the house with interesting antiques and dispense a very genuine kind of welcome. Jeremy Buckingham, the Head Chef, is justifiably proud of his *cuisine*, which draws its inspiration from the best ingredients and home-grown produce. A special feature is the ever changing menu, using unusual fish such as john dory, brill, sea bass, also succulent breast of duck or goose and local game, all complemented with an excellent wine cellar. We have been returning to this creeper-clad mellow stone house for some years now and can commend it unreservedly for a meal, a night or longer. The comfort is superb and the surroundings are so satisfying. Always beckoning one are the high peat moors, river valleys and broad reservoirs of Derbyshire's Dark Peak, just a short drive away. Country pursuits like fishing, climbing and walking, country customs, such as well dressing and sheepdog trials, and the impressive country houses of Chatsworth and Haddon Hall also draw people to the area. Roger and Sue Taylor's hotel will encourage them to stay.

Weekly Terms from £465.00 (Double)
Daily Terms from £63.75 (Double)
Bed and Breakfast from £80.00 (Double)
Lunch A La Carte. Sunday Lunch from £13.95 Table d'Hôte
Afternoon Tea from £3.50

Dinner £29.00. Gratuities at Guest's Discretion. Credit Cards–Access, American Express, Visa 4 Double, 7 Twin Bedrooms, 4 Four-poster Rooms (4 Rooms suitable for disabled)
All Rooms with Private Bath/Shower, TV,

Telephone, Radio, Baby-listening, Tea and Coffee-making Facilities Hairdryer, Trouser Press available. Open All Year. Fully Licensed. Full Central Heating. Cocktail Bar. Small Conference Facilities. Dogs by arrangement. Parking. Croquet

Section 4: Derbyshire

Bakewell–Milford House Hotel Mill Street, Bakewell, Derbyshire. DE4 1DA. Tel 0629 812130

For the holidaymaker, Bakewell is an excellent Peak District location in its own right and as a base for visiting Buxton to the north-west and Matlock to the south. For the more travelled businessman, Bakewell is equi-distant from the centres of Manchester, Stoke-on-Trent, Sheffield and Nottingham. Set in beautiful walled gardens laid out in the 19th century, Milford House is a family-run Georgian house lying peacefully back from the busy A6 road, offering spacious, well furnished accommodation. Justly proud of the fact that they have owned this hotel for thirty-eight years, the Hunt family runs Milford House with enthusiastic efficiency, specialising in traditional English home cooking. The hotel is open to non-residents for dinner every evening except Sunday, when lunch is available. We have received unsolicited good reports of the food, the service and the colourful furnishings from guests, confirmed in every respect by our inspectors. There is much to be seen in this small corner of Britain and, on request, the hotel will provide a packed luncheon to give you full freedom to explore the local scenery, country houses and gardens, castles and industrial archaeology. To the hotel's credit, they number many regulars and returning visitors amongst their *clientele*: a competitive tariff must be a factor here. Milford House is situated in Mill Street, only a few yards off the A6 at the Buxton end of Bakewell: take care not to miss the turning!

Weekly Terms from £268.00
Daily Terms from £39.00
Bed and Breakfast from £28.00
Bar Lunch from £4.50
Lunch from £10.50 Table d'Hôte
Afternoon Tea from £4.50
Dinner from £13.00 Table d'Hôte
No Credit Cards accepted

Gratuities at Guest's discretion. VAT extra
5 Double, 5 Twin, 2 Single Bedrooms
8 Private Bathrooms
4 Private Shower Rooms
All Rooms with TV, Tea and Coffee-making Facilities
Radio and Hairdryer available on request
Open from Easter to end October

Residential and Restaurant Licence
Full Central Heating. Cocktail Bar
Children over 10 years catered for
Dogs not allowed
Parking Facilities (including Car Ports)
Croquet. Nearby: Putting, Squash, Badminton, Sauna, Golf, Fishing, Riding, Clay-pigeon Shooting

Near Bakewell, Great Longstone–The Croft Country House Hotel
Great Longstone, Bakewell, Derbyshire. DE4 1TF. Tel 0629 640278

Once in a while we come across something special. Where the location is picturesque, the building has character, decor and furnishings are first-class, the welcome genuine, the service impeccable and the *cuisine* superb. Even with this said, there is more. Possibly it is the main hall with its galleried landing and lantern ceiling, leading to all bedrooms and general rooms, which is the catalyst producing an atmosphere of spontaneous friendliness between strangers. Allan and Lynne Macaskill have succeeded in maintaining the warmth and friendliness associated with a family home, whilst running a successful business. The Croft is just the right size for private dinner parties, wedding receptions and small conferences. It would be a delight for a family weekend. As the informative brochure suggests: 'Occupy most rooms and have the hotel to yourselves'. Although the decor and furnishings are in keeping with the Victorian period of the house, the modernisation includes a lift, and two of the bedrooms are suitable for a wheelchair. The charming and intimate dining-room is open to non-residents throughout the week and we have nothing but praise for every aspect of our meal. From The Croft the whole of Derbyshire is accessible: innumerable places of interest to visit, a wide choice of sporting activities, quality entertainment, caverns and mines, scenery to encourage walking, cycling or outings by car. Don't miss a great experience.

Weekly Terms from £350.00 per person
Bed and Breakfast from £80.00 per room
Dinner from £19.50 Table d'Hôte
Gratuities at Guest's discretion
VAT inclusive
Credit Cards–Access and Visa

2 Twin, 1 Single, 7 Double Bedrooms
5 Private Bathrooms, 4 Private Shower Rooms. All Rooms with TV, Radio, Tea and Coffee-making Facilities
Hairdryer available on request
Open from 1st March to 3rd January

Residential and Restaurant Licence
Full Central Heating. Lift. Cocktail Bar
TV Lounge. Conference Facilities
Children catered for. Guide Dogs only
Parking Facilities. Nearby: Tennis, Swimming, Golf, Fishing, Hang-gliding

Section 4: Derbyshire

Near Bakewell, Hassop—Hassop Hall Hotel Hassop, Near Bakewell, Derbyshire. DE4 1NS. Tel 0629 640488. Fax 0629 640577

It is a remarkable fact that Hassop Hall has been linked to only five families since its inclusion in the *Domesday Book* 900 years ago. The history of this impressive country residence is particularly well documented and, when one stays here, it is almost impossible not to reflect upon the events which have shaped it and upon the many stories it has to tell. Now that it is an hotel it is very easy, when reviewing its special qualities, to run out of superlatives. Its setting alone is truly magnificent. Step inside Hassop Hall and one is greeted not only by elegance, but also by the warmth of a home which continues to be lived in and is cherished. The photographs and literature which Mr and Mrs T Chapman have prepared do not in any way overstate the attractions of Hassop Hall. Indeed, what they modestly do not record is the assiduous attention given to the needs of each guest. The service shown to us was faultless and our bedroom was the epitome of good taste. Sunday luncheon was also an enjoyable experience, for not only was the food cooked and served to perfection, but the presence of several family parties in the dining-room created a very congenial atmosphere. We discovered that plans are in hand to restore the ballroom to cater for many functions, including concerts, and we have no doubt that this room will be as elegant as the rest of Hassop Hall. You will find this splendid establishment on the B6001 road between Bakewell and Calver.

All Terms pertaining to 1992
Room Rate from £65.00
Lunch from £8.75 (2 courses),
£12.95 (full) Table d'Hôte
Dinner from £19.95 weekdays,
£24.95 Saturday Table d'Hôte
Service Charge and VAT inclusive

Credit Cards—Access, American Express,
Diners Club, Visa
2 Family Rooms. 1 Suite
6 Double, 7 Twin Bedrooms
Double Rooms may be let as Singles.
13 Rooms with Private Bath/Shower Room
13 Rooms with TV, Telephone, Radio,
Hairdryer

Pressing Facilities available
Open all Year except few days at Christmas
Residential and Restaurant Licence
Full Central Heating. Lift. Cocktail Bar
Limited Conference Facilities
Dogs allowed at Proprietors' discretion
Parking Facilities. Helicopter Landing Pad
All-weather Tennis Court, Croquet

Buxton—The Lee Wood Hotel The Park, Buxton, Derbyshire. SK17 6TQ. Tel 0298 23002. Fax 0298 23228

We know this part of Derbyshire well. The valleys with their hide-and-seek rivers; those cross-country hikes over stone walls to Earl Sterndale (the Silent Woman) and to Flagg (the Bull-ith-Thorn); and the drives across the roof of England to the small villages of Peak Dale and Peak Forest. And always a return to the highest town in England, Buxton just over 1,000 feet above sea level. Here we are on more civilised terrain and we recommend The Lee Wood to those who appreciate a personal, family-run hotel in the three-star category. It is situated on the A5004 road, in its own grounds and within a few minutes' walk of the town. We always experience a sense of exhilaration up here, where the air is like champagne and one's mental cobwebs are quickly blown away. The Lee Wood Hotel is, to our minds, the perfect complement to these elements, for it is warm and comfortable and the food is exceptionally good. It has benefited enormously by also being a long-established family business. Mr John Millican is your host today and, like his parents before him, he prides himself on giving the best. The *Garden Room* conservatory restaurant provides a wide and varied selection of dishes on both the *table d'hôte* and *à la carte* menus. The Lee Wood is an excellent venue for conferences, receptions and private parties, and, all told, is a very impressive hotel. Nearby is the internationally acclaimed Buxton Opera House where there is a varied programme throughout the year.

Weekly Terms from £335.00
Daily Terms from £50.00
Bed and Breakfast from £35.00
Lunch from £9.50 Table d'Hôte
Afternoon Tea from £3.25
Dinner from £16.50 and A La Carte
Gratuities at Guest's discretion
VAT inclusive
Credit Cards–Access, American Express,

Diners Club, Visa
Some No Smoking Rooms
2 Family Rooms
15 Double, 13 Twin, 6 Single Bedrooms
All Rooms with Private Bathroom, TV,
Telephone, Radio, Baby-listening, Tea and
Coffee-making Facilities, Trouser Press,
HairdryerSome Rooms with Mini-bar.
Open All Year

Fully Licensed
Full Central Heating
Lift. Cocktail Bars. Games Room
Conference Facilities
Parking Facilities. Night Porter
Nearby: Tennis, Croquet, Putting, Squash,
Swimming Pool, Solarium, Sauna, Golf,
Fishing, Riding

Section 4: Derbyshire

Castle Donington—Priest House Hotel
Kings Mills, Castle Donington, DE7 2RR. Tel 0332 810649. Fax 0332 811141

We have watched this hotel, with interest and admiration, since the mid-summer of 1989. From then on, the resident owner, Philip Humphreys, has worked tirelessly and methodically to raise the standards in every respect until, now, it bears most clearly the marks of a perfectionist's ideals. No quick face-lift here: the decor, facilities, service and *cuisine* are all a match for the inherent charm of the buildings and their appealing situation. The Priest House is on a peaceful stretch of the Trent, with fishing rights, and is within easy reach of the East Midlands airport and the M1 motorway. In the locality are Elvaston Castle, Whatton Gardens, several museums and, of course, motor-racing. Mr Humphreys has transformed the accommodation offered in three respects. He has refurbished existing hotel rooms, converted a row of seventeenth-century cottages to modern standards of comfort, and built additional premises to bring the total complement of bedrooms to forty-five. It is, of course, the main building which is of most historic interest. Mentioned in the Domesday Book of 1087, it was originally a watermill, at one stage used as a Mint by King James I, the site of a Cromwellian battle and a chapel where the Wesleys once preached. A very popular venue for wedding receptions, with its *Riverside Suite* catering for up to 140 guests, the Priest House also has a restaurant offering *table d'hôte* and extensive *à la carte* menus embracing English and French food. For business meetings there are, additionally, three seminar rooms.

Bed and Breakfast from £65.00 Single, £75.00 Double. Bar Meal from £3.00 Lunch from £10.95 and A La Carte Afternoon Tea from £3.00 Dinner from £15.95 and A La Carte Service Charge inclusive

Credit Cards—Access, American Express, Diners Club, Visa 22 Family Rooms, 2 Suites 17 Double, 7 Single Bedrooms All Rooms with Private Bathroom, TV, Telephone, Radio, Tea and Coffee-making

Facilities, Hairdryer. 25 Rooms with Trouser Press. Open all Year. Fully Licensed. Full CH. Conference Facilities Children catered for. Dogs allowed. Parking Facilities. Night Porter. Coarse Fishing, Shooting, Canoeing

Near Matlock–Riber Hall
Matlock, Derbyshire. DE4 5JU
Tel 0629 582795. Fax 0629 580475

We are often asked what constitutes a successful hotel. Is it excellent *cuisine* and service backed up by friendly staff? Is it comfortable accommodation in an ideal setting, or is it perhaps the amenities which the hotel offers in general? Often it is a combination of all these attributes and one good case in point is Riber Hall. It is an enchanting Elizabethan manor, set in the peaceful backwater of Riber village, which is surrounded by grounds which feature a delightful walled garden and a flourishing orchard. Under the experienced direction of Mr Alex Biggin, Riber Hall has built up a fine reputation for its first-class restaurant, where you can relax in comfort and enjoy the best food and service with cut glass and bone china, in an intimate atmosphere which is enhanced by the fine period furniture and fireplaces. The bedrooms around the courtyard are equally delightful. Most of them contain antique four-poster beds, and all have central heating, private bathrooms (five with whirlpool baths), television, radios, telephones and small bars. Riber Hall is only twenty minutes' drive from Junction 28 of the M1 and is conveniently situated for Sheffield, Nottingham and Derby. Within twenty minutes' drive are three of England's finest stately homes, Chatsworth House, Haddon Hall and Hardwick Hall as well as the Peak National Park with its wealth of interesting features and pretty villages. To us, Riber Hall has all the ingredients which are part of a well-run hotel.

Bed and Continental Breakfast from £78.00 Lunch from £14.50. Afternoon Tea from £6.75. Dinner A La Carte Gratuities at Guest's discretion VAT inclusive. Credit Cards–Access, American Express, Diners Club, Visa

11 Double Bedrooms All Rooms with Private Bath/Shower Room, TV, Telephone, Radio, Tea and Coffee-making Facilities, Hairdryer, Trouser Press, Mini Bar. Open all Year. Residential and Restaurant Licence. Full

Central Heating. Cocktail Bar. Conference Facilities. Children over 10 years catered for. Dogs not allowed. Parking Facilities Hard Tennis Court. Nearby: Swimming Pool, Golf, Riding,Clay Pigeon Shooting

Section 4: Essex

Harwich, Dovercourt—Cliff Hotel Marine Parade, Dovercourt,
Harwich, Essex. CO12 3RD. Tel 0255 503345. Fax 0255 240358

This popular hotel makes an excellent base at which to stay a night or longer, when departing for or arriving from the Continent. As its name suggests, the hotel occupies a central position on the cliff, and it overlooks Dovercourt Bay. The hotel is no more than a five-minute drive from the ferries for Germany, Denmark and Holland. Our suggestion, then, is to rest awhile, before or after your trip, at this friendly hotel where the manager John Wade, will make you feel like one of the family. The hotel is warm and inviting throughout and you may relax in the comfort of the coffee lounge and restaurant. The *cuisine* is varied and of a high standard–both *table d'hôte* and *à la carte* menus are available, as well as an interesting wine list at reasonable prices. *Shades Bar*, which has recently been most attractively redecorated, is very popular for its bar food at lunchtime and as a meeting place in the evening. The bedrooms are well equipped: all have colour television and the majority have a private bath or shower room. In short, this late Victorian hotel offers the charm of the past combined with the amenities of today, and you are assured of a warm welcome and attentive service.

Bed and Breakfast from £43.00
Bar Lunch from £3.75
Lunch from £9.00 and A La Carte
Afternoon Tea from £1.50
Bar Supper from £3.50
Dinner from £10.75 and A La Carte
Gratuities at Guest's discretion
VAT inclusive. All Credit Cards accepted

6 Family Rooms. 1 Suite
9 Double, 11 Twin, 4 Single Bedrooms
27 Private Bathrooms
2 Private Shower Rooms
All Rooms with Colour TV, Telephone, Radio, Baby-listening, Tea and Coffee-making Facilities
10 Rooms with Hairdryer

Open all year. Fully Licensed
Full Central Heating. Cocktail Bar
TV Lounge. Dogs allowed
Parking Facilities
Conference Facilities. Night Porter
Nearby: Tennis, Putting, Squash, Badminton, Indoor Swimming Pool, Golf, Fishing, Riding, Sailing

Old Harlow—Churchgate Manor Hotel
Churchgate Street, Old Harlow, Essex. CM17 0JT. Tel 0279 420246. Fax 0279 437720

Although only one hour's drive from London, this area of Essex contains many delightful Tudor villages, whilst in the unspoilt Roding Valley are timbered cottages and moated farmsteads. Churchgate Manor Hotel is a luxurious complex built around a fine old Jacobean country manor house which today houses the *Manor Restaurant* and forms the focus of the picturesque village of Churchgate Street. Rarely is such an impressive range of facilities found combined with a friendly, relaxed atmosphere. The hotel comprises eighty-seven modern bedrooms, all with private bathrooms, most with hairdryers and electric trouser presses, some with computer points, jacuzzi baths, mini-bars and safes. There are seven function rooms, three of which are suitable for dinner-dances or for use as lecture rooms, and between them catering also for receptions, conferences, banquets and theatre-style presentations with a full range of supporting audio-visual equipment. Truly, a most comprehensive array of services in an accessible, attractive setting of landscaped gardens, paved terraces and floodlit fountains. Here one can wine and dine at any level from a bar snack to dinner in splendid surroundings. Guests can readily choose between quiet relaxation or a more active holiday taking advantage of the excellent facilities of the hotel's leisure centre. We need hardly add that the decor, furnishings and service are all of the very best quality and there is always a warm welcome awaiting guests.

Daily Terms from £49.00
(Weekend Break only)
Bar Lunch from £3.00
Lunch from £18.50 A La Carte
Afternoon Tea from £2.50
Dinner from £16.50 and A La Carte
Gratuities at Guest's discretion
VAT inclusive
Credit Cards—Access, American Express, Diners Club, Visa

7 Family Rooms. 6 Suites
25 Double, 27 Twin, 22 Single Bedrooms
All Rooms with Private Bathroom, TV, Telephone, Radio, Tea and Coffee-making Facilities, Hairdryer
60 Rooms with Trouser Press
21 Executive Rooms with Jacuzzi Bath

Open All Year. Fully Licensed

Full Central Heating. Cocktail Bar
Conference Facilities
Children catered for. Dogs allowed
Parking Facilities. Night Porter
Indoor Swimming Pool, Solarium, Sauna
Nearby: Squash, Badminton, Golf, Fishing, Riding

Section 4: Essex

Saffron Walden—The Saffron Hotel 10 High Street,
Saffron Walden, Essex. CB10 1AY. Tel 0799 522676. Fax 0799 513979

The M11 motorway has been a boon for tourists. Now Cambridge can be considered a day's excursion from London. The discerning, however, know that a short distance from the fast lanes are some of the most ancient and interesting towns in Britain. Saffron Walden, for instance, is an absolute gem and this aptly named hotel is an excellent choice. It has been part of the High Street since the sixteenth century, but, whilst many of its original features remain, it has been modernised to a high degree. This popular hotel is run by Nigel Hudson who recently completely redecorated the hotel. This influence is certainly used to good effect for we have never seen the hotel in better heart. It has always been a social centre for the town and the lounge bar, which has an excellent bar menu, is a convivial place for both guests and locals. Do try, however, to engage one of the bedrooms, for not only will you find great comfort here, but you will also be able to enjoy the excellent *table d' hôte* menu and *à la carte* specialities in the new *Garden Restaurant* at the leisurely pace they deserve. For an economical break, a celebration or as part of a touring holiday, The Saffron is our choice in the town.

Weekly Terms on Application
Bed and Continental Breakfast from £30.00
Bar Meal from £2.50
Lunch from £13.50 and A La Carte
Dinner from £13.50 and A La Carte
Service Charge at Guests' Discretion
VAT inclusive. Credit Cards—Access, American Express, Diners Club, Visa

2 Family Rooms, 3 Bridal Suites
11 Double, 5 Twin, 5 Single Bedrooms
18 Private Bathrooms
2 Private Shower Rooms
All Rooms with TV, Telephone, Radio, Tea and Coffee-making Facilities, Baby-listening. 4 Rooms with Hairdryer
Open all Year. Fully Licensed

Full Central Heating
Conference Facilities
Dogs allowed
Parking Facilities
Nearby: Tennis, Squash, Badminton, Indoor Swimming Pool, Sauna, Golf

Thorpe Bay–Roslin Hotel
Thorpe Esplanade, Thorpe Bay, Essex. SS1 3BG. Tel 0702 586375. Fax 0702 586663

A 'wag' once penned the following anecdote, 'An hotel on the moon would be fine, but would it have any atmosphere?' Amusing enough, but it does underline the importance of hospitality and a warm and friendly service. At the Roslin Hotel, situated on the Esplanade, it was the atmosphere and cleanliness which charmed us immediately and left a lasting impression. The Oliver family have been attracting guests to this *cul-de-sac* of contentment for over twenty-five years and, following our recent visits, we can appreciate why guests return year after year to enjoy Roslin food, accommodation and views. The hotel sits on the sea-front and boasts one of the finest views of the Thames Estuary. The panoramic windows in the lounges keep one in constant touch with the comings and goings of the river's activities and the Continental-style terrace is an outstanding feature of the hotel. The restaurant also overlooks the estuary and it was through reports of the Olivers' kitchen crafts that we were initially brought to their hotel. From what we have seen, heard and experienced the Roslin offers a varied menu and wine list, both enhanced by friendly service. Above stairs, all the bedrooms have a private bath or shower room and fulfil the prerequisites for a comfortable stay. All hotel residents are given temporary membership of the local leisure centre. The hotel is a delight at any time of the year and, as a sampler, many guests take advantage of its special 'Weekend Break' tariff which operates all year.

Weekly Terms from £255.00
Bed and Breakfast from £38.00 Single, £30.00 Double
Bar Meal from £4.00
Lunch from £9.50 and A La Carte
Dinner from £13.00 and A La Carte
Gratuities at Guest's discretion
VAT inclusive

All major Credit Cards accepted
6 Family Rooms. 14 Double, 10 Twin, 15 Single Bedrooms. 35 Private Bathrooms. 10 Private Shower Rooms.
All Rooms with TV, Telephone, Radio, Baby-listening, Tea and Coffee-making Facilities, Hairdryer. Open all Year Residential and Restaurant Licence

Full Central Heating. Cocktail Bar
Conference Facilities. Dogs allowed
Parking Facilities. Night Porter
Nearby: Tennis, Putting, Squash, Badminton, Swimming Pool, Sauna, Golf, Fishing, Riding, Sailing, Windsurfing, Water Skiing

Section 4: Gloucestershire

Ampney Crucis—The Crown of Crucis
Ampney Crucis, Cirencester, Gloucestershire. GL7 5RS. Tel 0285 851806. Fax 0285 851735

There are four Ampneys scattered in the countryside to the east of Cirencester: Down Ampney, Ampney St. Peter; Ampney St. Mary; and the delightfully named Ampney Crucis, whose jewel in the crown is this former coaching inn, now a thriving and popular hotel. In time-honoured tradition, it serves the needs of the wayfarer, be that for refreshment, repast, or rest. We stayed overnight and, therefore, enjoyed all three, and, so satisfying and comfortable did we find the Crown, that we would have happily put down roots there for a few days, or more. The bedrooms surround an attractive garden courtyard and most have pleasant views across the gently flowing Ampney Brook and the local cricket ground. All the rooms have modern facilities. They are also deliciously quiet and away from traffic noise. The passing motorist is lured to the Crown with an extensive and varied menu, featuring several home-made dishes and specials, whilst, clearly, the restaurant also has a devoted following. It offers the best of English food on its *à la carte* menu, but of more interest is the fact that the original dishes are cooked to order and that only the freshest produce is used. In winter, roaring log fires enhance the conviviality of the Crown, but it is always friendly and welcoming. We felt a real interest was taken in our well being, and all those little things which make one feel especially at ease were done so well. All this reflects the enthusiasm and zeal of the owners, Ken and Tessa Mills, whose influence is everywhere. They even have a function room for up to 100 people.

All Prices pertain to 1992
Bed and Breakfast from £49.00 Single, £60.00 Double. Bar Lunch from £2.95
Afternoon Tea from £2.25
Bar Supper from £3.80
Dinner from £13.00 and A La Carte

Gratuities at Guest's discretion
VAT inclusive. Credit Cards–Access, American Express, Visa
2 Family, 8 Double, 16 Twin Bedrooms
All Rooms with Private Bathroom, TV, Telephone, Baby-listening, Tea

and Coffee-making Facilities, Hairdryer
Radio available on request
Open all Year except Christmas Day
Fully Licensed. Full Central Heating
Conference Facilities. Children catered for
Dogs allowed. Parking Facilities

Bourton-on-the-Water—Dial House Hotel
The Chestnuts, High Street, Bourton-on-the-Water, Gloucestershire. GL54 2AN. Tel 0451 22244

'Little Venice of the Cotswolds' has been appended to Bourton-on-the-Water, because of the river Windrush which meanders gently through the village under quaint bridges. In this picturesque village lie the famous Birdland Zoo, a perfumery, motor museum and a model village. Here also, within a secluded garden setting, stands the 1698 Dial House, combining all the facilities of a modern hotel with the charm and elegance of a bygone era. The warm hospitality and individual attention accorded to guests in this ten-bedroom country house is engendered by the charming hosts Lynn and Peter Boxall. Their twenty-six years' experience within the hotel industry is reflected in the efficient service, putting visitors at their ease. Oak beams and an inglenook fireplace in the restaurant create the aura of old England, a comfortable and homely setting in which to enjoy the imaginative *cuisine* based on fresh traditional ingredients. A cosy bar and the open log fire in the stylish lounge offer opportunities to chat with one's fellow guests over an aperitif or coffee and liqueurs. No less than three of the *en suite* rooms have four-poster beds, another has a half-tester, and several overlook the garden. Here one may enjoy a game of croquet on the lawns, or lounge with a drink or coffee by the ornamental pool. Because Bourton-on-the-Water lies close to the Gloucestershire/Oxfordshire boundary, with Warwickshire and Wiltshire within easy reach, one has a host of historic buildings, museums and nature reserves to visit locally.

Weekly Terms from £224.00 (Bed and Breakfast). Daily Terms from £86.75 for two Bed and Breakfast from £32.00
Bar Lunch from £2.50
Lunch from £8.50 and A La Carte
Dinner A La Carte

Gratuities at Guest's Discretion
VAT inclusive. Credit Cards–Access, American Express, Visa
1 Single, 6 Double, 3 Twin Bedrooms
6 Private Bathrooms. 4 Private Shower Rooms. All Rooms with TV, Telephone,

Radio, Tea and Coffee-making Facilities, Hairdryer. Trouser Press available
Open all Year. Residential and Restaurant Licence. Full Central Heating. Cocktail Bar.
Conference Facilities. Dogs not allowed
Parking Facilities. Croquet

Section 4: Gloucestershire

Bibury—The Swan Hotel
Bibury, Gloucestershire, GL7 5NW
Tel 0285 740695. Fax 0285 740473

Victorian artist William Morris regarded Bibury as England's most beautiful village and, for centuries, there has been an inn or hostelry on the north side of the river Coln where Bibury meets the village of Arlington. A watercolour hanging in the writing room of the hotel is mentioned in the deeds and shows the hotel as it was in 1650. Very recently, The Swan was closed for a whole year during which it underwent a comprehensive programme of restoration, renovation and refurbishment. We now rate the hotel as quite exceptional on all counts. The eighteen en suite bedrooms are individually furnished to the highest standards of comfort: chintzy fabrics, most of the furniture antique, Egyptian cotton sheets and wool blankets on the beds, fluffy white towels and towelling robes complemented by fine fragrances and soaps. An air of tasteful luxury pervades every room, from the glittering chandeliers in the dining room to the cosy sofas in the parlour. At dinner, a daily changing table d'hôte menu complements the more embracing à la carte menu. We lunched here and rate the Swan as one of the homes of great English cooking. The picturesque village, with its trout stream and the delightful cottages of Arlington Row, is the ideal central point from which to explore the natural and historic beauty of the Cotswolds. There is a mechanical music museum at Northleach and, in Cirencester, the enlarged Norman church of St John the Baptist has a peal of twelve bells, the oldest in Britain.

Daily Terms from £99.50
Bed and Breakfast from £70
Bar Lunch from £3.50
Lunch from £17.50 Table d'Hôte
Afternoon Tea from £3.65
Brasserie A La Carte
Dinner from £29.50 and A La Carte
Service Charge and VAT inclusive
Credit Cards—Access, Visa
1 Family Room

1 Single, 9 Double, 7 Twin Bedrooms
17 Private Bathrooms
1 Private Shower Room
All Rooms with TV, Telephone, Radio, Trouser Press, Hairdryer, Mineral Water, Biscuits
Baby-listening, Tea and Coffee-making Facilities on request
Open from 7 January to 23 December
Fully Licensed

Full Central Heating
Lift. Cocktail Bar
Conference Facilities
Children catered for
Dogs not allowed
Parking Facilities
Fishing
Nearby: Tennis, Golf, Riding, Sailing, Windsurfing, Water Skiing, Shooting

Section 4: Gloucestershire

Bourton-on-the-Water—Finden Lodge Hotel Cirencester Road, Bourton-on-the-Water, GL54 2LE. Tel 0451 20387. Fax 0451 21635

Superb comfort and outstanding cuisine in a converted Cotswold farmhouse, splendid walks starting on the doorstep and, within a fourteen-mile radius, a veritable wealth of interesting, scenic and historic places to visit. This is Finden Lodge, a family run hotel in the famous and delightful Gloucestershire village of Bourton-on-the-Water, close to the county boundary of Oxfordshire. Janet and Paul Finden-Smart extended and upgraded a neglected premises and, in October 1989, opened it as a superior hotel with twelve spacious *en suite* bedrooms. With their sons Adrian and Stephen, they provide a welcoming, warm and relaxing atmosphere in which guests receive every consideration. Early recognition was accorded to their two-room Wedgwood Fayre Restaurant (one room reserved for non-smoking guests) in which local specialities are prepared naturally from fresh produce. Socialising comes naturally in the convivial bar where lunch and evening buffet meals are of an exceptionally high standard and, in the residents' lounge, the charm and style of the setting encourages discussion of the many local places to be seen. Within an area embracing Cirencester, Gloucester, Cheltenham, Tewkesbury and Evesham there are enough view points, museums, golf courses, castles, parks, galleries, hill forts, potteries, stately homes and gardens, zoos, an amphitheatre, polo ground, preserved railway, motor-museum, race-course and bird park to provide many really worth-while tours to suit every inclination. Fishing and riding are available locally. Your friendly hosts will be happy to advise you on these many activities.

Special Breaks available
Weekly Terms 10% discount
Bed and Breakfast from £62.00 per room
Bar Meal from £4.00
Lunch from £13.50 and A La Carte
Afternoon Tea from £3.50

Dinner from £13.50 and A La Carte
Gratuities at Guest's Discretion
VAT inclusive. Credit Cards—Access,
American Express, Visa
2 Family Rooms, 10 Double Bedrooms
All Rooms with Private Bathroom, TV,

Telephone, Radio, Tea and Coffee-making Facilities. Hairdryer available
Open all Year. Fully Licensed
Full Central Heating. Conference Facilities
Children catered for. Dogs allowed
Parking Facilities

Cheltenham—On the Park Evesham Road, Cheltenham, Gloucestershire. GL52 2AH. Tel 0242 518898

'A beautiful old house of very gracious proportions' is how our inspector describes On the Park. It was acquired some two-and-a-half years ago by Mr and Mrs Gregory and has been transformed by them: they both have a tremendous flair for interior design and decor. Nor is Darryl Gregory a newcomer to the hotel trade or to our Guide. At two previous locations he has won awards for running best-kept hotels. Within this latest hotel, a classic example of a Regency villa which overlooks Cheltenham's beautiful Pittville Park, is the nationally acclaimed *Epicurean Restaurant* gives guests the opportunity to sample some of the best modern British cooking on offer today. Each of the eight *en suite* bedrooms is individually decorated, furnished with antiques and equipped with modern amenities including remote control satellite television and direct-dial telephones. In some parts of the hotel the plaster work has been exquisitely hand-painted by Mrs Gregory. Everywhere the decor is more than a match for the surroundings outside. In 1883, Scottish writer Catherine Sinclaire described her visit to 'Pittville in the suburbs of Cheltenham, a scene of gorgeous magnificence.....with houses of every size, shape and character... so fresh and clean, you would imagine they were all blown out at once, like soap bubbles'. Cheltenham's medicinal spring waters still flow in Pittville Pump Room.

Weekly Terms on application
Daily Terms from £49.50
Bed and Breakfast from £32.00
Lunch from £12.50 and A La Carte
Afternoon Tea from £4.50
Dinner from £17.50 and A La Carte

VAT inclusive. Credit Cards—Access,
American Express, Visa
4 Double, 4 Twin Bedrooms
All Rooms with Private Bathroom, TV,
Telephone, Radio, Tea and Coffee-making Facilities, Hairdryer

Open all Year
Residential & Restaurant Licence
Full Central Heating. Cocktail Bar
Children over 8 years catered for
Dogs allowed by arrangement
Parking Facilities

Section 4: Gloucestershire

Cheltenham–Prestbury House Hotel and Restaurant
The Burgage, Prestbury, Cheltenham, Gloucestershire. GL52 3DN
Tel 0242 529533. Fax 0242 227076

This imposing Georgian mansion, fashioned from the famous honey-coloured stone, promises the visitor the epitome of elegant country living. It is also a house of history, and we are convinced it has a happy past, for there is a friendly feeling from the moment one arrives. Indeed, just two families have been charged with its care since the house was built in 1700. The first kept it as a private residence until thirty years ago. Since then, two generations of the same hotel family have brought the story up-to-date. Unlike many of our country houses which have been adapted for hotel purposes, Prestbury House gives the impression of having been blended. There is a sense of good taste, in the well-proportioned rooms with their apposite furnishings. The gardens, complete with croquet lawn, are like the house; full of English charm. Call at Prestbury House for a meal, as we did, and before you leave we wager you will sense a feeling of having put the rest of the world in abeyance. So, to stay for a night or longer must be a panacea! You will notice a cocktail bar, reminiscent of a comfortable study; a dining room notable for its bay windows and elegant Adam fireplace; and a smaller dining room, *The Oak Panelled Room*, where we dined. The menus and cellar offer a selection which caters for all tastes, and the preparation and presentation of the *cuisine* is first class. Conference facilities are available in beautiful oak panelled rooms. Above stairs the bedrooms reflect the rest of the house–tastefully comfortable to a sumptuous four-poster room. As a perfect bolt-hole, you could simply relax totally, of course, or, do the opposite and walk from here to the heights of Cleeve Hill, the highest point of the Cotswold Way.

Weekly terms from £495.00 (6 nights)
Bed and breakfast from £53.00
Bar Meal from £2.50
Lunch from £8.50 (Business),
£16.50 Table d'Hôte
Afternoon Tea from £3.00
Dinner from £16.50 and A La Carte
Service Charge and VAT inclusive
Credit Cards—Access, American Express, Visa

3 Family Rooms
1 Single, 5 Double, 11 Twin Bedrooms
All Rooms with Private Bathroom, TV, Telephone, Radio, Baby-listening, Tea and Coffee-making Facilities, Trouser Press, Hairdryer
Open all Year
Fully Licensed. Full Central Heating
Cocktail Bar
TV Lounge

Conference Facilities
Children catered for
Guide Dogs only allowed
Parking Facilities
Croquet, Riding, Shooting
Nearby: Tennis, Putting, Squash, Badminton, Swimming, Solarium, Sauna, Golf, Fishing, Hill Walking

Section 4: Gloucestershire

Chipping Campden–Noel Arms Hotel
High Street, Chipping Campden, Gloucestershire. GL55 6AT. Tel 0386 840317. Fax 0386 841136

The Noel Arms dates back some 600 years when guests varied from international wool merchants who traded in the market, to King Charles II who rested at the hotel after the famous battle of Worcester in 1651. The hotel, with twenty six *en suite* bedrooms, has been recently extended to provide the highest of quality for guests' comfort within traditional surroundings with modern facilities. All rooms are decorated and furnished to a high standard with those rooms in the older part of the hotel having antique furniture and original paintings. The muskets, swords and armour covering the walls of the bar and lounge give the Noel Arms the atmosphere of one of the great halls of the Cotswolds. Here you can enjoy morning coffee, a bar meal or a Cotswold tea with home-made biscuits and other delights, In the oak panelled *Gainsborough Restaurant*, named after the famous family who once owned the Noel, one can choose a roast from the carvery or a selection from the extensive *à la carte* menu, complemented by a fine international wine list. Coffee can be taken in the conservatory or, in winter, in front of a roaring fire. The chef's high standards allow only the freshest local produce to be used. A warm welcome is certain from Mr Neil John and his friendly staff whether you stay overnight or just pop in for morning coffee. The Noel Arms makes an excellent centre for the many attractions of this area, whilst golf, riding, fishing and other activities can be arranged for the sportsman.

Bed and Breakfast from £78.00 Double
Bed and Breakfast from £58.00 Single
Bar Lunch from £2.00
Dinner from £12.75 and A La Carte
Gratuities at Guest's discretion
VAT inclusive

Credit Cards–Access, American Express, Visa
13 Double, 11 Twin Bedrooms
2 4-poster Rooms
All Rooms with Private Bath/Shower Room, TV, Radio, Tea and Coffee-making Facilities. Hairdryer available

Open all Year
Fully Licensed
Full Central Heating. Conference Facilities
Dogs not allowed. Ample Parking
Nearby: Tennis, Squash, Swimming Pool, Solarium, Sauna, Golf, Riding, Shooting

Cirencester—Corinium Court Hotel and Restaurant
12 Gloucester Street, Cirencester, Gloucestershire. GL7 2DG. Tel 0285 659711. Fax 0285 885807

Corinium Court Hotel is situated in the old part of Cirencester and was originally built, in 1595, as the town house of a wool merchant. There are sixteen well-appointed and comfortable bedrooms, all with a private bathroom or shower, the majority of which overlook the courtyard or the walled-in garden and are therefore quiet. All rooms are fitted with television, direct-dial telephone and radio and fire precautions have been installed throughout. The *Courtyard Bar* is comfortable and here one may enjoy a quiet drink by a log fire or on the adjoining patio. Tea, coffee and light lunches are served on the patio in the summer season. There is a wide selection of tasty bar snacks and a delicious hot and cold table is also available. The old barn and stabling have been converted into an exceptional restaurant which overlooks the well-tended gardens. The menu is varied and adventurous and great attention is paid to the quality and presentation of the food, both in the kitchen and in the restaurant. There is a large car park accessible from Spitalgate Lane. Corinium Court is an ideal centre from which to explore the picturesque Cotswold villages and many places of interest are within a thirty-five-mile radius. It is an oasis in the centre of the Cotswolds, where hospitality is the motto.

Weekly Terms from £315.00 Single
Bed and Breakfast from £45.00 Single
Bar Lunch from £2.50
Lunch from £5.50 and A La Carte
Afternoon Tea from £1.50
Dinner from £14.00 and A La Carte
Gratuities at Guest's discretion
VAT inclusive

Credit Cards—Access, American Express, Visa
1 Family Room
2 Single, 10 Double, 4 Twin Bedrooms
All Rooms with Private Bathroom, TV, Telephone, Radio, Baby-listening
Open all Year.
Fully Licensed
Full Central Heating

Dogs allowed
Ample Parking
Nearby: Tennis, Putting, Squash, Badminton, Swimming Pool, Solarium, Sauna, Golf, Fishing, Riding, Sailing, Windsurfing, Water Skiing

Section 4: Gloucestershire

Near Coleford—Lambsquay House Hotel Royal Forest of Dean, Coleford, Gloucestershire. GL16 8QB. Tel 0594 833127. Fax 0594 833127

Built on the site of the ancient Lambsquay iron mine, this delightful seventeenth century Georgian mansion truly reflects the unhurried and unspoilt character of this area. Lambsquay House would be an excellent choice as a base for exploring this fascinating area, for the standards throughout are extremely high and the owners, Peter Waite and his Swiss/Italian wife, Serena, offer genuine warm hospitality to all who stay there. It seemed to us that this little Forest of Dean showpiece would be an ideal place in which to 'wind down' for a few days. The views hereabouts are of gentle meadows and far-reaching woodlands. Ancient hedges and farmlands sculpture this pleasant landscape. With a little luck you may see deer and peregrine falcons and, of course, the Forestry Commission has created many walks, picnic glades and viewing points. Lambsquay fits perfectly into the scene. Nine spacious and comfortable bedrooms, each complete with private bathroom, colour television, radio/telephone and beverage-making facilities. A welcoming Victorian lounge bar with a generous supply of good magazines emphasises the country house appeal. The restaurant which overlooks the garden and pond, serves traditional English and interesting continental *cuisine*, including vegetarian dishes. We hardly need say more for, surely, you can guess the rest. Remember that the Wye valley, the Welsh borders, pony trekking, fishing and golf are all at hand. In short, here is an hotel of contentment in rural England's heart.

All Prices pertain to 1992
Weekly Terms from £34.00 p.p. per night
Bed and Breakfast from £24.00
Afternoon Tea from £2.00
Dinner from £14.00 and A La Carte
Gratuities at Guest's discretion
VAT inclusive

Credit Cards—Access, American Express, Diners Club, Visa
1 Suite/Family Room
1 Single, 5 Double, 2 Twin Bedrooms
8 Private Bathrooms. 1 Private Shower Room. All Rooms with TV, Telephone, Radio, Baby-listening, Tea and Coffee-making Facilities

Open from February to December
Fully Licensed. Full Central Heating
Cocktail Bar. Small Conference Facilities
Children catered for
Dogs allowed
Parking Facilities
Nearby: Golf, Fishing, Riding, Walking

Near Moreton-in-Marsh—The Crown Inn & Hotel High Street, Blockley, Moreton-in-Marsh, Gloucs. GL56 9EX. Tel 0386 700245. Fax 0386 700247

The centuries have been kind to the Crown Inn & Hotel at Blockley for, like good wine, this fifteenth century coaching inn has aged to perfection. It maintains its role in the heart of this little Cotswold community, although all its facilities have been upgraded to ensure that they satisfy the most fastidious of modern day travellers. The cobbled courtyard has been replaced by a patio where guests may read their morning newspapers and local people and their friends can enjoy coffee or afternoon teas. The hotel's twenty-one comfortable *en suite* bedrooms have modern facilities. The hotel has three resident lounges; the first where one may sit in comfort in front of a blazing log fire. The second lounge contains a guest library and games for those who want to relax and the third lounge is just inside the garden. The hotel is owned and run by the Champion family and has an informal and relaxed atmosphere with a personal touch, whilst still maintaining an efficient and courteous service throughout. The hotel has two restaurants, *La Couronne*, a candle-lit French restaurant which serves a four course evening meal, and an *à la carte Bistro* which specialises in fresh fish and brasserie. Both restaurants serve the best of international and English *cuisine* freshly and individually prepared for its guests. Sweet buffs may like to try the hotel's home-made sweets, including its speciality Icky Sticky Toffee Pudding. Whilst the Crown Inn reflects the tranquil nature of Blockley with walks along bridle paths, bowls on the village green and horse riding from local stables, there is a great deal for visitors to see and do in this corner of the Cotswolds.

Weekly Terms from £273.90
Bed and Breakfast from £36.00
Lunch from £2.25 A La Carte
Dinner from £16.95 Table d'Hôte and A La Carte. Gratuities at Guest's discretion
VAT inclusive. Credit Cards—Access,

American Express, Visa
3 Suites (2 Four-Poster). 3 De Luxe Rooms (2 Family)
2 Four-Poster, 9 Double, 4 Twin Bedrooms
Doubles can be let as Singles
18 Private Bathrooms. 3 Private Shower

Rooms. All Rooms with TV, Telephone, Radio, Tea and Coffee-making Facilities, Hairdryer. Open all Year
Fully Licensed. Full Central Heating
Conference Facilities. Dogs allowed in some rooms. Parking Facilities

Section 4: Gloucestershire

Forest of Dean—Clearwell Country House Hotel
Royal Forest of Dean, Gloucestershire, GL16 8LG
Tel 0594 832320. Fax 0594 835523

Originally the site of a Roman villa, next a manor as home for the thirteenth century crusader Sir John Joce, and later an Elizabethan mansion in which it is believed Sir Walter Raleigh claimed Bess Throckmorton as his bride; then, in 1727, Roger Morris designed Clearwell Castle, the first building to be created in the Gothic Revival style. A disastrous fire in 1929 reduced the castle to an empty shell, since when several phases of restoration have brought the building back to its former splendour. Parts of the Elizabethan structure can still be seen in the banqueting hall and on the ground floor. Nothing is ostentatious here: the grandeur, dignity and spaciousness are all in keeping with the imposing nature of the building and its superb surroundings. A most magnificent reception hall, with its high figured ceiling, polished floor, sparkling chandelier and arched recesses sets the pattern for a majestic ambience that pervades all parts of this quite exceptional luxury hotel. Decor, furnishings and the service are of the very highest standards. Whether you plan a prestigious business seminar, a major social celebration or a personal holiday, Clearwell Castle offers every facility and comfort to guarantee a memorable occasion. In addition to the rich history of the hotel, there lies close by a wealth of interesting sites, structures, gardens and museums extending from Ross-on-Wye to Chepstow. Also on your doorstep is all the natural beauty of the Forest of Dean.

Daily Terms from £57.50	2 Family, 1 Single, 9 Double,	Cocktail Bar
Bed and Breakfast from £55.00 Single,	2 Twin Bedrooms	TV Lounge
£60.00 Double	14 Private Bathrooms	Conference Facilities
Lunch from £9.95 Table d'Hôte	2 Private Shower Rooms	Children catered for
Afternoon Tea from £1.50	All Rooms with TV, Telephone, Radio,	Dogs allowed
Dinner from £17.50 and A La Carte	Tea and Coffee-making Facilities	Parking Facilities
Gratuities at Guest's discretion	Hairdryer available	Shooting
VAT inclusive	Open all Year	Nearby: Squash, Badminton, Swimming,
Credit Cards—Access, American Express,	Fully Licensed	Golf, Fishing, Riding
Diners Club, Visa	Part Central Heating and open fire	

Section 4: Gloucestershire

Stonehouse–Stonehouse Court Hotel Bristol Road, Stonehouse, Gloucestershire. GL10 3RA. Tel 0453 825155. Fax 0453 824611

Stonehouse Court sits in a level tract of land between the River Severn and the Cotswold hills and is another example of how Britain's heritage can be experienced and not just observed. There is a timeless quality to this well-preserved house, built in the early part of the seventeenth century, and to its six acres of secluded grounds. Oak panelling, ornate ceilings, stone fireplaces and gleaming chandeliers evoke the spirit of an elegant home. Everywhere the theme continues–you will find a discreetly sociable air, gracious surroundings, professional service and *haute cuisine*. Our visit here was sufficient to arouse our interest, tempt our palates and instil in us a commitment to return at the earliest opportunity. Although a private bathroom, colour television and a telephone are standard equipment in the bedrooms, each room has a distinctive style of its own. The cosy restaurant, with its classic French and English dishes, attracts an interesting clientele of lovers of good food. In the grounds are two small pools and a croquet lawn. The *Crellin Room*, overlooking the gardens, is used for private luncheons, family celebrations and conferences. With an hotel which offers so much, one is obliged to list its amenities, but we do hope you will sample Stonehouse Court, for guests are made to feel truly cherished. It is also ideally positioned for visiting Slimbridge Wild Fowl Trust, the Cotswolds and Wales.

Bed and Breakfast from £72.50 Single, £49.00 (sharing Twin/Double)
Lunch from £14.00 and A La Carte
Afternoon Tea from £4.50
Dinner from £20.00 and A La Carte
Gratuities at Guest's discretion

VAT inclusive. Credit Cards–Access, Visa
1 Suite. 23 Double, 7 Twin, 6 Single Bedrooms. All Rooms with Private Bathrooms, TV, Telephone, Radio, Baby-listening, Tea and Coffee-making Facilities, Trouser Press,

Hairdryer. Open all Year. Fully Licensed
Full Central Heating
Cocktail Bar. Conference Facilities
Children catered for. Parking Facilities
Helipad. Dogs not allowed. Night Porter
Croquet, Fishing

Stow-on-the-Wold–Stow Lodge Hotel The Square, Stow-on-the-Wold, Cheltenham, Gloucs. GL54 1AB. Tel 0451 830485

This friendly hill-top town is notable for its large market square, its clusters of old houses, the glorious scenery which surrounds it and the Stow Lodge Hotel. The hotel is reached by a shady path which will lead you to a gracious garden spacious enough to afford complete tranquillity. Jim and Vera Jux and their daughter and son-in-law, Val and David Hartley, have given the hotel a reputation for the warmth of its hospitality and we are delighted to learn that this family involvement has been enhanced by the Juxs' grandsons joining the business. During a recent visit to Stow Lodge we were reminded of its finer points. The tastefully furnished bedrooms are well equipped with a private bathroom, colour television, radio and beverage-making facilities. The attractive lounge, with its open fire and genuine priest hole, has an old-world charm and it is a delight to enjoy bar meals at tables neatly spaced out on the lawn. The traditional English home cooking relies on fresh local produce and prime ingredients, all soundly prepared and served by welcoming staff. It seemed to us that everything possible is done to make your stay at this happy family hotel a memorable one. You will find the hotel beside the A429 road, near to its junction with the A436.

Terms on Application
Breakfast: English £8.00
Breakfast: Continental £5.00
Bar Lunch from £3.00
Bar Supper from £7.00
Dinner from £13.00 and A La Carte
Gratuities at Guest's discretion

VAT inclusive
Credit Cards–American Express, Diners Club
1 Single, 10 Double, 8 Twin Bedrooms
2 Family Rooms. 1 Four-Poster Room
All Rooms with Private Bathroom, TV, Intercom, Radio,
Tea and Coffee-making Facilities

Hairdryer available on request
Open from mid-January to 20th December
Fully Licensed. Full Central Heating
Cocktail Bar. Dogs not allowed
Children over 5 years catered for
Parking Facilities. Night Porter
Nearby: Riding, Golf

Section 4: Gloucestershire

Near Stroud, Amberley–The Amberley Inn Amberley, Stroud, Gloucestershire. GL5 5AF. Tel 0453 872565. Fax 0453 872738

This part of the Cotswolds is not as well known as the northern uplands, but it is here that one finds the lovely deep valleys. The Amberley Inn has fine views of the Woodchester Valley and stands on the edge of Minchinhampton Common, an area of National Trust common land where cattle and horses roam freely. Adjacent to the hotel is Minchinhampton's old golf course. We were pleased to find that a recent extension to the inn had been constructed with such skill and taste that it enhanced the appearance of the attractively gabled Cotswold-stone building. Inside, one finds the charming *Culver Room*, furnished, like the restaurant, with brightly polished tables and this is an excellent setting for a private dinner party. Above this room, a spacious new bedroom has, like the other rooms, a bathroom, radio, telephone, television and beverage-making facilities. The atmosphere of the hotel is, however, still that of a traditional country inn, with large open fireplaces, oak panelling, cheery conviviality in the bars and friendly service. The standard of the food is consistently good. Sunday lunch here is a great social occasion and the *Amberley Bar* and the *Lounge Bar* are pleasant venues for meeting friends and enjoying light meals. The Amberley Inn is owned by the Price family, who also own The Hare and Hounds Hotel at Westonbirt. You will find the inn half a mile from the A46 Bath/Cheltenham road and seven miles from Junction 13 of the M5. The inn's 'Getaway Breaks' tariff and its golf, ballooning and riding packages are excellent value.

Weekly Terms from £315.00
Daily Terms from £46.00
Bed and Breakfast from £35.00
Bar Meal from £3.50
Lunch from £7.50 and A La Carte
Afternoon Tea from £1.25

Dinner from £15.50 and A La Carte
Service and VAT inclusive
Credit Cards–Access, American Express, Visa
4 Double, 7 Twin, 3 Single Bedrooms
All Rooms with Private Bathroom, TV,

Telephone, Radio, Baby-listening, Tea and Coffee-making Facilities. Hairdryer available on request. Open all year. Fully Licensed. Full Central Heating
Conference Facilities. Dogs allowed. Parking Facilities

Near Tetbury, Westonbirt–The Hare and Hounds Hotel
Westonbirt, Tetbury, Gloucestershire. GL8 8QL. Tel 066 688 233. Fax 066 688 241

Westonbirt, set in the southern Cotswolds, has many attractions. The world-famous arboretum, which has one of the finest collections of trees in the country, is a picture of flowering rhododendrons in the spring and a blaze of autumn colour in October. It lies close to the striking Hare and Hounds Hotel, which was established as an inn during the nineteenth century. The hotel is conveniently located off the A433 road in ten acres of woodland, trim lawns and gardens and has two all-weather tennis courts and a good squash court. Within, the tasteful decoration and distinctive furnishings of the front hall produce a warm and welcoming atmosphere. Under the active direction and professional expertise of the owners, Jeremy and Martin Price, everything runs smoothly at the hotel. Stay here and enjoy one of the excellent English or Continental speciality dishes in the relaxing atmosphere of the imposing restaurant, relish a choice drink from the balanced list of vintage wines and appreciate the consistently good service of the helpful staff. Many of the bedrooms have delightful views and all have private bathrooms. There are eight particularly pleasant rooms in the attractive garden cottage and adjacent coach house, just seventy-five yards from the main hotel entrance. Special rooms are available for dinner-dances, wedding receptions, family celebrations and seminars. A good choice of short-break holidays, including activities such as golf, riding and gliding, is offered.

Weekly Terms from £353.00
Daily Terms from £52.00
Bed and Breakfast from £39.50
Bar Meals from £3.50
Lunch from £10.75 and A La Carte
Dinner from £17.75 and A La Carte
Service and VAT inclusive
Credit Cards–Access, American Express, Visa

2 Family Rooms
12 Double, 12 Twin, 4 Single Bedrooms
All Rooms with Private Bathroom, TV,
Telephone, Radio, Baby-listening,
Tea and Coffee-making Facilities, Hairdryer
Open all Year.
Fully Licensed
Full Central Heating
Cocktail Bar

Games Room
Conference Facilities
Dogs allowed
Parking Facilities
Tennis, Croquet, Squash
Nearby: Golf, Fishing, Riding, Windsurfing, Jetskiing

Section 4: Hereford & Worcester

Chaddesley Corbett–Brockencote Hall Country House
Chaddesley Corbett, Nr Kidderminster, Worcs. DY10 4PY. Tel 0562 777876. Fax 0562 777872

'Visitors feel that they are welcomed to share the rich treasures, the outstanding *cuisine* and comfort of a most magnificent house which is a feast for the eyes, the mind and the palate'. No, not a quote from the hotel's brochure: the words of one of our seasoned inspecting couples. First credit for such a glowing report must go to Brockencote's owners, Alison and Joseph Petitjean (English and French, respectively), whose warm personalities are backed by their experience of managing some of Europe's leading hotels. Secondly, the quality of the accommodation-architecture, decor, furnishings and a relaxed, impeccable service-is of the highest possible standard. The third factor is the superb lakeside setting within seventy acres of landscaped grounds. As for location, nowhere can claim a more central position in England, offering easy day-tour exploration of no less than six counties. Between them, they provide a fascinating cross-section of historic buildings, a variety of picturesque terrains and numerous interesting centres ranging from quaint villages to large towns with shops and industries of equal value to tourists and business people. Not that one has to leave Chaddesley Corbett itself to sample the English heritage of this countryside. The village has its own general store, school, doctor, post office, butcher and blacksmith; Brockencote estate has been in existence for more than three hundred years. A perfect choice for the special sojourn of a lifetime.

Two Day Break from £125.00
Bed and Breakfast from £75.00
Lunch from £15.50 Table d'Hôte
Afternoon Tea from £1.50
Dinner from £19.50 Table d'Hôte
VAT inclusive

Credit Cards–Access, American Express, Diners Club, Visa. 1 Family Room
1 Single, 6 Double, 2 Twin Bedrooms
7 Private Bathrooms, 1 Private Shower Room. 8 Rooms with TV, Telephone, Radio, Baby-listening

Open from third week January to 26th December inclusive. Fully Licensed
Full Central Heating. Cocktail Bar
Conference Facilities. Children catered for
Dogs not allowed. Parking Facilities
Nearby: Golf, Riding, Shooting

Evesham–The Mill at Harvington
Anchor Lane, Harvington, Evesham, Worcestershire. WR11 5NR. Tel 0386 870688

Give or take a few miles, Evesham is equi-distant from Worcester, Cheltenham and Stratford-upon-Avon, and the National Exhibition Centre, next to Birmingham International Airport, is only thirty minutes away. Owners Simon and Jane Greenhalgh were known to us as skilful and enthusiastic hoteliers before they acquired and transformed this superior Georgian mansion into an attractive hotel, where all the comforts of gracious living are available to guests. Our inspector's report on this hotel is one of unqualified praise, including the statement that 'everything in the brochure is true'. Nestling in the fertile Vale of Evesham, the setting for the Mill at Harvington could hardly be more idyllic. The comfortable bedrooms overlook the gardens and river, abounding with wild life. The excellent menus are changed frequently, taking advantage of the bountiful local produce: indeed, the restaurant is already renowned for the excellence of its award winning *cuisine*. The charming dining room opens out on to the lawn and gardens which stretch down to the River Avon with rolling meadows beyond. The area is rich in history with many interesting places to visit whilst the Cotswold villages tempt the traveller to linger and explore. There is something for everyone in this quiet, civilised hotel–a perfect place for recharging one's batteries.

Weekly Terms on Application
Daily Terms from £46.50 (sharing Double/Twin, 2 or more nights)
Bed and Breakfast from £42.50 (sharing Double/Twin)
Lunch from £10.95
Dinner from £19.75 Table d'Hôte
Gratuities at Guest's discretion
VAT inclusive

Credit Cards–Access, American Express, Visa
12 Double, 3 Twin Bedrooms
All Rooms with Private Bathroom, TV, Telephone, Radio, Baby-listening, Tea and Coffee-making Facilities, Hairdryer, Books, Games, Mineral Water
Open all Year except Christmas
Residential and Restaurant Licence

Full Central Heating
Conference Facilities
Children over 10 years catered for
Dogs not allowed
Parking Facilities
Hard Tennis Court, Croquet, Outdoor Heated Swimming Pool, Fishing
Nearby: Golf, Riding

Section 4: Herefordshire & Worcester

Near Hereford, Much Birch–The Pilgrim Hotel Much Birch, Hereford. HR2 8HJ. Tel 0981 540742. Telex 35332 PILGRIM HOTEL

Tucked away in the shadow of the Black Mountains, between the Golden Valley of the River Dore and the winding splendour of the Wye, is one of the best country-house hotels in Herefordshire–The Pilgrim Hotel. Its name is derived from the ancient route (now the A49 road) which took pilgrims to the shrine of St Ethelbert at Hereford. The hotel stands well back from this road, in four acres of rich pastureland. Under the personal direction of the Gray family, the hotel provides a warm welcome, very comfortable accommodation and enticing dishes on the menus. You are given the opportunity to eat well from a fixed-price menu or you can choose one of the more exotic dishes on the à la carte menu. The lounge and dining-room, as well as the bedrooms, offer superb views of the surrounding rolling countryside. French doors open onto the well-kept lawns, which include a pitch-and-putt course, a putting green, a badminton court and a croquet lawn. Guests enjoy the personal service which the young and friendly staff enjoy giving and the hotel is a perfect place to stay for those who enjoy walking, playing golf and exploring the charming Herefordshire countryside. The spacious bedrooms are well appointed and are a good example of the enterprise of the proprietors, being fully equipped with modern amenities. This hotel is a gem to be enjoyed at any time of the year.

Golf Package Terms on Application	Gratuities at Guest's discretion	Open all Year. Fully Licensed
Weekly Terms from £247.00	VAT inclusive. Credit Cards–Access,	Full Central Heating. Cocktail Bar.
Daily Terms from £39.50	American Express, Diners Club, Visa	Conference Facilities
Bed and Breakfast from £52.00	3 Family Rooms, 2 Four Poster Rooms	Dogs allowed. Parking Facilities
Bar Lunch from £2.65	1 Single, 9 Double, 10 Twin Bedrooms	Croquet, Putting, Badminton, Golf
Lunch from £8.75 Table d'Hote	All Rooms with Private Bath/Shower	Nearby: Tennis, Squash, Swimming Pool,
Afternoon Tea from £1.50	Room, TV, Telephone, Radio,	Solarium, Sauna, Golf, Fishing, Riding,
Bar Supper from £3.50	Baby-listening, Tea and Coffee-making	Sailing, Shooting, Hang-gliding
Dinner from £18.50 and A La Carte	Facilities, Trouser Press, Hairdryer,	

Near Hereford, Ullingswick–The Steppes Ullingswick, Near Hereford. HR1 3JG. Tel 0432 820424

Set in the delightful Wye Valley, this tranquil seventeenth century country house hotel continues to delight our readers with its ancient timbers, inglenook fireplaces and low ceilings, skilfully combined with all the modern comforts expected from a first class establishment. The house is furnished throughout with good quality period furniture in keeping with its farmhouse origins. The bedrooms, each with *en suite* facilities, are individual in style and furnishings and provide every comfort for a warm and restful stay. The chef, whose reputation for culinary skill is now worldwide, offers imaginative dishes which range from medieval royal recipes through revived local dishes and Mediterranean delights to sophisticated modern French *cuisine*. Each candlelit dinner is memorable. However, a full *à la carte* menu of more familiar and vegetarian dishes is also available by prior arrangement. Particular emphasis is placed on presentation and the originality of the vegetable courses. A fine wine list complements the range of the menu. Many readers have spoken of the generous breakfasts including the extensive and interesting selection of cooked items. Ullingswick is an ideal centre from which to visit the lovely and historic Welsh Marches, the Black Mountains, Elgar's beloved Malvern Hills and numerous black and white villages and ancient churches. The nearby 'three choirs' cathedral cities of Hereford, Worcester and Gloucester provide a further wealth of interest. The resident proprietors of The Steppes are Henry and Tricia Howland.

Weekly Terms from £280.00	Facilities, Hairdryer, Personal Bar	Dogs allowed
Daily Terms from £40.00	Open from mid January to mid December,	Parking
Service Charge and VAT inclusive	Christmas and New Year	Nearby: Putting, Squash, Badminton,
1 Twin, 5 Double Bedrooms	Restaurant Licence	Swimming Pool,
All Rooms with Private Bathroom, TV,	Full Central Heating and Log Fires	Solarium, Golf, Fishing, Riding
Telephone, Radio, Tea and Coffee-making	Cocktail Bar	

Section 4: Herefordshire & Worcester

Ledbury—The Feathers Hotel High Street, Ledbury, Herefordshire. HR8 1DS. Tel 0531 2600/5266. Fax 0531 2001

It is so well preserved that one can hardly believe The Feathers to be genuine. Yet it was originally an Elizabethan house, to which a Jacobean top storey was added, an adjacent seventeenth-century manor house incorporated in Georgian times, and a wing built at the back during the Cromwellian period. Two hundred years ago it became a famous coaching inn and mail coaches were still stopping there in 1876. The guardians of this fine old inn have done a marvellous job in restoring and incorporating modern amenities into its ancient structure. Up deep carpeted stairs one finds eleven bedrooms, all *en suite* and modernly equipped, yet each full of individual character. To dine at The Feathers is to appreciate the more its mellow past. On an outward journey we enjoyed home-made soup and grilled darne of salmon in the oak-beamed *Fuggles Bar* (after John Fuggles who made Herefordshire famous with his hops). When returning a few days later we made our way to the elegant restaurant, with its excellent modern *cuisine*, impeccable service and award winning wines. It is quite clear that all the time-honoured arts of cooking, hospitality, cheerfulness and personal attention are given free rein at The Feathers. The market town of Ledbury was greatly loved by poets Browning and Wordsworth. John Masefield was born there and described it 'pleasant to the sight, fair and half-timbered houses black and white'. The Malvern Hills beckon walkers and ramblers and Hereford, Gloucester and Worcester are all equi-distant from here.

Bed and Breakfast from £59.50
Breakfast: English £5.50
Bar Meal from £4.95
Sunday Lunch from £11.00
Afternoon Tea from £2.75
Dinner from £12.00 and A La Carte

No Service Charge. VAT inclusive
Credit Cards—Access, American Express, Diners Club, Visa. 2 Family Rooms
6 Double, 5 Twin Bedrooms
All Rooms with Private Bathroom, TV, Telephone, Radio, Tea and Coffee-making

Facilities, Trouser Press, Hairdryer
Baby-listening on request
Open all Year. Fully Licensed
Full Central Heating. Conference Facilities
Children catered for. Dogs allowed
Parking Facilities. Night Porter

Ross-on-Wye—The Chase Gloucester Road, Ross-on-Wye, Herefordshire. HR9 5LH. Tel 0989 763161. Fax 0989 768330

'Behind the formal splendour of the architecture....you will know you are in a house where the elegance and craftsmanship of the past is valued'. These words are abstracted from the hotel's brochure which, incidentally, includes colour photographs whose reproduction is quite superb: and rightly so. Referring to the total restoration and refurbishment, our inspector wrote '....the whole concept shows not only excellent taste but also reflects the high skills of all those who worked to make it such a truly beautiful hotel'. Just a few minutes' walk from the centre of Ross-on-Wye, an attractive market town set on a red sandstone cliff, overlooking a dramatic bend of the river Wye, The Chase is a handsome Regency mansion standing in pleasant grounds. A rich and restful splendour throughout the hotel is nowhere more impressive than in the dining-room. Their chef favours a modern British approach with a continental influence and, whether your tastes lie towards Herefordshire beef and Barbary duckling, or towards mushroom and spinach strudel, you are assured of succulent and imaginative dishes based on the freshest possible ingredients. A warm informality is the keynote of the decor in the luxurious *en suite* bedrooms with their comprehensive modern amenities. Places to visit in this area, and the numerous activities available, are most usefully summarised in The Chase brochure. They range from candle-making to country craft museums, bird and butterfly parks to ballooning, railway centres, fishing, golfing, and walking in 'a landscape of infinite variety'. Altogether a rare treat.

Weekly Terms on Application
Daily Terms from £65.00
Bed and Breakfast from £50.00
Bar Lunch from £5.00
Lunch from £12.50 and A La Carte
Afternoon Tea from £2.50

Dinner from £19.50 and A La Carte
Gratuities at Guest's discretion. VAT inclusive. Credit Cards—Access, American Express, Diners Club, Visa
1 Family, 23 Double (2 Four Poster), 15 Twin Bedrooms. All Rooms with Private

Bathroom, TV, Telephone, Radio, Baby-listening, Tea and Coffee-making Facilities, Hairdryer. 8 Rooms with Trouser Press. Open all Year. Fully Licensed
Full CH. Conference Facilities
Children catered for. Dogs not allowed

Section 4: Hereford & Worcester

Near Ross-on-Wye,–The Old Court Hotel Symonds Yat West, Ross-on-Wye, Herefordshire. HR9 6DA. Tel 0600 890367. Fax 0600 890964

Note firstly the 'West' part of the address: two settlements, Symonds Yat East and West, are separated by the Wye and there is no bridge over the river at this point. Easily accessible, however, is this lovely Cotswold stone and creeper clad house (circa 1570), which lies within a few hundred yards of the A40 trunk road. If the house spells restfulness within, the three acres of landscaped gardens, with colourful flower beds, rookery and heated swimming pool, ensure seclusion. The Old Court Hotel was once the home of John Graves Simcoe, Governor General of Upper Canada and the founder of Toronto, and fittingly the rooms are beautifully proportioned and full of character. To complement these finer points, John and Elizabeth Slade, who also own The Paddocks Hotel nearby, have equipped three of the well appointed guest rooms with four-poster beds, and have added to the hotel an attractive conservatory and patio area. The original medieval *Court Room*, once the scene of raucous banquets, is now renowned for distinguished modern English *cuisine*, prepared with care by *Cordon Bleu* chef, Karen Jenkins. Her three-course candle-lit dinner menus are changed daily, reflecting the freshness of the ingredients she uses, and we found it impossible to resist freshly caught Wye Valley trout with prawns, almonds and pineapple, together with a bottle of the hotel's own label French dry white wine. Altogether a most excellent centre from which to explore the surrounding countryside.

Daily Terms from £37.50
Bed and Breakfast from £26.00
Breakfast: English £9.00
Bar Meal from £3.00
Afternoon Tea from £2.00
Dinner from £18.50
Service and VAT inclusive

Credit Cards—Access, American Express, Diners Club, Visa
17 Double, 3 Twin Bedrooms
14 Private Bathrooms
All Rooms with TV, Telephone, Radio, Tea and Coffee-making Facilities
Open all Year
Fully Licensed

Full Central Heating
Conference Facilities
Dogs allowed. Parking Facilities
Outdoor Swimming Pool
Nearby: Tennis, Croquet, Putting, Golf, Fishing, Riding, Sailing, Windsurfing, Water Skiing

Near Ross-on-Wye–Pengethley Manor Harewood End, Near Ross-on-Wye, Herefordshire. HR9 6LL. Tel 0989 87211. Fax 0989 87238

There are so many things we like about this expertly run country-house hotel that we cannot catalogue all of them. From its hillside position it commands magnificent views and is ideally situated for touring the Wye Valley, the Black Mountains and the Royal Forest of Dean. It is a fine Georgian building situated in fifteen acres of beautiful gardens and grounds which incorporate an outdoor heated swimming pool, nine hole golf course and a trout lake. Within, all is spotless and in the very best of taste. There is an old library and a cocktail bar. In the attractive restaurant modern English presentation service and crystal wine glasses complement the high-quality *cuisine*, which features fresh local produce, such as Herefordshire beef, Wye salmon and vegetables from the hotel's gardens. A *la carte* and *table d' hôte* menus are available seven days a week and the cellar contains a selection of around 150 wines. Some of the bedrooms bear names rather than numbers: The *Seymour Room* has a beautiful four-poster bed and the spacious *John Powell Room* has lovely antique furniture. In *Hentland House*, adjoining the main hotel, there is a ground-floor room, with a double and a single bed and a bathroom *en suite*, designed for disabled guests. The proprietors and their expert team, are indefatigable in anticipating the needs and comforts of their guests. Pengethley Manor is quietly situated four miles from Ross off the main Hereford road.

Weekly Terms from £385.00
Daily Terms from £65.00
Bed and Breakfast from £50.00
Bar Lunch from £3.50
Lunch from £16.00
Afternoon Tea from £2.50
Dinner from £21.00 and A La Carte
Service Charge and VAT inclusive

Credit Cards–Access, American Express, Diners Club, Visa
3 Family Rooms. 3 Suites
11 Double, 7 Twin Bedrooms
(4 Rooms with 4-poster Bed)
All Rooms with Private Bathroom, TV, Telephone, Radio, Baby-listening, Hairdryer
Open all year. Fully Licensed

Full Central Heating. Cocktail Bar
Conference Facilities. Dogs allowed
Parking Facilities. Croquet, Putting,
Outdoor Swimming Pool, Fishing
Nearby: Tennis, Squash, Badminton, Swimming Pool, Golf, Fishing, Riding, Shooting

Section 4: Hereford & Worcester

Near Ross-on-Wye, Wilton—Orles Barn Hotel and Restaurant
Wilton, Ross-on-Wye, Herefordshire. HR9 6AE. Tel 0989 62155

This seventeenth-century country house has a quiet appeal to those seeking a restful break in pleasant surroundings. The one and a half acres of attractive well-kept gardens and lawns and the open-air swimming pool make a picturesque setting. Inside, everything is immaculately maintained, from the main lounge and dining-room to the nine bedrooms, all of which have a private bath or shower room. The accent is on good English or continental cooking, using fresh local produce, and specialities include sirloin steak garni, baked trout with almonds, Herefordshire beef, Wye salmon and Spanish paella. Forty well-chosen wines, including a selection of fine Spanish Riojas are offered in the inviting cocktail bar. The friendly hosts, Julio and Marion Contreras, have established a reputation for providing a perfect rendezvous for families and friends who want to meet for a reunion or a celebration. The standards Mr and Mrs Contreras maintain are high and visitors to Orles Barn Hotel are enthusiastic about all the dishes, the reliable service, the fair prices and the unhurried atmosphere, which relaxes the most restless traveller. Overlooking the River Wye and, farther afield, the Welsh hills, the hotel is a paradise for anglers, walkers and for those who wish to explore this gracious area with its old timbered houses and historic villages. The castles of Goodrich, Raglan, Skenfrith and Chepstow are an easy car journey away.

Weekly Terms from £250.00	VAT inclusive. Credit Cards—Access,	Residential and Restaurant Licence
Bed and Breakfast from £35.00	American Express, Visa. 1 Family Room. 5	Full Central Heating. Cocktail Bar
Lunch from £9.95 Table d'Hôte	Double, 1 Single, 2 Twin Bedrooms. 5	Conference Facilities
Afternoon Tea from £5.00	Private Bathrooms. 3 Private Shower	Dogs allowed by arrangement
Bar Supper from £4.50	Rooms. All Rooms with TV, Tea and	Parking Facilities. Night Porter
Dinner from £10.50 and A La Carte	Coffee-making Facilities, Baby-listening,	Outdoor Heated Swimming Pool
Gratuities at Guest's discretion	Trouser Press, Hairdryer	Nearby: Tennis, Putting, Golf, Fishing,
	Open from December to October inclusive	Riding, Windsurfing

Upton-upon-Severn—The White Lion Hotel High Street,
Upton-upon-Severn, Worcester. WR8 0HJ. Telephone 06846 2551

Upton, about ten miles south of Worcester, is a pleasant market town with Saxon origins. A large white lion looks down from the impressive portico of The White Lion Hotel onto the High Street. The hotel's eighteenth-century facade is rather deceptive though, for the building does, in fact, date back to 1510 and retains the original oak beams. It is said to be the place where Sarah Siddons, the famous tragic actress, appeared in Upton. The convivial lounge bar contains fascinating military and local prints and the artistic theme continues with hunting and sporting prints in the peaceful residents' lounge. Old inn scenes are a feature of the *Tudor Restaurant*. Local specialities, such as Royal Double Gloucester omelette filled with smoked salmon, Avon trout with orange and herb stuffing and Fillets of Veal Tewkesbury, feature on the 'Bill of Fayre' menu. Fresh vegetables accompany these dishes and meals are rounded off with delicious home-made sweets, coffee and truffles. Vegetarian meals are also available. Appetising snacks and salads are served in the lounge, where maps and framed newspaper and magazine articles provide an interesting diversion. The ten comfortable and individual bedrooms are well equipped with private facilities. In the Georgian part of the hotel there is a suite with a splendid antique four-poster bed. The enthusiastic resident proprietors, Mr and Mrs R L Withey, ensure that guests receive professional service and the best traditional hospitality. The hotel is ideally situated for touring the Cotswolds, Malvern hills and Welsh Marches, as well as Tewkesbury and the city of Worcester.

Weekly Terms from £300.00	Gratuities at Guest's discretion	Telephone, Radio, Tea and Coffee-making
Daily Terms from £43.00 (Half Board)	VAT inclusive. Credit Cards—Access,	Facilities. Hairdryer available on request
Bed and Breakfast from £33.90	American Express, Diners Club, Visa	Open all year except Christmas
Lunch from £14.50 and A La Carte	5 Double, 1 Single, 4 Twin Bedrooms	Day/Boxing Day. Fully Licensed. Full
Afternoon Tea from £2.60	8 Private Bathrooms. 2 Private Shower	Central Heating. Cocktail Bar. Conference
Dinner from £14.50 and A La Carte	Rooms. All Rooms with Colour TV,	Facilities. Dogs allowed. Parking Facilities

Section 4: Hereford & Worcester

Vowchurch—The Croft Country House Hotel
Vowchurch, Herefordshire. HR2 0QE.. Tel 0981 550 226

Surrounded by stud farms, with superb views across the Golden Valley and wooded hillsides to the Black Mountains, this is a near-perfect example of the English country house. Situated in Vowchurch, so perilously near the boundary that Wales nearly claimed it, The Croft is a charming Country House Hotel of warmth and welcome, dating from the eighteenth century. It is a dream of a place and the Molinary family who run it are dedicated to good food, comfort and those little touches which make all the difference. There are two *table d'hôte* menus reflecting variety and the best of traditional British and modern *cuisine*. All dishes and sauces are freshly prepared and cooked to order, most of the vegetables and fruit being grown in their gardens and orchard. They are able to offer a comprehensive selection of wines and spirits to complement the meals as well as draught ale and lager from their small bar. Probably you will feel like staying there a while ... the most comfortable beds, pretty duvets, fitted carpets, period furniture and all those notions of modern refinement, including one's own bathroom. The gardens and paddocks are a special feature with mature trees, herbaceous borders, lawns, summer house and lily pond. It is all very restful and the views and sunsets are quite spectacular. In the heart of the Golden Valley, orchards, meadows and half-timbered farmsteads are flanked by gentle hills to the east and the Black Mountains to the west. You will find the Croft Country House Hotel ten miles west of Hereford on the B4348 Ross-on-Wye to Hay-on-Wye road.

Bargain Breaks available
Daily Terms from £34.50
Bed and Breakfast from £22.00
Packed Lunch upon request
Dinner from £12.50 Table d'Hôte
Gratuities at Guest's Discretion

VAT inclusive. Credit Cards–Access, Visa
1 Family Room/Half Tester Room
1 Suite, 2 Twin, 5 Double Bedrooms
All Rooms with Private Bathroom, TV, Radio, Tea and Coffee-making Facilities, Hairdryer, Mineral Water. Ironing Facilities

upon request. Open All Year. Residential and Restaurant Licence
Full Central Heating. Cocktail Bar
Guide Dogs only allowed. Parking Facilities
Tennis, Croquet. Nearby: Swimming Pool, Golf, Riding, Fishing

Worcester—The Diglis Hotel
Severn Street, Worcester. WR1 2NF. Tel 0905 353518

Diglis House was the family home of Benjamin Williams Leader, the Royal Academy artist (1831-1923) whose famous painting "February Fill Dyke" is a scene now often used on Christmas cards. John Constable, the famous landscape artist, was a close friend of the family and stayed regularly at Diglis House. Superbly situated on the banks of the River Severn, with terraced gardens and mature trees, the inherent charm of the beautiful surroundings must appeal to everyone. A few minutes' walk away is the magnificent cathedral, the celebrated Royal Worcester porcelain factory and, in either direction, riverside paths near the famous county cricket ground which are reached without crossing any bustling city roads. The Steamer Company offers river trips from April to December and the country house hotel, with its own moorings, welcomes families including their children and any pets, throughout the year. Currently, a major programme of refurbishment and alteration is taking place. In Worcester itself, without having to walk too far, the historic buildings to be seen include the timbered fifteenth-century Greyfriars Franciscan house and the eighteenth-century Guildhall with Civil War armour used in the battle of Worcester in 1651. Explore the surrounding countryside and see the hop fields, cider apple orchards and meadows grazed by burly Hereford cattle and then return to the excellent *cuisine* at the Diglis, with the spotless napery, fresh flowers and a staff to whom nothing is too much trouble.
Weekend Breaks Terms on Application

Daily Terms from £41.00 Single, £69.50 Double/Twin. Bed and Breakfast from £32.50 Single, £52.50 Double/Twin
VAT inclusive. 1 Family Room
2 Double, 5 Twin, 4 Single Bedrooms
3 Private Bathrooms

2 Private Shower Rooms
All Rooms with TV, Radio, Tea and Coffee-making Facilities
Open all Year. Fully Licensed
Full Central Heating
Conference Facilities. Children catered for

Dogs allowed at Management's discretion
Parking Facilities
Nearby: Tennis, Putting, Squash, Badminton, Swimming, Solarium, Sauna, Golf, Riding, Sailing

Section 4: Hertfordshire

Near Hitchin, Redcoats Green—Redcoats Farmhouse Hotel
Redcoats Green, Near Hitchin, Herts. SG4 7JR. Tel 0438 729500. Fax 0438 723322

Having read the word 'farmhouse' you may have decided that this is a place of simplicity and basic comforts. If you have, you will not be further from the truth. Redcoats is a hive (or rather, a series of hives) of industry. The farmhouse itself is a remarkable timber-framed structure, with lovely weathered tiles. The rich mouldings on the principal fireplace date Redcoats to the second half of the fifteenth century. Another 'bit' of Redcoats is the stable block, where eight of the bedrooms are located, fully equipped with colour television, direct-dial telephone and hospitality tray for beverages. The nodal point of the whole place, however, is the kitchen, constantly busy and the birthplace of some of the finest food you will find this close to London. In the lively lounge, full of rural artefacts and harness, and a profusion of roses, one can dine on the most satisfying traditional dishes complemented with wine by the glass. In the dining room or *Oak Room*, however, it is absolutely essential to book in advance. Diners travel for miles to enjoy the English specialities and continental *cuisine*. Fresh Scottish salmon, roast duck, fillet steak stuffed with smoked oysters, local game and more were all on offer whilst we were there. A splendid conservatory has just been added where where one can partake of breakfast, lunch or sample the new evening menu with its emphasis on shellfish. Peter Butterfield and his sister, Mrs Jackie Gainsford, the proprietors, could hardly be more kindly and welcoming, and their hotel, although it is close to the A1(M) exudes an air of peace and tranquility.

Bed and Breakfast from £48.00
Club Lunch from £10.50
Lunch from £23.00 A La Carte
Dinner from £23.00 and A La Carte
Gratuities at Guest's discretion
VAT inclusive. Credit Cards—Access, American Express, Diners club, Visa

2 Family Rooms. 1 Single, 9 Double, 2 Twin Bedrooms. 9 Private Bathrooms
3 Private Shower Rooms. All Rooms with TV, Telephone, Baby-listening, Tea and Coffee-making Facilities
2 Rooms with Radio, Hairdryer
3 Rooms with Trouser Press

Open All Year except Christmas. Fully Licensed. Full Central Heating
Cocktail Bar. Small conference Facilities
Children catered for. TV Lounge
Dogs allowed by arrangement
Parking Facilities
Nearby: Tennis, Squash, Swimming, Golf, Riding, Shooting, Gliding

St Albans-Sopwell House Hotel & Country Club
Cottonmill Lane, Sopwell, St. Albans, Hertfordshire. AL1 2HQ. Tel 0727 864477. Fax 0727 44741

Although only minutes away from the M1, M10 and M25 motorways, this luxurious and peaceful retreat has recently undergone additional refurbishment and redevelopment, making it a unique destination hotel. Within its twelve acres of grounds and landscaped gardens, there is now a Country Club with unparalleled health and leisure facilities, ranging from an ozone-purified indoor pool and fitness centre through to extensive treatments by highly qualified therapists. These comprehensive services are central to special interest breaks such as 'Stressbuster' and 'Romance and Rejuvenation', with facials and body treatments available. Whether or not these therapies are sought, the hotel offers unsurpassed levels of elegance and comfort in a true country house character. One may dine in style in their award-winning *Magnolia Conservatory* restaurant, or take a light healthy meal in *Bejerano's Brasserie*, overlooking the pool. For social occasions or business functions there are six private suites and the magnificent *St Albans* ballroom, catering for small parties or hundreds of guests. For relaxation, choose between croquet on the lawns or a browse through the well stocked library in the Music Room Lounge. We now commend Sopwell House even more highly than in previous years.

Room Rate from £67.50
Breakfast: English £7.95
Breakfast: Continental £5.95
Bar lunch from £2.75
Lunch from £14.75 and A La Carte
Afternoon Tea from £7.45
Dinner from £18.50 and A La Carte
Gratuities at Guest's discretion
VAT inclusive

Credit Cards–Access, American Express, Diners Club, Visa
92 Luxury Bedrooms (many with four-posters)
All Rooms with Private Bathroom, TV, Telephone, Radio, Tea and Coffee-making Facilities, Trouser Press, Hairdryer
Open all Year. Fully Licensed
Full Central Heating

Cocktail Bar. Conference Facilities
Children catered for. Dogs allowed.
Parking Facilities. Night porter
Indoor Swimming Pool, Sauna, Steam Room, Spa Bath, Fitness Studio, Health & Beauty Centre, Snooker, Hairdressing Salon. Nearby: Tennis, Squash, Golf, Riding

Section 4: Hertfordshire

St Albans–St Michael's Manor Hotel
Fishpool Street, St Albans, Hertfordshire. AL3 4RY
Tel 0727 864444. Telex 917647. Fax 0727 48909

The distinctive ecclesiastical history of St Albans, called 'Verulamium' by the Romans, gives the city a special appeal. St Alban was a Roman soldier who was beheaded for protecting a Christian fugitive and became known as Britain's first Christian martyr. The only English pope, Nicholas Breakspear, was born locally and educated in St Albans and the city has a cathedral and numerous pretty churches. This charming sixteenth-century manor house takes its name from the nearby church of St Michael and celebrated 400 years of history in 1986. It lies in five acres of grounds between the river and Fishpool Street, at the heart of this old city, but the views from the house are of sweeping lawns, of specimen trees and of a private lake with swans, mallard and coots. The situation, the architecture and the atmosphere of St Michael's Manor make it one of the loveliest hotels in England. Expert chefs and a team of highly trained staff are also important ingredients. So, too, is the eye for elegance which is apparent in the continual updating of the hotel. The main lounge and the restaurant are beautifully decorated with a Victorian conservatory extension to the restaurant and all the bedrooms have *en suite* facilities, colour television, radio, telephone, hairdryer and a wide range of thoughtful items designed to make one feel totally cosseted. Michael and Gladys Newling Ward, their Resident Director, Martin Richardson and Manager Andrew Billington, maintain an hotel of charm and contentment just twenty miles from London.

Bed and Breakfast from £80.00
Lunch from £17.00 and A La Carte
Dinner from £19.75 and A La Carte
Sunday Night Buffet Supper £14.00
Gratuities at Guest's discretion
VAT inclusive
Credit Cards–Access, American Express, Diners Club, Visa

12 Double (4 with 4-poster Bed), 7 Twin, 3 Single Bedrooms
All Rooms with Private Bathroom, TV, Telephone, Radio, Hairdryer, Trouser Press
Open all Year
Fully Licensed
Full Central Heating
Cocktail Bar.

TV Lounge
Conference Facilities
Children over 10 catered for
Small dogs allowed by arrangement
Parking Facilities
Night Porter
Nearby: Tennis, Putting, Indoor Swimming Pool, Solarium, Sauna, Golf

Section 4: Hertfordshire

Near Tring, Aldbury—Stocks Hotel & Country Club
Stocks Road, Aldbury, Near Tring, Hertfordshire. HP23 5RX
Tel 044285 341. Fax 044285 253

In a setting of refined luxury, the leisure amenities here are second to none. Four all-weather tennis courts (one floodlit), a full-size cricket pitch, greens for croquet and bowls, stables and three qualified groom/trainers for fifteen horses, a squash court, heated outdoor swimming pool, full-size snooker table, modern gymnasium with six machines, table tennis and the largest indoor heated jacuzzi in England, complete with solarium, sunbeds and sauna. The tariff here includes free use of all leisure facilities. Incredibly, within its twenty acres of parkland—surrounded by ten thousand acres of National Trust Estate—Stocks offers more! Balloon flights, blindfold driving, laser shooting and archery can be arranged, with corporate hospitality packages a speciality. Located in the heart of the Chiltern Hills, the hotel dates back to 1176 and, relatively recently, was for a time used as a training school by entrepreneur Victor Lownes for his Playboy 'Bunny' girls. Under the present ownership, extensive development has added conference facilities and an eighteen-hole (7,185 yards) golf course scheduled to come into full-time use in the spring of 1994. Complementing all these recreational possibilites are first-class comfort and a most excellent *cuisine*, including classical dishes, regional specialities, continental courses and special meals for light healthy eating and for vegetarians. After dinner, relax with a brandy by an open fire before retiring to one of the spacious, beautifully furnished bedrooms with every conceivable comfort. Everything is here for re-vitalising the busy executive and for relaxing the energetic holidaymaker.

Bed and Breakfast from £70.00
Bar Meal from £3.50
Lunch from £18.50 and A La Carte
Afternoon Tea from £3.50
Dinner from £18.50 and A La Carte
Service Charge 8% Food and Beverage
VAT inclusive
Credit Cards—Access, American Express, Diners Club, Visa

5 Suites. 1 Single, 3 Double, 9 Twin Bedrooms
13 Private Bathrooms
5 Private Shower Rooms
All Rooms with TV, Telephone, Radio, Hairdryer, Bathrobes in Suites
Open all Year. Fully Licensed
Full Central Heating
Cocktail Bar. TV Lounge. Games Room

Conference Facilities
Children catered for
Dogs not allowed
Parking Facilities
Night Porter
Tennis, Croquet, Squash, Outdoor Pool, Jacuzzi, Solarium, Sauna, Riding.
Shooting by arrangement
Nearby: Golf, Fishing

Section 4: Lincolnshire

Near Lincoln, Branston–Moor Lodge Hotel
Branston, Lincoln. LN4 1HU.
Tel 0522 791366. Fax 0522 794389

Drive northwards from Branston and one is soon enjoying splendid views of the twin spires of Lincoln's cathedral rising above the fens. Tens of thousands of tourists visit this ancient city each year (it was the fourth most important town in the realm at the time of the Norman Conquest) to view its historic castle, its walls and gates and the many lovely old houses. Branston is conveniently nearby, yet it seems remote from the crowds, and the Moor Lodge Hotel is a welcome discovery for anyone seeking a wide range of facilities and high standards in this pleasant district. The hotel is privately owned by Mr W Craddock and managed by Mr Bob Walker, who has done a remarkable job in reviving the hotel's fortunes. His ideas on furnishings and décor are in the best taste and we have little doubt that his ambition to move Moor Lodge into the four-star category will soon be achieved. We certainly look forward to returning there and enjoying once more the friendly environment and the very personal service. The *Arnhem Room* restaurant provides a tasteful setting for the excellent food and the well stocked wine cellar will delight connoisseurs. The hotel's facilities are exceptional for the area and include a large ballroom (attractively decorated in an ivory and gold motif), a good conference area and twenty-five well-equipped bedrooms. You will find this up-and-coming hotel three miles south east of Lincoln, on the B1188 road in the attractive village of Branston, with its stone cottages and small Saxon church.

Weekly Terms from £415.00
Bed and Breakfast from £59.50
Bar Lunch from £5.00
Lunch from £9.75 and A La Carte
Afternoon Tea from £4.60
Dinner from £16.30 and A La Carte
Gratuities at Guest's discretion

VAT inclusive. Credit Cards–Access, American Express, Diners Club, Visa
2 Family Rooms
10 Double, 9 Twin, 4 Single Bedrooms
22 Private Bathrooms
3 Private Shower Rooms
All Rooms with TV, Telephone, Tea and Coffee-making Facilities

5 Rooms with Hairdryer and Trouser Press
Open all Year. Fully Licensed
Full Central Heating. Cocktail Bar
Conference Facilities. Dogs allowed
Parking Facilities
Nearby: Tennis, Squash, Badminton, Swimming Pool, Sauna, Golf, Fishing

Section 4: Lincolnshire

Stamford—Garden House Hotel St. Martin's, Stamford, Lincolnshire. PE9 2LP. Tel 0780 63359. Fax 0780 63339

Although easily accessible from the A1 road, the whole of Stamford is a conservation area whose narrow streets and picturesque squares retain many fine stone buildings, predominantly in the Georgian style. In spite of pressures from the larger urban centres in the region, the town, once capital of the Fens, is largely a self-contained entity whose engineering products are well-known in many countries of the world. As its name suggests, there is a peaceful garden at the rear and a delightful flower filled conservatory, an ideal venue for wedding receptions. Parts of the Garden House Hotel date back to 1796 but it was only in 1985 that Richard and Janet Gorrie acquired an adjoining property enabling them to enlarge their hotel to twenty bedrooms, all with a private bathroom. Some of the larger rooms make ideal family accommodation, and children are made especially welcome. Because of the location, with a network of 'A' roads and so many attractive sites nearby, the hotel is as valuable to the travelling businessperson as it is appealing to the touring holidaymaker. Catering is to a very high standard on a most moderate tariff, with an excellent vegetarian choice, and carefully selected wines to complement the appetising traditional food. Back-up facilities are available for such business functions as conferences and seminars. Lovers of the great outdoors, sports enthusiasts, photographers and historians will all find much of exceptional interest all around Stamford, most notably the magnificent Burghley House, and your hosts are more than happy to assist with any information. For those with a sense of adventure, the Peterborough Parachute Club holds week-end courses at Sibson!

Weekend breaks (min 2 nights), all August, £35 per night incl. £10 towards a la carte menu. Bed and Breakfast from £40.00. Bar Meal from £2.65. Lunch from £17.15 A La Carte. Afternoon Tea from £3.45. Dinner from £17.15 A La Carte	Gratuities at Guest's discretion VAT inclusive. Credit Cards—Access, American Express, Visa 1 Family Room. 9 Double (1 4-poster), 8 Twin, 2 Single Bedrooms All Rooms with Private Bathroom, TV,	Telephone, Radio, Baby-listening, Tea and Coffee-making Facilities, Hairdryer. 2 Rooms with Trouser Press Open all Year. Fully Licensed. Full Central Heating. Cocktail Bar. Conference Facilities Children catered for. Dogs allowed

Near Lincoln, Washingborough—Washingborough Hall Country House Hotel
Church Hill, Washingborough, Lincoln. LN4 1BE. Telephone 0522 790340

The cathedral city of Lincoln lies just a few minutes' drive away, yet here, in flat farmland, through which runs the River Witham, one could not wish for a more rural outlook. At Washingborough Hall, Brian and Mary Shillaker have created a most comfortable and charming hotel in what was originally the manor house and later the rectory of this lovely Lincolnshire village. It is quite clear to all who call here that these caring owners take a very keen interest in the welfare of their guests. The menu is varied, the wine list is very good and the atmosphere throughout is most relaxing. The surrounding gardens are also quite beautiful and are the pride of Mary Shillaker. She takes a particular interest in fuchsias and there are many varieties to admire. The grounds cover three acres in all and include lawns, woodland and a heated open-air swimming pool. Within this house of character, each room has an individual charm, the four-poster suite with its beautiful bathroom featuring a corner spa bath, and the *Bamboo Suite* being especially delightful. Any guest staying here will be most comfortable, for the bedrooms are well equipped, with a private bath or shower, colour television, radio, telephone, hairdryer and beverage-making facilities. Washingborough Hall can be highly recommended to those who seek good standards, a restful environment and a very personal welcome. There is fishing, golf and walking in the vicinity and Belvoir Castle, Market Rasen, Burleigh House and, of course, Lincoln are all within easy reach.

Weekly Terms from £280.00 Bed and Breakfast from £34.50 Bar Meal from £5.95 Lunch from £7.50 Afternoon Tea from £1.50 Dinner from £13.50 and A La Carte	Gratuities at Guest's discretion VAT inclusive. Credit Cards—Access, American Express, Diners Club, Visa 5 Double, 5 Twin, 2 Single Bedrooms 9 Private Bathrooms. 3 Private Shower Rooms. All Rooms with TV, Telephone,	Radio, Tea and Coffee-making Facilities, Trouser Press, Hairdryer Open all Year. Fully Licensed Full Central Heating. Conference Facilities Dogs allowed. Parking Facilities Croquet, Outdoor Swimming Pool

Section 4: Norfolk

Blakeney—The Blakeney Hotel Blakeney, Holt, Norfolk. NR25 7NE
Tel 0263 740797. Fax 0263 740795

There are not many hotels on the Norfolk coastline with such an animated marine outlook. The Blakeney Hotel is a traditional, privately owned, friendly hotel with magnificent views across the estuary and salt marshes to Blakeney Point, which is an area of outstanding natural beauty owned by the National Trust. From the restaurant, the main lounge and many of the bedrooms, the holiday scene is of multi-coloured craft either bobbing and tugging at their moorings or gliding in and out past Blakeney Point. The hotel offers a wide choice of accommodation. All rooms have private bathroom, colour television and tea and coffee-making facilities. The cocktail bar and restaurant, which serves a good fresh food, both overlook the quay. There are comfortable lounges and fine south-facing private gardens in which to relax, whilst, for the more energetic, there is a heated indoor swimming pool, spa bath, sauna and mini-gym. Other facilities include snooker and a games room. There is a whole host of recreations at Blakeney to suit the family on holiday, including birdwatching, although water sports (sailing, fishing and swimming) are main activities. Judging by the number of golf clubs one sees at the hotel, it is obvious that this area also has great appeal for the golfer. North Norfolk has sandy beaches, pretty villages and market towns, Sandringham and other stately homes and the lovely city of Norwich is only an hour's drive away.

Weekly Terms from £343.00 Daily Terms from £54.00 (min 2 nights) Bed and Breakfast from £47.00 Lunch from £7.50 Dinner from £16.00 Gratuities at Guest's discretion VAT inclusive. Credit Cards–Access, American Express, Diners Club, Visa	2 Family Rooms. 2 Suites 23 Double, 25 Twin, 10 Single Bedrooms 58 Private Bathrooms. 2 Private Shower Rooms. All Rooms with TV, Telephone, Radio, Baby-listening, Tea and Coffee-making Facilities. 30 Rooms with Trouser Press and Hairdryer. Open all Year. Fully Licensed. Full Central Heating.	Cocktail Bar Games Room. Conference Facilities Children catered for. Dogs allowed Parking Facilities. Night Porter Indoor Heated Swimming Pool, Sauna, Spa Bath, Mini-gym, Billiards Nearby: Tennis, Squash, Badminton, Golf, Fishing, Riding, Sailing, Windsurfing,

Blakeney—Manor Hotel Blakeney, Holt, Norfolk. NR25 7ND.
Tel 0263 740376

This peaceful sixteenth-century manor, overlooking a free harbour and saltings, lies mid-way between Wells-next-the-Sea and Sheringham on Norfolk's north coast. It offers safe bathing for the children, sea fishing trips, enjoyable walks and is the natural sanctuary for a profusion of wild birds. Also widely patronised are the nearby riding stables and three golf courses. For the 'nineteenth hole' one could not wish for a more convivial setting than the hotel's Manor Bar, blessed with Real Beer from an air-conditioned cellar. The dining areas with warm decor are enhanced by attractive views through a number of windows. The restaurant is a relaxing room in which to enjoy local fish, crustaceans and free-range poultry. Ancient flint walls afford some privacy for guests sitting out or strolling round the well-kept hotel gardens; at the same time one can delight in expansive vistas over the quays, creeks and dunes. The free harbour in front of the Manor Hotel makes it wholly feasible for guests to bring their sailing boats with them, the varied coastline and Blakeney Point adding interest to this popular sport. For those preferring to explore by land, there are the interest and appeal of Holkham Hall, Walsingham Abbey and-close by-the Shirehall Museum, Kelling Park, Felbrigg Hall and the Shell Museum. When finally you wish to put your feet up, every one of the *en suite* bedrooms has a colour television installed.

Bed and Breakfast from £27.00 Bar Lunch from £1.85 Dinner from £13.50 and A La Carte Service Charge and VAT inclusive No Credit Cards accepted 2 Family Rooms 8 Double, 21 Twin, 5 Single Bedrooms 34 Private Bathrooms	2 Private Shower Rooms All Rooms with TV, Telephone, Radio, Tea and Coffee-making Facilities Open All Year except for three weeks including Christmas Fully Licensed Full Central Heating Small Conference Facilities	Children over 10 years catered for Dogs allowed Parking Facilities Sailing, Windsurfing, Water Skiing, Shooting Nearby: Tennis, Badminton, Fishing, Riding, Sailing, Bowling

Section 4: Norfolk

Gorleston-on-Sea—The Cliff Hotel Cliff Hill, Gorleston-on-Sea, Great Yarmouth, Norfolk. NR31 6DH. Tel 0493 662179. Fax 0493 653617

At certain times of the year Great Yarmouth does not seem to rest, but across the River Yare there is a quieter place to stay, namely, Gorleston-on-Sea. There is a pleasant golf course here and the sands are broad and clean. Gorleston's greatest attraction for us, however, is the aptly named Cliff Hotel, which has a superb elevated position overlooking the harbour mouth and the sea. Quiet, comfortable and up to date, the hotel has a wide range of very stylish facilities which attract the holidaymaker, the businessman and those seeking a venue for a special occasion. The bedrooms are equipped with all the expected modern facilities, such as bath or shower rooms *en suite*, colour television, telephones, baby-listening and hairdryers, and VIP room service is available twenty-four hours a day. The *Chandelier Dining Room*, which epitomises the elegance one finds throughout the public rooms, is served by a team of chefs who use the freshest produce and offer a wide selection of English dishes. A comfortable lounge and luxury bedroom extension have just been opened whilst conference rooms for up to 200 people and three bars complete the comprehensive range of amenities to be found at The Cliff Hotel. All year round the hotel welcomes a steady flow of people seeking good food, comfort and value for money. To assist this trend the hotel offers special weekend terms and 'Getaway Breaks'. The Cliff Hotel at Gorleston-on-Sea is a most hospitable place–you will be happy here, for Mr R Scott and his team will do everything in their power to see that you are.

Weekly Terms from £271.00
Bed and Breakfast from £62.00
Lunch from £13.50 and A La Carte
Dinner from £13.50 and A La Carte
Gratuities at Guest's discretion
VAT inclusive
Credit Cards–Access, American Express, Diners Club, Visa
1 Suite, 5 Family Rooms

14 Double, 6 Twin, 12 Single Bedrooms
33 Private Bathrooms
6 Private Shower Rooms
All Rooms with TV, Telephone, Radio, Baby-listening, Tea and Coffee-making Facilities, Hairdryer. 20 Rooms with Trouser Press
Open all Year. Fully Licensed
Full Central Heating. Cocktail Bar

Small Conference Facilities
Dogs not allowed
Parking Facilities. Night Porter
Nearby: Tennis, Croquet, Putting, Squash, Badminton, Swimming, Solarium, Sauna, Golf, Fishing, Riding, Sailing, Windsurfing, Water Skiing, Shooting

Near Hunstanton–Titchwell Manor Hotel Titchwell, Brancaster, King's Lynn, Norfolk. PE31 8BB. Tel 0485 210221. Fax 0485 210104

Lovers of the great outdoors will be well suited here, whether historians, walkers, cyclists, sportsmen, artists or photographers. This is an area boasting above average sunshine and below average rainfall, even in winter. In their helpful brochure, the hotel itemises the numerous stately homes, golf clubs, bird and wildlife reserves in the area, together with details of horse riding, theatres and places of historic interest. The resident proprietors offer caring attention for the disabled, the ground-floor rooms being suitable for wheelchairs. With its large walled garden, and glorious views of the beach and sea, this hotel is ideally situated for those wishing to explore all the history and natural beauty of Norfolk's north-west coast. The extensive menus in the dining-room offer true English fare, using fresh produce, and local game and seafood in season. Packed lunches and attractive bar meals are also available. We have received good reports of the catering from local residents as well as from visitors. 'Getaway Breaks' are bookable throughout the year (excluding, of course, Bank Holiday weekends) and on these, as for normal reservations, children and pets are made welcome. Inside the hotel, a bright and unpretentious decor is complemented by the informal but efficient service given by the staff. When staying at Titchwell Manor, be sure to visit the country home of HM The Queen at Sandringham, only ten miles away. Also note that every church in the area is of architectural and historic interest.

Weekly Terms from £300.00
Daily Terms from £42.00
Bed and Breakfast from £35.00
Room Rate from £30.00
Bar Meal from £3.95
Afternoon Tea from £1.50
Dinner from £15.95 and A La Carte
Gratuities at Guest's discretion
VAT inclusive

Credit Cards–Access, American Express, Diners Club, Visa
2 Family Rooms. 5 Double, 6 Twin, 3 Single Bedrooms
10 Private Bathrooms, 6 Private Shower Rooms. All Rooms with TV, Telephone, Radio, Baby-listening, Tea and Coffee-making Facilities, Hairdryer
Open All Year. Fully Licensed

Full Central Heating
Cocktail Bar
Children catered for
Dogs allowed by arrangement
Parking Facilities
Nearby: Golf, Fishing, Riding, Sailing, Windsurfing, Water Skiing, Birdwatching

Section 4: Norfolk

Near King's Lynn, South Wootton—Knights Hill Hotel
South Wootton, King's Lynn, Norfolk. PE30 3HQ.. Tel 0553 675566. Fax 0553 675568

There is a self-sufficiency about Norfolk and Norfolk people. It is one of the few counties in England which one does not naturally pass through on the way to somewhere else. Knights Hill Hotel is unusual, too. In fact, there are few places like it in the whole country. It is simply... a village, but in miniature, which comprises a country-house hotel and *Garden* restaurant; the *Farmer's Arms* pub and restaurant; *Knights Barn*—a conference, banqueting and exhibition centre; and the *Knights Hill Health and Leisure Club*. Within this self-sufficient village there is enough choice to satisfy almost every taste and temperament. The hotel provides accommodation in a country-house style, whilst the courtyard appartments behind the *Farmer's Arms* have a more traditional appeal. All, however, boast an integral bathroom, colour television, radio, direct-dial telephone, hairdryer, trouser press and beverage-making facilities. We noted that children under the age of fifteen are accommodated free when sharing their parents' room. Choice is also the keyword with the catering, with Real Ales and tasty pub meals being available in the *Farmer's Arms*, traditional fare in the restaurant, and a fine range of dishes on offer in the *Garden Restaurant*. Guests staying in any of the accommodation automatically receive temporary membership of the Health and Leisure Club. With its all-weather tennis courts, indoor swimming pool, sauna, spa bath and fitness studio, the club offers something for everyone. The conference, banqueting and exhibition centre has a suite of rooms so flexible they can serve from four to 400 people.

Bed and Breakfast from £46.00 per person
Bar Meal from £3.75. Lunch from £10.00
Dinner from £14.25 and A La Carte
No Service Charge. VAT inclusive
Credit Cards—Access, American Express, Diners Club, Visa

39 Double, 13 Twin, 6 Single Bedrooms
All Rooms with Private Bathrooms, TV, Telephone, Radio, Tea and Coffee-making Facilities, Trouser Press, Hairdryer
Open all Year
Fully Licensed

Full Central Heating
Cocktail Bar
Conference Facilities
Children catered for
Dogs allowed by arrangement. Parking Facilities. Extensive Leisure Facilities

Near King's Lynn —Congham Hall Country House Hotel
Grimston, King's Lynn, PE32 1AH. Tel 0485 600250. Fax 0485 601191

Do try to visit Congham Hall. Spend two days here for refreshment or a week for complete relaxation. Set in country which is flat and where the dominating feature is the sky, Congham Hall's forty acres of private parkland are verdant and full of interest. There are paddocks, orchards and herb gardens, and at the centre is the lovely Georgian manor house, which Christine and Trevor Forecast have converted into one of the best country-house hotels in Britain. They have created a small elegant retreat, very English in character, where they provide the highest standards of *cuisine* and service. Breakfasts are entirely English (there is no Continental-style breakfast) and lunch can be taken in the restaurant or, on fine days, one can enjoy the hotel's popular 'Pimms on the Lawn' salad lunch. The dinner menus created by Murray Chapman are most imaginative. His speciality dishes are quite outstanding and one cannot eat here without feeling a sense of occasion. The hotel itself is most tastefully decorated and provides a high degree of comfort and amenities. The house contains a superb board room for meetings, a spacious cocktail bar and lounge and even a jacuzzi. Christine and Trevor Forecast's policy of never accepting less than the best has brought their hotel international recognition in a remarkably short period of time. Congham Hall lies close to the village of Grimston, which you should head for in preference to Congham village itself.

Weekend Breaks available
Bed and Breakfast from £80.00 Single
Bar Lunch from £5.00
Lunch from £13.50 and A La Carte
Dinner from £30.00 and A La Carte
Gratuities at Guest's discretion

VAT inclusive. Credit Cards—Access, American Express, Diners Club, Visa
2 Suites. 1 Single, 4 Double, 7 Twin Bedrooms. All Rooms with Private Bath/Shower Room, TV, Telephone, Radio, Hairdryer, Books, Fresh Fruit. Open all Year.

Residential and Restaurant Licence
Full Central Heating. Cocktail Bar
Conference Facilities. Children over 12 years catered for
Dogs allowed in kennels only
Parking Facilities. Night Porter

Section 4: Norfolk

North Walsham—Beechwood Hotel 20 Cromer Road, North Walsham, Norfolk. NR28 0HD. Tel 0692 403231

In every county with a seaboard we look for one or more towns which are an easy car drive from the sea. The old market town of North Walsham, dominated by the ruined tower of its church, is just five miles from the coast, seven miles from the Broads and fourteen miles from the cathedral city of Norwich. Being such a nodal point, it is not surprising that it caught our eye, as did the Beechwood Hotel, which is only a few minutes' walk from the town centre. The setting of the hotel in a garden of beautifully maintained shrubs and trees is most attractive. The Beechwood is a spacious Georgian house, built at the turn of the eighteenth century, which has been developed and extended over the years. Ernest and Jenny Townsend came here in 1972, saw the possibilities and converted the house into a small hotel. They have been attracting discerning guests ever since. There are just eleven bedrooms, all with pleasing views and modernised for comfort. First-class home cooking is a feature of the four-course dinners and the full English breakfasts are ample by any standard. Because of its relaxed and convivial atmosphere the Beechwood Hotel struck us as being an excellent place for families and, outside the school holidays, ideal for those wanting a peaceful and refreshing time.

Weekly Terms from £148.00
Daily Terms from £28.00
Bed and Breakfast from £22.00
Dinner from £10.00 Table d'Hote
Gratuities at Guest's discretion
VAT inclusive
5 Family Rooms
1 Single, 2 Double, 3 Twin Bedrooms

3 Private Bathrooms
4 Private Shower Rooms
All Rooms with Tea and Coffee-making Facilities
Hairdryer available on request
Open all Year except Christmas
Residential Licence
Full Central Heating

TV Lounge
Games Room
Children over 5 years catered for
Dogs allowed
Parking Facilities
Nearby: Tennis, Squash, Golf, Fishing, Riding

Norwich—The Annesley House Hotel
6-8 Newmarket Road, Norwich, Norfolk. NR2 2LA. Tel 0603 624553

Recently extended, this excellent and friendly hotel in a pretty, conservation area of Norwich now has a total of twenty-four bedrooms. It comprises three historic Grade 2 listed Georgian buildings, two of which are connected by a conservatory which houses a fifty year old grape vine. During their seven year ownership, David and Jill Reynolds have made numerous changes and improvements, the latest being further upgrading of all bedrooms to an exceptionally high standard. The *en suite* bedrooms have co-ordinated fabrics and wall coverings and are comprehensively equipped with all modern comforts. In their independently commended restaurant with its softly contrasting colours and thoughtful lighting scheme, diners have an extensive choice from *à la carte* and *table d'hôte* menus, all at most reasonable prices. A wide selection of snacks in the comfortable lounge bar awaits those not dining in the restaurant. Conveniently close to the city centre, the location is also ideal as a base for exploring the Norfolk Broads or visiting some of the many coastal resorts. Opposite the Hotel is the Norfolk and Norwich Hospital, Norwich City College is within easy walking distance and the University of East Anglia is only a few minutes' away by car. On your return to Annesley House, according to the time of year, enjoy the sunny and secluded patio or relax by the warmth of a log fire.

Bed and Breakfast from £50.00
Bar Meal from £5.50
Dinner from £13.50 and A La Carte
Gratuities at Guest's discretion
VAT inclusive
Credit Cards—Access, American Express,

Diners Club, Visa
3 Family Rooms
12 Double, 2 Twin, 7 Single Bedrooms
All Rooms with Private Bathroom, TV, Telephone, Hospitality Tray, Trouser Press, Iron and Board, Hairdryer

Open all Year
Residential and Restaurant Licence
Full Central Heating. Cocktail Bar
Dogs not allowed. Parking Facilities
Nearby: Putting, Squash, Badminton, Swimming, Solarium, Sauna, Golf, Fishing

Section 4: Norfolk

Norwich—Hotel Nelson Prince of Wales Road,
Norwich, Norfolk. NR1 1DX. Tel 0603 760260. Fax 0603 620003

The waters of the Wensum wash against its foundations, for Hotel Nelson, named after Norfolk's greatest son, Admiral Horatio Nelson, stands on the riverbank opposite Norwich's railway station. In this very English of cities, with its castle, cathedral and thousand years of history, Hotel Nelson is uncompromisingly modern, yet it in no way seems out of place. Perhaps, this is because it looks so welcoming. One certainly receives traditional high standards of service there, and, of course, East Anglian folk do make very good hosts. It did not surprise us at all when the hotel won top place in our competition, judged in conjunction with the British Tourist Authority, to find the hotel in Britain which is doing more than any other to make its overseas visitors feel especially welcome. On the material side, the hotel offers bedrooms equipped with private bathroom and just about every other piece of up-to-date paraphernalia one associates with contemporary comfort, including refrigerators with fresh milk. Some of the rooms even boast balconies and spa baths! The theme continues in the air-conditioned *Trafalgar Room*, which has a broad range of dishes, from vegetarian to traditional English. The *Quarter Deck Buttery* serves light meals and is most attractive, with its outlook directly onto the river. Conferences and receptions are accommodated in a medley of five banqueting rooms, each well equipped.

Daily Terms from £45.00
Bed and Breakfast from £74.00
Bar Meal from £4.00
Lunch from £9.95 and A La Carte
Afternoon Tea from £3.50
Dinner from £13.50 and A La Carte
Service and VAT inclusive

Credit Cards—Access, American Express, Diners Club, Visa
3 Four-poster Suites
42 Double, 50 Twin, 26 Single Bedrooms
All Rooms with Private Bathroom, TV, Telephone, Radio, Baby-listening, Tea and Coffee-making Facilities, Refrigerator, Fresh Milk, Hairdryer, Trouser Press

Open all Year. Fully Licensed
Full Central Heating. 3 Lifts
2 Cocktail Bars
Conference Facilities
Children catered for
Dogs not allowed
Parking Facilities. Night Porter
Private River Quay

Sheringham—The Beacon Hotel
1 Nelson Road, Sheringham, Norfolk. NR26 8BT. Tel 0263 822019

The geography of Norfolk's northern coast changes at Sheringham. To the east is high ground where the land ends abruptly to form tumbling cliffs, whilst westwards are the salt marshes, teeming with bird life and a magnet to ornithologists. We, however, like most other visitors to Sheringham, come for the equable climate and the resort's safe bathing and excellent golf courses. The Beacon Hotel is also a major inducement, for it is situated in its own grounds by the sea (the views are superb) and yet the town is only a few minutes' walk away. There are only six bedrooms, a small pleasing bar, a lounge with colour television and a most attractive dining-room for twelve diners. Mr and Mrs Richard Gausden provide the atmosphere of friendliness and efficiency and the personal attention which mean so much. They sum up their aims by the alliterative: 'cleanliness, comfort and *cuisine*' and we would say they achieve these aims. We would also stress the hotel's prime cliff-top situation, which provides such a memorable vista and the relaxed house-guest feeling one enjoys within. Although we tend to travel constantly with professional aims in mind, the coastal strip between Weybourne and Cromer will invariably induce us to take a breather from our wanderings: the Poppy Line, between Weybourne and Sheringham, puffs away for enthusiasts, Cromer offers all the pleasures of a charming resort and the Runtons sit between the sea and the highest ground in Norfolk.

Weekly Terms from £189.00

Daily Terms from £30.00
Gratuities at Guest's discretion
Credit Cards–Access, Visa
3 Double, 2 Twin Bedrooms
2 Single Bedrooms
4 Private Shower Rooms

All Rooms with Tea and Coffee-making Facilities
Open from May to September
Residential Licence
Full Central Heating
Cocktail Bar. TV Lounge

Children not catered for
Dogs not allowed. Parking Facilities
Nearby: Putting, Swimming, Golf, Fishing, Riding, Sailing, Water Skiing, Windsurfing, Birdwatching

Section 4: Norfolk

Old Hunstanton—Caley Hall Motel and Restaurant
Old Hunstanton, Norfolk. PE36 6HH
Tel 0485 533486

A ten-minute walk from Caley Hall takes one to the wide beaches of Old Hunstanton, on the very tip of the north-west coast of Norfolk, some one and a half miles from the busier town of Hunstanton itself. Carolyn and Clive King, no newcomers to 'Let's Halt Awhile', have developed their motel from a seventeenth-century manor house, whose outbuildings are now the restaurant and bar, and to which have been added twenty-five chalet rooms. Most of these, and the associated amenities, are at ground level and suitable for wheelchairs. Exceptionally good standards are maintained in this motel, with a relaxed and friendly atmosphere throughout. Their intimate restaurant, which is under the personal direction of Clive King, offers a three course *table d'hôte* dinner menu at a most moderate cost. All chalets have television, private bathrooms, tea-making facilities, fitted carpets and full heating. Four of them, for family occupation, have two interconnecting rooms. Caley Hall, is a convenient and comfortable base from which to visit the many attractions of this area. The Queen's country estate, at Sandringham, is just seven miles away. Also within easy reach is the boyhood home of Lord Nelson at Burnham Thorpe, the magnificent Palladian home of the Earl of Leicester-Holkham Hall, the historic architecture and Tuesday market at King's Lynn, and the famed National Trust bird sanctuary on Scolt Head Island, accessible from Brancaster Staithe.

Weekly Terms from £234.00
Daily Terms from £39.75
Bed and Breakfast from £27.00
Lunch £12.75 Table d'Hôte
Dinner £12.75 Table d'Hôte

Gratuities at Guest's discretion
VAT inclusive
Credit Cards—Access, Visa
4 Family Rooms
8 Double, 8 Twin, 4 Single Bedrooms
All Rooms with Private Bathroom,

TV, Tea and Coffee-making Facilities
Open all Year
Full Central Heating
Children catered for
Parking Facilities

Section 4: Norfolk

Sheringham–The Beaumaris Hotel
15 South Street, Sheringham, Norfolk. NR26 8LL. Tel 0263 822370

Fishing boats colour the sand and shingle beach at Sheringham, a town well known for its Poppy Line private railway and its golf course–the finest in Norfolk. If you would rather not live there like Canute, with the waves lapping at your feet, we would strongly recommend this very pleasant hotel, which is situated in South Street. It is very easily one of the most attractive small hotels we have visited. Three generations of the same family have ensured that The Beaumaris Hotel has maintained its up-to-the-minute appeal and a warm friendly atmosphere. Most of the bedrooms have *en suite* facilities, the dining room and lounge bar are very attractive rooms, the kitchens are a pleasure to visit and the whole place is beautifully furnished and scrupulously clean. The ground floor suites have been specially designed to accommodate wheelchairs and, as an adjunct to the English *cuisine*, special diets are catered for. We called here recently for lunch. The food was very good, deftly served and reasonably priced and was made all the more enjoyable by the pleasant view of the hotel's well tended garden. Being situated very near the town centre and the sea, but tucked away in a quiet road, The Beaumaris makes for a restful holiday.

All Prices pertain to 1992	Credit Cards—Access, American Express,	Fully Licensed. Full Central Heating
Weekly Terms from £245.00	Diners Club, Visa	Cocktail Bar. TV Lounge
Daily Terms from £36.00	5 Family Rooms. 9 Double, 9 Twin, 7	Conference Facilities
Bed and Breakfast from £30.00	Single Bedrooms	Children catered for
Bar Lunch from £1.60	17 Private Bathrooms	Dogs allowed
Lunch from £8.95	5 Private Shower Rooms	Parking Facilities
Afternoon Tea from £1.00	All Rooms with TV, Telephone, Radio,	Nearby: Tennis, Putting Squash,
Dinner from £13.95	Baby-listening, Tea and Coffee-making	Badminton, Swimming, Solarium Sauna,
Gratuities at Guest's discretion	Facilities	Golf, Fishing, Riding, Sailing, Windsurfing
VAT inclusive	Open from 1st February to 18th December	

Have you returned your membership form?
By simply completing and returning to us the registration card inserted in this book you will automatically become a 1993 member of the Ashley Courtenay Circle , an invaluable link between author and reader. For members, we compile and revise each year special listings of hotels which offer particular amenities, such as a sauna, swimming pool, golf course (or adjacent), four-poster beds, facilities for the disabled, special Christmas programmes, vegetarian dishes, non-smoking areas and self-catering facilities. We can even direct you to hotels which are especially pleased to receive young children and dogs. These lists are free of charge. Just send a stamped addressed envelope.

Section 4: Northamptonshire

Near Northampton, Weston Favell—Westone Moat House
Ashley Way, Weston Favell, Northampton. NN3 3EA. Tel 0604 406262. Fax 0604 415023

Set in its own grounds overlooking a picturesque terrace and lawn, is Westone Moat House-a fine country house which was built at the turn of the century as a home for the Sears family. It is now a lovely hotel providing sixty six luxury bedrooms, all of which have a private bathroom, satellite colour television with video channel, telephone, radio, trouser press, hairdryer and tea and coffee-making facilities. From the lounge, guests can enjoy lovely views across the lawns where one can play croquet on fine afternoons. On more chilly evenings a cosy fire creates the perfect atmosphere to enjoy preprandial drinks before tasting the culinary delights served in the *Westone Restaurant*. There are both *table d' hôte* and a more extensive *à la carte* menus available and judging from our fellow guests, this restaurant is also very popular amongst the locals. Other facilities at this hotel include a putting green, sauna, solarium, and a small gymnasium. Special weekend breaks are on offer here making this an ideal base for visiting Althorp House, Stoke Bruerne, Silverstone and Rockingham Castle. The Westone Moat House is located only ten minutes from junction 15 on the M1 motorway and Northampton town centre thus making it a quiet, relaxed setting yet very accessible. Service is attentive and the staff always have the comfort of the guests in mind.

Bed and Breakfast from £27.00 (w/end),
£66.50 (midweek)
Lunch from £10.75 and A La Carte
Dinner from £12.25 and A La Carte
Service Charge and VAT inclusive
Credit Cards—Access, American Express, Diners Club, Visa. 3 Suites
9 Double, 26 Twin, 27 Single Bedrooms

(3 Rooms can be let as Family Rooms)
All Rooms with Private Bath/Shower Room, TV, Telephone, Radio, Baby-listening, Tea and Coffee-making Facilities, Trouser Press, Hairdryer
Open from 1st January to 24th December
Fully Licensed
Full Central Heating. Lift

Cocktail Bar
TV Lounge
Conference Facilities
Dogs allowed but not in Public Rooms
Parking Facilities. Night Porter
Croquet, Putting, Solarium, Sauna, Mini Gym

Near Wellingborough—The Tudor Gate Hotel
35 High Street, Finedon, Northants, NN9 5JN. Tel 0933 680408. Fax 0933 680745

Transforming this lovely seventeenth-century farmhouse into an hotel, in 1967, was a good idea which has really worked. Thanks to Stuart and Gill Andrews, The Tudor Gate is a happy home-from-home where the friendly staff are able to act like part of the family. The philosopy here is simple–provide a superb *à la carte* menu with dishes which are professionally prepared, offer an abundant wine list suitable for every taste, give real value for money and, above all, ensure that guests receive friendly service. The Tudor Gate has a motto: 'The Gate hangs and hinders none, Refresh and Pay and Travel on, But if perchance a storm appear, Furl up your sail and anchor here.' The poetry may be dubious, but the intention is clear and was well demonstrated in the genuine hospitality which we received. All bedrooms are *en suite*, with satellite television and three with four-poster beds. The immaculately clean kitchens and the hotel's modern features in no way detract from its old-world charm, the splendour of the original oak beams and the Tudor influence sustained by the furniture and décor in the attractive restaurant. As we have indicated, the catering here is a strong suit. Scotch salmon is available in season, ribs of English beef are offered for Sunday luncheon and the various speciality dishes are changed daily. The Andrews set out to provide something a little bit special and their hotel's popularity is a measure of their success.

Bed and Breakfast from £25.00 pp sharing,
£40.00 Single (weekends)
Lunch from £10.00 and A La Carte
Afternoon Tea from £3.00
Dinner from £10.00 and A La Carte
Gratuities at Guest's discretion
VAT inclusive
Credit Cards–Access, American Express, Diners Club, Visa

1 Family Room
10 Double, 1 Twin, 4 Single Bedrooms
(3 Rooms with Four Poster)
11 Private Bathrooms
5 Private Shower Rooms
All Rooms with TV, Telephone
Open all Year
Residential and Restaurant Licence
Full Central Heating. Cocktail Bar

Conference Facilities
Dogs allowed by arrangement.
Parking Facilities
Nearby: Tennis, Squash, Badminton
Swimming Pool, Solarium, Sauna, Golf, Fishing, Riding, Sailing, Windsurfing, Water Skiing

Section 4: Oxfordshire

Burford—Cotswold Gateway Hotel Cheltenham Road, Burford, Oxfordshire. OX18 4HX. Tel 0993 822695/823345. Fax 0993 823600

Starting life in the eighteenth century as the 'Bird in Hand' inn, a prosperous period began in 1812 when the lane which ran along the top of the Windrush Valley was made into a coach road, all travellers between Cheltenham and London breaking their journey here. Towards the end of the nineteenth century the building started a fifty-year spell as a boys' boarding house for Burford Grammar School, re-opening in 1928 as the Cotswold Gateway Hotel. However, the stunning beauty of the small town owes more to the wealth of the wool merchants of the fifteenth and sixteenth centuries. In November 1988, after twelve months of alteration and refurbishment, Mr and Mrs Ray Ford opened the hotel as an impressive follow-up to their development of the Cotswold Gateway Antique Centre next door. With a dozen or more antique shops contributing to the good shopping, Burford also boasts a range of excellent restaurants, a vigorous musical life and a varied range of local craft businesses. Not that one will wish to miss the distinctive catering at the hotel by the head chef and his team. They specialise in the lighter style of cooking where natural and delicate flavours of the best fresh ingredients are skilfully preserved in individually prepared dishes. An extensive wine list includes bottles from the New World. A splendid all-seasons hotel in a fascinating town with excellent road communication in every direction.

Bed and Breakfast from £55.00
Bar Lunch from £3.50
Lunch from £14.95 and A La Carte
Afternoon Tea from £1.75
Dinner from £14.95 and A La Carte
Gratuities at Guest's discretion
VAT inclusive
All Major Credit Cards accepted

4 Family Rooms
9 Double, 1 Single, 2 Twin Bedrooms
All Rooms with Private Bathroom, TV,
Telephone, Radio, Baby-listening, Tea and
Coffee-making Facilities, Trouser Press,
Hairdryer. Open all Year
Fully Licensed
Full Central Heating

Conference Facilities
Children catered for
Dogs allowed
Parking Facilities
Nearby: Squash, Badminton, Swimming
Solarium, Sauna, Golf

Burford—The Golden Pheasant Hotel High Street, Burford, Oxfordshire. OX8 4RJ. Tel 099382 3223/3417. Fax 0993 822621

Burford is a delightful Cotswold town, with honey coloured stone-built houses lining the steep High Street which descends to a fine old bridge across the river Windrush. Nestling snugly in the centre stands the Golden Pheasant, one of the town's earliest coaching inns. This charming hotel is extremely comfortable by modern standards yet retains an old-fashioned air of peace and tranquility. Our room was vast with genuinely old beams but was superbly equipped and decorated. Each of the twelve bedrooms (two with four-poster beds and all with private bath or shower room) has an individual character. The intimate candlelit restaurant has a well deserved reputation for excellent food and one can choose from a wide variety of unusual and mouth-watering English and French country dishes, cooked to perfection and complemented by wine selected from a comprehensive list. Light weekday lunches, traditional Sunday lunches and Cotswold cream teas are also on offer. All guests are made to feel truly welcome by the owners, Daniel and Helen Holmes and, indeed, The Golden Pheasant is a most comfortable and convenient hotel from which to visit historic Oxford, Blenheim Palace, Shakespeare's country, Bath and neighbouring Cotswold villages. There is excellent shopping at Cheltenham and near at hand there is a variety of outdoor pursuits and the famous Cotswold Wildlife Park. The hotel even provides bicycles for those wishing to explore the uncrowded lanes of this lovely corner of Britain.

Bed and Breakfast from £57.00 (Single),
£80.00 (Double/Twin)
Bar Lunch from £2.25
Afternoon Tea from £1.60
Dinner from £15.95
Gratuities at Guest's discretion

VAT inclusive. Credit Cards–Access,
American Express, Visa
8 Double (2 Four-poster), 4 Twin Bedrooms
8 Private Bathrooms
4 Private Shower Rooms
All Rooms with TV, Telephone, Radio,

Baby-listening, Tea and Coffee-making
Facilities, Hairdryer. Open all Year
Fully Licensed. Full Central Heating
Conference Facilities (up to 16)
Children catered for. Dogs allowed by
arrangement. Parking Facilities

Section 4: Oxfordshire

Deddington—The Holcombe Hotel and Restaurant
High Street, Deddington, Oxfordshire. OX5 4SL. Tel 0869 38274

Our inspectors have dubbed this the 'Welcome Hotel', so hospitable and friendly is it. It is also utterly charming. A delightful family-run, seventeenth century hotel, with highly professional and personalised attention from the proprietors and caring staff. The Holcombe Hotel is perfect for anyone seeking a rural setting in the heart of some of the most beautiful of Cotswold countryside. Yet, since the attractive former market town of Deddington lies literally in the the heart of England and only five miles from the newly opened M40, this is a grand spot from which to tour: Woodstock, Blenheim Palace, Warwick Castle, Cotswold villages and country houses, and many places of interest are within easy reach. The Holcombe's attractions include the comfortable *Cottage Bar* and the highly recommended restaurant, both noted for their pleasant ambiance. The menu offers a wide range of dishes, with special emphasis on fresh produce and game in season. Relaxation is the keynote of this hotel and the comfortable bedrooms reflect this. They are all individually decorated and have a private bath or shower. Each also has colour television, telephone, radio, tea-making facilities, trouser press and hairdryer. Cotswold stone walls, open fireplaces and the original beams add character to this 300-year old Cotswold inn, which has been modernised in just the right way and totally refurbished to a very high standard. Carol and Chedly Mahfoudh are the resident proprietors of this house of welcome.

Weekly Terms from £300.00
Daily Terms (Getaway Break) from £45.00
Bed and Breakfast from £57.00 Single, £69.00 Double, £85.00 de Luxe
Bar Meal from £3.95
Lunch from £14.50 and A La Carte
Dinner from £17.95 and A La Carte
Gratuities at Guest's discretion

VAT inclusive
Credit Cards—Access, American Express, Visa
2 Family Rooms. 1 Suite
9 Double, 2 Single, 6 Twin Bedrooms
14 Private Bathrooms. 3 Private Shower Rooms. All Rooms with TV, Telephone, Radio, Baby-listening, Tea and

Coffee-making Facilities, Hairdryer, Trouser Press. Open all Year
Fully Licensed. Full Central Heating.
Cocktail Bar
Conference Facilities. Children welcome
Dogs allowed in some rooms
Parking Facilities

Milton Common–The Belfry Hotel
Brimpton Grange, Milton Common, Oxford. OX9 2JW. Tel 0844 279381. Fax 0844 279624

There are degrees of roadside hotels. Those which are essentially pubs, others which cater for visitors who just want to put their heads down for the night, and the few which strive for very high standards and offer every comfort, imaginative food and great friendliness to the stranger. In the latter category is the well-established Belfry, set back from the A40 London/High Wycombe/Oxford road. The roar of heavy traffic past the hotel's gates may have subsided, but it is a simple matter to dip off the new M40 motorway at Junction Seven and find The Belfry waiting, welcoming and very friendly. Hotels elsewhere may be recession hit, but The Belfry seems always to be a hive of activity. Yet, even at its most busy, it is restful, too. What a pleasure it is to settled down into a comfortable back-easing chair and order one's favourite refreshment! After a drink, a little exploration. An oak-panelled restaurant looking absolutely splendid; the *Tudor Bar* a hubbub of conversation; a peek into some of the modernly equipped bedrooms, executive rooms and suites; and a tour of the hotel's leisure complex, with its magnificent indoor swimming pool, sauna, solarium, mini-gym and areas for relaxation. A purpose-built conference and exhibition suite is also an important aspect of The Belfry's services, and once again the facilities are of the highest order. And allied to all this is a management and staff to whom courtesy seems to come quite naturally. If you can stay at The Belfry for a while you will be in the very heart of South Oxfordshire and the opportunities for exploration are, therefore, endless.

Bed and breakfast from £70.00 Single, £85.00 Double
Bar Lunch from £3.50. Lunch from £14.50
Dinner from £17.50
Gratuities at Guest's Discretion
VAT inclusive. Credit Cards–Access,

American Express, Diners Club, Visa
3 Suites. 29 Double, 34 Twin, 11 Single Bedrooms. 70 Private Bathrooms, 7 Private Shower Rooms
All Rooms with TV, Telephone, Radio, Tea and Coffee-making Facilities

20 Rooms with Hairdryer
Open from 31st Dec 1992 to 24th Dec 1993
Fully Licensed. Full Central Heating
Cocktail Bar. Conference Facilities
Children catered for. Dogs allowed
Parking Facilities. Night Porter

Section 4: Oxfordshire

Shipton-under-Wychwood—The Shaven Crown Hotel
Shipton-under-Wychwood, Oxfordshire. OX7 6BA. Tel 0993 830330

The present proprietors of this lovely fourteenth-century inn are full of enthusiasm and give personal attention to the needs of their guests. Trevor Brookes and his wife, Mary, are ably supported by their son, Justin who gained valuable experience in a first-class hotel in Canada. The Shaven Crown was built as a hospice to the twelfth-century Bruern Abbey and it retains many of the original features, including the *Great Hall*, which has a magnificent fourteenth-century roof, a medieval archway, sturdy oak beams and a huge fireplace. The hotel is built round an attractive courtyard garden, where afternoon tea is served on tables with gaily coloured umbrellas. A team of three chefs prepares dishes based on the freshest ingredients, including fish, game, meat and chicken. Specialities such as fillet of pork *Savoyarde* and roast rack of lamb with rosemary and garlic are a connoisseur's delight. The crowning glory of your meal could be a blackberry bombe! A handsome oak staircase leads up to the bedrooms, which are comfortably appointed with period furniture. Whether you choose to dine or stay here, you will soon discover that the tradition of hospitality established by the hospice's fourteenth-century founders is well maintained today.

Weekly Terms from £208.00
Bed and Breakfast from £33.00
Breakfast: English £6.75
Breakfast: Continental £3.75
Bar Meal from £3.85
Sunday Lunch from £14.50 Table d'Hôte
Afternoon Tea from £1.65
Dinner from £18.50 Table d'Hôte

VAT inclusive
Credit Cards—Access, Visa
1 Family Room
1 Single, 5 Double, 2 Twin Bedrooms
3 Private Shower Rooms
All Rooms with Private Bathroom, TV, Tea and Coffee-making Facilities
Hairdryer available on request

Open all Year
Fully Licensed
Full Central Heating
Dogs not allowed
Parking Facilities
Nearby: Tennis, Golf, Fishing

Thame—Thatchers 29-30 Lower High Street,
Thame, Oxfordshire. Tel 084421 2146/3058. Fax 084421 7413

We love old inns, but not the type which rely heavily on faked 'olde worlde' atmosphere. Thatchers, however, is the genuine article and is one of the best small hotels in the country. It stands, long, low and part-thatched, in Thame's Lower High Street. We go out of our way to eat here, but, because of its popularity and the fact that it has only ten bedrooms, securing accommodation can sometimes be difficult. The bedrooms, like the rest of the hotel, are full of genuine charm and character. No two rooms are the same and most display original features such as old beams, as well as being equipped with modern amenities such as private bathrooms. Four of the rooms have four-poster beds and open log fires. Thatchers even has a sauna, a solarium and a Californian hot tub with jacuzzi jets. The *cuisine* at Thatchers is based upon the best ingredients: fresh fish and vegetables arrive daily from London's markets, the finest meats are purchased from various butchers, game is shot locally. The creative chefs produce memorable and imaginative dishes from these raw materials. The combination of history, excellent food, comfort and a friendly home-from-home environment has given this small hotel a large reputation.

Bed and Breakfast from £49.50
Lunch from £13.50 and A La Carte
Dinner from £13.50 and A La Carte
Gratuities at Guest's discretion
VAT inclusive
Credit Cards—Access, Visa
1 Family Room

1 Twin, 4 Double Bedrooms
4 Single Bedrooms
All Rooms with Private Bathroom, TV, Telephone, Welcome Packs and Baby-listening
Open all Year. Fully Licensed
Full Central Heating

Cocktail Bar. Dogs allowed
Solarium, Sauna, Jacuzzi
Nearby: Tennis, Croquet, Putting, Squash, Badminton, Swimming Pool, Golf, Fishing
Riding, Shooting, Hang-gliding

Section 4: Shropshire

Near Bridgnorth—Cross Lane House Hotel
Astley Abbots, Bridgnorth, Shropshire. WV16 4SJ
Tel 0746 764887. Fax 0746 766869

It could be that whilst Bridgnorth may sound attractive-and indeed it is, you might prefer, as a country lover, to be outside the town. That being so, you should ascend the Severn valley by way of the B4373 road and after about a mile Cross Lane House Hotel will be found set back on the right hand side. Already the air has become clearer and invigorating, the scenery totally unspoilt and you are likely to feel on top of the world. But then, at Astley Abbots you very nearly are! By sheer coincidence, we knew this imposing mellow brick farmhouse during the Thirties, when our 'Uncle' Tom lived there and we used to visit on Sunday afternoons to enjoy enormous country teas in the large gardens. Cross Lane House became an hotel just a few years ago, but, since it has always been such a happy and hospitable place, it is especially suited for its new role. The owners, Diane and Robert Cleal, have enhanced the original features of the house ... inglenook and open fires, ancient beams and William IV entrance hall ... and have furnished the house in an appropriate manner, even to the extent of incorporating a full-tester bed and an Edwardian bathroom in one of the eight bedrooms. We were accommodated in the Coach House Room, situated across the gravel driveway from the house, and which, like all the rooms, is beautifully equipped and enjoys lovely views. The meals are prepared by Diane Cleal and her dishes are quite outstanding. There is no written menu, but she uses the freshest local ingredients to such good effect that Cross Lane House has become known for its good food.

Weekly Terms from £262.50
Daily terms from £37.50
Bed and Breakfast from £27.50
Lunch from £14.50 Table d'Hôte
Dinner from £23.50 Table d'Hôte
Gratuities at Guest's discretion
VAT inclusive
Credit Cards—Access, Visa

4 Double, 2 Twin, 3 Single Bedrooms
8 Private Bathrooms
1 Private Shower Room
All Rooms with TV, Radio, Tea and Coffee-making Facilities, Trouser Press.
Hairdryer available on request
Open all Year
Residential and Restaurant Licence

Full Central Heating
Conference Facilities
Children catered for. Dogs allowed
Parking Facilities. Croquet
Nearby: Tennis, Putting, Squash, Badminton, Swimming, Solarium, Sauna, Golf, Fishing, Riding, Sailing, Hang-gliding

Section 4: Shropshire

Near Bridgnorth, Worfield—The Old Vicarage Hotel
Worfield, Bridgnorth, Shropshire. WV15 5JZ. Tel 07464 497. Fax 07464 552

Where shall we begin? Here is exceptional accommodation in an area of outstanding beauty, steeped in history and centrally located for visits to numerous places of interest. Shropshire is a fascinating county in the dramatic countryside of the Welsh Borderland. All around there lies evidence of past events, from Border conflicts of Celt, Roman, Saxon and Norman, to the many changes when the Industrial Revolution was born in Shropshire. It is in this rich setting that Christine and Peter Iles discovered an Edwardian Parsonage in 1979, and transformed it into what may justifiably be described as one of the finest country house hotels in the United Kingdom (a finalist in the ETB's Hotel of the Year 1991 competition). This is a place for the discerning traveller who values the best of food and wine, period furnishings and an atmosphere of efficient informality. If further praise be needed, the high proportion of guests making repeated return visits testifies to the quality of the hospitality. At The Old Vicarage one may choose quiet seclusion or friendly company and, in the bar where friendships are often first formed, there is an extensive range of aperitifs, single malts, international beers and low or non-alcoholic drinks. Amongst the silver and cut-glass of the dining-rooms there is a cuisine with an emphasis on the fresh and natural. Shell and sea fish from the West Country, wild salmon from the Severn and Wye, Welsh lamb, local game, traditionally reared pork, beef and poultry. Here, then, is somewhere to halt for a long while.

Leisure Breaks from 1st March 1993
Standard £64.50, Luxury Room £74.00 per person per day
Weekly Terms from £777.00 Double
Daily Terms from £137.50 Double
Bed and Breakfast from £78.50 (for two)
Lunch from £17.50 (prior booking only)
Dinner £19.50 and £27.50

Service Charge at Guest's discretion
VAT inclusive
Credit Cards—Access, American Express, Diners Club, Visa
9 Double, 5 Twin Bedrooms
All Rooms with Bath/Shower Room, TV, Telephone, Radio, Tea and Coffee-making Facilities, Hairdryer, Fruit, Minibar

Coach House Rooms with Jacuzzi
Open all year except 21 December to 3rd January. Residential and Restaurant Licence. Full Central Heating
Conference Facilities. Dogs allowed
Parking Facilities
Nearby: Tennis, Squash, Badminton, Swimming Pool, Golf, Riding, Shooting

Cleobury Mortimer, Near Kidderminster—The Redfern Hotel
Cleobury Mortimer, Shropshire. DY14 8AA. Tel 0299 270395. Fax 0299 271011

The building which now houses The Redfern Hotel was once one of Cleobury Mortimer's twenty-three public houses. Having been carefully modernised and extended with the assistance of the English Tourist Board, The Redfern Hotel has the charm and warmth of the past plus all the comforts expected by today's travellers. There are eleven bedrooms, all with either a private bathroom (two with whirlpool baths) or shower room, and most of the modern sophistications one could wish for. One room also boasts a four-poster bed. Prompt personal service, a comfortable environment and high standards of culinary achievement are the hallmark of Jon and Liz Redfern with their son Richard. Breakfast is served in the delightful first floor conservatory with views of the local countryside. Their very reasonable summer rates are reduced if one takes advantage of the hotel's off-season weekend breaks. The hotel is a delightful retreat in an area with a reputation for Hereford beef, Shropshire sheep and Severn salmon. The old market town of Cleobury Mortimer is just eleven miles from Ludlow and the same distance from Kidderminster, whilst among the many attractions within easy driving distance, are the Ironbridge Gorge Museum and Severn Valley Railway. Enjoy the hospitality of The Redfern Hotel and you will leave refreshed and happy.

Weekly Terms from £220.00
Daily Terms from £38.50
Bed and Breakfast from £30.00
Lunch from £5.00 and A La Carte
Bar Snacks from £3.50
Dinner from £14.75 and A La Carte
Service Charge and VAT inclusive
Credit Cards–Access, American Express, Diners Club, Visa

2 Family Rooms
5 Double, 4 Twin Bedrooms
5 Private Bathrooms
6 Private Shower Rooms
All Rooms with TV, Telephone, Radio, Baby-listening, Tea and Coffee-making Facilities, Hairdryer
Open all Year
Residential and Restaurant Licence

Full Central Heating
Cocktail Bar
Conference Facilities
Dogs allowed
Parking Facilities
Nearby: Golf, Fishing, Riding, Shooting

Section 4: Shropshire

Little Stretton—Mynd House Hotel
Little Stretton, Shropshire, SY6 6RB
Tel 0694 722212. Fax 0694 724180

The A49 winds along midway between Shrewsbury and Ludlow where the brown and blue hills suddenly sweep down all around. This is the Stretton Gap, where the Longmynd, Caradoc and Ragleth Hills hover over the old Roman Watling Street. The 'Strettons' beckon and at the narrowest point on the Gap the sign for Little Stretton invites exploration. This delightful small hamlet with its thatched church and rural street scene, is protected as a Conservation Area enclosed by an Area of Outstanding Beautya delight at any time of the year, as are the Stretton hills in general. Walks radiate in all directions. Narrow, unfrequented roads wind along the valleys with ever-changing views of the hills and batches, many leading to the plateau of the Longmynd, 5,000 acres of dissected moorland owned by the National Trust. The rather severe Edwardian exterior of Mynd House belies the intimate interior which has been enhanced with period furniture and decor. No reception or room numbers here, you are received as a guest in an Edwardian country house. The eight bedrooms provide delightful accommodation and there are luxury suites for those special occasions including sitting room and spa bath. In the lace fringed restaurant interesting cuisine without extremes is achieved, using the best of local meat, fish, game and cheeses. As you would expect from the UK winner of the Mercier Prix d'Elite, the wine list is outstanding with over 300 bottle selection and an incredible 100 half bottle choice along with many ports and dessert wines by the glass.

Short Breaks all year (any 2 days or more) from £38.50 pp per day
Daily Terms from £46.00 Single, £77.00 Double
Bed and Breakfast from £55.00 (for two)
Lounge Lunch from £5.00
Dinner £18.00 and £27.00
Gratuities at Guest's discretion

VAT inclusive
Credit Cards—Access, American Express, Visa. Debit Cards—Switch, Connect
2 Suites (one Four-Poster and double Spa Bath). 1 Single, 5 Twin/Double Bedrooms.
All Rooms with Private Bathroom, TV, Telephone, Radio, Tea and Coffee-making Facilities, Hairdryer

Open all year except Christmas, January and one week August
Residential and Restaurant Licence
Full Central Heating, Log Fire
Children catered for
Dogs allowed (not in all bedrooms).
Parking Facilities

Section 4: Shropshire

Ludlow—Dinham Weir Hotel and Restaurant
Dinham Bridge, Ludlow, Shropshire. SY8 1EH. Tel 0584 874431

Ludlow lies in the beautiful rolling countryside of Shropshire, although it is almost captured by a northward excursion of the Hereford and Worcester county boundary. In this historic town, by the tranquil waters of the River Teme, is the Dinham Weir Hotel and Restaurant. It occupies the site of the original Castell Myll dating back to the seventeenth century, recorded as being worked as an iron foundry until the late nineteenth century. Here one may wine and dine by candlelight in a restaurant which may well be the closest to a river of any in South Shropshire. Traditional English *cuisine* is based on quality steaks, farm-fresh poultry and selected fish, all so prepared as to enhance their innate flavours without overwhelming them. A vegetarian menu is also available. From the dining-room, glass doors lead to a small patio above the weir. Views of this, and of the river, can be seen from the six *en suite* bedrooms. Externally, the hotel presents a pleasing and impressive image and, inside, rooms are cosy with adequate space in the thirty-cover restaurant. Landscaped gardens add to the peaceful charm of the lovely surroundings, beyond which lie Wenlock Edge and the river Corve in Corve Dale, a Farming Museum in Ape Dale, Shipton Hall, the Whitehouse Museum and several castles. Ludlow itself has much that is of historic interest and, mainly towards the Welsh border, numerous forts remain as objectives for short excursions in this open territory.

Special 2/3 Day Breaks available
Weekly Terms from £265.00
Daily Terms from £42.00
Bed and Breakfast from £30.00
Bar Lunch from £2.60
Lunch from £10.50 and A La Carte
Dinner from £10.50 and A La Carte
Gratuities at Guest's Discretion

VAT inclusive
Credit Cards—Access, American Express, Diners Club, Visa
1 Four Poster Suite
3 Double, 2 Twin Bedrooms
1 Private Bathroom, 5 Private Shower Rooms
All Rooms with TV, Telephone, Radio, Tea

and Coffee-making Facilities. Hairdryer, Trouser Press available on request.
Open all Year. Residential and Restaurant Licence. Conference Facilities. Children over 5 years catered for.
Dogs not allowed. Parking Facilities Nearby: Tennis, Putting, Swimming, Golf, Fishing, Riding, Shooting

Ludlow–Overton Grange Hotel
Ludlow, Shropshire. SY8 4AD. Tel 0584 873500

Nestling in the scenic Shropshire countryside, Overton Grange lies approximately one and a half miles south of Ludlow, about one mile after the bridge over the Teme; the drive is on the right. Once the Edwardian mansion of the Betton-Foster family, the impressive frontage and superb setting, including two-and-a-half acres of lovely garden, retain an old world character and charm. Now that refurbishing has been completed all rooms are *en suite*, each one with its own individual décor and most with lovely commanding views of the surrounding countryside. A spacious conservatory adjoining the residents' lounge and bar is a relaxing and casual venue for light meals, whilst serving extensive *à la carte* and *table d'hôte* menus for lunch and dinner in the oak panelled restaurant. A self-contained *Garden Suite* with French window opening on to the lawns at the rear of the hotel is available for large parties of up to 200 covers. Mr. Ingrassia puts a great emphasis on good food and wines and during the winter months a warm welcome awaits with open log fires. There is much of interest in this peaceful part of the Marches where time seems to stand still. In Ludlow itself an eleventh-century castle, one of the thirty-two built to guard the Welsh borders, stands on a low cliff above the river. It is just one of the many historic, sporting or scenic attractions in this part of Shropshire.

Weekly and Daily Terms on Application
Bed and Breakfast from £31.00
Bar Snacks from £2.50
Lunch from £12.50 and A La Carte
Dinner from £14.95 and A La Carte
Gratuities at Guest's discretion
VAT inclusive
Credit Cards–Access, American Express,

Diners Club, Visa
1 Family Room. 2 Suites
8 Double, 4 Twin Bedrooms
11 Private Bathrooms. 4 Private Shower Rooms. All Rooms with TV, Telephone, Radio, Baby-listening, Tea and Coffee-making Facilities
Hairdryer available on request

Open all Year. Fully Licensed
Cocktail Bar. Conference Facilities
Dogs not allowed
Parking Facilities. Croquet
Nearby: Tennis, Indoor Swimming Pool, Solarium, Sauna, Golf, Fishing, Riding, Shooting

Section 4: Shropshire

Near Oswestry—Pen-y-Dyffryn Hall Hotel
Rhydycroesau, Near Oswestry, Shropshire. SY10 7DT. Tel 0691 653700

Rhydycroesau (Rud-uh-croy-sigh) which translates as 'The Ford of the Crossings' is a sleepy little hamlet just three miles west of the ancient market town of Oswestry and it straddles the border between England and Wales. The river marking the border runs alongside the hotel gardens. Pen-y-Dyffryn (Pen-uh-Duf-rin) means 'The Head of the Valleys' and the original building was a Georgian rectory. To do justice to the charm of this lush and peaceful area we should have a poet draft the text. A E Housman, on the Border Country, wrote 'A country for easy livers, the quietest under the sun'. It is where the lovely Welsh hills rise above the most unspoilt parts of old rural England. We are quoting from the hotel's own brochure but need not apologise: it is factual and we have seen for ourselves the magnificent scenery, the quality of the stone Grade II listed building, sampled the superb *cuisine* and experienced the warmth and comfort of the hospitality. All seven of the large *en suite* bedrooms are fully equipped and all have breathtaking views of the Welsh hills beyond the attractively terraced hotel gardens. Guests here are surrounded by a wealth of mountains, rivers and lakes, they can visit old pubs and even older castles, go pony trekking, play golf on the three eighteen-hole courses within ten miles of the hotel, or make a short excursion to the Snowdonia National Park. Your hosts, Miles and Audrey Hunter, can arrange local fishing, horse riding, guided walks and golfing weekends.

Weekly Terms from £260.00	1 Family Room. 1 Single, 3 Double,	Full Central Heating. Conference Facilities
Daily Terms from £41.00	2 Twin Bedrooms	Children catered for. Dogs allowed
Bed and Breakfast from £31.00	5 Private Bathrooms	Parking Facilities. Fishing
Bar Supper from £6.95	2 Private Shower Rooms	Nearby: Tennis, Squash, Badminton,
Dinner from £12.95 and A La Carte	All Rooms with TV, Radio, Tea and	Swimming, Solarium, Sauna, Golf, Riding,
Gratuities at Guest's discretion	Coffee-making Facilities, Trouser Press,	Sailing, Windsurfing, Shooting, Hot Air
VAT inclusive. Credit Cards—Access,	Hairdryer, Baby-listening	Ballooning, Walking
American Express, Visa	Open All Year. Fully Licensed	

Near Oswestry, Trefonen—Ashfield Country Hotel
Llwyn-y-Maen, Trefonen, Oswestry, Shropshire. SY10 9DD. Tel 0691 655200

Ashfield Country Hotel is situated on the Trefonen road, in fifteen acres of its own grounds, one and a half miles from Oswestry. Less than half a mile away, across the fields, is a fine stretch of the Offa's Dyke path. Bill and Barbara Lewis, the resident owners of the hotel, offer friendly personal service and home cooking, making good use of fresh local produce. They serve a full English breakfast, which includes locally baked bread and free-range eggs. Their dinners are equally mouthwatering, with specialities such as roast beef, Welsh lamb, roast chicken, fresh salmon and trout and home-baked ham. Vegetarian and special diets can be catered for upon request and light lunches are available to residents only. Whilst lunching or dining, one can enjoy pleasant views through the patio windows, over the Candy Valley and the nearby wooded hills. Attractive polished beech floors are a feature of the public rooms and bedrooms. There are just twelve bedrooms, comfortably furnished and kept spotlessly clean. All of them have private bathrooms, colour television, telephone and tea and coffee-making facilities. The hotel's two-night 'Mini Breaks' and special weekly terms are most reasonable and are a tempting prospect for those who seek a quiet holiday touring, pony trekking or walking in the Welsh border country. Three National Trust properties are within easy reach of the hotel.

Weekly Terms from £245.00	VAT inclusive	Coffee-making Facilities
Bed and Breakfast from £60.00	2 Family Rooms	2 Rooms with Hairdryer
Afternoon Tea from £3.00	5 Double, 4 Twin Bedrooms	Open all year. Fully Licensed
Bar Supper from £5.00	1 Single Bedroom	Full Central Heating
Dinner from £12.00 and A La Carte	All Rooms with Private Bathroom, TV,	Conference Facilities
Gratuities at Guest's discretion	Telephone, Radio, Tea and	Dogs allowed

Section 4: Staffordshire

Burton-upon-Trent—The Riverside Hotel & Restaurant
Riverside Drive, Branston, Burton-upon-Trent, Staffs. DE14 3EP. Tel 0283 511234

Here is an inn which is a model of enterprise. It began in a modest way, but has become one of the most flourishing hotels in the county, with excellent all-round comfort and a marvellous name for food. It stands on the outskirts of Burton, half a mile from the A38, and has an attractive terraced garden stretching down to the River Trent, which offers a fascinating view of the bird sanctuary on the opposite bank. It is a lovely setting and the atmosphere within is equally peaceful and relaxing. The twenty-two bedrooms, many of which have river views, are all provided with *en suite* bathrooms, colour television, radios, baby-listening and beverage-making facilities. The elegant restaurant with views over the river serves an extensive *à la carte* menu as well as a good selection from the *table d'hôte* menu. Impressive, too, is the large selection of *hors-d'oeuvres*, the mouthwatering sweets and savouries and, what the hotel claims is the best selection of brandies in the Midlands! The extensive cellar holds some very fine wines. The Riverside Hotel also caters for a wide range of business and social occasions, including conferences, seminars, wedding receptions and banquets. Golf can be arranged at the affiliated golf course which is within a wood's drive of the hotel. Burton-upon-Trent is, of course, renowned as the centre of Britain's brewing industry and a trip to the Bass Museum, which illustrates 200 years of brewing history, is well worth while. The Riverside Hotel is personally run by Bruce Elliott-Bateman

All Terms pertaining to 1992 Weekly Terms from £333.00 Bed and Breakfast from £60.00 Bar Meal from £2.95 Lunch from £9.95 A La Carte Afternoon Tea from £1.25	Dinner from £14.95 and A La Carte Gratuities at Guest's discretion VAT inclusive. Credit Cards—Access, American Express, Visa 6 Double, 5 Twin, 11 Single Bedrooms All Rooms with Private Bath/Shower	Rooms, TV, Telephone, Radio, Baby-listening, Tea and Coffee-making Facilities. Trouser Press and Hairdryer available. Open all year. Fully Licensed Full Central Heating. Cocktail Bar Conference Facilities

Lichfield—Angel Croft Hotel Beacon Street, Lichfield, Staffordshire. WS13 7AA. Tel 0543 258737. Fax 0543 415605

Dr Samuel Johnson, who was born in Lichfield, described the city's inhabitants as 'The most sober, decent people in England'. The city itself has remained a peaceful and genteel place, with a majestic cathedral and acres of open parkland. The Angel Croft Hotel reflects this atmosphere perfectly, for it has a most delightful garden and is flanked on one side by the towering spires of the cathedral and on the other by the green expanse of Beacon Park. Consequently, it has a feeling of spaciousness which is uncommon in a town hotel. It is also one of the most friendly hotels we know, for the family owners are actively involved in most of its departments. The entrance hall of the hotel is most impressive, with a winding staircase typical of Lichfield's Georgian houses. The *Knight's Bar and King's Restaurant* is also notable, for it is housed in what was probably a wine cellar and offers excellent food, served by friendly, efficient staff. The owners have recently purchased a Georgian town house nearby, *Westgate House*, which they have skilfully renovated to provide further accommodation. These rooms are most tastefully equipped and include two *de luxe* executive suites which have superb views of the west front of the cathedral. Lichfield's first cathedral was consecrated in 700AD and the present cathedral library contains some of the finest illuminated manuscripts in Europe. The Roman bath house three miles to the south west of the city, on Watling Street, is also well worth visiting.

Terms on Application Gratuities at Guest's discretion VAT inclusive Credit Cards—Access, Diners Club, Visa 2 Family Rooms. 2 Suites 5 Double, 10 Twin, 2 Single Bedrooms	11 Private Bathrooms 5 Private Shower Rooms All Rooms with TV, Telephone, Radio, Baby-listening, Tea and Coffee-making Facilities. Hairdryer available on request Open all year except 25th and 26th	December. Fully Licensed Full Central Heating. Cocktail Bar Conference Facilities. Dogs not allowed Parking Facilities Nearby: Tennis, Putting, Squash, Badminton, Swimming, Solarium, Sauna,

Section 4: Suffolk

Aldeburgh—Uplands Hotel
Victoria Road, Aldeburgh, Suffolk. IP15 5DX. Tel 0728 452420

The North Sea nibbles voraciously at Suffolk's sea-board, ensuring that the county has no coastal road. Aldeburgh's famous half-timbered Moot Hall, which now stands on the beach, was, when it was built in the sixteenth century, separated from the sea by three roads which have long since been washed away. These incursions have kept Suffolk seaside towns delightfully natural and unspoilt. Aldeburgh is especially attractive, with Georgian houses and a fish market. Another of the town's well-established landmarks is the Uplands Hotel, which stands at the top of the hill opposite the old church. Catering has always been a strong suit at Uplands and Robert, Patricia and Nichola Tidder, the owners, rigorously maintain the high standards. We always enjoy dining here, for the meals are cooked with finesse and there is always a good selection of wines available. House guests will tell you that not only are the bedrooms well equipped and the public rooms comfortable, but the warm and friendly atmosphere within the hotel makes it a very hospitable home-from-home. The town is famous throughout the musical world for the annual Aldeburgh Festival, although the concerts are actually held at Snape, which is some six miles inland. To the south of Aldeburgh, one may launch sailing craft on the River Alde and to the north is the unique holiday village of Thorpeness, built around a sixty-five acre lake. Do consider Uplands Hotel when you next plan an East Anglian holiday, it is expertly run and most hospitable.

Weekly terms £275.00
Daily Terms from £42.00
Bed and Breakfast from £26.00
Dinner from £15.00 and A La Carte
Gratuities at Guest's discretion
VAT inclusive

Credit Cards–Access, American Express, Diners Club, Visa. 2 Family Rooms
5 Double, 9 Twin, 4 Single Bedrooms
16 Private Bathrooms. 1 Private Shower Room. All Rooms with TV, Tea and Coffee-making

Facilities, Telephone, Baby-listening
Open all Year. Residential and Restaurant Licence. Full CH. Cocktail Bar Conference Facilities. TV Lounge. Parking Facilities
Nearby: Tennis, Putting, Squash, Badminton, Golf, Fishing, Riding, Sailing

Clare—The Bell Hotel
Market Hill, Clare, Sudbury, Suffolk. CO10 8NN. Tel 0787 277741. Fax 0787 278474

For years we have been acclaiming the rural charm of this part of East Anglia, where Essex, Suffolk and Cambridgeshire are as interwoven as a lovers' knot. The valley of the Stour is particularly attractive, for strung along the valley road (the A1092) are three very pretty villages–Cavendish, Clare and Stoke-by-Clare. This famous white-faced and half-timbered inn stands close to the main entrance of the castle in Clare. Dating from about 1585, The Bell may at one time have been an alehouse, but it later became a renowned posting house. We derive great pleasure from visiting The Bell, for, although it has been carefully modernised where necessary, its mellowness remains unaltered and one experiences that feeling of well-being which is associated with exposed beams and open fireplaces. The current custodians of this lovely house are Brian and Gloria Miles. Under their direction, The Bell has many virtues–friendliness, comfort, cleanliness and excellent fare all immediately spring to mind. The bedrooms, whether in the original part of the hotel or set around the *Dickensian Courtyard*, are full of character and appropriately furnished. Many of the rooms have four-poster beds and some others have half-testers. Our room was so well equipped and the bed comfortable. The restaurant serves superb *cuisine* and offers a choice of over 100 wines to complement one's meal, with after dinner coffee being taken in the large comfortable conservatory. The *Wine Bar* serves dishes of a more modest nature.

Weekly Terms On Application
Bed and Breakfast from £38.50 Single, £56.50 Double
Bar Meal from £4.50
Lunch from £11.00 and A La Carte
Afternoon Tea £2.95
Dinner from £15.95 and A La Carte
Gratuities at Guest's discretion
VAT inclusive
Credit Cards–Access, American Express,

Diners Club, Visa
2 Family Rooms
19 Double, 2 Single, 4 Twin Bedrooms
18 Private Bathrooms
1 Private Shower Room
20 Rooms with TV, Telephone, Radio, Tea and Coffee-making Facilities, Baby-listening, Hairdryer
Trouser Press available on request

Open all Year. Fully Licensed
Full Central Heating
Conference Facilities
Dogs allowed. Parking Facilities
Nearby: Tennis, Swimming Pool, Golf, Fishing, Riding

Section 4: Suffolk

Felixstowe—Marlborough Hotel
Sea Front, Felixstowe, Suffolk. IP11 8BJ. Tel 0394 285621. Telex 987047

Felixstowe sits at the end of a peninsula which is bounded by the sea to the south and by the rivers Deben to the east and Orwell to the west. Visitors come to this resort either to enjoy its cliff-top situation or to take the direct car-ferry service to Zeebrugge. The Marlborough Hotel is an imposing building situated in a superb position on Felixstowe's seafront, many of its forty-seven bedrooms having sea views. Ideal for that overnight stop or weekend break and well placed for touring the famous areas of Suffolk and Essex, including East Bergholt where the artist John Constable lived or the cultural centre of Aldeburgh and Snape. Michael Hollman, General Manager, ensures that both travellers and tourists are well catered for–the *L'Aperitif Lounge* or residents' bar, ideal for that pre-dinner drink or after dinner relaxation with coffee and liqueurs. The Rattan Restaurant boasts an excellent carvery which is included as a choice in the *table d'hôte* menu and there is an *à la carte* menu for that special occasion. In addition the comfortable *Flying Boat Bar* offers a good selection of bar meals. The *Sea Breeze Suite* has been created for those who would enjoy a romantic weekend: it has a four-poster bed and a magnificent double whirlpool bath. The hotel also caters for banquets, dances, wedding receptions, conferences and exhibitions. Hotel guests can enjoy a round of golf at the Felixstowe Ferry Golf Club, a superb par-72 links course, for half the normal green fees.

Weekly Terms from £250.00
Bed and Breakfast from £25.00 (sharing)
Lunch from £7.25 and A La Carte
Dinner from £11.95 Table d'Hôte
Gratuities at Guest's discretion
VAT inclusive. Credit Cards–Access, American Express, Diners Club, Visa
1 Family Room

19 Double, 21 Twin, 5 Single Bedrooms
All Rooms with Private Bath/Shower Rooms, TV, Telephone, Radio, Tea and Coffee-making Facilities
Trouser Press and Hairdryer available
Open all Year. Fully Licensed
Full Central Heating. Lift
Cocktail Bar. TV Lounge

Conference Facilities. Dogs allowed
Parking Facilities. Night Porter
Nearby: Tennis, Croquet, Putting, Squash, Swimming Pool, Solarium, Sauna, Golf (50% discount on green fees for Residents), Sea Fishing, Windsurfing, Flying

Sudbury—The Mill Hotel
Walnut-Tree Lane, Sudbury, Suffolk. CO10 6BD. Tel 0787 375544. Telex 987623

In the Domesday Book, it records of Sudbury in 1086 that 'there is a mill', and tradition has it that the hotel stands on this original site. The mill wheel still working today, embodied within the building, was made in Suffolk in 1889. Sudbury itself is the birthplace of Thomas Gainsborough, the famous portrait artist, and his nearby house is now a museum and art gallery. Many of the unspoiled medieval villages and magnificent churches in this part of England have been immortalised by Constable. Flatford Mill, the subject of one of his most famous paintings, lies just a few miles to the south. Collectors will wish to spend hours browsing in the excellent local antique shops. At the Mill Hotel, which has recently been totally refurbished, we enjoyed a reasonably priced and wholly excellent meal in the oak beamed restaurant, overlooking the terrace with its riverside setting. In keeping with the peaceful setting, the fifty bedrooms are quiet, centrally heated and each with its own bathroom. There is a *Meadow Bar* which overlooks the mill pond and is surrounded by acres of tranquil water meadow. The hotel has fishing rights on the adjacent stretch of the River Stour which provides some of the best coarse fishing in England. An extensive *à la carte* menu–with daily specialities—is provided in the restaurant which is in the old millhouse, dating back nearly 300 years. For conferences and receptions, the *Gainsborough Room* and the *Drawing Room* can accommodate up to 100 guests. Altogether an ideal holiday or business centre for East Anglia.

Daily Terms from £f38.50 pp (min 2 nights sharing Twin)
Bed and Breakfast from £50.00 Single, £39.00 Double pp
Lunch £10.50. Dinner £17.50
VAT inclusive. Gratuities at Guest's discretion. Credit Cards—Access, American Express, Diners Club, Visa
2 Family Rooms, 1 mini Suite, 1 Four-Poster Room
28 Double, 11 Twin, 5 Single Bedrooms
45 Private Bathrooms. 3 Private Shower Rooms. All Rooms with TV, Radio, Telephone, Tea and Coffee-making Facilities, Baby-listening, Hairdryer
Open all Year. Fully Licensed. Full Central Heating. Cocktail Bar. Dogs allowed
Parking Facilities Night Porter

Section 4: Suffolk

Near Woodbridge—Seckford Hall
Near Woodbridge, Suffolk. IP13 6NU. Tel 0394 385678. Fax 0394 380610

Those interested in the preservation of our ancient heritage will be most pleased to see how this, one of our finest specimens of Tudor architecture–so happily furnished with genuine period pieces–has been adapted for hotel use. It is a lovely building nestling in grounds which comprise a willow-fringed lake, lawns, a terrace and walled gardens. Seckford Hall, with its attractive cocktail bar and newly extended and refurbished dining-room, is much in vogue for lunches and dinners. The homarium (lobster pond) in the hall displays the fresh seafood, which is a speciality. The bedrooms are all furnished to a high standard, each with a bathroom *en suite* and colour television with teletext. *The Courtyard* is an exciting development of luxury suites, an indoor swimming pool and buttery. The complex is located adjacent to the main hotel. The hotel is, therefore, a comfortable base for motorists wishing to tour the Suffolk countryside and coast, as well as for those wishing to stay put and relax in contentment for a few days. The resident owners are Mr and Mrs Michael Bunn and Seckford Hall has been in the same family ownership for forty years. It remains ever inviting within and without. Motorists should avoid the turning to the town of Woodbridge and continue along the by-pass (A12) until they see the hotel sign to the left.

Weekly Terms from £415.00
Bed and Breakfast from £85.00 (two persons sharing)
Bar Lunch from £3.95
Lunch from £11.50 and A La Carte
Dinner from £21.00 A La Carte
Service Charge and VAT inclusive
Credit Cards–Access, American Express,

Diners Club, Visa
15 Double 14 Twin, 5 Single Bedrooms
All Rooms with Private Bathroom, TV, Telephone, Radio, Baby-listening, Tea and Coffee-making Facilities
Open all Year except Christmas Day
Fully Licensed. Full Central Heating
Cocktail Bar . Conference Facilities

Children catered for. Dogs allowed
Parking Facilities. Night Porter
Indoor Heated Swimming Pool, Solarium, Spa Bath, Exercise Room, Trout and Coarse Fishing in Hotel Lake, 9-hole Golf Course. Nearby: Tennis, Squash, Sauna, Riding, Sailing, Windsurfing, Tenpin Bowling, Karting

---

Infallible?
The answer is no because even as these lines are being written, hotel ownership, management and staff are changing somewhere. Invaluable? Yes, because by joining the Ashley Courtenay Circle (no extra charge) you can check up with us at any time during the current season.

A reminder.
Some of the tariffs in this book are those quoted for 1992. As prices will probably have changed for 1993 please check before booking. Please also note that the weekly and daily hotel rates shown in this book are for half board only (dinner, room and breakfast) unless otherwise stated.

Section 4: Warwickshire

Berkswell—Nailcote Hall Hotel & Restaurant Nailcote Lane, Berkswell, Warwickshire. CV7 7DE. Tel 0203 466174. Fax 0203 470720

Rarely does a hotel have the facilities to accommodate banquets, conferences and meetings so comprehensively and yet maintain the personal touch that means so much to private guests. Whether you seek audio-visual facilities for a presentation, or soft live music for a romantic occasion, this hotel is ready to oblige. Whatever the event, the superb *cuisine* in their *Oak Room Restaurant*, complemented by a wine list of distinction, will make your visit most memorable. The word 'Nailcote' is believed to be derived from the Norman French word for armourer and there has been a dwelling on the site of this hotel since the time of the Norman conquest. The location, between Coventry and Birmingham, is obviously valuable for commerical and business promotions. At the same time, the setting in eight acres of garden and parkland ensures a peaceful break from the world of commerce and, for the tourist, a luxurious centre from which to visit Stratford-upon-Avon and the Cotswolds. Nailcote Hall is of sixteenth-century origin but, in 1780, it was much altered and the Georgian wing was added. Recently, a further Georgian-style wing was completed. Under its new owner in 1991, a major programme of refurbishment and upgrading has introduced many new amenities whilst retaining the warm and friendly ambience. Tasteful colour schemes in particular caught our eye. The leisure facilities here include a three-hole practice golf course with putting green, tennis court, pétanque and croquet.

Weekly and Daily Terms on Application
Bed and Breakfast from £95.00 Single, £115.00 Double
Lunch from £22.50 and A La Carte
Business Lunch from £16.00
Afternoon Tea from £4.00
Dinner from £23.50 and A La Carte
Gratuities at Guest's discretion

VAT inclusive. Credit Cards—Access, American Express, Diners Club, Visa
4 Executive, 14 Double, 2 Twin Bedrooms
All Rooms with Private Bathroom, TV, Telephone, Radio, Tea and Coffee-Making Facilities, Trouser Press, Hairdryer
Open All Year. Residential and Restaurant Licence. Full Central Heating

Cocktail Bar. TV Lounge
Conference Facilities
Children catered for
Dogs not allowed
Parking Facilities. Night Porter
Hard Tennis Court, Croquet, Putting
Nearby: Golf, Fishing, Riding, Shooting

Stratford-upon-Avon—Stratford House Hotel Sheep Street, Stratford-upon-Avon, Warwickshire. CV37 6EF. Tel 0789 268288. Fax 0789 295580

Only one hundred yards from the world renowned Royal Shakespeare Theatre, you can step through an open door from Sheep Street into the welcoming comfort of this hotel's very pretty lounge. Walk through the reception area and a cosy bar, and you are greeted by the light decor of the spacious *Shepherd's Garden Restaurant*, overlooking the soft greens of the walled garden beyond. Indoors or out, the tranquil setting is immediately conducive to relaxed enjoyment of a drink or a meal. Lunch and dinner menus offer a splendid choice of mouth-watering dishes, realistically priced and served most courteously and efficiently. Only fresh ingredients are used, pre-theatre dinners are bookable and, once a quarter, very popular gourmet dinners are prepared by a guest chef. Their wine list extends to over fifty bins, with many of these most usefully available in half bottles. This restaurant is a delightful setting for small wedding receptions and private functions. For senior executive policy meetings, the Georgian Lounge is ideal, patrons here sometimes taking over the entire hotel for two or three days of complete privacy, supported by twenty-four hour service. Superior quality furnishings, absolutely spotless cleanliness and elegant furniture all confirm that the standards maintained here are of the very highest. For home and overseas visitors, this select hotel is the perfect centre for touring the Heart of England with the beauty of the Cotswold countryside and its picturesque villages nearby.

Weekly Terms on application
Bed and Breakfast from £27.00
Lunch from £9.50 A La Carte
Dinner from £13.50 A La Carte
Gratuities at Guest's discretion
VAT inclusive. Credit Cards–Access,

American Express, Diners Club, JCB, Visa
1 Family Room, 1 Single, 4 Double, 5 Twin Bedrooms. 8 Private Bathrooms.3 Private Shower Rooms. All Rooms with TV, Telephone, Radio, Tea and Coffee-making Facilities. Hairdryer available. Baby Sitting

arranged. Theatre Booking Service
Open all Year except Christmas
Residential and Restaurant Licence
Full CH. Cocktail Bar. Children over 4 catered for. Dogs not allowed
Car Parking arrangement

Section 4: Warwickshire

Stratford-upon-Avon—Welcombe Hotel and Golf Course Warwick Road, Stratford-upon-Avon, Warwickshire. CV37 0NR. Tel 0789 295252. Fax 0789 414666

One of the many attributes of this superior hotel is that desirable ingredient so often missing in newer hotels–space. There is spaciousness both inside and outside this imposing nineteenth-century country house. It stands in 157 acres of parkland which slopes gently towards the River Avon and contains an eighteen-hole, par-70 golf course. The present mansion was built in 1869 by Mr Mark Philips, remaining with the Philips family for many years and then was left by Mr R N Phillips to his daughter Caroline, the wife of the late Rt Hon Sir George Trevelyan. One of its many distinguished visitors was Theodore Roosevelt, who stayed here in 1910. Today, it is one of the leading hotels in this famous area and preserves an atmosphere of gracious living. Whether you stay in one of the spacious bedrooms in the original house, with its antique furnishings, or in the garden wing, you will find your room well planned with a bathroom *en suite*, colour television, radio, a telephone, beverage-making facilities, a trouser press and a hairdryer, and twenty-four-hour room service is available. The food is excellent and the *haute cuisine à la carte* menu offers many specialities. On Sundays a special luncheon menu is offered, with roast beef carved from a trolley. We have visited the hotel on many occasions and at all times of the year. A stay here is certainly very agreeable and readers should note that the hotel is now operated by Orient Express Hotels.

Bed and Breakfast from £90.00
Lunch from £17.50 and A La Carte
Afternoon Tea from £7.50
Dinner from £27.50 and A La Carte
Service Charge and VAT inclusive
Credit Cards–Access, American Express,

Diners Club, Visa
34 Double, 40 Twin, 2 Single Bedrooms
(inc 10 Suites, 15 Family Rooms). All
Rooms with Private Bath/Shower
Rooms, TV, Telephone, Radio,
Baby-listening, Trouser Press, Hairdryer

Tea and Coffee-making Facilities upon request. Open all Year except 28 December to 3 January
Fully Licensed. Full Central Heating
2 Cocktail Bars. Games Room
Dogs allowed. Parking Facilities

Near Stratford-upon-Avon, Alcester—Kings Court Hotel Kings Coughton, Near Alcester, Warwickshire. B49 5QQ. Tel 0789 763111. Fax 0789 400242

One of King's Coughton's claims to fame is its notoriety in connection with the Gunpowder Plot, a conspiracy to blow up the English Parliament and James I on the fifth of November, 1605. A more relevant claim, to us, is the excellence of the Kings Court Hotel, a newly refurbished Tudor lodge and Georgian farmhouse, together with a bedroom extension offering the most comfortable rooms. Naturally all the bedrooms have *en suite* facilities but some are really like suites since each has its own sitting area. The Tudor bedrooms, named after Shakespeare's characters, are full of interest with original oak beams. Throughout the hotel the decoration can only be described as exquisite with furnishings of an extremely high standard. Overlooking the garden courtyard and fountain, the spacious and finely decorated restaurant offers an extensive and varied *à la carte* menu, featuring home-made dishes and specialities available at lunch time and in the evening. A mouthwatering selection of desserts ensures that you have a memorable meal. An open fire and friendly atmosphere draw you into the bar known as the *Twisted Boot* where you can enjoy good drink, convivial company and excellent bar meals. There are three rooms available for private parties, weddings and conferences of up to 100 guests. The owners, Robert and Kerryn Beverley and their staff can be justifiably proud of the efficiency and pleasant hospitality at this delightful hotel. Kings Court is ideally situated for visiting Stratford-upon-Avon, Warwick and the Cotswolds, and is only twenty-five minutes from the NEC, ICC and Birmingham city centre.

Bed and Breakfast from £49.00 Single, £60.00 Double. Bar Meal from £2.95
Lunch from £7.00 and A La Carte
Afternoon Tea from £1.50
Dinner from £12.00 and A La Carte
Service Charge and VAT inclusive

Credit Cards–Access, American Express, Visa. 1 Family Room
11 Double, 2 Twin, 6 Single Bedrooms
All Rooms with Private Bathroom, TV, Telephone, Radio, Tea and Coffee-making Facilities, Hairdryer. Open all Year

Fully Licensed. Full Central Heating
Conference Facilities
Children catered for. Dogs allowed
Parking Facilities. Nearby: Tennis, Squash, Badminton, Swimming, Solarium, Sauna
Golf, Fishing, Riding, Sailing

Section 4: Warwickshire & West Midlands

Near Stratford-upon-Avon, Billesley—Billesley Manor Hotel and Restaurant
Billesley, Alcester, Warwickshire. B49 6NF. Tel 0789 400888. Fax 0789 764145

Billesley Manor's history started long before the *Domesday Book* was compiled. In 1066 William I granted the property to the Trussell family. The present impressive building, which stands back from the A46 road three miles from Stratford-upon-Avon, was developed by Sir Robert Lee, Lord Mayor of London, towards the end of the sixteenth-century. The house is surrounded by a garden with fantastic topiary work and the eleven acres of grounds encompass two tennis courts, croquet and boules, a pitch-and-putt course and a delightful heated indoor swimming pool where in warm weather, doors can be opened onto the patio. Inside the house is elegance which one associates with our finest architecture–high moulded ceilings, graceful chandeliers, fine oak panelling and carved fireplaces. There are forty-one bedrooms including suites and four-poster rooms and many have been attractively refurbished in 1991 to a very high standard. To lunch or dine here is a memorable occasion: superb English dishes and French *entrees* vie for one's attention. For connoisseurs of wine it can be a heady experience choosing and enjoying some of the hundred or so listed wines. Here, then, is an hotel of great stature in an excellent location for touring the Cotswolds and Shakespeare country. There are special facilities for banquets and conferences for up to eighty people. If you appreciate history and high standards, excellent service and good value, together with the simple pleasures like home-made bread and fudge, you will wish to return here often.

Bed and Breakfast from £99.00 Single, £128.00 Twin
Bar Lunch from £3.50
Lunch from £17.00 and A La Carte
Afternoon Tea from £6.50
Dinner from £27.00 and A La Carte
Gratuities at Guest's discretion

VAT inclusive. Credit Cards—Access, American Express, Diners Club, Visa
3 Four Poster Rooms. 2 Suites
17 Double, 1 Single, 18 Twin Bedrooms
All Rooms with Private Bathrooms, TV, Telephone, Radio, Baby-listening, Hairdryer, Trouser Press. Room Service
Open all Year. Fully Licensed

Full Central Heating and Log Fires
Cocktail Bar. Conference Facilities
Children catered for. Dogs not allowed.
Parkiing Facilities. Night Porter
Tennis, Croquet, Pitch & Putt, Pool
Nearby: Golf, Fishing, Riding, Shooting, Royal Shakespeare Theatre

Aldridge—The Fairlawns at Aldridge Little Aston Road, Aldridge,
Birmingham, West Midlands. WS9 0NU. Tel 0922 55122. Fax 0922 743210

Away from the hustle and bustle of the city centre, and yet within easy reach of central Birmingham, this outstanding establishment is a winner on many counts. The situation is superb. Seventy acres of open countryside surround The Fairlawns' large landscaped gardens and from here the NEC International Arena, the old English towns of Warwick and Kenilworth, and many beautiful Cotswold villages are all in compass. The hotel's proprietor is John Pette and his warm Yorkshire friendliness sets a pattern of welcome and hospitality which would beguile any visitor. Little wonder The Fairlawns is such a magnet of attraction hereabouts. The air-conditioned restaurant plays its part, too, for here there is something to suit every taste. From a light meal with freshly baked rolls, seasonal main courses created by *chef de cuisine* Stefan Wilkinson, home-made sweets and freshly brewed Colombian coffee with hand-made chocolates. The extensive cellars offer wines from around the world, which range from *vin ordinaire* to the connoisseur's choice. The next time we visit The Fairlawns it will be to stay, not simply because then each night the restaurant will be just a corridor away, but because we know we shall be extremely comfortable in any of the spacious bedrooms. They are all so beautifully equipped, be they standard rooms, one of the luxury suites or the honeymoon suite with its romantic tester bed. The hotel also has a number of private dining rooms which are in constant demand for conferences, seminars and family celebrations.

Bed and Breakfast from £42.50
Bar Lunch from £2.20
Lunch from £12.95 and A La Carte
Dinner from £18.95 and A La Carte
Service Charge and VAT inclusive
Credit Cards—Access, American Express,

Diners Club, Visa
1 Family Room. 5 Suites
20 Double, 5 Twin, 4 Single Bedrooms
All Rooms with Private Bathroom, TV, Telephone, Radio, Baby-listening, Tea and Coffee-making Facilities, Trouser Press,

Hairdryer. Open All Year
Residential and Restaurant Licence
Full Central Heating
Cocktail Bar. Conference Facilities
Children catered for. Dogs allowed
Parking Facilities. Night Porter

Section 4: West Midlands

Birmingham, King's Norton—Norton Place Hotel
180 Lifford Lane, King's Norton, Birmingham B30 3NT
Tel 021 433 5656. Fax 021 433 3048

Standing in beautiful walled gardens, Norton Place is unquestionably one of the most exclusive hotels in the West Midlands. All ten bedrooms have en suite bathrooms with marble walls and floors, as well as showers, Crabtree & Evelyn toiletries and all of those small personal touches you would expect to find in an hotel of this standard. Throughout the hotel a charming originality of design is expressed in the finest furnishings and fabrics, setting standards of unrivalled comfort and modern luxury, together with personal attentive service. Norton Place is a prestigious venue for both formal and informal conferences with six purpose-designed conference suites to hold up to 150 delegates. The Lombard Room Restaurant has built up an enviable reputation for its excellent cuisine chosen from only the finest ingredients, and a standard of service that is unsurpassed, combined with one of the country's most extensive wine lists. The restaurant is open for lunch and dinner seven days a week. To enhance your stay even further, a luxury swimming pool and leisure facilities have just been completed. In conjunction with all this is Autoworld, a unique collection of cars and associated displays in period sets up to the present day. All of this is located just fifteen minutes' drive away from the centre of Birmingham or the NEC.

Daily Terms from £90.00
Breakfast: English £8.50
Lunch from £12.95 and A La Carte
Afternoon Tea from £6.00
Dinner from £18.00 and a La Carte
VAT inclusive
Credit Cards—Access, American Express, Diners Club, Visa
1 Suite. 9 Double/Twin Bedrooms

(All Rooms can be let as Singles)
All Rooms with Private Bathroom, TV, Telephone, Radio, Trouser Press/Iron, Hairdryer, Mini Bar, Safe, Video/Book Library, 24 hr Room Service
24 hr Valet Service
Open all Year. Fully Licensed
Full Central Heating. Cocktail Bar
Conference Facilities

Children over 10 years catered for
Dogs not allowed
Parking Facilities. Night Porter
Simulated Clay Pigeon Shooting, Fitness Centre
Nearby: Tennis, Putting, Squash, Badminton, Swimming, Solarium, Sauna, Golf, Fishing, Riding

Section 4: West Midlands

Coventry—Hylands Hotel 153 Warwick Road, Coventry, West Midlands. CV3 6AU. Tel 0203 501600. Fax 0203 501027

When many hotels situated in the spreading conurbations have been built with little character or have lost their identities, it is good to find, in quiet parkland surroundings, a personally run hotel such as the Hylands. We had anticipated the ample comfort and good food here, but our major recollections are of a warm welcome and of assiduous service throughout our stay. The catering, too, is a memorable experience. The chef takes pleasure in cooking and a pride in presentation, and the produce, which he turns into a varied selection of dishes, is obviously of good quality. A distinctly modern accommodation wing includes bedrooms which are contemporary in design and have private bathrooms, colour television, radio, direct-dial telephone and beverage-making facilities. As one would expect of an hotel in such a location, there are comprehensive facilities for small conferences, seminars and special functions for up to sixty people. Coventry itself is a fascinating city, with a long history. Its centre, much of it pedestrianised and dotted with parks, is a combination of the medieval and the modern. Learn more about the city's most famous character, Lady Godiva, and why such phrases as 'true blue' and 'sent to Coventry' have passed into our language. There is a lot more to Coventry than you might suppose. The Hylands Hotel offers a particularly attractive and comprehensive bargain weekend tariff, so we hope we have whetted your appetite.

All Prices pertain to 1992	4 Family Rooms. 1 Suite. 1 Triple Room	Residential and Restaurant Licence
Bed and Breakfast from £59.00	11 Double, 6 Executive Double, 10 Twin	Full CH. Conference Facilities
Lunch from £10.95 Table d'Hôte	8 Executive Single, 14 Single Bedrooms.	Dogs allowed in Bedrooms only
Dinner from £13.75 Table d'Hôte	All Rooms with Private Bath/Shower	Parking Facilities. Night Porter
Gratuities at Guest's discretion	Room, TV, Telephone, Radio,	Nearby: Tennis, Putting, Squash,
VAT inclusive. Credit Cards–Access,	Baby-listening, Tea and Coffee-making	Badminton, Swimming, Solarium, Sauna,
American Express, Diners Club, Visa	Facilities, Trouser Press, Hairdryer	Golf, Riding
	Open all Year except Christmas	

Sutton Coldfield—Sutton Court Hotel 60-66 Lichfield Road, Sutton Coldfield, West Midlands. B74 2NA. Tel 021 355 6071. Fax 021 355 0083

Seven miles from the centre of Birmingham is one of the West Midland's prettiest towns, the Royal Borough of Sutton Coldfield, which enjoys the well known Sutton Park, frequented by King Charles II. The nearby Wyndley Leisure Centre is set in thirty two acres, part of 2,400 acres of natural parkland which is just two minutes' walk from the hotel. Adjacent to the A5127 Lichfield Road is this popular enterprising hotel which has kept the elegance of the fine Victorian building. We have enjoyed Sutton Court's hospitality on a number of occasions recently and each visit has whetted our appetites to discover more about this privately owned hotel. The spacious bedrooms are all individually designed with private bathroom, colour television, in-house movies, hairdryer, trouser press, direct dial telephone and refreshment trays, and there are 24-hour room service facilities. Several of the executive suites with their kingsize beds are especially delightful. The food here is also a major attraction, with a selection of time-honoured and original dishes available, all beautifully prepared and presented. During our last visit to the hotel we sampled one of the vegetarian alternatives and found it very flavoursome. The overall impression is of that *rara avis* of modern times, truly personal service. The staff of the *Courtyard Restaurant*, in their distinctive dress, are unfailingly courteous, the housekeeper will happily assist those with special needs and who require extra comforts, and the bellboys and porters are always on hand to carry one's luggage. It is all part of the service in this relaxed and cheerful hotel

Weekly Terms from £510.00 Single,	Lunch from £9.95 and A La Carte	22 Twin, 17 Single Bedrooms. All Rooms
£737.00 Twin	Dinner from £15.95 and A La Carte	with Private Bath/Shower Room, TV,
Daily Terms £92.50 Single, £120.00 Twin	Gratuities at Guest's discretion. VAT	Telephone, Radio, Baby-listening, Tea and
(Fri-Sun £39.50 Room only)	inclusive. Credit Cards–Access, American	coffee-making Facilities, Trouser Press,
Bed and Breakfast from £72.00 Single,	Express, Diners Club, Visa	Hairdryer. Open all Year
£89.00 Twin (Fri-Sun £35.00 Room only)	8 Family Rooms/Suites, 17 Double,	Residential and Restaurant Licence

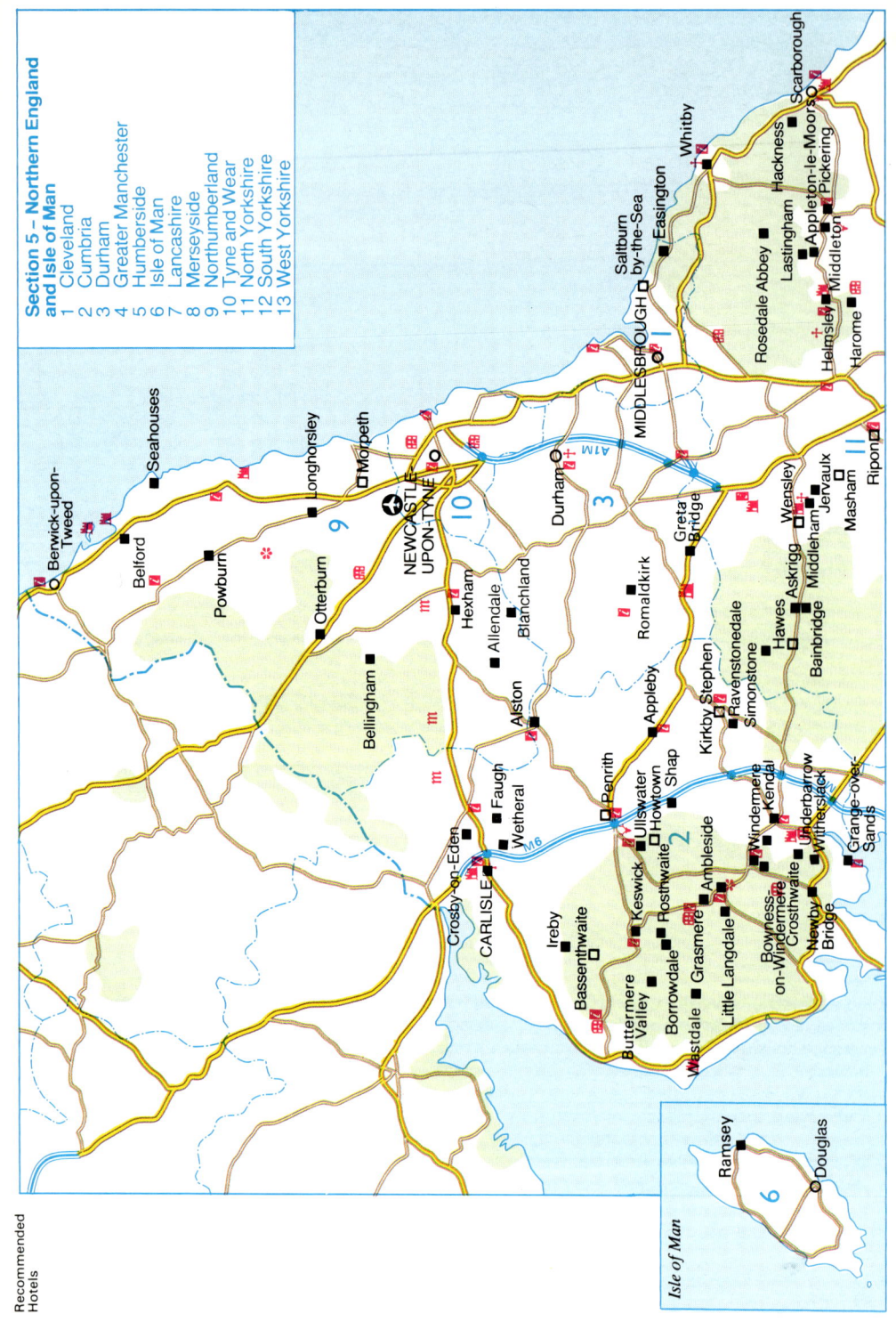

NORTHERN ENGLAND

Derwentwater, Cumbria

Section 5 - Northern England

Cleveland, Cumbria, Durham, Greater Manchester, Northumberland, Isle of Man, Tyne and Wear, North and South and West Yorkshire.

Cleveland

The busy estuary of the River Tees divides this small county into two halves. Although it is difficult to ignore the heavy industrial areas of Middlesborough, there are occasional quiet havens to be explored. Captain Cook's father was buried at Marske-by-the-Sea, unaware that his son had died six weeks earlier. The coast is all fine sand and at Redcar one may see racehorses exercising along the beach.

Cumbria

The Lake District is Britain's biggest National Park. It contains England's largest lake, Windermere, and her loftiest mountain, Scafell Pike. When writing of this area one is mindful of being in illustrious company, for Wordsworth, Coleridge, Ruskin, Beatrix Potter, Southey, Sir Hugh Walpole and many other eminent writers have tried to capture the spirit of this spectacular region in poetry and prose. In many ways its splendour is overwhelming and is certainly not diminished by the countless tourists who flock there every summer. Even so, we ourselves would choose to go there out of the high season, for not even an autumn mist can fully blot out Cumbria's beauty.

Lindisfarne Castle, Northumberland

Durham

The crowning glory of this northern county is Durham Cathedral, which commands an impressive curve of the River Wear. Note the waterfalls of High Force and Cauldron Snout, the range of northern Pennines, rising to 2,000 feet and more, the moorland road from Barnard Castle which runs above the Derwent valley into Northumberland and the Saxon churches of Escomb and Monkwearmouth.

Greater Manchester

Although small in area, this county is not small in population, for it encompasses the city of Manchester, together with its immediate neighbours Oldham, Wigan and Stockport. It is a region which has associations with the Industrial Revolution and the cotton industry. However, it has links with ancient history, too, for early Britons lived here and the Romans built a road between Manchester and York, traces of which still remain.

Humberside

The mighty River Humber is a great natural barrier between the north and south of this county. Before the imposing Humber suspension bridge was built, motorists had to cross the river by ferry or drive round via Goole. Now it is a county which is easily explored. Its distinguishing features are, commercially, the city of Hull and, architecturally, Beverley Minster. In addition, both Cleethorpes and Bridlington are excellent seaside resorts.

Isle of Man

Although only thirty-two miles long by thirteen miles at its widest point, the Isle of Man is noted for its independence and individuality. Its three-legged coat of arms, the TT motorcycle races and its tailless variety of cat, the Manx, are famous throughout the world. The island also has the oldest parliament in the world. Just thirty miles from both England and Ireland, the Isle of Man is easily reached by steamer or air.

Lancashire

Motorists passing through the county north/south on the M6 will miss much if they ignore the Trough of Bowland and the Lune and Ribble valleys. The Lancashire sea-board provides healthy resorts for its industrial centres - Lytham St Anne's, Blackpool and Morecambe are all worth visiting.

Merseyside

This is an oddly-shaped county, the main body of which is almost circular and takes in the city of Liverpool and neighbouring Kirkby and St Helens. To this area is added an elongated strip of land which follows the coast northwards to the Ribble estuary and takes in the popular holiday resorts of Southport and Formby.

Embleton Bay, Northumberland

Northumberland

In years gone by border warfare was rife in this large county. Hence there are many remarkable ruined castles and fortified parsonage houses at Elsdon and Embleton, and, of course, there is Hadrian's Wall. Much of the coastline is well worth visiting. See the Farne Islands near Bamburgh and the holy island of Lindisarne. Other interesting places are Alnwick, Blanchland and Morpeth. For the most spectacular first view of Scotland take the A68 from Scotch Corner to Carter Bar.

Tyne and Wear

Tyneside and Wearside and, further to the south, Teeside, have become industrial ports. Between these ports the coast is largly unspoilt with long stretches of often deserted sands and dunes. Druridge Bay is a marvellous example, with white sands backed by dunes and open country. The people of Tyneside can travel to the coast on the sleek trains of the Metro.

North, South and West Yorkshire

Each of these three counties has special charms of its own, but it is North Yorkshire which has been most popular with tourists during the post-war period. Fortunately the county is large - it covers most of the rural areas of the North and West Ridings, together with a medley of coastal villages such as Robin Hood's Bay and Staithes - so that it accommodates all who go there without being spoilt. For touring purposes, Yorkshire can be divided into three areas - the western dales and uplands, the central plain and the eastern sea-board, together with the North Yorkshire moors.

Section 5: Cleveland and Cumbria

Near Saltburn-by-the-Sea, Easington—Grinkle Park Hotel
Easington, Saltburn-by-the-Sea, Cleveland. TS13 4UB. Tel 0287 640515. Fax 0287 641278

Whilst motoring around the Cleveland Hills we were attracted once again to this lovely country-house hotel. We called in to look at some of the rooms, with their attractive new décor and we wandered round the gardens, where rhododendrons, azaleas and laburnum added colour. Above stairs, the immaculate bedrooms are individually named. If you choose to stay here you will be given *Skylark, Azalea, Baysdale* or some other reminder of rural life, rather than a number. As we enjoyed the home-made refreshments provided for us, our thoughts turned to that passage in Longfellow's *Masque of Pandora*, 'The atmosphere breathes rest and comfort, and the many chambers seem full of welcomes.' The food at Grinkle Park is varied and of a gourmet standard. At lunchtime, for instance, you will be offered a choice of bar snacks in the attractive sun lounge, and a *table d' hôte* menu of notable value. In the evening an *à la carte* selection is also available. A thoughtfully compiled wine list complements the food. The other facilities at Grinkle Park reinforce the impression of a country-house life-style. Snooker, croquet and clay-pigeon shooting are all at hand and thirty-five acres of grounds ensure complete seclusion. You will find this excellent country-house hotel just four miles from the coast. The imaginative refurbishment which has taken place here and the guidance of Mrs. Jane Norton, the manageress, have made Grinkle Park a warm and welcoming place to stay.

Weekly Terms from £327.25
Bed and Breakfast from £65.00 (Single) £80.00 (Double)
Bar Lunch from £3.50
Lunch from £9.95 (2 courses)
Dinner from £15.50 and A La Carte
Gratuities at Guest's discretion
VAT inclusive

Credit Cards—Access, American Express, Diners Club, Visa
7 Double (2 with 4-poster Bed), 6 Twin, 7 Single Bedrooms. 14 Private Bathrooms
6 Private Shower Rooms
All Rooms with TV, Telephone, Baby-listening, Tea and Coffee-making Facilities, Trouser Press

6 Rooms with Hairdryer
Open all Year. Fully Licensed
Conference Facilities
Children catered for. Dogs allowed
Parking Facilities
Tennis, Croquet, Clay-pigeon Shooting, Fishing

Alston—Lowbyer Manor
Alston, Cumbria. CA9 3JX. Telephone 0434 381230

'But for the modern dress of the people, you would imagine yourself to have gone back in time one hundred years'. This is written of Alston in the brochure for this Country House Hotel and Restaurant. At one time owned by the Earl of Derwentwater, The Manor dates from the seventeenth century and has been thoughtfully converted to provide quiet, comfortable accommodation. Everywhere the original atmosphere persists: exposed natural stone walls, oak beams and an inglenook fireplace. Dinner *à la carte* is served in their *Derwent* Restaurant, offering predominantly English dishes. A sense of history pervades not only The Manor and the steep cobbled streets of Alston, it extends to the wild unspoilt fells and peaks of the High Pennines. The Romans passed this way and created the Maiden Way, their western route to Hadrian's Wall and Whitley Castle, a huge fort north of Alston. There are many interesting walks to be taken, ranging from a gentle riverside stroll to more strenuous expeditions to the summit of one of the nearby fells; Alston, of course, is on the Pennine Way. Much exists to interest the botanist and the ornithologist out on the moors where, also, you may discover ancient quarries and mine workings. Because Alston is the meeting-point for five roads it is uniquely suitable as a base for touring northern England and southern Scotland, the Lake District, Northumbria, County Durham and North Yorkshire. Consequently, you will have easy access to a wide variety of activities including golf, fishing, shooting, riding and, in the winter-time, skiing.

Weekly Terms from £280.00
Bed and Breakfast from £29.95
Afternoon Tea from £2.25
Dinner from £14.50 A La Carte
Gratuities at Guest's discretion
VAT inclusive. Credit Cards—Access,

American Express, Diners Club, Visa
6 Double, 1 Single, 5 Twin Bedrooms
7 Private Bathrooms
5 Private Shower Rooms
All Rooms with TV, Radio,
Tea and Coffee-making Facilities

Hairdryer, Iron, Drying Facilities available on request. Open all Year
Residential and Restaurant Licence
Full Central Heating. Cocktail Bar
Conference Facilities. Children catered for
Dogs allowed by arrangement

Section 5: Cumbria

Near Alston—Lovelady Shield Country House Hotel
Nenthead Road, Near Alston, Cumbria. CA9 3LF. Tel 0434 381203. Fax 0434 381515

So many people have written to us in praise of this exquisite country house, we cannot possibly claim it as one of our 'discoveries'. One reader has written, 'without any hesitation or shadow of a doubt I recommend Lovelady Shield Country House Hotel to tourists and British friends.'. Another reader's comments were less flamboyant. 'Such a pleasant hotel, such good service, food and accommodation'. Personal recommendation has alone brought fame to Lovelady Shield and we are happy to add our note of appreciation, too. Here, Kenneth and Margaret Lyons run their hotel as a labour of love. They provide the finest English food and excellent speciality dishes to tempt the appetite. The exceptional selection of cheeses is also praised. If all this and the hotel's name are not temptation enough to stay there, think of days spent exploring the Lake District, the Scottish borders and the magnificent countryside either side of Hadrian's Wall. Then consider the absolute tranquility of this lovely corner of Cumbria, where the Lyons have established a comfortable rural retreat of the highest standard–in fact the hotel has now been awarded four crowns and highly commended by the ETB. All the bedrooms are equipped with *en suite* bathroom or shower room and the latest notions of comfort. The four and a half acres of gardens are bounded on one side by the River Nent and contain a hard tennis court and a trim croquet lawn. Two and a half miles to the west, along the A689 road, is Alston, the highest market town in England.

Weekly Terms from £368.00	1 Four-Poster Suite	Full Central Heating
Daily Terms from £60.00	5 Double, 4 Twin, 2 Single Bedrooms	Cocktail Bar
Bed and Breakfast from £37.50	8 Private Bathrooms	Dogs allowed
Sunday Lunch £12.00	4 Private Shower Rooms	Parking Facilities
Dinner £22.50	All Rooms with TV, Radio, Telephone,	Tennis, Croquet
Gratuities at Guest's discretion	Baby-listening, Hairdryer, Electric Blankets	Nearby: Golf, Fishing, Riding, Shooting
VAT inclusive. Credit Cards—Access,	Open from 20th February to 2nd January	
American Express, Diners Club, Visa	Residential and Restaurant Licence	

Ambleside—Compston House Hotel
Compston Road, Ambleside, Cumbria. LA22 9DJ. Tel 05394 32305

This is a small and friendly hostelry, right in the centre of Ambleside, enjoying lovely views of the surrounding fells and just a ten minute walk away from the shore of Lake Windermere. Built of local stone in typical Lakeland style, Compston House fits in well in this quaint village full of charm and character. If personal service means anything at all in these days of hackneyed phrases, it means a great deal here. Recent extensive improvements have been most successfully completed and all rooms have been refurbished and redecorated to a high standard. Each comfortable room is centrally heated and has its own private facilities together with colour television and tea and coffee-making equipment. You could try that romantic four poster for that special occasion or the beautiful king size room which boasts an extra large bed and sofa area for added luxury. Delicious four course breakfasts are a speciality and, from time to time, excellent home-cooked evening meals are available. Numerous good restaurants and pubs are within five minutes' walk so eating out is both very easy and enjoyable. A cosy licensed bar and comfortable lounge tempt you to linger and enjoy the beautiful views but if your interests include tennis, croquet, bowls and putting, you will be ideally situated at Compston House, for all these activities are to be found in the pretty park opposite the hotel. If, on the other hand, you prefer a day's sightseeing, rock climbing, sailing or hill walking, Ann and Graham Smith will be happy to send you off with a substantial packed lunch.

Weekly Terms from £205.00	1 Twin, 6 Double Bedrooms	Residential and Restaurant Licence
Daily Terms from £30.00	All Rooms with Private Bathroom, TV, Tea	Full Central Heating. Cocktail Bar
Bed and Breakfast from £19.50	and Coffee-making Facilities	Children over 5 catered for. Dogs not
Bar Meal from £3.50. Dinner from £10.50	Hairdryer, Iron and Shoe Cleaning	allowed. Car Park nearby. Nearby: Tennis,
Table d'Hôte. Gratuities at Guest's	available on request	Croquet, Putting, Squash, Badminton,
discretion. VAT inclusive. 1 Family Room	Open all Year except for 4 weeks	Swimming, Solarium, Sauna, Fishing

Section 5: Cumbria

Ambleside—The Fisherbeck Hotel
Lake Road, Ambleside, Cumbria. LA22 0DH. Tel 05394 33215

Whatever your interests, this hotel will provide you with an ideal base. Your hosts, Brian and Kathleen Barton will enjoy telling you the intriguing history of their hotel–parts of the building have been used as a tannery and a school. If you are approaching from the south, leave the M6 at Junction 36, signposted A590 South Lakes, and follow the signs for the A591 to Windermere. Keep to the A591 at Windermere for Ambleside. As you enter Ambleside bear right at Waterhead and you will find the hotel on the right in about 700 yards. If you are approaching from the north, follow the main A591 road through Ambleside town centre towards Windermere. The hotel is on the left as you leave Ambleside. There is a choice of twenty bedrooms, eighteen with private facilities, which have been attractively furnished and decorated. The pleasant lounge has magnificent views towards Loughrigg Fell and is an ideal place to relax and chat with other visitors. Kathleen Barton personally supervises the cooking, providing a varied menu of outstanding quality. We particularly enjoyed her roast leg of pork with spicy orange sauce and *suprême* of chicken with a mild creamy ginger sauce. The hotel has an extensive although inexpensive wine list to complement your meal. The hotel stands in its own grounds and provides magnificent views of the surrounding fells. Arrangements have been made for residents to fish on several of the nearby tarns and rivers. There is so much to see and do and the local Tourist Information Centres are a mine of information. Just ask. Cumbrian hospitality and friendliness will do the rest.

Special Breaks from Nov to end March
Weekly Terms from £225.00
Daily Terms from £35.00
Bed and Breakfast from £24.50
Bar Meal from £4.00. Lunch from £8.00
Dinner from £15.50

Gratuities at Guest's discretion
VAT inclusive. Credit Cards–Access, Visa
3 Family Rooms. 1 Single, 14 Double, 2 Twin Bedrooms. 8 Private Bathrooms. 9 Private Shower Rooms
All Rooms with TV, Telephone, Tea

and Coffee-making Facilities
Open from January to December
Fully Licensed. Full Central Heating
Cocktail Bar. Dogs not allowed
Parking Facilities. Children catered for
Nearby: Tennis, Putting, Squash

Ambleside—Kirkstone Foot Country House Hotel
Kirkstone Pass Road, Ambleside, Cumbria. LA22 9EH. Tel 05394 32232

Here, in the Lake District's beautiful vale of the Rothay, lies Kirkstone Foot, a truly delightful place to stay. Hidden away, in tranquil gardens where one can stroll peacefully, yet it is only five minutes' walk from the centre of Ambleside. Under the able management of Andrew and Annabel Bedford this seventeenth century manor house offers a typical lakeland centre for all the diverse attractions of this area. News of their excellent reputation has spread far and wide, as visitors from the USA and Australia were there when we stayed. Andrew welcomed us and showed us around. We made our choice for the delicious five course dinner and, as did everyone, went for a drink before dinner at 7.30 p.m. The mouth-watering fare is English cooking at its best complemented by an extensive wine list with a selection from nearly every wine producing country in the world. Unique as far as we know, Kirkstone Foot, as well as being a delightful hotel, has seventeen self-catering apartments for two to eight persons. For disabled visitors a ground floor apartment can be arranged and the hotel facilities are available to all guests. From the hotel the narrow steep road to the summit of Kirkstone Pass (1500 feet) is known locally as *The Struggle* but staying at Kirkstone Foot Country House Hotel is no struggle at all!

Weekly Terms from £285.50 High Season
Daily Terms from £39.50 High Season
Packed Lunches available on request
Afternoon Tea from £1.20
Dinner from £18.25 Table d'Hôte
Gratuities at Guest's discretion
VAT inclusive
Credit Cards—Access, American Express,

Diners Club, Visa
2 Family Rooms
1 Single, 6 Double, 6 Twin Bedrooms
15 Self-catering Apartments
All Rooms with Private Bathroom
(2 with Shower), TV, Telephone,
Radio, Tea and Coffee-making Facilities,
Hairdryer. Baby-listening available

Open from February to December, also Christmas and New Year
Residential Licence. Full Central Heating
Dogs allowed in Apartments only
Parking Facilities. Nearby: Tennis, Croquet, Putting, Squash, Swimming, Golf Fishing, Riding, Sailing, Windsurfing, Water Skiing

Section 5: Cumbria

Ambleside—Rothay Garth Hotel
Rothay Road, Ambleside, Cumbria. LA22 0EE. Tel 05394 32217. Fax 05394 34400

The most valid commendation for any hotel is a high proportion of guests making return visits. The proportion here is very considerable as a result of sustained high standards and attention to detail. There is an annual programme of improvements and all rooms, bedrooms and public rooms are furnished and decorated luxuriously. The beautiful and elegant *Loughrigg Restaurant* overlooks the water garden and the mountain of Loughrigg beyond. Chefs Philip Taylor and Susan Crosby take pride in the preparation and presentation of the *table d'hôte* menus. Fresh local produce is the basis for the highly acclaimed menus which give an excellent individual choice and change every night. The imaginative dishes are well supported by a wide range of carefully selected wines. Personal attention by proprietors, Doreen and David Clark, leaves guests free to enjoy to the full the charm and scenic beauty of the area. Ambleside village, with its quality shops, museums, craft centres, arts and entertainment, enjoys a central location at the northern end of Lake Windermere and is ideal for a holiday at any time of the year. Hotel staff are happy to arrange activities ranging from cultural visits, coach and lake tours, fishing, pony trekking and the popular guided walks. For the visitor staying a week, an excursion or activity is offered free giving you the opportunity to make the most of your time in this peaceful yet exhilarating region. The hotel offers splendid value breaks throughout the year.

Weekly Terms (including day on lake or scenic tour) from £238.00 (winter), £320.00 (summer)
Bed and Breakfast from £27.00 (winter), £36.00 (summer)
Lunch from £9.50 and A La Carte
Dinner from £19.00 Table d'Hôte
Gratuities at Guest's discretion

VAT inclusive. Credit Cards—Access, American Express, Diners Club, Visa
2 Family Rooms. 1 Suite
9 Double, 2 Single, 2 Twin Bedrooms
8 Private Bathrooms. 6 Private Shower Rooms. All Rooms with TV, Telephone, Radio, Baby-listening, Tea and Coffee-making Facilities, Hairdryer, Fruit,

Stationery. Open all year
Residential and Restaurant Licence
Full Central Heating. Cocktail Bar
TV Lounge. Conference Facilities
Special Diets catered for
Dogs allowed by arrangement
Parking Facilities
Windsurfing, Canoeing, Guided Walks

Ambleside—Rothay Manor Hotel
Rothay Bridge, Ambleside, Cumbria. LA22 0EH. Tel 053 94 33605. Fax 05394 33607

One of the best compliments we can pay this lovely hotel is to say that even when it has a full complement of guests it appears to be no more than 'quietly busy'. When we called here recently, our lunch was simple, yet mouthwatering, the service was most efficient, yet discreet, and the surroundings were elegant, yet sublimely comfortable. Within this Regency house, situated at the head of Lake Windermere and flanked by the fells of Loughrigg and Wansfell, you will find comfortable bedrooms, each fully equipped with private bathroom, colour television, telephone and central heating. Some rooms have balconies overlooking the garden. A lodge in the grounds (just fifty yards from the front door of the hotel) has been converted into two suites, one especially designed for honeymooners and the other, with three bedrooms leading off a lounge, for families. One ground floor room has been enlarged and refurbished and is now suitable for disabled guests. Almost every visit to Rothay Manor reveals further refinements which add to guests' comfort and well-being. Above all there is the exquisite food. Quite why so many good chefs gravitate to Cumbria we do not know, but guests at Rothay Manor enjoy a tradition of culinary excellence. The menus are not large, but they are changed every evening and the dishes are a lesson in imagination. With each main course a complementary wine is suggested. Ambleside lies at the heart of Lakeland and from here one can travel southwards around the perimeter of Lake Windermere or visit the northern lakes and the unspoilt grandeur of the craggy passes and fells.

Bed and Breakfast from £52.00
Buffet Lunch from £6.00
Sunday Lunch £13.25
Afternoon Tea from £6.50
Dinner from £20.00 Table d'Hôte
Gratuities at Guest's discretion

VAT inclusive. Credit Cards—Access, American Express, Diners Club, Visa
5 Family Rooms. 3 Suites
3 Twin, 5 Double, 2 Single Bedrooms (2 Rooms suitable for Disabled Guests)
All Rooms with Private Bathroom, TV,

Radio, Telephone. Open from February to 1st week January. Residential and Restaurant Licence. Full Central Heating. Cocktail Bar. Conference Facilities
Dogs allowed in grounds only
Parking Facilities. Croquet

Section 5: Cumbria

Ambleside—Wateredge Hotel
Borrans Road, Ambleside, Cumbria. LA22 0EP. Tel 05394 32332

Situated in an unrivalled position at the head of Windermere and on the outskirts of the picturesque town of Ambleside, stands the Wateredge. This family run hotel was originally two seventeenth century fishermen's cottages, whose character now forms the basis of the charm of the whole building. The well-maintained hotel gardens run down to the edge of the water and afford unsurpassed views of Lake Windermere and the Lakeland Fells. Here, guests can enjoy morning coffee, light lunches and afternoon teas on the garden patio or, perhaps, venture out in the hotel's own rowing boat from the small jetty. All the public rooms have a bright and welcoming décor, many being furnished with antiques, local books and novels, offering interesting relaxation. Dining at the Wateredge is an occasion in itself. The dining area, set within the original cottages, creates its own particular ambiance under oak-beamed ceilings with the glow of a warm log fire in winter time. The traditional six course dinners are prepared with flair and imagination using only fresh produce of the highest quality and a truly mouthwatering choice of dishes is offered. At the Wateredge you may choose to stay in one of the hotel's elegant bedrooms, all with full bathroom facilities, or in one of the five spacious luxury suites with either balcony or patio. Travelling northwards on the A591, fork left just after the Ambleside sign, skirt Lake Windermere for a few hundred yards and look for Wateredge on your left behind a neat hedge.

Terms on Application
Gratuities at Guest's discretion
VAT inclusive. Credit Cards—Access, American Express, Visa
1 Family Room. 5 Suites. 8 Double, 6 Twin, 3 Single Bedrooms
18 Private Bathrooms. 5 Private Shower Rooms. All Rooms with TV, Telephone.

Radio, Tea and Coffee-making Facilities, Hairdryer. Open from Early February to Mid-December. Residential and Restaurant Licence. Full Central Heating and Log Fires Cocktail Bar. TV Lounge
Conference Facilities
Children over 7 years catered for

Dogs by arrangement but not in Public Rooms or Suites
Parking Facilities. Fishing, Rowing Nearby: Tennis, Croquet, Putting, Swimming, Golf, Fishing, Riding, Sailing, Windsurfing, Water Skiing

Ambleside, Barngates—The Drunken Duck Inn
Barngates, Ambleside, Cumbria. LA22 0NG. Tel 05394 36347

When we were young blades, between the wars, we used to visit this mellow inn and we remember the food we got there suited our voracious appetites and that the story of how the inn gained its name hung on the wall of the small lounge bar. Many years before, the landlady found that she had run short of rations. Remote from any shop and fretting over her empty larder, she looked out of the window and saw what appeared to be six dead ducks at her door. Praising Providence for such unexpected manna, she commenced plucking them and hardly had she completed her task when all six started to show signs of life. The ducks were not dead, but dead drunk, having imbibed too freely of a leaking cask of beer. Filled with remorse, the landlady promptly knitted them a red jacket apiece, and the Barngate Inn has been known as The Drunken Duck ever since. It is a good story and we recounted it in the bar with some locals when we stayed at the inn recently. The victuals here were everything we remembered them to be–honest, man-size amounts of hearty Cumberland food, which recognised the needs of walkers and fishermen who have been out in the fresh air all day. After a bottle of good Mosel inside us and a good night's sleep, we were almost prepared to do justice to the enormous breakfast the following morning! The bedrooms are very well equipped and the new dining room is quite delightful. Yet, this has all the characteristics and atmosphere of a traditional lakeland inn. It stands sentinel at the crossroads on the Ambleside—Coniston road, and you should stop there.

Weekly and Daily Terms on Application
Bed and Breakfast from £45.00 Single, £65 Double. Bar Lunch from £4.00
Bar Supper from £6.00
Dinner from £20.00 Table D'Hôte
(Residents only)

VAT inclusive. Gratuities at Guest's Discretion. Credit Cards—Access, Visa
1 Twin, 9 Double Bedrooms
(Doubles can be let as Singles)
8 Private Bathrooms
2 Private Shower Rooms

All Rooms with TV, Telephone, Tea and Coffee-making Facilities, Hairdryer
Open All Year. Fully Licensed
Full Central Heating
Small Conference Facilities
Dogs allowed. Parking Facilities

Section 5: Cumbria

Ambleside, Rothay Bridge—Riverside Hotel
Near Rothay Bridge, Ambleside, Cumbria. LA22 9LJ
Tel 05394 32395

Ambleside is a town which must sooner or later figure in one's lakeland explorations, so make a note of the Riverside Hotel. Since the little town is much frequented, especially in summer, it can be advantageous to stay just outside—follow the beautiful, quiet lane which runs alongside the River Rothay and you will find the hotel and its extensive grounds. A 100-yard stretch of the river belongs to the hotel and there is direct access from the grounds onto Loughrigg Fell. Tasteful modernisation has given all the bedrooms central heating, en suite bathroom, colour television, direct-dial telephone, hairdryer and beverage-making facilities. James and Jean Hainey are the owners and they work hard to ensure that there is a feeling of warmth and a friendly atmosphere at the Riverside. Mr Hainey is a professional chef and was a part-time lecturer at a catering college. He also gained a high reputation at one of Blackpool's leading hotels, which he owned for twenty-four years. Now, he and his wife have chosen the quiet and peace of this small hotel, which has been sought out by people from all over the world. The catering is very good and Mr Hainey is happy, as far as possible, to cater for the special tastes of his guests, including vegetarians. An ideal spot, indeed, is the Riverside for those wanting to spend their holidays amid lakeland's unparalleled natural advantages, but also want to escape from the crowds. The hotel has been awarded four crowns highly commended by the English Tourist Board.

Weekly Terms from £280.00
Daily Terms from £40.00
Bar Lunch from £5.00
Afternoon Tea from £5.00
Dinner from £18.00 and A La Carte
Gratuities at Guest's Discretion
VAT inclusive
Credit Cards—Access, Visa

6 Double, 4 Twin Bedrooms
7 Private Bathrooms
3 Private Shower Rooms
All Rooms with TV, Telephone, Radio, Tea and Coffee-making Facilities, Hairdryer
Open from February to November
Residential and Restaurant Licence
Full Central Heating

TV Lounge. Conference Facilities
Cocktail Bar. Dogs not allowed
Parking Facilities. Fishing
Nearby: Tennis, Putting, Squash, Badminton, Swimming Pool, Sauna, Golf, Riding, Sailing, Windsurfing, Water Skiing, Shooting

Section 5: Cumbria

Near Ambleside—Skelwith Bridge Hotel
Skelwith Bridge, Near Ambleside, Cumbria. LA22 9NJ. Tel 05394 32115. Fax 05394 34254

Those in pursuit not only of the quiet life but of the good life will be charmed by this lovely traditional seventeenth century lakeland inn situated in the heart of the Lake District National Park and surrounded on all sides by splendidly dramatic scenery.. Set in pretty woodlands a little way back from a bridge over the River Brathay, it has been a pivotal point for tourists and holidaymakers to this area for as long as we have known it. Well appointed *en suite* bedrooms offer all the modern facilities expected by today's travellers and most rooms have good views of the fells and woodlands. Across the hotel forecourt is the *Lodge*–ideal for those seeking separation without isolation. Below stairs an abundance of oak beams and original features create a unique atmosphere in the lounges and library bar, ideal places for relaxation after a day spent exploring this beautiful area. The Bridge Restaurant which overlooks the woods and affords a glimpse of the river beyond, is a setting equal to the fine *cuisine* which is served there. To the rear of the hotel you will find *The Talbot* where food and drinks have been served to travellers for over 300 years. The Lake District charms may vary with each season but Skelwith Bridge Hotel is highly recommended for its cheer, comfort and personal welcome at any time of the year.

Terms on Application
No Service Charge
VAT inclusive
Credit Cards—Access, Visa
3 Family Rooms. 2 Four Poster Rooms
9 Double, 10 Twin, 5 Single Bedrooms
23 Private Bathrooms
6 Private Shower Rooms

All Rooms with TV, Radio, Telephone,
Tea and Coffee-making Facilities,
Baby-listening, Hairdryer
Open all year
Fully Licensed
Central Heating and Log Fires
Cocktail Bar
Conference Facilities

Dogs allowed
Parking Facilities
Fishing
Nearby: Tennis, Croquet, Putting, Squash,
Swimming, Sauna, Golf, Riding, Sailing,
Windsurfing, Water Skiing, Shooting

Near Ambleside, Clappersgate—Nanny Brow Country House Hotel
Clappersgate, Ambleside, Cumbria. LA22 9NF. Tel 05394 32036. Fax 05394 32450

The Lake District National Park is an extensive region encompassing virtually every type of land and water mass to delight the sight-seer, sportsman or explorer. Centrally placed in this Park, close to the northern end of Lake Windermere, Clappersgate is an area abundant in lovely houses and is well served by minor and main roads offering scenic excursions in every direction. Within five acres of peaceful gardens, terraces and stepped lawns, stands the white-painted Nanny Brow, the garden wing blending well with the original 1908 country house. Built and designed by a London architect for his own use, the careful conversion to an elegant hotel began in 1952. The interior of the whole exhibits a restrained use of quietly contrasting soft colours in a spacious arrangement enhanced by picturesque views through leaded-light windows. In winter, warm log fires burn in the lounge and entance hall. Within the garden wing there are luxury suites, a spa bath and solarium. To the credit of the friendly proprietors, Michael and Carol Fletcher, many of their guests make return visits and would be reluctant to stay anywhere else in Lakeland. The hotel brochure describes Nanny Brow as 'An Oasis of Elegance' which is most apt. All the *en suite* bedrooms have modern facilities including colour television with free satellite channels. Guests can return from fell-walking or fishing to excellent food in the elegant dining-room. The *cuisine* has earned a number of independent commendations, whilst the hotel is now 4 crowns highly commended.

Weekly Terms from £346.00
Daily Terms from £55.00
Bed and Breakfast from £40.00
Afternoon Tea from £5.50
Dinner from £18.50 Table d'Hôte
Gratuities at Guest's discretion
VAT inclusive. Credit Cards—Access,
American Express, Visa
3 Family Rooms. 6 Suites (2 Four-posters)
5 Double, 4 Twin Bedrooms

18 Private Bathrooms
1 Private Shower Room
All Rooms with TV, Telephone, Radio,
Baby-listening, Tea and Coffee-making
Facilities, Hairdryer, Mini-bar
7 Rooms with Trouser Press
Open All Year. Fully Licensed
Full Central Heating
Cocktail Bar. Conference Facilities

Children catered for
Dogs allowed. Parking Facilities
Croquet, Putting, Solarium, Fishing
Nearby: Tennis, Squash, Badminton,
Swimming, Sauna, Golf, Riding, Sailing,
Windsurfing, Water Skiing

Section 5: Cumbria

Near Ambleside—Eltermere Country House Hotel Elterwater, Near Ambleside, LA22 9HY. Tel 09667 207 (from Spring 1993 05394 37207)

Following our visit to this quite delightful country-house hotel we carried out a survey amongst some of our well-travelled friends. More than half of them had not heard of the village of Elterwater at all. Others recalled the name, but could not place the location. The village actually lies just a few miles from the head of Lake Windermere, but it is well sheltered in the valley of Langdale and is deliciously unspoilt. If you thrill to magnificent mountain scenery or if you love a secluded garden and peaceful countryside, then the Eltermere Country House Hotel is a marvellous place to stay. It appeals to those who enjoy a very personal welcome, home-cooked food and country-style comforts. Neil and Shelagh Stephenson and family took over Eltermere three years ago and run it in conjunction with the Three Shires Inn at Little Langdale. We loved our bedroom, where the *en suite* bathroom was reached via a flight of stairs leading from the sleeping area. Also impressive in this listed building of great character are the elegant dining-room and the residents' bar. Behind the hotel the craggy Langdale Pikes rise to almost 2,500 feet and to the fore Great Langdale Beck splashes into Elterwater, and then continues southwards for about a mile to Skelwith Bridge, where it forms an impressive waterfall. Whatever else you may do when you stay here, be sure to climb the hill behind the village, for it is a wonderful scenic vantage point.

Weekly Terms from £272.00 High Season
Daily Terms from £33.00 Low Season, £47.00 High Season
Bed and Breakfast from £27.50
Dinner from £16.00 Table d'Hôte
Gratuities at Guest's discretion
VAT inclusive

No Credit Cards accepted
8 Double, 7 Twin,3 Single Bedrooms
8 Private Bathrooms
7 Private Shower Rooms
All Rooms with TV, Tea and Coffee-making Facilities. Open from January to December
Residential and Restaurant Licence

Full Central Heating
Cocktail Bar
Parking Facilities
Dogs not allowed in hotel
Putting. Nearby: Tennis, Fishing, Riding Walking

Near Ambleside, Little Langdale—Three Shires Inn Little Langdale, Ambleside, Cumbria. LA22 9NZ. Tel 09667 215 (from Spring 1993 05394 37215)

Situated in one of the most beautiful and unspoilt valleys of the Lake District, the Three Shires Inn is ideally located for those wanting lovely walks from the doorstep, sporting activities or scenic drives in the immediate surroundings. Owned and run by the Stephenson family now in their eleventh year here, this nineteenth century slate inn with modern facilities and comforts has gained a fine reputation as a country hotel and restaurant. Everyone can be assured of a warm welcome and the personal care of the Stephenson family. All rooms have delightful views. Each is cosily decorated and most have *en suite* facilities. The dining room, where an outstanding five course dinner is served each evening, commands picturesque views of the surrounding fells. The *Slaters Bar* features a polished stone floor of local green Westmorland slate, and genuine oak beams. Here the hungriest walkers will have their appetites satisfied by delicious and imaginative bar meals. In summer meals can be taken in the garden by the stream while enjoying the delightful view to the south. Just off the beaten track at the eastern foot of Wrynose Pass but only five miles from Ambleside, in one of the prettiest valleys of the area, lies the Three Shires Inn. It is two miles from Elterwater in great Langdale where our second hotel, The Eltermere Country House Hotel, is located.

Weekly Terms from £240.00
Daily Terms from £34.00
Bed and Breakfast from £26.00
Bar Meal from £2.50
Lunch A La Carte
Afternoon Tea from £1.00
Dinner from £16.00 and A La Carte
Service Charge and VAT inclusive
1 Family Room

1 Single, 5 Double, 5 Twin Bedrooms
7 Private Bath/Shower Rooms
Tea and Coffee-making Facilities and Hairdryer available
Open February to mid-November
Weekends only mid-November to February and New Year week
Fully Licensed. Full Central Heating
2 Cocktail Bars

TV Lounge
Children catered for
Dogs allowed in public bar only
Parking Facilities
Nearby: Tennis, Croquet, Putting, Swimming, Golf, Fishing, Riding, Sailing, Windsurfing, Water Skiing, Fell Walking, Climbing

Section 5: Cumbria

Appleby-in-Westmorland–Appleby Manor Country House Hotel
Roman Road, Appleby-in-Westmorland, Cumbria. CA16 6JD.
Tel 07683 51571. Fax 07683 52888

From the fine marble fireplaces to the dramatic views of the highest Pennine peaks, here is a quality of life appropriate to a fertile valley in which flows a River Eden. The Manor at Appleby-'the place of the apple tree'-stands serenely overlooking a superb seventeenth century castle and Norman keep and, within, boasts a galleried first floor, panelled ceiling and an indoor leisure club. Weight-watching guests can choose between the heated swimming pool, solarium, sauna, steam room, jacuzzi or mini-gym to justify indulgence in the superb cuisine of the restaurant. However, the increasing prestige here must, in part, be due to the inclusion of several appetising dishes suitable for those on vegetarian or health-conscious diets. Following an evening's relaxation over a malt whisky in the main lounge and a night's sleep in one of the thirty luxurious en suite bedrooms, visitors can plan a new day around local tennis, squash, golf, fishing, shooting, riding, sailing, windsurfing or falconry. The Lakeland Fells and Yorkshire Dales are only twenty minutes' drive away and there are numerous other touring opportunities in the district. Appleby itself averages only one third of the rainfall recorded in the centre of the Lake District, making walks here in this historic county town of Westmorland exceptionally pleasant. Pass the old Moat Hall and, from the top of the castle keep, gaze over a panoramic view stretching from the Rare Breeds Conservation Centre to the peaks of the Lakeland Fells.

Weekly Terms from £285.00
Daily Terms from £45.00
Bed and Breakfast from £39.00
Lunch from £16.00 and A La Carte
Dinner from £16.00 and A La Carte
No Service Charge. VAT inclusive
Credit Cards–Access, American Express, Diners Club, JCB, Visa

8 Family Rooms. 2 Four Poster Rooms
9 Double, 11 Twin Bedrooms
All Rooms with Private Bathroom, TV, Radio, Baby-listening, Telephone, Tea and Coffee-making Facilities, Hairdryer
Open all year. Fully Licensed
Full Central Heating
Cocktail Bar. Games Room

Conference Facilities
Dogs allowed in Coach House only.
Parking Facilities
Croquet, Indoor Swimming Pool, Solarium, Sauna, Steam Room, Jacuzzi, Mini-Gym
Nearby: Tennis, Squash, Swimming, Golf, Fishing, Riding, Sailing, Windsurfing, Shooting, Falconry

Section 5: Cumbria

Barrow-in-Furness–Abbey House Hotel
Abbey Road, Barrow-in-Furness, Cumbria. LA13 0PA. Tel 0229 838282. Fax 0229 820403

This most impressive red sandstone building is a superb and slightly unusual example of the work of the eminent English architect, Sir Edwin Lutyens. It was completed in 1914 as a business guest house and, in its conversion to a graceful hotel of the very highest calibre, virtually all of the magnificently-proportioned rooms have adapted to their new role with minimal disturbance. There is an inherent grandeur and quiet dignity about the hotel equalled only by the fourteen acres of grounds comprising a beautifully balanced mixture of formal gardens and wooded copses. Beyond these lies a splendid vista of mature woodland and meadow interspersed with established walkways which lead to the ruins of nearby Furness Abbey. In less than half-an-hour's drive you are in the centre of the English Lake District with all the historic and picturesque places of interest in and around Grizedale Forest. Barrow-in-Furness lies on a peninsula with a road bridge to the Isle of Walney, and some tiny isolated islands in and around sheltered bays. Sailing craft complete the coastal picture: inland excursions bring you to the tarns, fells and pikes of the Cumbrian Mountains. Abbey House offers impeccable accommodation for business and holiday visitors alike, and the finest *à la carte* French *cuisine* of the *Abbey Restaurant* is available to residents and non-residents. Excellent conference and banqueting facilities can be provided.

1992 Terms
Bed and Breakfast from £69.50 Single, £84.50 Twin/Double
Bar Lunch from £3.50
Lunch from £9.95 and A La Carte
Afternoon Tea from £2.50
Dinner from £16.95 and A La Carte
Gratuities at Guest's discretion

VAT inclusive
Credit Cards–Access, American Express, Switch, Visa
3 Family Rooms. 6 Suites
11 Double, 3 Single Bedrooms
All Rooms with Private Bathroom, TV, Telephone, Radio, Baby-listening, Tea and Coffee-making Facilities, Hairdryer,

Trouser Press
Open all year. Fully Licensed
Full Central Heating. Lift. 2 Cocktail Bars
Conference Facilities
Dogs allowed. Parking Facilities
Night Porter. Croquet, Putting
Nearby: Tennis, Squash, Swimming, Solarium, Sauna, Golf, Fishing, Riding,

Near Bassenthwaite, Ireby—Overwater Hall
Ireby, Carlisle, Cumbria. CA5 1HH. Tel 07687 76566

This treasure nestles in a peaceful valley some two and a half miles to the east of the northern end of Bassenthwaite Lake. The area is famed as the hunting ground of John Peel, whose grave is in the village of Caldbeck. The hotel is near and yet remote from the more crowded centres of the Lake District. Surrounded by twenty acres of mature woodland, this beautiful country house has been designated as a building of architectural and historic interest. It is now owned by Joyce and Arthur Kent and their family and is given their very personal care. The hall has been tastefully and comfortably refurnished and, since it is centrally heated throughout, is cosy and warm. All of the bedrooms have a bathroom *en suite* and have a colour television and radio. The food is truly superb: the *table d'hôte* dinners include ample individually prepared dishes. Mr and Mrs. Kent also cater for small parties. Around the hotel there are many tempting walks, through the pastures and woods of the valley or on the foothills and higher ridges of Skiddaw. In addition, fishing and riding can be enjoyed nearby. This haven of peace can be reached from the M6 by leaving at Junctions 40 or 41 near Penrith. The Kents will be happy to supply complete directions upon request. Overwater Hall is, indeed, worth finding.

Weekly Terms from £275.00
Daily Terms from £44.00
Bed and Breakfast from £32.00
Dinner from £17.00 and A La Carte
Gratuities at Guest's discretion
VAT inclusive
Credit Cards—Access, Visa
3 Family Rooms

1 Single, 6 Double, 3 Twin Bedrooms
10 Private Bathrooms
3 Private Shower rooms
All Rooms with TV, Radio, Baby-listening, Tea and Coffee-making Facilities, Hairdryer
Open from 12th February to 24th December
Residential and Restaurant Licence

Full Central Heating
Cocktail Bar
Games Room. Dogs allowed
Parking Facilities
Nearby: Tennis, Putting, Squash, Swimming, Golf, Fishing, Riding, Sailing, Walking

Section 5: Cumbria

Borrowdale, Rosthwaite—Scafell Hotel
Rosthwaite, Borrowdale, Near Keswick, Cumbria. CA12 5XB.
Tel 07687 77208. Fax 07687 77280

If imposing mountain scenery and outdoor activities appeal to you, we suggest that you should plan your itinerary to include a stay of a few days at the Scafell Hotel, for it is situated in the very heart of Borrowdale, almost at the foot of Great Gable and Scafell Massif and is, therefore, an excellent headquarters for climbers and hill walkers. Keen anglers, too, will appreciate the Scafell Hotel, for there is excellent fly fishing on the River Derwent and in Derwentwater. Those who are content with gentle rambling or just lazing on restful lawns fringed by trees amidst imposing scenery will be equally happy staying here. The comfortable bedrooms, beautifully decorated and some furnished with traditional antique furniture, are all equipped with private facilities, radio and tea and coffee-making facilities. The public rooms have been tastefully furnished and in the elegant restaurant one can enjoy excellent fare prepared by skilled chefs. Flambé dishes are a speciality and, in addition to the table d'hôte and à la carte dinner menus, the hotel now offers a selection of supper dishes. Excellent bar lunches are served in the pleasant bar lounge where old prints and photographs adorn the walls and a fire adds extra warmth on cold days. Packed lunches are available for those who wish to spend the day out on the fells or touring. Under the direction of the owner, Miles Jessop, and the management of Mrs Judith Figg, the staff of the Scafell Hotel offer efficient and friendly service, thus making this comfortable hotel an ideal base for exploring the heart of Lakeland.

Weekly Terms from £312.25
Daily Terms from £38.50
Bed and Breakfast from £33.50
Dinner from £17.75
Gratuities at Guest's discretion
VAT inclusive
Credit Cards–Access, Visa

6 Double, 12 Twin, 3 Single Bedrooms
3 Family Rooms. 24 Private Bathrooms
1 Private Shower Room
All Rooms with TV, Radio, Telephone, Baby-listening, Tea and Coffee-making Facilities
Open from 7th February to 2nd January

Fully Licensed
Full Central Heating
Cocktail Bar. Dogs allowed
Parking Facilities
Nearby: Squash, Golf, Fishing, Sailing, Windsurfing, Fell Walking and Climbing

Section 5: Cumbria

Borrowdale, Near Keswick—Greenbank
Borrowdale, Keswick, Cumbria. CA12 5UY. Tel 07687 77215

It is known simply as 'Greenbank'–nothing more–and is reached by way of a long curving driveway. This approach is worth negotiating, for here is one of the friendliest little hotels in Lakeland. Greenbank is owned and personally run by Trevor and Jennifer Lorton, who have happily forsaken other lifestyles for the magic air and scenery of Lakeland's fells. We found it refreshing to meet two people so proud of their hotel and so enthusiastic about the surrounding country. We were shown every nook and cranny of this ten-bedroomed, modernly equipped house and, instinctively, in many of the rooms, we turned to the windows to admire the unbroken views of Derwentwater and Skiddaw and the Borrowdale Valley. Immediately Greenbank comes into view it spells promise, and once inside there is a tray of tea waiting to welcome the new visitor. Each bedroom is attractively decorated and equipped with either an *en suite* bath or shower, whilst downstairs, on chilly evenings, the two lounges crackle with the sound of blazing logs from open fires. There is a four-course dinner every evening and a full breakfast before you set out for the day. The menus provide English traditional cooking at its best using lots of fresh produce and the owners are very happy to prepare for you a packed lunch on request. We liked Greenbank a great deal, it was just like a home from home. You will find the hotel high up on wooded slopes in the heart of Borrowdale, just three and a half miles from Keswick. Fell walking, climbing and sightseeing are, therefore, natural pursuits to be followed from Greenbank.

Weekly Terms from £192.50
Daily Terms from £31.50
Gratuities at Guest's discretion
VAT inclusive
1 Family Room. 1 Single Room
6 Double, 2 Twin Bedrooms

9 Private Bathrooms
1 Private Shower Rooms
All Rooms with Radio, Tea and Coffee-making Facilities, Hairdryer
Open from February to November
Residential Licence

Full Central Heating. TV Lounge
Children catered for. Dogs not allowed
Parking Facilities
Nearby: Tennis, Putting, Badminton, Squash, Swimming, Golf, Fishing, Riding, Sailing, Windsurfing

Bowness-on-Windermere—The Burn How Garden House Hotel
Back Belsfield Road, Bowness-on-Windermere, Cumbria. LA23 3HH. Tel 05394 46226P255D

For the peace and tranquility of its garden setting, yet only a short walk to Lake Windermere and the centre of Bowness, it would be hard to find a finer hotel than Burn How. It is a unique combination of elegant Victorian houses, modern chalets and family rooms. Whichever you choose you will find the same high standards throughout-all are luxuriously appointed with private bathroom, colour television, radio, hairdryer, direct-dial telephone and tea and coffee-making facilities. Many of the rooms have private sun balconies and, for the romantically inclined, four-poster beds. The family chalets have baby listening services and six have been designed with the disabled in mind. A children's menu and room service is available for any meal. The highly acclaimed restaurant in the main house is a tasteful combination of Victorian and Georgian furnishings, but with any restaurant it is the food that matters most and here you will find dishes best described as 'English with French connections'-the finest of fresh market produce with caring service. It is evident that the owner, Michael Robinson, and his staff take pride in offering first class food and friendly service. The advantages of Burn How do not end here–there is a sauna and solarium for your enjoyment and ample car parking just by your accommodation. Above all you will enjoy the excellent meals and the obvious desire of all concerned to ensure that your stay is truly memorable.

Weekly Terms from £190.00
Daily Terms from £43.00
Bed and Breakfast from £33.00
Bar Lunch from £3.00
Dinner from £17.50 and A La Carte
Gratuities at Guest's discretion
VAT inclusive. Credit Cards–Access, American Express, Visa

10 Family Rooms
6 Double, 6 Twin, 4 Single Bedrooms
All Rooms with Private Bathroom, TV, Telephone, Radio, Tea and Coffee-making Facilities, Hairdryer, Baby-listening
Open All Year
Residential and Restaurant Licence
Full Central Heating

Cocktail Bar
Conference Facilities
Dogs not allowed
Parking Facilities. Solarium, Sauna
Nearby: Tennis, Croquet, Putting, Squash, Badminton, Swimming, Golf, Fishing, Riding, Sailing, Windsurfing, Water Skiing

Section 5: Cumbria

Bowness-on-Windermere—Linthwaite House Hotel
Kendal Road, Bowness-on-Windermere, LA23 3JA.
Tel 05394 88600. Fax 05394 88601

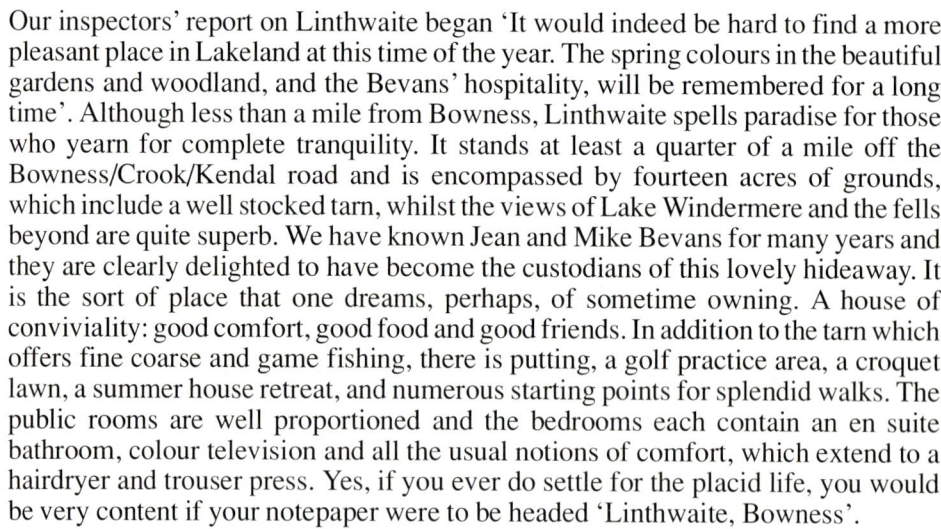

Our inspectors' report on Linthwaite began 'It would indeed be hard to find a more pleasant place in Lakeland at this time of the year. The spring colours in the beautiful gardens and woodland, and the Bevans' hospitality, will be remembered for a long time'. Although less than a mile from Bowness, Linthwaite spells paradise for those who yearn for complete tranquility. It stands at least a quarter of a mile off the Bowness/Crook/Kendal road and is encompassed by fourteen acres of grounds, which include a well stocked tarn, whilst the views of Lake Windermere and the fells beyond are quite superb. We have known Jean and Mike Bevans for many years and they are clearly delighted to have become the custodians of this lovely hideaway. It is the sort of place that one dreams, perhaps, of sometime owning. A house of conviviality: good comfort, good food and good friends. In addition to the tarn which offers fine coarse and game fishing, there is putting, a golf practice area, a croquet lawn, a summer house retreat, and numerous starting points for splendid walks. The public rooms are well proportioned and the bedrooms each contain an en suite bathroom, colour television and all the usual notions of comfort, which extend to a hairdryer and trouser press. Yes, if you ever do settle for the placid life, you would be very content if your notepaper were to be headed 'Linthwaite, Bowness'.

Weekly Terms from £350.00
Daily Terms from £55.00
Afternoon Tea from £2.00
Dinner from £25.00 Table d'Hôte
Service Charge and VAT inclusive
18 Double/Twin Bedrooms

All Rooms with Private Bathroom, TV, Telephone, Radio, Tea and Coffee-making Facilities, Hairdryer, Trouser Press
Open All Year
Residential and Restaurant Licence
Full Central Heating
Children catered for

Dogs not allowed
Parking Facilities
9-hole Putting, Trout Fishing, Croquet
Nearby: Tennis, Swimming, Golf, Walking Fishing, Sailing, Windsurfing, Water Skiing, Leisure Club

Section 5: Cumbria

Buttermere Valley—Pickett Howe
Brackenthwaite, Buttermere Valley, Cumbria. CA13 9UY. Tel 0900 85444

Dating from around 1650, this Grade II listed farmhouse sits peacefully amidst the stunning natural beauty of the Lake District. Surrounded by fifteen acres of hillside, wood and pasture, entered by a private track, it marks the confluence of the Buttermere, Loweswater and Lorton valleys. Since purchasing Pickett Howe in 1990 David and Dani Edwards have extensively renovated their Lakeland statesman's long house, retaining the flagged floors, oak beams, mullioned windows and provision for log fires. By summer 1992 they received the coveted English Tourist Board's 'De Luxe' status together with other national awards. The three double and one twin bedroom all include whirlpool baths or power showers in their *en suite* facilities, as well as the antiques and quality furnishings which grace the whole hotel. Candlelight and chamber music welcome you into the dining room, where Cumbria crystal and silver dinner settings sparkle on oak tables. Delightfully different dishes appear on the menu, offering an interesting and well balanced five course meal, the main course selection always including appetising meat, fish and vegetarian choices. A quite superb and comprehensive breakfast menu also offers many alternatives for a healthy and satisfying start to the day. Real personal attention from the proprietors not only meets your every need in the hotel, but Mr and Mrs Edwards will also see to it that their advice, maps and books assist you in making the very best of your time in this lush and lovely part of England.

Weekly Terms from £322.00
Daily Terms from £46.00
Bed and breakfast from £29.00
Dinner from £17.00 Table d'Hôte
1 Twin, 3 Double Bedrooms
3 Private Bathrooms

1 Private Shower Room
All Rooms with TV, Telephone, Radio, Tea and Coffee-making Facilities, Hairdryer
Trouser Press available
Open April to October
Residential Licence

Full Central Heating
Children over 10 years catered for
Parking Facilities
Nearby: Tennis, Squash, Badminton, Indoor Pool, Golf, Fishing, Riding, Sailing, Windsurfing

Carlisle—Cumbrian Hotel
Court Square, Carlisle, Cumbria. CA1 1QY. Tel 0228 31951. Fax 0228 47799

The ancient town of Carlisle fits perfectly into any pattern of touring Britain. It is a gateway to Scotland, is ideally placed for following the Roman legacies of Hadrian or discovering the delights of the Solway Firth, whilst its own 2,000 year-old history makes for fascinating exploration, whilst the excellent traffic-free shopping centre is an added bonus. Good accommodation in the city, however, is limited, so the emergence of the Cumbrian Hotel as a first class establishment is a boon to weary travellers and its location, next to the station, is ideal for those travelling by rail as well as the motorist. We stopped at the Cumbrian for dinner on one trip and liked it so much we returned during the next to stay the night. How pleasant to be able to sleep away from all traffic noise, to enjoy one's meal with elbow room in an attractive restaurant, to find first class bedroom facilities, *and to be given so much personal attention!* A Victorian theme is being developed at the Cumbrian Hotel, even to a doorman and pages, and this attention to detail is impressive. There is a public bar and a coffee shop adjacent to the hotel but separate from it, and the service and standards here, too, are excellent. In fact, whether you seek respite, or refreshment, a good dinner, or a comfortable base for a few days, and all allied to *the* most friendly service, you will want for nothing at the 'new' Cumbrian Hotel. A good resting place too for the disabled since wheelchair assistance is always available and some rooms are near the lift. The hotel also has conference, banqueting and ballroom facilities, as well as garage parking.

Daily Terms from £50.00
Room Rate from £79.50
Bar Lunch from £4.00
Lunch from £9.75 Table d'Hôte
Afternoon Tea from £4.00
Dinner from £14.95 Table d'Hôte

All Major Credit Cards accepted
33 Double, 31 Twin, 30 Single Bedrooms
All Rooms with Private Bathroom, TV, Telephone, Radio, Baby-listening, Tea and Coffee-making Facilities, Trouser Press, Hairdryer. Open all Year. Fully Licensed

Lift. Cocktail Bar. TV Lounge
Conference Facilities
Children catered for. Dogs allowed
Parking Facilities. Night Porter
Nearby: Tennis, Putting, Squash, Badminton, Swimming Pool, Solarium,

Section 5: Cumbria

Near Carlisle, Crosby-on-Eden–Crosby Lodge
High Crosby, Crosby-on-Eden, Near Carlisle, Cumbria. CA6 4QZ. Tel 0228 573 618

Travellers seeking a base for exploring the English Lake District, the Scottish Lowlands and Hadrian's Wall should consider this country-house hotel, conveniently situated on the A689 (formerly B6264) road from Carlisle to Brampton and only a five-minute drive away from Exit 44 of the M6. There is a feeling of tranquillity in the pastoral landscape which is the setting for the parkland and delightful gardens surrounding Crosby Lodge. The smiling welcome of the hosts, Pat and Michael Sedgwick, will heighten your expectations of a memorable sojourn here. Their kindness and personal attention will ensure your total comfort. Michael was trained at Brown's Elegant Hotel, London, with its accent on French *cuisine*, and in Switzerland. This border-country hotel, therefore, offers a distinctive menu of French and traditional British dishes, including Dover Sole *Meunière*, roast farm duckling and mussels cooked in their shells with dill sauce. An unusual and varied selection, entirely home-made, is available from the sweet trolley. In addition, a wide range of snacks is available in the well-stocked lounge bar. Guests enjoy coffee and *petit-fours* after their meals in the peaceful atmosphere of the residents' lounge. On Sunday evenings a *table d'hôte* menu is provided for residents. The eleven elegant and spacious bedrooms have bath and shower rooms *en suite* and morning tea is brought to your room if required. Throughout the day life runs smoothly and cheerfully and guests leave refreshed by the warm-hearted hospitality.

Weekly Terms from £350.00
Daily Terms from £69.00 (sharing Double)
Bed and Breakfast from £65.00 (Single)
Bar Lunch from £4.75
Lunch from £15.50 and A La Carte
Dinner from £25.00 and A La Carte

Gratuities at Guest's discretion
VAT inclusive. Credit Cards–American Express, Visa
2 Family Rooms. 1 Single Bedroom
3 Double, 5 Twin Bedrooms
10 Private Bathrooms. 1 Private Shower

Room. All Rooms with TV, Telephone, Radio, Baby-listening, Hairdryer
Open from mid-January to Christmas Eve
Residential and Restaurant Licence
Full Central Heating. Cocktail Bar
Dogs allowed by arrangement

Faugh, Heads Nook, Near Carlisle—The String of Horses Country Inn
Faugh, Heads Nook, Carlisle, Cumbria. CA4 9EG. Tel 0228 70297/509. Fax 0228 70675

A friend of ours used to spend much of his time in an internationally known hotel in Park Lane, Mayfair. Finding himself in the Carlisle area, he pulled into The String of Horses for overnight accommodation. To his surprise, he found that in his bedroom, fresh fruit and flowers plus a miniature sherry greeted him and in the bedside refrigerator he found chilled champagne, Perrier water, ice and so on. His bathroom was luxury itself—a double circular bath with gold fittings. The friendly and personal reception he received, together with the excellent *cuisine* and comprehensive wine list with many rare and expensive wines, convinced him that Mayfair still had a lot to learn! On hearing his comments, curiosity got the better of us—so off we went to Faugh and there, to our pleasure, found everything precisely as our eclectic friend had described. It is good to find an inn exuding obliging service, good food and a lot of imagination. The attractions of The String of Horses do not end there, however, for there is an outdoor heated swimming pool, a solarium, a sauna, a whirlpool spa and an ergometer for the sole use of residents. The inn is under the very personal direction of Eric and Anne Tasker and is a grand spot with plenty of interest. Corby Castle towers above the trees by the River Eden, there is racing at Carlisle and to the north, near Lanercost Priory, Hadrian's Wall begins its almost unbroken journey to Newcastle-upon-Tyne.

Bed and Breakfast from £58.00 Single, £65.00 Double
Bar Meal from £3.25
Lunch from £10.95 and A La Carte
Dinner from £16.95 and A La Carte
Gratuities at Guest's discretion. VAT inclusive. Credit Cards—Access, American Express, Diners Club, Visa
4 Suites. 8 Double, 2 Twin Bedrooms

(Doubles can be let as Singles)
9 Private Bathrooms. 5 Private Shower Rooms. All Rooms with TV, Telephone, Radio, Baby-listening, Tea and Coffee-making Facilities, Ionisers, Trouser Press, Hairdryer, Mini-Bar, Clock, Fresh Fruit. Open all year. Fully Licensed
Full Central Heating
Conference Facilities. Cocktail Bar

Dogs allowed by arrangement
Parking Facilities. Night Porter. Swimming Pool, Solarium, Sauna, Whirlpool Spa Bath, Exercise Machines
Nearby: Tennis, Putting, Squash, Badminton, Golf, Fishing, Riding, Sailing, Windsurfing, Water Skiing, Shooting

Section 5: Cumbria

Grange-in-Borrowdale—Borrowdale Gates Country House Hotel
Grange-in-Borrowdale, Keswick, Cumbria. CA12 5UQ. Tel 07687 77204

This charming Lakeland Victorian house nestles peacefully in almost two acres of wooded gardens on the edge of the ancient hamlet of Grange. It is surrounded by the breathtaking scenery of the Borrowdale Valley and is close to Derwentwater, often referred to as the 'Queen of the English lakes'. In last year's guide we reported on a programme of improvements by the resident proprietors, Terry and Christine Parkinson. More recently the ground floor areas have been re-schemed affording magnificent views from the bar and lounges and from the newly created and refurbished restaurant. Cooking is by Chef Patron Terry Parkinson, with superb *cuisine* offering a new menu each day which is complemented by a wine list of outstanding variety. The hotel, which has six of its bedrooms on the ground floor, is situated in one of the most beautiful valleys in the Lake District National Park. This entire region presents a feast of places possessing superb views for walkers, numerous buildings of literary and historical interest to the tourist, within leisurely mooring distance, frequently tempting the traveller to abandon his car and explore on foot. Borrowdale Gates is surrounded by rugged charm on all sides and within, with its antiques and log fires, offers an atmosphere of tranquillity and relaxation.

Weekly Terms from £341.50 April-October
Daily Terms from £42.50 Low Season, £59.00 High Season (Double/Twin)
Bed and Breakfast from £29.00 Low Season, £45.50 High Season (Double/Twin)
Bar Lunch from £4.50 (Mon-Sat incl.)
Sunday Lunch from £10.00 Table d'Hôte

Dinner from £18.75 Table d'Hôte
Gratuities at Guest's discretion
VAT inclusive
Credit Cards—Access, Visa
2 Family Rooms. 9 Double, 8 Twin, 4 Single Bedrooms
19 Private Bathrooms. 4 Private Shower Rooms. All Rooms with TV, Telephone,

Radio, Tea and Coffee-making Facilities
Baby-listening, Hairdryer available. Open All Year. Residential and Restaurant Licence. Full Central Heating
Cocktail Bar. Children catered for. Dogs not allowed. Parking Facilities.
Nearby: Tennis, Putting, Swimming, Solarium, Sauna, Golf, Fishing

Grange-over-Sands–Hampsfell House Hotel
Hampsfell Road, Grange-over-Sands, Cumbria. LA11 6BG. Tel 05395 32567

We were impressed–but not surprised–when Hugh and Mary Sharrock achieved many improvements here within a short time of assuming resident ownership in November 1990. Our lack of surprise was due to our experience of the efficient running of their earlier enterprise, a hotel in Perthshire which earned a place in 'Let's Halt Awhile'. Refurbishment of Hampsfell House has resulted in an hotel whose comfort and scenic setting, in an area renowned for its temperate climate, now offers exceptional value for money. It stands in about two acres of private grounds and woodland, on the fringe of Eggerslack Woods. To the south lie the extensive sands of Morecambe Bay and to the north the vast appeal of the Lake District. In the immediate vicinity there are many colourful gardens, abundant wildlife, sporting facilities and walks to suit young and old alike. Despite these many attractions, the hotel enjoys a quiet, gently elevated position, away from main roads and railway lines. A few minutes' walk brings one to the centre of Grange-over-Sands, to the promenade and all local amenities, whilst only a short drive away is the network of minor roads threading through Grizedale Forest, lying between Coniston Water and Lake Windermere. At the end of a day's touring, guests will return to a home-cooked dinner, complemented by a choice of fine wines. On cooler evenings there is a cheery fire in the bar, which opens onto the terraced garden and, from the lounge, the view is into a sheltered, walled garden at the side of the hotel.

Weekly Terms from £220.00
Daily Terms from £36.00
Bed and Breakfast from £22.50
Bar Lunch from £6.50
Lunch from £7.85 Table d'Hôte
Afternoon Tea from £2.25

Dinner from £14.00 Table d'Hôte
Gratuities at Guest's discretion
VAT inclusive. Credit Cards–Access, Visa
1 Family Room. 4 Double, 4 Twin Bedrooms. 4 Private Bathrooms
3 Private Shower Rooms

All Rooms with TV, Tea and Coffee-making Facilities, Hairdryer
5 Rooms with Trouser Press
Open all Year except Christmas
Fully Licensed. Full central Heating
Cocktail Bar. Children catered for

Section 5: Cumbria

Grange-over-Sands—Graythwaite Manor
Fernhill Road, Grange-over-Sands, Cumbria. LA11 7JE
Telephone 05395 32001

Blue-green waters flow rapidly out of Morecambe Bay twice a day to reveal a vast expanse of glistening sands. Grange-over-Sands lies on the bay's north-western flank and because of its position, sheltered from westerly winds and crowned to the north by Hampsfell, it is a gardener's paradise. Some of the most beautiful formal, ornamental gardens of the town are to be found in the eight acres of grounds which surround Graythwaite Manor. The skilfully landscaped grounds and the fine creeper clad manor house create a very restful country house environment. What a pleasant sight will greet you as you step into the square lounge hall—oak panelling, a feeling of space and fresh flowers. There is a range of tastefully furnished bedrooms, many with splendid views and each with a private bathroom, colour television, a telephone, an electric blanket and beverage-making facilities. Graythwaite Manor is a warm and inviting place in every respect, with central heating and log fires on chilly days. Here one could well settle down for life, for the views are superb, the surroundings are satisfying and the Blakemore family, who have always owned the hotel, could not be more kindly and hospitable. When you call in for a meal, go in time to appreciate the ambience of the lounges and the cocktail bar. In the latter an extensive range of bar snacks is available. Excellent *table d'hôte* lunches and dinners are served in the attractive dining room. This is an excellent base from which to explore the Cumbrian coastline, and the many other attractions of the area. There is more than mere comfort in Graythwaite Manor. It is an hotel which, by recommendation, attracts the discerning.

Weekly Terms from £315.00
Daily Terms from £45.00
Bar Lunch from £1.50. Lunch from £10.00
Afternoon Tea from £2.50
Dinner from £18.50
VAT inclusive. Credit Cards—Access, Visa
1 Family Room
3 Double, 14 Twin, 5 Single Bedrooms

All Rooms with Private Bath/Shower
Room, TV, Telephone, Radio, Tea and Coffee-making Facilities, Electric Blankets, Hairdryer, Baby-listening
Open all year. Fully Licensed
Full Central Heating. Log Fires and Electric Fires
Cocktail Bar. Billiard Room

Guide Dogs only allowed
Conference Facilities
Parking Facilities
Tennis, Putting
Nearby: Squash, Badminton, Swimming, Golf, Fishing, Riding, Sailing, Windsurfing, Water Skiing, Birdwatching

Section 5: Cumbria

Grange-over-Sands—The Netherwood Hotel
Grange-over-Sands, Cumbria. LA11 6ET. Tel 05395 32552. Fax 05395 32552

Majestic externally and warmly relaxing internally—with superb oak panelling throughout, executed by Waring and Gillows of Lancaster—this is a place for the discerning tourist. Owned and run by the Fallowfield brothers, there is an authentic atmosphere of old world luxury skillfully blended with modern comforts. The Netherwood was built in the latter part of the nineteenth century as a private home for the Deakin family and stands above wooded slopes facing southwards over Morecambe Bay Estuary. Despite the spaciousness of the various communal rooms there is a very strong homely feeling here, as in the bedrooms. From the beautiful gardens the views are breathtaking. Lunch and dinner menus offer an excellent choice of honest wholesome foods, with a wide selection of wines available, at remarkably modest overall prices. Proper attention is given to local produce, one of the house specialities being poached Morecambe Bay salmon in shrimp sauce. From this distinctive hotel in a quiet resort there are many and varied sporting, cultural and sight-seeing activities to suit all tastes. Inland are Coniston Water and Lake Windermere with their associated cluster of villages and beauty spots. Several noted vantage points will appeal to naturalists, to photographers and to all who take pleasure in the combined scenery of mountains, woodland, sea and lakes.

Weekly Terms from £388.75	VAT inclusive. Credit Cards accepted	Coffee-making Facilities. Trouser Press
Daily Terms from £56.25	5 Family Rooms. 10 Superior Double/Twin	and Hairdryer on request. Open all year.
Bed and Breakfast from £40.75	1 Honeymoon Suite. 1 Family Room	Fully Licensed. Full Central Heating. TV
Bar Meal from £3.00	suitable disabled	Lounge. Lift. Conference Facilities.
Lunch from £10.75 and A La Carte	6 Double, 5 Twin, 4 Single Bedrooms	Children catered for. Dogs allowed.
Afternoon Tea from £1.95	27 Private Bathrooms. 2 Private Shower	Parking Facilities. Night Porter. Heated
Dinner from £18.25 and A La Carte	Rooms. All Rooms with TV, Telephone,	Indoor Swimming Pool, Solarium, Spa
Gratuities at Guest's discretion	Radio, Baby-listening, Tea and	Bath, Steam Room, Fitness Room

Grasmere—Gold Rill Country House Hotel
Red Bank Road, Grasmere, Cumbria. LA22 9PU. Tel 09665 486

This is one of our earliest recommendations in the Lake District. We are glad to say it is still one of the best. We must know every nook and cranny of this well-equipped house, yet, instinctively, our thoughts always turn to its unbroken views of crags, fells, tarns and lake. The peak of Silver Howe rises behind, whilst Grasmere Lake stretches away in the fore towards Rydal Water. Two acres of gardens bloom and blaze with colour and afford recreation in the form of putting, croquet and a screened outdoor heated swimming pool. The hotel even has its own pier, where one may laze, fish or paddle a canoe. Gold Rill is owned by Paul and Cathy Jewsbury, who forsook other considerations for the clean air and magical scenery of this very central spot in Lakeland. From the onset, they set about their newly acquired venture with great enthusiasm and it is clear this has become a labour of love. Comfortable, cosy and complete sums up their hotel today. In the bedrooms one could settle down for life, so well equipped are they, whilst the lounge, cocktail bar and dining room could hardly be more comfortable. As to matters of the table, their beautifully presented, modern English *cuisine* has become the background to the hotel's success. Gold Rill is open all year and offers some very attractive seasonal tariffs: Spring Time when the daffodils are blooming; Summer Days for family holidays; Autumn Colours for restful breaks; and Winter Walks, which speak for themselves. Of course, the village is just 300 yards away, with its boat hire, church and Wordsworth's home.

Daily Terms from £39.00	Credit Cards—Access, Visa	Fully Licensed. Full Central Heating
Bed and Breakfast from £31.00	11 Double, 6 Twin, 3 Single Bedrooms	Cocktail Bar. Children catered for
Bar Lunch from £3.00	All Rooms with Private Bathroom, TV,	Dogs allowed. Parking Facilities
Dinner from £18.00 Table d'Hôte	Telephone, Radio, Baby-listening, Tea and	Croquet, Putting, Outdoor Swimming Po
Gratuities at Guest's discretion	Coffee-making Facilities, Hairdryer	Nearby: Golf, Fishing, Riding, Sailing,
VAT inclusive	Open from February to December	Windsurfing, Water Skiing

Section 5: Cumbria

Near Grange-over-Sands — The Old Vicarage
Witherslack, Near Grange-over-Sands, Cumbria. LA11 6RS
Tel 044 852 381. Fax 044 852 373 (From Spring 93 05395 52381 Fax 52373)

The scenic attractions of the Lake District are well known. If you seek somewhere really secluded, out of the mainstream of life, we have good reason to lead you to Witherslack in the Winster Valley. By the church green, in five acres of gardens and woodland, is this utterly delightful Georgian vicarage, now a very elegant hotel. Before making your way there, however, do try to obtain a copy of the hotel's brochure. We have voted it the most attractive publication of its kind to have come into our offices for a long time. It raises high expectations, which, we are happy to confirm, are more than fulfilled when one visits The Old Vicarage. It has a quite delightful ambience, with every piece of furniture carefully chosen to enhance the character of the house. The bedrooms are well equipped with either a bath or a shower room. Downstairs there are two comfortable lounges, one with French windows which open out onto the garden where squirrels, deer and other wild animals are often seen. The resident proprietors, Jill and Roger Burrington-Brown and Irene and Stanley Reeve, are ably assisted by some very friendly Cumbrian staff and between them all they have created a happy and truly relaxing atmosphere at The Old Vicarage. When we called at the hotel Mr Burrington-Brown was busy baking in the kitchen. The hotel has collected accolades and commendations from many sources for its cuisine and excellent wine list. Vegetarians and people with special diets can be certain that their needs will be met. It is all freshly cooked and home made and the carefully planned five-course dinners are justly regarded as some of the best in Cumbria.

Weekly Terms from £175.00
Bed and Breakfast from £25.00
Dinner from £19.50 Table d'Hôte
Gratuities at Guest's discretion
VAT inclusive
Credit Cards—Access, American Express, Visa

1 Single, 12 Double, 3 Twin Bedrooms
All Rooms with Private Bathroom, TV, Telephone, Radio, Tea and Coffee-making Facilities, Hairdryer
Open all Year. Fully Licensed
Full Central Heating. Children catered for
Dogs allowed by arrangement

Parking Facilities
All-weather Tennis Court
Nearby: Tennis, Squash, Badminton, Swimming, Solarium, Sauna, Golf, Fishing, Riding, Sailing, Windsurfing, Water Skiing, Fell Walking, Birdwatching

Section 5: Cumbria

Near Kendal—Heaves Hotel
Levens Bridge, Near Kendal, Cumbria. LA8 8EF. Tel 05395 60396/60269

You will have to travel a long way to find a more caring and courteous host than Mrs M L Southwell, who keeps a constant eye on all that goes on in this wondrous mansion. The rooms are lovely in proportion and size, whilst the gardens are festooned with flowers for most of the year. Heaves Hotel is very reasonably priced, deliciously quiet, but extremely accessible for motorists. It lies four miles south of Kendal with access from the A6 half a mile south of the junction with the A591, which is three miles from exit 36 of the M6. Around the hotel are ten acres of gardens and woodlands, which afford outstanding views of the Pennines, Morecambe Bay and Lakeland hills. Inside the house, note the Adam-style staircase and the well stocked library with its mantelpiece and overmantel, thought to be the work of Grinling Gibbons. Whilst Heaves Hotel is naturally busy in the summer season, Mrs Southwell has, through personal recommendations, built up a most flourishing winter business. So if you are seeking sanctuary from the vagaries of the English climate, remember this country hotel, where within you will find great comfort, a billiards room, fires to cheer and central heating... and one's experience of winter may be confined to the weather reports. The cooking—*cuisine* is too pretentious a word here—is excellent. Heaves has a fine reputation for the variety and quality of its food. So many people have found Heaves Hotel to their liking and return there year after year. It offers friendliness, quietitude; there is room to rove... and to breathe!

Weekly Terms from £196.00
Daily Terms from £28.00
Bed and Breakfast from £19.00
Lunch from £7.00
Afternoon Tea from £2.50
Dinner from £9.00 Table d'Hôte

Service Charge and VAT inclusive
Credit Cards–Access, American Express, Diners Club, Visa. 3 Family Rooms. 3 Suites. 5 Double, 4 Twin, 4 Single Bedrooms. 8 Private Bathrooms. 2 Private Shower. Rooms. 6 Rooms with TV,

Telephone, Hairdryer. Open all year except 4 days at Christmas. Residential and Restaurant Licence. Chair Lift. TV Lounge. Games Room. Part Central Heating. Dogs allowed. Conference Facilities. Parking Facilities. Putting

---

Have you returned your membership form?
By simply completing and returning to us the registration card inserted in this book you will automatically become a 1993 member of the Ashley Courtenay Circle , an invaluable link between author and reader. For members, we compile and revise each year special listings of hotels which offer particular amenities, such as a sauna, swimming pool, golf course (or adjacent), four-poster beds, facilities for the disabled, special Christmas programmes, vegetarian dishes, non-smoking areas and self-catering facilities. We can even direct you to hotels which are especially pleased to receive young children and dogs. These lists are free of charge. Just send a stamped addressed envelope.

Section 5: Cumbria

Keswick—Chaucer House Hotel
Ambleside Road, Keswick, Cumbria. CA12 4DR. Tel 07687 72318

Keswick lies in a beautiful position below the towering bulks of Skiddaw and Saddleback. It is a town with an almost magical quality and its beauty has attracted poets, artists and visitors from all over the world. The town is attractive in itself—narrow streets and buildings of old grey stone. Keswick straddles a natural convergence of roads which makes it an excellent centre for tours to the other parts of Lakeland. The town is best seen on foot and a short walk takes one down a pleasant road below The Heads to the edge of Derwentwater, where the landing stages offer cruises, motor boats and rowing skiffs. Chaucer House Hotel has thirty-five bedrooms, most *en suite* and all tastefully refurbished to a high standard with comfort in mind and to guarantee a good night's sleep. All bedrooms have tea and coffee making facilities. There are several lounges and a cocktail bar furnished and decorated in Victorian style with an abundance of interesting pictures and paintings, ornaments and antiques. There is a breakfast to suit every appetite, including the famous Cumberland sausage, black pudding and kippers. In the evening relax over a candle-lit dinner with mouth-watering dishes where only fresh local produce is used, and afterwards coffee can be taken in the lounges or the bar. The hotel is ideally and peacefully situated only a few minutes' walk from the town centre, with splendid views of the lake and surrounding fells. You will eat so well in this hotel that you will need to walk it off!

Weekly Terms from £228.00
Daily Terms from £31.50
Bed and Breakfast from £29.50
Lunch (residents) from £5.50 and A La Carte. Afternoon Tea from £3.00
Dinner from £11.55 and A La Carte

Gratuities at Guest's discretion. VAT inclusive. Credit Cards—Access, American Express, Diners Club, Visa
4 Family Rooms. 13 Double, 10 Twin, 8 Single Bedrooms. 6 Private Bathrooms. 31 Private Shower Rooms. All Bedrooms with

TV, Radio, Tea and Coffee-making Facilities, Electric Blankets. Hairdryer available on request
Open from February to December. Residential and Restaurant Licence
Cocktail Bar. TV Lounge. Lift

Keswick–The Grange Country House Hotel
Manor Brow, Ambleside Road, Keswick, Cumbria. CA12 4BA. Tel 07687 72500

Keswick is one of the principal centres of the Lake District, and it is easy to see why. It lies on the Greta, is sheltered by Skiddaw and stands only half a mile from Derwentwater. The latter is one of the most satisfying of all the lakes of England–its banks are a medley of wooded slopes, green fells and abrupt crags and its surface is dotted with charming islets. With Keswick's popularity as a touring and walking centre we were especially pleased when we dicovered this hotel situated on 'Manor Brow', just off the A591 to Grasmere. Set high up and secluded in most charming surroundings, The Grange offers both solitude and accessibility. If the location is appealing, once you have stepped inside The Grange you will be completely won over. Duncan and Jane Miller who are caring and considerate hosts have furnished it beautifully with a wealth of antiques, but with the accent on comfort rather than formality. The bedrooms are individually decorated, some contain half-tester beds and all are equipped with attractive *en suite* bathrooms/showers. Another delight at the Grange are the 'Special Occasion Breaks' which have many thoughtful extras for your pleasure, including a well stocked picnic basket with wine for that lazy day in the country. The restaurant, the quiet reading lounge and the coffee lounge are some of the nicest rooms we have seen, and each has magnificent views of the garden, the valleys, the lakes and the surrounding mountains. The standards of food, comfort and welcome are consistently high and, whatever the season, Lakeland is never less than spectacular.

Weekly Terms from £283.50
Daily Terms from £43.75
Bed and Breakfast from £34.50
Lounge Snacks from £3.50
Afternoon Tea from £2.50
Dinner from £16.25 Table d'Hôte

Gratuities at Guest's discretion
VAT inclusive. Credit Cards–Access, Visa
7 Double, 3 Twin Bedrooms. 5 Private Bathrooms. 5 Private Shower Rooms
All Rooms with TV, Telephone, Radio, Tea and Coffee-making Facilities, Hairdryer

Open from March to November
Residential Licence. Full Central Heating and Log Fire. Children catered for. Dogs allowed by arrangement. Parking Facilities Nearby: Tennis, Putting, Squash, Swimming, Solarium, Golf, Fishing

Section 5: Cumbria

Keswick—Ladstock Country House Hotel
Thornthwaite, Keswick, Cumbria. CA12 5RZ. Tel 07687 78210D

A host of golden daffodils greets the visitor in the spring, which is only right and proper since we are right in the middle of Wordsworth country. Our hotel is in a quiet and peaceful setting amid sylvan beauty. Rhododendrons fill the garden with colour in the summer, providing a friendly charm of their own. This lovely country house is only three miles from Keswick, set on a hillside in twelve acres of superbly wooded grounds, with lawns and terraced gardens overlooking Bassenthwaite Lake and the majestic slopes of Skiddaw. Originally a vicarage, the main structure was enlarged at the beginning of this century by a well known architect. The spacious rooms of this listed building are richly furnished with both antique and modern furniture. The spacious four-poster or half-tester rooms are ideal for honeymoons, VIP guests and weekend breaks, or just for people who want to spoil themselves with the good things in life. Each room has either bath or shower *en suite*, a colour television, as well as coffee and tea making facilities. Mr and Mrs J T Sandham are your hosts and have spent twenty-one years creating a peaceful retreat. The dining room is magnificent with a superb set menu offering three or four alternatives for each course. To get there leave the M6 at Penrith, join the A66 until Keswick. Keep Derwentwater on your left, Skiddaw on your right, leave the A66 first turning after Braithwaite signed Thornthwaite and you will find the hotel three quarters of a mile on the left hand side.

Daily Terms from £40.00
Bed and Breakfast from £23.00
Bar Meal from £5.00
Lunch (residents) from £8.50 and A La Carte
Dinner from £17.50 and A La Carte
Credit Cards—Access, Visa
Gratuities at Guest's discretion

VAT inclusive. 3 Family Rooms
13 Double, 6 Twin Bedrooms
Single Bedrooms available if required
18 Private Bathrooms
4 Private Shower Rooms
All Rooms with TV, Telephone, Tea and Coffee-making Facilities
Hairdryer available on request

Open from February to January
Fully Licensed. Full Central Heating
TV Lounge. Conference Facilities
Children catered for
Dogs not allowed. Parking Facilities
Nearby: Tennis, Putting, Squash, Badminton, Swimming, Golf, Fishing.

Keswick, Underskiddaw—Red House Hotel
Underskiddaw, Near Keswick, Cumbria. CA12 4QA. Tel 07687 72211

At 3,054 feet, Skiddaw is one of the loftiest peaks in Lakeland, yet the ascent offers the climber a safe and easy day on the fells. We have been up and down in under five hours, and, having chosen a splendid day, we were able to identify Grisdale Pike, the Cumbrian Coast and even gain a glimpse of Ireland. It is also an easy matter to pick out the Red House Hotel from up there, for this comfortable Victorian house nestles between Bassenthwaite Lake and Skiddaw's western slopes. So, the Red House offers a secluded and essentially private base in easy reach of Keswick and the northern lakes. It is warm and friendly, not the least bit impersonal, and, therefore, ideal for relaxing holidays. Yet, these aspects, and the delicious food–traditionally associated with such a country house–are not in themselves, the only reasons we single out this hotel. There is another ingredient, which we will call the Moor's touch. Nicholas and Elaine Moor, the resident proprietors, have been beavering away at the Red House to such good effect that now one could hardly wish for a more comfortable country house hideaway. The ground floor has seen a great deal of refurbishment in the most attractive manner, and most of the bedrooms have received the same treatment. All the essentials are there: private bathrooms and modern et ceteras upstairs; a bar, drawing room, lounge, dining room; and a cellar games room below. The eight acres of grounds have a natural beauty, which is also being enhanced. Relaxation and good food are the keynotes here.

Tariff and Special Breaks upon Application
Daily Terms from £42.00
Bed and Breakfast from £30.00
Gratuities at Guest's discretion
VAT inclusive. Credit Cards—Access, Visa
2 Family Rooms. 8 Double, 7 Double/Twin,

2 Twin, 2 Single Bedrooms
All Rooms with Private Bathroom, TV, Tea and Coffee-making Facilities
Baby-listening available
Open all Year
Residential and Restaurant Licence

Full Central Heating
Cocktail Bar. TV Lounge
Games Room. Conference Facilities
Children catered for.
Well behaved Dogs allowed
Parking Facilities. Putting, Outdoor Pool

Section 5: Cumbria

Near Keswick, Thornthwaite—Thwaite Howe
Thornthwaite, Near Keswick, Cumbria. CA12 5SA.
Tel 07687 78281

There can be few hotels in Lakeland with views more magnificent than those which greet guests to Mike and Penny Sutton's lovely stone-built Victorian country house standing on an elevated site in grounds extending to two-and-a-half acres. Skiddaw at over 3,000 feet lies directly opposite, across the Derwent valley and the panorama extends round past Blencathra to Helvellyn. In spring, the display of daffodils is superb, whilst the summer sunsets and the autumn colours on the fells are a joy to behold. Immediately behind the hotel lies Thornthwaite forest with its profusion of wildlife and forest walks. Since escaping from the pressures of professional life some years ago, Mike and Penny have built up a regular clientele in Lakeland and, as resident owners, place great emphasis on providing a personal service (Penny produces the five course dinners, whilst Mike provides breakfasts which will satisfy the heartiest of appetites) at value-for-money prices in a totally relaxed and informal atmosphere. Since acquiring the hotel, Mike and Penny have made many improvements, including the installation of full central heating, although you will still find a log fire burning in the lounge in inclement weather. They are also delighted to have been awarded a commendation by the English Tourist Board. So if you are looking for a peaceful holiday base in a quiet yet central part of Lakeland, just four miles from Keswick, then Thwaite Howe is an ideal choice.

Weekly Terms from £238.00
Daily Terms from £36.00
Bed and Breakfast from £25.00
Dinner from £12.50 Table d'Hôte
Gratuities at Guest's discretion
VAT inclusive
4 Double, 4 Twin Bedrooms

All Rooms with Private Bathrooms,
Telephone, TV, Radio, Tea and
Coffee-making Facilities, Hairdryer
Open from March to November
Residential and Restaurant Licence
Full Central Heating
Cocktail Bar

Children over 12 catered for
Parking Facilities
Dogs welcome
Nearby: Tennis, Swimming, Golf, Fishing, Riding, Sailing, Windsurfing, Water Skiing, Shooting, Hang-gliding

Section 5: Cumbria

Near Kirkby Stephen, Ravenstonedale—The Black Swan
Ravenstonedale, Kirkby Stephen, Cumbria. CA17 4NG. Tel 05396 23204

Ravenstonedale (pronounce it 'Rassendale' and you will not be marked out as a foreigner) has infinite possibilities as a holiday centre, for it is situated mid-way between the Lake District and the Yorkshire Dales. Only a ten minue drive from junction 38 of the M6, a short journey indeed, but you will arrive in another world. Here is a village which seems untouched by time... and very sleepy, as if the moorland air had got the better of it! Fortunately, too, Ravenstonedale has a very good hotel in The Black Swan. It was built of lakeland stone around the turn of the century and is one of those hostelries of which the north of England can be proud. If there is an industry in the village it is The Black Swan. It attracts people who love unrivalled walking country, observing spectacular birdlife or excellent fishing. The hotel has access to a private stretch on the Eden as well as its own lake for brown trout. After nightfall there are comfortable lounges, good books and magazines, log fires, a quaint stone-walled lounge bar and a handsome dining room. Above stairs the bedrooms, both in equipment and furnishing, will appeal to you. All but two have a private bathroom, whilst there are a number of thoughtful items, such as electric blankets and hairdryers, which are standard throughout. But given these assets, and the unique character of The Black Swan, the owners work hard on that other essential good food. Home-made dishes; local beef, lamb and game; traditional cheeses; fine wines and ports. No wonder we wake up here each morning with that 'glad to be alive' feeling and breathe in great gulps of the marvellous air.

Weekly Terms from £290.00
Daily Terms from £63.00 Double, £45.00
Single. Bed and Breakfast from £45.00
Bar Meal from £4.50
Lunch from £8.50 Table d'Hôte
Afternoon Tea from £3.00

Dinner from £20.00 and A La Carte
Gratuities at Guest's discretion. VAT inclusive. Credit Cards—Access, American Express, Diners Club, Visa
8 Double, 6 Twin Bedrooms
(3 Rooms with Ground Floor Access)

13 Private Bathrooms
All Rooms with Telephone, Tea and Coffee-making Facilities, Baby-listening, Hairdryer, Electric Blankets
Open All Year. Fully Licensed. Full CH
Children catered for. Dogs allowed

Newby Bridge—Swan Hotel
Newby Bridge, Near Ulverston, Cumbria. LA12 8NB. Tel 05395 31681. Fax 05395 31917

Here, one is spoiled for choice with so many places of historical interest, vast areas of diverse natural beauty, and a local setting of charm and tranquillity. Arthur Ransome wrote his famous novel *Swallows and Amazons* whilst staying in this Cumbrian village on the River Leven. Overlooking a fine stone bridge, the Swan Hotel has been providing shelter and refreshment to travellers since the seventeenth century, when it was one of the foremost coaching inns of the area. Today, it is managed by Mr and Mrs J Bertlin and has achieved quite exceptional standards of graceful, modern comfort. Every one of the thirty-six bedrooms has a private bathroom and includes a trouser press in the range of facilities. Many of them have views of Newby Bridge and the river, an idyllic scene which is also visible from the first-floor *Tithe Barn Restaurant*. As elsewhere in the Swan, the decor here has an elegance to suit the function of the room and undoubtedly contributes much to the continuing good reputation accorded by diners. In the traditional surroundings of *The Mailcoach* wine bar, in addition to informal lunches, afternoon teas and evening meals, a special children's menu is available. The hotel provides family board games, darts and table tennis, plus a croquet lawn and golf swing practice net in the summer months. A range of quality merchandise and souvenirs are available in the hotel's shop (March to December). Staff are ready to advise on the numerous outdoor activities which abound in the Lake District National Park area. To find the hotel leave the M6 at junction 36, follow the A590 for sixteen miles. Soon after passing the Newby Bridge sign, the Swan Hotel will be seen on the right hand side.

Daily Terms from £58.00 (min 2 nights)
Bed and Breakfast from £45.00 (sharing Double/Twin). Bar Lunch from £6.00.
Lunch from £10.50 Table d'Hôte
Dinner from £19.25 and A La Carte
Gratuities at Guest's discretion. VAT

inclusive. Credit Cards—Access, American Express, Diners Club, Switch, Visa
8 Family Rooms. 1 Suite
4 De luxe Double Bedrooms
6 Double, 10 Twin, 7 Single Bedrooms
All Rooms with Private Bathroom, TV,

Telephone, Radio, Tea and Coffee-making Facilities, Trouser Press, Hairdryer
Most rooms with Baby-listening
Closed 4th to 13th January 1993 inclusive
Fully Licensed. Full CH. Cocktail Bar.
Conference Facilities. Dogs not allowed

Section 5: Cumbria

Shap, Near Penrith—Shap Wells Hotel
Shap, Near Penrith, Cumbria. CA10 3QU. Tel 09316 628/744. Fax 09316 377

The A6 road ducks beneath and weaves above the M6 between Junctions 39 and 40 of the motorway. We had left Ullswater late in the afternoon and, in the company of two hoteliers, had decided to travel south by means of the former road. Just south of the link road to Junction 39 we saw to our right a sign indicating the way to Shap Wells Hotel, down a narrow country road. We took it, travelled past sheep nibbling at the verges, drove under a bridge and there, in the gloomy winter's mist, appeared this large hotel, with an inviting glow emanating from its reception lounge. Once inside, our chairs were drawn up around a huge coal fire within a matter of minutes, ample refreshments were brought to us and we began to marvel at the layout of this former shooting lodge, once owned by the Earl of Lonsdale. Shap Wells is the sort of place which begs investigation. The epitome of Victorian elegance, the rooms, hallways and passages are spacious and full of interest. There is accommodation to suit the needs of tourists, walkers and those *en route* to and from Scotland. The dining-room is also a favourite of ours—not only are the *à la carte* menus imaginative and the buffet menus extensive, but also the service is quick, cheerful and attentive. There is nowhere else we know which is quite like the Shap Wells Hotel, for it is similar to an ocean liner in a sea of tranquillity and it is most personally run by Mr and Mrs Geoffrey Metcalfe.

Weekly Terms from £250.00
Daily Terms from £36.00
Bed and Breakfast from £29.50
Bar Meals from £3.00. Lunch from £6.50
Dinner from £12.50 and A La Carte
No Service Charge. VAT inclusive
Credit Cards—Access, American Express, Diners Club, Visa

6 Family Rooms
31 Double, 43 Twin, 8 Single Bedrooms
All Rooms with Private Bathroom, TV, Telephone, Radio, Baby-listening, Tea and Coffee-making Facilities
20 Rooms with Hairdryer
Open from 15 February to 2 January
Fully Licensed

Full Central Heating
Cocktail Bar. TV Lounge
Games Room
Conference Facilities
Dogs allowed. Parking Facilities
Hard Tennis Court,
Shooting (by arrangement)

Wasdale—Wasdale Head Inn
Wasdale Head, Near Gosforth, Cumbria. CA20 1EX. Tel 09467 26229. Fax 09467 26334

England's highest point, Scafell Pike, stands amongst the crags of the most majestic part of the Lake District. In the summer, many walkers pick their way up to the summit, where they can pause to admire the views of Windermere, Derwentwater and Wastwater, the deepest lake in England. Nestled beneath the austere crags is Wasdale church, which is claimed to be the smallest in the country, and the famous Wasdale Head Inn. In 1856, Will Ritson, the first landlord, was granted a licence: he was known as 'the biggest liar in England' because of the tall stories he told to his fellow climbers. *Ritson's Bar* is, however, not just a haven for climbers, but attracts all lovers of magnificent scenery and real ale. Here one can relish appetising home-made snacks and the warmth of log fires on cold days. There are ten snug pine-panelled bedrooms, with attractive Continental quilts, direct-dial telephone and tea and coffee-making facilities, with fresh milk if requested. Eight of the rooms have private bathrooms and two have a shower room. The views from the windows are of the massive pyramid of Great Gable and of rich green valleys with waterfalls. The generous breakfasts and roast joints with fresh vegetables are irresistible. Neither have the helpful extra facilities been forgotten—packed lunches and flasks, a drying room and the *Barn Door* shop, with a wide range of outdoor equipment, books and food supplies, satisfy the needs of fell walkers. There are also some self-catering cottages under the same ownership nearby, making this hotel a perfect place to unwind in the company of a host of friendly people.

All Prices pertain to 1992
Weekly Terms from £350.00
Daily Terms from £53.00
Bar Meal (3 course) from £5.00
Dinner from £20.00 Table D'Hôte
No Service Charge. VAT inclusive

Credit Cards—Access, Visa
2 Family Rooms. 4 Double, 2 Twin, 2 Single Bedrooms. 8 Private Bathrooms
2 Private Shower Rooms
All Rooms with Telephone, Tea and Coffee-making Facilities

Baby-listening available on Request
Open from Mid March to Mid November
Fully Licensed. Full Central Heating
Cocktail Bar. Dogs allowed. Parking Facilities. Nearby: Swimming, Solarium, Sauna, Golf, Riding, Fell Walking,

Section 5: Cumbria

Ullswater—Sharrow Bay Country House Hotel
Ullswater, Penrith, Cumbria, CA10 2LZ
Tel 07684 86301/86483. Fax 07684 86349

Reputedly the first true country house hotel, Sharrow Bay is everything a lover of hotels could wish for. In location, comfort, atmosphere and cuisine it is as near perfection as one could find. Brian Sack and Francis Coulson have been working partners in Sharrow Bay Hotel for forty-four years and, in that time, they have created an hotel which is surely unique. They have also worked tirelessly to keep commercialism away from Ullswater, with the result that it is, perhaps, the most peaceful and beautiful lake in Cumbria. Yet, for all the hotel's inherent advantages, its worldwide fame has primarily been the result of the outstanding cuisine. In recent years Brian and Francis received the prestigious Sunday Times 'Taste of England' award for their food, an addition to an already impressive list of accolades. You will find Sharrow Bay just north of Howtown, surrounded by twelve acres of gardens and woodlands and claiming half a mile of lake shore. Inside, the décor and furnishings never fail to please the eye, the two lounges are a lesson in comfort, a luxurious conservatory gives a wonderful view of Barton Fell, the drawing-room affords glorious views and the appointments in the dining-room are a fitting setting for the cuisine. As the fame of Sharrow Bay has spread, the Lodge, at the gates of the hotel, about 400 yards from the main house, and Bank House, about a mile away along the lake, have been adapted to provide additional accommodation. Having known the owners for so long, we share their sense of pride in what has been achieved at Sharrow Bay.

Daily Terms from £90.00
English Breakfast £14.50
Lunch from £28.50 Table d'Hôte
Afternoon Tea from £10.00
Dinner from £39.50 Table d'Hôte
Service Charge and VAT inclusive
6 Suites
7 Double, 11 Twin, 5 Single Bedrooms

24 Private Bathrooms
1 Private Shower Room
All Rooms with TV, Telephone, Radio, Trouser Press, Hairdryer
4 Rooms with Tea and Coffee-making Facilities. Open from early March to early December. Residential and Restaurant Licence

Full Central Heating
Small Conference Facilities
Children not catered for.
Dogs not allowed
Parking Facilities
Lake Swimming
Nearby: Riding, Sailing, Fell Walking

Section 5: Cumbria

Windermere—The Dalegarth Hotel
Lake Road, Windermere, Cumbria. LA23 2EQ. Tel 05394 45052/46702

You have only to step out of the front door of this hotel to begin a scenic woodland walk, leading on to a footpath beside Lake Windermere and to the Steamboat Museum. Dalegarth is a handsome, traditional Lakeland stone house, built over one hundred years ago in a slightly elevated position between Windermere and the village of Bowness. Proprietors Will and Liz Howarth have clearly achieved a major improvement in the facilities. We were able to see extensive, tasteful refurbishment and admire the four-poster water beds, spa baths and sun beds in the Honeymoon Suites. A sauna and small exercise area have also been included within the hotel and guests may use the swimming pool and leisure facilities at the nearby *Spinnaker Club* overlooking the lake. The hotel dining-room offers a selection of traditional home cooking and Cumbrian fare, all personally supervised by the proprietors, and complemented by an extensive wine list. It was pleasant to note that the communal rooms have the attractive quality of being light and airy by day and warmly intimate in the dark evenings. A large proportion of the hotel's trade is made up of regular clientele who return to enjoy the high standard of *cuisine*, service and comfort offered. We have mentioned the local footpaths and to discover new routes you can join in organised fell walks. Other outdoor activities in this beautiful area of lakes and rolling wooded hills include golf, riding, boating, water skiing, lake cruises and swimming. Local shops, restaurants and museums have a distinctive character and a Craft Centre is of particular interest.

Weekly Terms from £120.00	Credit Cards—Access, Visa	Coffee-making facilities, Hairdryer
Daily Terms from £20.00	1 Family Room. 4 Honeymoon Suites	Open all Year. Residential Licence
Bed and Breakfast from £19.00	3 Special Occasion Rooms	Full Central Heating
Dinner from £13.50 Table d'Hôte	1 Twin, 1 Single, 2 Double Bedrooms	Conference Facilities
Gratuities at Guest's discretion	All Rooms with Private Bathroom, TV,	Dogs allowed. Children catered for
VAT inclusive	Video, Telephone, Radio, Tea and	Parking Facilities. Solarium, Sauna

Windermere–Fir Trees
Lake Road, Windermere, Cumbria. LA23 2EQ. Tel 05394 42272

If you wish to stay in the Lake District on a bed and breakfast basis, you really could not do better than the Fir Trees, which is a charming guest house of considerable character and, in keeping with its Victorian origins, is furnished with antiques throughout the premises. Well situated half-way between the resort villages of Windermere and Bowness, it reflects standards which are normally associated with good quality hotels. The bedrooms are both spacious and beautifully furnished and each is equipped with a bath or shower room *en suite* and a colour television. A few of these rooms, because of their size, are particularly suitable for families. The catering takes the form of ample English breakfasts, the sort that set you up for most of the day. Since Windermere and Bowness boast an immense number of eating places, an increasing number of visitors to the area are seeking accommodation on bed and breakfast terms. At Fir Trees guests can enjoy the benefits of this arrangement and forego none of the luxury one expects of an hotel of good quality. The success and high reputation which Ira and Allene Fishman, the friendly and hospitable owners, have gained here proves that this is a winning combination. In short, Fir Trees is undoubtedly one of the best bed and breakfast establishments in the area, a place to which you are bound to return time and time again. It is an excellent base for those who wish to explore the whole of the Lake District by car or for those whose main activity is walking.

Bed and Breakfast only	1 Family Room. 5 Double, 1 Twin	Open all Year. Unlicensed
Weekly Terms from £125.00	Bedrooms. 1 Private Bathroom	Full Central Heating. Dogs not allowed
Bed and Breakfast from £18.50	6 Private Shower Rooms	Children catered for. Parking Facilities
Gratuities at Guest's discretion	All Rooms with TV	Nearby: Tennis, Putting, Squash,
VAT inclusive. Credit Cards–Access,	Tea & Coffee-making Facilities on request	Badminton, Swimming Pool, Solarium,
American Express, Visa	Baby-listening by arrangement	Sauna, Golf, Fishing, Riding, Sailing

Section 5: Cumbria

Near Windermere, Ecclerigg—Merewood Country House Hotel
Ecclerigg, Windermere, Cumbria. LA23 1LH. Tel 09662 6484. Fax 09662 2128

And now for an exciting hotel discovery in Lakeland, easily accessible, yet seemingly off the beaten track. Most of the hotels in this region crane their necks to claim a glimpse of one or other of the lakes, but Merewood, although it enjoys magnificent views of Lake Windermere, is more a country house, and in the truest sense—quintessentially English, preserved from the holiday throng and utterly peaceful. It lies three miles beyond Winderemere village, off the A591 road to Ambleside, and at the end of a long wooded drive. One senses that here the art of good living has been exercised for many years; a tradition diligently maintained today. The conversion from private house to *luxury* hotel has been carried out with such impeccable good taste that we felt the desire to abandon our tours, there and then, and simply drop out for a few days in these classical surroundings. The hotel certainly puts every temptation in one's path—*cuisine* in the modern French style; a wine list compiled by General Manager Bernard Bloodworth; rooms which are full of interest and fine period furniture; and lovely *en suite* bedrooms, each named after local literary figures and decorated with great flair in Laura Ashley designs. The *Byron* and *Tennyson* suites have the added luxury of spa pool baths. And all this is wrapped up in twenty acres of landscaped grounds, which afford 'Royal Box' views. It it all so idyllic.

Special Weekend Breaks from £95.00
Bed and Breakfast from £45.00
Bar Lunch from £3.50
Lunch from £8.95 Table d'Hôte
Afternoon Tea from £2.50
Dinner from £17.50 Table d'Hôte
Service and VAT inclusive
Credit Cards—Access, American Express, Visa
2 Family Rooms. 4 Suites
2 Twin, 14 Double Bedrooms
All Rooms with Private Bathroom, TV, Telephone, Radio, Baby-listening, Tea and Coffee-making Facilities, Hairdresser
Trouser Press in Suites. Open All Year
Residential and Restaurant Licence
Full Central Heating. Cocktail Bar
Conference Facilities
Children catered for
Dogs allowed by arrangement
Parking Facilities. Nearby: Putting, Squash, Badminton, Swimming, Solarium, Sauna, Golf, Fishing, Riding, Sailing, Windsurfing, Water Skiing, Shooting

Near Windermere—Langdale Chase
Windermere, Cumbria. LA23 1LW. Tel 05394 32201. Fax 05394 32604

It was a sunny afternoon in early May when we first called at this Lakeland hotel and were refreshed anew with the magnificent views of lake and mountains, including Langdale Pikes, Scafell and Coniston Old Man. From the windows and terrace one looks across smooth green lawns and flowerbeds to Lake Windermere, with Langdale Pike in the distance. Popular with overseas visitors, particularly Americans, Langdale Chase maintains the atmosphere of a comfortable country house, although the most modern necessities are incorporated in the thirty-one bedrooms, all of which have bath or shower rooms *en suite* and six are in a Lakeland-stone garden bungalow opening onto a wide terrace facing the lake. Car parking is adjacent. We were equally impressed with the variety of the menu presented to us in the restaurant. The excellent, extensive wine list was a fitting complement to the food in this aristocrat of Lakeland hotels. Out of doors are grass tennis courts, a putting course, a croquet lawn and a rowing boat operating from the hotel's jetty. During a recent visit, a pleasant lunch on the terrace was followed by a stroll through the grounds. The last colour of the rhododendrons was giving way to a display of peonies and to the roses of early summer. All, from the kitchen garden to the fine specimen trees, was obviously tended with care. Here, indeed, is gracious living.

All Prices pertain to 1992
Bed and Breakfast from £51.00
Bar Lunch from £3.50
Lunch from £10.75 Table d'Hôte
Afternoon Tea from £7.00
Dinner from £22.00 Table d'Hôte
Service Charge and VAT inclusive
Credit Cards—Access, American Express, Diners Club, Visa
13 Double, 10 Twin, 7 Single Bedrooms
1 Family Room
All Rooms with Private Bathroom, TV, Telephone, Tea and Coffee-making Facilities, Baby-listening, Hairdryer
Open all Year
Fully Licensed
Central Heating. Cocktail Bar
Conference Facilities
Dogs allowed. Parking Facilities
Night Porter
2 Grass Tennis Courts, Croquet, Putting
Nearby: Swimming, Golf, Fishing, Riding, Sailing, Water Skiing, Adjacent Leisure Club Membership

Section 5: Durham

Greta Bridge, Rokeby—The Morritt Arms Hotel
Greta Bridge, Barnard Castle, Co. Durham. DL12 9SE. Tel 0833 27232/27392

The old English wayside inn is still one of our romantic delights, inviting us into the flavour of a Dickensian past. The Morritt Arms Hotel is the sole survivor of three old coaching inns at Greta Bridge and it was, in fact, at one of the inns (he never said which one) that Charles Dickens stayed the night of 31st January 1838, having arrived by coach from London when visiting Yorkshire to research his novel Nicholas Nickleby. The hotel is still full of character and the owners, twin brothers David and John Mulley, run it as if it were a home for themselves. To enhance the atmosphere of peace and quiet there is no background music and functions are restricted. They are also dedicated to good food, a friendly atmosphere and modern hotel comforts, with the proviso that these are in keeping with the inherent charm of this old house. Thus, you will find individually styled bedrooms, all with *en suite* facilities, and all are of a good size. Bar meals are served at lunchtime; there is an attractive beer garden and ample parking. Make The Morritt Arms your headquarters and you can easily visit Egglestone Abbey, Barnard Castle, The Bowes Museum, the confluence of the Tees and Greta and the graceful Greta Bridge. Since it has been bypassed this famous inn is peacefully situated, undisturbed by the noise of traffic and remains a very pleasant place in which to pass any time of the day.

Special Breaks available all Year
Bed and Breakfast from £50.00 Single, £72.00 Double/Twin
Bar Lunch from £2.00
Sunday Lunch from £12.00
Dinner £19.50 Table d'Hôte

Credit Cards—Access, American Express, Diners Club, Visa
3 Single, 8 Double, 6 Twin Bedrooms
All Rooms with Private Bathroom, TV, Telephone, Tea and Coffee-making Facilities, Trouser Press

Open All Year.
Fully Licensed
Part central Heating
Dogs allowed
Parking Facilities
Nearby: Golf, Fishing, Riding

Romaldkirk—Rose and Crown Hotel
Romaldkirk, Barnard Castle, Co Durham. DL12 9EB. Tel 0833 50213. Fax 0833 50828

Considered by many to be one of the prettiest villages in Teesdale, Romaldkirk derives its name from St Rumwald, a prodigious infant saint whose memory is enshrined in the cruciform Norman church of St Romald, known as the 'Cathedral of the Dale'. We approached this unspoilt village from Bowes, the twisting road taking us over several narrow streams and through wild heather. On entering Romaldkirk, with its water pump and stocks on the village green, the atmosphere is one of days gone by. The Rose and Crown is a beautiful old house, the accommodation offered by its seven comfortable bedrooms being supplemented by a number of private courtyard rooms at the rear of the hotel. Stone and timbers set the scene for the two charming bars and the dining room. Resident owners Christopher and Alison Davy run the Rose and Crown with evident pride and from their spotless kitchen produce a choice of succulent dishes to satisfy the most demanding diner. Immediate surroundings to Romaldkirk are rolling farmland, but this is an area of contrasts. Hamsterley Forest, The Pennines, England's largest waterfall (High Force), Bowes and Barnard Castles, rivers and reservoirs and, in Bowes Museum, one of the greatest collections of art treasures in Europe. The area offers shooting, fishing, riding, golf, water sports and planned walks. But do take a second look at the church: its windows and escutcheon are steeped in history.

All Prices pertain to 1992
Weekly Terms on Application
Bed and Breakfast from £45.00
Bar Lunch from £5.00
Lunch from £10.25 Table d'Hôte
Bar Supper from £4.00
Dinner from £22.00 Table d'Hôte
Service and VAT inclusive

Credit Cards—Access, Visa
1 Family Room. 2 Suites
1 Single, 3 Double, 4 Twin Bedrooms
All Rooms with Private Bathroom, TV, Telephone, Radio, Baby-listening, Tea and Coffee-making Facilities
Open All Year except Christmas Day and Boxing Day.

Fully Licensed
Full Central Heating
Conference Facilities
Children catered for. Dogs allowed
Parking Facilities
Nearby: Squash, Solarium, Sauna, Golf, Fishing, Riding, Sailing, Shooting

Section 5: Greater Manchester

Ashton-under-Lyne—York House Hotel York Place, off Richmond Street, Ashton-under-Lyne. OL6 7TT. Tel 061 330 5899. Fax 061 343 1613

York House Hotel, which lies just north-west of the town centre, has been described as 'an oasis in Ashton-under-Lyne'. With thirty-four *en suite* bedrooms, discreetly separated function room for business or social occasions, spacious gardens ideal for wedding photographs and an exceptionally fine restaurant, this flourishing 1800's property is immeasurably more than a mere watering-place. First mention must go to the *Seasons Restaurant*, which offers a fixed-price lunch menu, plus a seasonal menu and classic *à la carte* menu, available at lunch-time and in the evenings. On the classic menu alone, the gourmet is spoiled for choice: with the seasonal menu, which is changed monthly, the creativity of the *cuisine* is extended to utilise currently available ingredients. Unusually for an hotel of this size, it is privately owned and family-run, staff not actually related to the proprietor having served for many years. There is an evident pride taken in the high level of personal attention and courteous efficiency to be found throughout the hotel. Also, the tariff is set at commendably realistic prices. We can well imagine that persons attending mid-week conferences or seminars will wish to make return visits privately at weekends. Certainly it offers a convenient and lavish setting for those special social functions. Staff offer comprehensive services and practical advice on all aspects of wedding receptions. A suite seating seventy people for a meal (or 100 for a buffet) is complemented by facilities for an evening disco. There is a boardroom for confidential business discussions. Whatever the occasion, York House will serve you well.

Bed and Breakfast from £47.50
Lunch from £9.50 and A La Carte
Dinner A La Carte
10% Service Charge
VAT inclusive. Credit Cards—Access, American Express, Diners Club, Visa

2 Family Rooms
19 Double, 5 Twin, 8 Single Bedrooms
All Rooms with Private Bath/Shower Room, TV, Telephone, Radio, Tea and Coffee-making Facilities, Hairdryer
1 Room with Trouser Press

Open All Year. Residential and Restaurant Licence. Full Central Heating
Cocktail Bar. Conference Facilities
Children catered for. Dogs allowed
Parking Facilities. Night Porter

Near Bury, Ramsbottom—The Old Mill Hotel Springwood Street, Ramsbottom, Lancashire. BL0 9DS. Tel 0706 822991. Fax 0706 822291

The once industrious stream is now reduced to a picturesque trickle and the mighty water-wheel has yet to be repaired and reinstated, but there is no doubting that this Old Mill is the genuine article. It once served the inhabitants of the small cotton town of Ramsbottom, which is set amidst lovely Lancashire moorland scenery. The grist to the mill today, however, are two excellent restaurants; a medley of guest rooms, including connecting family rooms, those with king-size beds and one with a four-poster; and a superbly appointed leisure complex, with indoor pool, whirlpool bath, sauna, solarium and gymnasium. From what was a rather neglected hotel a few years ago, The Old Mill is now a model of its kind. The *Trattoria da Nicola* restaurant serves a good selection of top-quality Italian dishes and wines. We, however, elected to dine in the *Garden Restaurant*, which is situated on the first floor and affords superb views across the gardens, the town and adjacent countryside. And our verdict? Rarely have we visited an hotel where we were made to feel more at home, better fed, or where the service was speedier. For all this we have to thank Karen Sacco, who has done a tremendous job here since acquiring The Old Mill. It seems almost superfluous to say that the bedrooms are fully equipped and the whole place is very comfortable, and that we felt our visit was too fleeting. To make amends for the latter we are making arrangements to return to The Old Mill with friends, to enjoy the hotel's very competitive weekend rates and take full advantage of the leisure facilities.

Weekly Terms from £290.50 Single
Bed and Breakfast from £31.50
Bar Lunch from £2.75
Lunch from £7.50 and A La Carte
Afternoon Tea from £3.00
Dinner from £12.50 and A La Carte

Gratuities at guest's discretion
All Major Cards accepted. VAT inclusive
3 Family Rooms. 12 Double, 12 Twin, 12 Single Bedrooms. All Rooms with Private Bath/Shower Room, TV, Telephone, Radio, Tea and Coffee-making Facilities, Trouser Press, Hairdryer, Fruit
Open All Year. Fully Licensed
Full Central Heating
2 Cocktail Bars. Conference Facilities
Children catered for. Dogs not allowed
Parking Facilities. Night Porter

Section 5: Greater Manchester

Manchester Airport—Etrop Grange Hotel
Outwood Lane, Manchester Airport, M22 5NR
Tel 061 499 0500. Fax 061 499 0790

Etrop Grange is a rare find. Tucked away in over an acre of quiet and secluded gardens, one would never guess that this beautiful country house hotel and restaurant lies just a few minutes from Manchester Airport and the motorway network. Built in 1780, this elegant Grade II listed building was once owned by an eccentric who filled the house with wax dummies, and later by a wealthy banker who wanted to own 'the finest house in Cheshire'. The proprietors, John and Susan Roebuck have transformed this family home into a family-run hotel and restaurant with the emphasis firmly on comfort, delicious food and traditional hospitality. Each bedroom has been individually designed and furnished under the careful guidance of Susan Roebuck to reflect the history of this fine country house. The four-poster rooms make Etrop Grange the ideal venue for honeymooners and special rates are available. The hotel is popular with business visitors and excellent conference and banqueting facilities are provided. The weekend is a perfect opportunity to stay at Etrop Grange and take advantage of special accommodation tariffs. Come and explore the North West of England, the rolling Cheshire countryside, Manchester city centre with its wealth of theatres, galleries and shops. Lancashire offers many beautiful coastal resorts and a step further takes you into the splendour of the Lake District, all of which are easily accessible from the hotel with its excellent motorway and road links. Etrop Grange has just been nominated as Cheshire Life Hotel of the Year

Terms from September 1992
Room Rate from £85.00 Single (W/end £54.50)
£89.50 Double (W/end £54.50)
Suites from £125.00
Lunch from £11.50
Dinner from £19.50
VAT inclusive
Credit Cards—Access, American Express, Diners Club, Visa

4 Family Rooms. 2 Suites
8 4-poster Master Bedrooms
3 Single, 24 Double Bedrooms
1 Room suitable for disabled
All Rooms with Private Bathroom, TV, Telephone, Radio, Baby-listening, Tea and Coffee-making Facilities, Trouser Press, Hairdryer, Private Bar, Newspapers
Open all Year
Fully Licensed

Full Central Heating
8 Conference Suites
Cocktail Bar
Children catered for
Dogs allowed
Courtesy Car to and from Airport
Parking Facilities. Night Porter
Nearby: Golf, Fishing, Riding, Windsurfing, Water Skiing, Shooting

Section 5: Humberside

Driffield—The Bell in Driffield
Market Place, Driffield, Humberside. YO25 7AP. Tel 0377 46661. Fax 0377 43228

'A place where intending managers and owners of Georgian-style hotels should be forcibly dragged and shown how to do it properly.' So wrote the Yorkshire Post, of The Bell in Driffield. This classical Georgian building, Grade 2 listed, was 250 years old in 1992. Anyone with a feeling for history will find much of interest in this distinctive three-storey hotel. Maps, prints and pictures adorn the walls, with muskets hanging protectively alongside original photographs. A successful blend of the traditional and modern is evidenced by the presence of a grandfather clock, a grand piano and a useful illuminated display showing local places of interest. Residents and non-residents have praised the quality of the lunches, the menu being changed daily. To complement the excellent food, the Bell stocks no less than 190 whiskies, of which 130 are malt. There is also draught Guinness and a choice of three traditional beers. An extension to the rear of the Inn has stone flagging, original exposed brick, a preserved well (one of three which used to supply the hotel) and, in this area, children are welcomed. Accommodation and service are provided in a warm and friendly atmosphere, with an adjoining converted Town Hall, also owned by Mr and Mrs Riggs, offering a range of recreational, social and conference facilities. The Bell in Driffield (correctly Great Driffield) lies on the A166 road between York and Bridlington. In recent years it has received a most impressive list of prestigious awards for excellence, to which we are pleased to add our considered heartfelt commendation.

Bed and Breakfast from £62.00	American Express, Diners Club, Visa	Full Central Heating. Conference Facilities
Bar Meal from £4.95	4 Double, 3 Twin, 4 Single Bedrooms	Children over 12 catered for
Lunch from £7.95 and A La Carte	5 Suites. All Rooms with Private Bathroom,	Parking Facilities
Dinner from £12.00 and A La Carte	TV, Telephone, Radio, Tea and	Squash, Swimming, Solarium, Sauna,
Gratuities at Guest's discretion	Coffee-making Facilities, Trouser Press,	Steam Room, Gymnasium
VAT inclusive. Credit Cards—Access,	Hairdryer. Open all Year. Fully Licensed	Nearby: Golf Fishing, Riding

Nafferton—Wold House Country Hotel
Wold Road, Nafferton, Driffield, Humberside. YO25 0LD. Tel 0377 44242

To paraphrase our Inspector's comment: 'this hotel is set in a part of Humberside almost undiscovered by motorists'. Wold House is a country hotel situated within its own spacious grounds, which include an eighteen-hole putting green and a sheltered, heated, outdoor swimming pool. A recent addition is the provision of a full size snooker table and, in the large sun lounge, table tennis can be played. Within easy reach there are the golf courses at Driffield and Ganton; for the fisherman and boating enthusiast, Filey Bay and Bridlington Bay are accessible by road or by rail; on the doorstep is Great Driffield, the capital of the Wolds, a market town with excellent shopping facilities and a stake in history. House and gardens to be visited include Burton Agnes Hall and Sledmere, there is a pottery at Hornsea and the motor racing circuit at Carnaby. At Nafferton, one is close to North Yorkshire with its open moors and delightful dales. All these outdoor diversions should generate healthy appetites which will be well satisfied by the home cooking for which Wold House is noted. Their luncheon and dinner menus, both of which are competitively priced, offer a wide choice of wholesome fare. Pre-dinner drinks can be taken in the popular rendezvous of the cocktail lounge. The hotel has a residents' lounge and separate television lounge, although television sets are also provided in those rooms with *en suite* facilities. In summary: a good hotel, in beautiful secluded countryside, and an owner who is keen to meet the requirements of his guests.

Weekly Terms from £250.00	VAT inclusive. Credit Cards—Access, Visa	Hairdryer available on request
Daily Terms from £38.00	5 Double, 4 Twin, 2 Single Bedrooms	Open all Year except Christmas
Bed and Breakfast from £32.00	(4 Rooms can be let as Family Rooms)	Residential and Restaurant Licence
Lunch from £7.50 Table d'Hôte	4 Private Bathrooms. 4 Private Shower	Part central Heating. Cocktail Bar. TV
Dinner from £13.50 Table d'Hôte	Rooms. All Rooms with TV, Radio, Tea and	Lounge. Games Room
Gratuities at Guest's discretion	Coffee-making Facilities	Children catered for. Dogs allowed.

Section 5: Isle of Man

Ramsey—Grand Island Hotel
Ramsey, Isle of Man Tel 0624 812455. Fax 0624 815291

We drove northwards from Douglas to Ramsey and as we negotiated those twin road hazards, *Gooseneck* and *Hairpin*, were more than glad that our visit did not coincide with the island's famous T T motorcycle race. Ramsey proved to be a most pleasant find: quieter than Douglas and with a Victorian air. It lies on a shallow bay which stretches between Maughold Head and Point of Ayre, and with its background of mountains and the majestic estuary of the Sulby, Man's greatest river, running through the town, the environs are most pleasant. We strongly recommend that you visit the Grand Island Hotel. Undoubtedly, there is now a well-established trend of improvements here. A major innovation is an attractive indoor heated swimming pool and health complex. As befits an hotel of this calibre, the refurbishment throughout is to a high standard, and we received friendly and helpful assistance from all the staff with whom we had contact. A sauna is provided on the premises and, continuing the health theme, we noted that a number of vegetarian dishes are available on the well-balanced menus. Mr Andrew Gibson, the manager, explained that special arrangements with reduced green fees are available for their golfing visitors to use the local golf course which is just one mile away. We think you will find that this hotel more than lives up to its name–it is pleasant and comfortable, without in any way being grandiose. Ramsey has good roads radiating to all parts of the Isle, making the Grand Island Hotel a valuable summer-time base and a snug winter retreat.

Bed and Breakfast from £65.00
Bar Lunch from £3.50
Afternoon Tea from £3.50
Dinner from £13.00 and A La Carte
Gratuities at Guest's discretion
VAT inlusive. Credit Cards—Access,

American Express, Diners Club, Visa
4 Family Rooms. 8 Suites
13 Double, 24 Twin, 6 Single Bedrooms
All Rooms with Private Bathrooms, TV, Telephone, Radio, Baby-listening, Tea and Coffee-making Facilities

Open all Year. Fully Licensed
Full Central Heating. Lift. Cocktail Bar
Conference Facilities
Small Dogs allowed
Parking Facilities. Night Porter

Infallible?
The answer is no because even as these lines are being written, hotel ownership, management and staff are changing somewhere. Invaluable? Yes, because by joining the Ashley Courtenay Circle (no extra charge) you can check up with us at any time during the current season.

A reminder.
Some of the tariffs in this book are those quoted for 1992. As prices will probably have changed for 1993 please check before booking. Please also note that the weekly and daily hotel rates shown in this book are for half board only (dinner, room and breakfast) unless otherwise stated.

Section 5: Lancashire

Blackpool—The Headlands Hotel
611-13 South Promenade, Blackpool, Lancashire. FY4 1NJ. Tel 0253 41179

A visit to Blackpool has become a British tradition, yet as well as the almost endless entertainments to be found here, there are quieter sides to this happy resort—spacious parks, flower-decked gardens, bowling greens and golf courses. The Headlands, which looks directly onto the South Promenade and the sea, has a delightful southern aspect over restful and well-tended gardens. For over half a century The Headlands has been in the same family ownership and there is, therefore, a well-established tradition of quality in its comfort, catering and service. Traditional, too, is the style of its all-embracing tariff. It is one of the few remaining hotels offering completely inclusive terms: bedroom, full English breakfast, four-course luncheon, afternoon tea and seven-course dinner. The value is quite remarkable. The majority of the bedrooms face the sea and all have *en suite* facilities. If you are a particularly light sleeper you may prefer to stipulate a side room. Whether you are upstairs or downstairs, you will find that the hotel is tastefully carpeted and furnished, including the attractive oak-panelled dining room, the *West Lounge* residents' bar, the games room and the colour television lounge. The hotel has a resident organist during the high season and special tariffs for the Christmas and New Year periods. Further facilities include a lift to all floors and ample provisions for parking. Above all, the partners, Michael Simkin and Charles Ruppert, have the right psychology for hotelkeeping.

Weekly Terms from £211.00
Daily Terms from £30.45
Bed and Breakfast from £23.10
Bar Meal from £2.50
Lunch from £8.95 Table d'Hôte
Afternoon Tea from £0.90
Dinner from £13.10 Table d'Hôte
Gratuities at Guest's discretion

VAT inclusive. Credit Cards—Access, Visa
11 Family Rooms. 43 Suites
8 Double, 14 Twin, 10 Single Bedrooms
All Rooms with Private Bath/Shower Room, TV, Radio, Telephone, Baby-listening, Tea and Coffee-making Facilities.
Hairdryer available on request

Open from 17 January to 2 January
Residential Licence. Full Central Heating
Lift. Cocktail Bar. TV Lounge. Games Room
Conference Facilities. Parking Facilities
Dogs allowed at Management's discretion. Solarium. Nearby: Tennis, Putting, Squash, Badminton, Swimming

Catterall—The Pickerings Country House Restaurant and Hotel
Catterall, Garstang, Lancashire. PR3 0HA. Telephone 0995 602133

Some places are worth visiting, others are worth going out of one's way to visit. The Pickerings at Catterall falls clearly into the latter category and not just because of its celebrated food. The Pickerings is a good spot for the traveller, too, for it sits in a pleasant island of rurality with the main A6 road to the west and the M6 motorway to the east. However, within the peaceful confines of this originally seventeenth century house and its two acre garden one can feel a hundred miles from traffic and transportation. Currently the accommodation comprises sixteen bedrooms, including two on the ground floor, and the standards are extremely high. Three rooms boast four-poster beds, two contain whirlpool baths and all have *en suite* facilities. It is essential that you book well ahead to avoid disappointment. The same can be said to be true of the restaurant, for the two dining rooms are in constant demand, particularly when the hotel holds its special gourmet occasions, or when *The Pickerings Wine Club* meets for its regular tastings and dinner parties. The regular catering is based on five course dinners, offering a wide range of mouth-watering specialities and some imaginative vegetarian dishes. The fine wines include an excellent house champagne. As one reader put it 'dining at The Pickerings is less an occasion and more a celebration'. Conference secretaries should also make note of the *Garden Room* which can accommodate up to twenty people on an excellent daily room and refreshment rate..

Special Breaks available
Bed and Breakfast from £40.00
Lunch from £12.50 Table d'Hôte
Dinner from £19.00 Table d'Hôte
Service Charge and VAT inclusive
Credit Cards—Access, Visa

1 Family Room. 1 Suite
12 Double, 2 Twin, 2 Single Bedrooms
All Rooms with Private Bath/Shower Room, TV, Telephone, Tea and Coffee-making Facilities, Trouser Press, Hairdryer, Flowers, Fruit

Open All Year. Residential and Restaurant Licence. Full Central Heating
Cocktail Bar. Conference Facilities
Children catered for. Dogs allowed
Parking Facilities
Nearby: Tennis, Squash, Swimming

Section 5: Lancashire

Near Clitheroe, Slaidburn—Parrock Head Hotel
Slaidburn, Near Clitheroe, Lancashire. BB7 3AH.
Tel 02006 614

This seventeenth-century farmhouse stands in the rolling pastures of the upper Hodder Valley, about a mile to the north west of the delightful village of Slaidburn in the midst of the glorious countryside of the Forest of Bowland. There are extensive views in all directions of a ring of fells and woodland and an infinite variety of walks can be undertaken. Owned and personally hosted by Richard and Vicky Umbers, Parrock Head offers comfortable, relaxing seclusion. The farmhouse has been carefully renovated to give modern facilities whilst retaining the original character. All the rooms have private bathrooms. Two cottages have been built alongside the house to provide a further six beautifully furnished rooms. At the time of our visit there was a nip in the air, but the heating compensated for this. We chose dinner from an attractive, reasonably priced à la carte menu, whilst enjoying a drink at the small bar. The menu is changed daily and Mrs Umbers believes that she is able to provide guests with the choice they desire–for instance, guests may select two starters and omit the main course. Our meal was superbly cooked and served and Mr Umbers gave us knowledgeable advice on selection from an exclusive and imaginative wine list. After dinner, we climbed the short flight of stairs to the lounge and found we were able to browse through the Umbers' wide-ranging library and retire to deep chairs in front of a blazing fire. To reach Slaidburn and the Parrock Head Country Hotel we suggest leaving Clitheroe on the B6478 and driving via Waddington and Newton–but do make a reservation.

Weekly Terms from £320.00 Single, £515.00 Double
Bed and Breakfast from £37.50 Single, £55.00 Double
Bar Lunch from £2.50
Dinner from £13.50 A La Carte
Gratuities at Guest's discretion

VAT inclusive. Credit Cards—Access, American Express, Visa
2 Suites. 4 Double, 4 Twin Bedrooms
All Rooms with Private Bathroom, TV, Tea and Coffee-making Facilities
Hairdryer available on request
Open All Year

Residential and Restaurant Licence
Part Central Heating and Electric Heaters
Children catered for
Dogs allowed by arrangement
Parking Facilities
Nearby: Golf, Fishing, Walking, Birdwatching

Section 5: Lancashire

Goosnargh, Near Preston—Ye Horns Inn Horns Lane, Goosnargh, Near Preston, Lancashire. PR3 2FJ. Telephone 0772 865230. Fax 0772 864299

Although set in beautiful rolling countryside in the lee of fells and moors, and roughly equidistant from Inglewhite, Goosnargh and Longridge, this 200-year old inn is not difficult to find and is well worth seeking out. You should leave the A6 at Broughton traffic lights, just north of Preston, and take the B5296 road which is signed to Longridge. Then, where the road takes a very sharp right-hand bend, continue straight on and after a few minutes this delightful old black and white inn can be seen at the crossroads. Ye Horns Inn is under the ownership of Mrs E Woods, who is ably assisted by her daughter Elizabeth, her son Mark and his wife Denise. The inn has a most pleasant atmosphere and is spotlessly clean. With the addition of six beautifully furnished *en suite* bedrooms Ye Horns can now offer a 'room at the inn'. The restaurant is well known for the excellent food, some prepared from the produce of local farms, which is served in the cheerful main dining-room and in the adjoining 'snug' dining-room, with only four tables. The latter must be particularly pleasant by candlelight in the evenings. Our enjoyable lunch was perfectly served and we noted the obvious satisfaction of other diners. Ye Horns Inn is, indeed, well worth your patronage and is well placed for those exploring the lovely Ribble Valley or the Forest of Bowland.

Bed and Breakfast from £65.00 Double, £45.00 Single	VAT inclusive	Open all Year
Bar Lunch from £1.70	Credit Cards—Access, American Express, Diners Club, Switch, Visa	Full Central Heating
Lunch from £9.50 Table d'Hôte	4 Double, 2 Twin Bedrooms	Fully Licensed
Dinner from £17.00 Table d'Hôte	All Rooms with Private Bathroom, TV, Telephone, Radio, Trouser Press, Hairdryer	Dogs not allowed
Gratuities at Guest's discretion		Parking Facilities
		Nearby: Tennis, Golf, Fishing, Shooting

Langho—Mytton Fold Farm Hotel Whalley Road, Langho, Near Blackburn, Lancashire. BB6 8AB. Tel 0254 240662. Fax 0254 248119

All praise is due to the third-generation owners for the full range of services in the bedrooms: not only the customary television, radio/alarm clock, tea or coffee facilities, direct-dial telephone and hairdryer, but a combination (unisex) trouser press, well-lit large mirrors, useful wide shelves for one's toilet impedimenta, ironing board and plenty of courtesy items. There is thoughtful consideration here, friendly and willing service everywhere. In the dining-room one of us chose smoked breast of goose from the long list of starters. It was delicious. Mixed grill as a main course may seem commonplace; here, in quality, variety and quantity it was quite outstanding, with many other dishes available as alternatives. To complement all this is a reasonably priced wine list. Nor is the businessman forgotten since there are now extensive conference/banqueting facilities. Mytton Fold, winner of the 1991 trophy for the Best Kept Hotel in Lancashire's Best Kept Village Competition, lies between the villages of Langho and Whalley, the gateway to the beautiful Ribble Valley. It is an area embracing several 'Best Kept' small villages, a number of golf courses around Blackburn, Accrington, Burnley and Nelson, an artificial ski slope at Pendleton and Nature Trails at Whalley and Great Harwood. A network of small roads makes interesting driving in the Trough of Bowland while those prepared to make an excursion can explore eastwards to the Yorkshire Dales. To reach this hotel leave the M6 at exit 31, follow A59 signposted Whalley and Clitheroe for eleven miles and at a roundabout take the minor road signed 'Whalley'. The gateway is 800 yards on your right.

Bed and Breakfast from £27.00 (weekends), £32.25 (Mon-Thurs)	inclusive. Credit Cards—Access, American Express, Visa. 2 Four Poster Rooms	Hairdryer. 15 Rooms with Ironing Boards
Bar Lunch from £4.00 (Monday to Friday)	11 Double, 14 Twin Bedrooms	Open All Year. Residential and Restaurant Licence. Full Central Heating. Cocktail Bar
Sunday Lunch from £7.95 Table d'Hôte	All Rooms with Private Bath/Shower Room, TV, Telephone, Radio, Tea and Coffee-making Facilities, Trouser Press,	Conference Facilities
Dinner from £12.00 and A La Carte		Children over 6 years catered for
Gratuities at Guest's discretion. VAT		Dogs not allowed. Parking Facilities

Section 5: Lancashire

Lytham St Anne's—Chadwick Hotel South Promenade, Lytham St Anne's, Lancashire. FY8 1NP. Tel 0253 720061

It was through one of our readers that we discovered this friendly hotel commanding a beautiful sea-front position. We can endorse his sentiments about the food, the clean and comfortable bedrooms and the warm welcome from the manager, Mr Miles Corbett, and his pleasantly efficient staff. Essentially a family-run hotel, the Chadwick is owned by Mr Corbett's mother and is one of the most comprehensively equipped hotels we have come across. The accommodation is excellent, for all the rooms provide either a private bath or shower with toilet, a direct-dial telephone, radio, colour television and trouser press. Two of the rooms have a four-poster bed. There is a health complex, which includes an indoor swimming pool with a theme of ancient Greece, a Turkish bath, a sauna, and a solarium. The lounge areas, overlooking the sea-front, are spacious and tastefully furnished and one can sit and enjoy a drink in the comfortable *Buggatti Bar*. The *Atlantis Lounge*, which gives a good view of the leisure pool and spa, is a recent addition to the hotel's amenities. It was our impression that the Corbetts' one desire is for visitors to have a comfortable and enjoyable holiday. The tariff also offers excellent value for money. Being open all year, the Chadwick is also ideal for those who like to take a holiday out of season.

Weekly Terms from £240.80
Daily Terms from £34.40
Bed and Breakfast from £22.50
Bar Lunch from £3.00
Lunch from £6.90 Table d'Hôte
Afternoon Tea from £3.00
Dinner from £12.50
No Service Charge. VAT inclusive
Credit Cards—Access, American Express, Diners Club, Visa

20 Family Rooms
12 Double, 30 Twin, 10 Single Bedrooms
65 Private Bathrooms (12 with spa bath)
7 Private Shower Rooms
All Rooms with TV, Telephone, Radio, Baby-listening, Trouser Press, Hairdryer and Tea and Coffee-making facilities
24 hour Food and Beverage Service
Open all year. Residential and Restaurant Licence. Full Central Heating. Lift

Cocktail Bar. Games Room. TV Lounge
Conference Facilities
Guide Dogs only allowed
Parking Facilities. Night Porter
Swimming, Solarium, Sauna
Nearby: Tennis, Croquet, Putting, Squash, Badminton, Golf, Fishing, Riding, Sailing, Windsurfing, Water Skiing

Morecambe, Bare Village—The Elms Hotel Bare Village, Morecambe, Lancashire. LA4 6DD. Tel 0524 411501. Fax 0524 831979

There are hotels worth seeing and there are hotels worth going to see, and we would put The Elms at Morecambe firmly in the latter category. The reason for this is that, under the management of Mr Eric Grindrod, the hotel is going through something of a renaissance. Every bedroom has an attractive *en suite* bathroom and all modern notions of comfort. The public rooms beg one to relax, whilst The Elms' restaurant has gained such a reputation for good food that the hotel is the focal point for many local occasions. There are four function rooms which can accommodate up to 250 guests, four private bars and in the grounds the hotel has its own pub, *The Owl's Nest*, with a small comfortable bar. Impressive, too, are the staff who, clearly touched by the manager's enthusiasm and warmth, treated us most kindly throughout our visit. The owner's dream of recreating an hotel of elegance and charm is nearing completion at The Elms! The hotel lies just off the sea front and coastal road, at the top of Lansdowne Road, and is singularly blessed by the landscaped gardens enfolding it. By whom and why is this section of Morecambe named Bare? Certainly it must have been before nature landscaped Morecambe Bay with the lakeland mountains as a background.

Bed and Breakfast from £46.00
Bar Lunch from £2.00
Lunch from £8.75 and A La Carte
Afternoon Tea from £4.00
Dinner from £12.50 and A La Carte
Gratuities at Guest's discretion
VAT inclusive
Credit Cards—Access, American Express,

Diners Club, Visa
1 Family Room. 1 Suite
19 Double, 14 Twin, 6 Single Bedrooms
All Rooms with Private Bathroom, TV, Telephone, Tea and Coffee-making Facilities, Trouser Press, Hairdryer
Open all Year. Fully Licensed
Full Central Heating

Lift. Cocktail Bar. TV Lounge
Conference Facilities. Dogs allowed
Parking Facilities. Night Porter
Nearby: Tennis, Putting, Squash, Badminton, Swimming, Solarium, Sauna, Golf, Fishing, Riding
Sailing, Windsurfing, Water Skiing

Section 5: Merseyside

Southport—The Crimond Hotel 28 Knowsley Road, Southport, Merseyside. PR9 0HN. Tel 0704 536456. Fax 0704 548643

In our previous commendations, we have described Pat and Geoff Randle's friendly and comfortable hotel as a 'miniature palace'. The couple now have their daughter and son-in-law involved fully in running the hotel and in planning further improvements. Already, every bedroom now has comprehensive *en suite* facilities with new furniture. Guests can enjoy a jacuzzi, sauna and an indoor heated swimming pool. Although only two minutes' drive from the centre of Southport, and five minutes from six championship golf courses, the hotel's setting is peaceful, with a quiet garden at the rear. Locals and guests have praised the well balanced menus which are changed daily and appeal strongly to those with hearty appetites. For business functions such as conferences, the provision for up to thirty persons boardroom style, or fifty in theatre style, is particularly valuable with the centre of Liverpool not far away. Also, the warm hospitality has established The Crimond as an attractive venue for wedding receptions and those special social occasions. Holiday guests have the extensive sandy foreshore and National Trust properties, including Rufford Old Hall, amongst numerous places to visit nearby. Our 'palace' description is now more valid than ever.

Weekly Terms from £210.00 Single, £350.00 Double
Bed and Breakfast from £25.00
Bar Lunch from £3.50
Dinner from £9.95 and A La Carte
Gratuities at Guest's discretion
VAT inclusive
Credit Cards—Access, American Express,

Diners Club, Visa
2 Family Rooms. 4 Single Bedrooms
5 Double, 5 Twin Bedrooms
12 Private Bathrooms
4 Private Shower Rooms
All Rooms with TV, Telephone, Radio, Tea and Coffee-making Facilities, Hairdryer
12 Rooms with Trouser Press

Open all Year
Residential and Restaurant Licence
Full Central Heating
Cocktail Bars
Conference Facilities
Dogs allowed. Parking Facilities
Swimming, Jacuzzi, Sauna

Near Southport—Tree Tops Country House Restaurant and Motel Southport Old Road, Formby, Near Southport, L37 0AB. Tel 07048 79651

Tree Tops is just to the south of Ainsdale near the A565 road. When travelling northwards on the A565, you will find the turning to the motel just at the end of the stretch of dual carriageway, amidst a prominent area of woodland. The motel is strategically situated amongst a variety of mature trees so that one has the feeling of being right out in the country. The Tree Tops is personally run by Lesley Winsland, ably assisted by an experienced staff whose dedication ensures the complete happiness and welfare of their guests. They have every right to be proud of their welcoming cocktail bar and lounge, from which you proceed to the most exquisitely furnished restaurant. Open for lunch Sunday to Friday with *table d'hôte* and *à la carte* menus: dinner is served from Sunday to Saturday with a full *à la carte* and *table d'hôte* menus. The menus and wine list are most impressive and it is not surprising, therefore, that the motel has built up an excellent reputation for its *cuisine* and cellar. In the grounds we inspected some delightful chalets, each with its own bath or shower, colour television, direct-dial telephone and tea-making facilities. The grounds, which contain an outdoor heated swimming pool, were well maintained, with perfectly cut lawns. We concluded that The Tree Tops was an excellent place to stay.

Bed and Breakfast from £39.00
Lunch from £8.50 and A La Carte
Dinner A La Carte
10% Service Charge
VAT inclusive
Credit Cards—Access, American Express, Diners Club, Visa
2 Family Rooms
2 Double, 2 Twin, 5 Single Bedrooms

All Rooms with Private Bathroom, TV, Telephone, Radio, Tea and Coffee-making Facilities, Trouser Press, Hairdryer
Open all year
Residential and Restaurant Licence
Full Central Heating
Cocktail Bar
Small Conference Facilities
Dogs not allowed

Parking Facilities
Outdoor Heated Swimming Pool
Nearby: Tennis, Croquet, Putting, Squash, Badminton, Solarium, Sauna, Golf, Fishing, Riding, Sailing, Windsurfing, Water Skiing, Shooting, Flying School

Section 5: Northumberland

Belford—Blue Bell Hotel
Belford, Northumberland. NE70 7NE. Tel 0668 213543

Mrs Jean Shirley personally supervises the management of the Blue Bell Hotel and the emphasis is on a friendly welcome and generous hospitality. Originally a coaching inn, the Blue Bell has been modernised, without losing its charming character, to provide up-to-date amenities. All the bedrooms have colour television, telephone, radio and tea and coffee-making facilities and all have a private bathroom. We had the pleasure of staying in a most pleasant room which looked out over the lovely garden and a putting green. Fresh fruit and vegetables from the hotel garden are put to good use in the preparation of meals served in the restaurant. Guests may mingle with local people in *The Belford Tavern* or enjoy the elegance of the hotel bar for *apéritifs* and after-dinner drinks. The creeper-clad Blue Bell has a most commanding position, facing south towards Belford's Market Cross. Just three-quarters of a mile from the A1, the village of Belford is an excellent base for exploring the Northumbrian coastline where several traditional fishing villages can still be found. The entire area is rich in history, beautiful buildings and dramatic scenery: to the north lies Berwick and to the south lies Alnwick. If you wish to see Lindisfarne, the Farne Islands and the finest beaches in the north east the Blue Bell would suit you perfectly.

Weekly Terms from £270.00
Daily Terms from £44.00
Bed and Breakfast from £34.00
Bar Meal from £3.50
Lunch from £7.00 Table d'Hôte
Afternoon Tea from £4.00
Dinner from £15.00 and A La Carte
Gratuities at Guest's discretion

VAT inclusive. Credit Cards—Access, American Express, Diners Club, Visa
1 Family Room. 1 Single, 7 Double, 8 Twin Bedrooms (1 suitable disabled)
13 Private Bathrooms. 4 Private Shower Rooms. All Rooms with TV, Telephone, Radio, Tea and Coffee-making Facilities, Hairdryer. Open All Year

Fully Licensed. Full Central Heating
Cocktail Bar. Games Room
Conference Facilities
Children over 6 years catered for
Dogs allowed at Management's discretion
Parking Facilities. Putting
Nearby: Tennis, Golf, Fishing, Riding, Sailing Windsurfing, Water Skiing, Shooting

Blanchland—The Lord Crewe Arms Hotel
Blanchland, Near Consett, Co Durham. DH8 9SP. Tel 0434 675 251. Fax 0434 675 337

From Hexham take the B6306 road over the moors and after about ten miles you will reach Blanchland, on the border between Northumberland and Durham. The existence of the village was first recorded in 1165, the date of the founding of a Premonstratensian abbey. Part of the abbey church was incorporated into the present parish church and next to the fifteenth-century abbey gateway is the village square, which was the centrepiece of a model village built in the eighteenth century by Lord Crewe. The main body of The Lord Crewe Arms dates back to the mid-thirteenth century (it was once the home of the Abbot of Blanchland), but the annexe was constructed circa 1740. Today, the annexe houses country-style bedrooms, all with private bathrooms, telephones, hairdryers, beverage-making facilities and, a nice touch, fresh flowers, complimentary sherry and fruit on arrival. Under the guidance of the owners, Mr A Todd, Mr P Gingell and Mr I Press, The Lord Crewe Arms is a peaceful, well-ordered hotel. One dines extremely well in the excellent *Lord Crewe Restaurant* on a variety of traditional English dishes and one can sit and enjoy a drink in the *Crypt Bar*, originally the abbey crypt. We consider Blanchland, in the secluded Derwent Valley, to be an ideal place for a quiet short break or a holiday. Conference organisers, too, should make a note of this delightful hotel, for it offers excellent facilities for day or residential conferences.

Bed and Breakfast from £47.00
English Breakfast £7.50
Bar Lunch from £3.50
Sunday Lunch from £12.50 Table d'Hôte
Afternoon Tea from £2.00
Dinner from £21.50 A La Carte
Gratuities at Guest's discretion
VAT inclusive

Credit Cards—Access, American Express, Diners Club, Visa
2 Family Rooms. 11 Double (1 Four Poster), 5 Twin Bedrooms
17 Private Bathrooms (2 with whirlpool baths). 1 Private Shower Room
All Rooms with TV, Telephone, Radio, Tea and Coffee-making Facilities, Trouser Press, Hairdryer, Ironing Centre

Open all Year. Fully Licensed
Full Central Heating
Conference Facilities
Dogs allowed
Parking Facilities
Nearby: Tennis, Golf, Fishing, Riding, Sailing, Windsurfing, Shooting, Walking

Section 5: Northumberland

Hexham—The Beaumont Hotel Beaumont Street, Hexham, Northumberland. NE46 3LT. Tel 0434 602331. Fax 0434 602331

A little local knowledge enabled us to enter Hexham by the 'old' road, now a sliproad off the A69, which leads one directly to Beaumont Street. Once arrived Hexham's great abbey comes into view. To the left pretty gardens descend through mature trees to a scurrying burn, whilst on one's right The Beaumont Hotel stands solid and inviting. Martin and Linda Owen have owned the hotel for seven years or so and really have achieved a great deal here. Their hotel is very clean and comfortable and has seen a great deal of refurbishment. We had an excellent dinner, slept like tops on the best of mattresses and the following morning enjoyed the most ample of English breakfasts. Yet, even more impressive, perhaps, is the fact that The Beaumont is privately owned, privately run and is one of the friendliest places you will find anywhere. Each of the twenty-three bedrooms has either a private bath or shower, colour television, radio, telephone and beverage-making facilities. There is a pleasant bar upstairs and an attractive restaurant on the ground floor. The ballroom is spacious enough to accommodate up to 120 people and there is a smaller room, the *Abbey Suite*, for more intimate occasions. The Beaumont clearly plays an important role in Hexham's social life. For visitors to the hotel, at least part of their time is usually spent tracking down the Roman relics which abound in this area, but Hexham itself also rewards investigation. Please note that there is no car park but ample street parking.

Self Contained Flat available
Bed and Breakfast from £47.00
Lunch from £8.50 and A La Carte
Dinner from £11.00 and A La Carte
Gratuities at Guest's discretion
VAT inclusive
Credit Cards—Access, American Express,

Diners Club, Visa
1 Family Room. 11 Double, 5 Twin
6 Single Bedrooms. 18 Private Bathrooms
5 Private Shower Rooms
All Rooms with TV, Telephone, Radio, Tea and Coffee-making Facilities, Trouser Press. Open all Year except Boxing Day and New Years Day

Fully Licensed
Full Central Heating. Cocktail Bar.
Conference Facilities. Lift
Dogs not allowed
Street Parking. Night Porter
Nearby: Tennis, Squash, Badminton, Swimming, Golf

Hexham—County Hotel Priestpopple, Hexham, Northumberland., NE46 1PS. Tel 0434 602030

The historic town of Hexham is bisected by one long street, which bears three names for different parts of its length—namely, Hencotes, Battle Hill and Priestpopple. On this last section stands the County Hotel, which must surely be one of the most hospitable establishments in the country. Not only is the County open 365 days of the year, but it also offers refreshment between 8am and 10pm every day. Coffee, tea and sandwiches are available in the lounge all day, an amazing array of bar lunches and suppers is offered and high teas are served. In addition, an *à la carte* menu, which includes excellent English dishes and Northumbrian specialities, is offered at dinnertime in the silver-service restaurant. The hotel was busy when we visited with people calling in to partake of the marvellous hospitality provided by Ken Watts and his family. The hunting prints and riding paraphernalia in the cocktail bar and the pictures of ornamental pheasants in the lounge give a clue to Ken Watts' off-duty activities—he hunts twice a week during the season and goes shooting and deer stalking. Riding, pony trekking, fishing and deer stalking can be arranged for guests. Alternatively, they may prefer to play golf, squash or tennis, try their hand at water skiing or sailing on Kielder Reservoir or spend their days visiting the numerous places of interest in the vicinity. After long days spent in the open air we are sure you will sleep soundly in this homely hotel's comfortable bedrooms.

Terms on Application
English Breakfast £5.50
Bar Meal from £2.75
Lunch from £7.00 A La Carte
Afternoon Tea from £3.30
Dinner from £12.00 A La Carte
Gratuities at Guest's discretion
VAT inclusive. Credit Cards—Access, American Express, Visa

3 Family Rooms
4 Double, 2 Single, 3 Twin Bedrooms
9 Private Shower Rooms
All Rooms with TV, Telephone, Radio, Baby-listening, Tea and Coffee-making Facilities, Hairdryer
Open all Year
Fully Licensed
Full Central Heating

Cocktail Bar
Conference Facilities
Dogs allowed
Street Parking
Night Porter
Nearby: Tennis, Putting, Badminton, Swimming, Golf, Fishing, Riding, Sailing, Windsurfing, Water Skiing, Shooting

Section 5: Northumberland

Near Hexham—Bishop Field Country House Hotel Bishopfield, Allendale, Hexham, NE47 9EJ. Tel 0434 683248. Fax 0434 683830

We cannot praise this hotel and its friendly owners, Kathy and Keith Fairless, too highly. The conversion of their charming eighteenth-century farmhouse into an hotel of high standards has been a resounding success. The latest features that they have introduced here include two ground floor bedrooms, an additional lounge for non-smokers and two dining rooms, where dinner is eaten in a candlelit atmosphere. One of the biggest attractions of Bishop Field is Kathy Fairless's catering. She uses only the best ingredients to produce excellent English and French dishes and there are special vegetarian dishes. The breakfasts, too, are superb and are obviously designed with the needs of those who intend to spend their days in the open air in mind. Guests can enjoy walking in the countryside, make use of four miles of salmon fishing or go canoeing. The majority of guests, though, probably enjoy grouse shooting on the nearby moors. Whatever one's interest however, one's instincts will lead one at the end of the day back to this rural retreat. All the bedrooms have *en suite* facilities and colour television. The elegant lounge and the dining rooms all have an informal, friendly atmosphere and it is always a pleasure to be welcomed by the charming Fairless family.

Special Breaks available
Daily Terms from £53.00
Bed and Breakfast from £38.00
Credit Cards—Access, Visa
1 Family Room
4 Double, 7 Twin Bedrooms
6 Private Bathrooms

5 Private Shower Rooms
11 Rooms with TV, Telephone, Radio,
Tea and Coffee-making Facilities, Hairdryer
Open all Year except Christmas
and New Year
Restaurant Licence
Full Central Heating

Conference Facilities
Dogs allowed by arrangement
Parking Facilities
Fishing, Shooting
Nearby: Tennis, Putting, Squash,
Swimming, Golf, Riding, Sailing,
Windsurfing

Near Hexham, Bellingham—Riverdale Hall Hotel Kielder Road, Bellingham, Northumberland. NE48 2JT. Tel 0434 220254. Fax 0434 220457

Formerly the home of Lord Strafford, Riverdale Hall was purchased by Mr and Mrs John Cocker in 1979 and converted into a charming country-house hotel. The house stands in extensive grounds overlooking the North Tyne river just ten minutes' drive from Kielder Water. The magnificent countryside hereabouts offers plenty of opportunities for outdoor activities of all kinds. The Pennine Way flanks the hotel grounds and there are many other interesting walks: along Hadrian's Wall and in and around the Kielder Forest. On Kielder Water, one can go sailing, canoeing, windsurfing or water skiing, or simply join one of the passenger cruises. In addition, guests can play golf on Bellingham Golf Course, opposite the hotel. However, one could quite happily spend one's days within the hotel grounds: there is a sauna, a large indoor swimming pool, which opens onto a sheltered sunbathing terrace, and a cricket field. The North Tyne skirts the grounds and offers excellent fishing. Salmon and trout caught from the river feature on the menus, together with regional specialities such as Northumbrian lamb and Kielder venison. The *cuisine*, prepared under the supervision of Mrs Cocker, is of a high standard, so much so that the hotel became the first in the county to have an award from the RAC for its restaurant food. It is also a winner of the 'Best Hotel in Northumberland' award 1991.

Weekly Terms from £265.00
Daily Terms from £49.00
Bed and Breakfast from £32.50
Bar Meal from £1.70
Lunch from £7.95 and A La Carte
Dinner from £16.50 and A La Carte
Gratuities at Guest's discretion
VAT inclusive
Credit Cards—Access, American Express,

Diners Club, Visa
5 Family Rooms
6 Double, 7 Twin, 2 Single Bedrooms
5 Rooms with Four Poster Beds
All Rooms with Private Bathroom, TV,
Telephone, Radio, Tea and Coffee-making
Facilities
Trouser Press and Hairdryer available
on request.

Open all Year
Fully Licensed
Full Central Heating
Conference Facilities. Games Room
Dogs allowed
Parking Facilities. Putting, Swimming Pool,
Sauna, Fishing, Cricket
Nearby: Tennis, Golf, Riding, Sailing,
Windsurfing, Water Skiing, Shooting

Section 5: Northumberland

Near Morpeth—Linden Hall Hotel Longhorsley, Morpeth, Northumberland. NE65 8XF. Tel 0670 516611. Fax 0670 88544

Travellers who know the journey to and from Scotland will tell you that one of the best routes, for speed and for scenery, utilises the A697 Coldstream road, which means plotting a course through Bedlington, Wooler and Cornhill-on-Tweed. This route also contrives to take one to a most elegant Northumbrian hotel—Linden Hall. In a county full of small roadside inns, this Georgian masterpiece, set in 300 acres of parkland and approached by a private drive three-quarters of a mile long, is a surprise indeed. Although Linden Hall was a private residence until quite recently, today, thanks to the enterprise of its owners, it wears a new look which is still dignified and has, therefore, attracted a distinguished clientele. Within the hotel there is a medley of ornate ceilings, chandeliers, a sweeping staircase, beautiful furnishings and a magnificent domed hall. Here is country-house grace with its attendant recreations . . . a billiard room, a library, a delightful conservatory, and croquet, putting and tennis in the gardens. There is, however, little formality and no stiffness in the service one receives. Part of the hotel's acreage is put to good use supplying fresh produce for the kitchens, which serve both the excellent *Dobson Restaurant* and the pleasant *Linden Pub*. Above stairs, the bedrooms are a delight. Each room is fully equipped with a private bathroom and shower, a hairdryer, a radio, colour television, a telephone and a baby-listening service. Ten further bedrooms and leisure centre are planned for Spring 1993.

Special Breaks from £67.50 Half Board
Bed and Breakfast from £89.50
Bar Meal from £4.25
Lunch from £16.50 Table d'Hôte
Afternoon Tea from £5.50
Dinner from £21.50 Table d'Hôte
Service Charge and VAT inclusive
Credit Cards—Access, American Express,

Diners Club, Visa
2 Single, 25 Double, 18 Twin Bedrooms
(Family Rooms available)
All Rooms with Private Bath/Shower Room, TV, Telephone, Radio, Baby-listening, Tea and Coffee-making Facilities, Hairdryer, Trouser Press, Bath Robes, Mini Bar, Fruit. Valet Service

available. Open all Year. Fully Licensed
Full Central Heating. Lift
Cocktail Bar. Games Room
Conference Facilities. Dogs allowed
Parking Facilities. Night Porter. Tennis,
Croquet, Putting, Solarium, Sauna, Clay
Shooting. Nearby: Squash, Badminton,
Swimming, Golf, Fishing, Riding, Sailing

Otterburn—Otterburn Tower Hotel
Otterburn, Northumberland. NE19 1NB. Tel 0830 20620

Northumberland has, over the centuries, been the setting for many armed conflicts between the Scots and the English and many fortresses were built in defence against the marauding Scots. One such fortress was Otterburn Tower, built in 1076 by 'Robert with the beard' (a cousin of William the Conqueror). Most of the present building was constructed as a Victorian country house, around the original tower. Near to Otterburn Tower is the battlefield of Chevy Chase, one of many in the vicinity, but today all is peaceful here. Reminders of the past remain, though—one enters the hotel by way of an imposing hall, where an armour-clad figure guards the receptionist and one dines in a delightful dining-room, with 500-year-old oak panelling. The dishes featured on the *à la carte* and *table d'hôte* menus are, for the most part, English in character and would satisfy the most discerning guest. A selection of tasty meals is available in the well-stocked bar. Peter and Dianne Harding, the owners, provide warm Northumbrian hospitality and ensure that each guest receives individual attention. They offer a range of spacious, comfortable bedrooms—from single rooms to rooms with attractive four-poster beds. Neither have the needs of families been neglected, for they offer family rooms, cots and high chairs. One can relax in peace when you stay at the Otterburn Tower—in front of a fire in the cosy lounge, wandering round the extensive grounds or fishing on the hotel's beat on the River Rede.

Weekly and Daily Terms on Application
Bed and Breakfast from £27.50
Bar Meal from £4.50
Lunch from £8.50 and A La Carte
Afternoon Tea from £3.00
Dinner from £14.00 and A La Carte
Gratuities at Guest's discretion

VAT inclusive
Credit Cards—Access, American Express, Diners Club, Visa
5 Family Rooms. 4 Double, 2 Twin Bedrooms. (2 with 4-poster Bed)
5 Private Bathrooms
3 Private Shower Rooms. 8 Rooms with TV
All Rooms with Tea and Coffee-making

Facilities. Hairdryer available upon request
Open all Year. Fully Licensed
Part Central Heating. Cocktail Bar
TV Lounge. Conference Facilities
Dogs allowed at Management's discretion
Parking Facilities. Fishing
Nearby: Riding, Sailing, Windsurfing

Section 5: Northumberland

Powburn—Breamish House Hotel
Powburn, Alnwick, Northumberland. NE66 4LL. Tel 066 578 266/544. Fax 066 578 500

If ever you needed an excuse to visit this most unspoiled and untrammelled county in England, then Alan and Doreen Johnson's very personally run hotel is inducement enough. Its atmosphere of peace, tranquillity and hospitality, and its friendly welcome are rarely rivalled, in our experience, anywhere in this country. In spring, the five acres of grounds are carpeted with daffodils and bluebells, whilst in early summer the rhododendrons are at their splendid best. Here, too, is a playground of kingfishers, dippers, water rails and herons, for the Powburn runs right through the grounds. The hotel itself, an elegant Georgian style house built originally as a hunting lodge to nearby Callaly Castle, has eleven sumptuous *en suite* bedrooms. Each has been very comprehensively equipped, and then the owners have added their final touches–fresh fruit, flowers and confectionery, home-made biscuits and, sheer luxury, thick king-size towels and terry towelling bath robes. Over the years the Johnsons have also won an enviable reputation for superb food. Game from nearby shoots, smoked salmon, eel and trout from Berwick on Tweed, and fish selected from the quay at Amble, are constant reminders of the owners' policy of using only fresh produce whenever it is possible. Furthermore, the garden offers abundant fresh fruit and vegetables in season, whilst the greenhouse ensures a constant supply of fresh herbs. As for the outlook, the Cheviot Hills sweep almost to the hotel's doorstep; Hadrian's Wall, Holy Island and literally miles of empty beaches await your exploration. Beamish Country House was recently voted 'Hotel of the Year for Northumberland'.

Terms on Application
Sunday Lunch £12.95 Table d'Hôte
Dinner from £19.95 Table d'Hôte
VAT inclusive
1 Single, 6 Double, 4 Twin Bedrooms
All Rooms with Private Bathroom, TV,

Telephone, Radio, Tea and Coffee-making Facilities, Hairdryer
Open all year
Residential and Restaurant Licence
Full Central Heating
Children under 12 years by arrangement

Dogs allowed by arrangement
Parking Facilities
Nearby: Golf, Fishing, Riding, Sailing, Shooting, Hang-gliding, Bird Watching, Walking

Seahouses—Beach House Hotel
Sea Front, St Aidans, Seahouses, Northumberland. NE68 7SR. Tel 0665 720337. Fax 0665 720921

The heroism of Grace Darling who, in 1838 bravely rescued the survivors of the stricken *Forfarshire*, brought fame to the busy little port of Seahouses and to the Farne Islands which lie off shore. Fishing is still a preoccupation at Seahouses, although today most of its seasonal visitors are attracted to the port's unspoilt charm and to the excellent sandy beaches stretching south towards Beadnell and Embleton Bay and northwards to Bamburgh's magnificent castle. Seahouses does have another claim to fame, however, in the shape of this 'wee' hotel, which recently won the 'Holiday Hosts Award', organised by the Northumberland Tourist Board and the local BBC radio station. From what began life as a pleasantly sited seaside bungalow, the proprietors, Mr and Mrs F R Craigs, have created one of the most friendly and satisfying hotels we know. They now have fourteen guest rooms and each is equipped with a private bath/shower room and a whole host of modern comforts, which extend to complimentary toiletries and hot drinks. The catering is home cooking and baking at its very best and the five course dinners and ample breakfasts are based on local produce from the sea and countryside. There are no less than three lounges—one with a cheery fire, another with a pool table and other gentle entertainments, and the snug hall/lounge which has a small bar. The Beach House is both spacious and homely. We have not the slightest doubt that anybody staying there will be comfortable, well fed and very well looked after.

Weekly Terms from £255.00
Daily Terms from £42.00
Bed and Breakfast from £28.00
Dinner from £18.50
Gratuities at Guest's discretion
VAT inclusive. Credit Cards—Access, Visa

2 Family Rooms. 1 Suite
3 Double, 6 Twin, 2 Single Bedrooms
7 Private Bathrooms
7 Private Shower Rooms
All Rooms with TV, Telephone, Radio, Tea and Coffee-making Facilities, Hairdryer.

Baby-listening by arrangement
Open from April to November
Residential and Restaurant Licence
Full Central Heating. Cocktail Bar. TV Lounge. Games Room. Dogs allowed.
Parking Facilities

Section 5: North Yorkshire

Appleton-Le-Moors—Dweldapilton Hall Hotel Appleton-Le-Moors, North Yorkshire. YO6 6TF. Tel 07515 227. Fax 07515 540

As seasoned hotel hunters we treat hotel advertising with a degree of scepticism, especially when it concerns an hotel converted in the late 1970s. Consequently, when we first saw notices about Dweldapilton a couple of years ago we did not venture forth to sample the comfort or the fare. The name intrigued us, but nothing more. Having now been there we just wish we had called earlier. Dweldapilton Hall, totally refurbished, has all the features we seek in an hotel—an interesting building in a lovely setting, an hospitable owner, furnishings and fittings to delight the eye, and good English food with some traditional dishes especially to tempt the palate. In a sunny, elegant room, where a log fire added to the cheer, we enjoyed home-made soup, a delicious joint of lamb, home-made treacle tart (fourteenth century recipe), trifle and lemon geranium ice-cream. We felt pampered and so well cared for that we wished we could engage one of the comfortable bedrooms. Every room has either a bathroom or a shower room *en suite* and is equipped with colour television, radio/alarm, direct-dial telephone and beverage-making facilities. What a prospect this hotel holds for quiet, calm holidays. Garden lovers will take pleasure in pottering around grounds on which so much care is bestowed. The Yorkshire moors begin almost at the doorstep and, so full of interest is this area, the hotel has a good stock of guide books and leaflets for the use of the visitor. An even greater attraction for some is that this area is deliciously unspoilt. We left Dweldapilton with a vow to return and stay for a while.

Off Season and Summer Short Breaks
Weekly Terms from £367.50
Bed and Breakfast from £39.50
Bar Lunch from £7.50
Afternoon Tea from £4.75
Dinner from £19.50 Table d'Hôte
Gratuities at Guest's discretion

VAT inclusive. Credit Cards—Access, American Express, Visa
2 Suites. 1 Four-poster Room
4 Double, 3 Twin, 2 Single Bedrooms
All Rooms with Private Bathroom, TV,Radio, Tea and Coffee-making Facilities, Hairdryer.

Open from February to December..
Residential and Restaurant Licence. Full Central Heating
Lift. TV Lounge. Children not catered for
Dogs allowed. Parking Facilities
Nearby: Golf, Fishing, Riding

Have you returned your membership form?

By simply completing and returning to us the registration card inserted in this book you will automatically become a 1993 member of the Ashley Courtenay Circle , an invaluable link between author and reader. For members, we compile and revise each year special listings of hotels which offer particular amenities, such as a sauna, swimming pool, golf course (or adjacent), four-poster beds, facilities for the disabled, special Christmas programmes, vegetarian dishes, non-smoking areas and self-catering facilities. We can even direct you to hotels which are especially pleased to receive young children and dogs. These lists are free of charge. Just send a stamped addressed envelope.

Section 5: North Yorkshire

Bainbridge—Rose and Crown Hotel
Bainbridge, Wensleydale, North Yorkshire. DL8 3EE
Tel 0969 50225

Bainbridge was originally a settlement in the forest of Wensleydale, and this memory lives on with the blowing of the Forest Horn each evening from Holy Rood (September 27th) to Shrovetide. The Horn was blown to guide travellers to the security of the village and, when not in use, it hangs in the panelled hall of the Rose and Crown. This fifteenth-century hotel, which has an old-established and enviable reputation as the 'Pride of Wensleydale', overlooks the village green complete with old stocks and flanked by mellow stone houses. To the north is Swaledale, to the south, Coverdale, but Wensleydale is perhaps the best known of the Yorkshire Dales. It is an ideal area for touring and walking, or simply enjoying the beautiful countryside of the Yorkshire Dales National Park. Rivers, castles, museums and fells can be discovered via steeply rising and falling minor roads, free of heavy traffic. Healthy appetites stimulated by outdoor excursions will be thoroughly appeased at the Rose and Crown. The emphasis here is on traditional food, using local produce with everything home-made in their own kitchens. A moderately priced wine list and traditional beer (kept in the time-honoured manner) complement the excellent cuisine and bar lunches. Everything is cosy and relaxed: log fires, original beamed ceilings, antique furnishings and four-poster beds in several of the bedrooms. Games facilities in one of the bars provide visitors with a congenial setting in which to meet and chat with local residents, and learn more of the history and places of interest in this splendid open countryside. Amongst the many dramatic sights in the Pennine hills, the renowned Aysgarth Falls are a mere five miles east of Bainbridge.

Weekly Terms £350.00
Daily Terms from £50.00
Bed and Breakfast from £36.00
Bar Lunch from £3.75
Lunch from £9.00 A La Carte
Afternoon Tea from £3.95
Bar Supper from £4.75
Dinner from £16.50 A La Carte

VAT inclusive. Credit Cards—Access, Visa
1 Family Room. 9 Double, 2 Twin Bedrooms
4 Private Bathrooms. 8 Private Shower Rooms
All Rooms with TV, Radio, Tea and Coffee-making Facilities, Hairdryer. Trouser Press available

Open all Year. Fully Licensed
Full Central Heating and Log Fires
Conference Facilities
Children catered for
Dogs allowed
Parking Facilities. Fishing
Nearby: Golf, Riding, Windsurfing, Shooting

Section 5: North Yorkshire

Harrogate—Old Swan Hotel Swan Road, Harrogate, North Yorkshire. HG1 2SR Tel 0423 500055. Fax 0423 501154

If you would like to enjoy a day of contrasts, you could do no better than to explore the pretty villages, burbling rivers and sheep-covered hills in the beautiful Yorkshire Dales, and then spend your evening in dignified Harrogate. As one approaches the town the dale becomes wide and park-like and Harrogate is one of England's urban splendours. Superbly situated in acres of private gardens, the ivy-clad Old Swan Hotel is located close to the heart of the town. All of the 135 bedrooms, which include eleven luxury suites, have bath or shower rooms en suite, colour television with free in-house video films, direct-dial telephones and beverage-making facilities. The intention was to preserve the Old Swan's Victorian features and skilfully blend them with modern amenities. *The Wedgwood Restaurant* remains a magnificent setting for any meal or special occasion and the spacious public rooms are very elegant. *The Library Restaurant* is a stylish *à la carte* restaurant in intimate surroundings. In addition, personal service and excellent *cuisine* are obviously the prime concern of Doreen Boulding, General Manager, and her team. Since Harrogate is a major conference and exhibition centre, the Old Swan has an extensive range of function rooms and suites. However, it matters little if you go there on business or, as we did, as travellers and tourists. The food, comfort and hospitality justify any journey to the Old Swan at Harrogate.

Daily Terms from £67.00	Express, Visa	Open all Year. Fully Licensed
Room Rate from £83.00 Single	11 Suites. 3 Studio Twin Rooms	Full Central Heating. Lift
Breakfast: English £9.25	37 Double, 44 Twin, 40 Single Bedrooms	2 Cocktail Bars
Breakfast: Continental £7.75	All Rooms with Private Bath or Shower	Conference Facilities
Lunch A La Carte	Room, TV, Telephone, Radio,	Dogs allowed. Parking Facilities
Dinner from £15.00 and A La Carte	Baby-listening, Tea and Coffee-making	Night Porter. Croquet, Putting
VAT inclusive	Facilities	Nearby: Squash, Badminton, Swimming,
Credit Cards–Access, American	Hairdryer available on request	Solarium, Sauna, Golf, Riding

Harrogate—The White House Hotel 10 Park Parade, Harrogate, North Yorkshire, HG1 5AH. Tel 0423 501388. Fax 04232 527973

Imposing externally and impressive within, this eleven-bedroom house is most tastefully decorated to the highest standards. Having first enjoyed an excellent evening meal in the charming dining-room, we were soon to discover the reason for the quality of the furnishings and the outstandingly attractive decor. Prior to entering the hotel trade, owner/manager Jennie Forster was an interior designer by profession. This is abundantly evident in all areas of the hotel, which was built in 1836 in the manner of a Venetian villa. Its exclusive heritage is reflected in every detail, from the luxurious fireplaces in the ground floor reception rooms to the intricate plasterwork ceilings and comfortable antique furnishings. Situated looking over Harrogate's beautiful Stray, it is a most memorable location for a wedding reception, private dinner party or other special occasion. Daily *à la carte* menus, for both lunch and dinner, utilise only fresh produce, expertly presented in a calm atmosphere created by starched tablecloths, silver and lead crystal. A magnificent bay window in the dining room contributes to the elegance of the surroundings. The White House is in the most picturesque part of the floral town of England, only a few minutes' walk from the town and the conference centre. Guests here are well placed for exploring the Yorkshire dales and moors, Bronte and Herriott country, whilst the east and west coasts and the Lake District are only one hour's drive away.

All Prices pertain to 1992	1 Family Room, 3 Double, 3 Single,	Full Central Heating. TV Lounge
Daily Terms from £55.00 Single,	4 Twin Bedrooms	Small Conference Facilities
£75.00 Double	All Rooms with Private Bathroom, TV,	Children catered for
Bed and Breakfast from £85.00	Telephone, Radio, Baby-listening, Tea and	Dogs allowed by arrangement
Bar Lunch and lunch Table d'Hôte	Coffee-making Facilities, Hairdryer, Bath	Parking Facilities. Sports Club Facilities
Afternoon Tea	Robes, Mineral Water, Fruit, Laundry	Nearby: Tennis, Putting, Squash,
Dinner A La Carte	Service	Swimming, Solarium, Sauna, Golf, Riding,
VAT inclusive. Credit Cards—Access,	Open all Year	Hang-gliding
American Express, Diners Club, Visa	Residential and Restaurant Licence	

Section 5: North Yorkshire

Near Hawes, Simonstone—Simonstone Hall
Simonstone, Hawes, North Yorkshire. DL8 3LY
Tel 0969 667255. Fax 0969 667741

Near the boundary between Yorkshire and Cumbria lies the small town of Hawes, the 'capital of Wensleydale', and one and a half miles to the north stands Simonstone Hall. The present owners, John and Sheila Jeffryes, restored the hall, formerly the home of the Earls of Wharncliffe, and converted it into a warm and welcoming country-house hotel. The house has been decorated and furnished in keeping with its origins, using pleasing colour schemes, original oil paintings and a wealth of antique furniture. We studied with great interest the montage of nineteenth-century maps of Yorkshire. There are just ten spacious bedrooms, so the friendly owners are able to pay personal attention to the needs of their guests. The gracious dining-room is the setting for excellent dinners, chosen from well-balanced table d'hôte, à la carte, diabetic or vegetarian menus, to which healthy choice options have now been added; these are complemented by an interesting and wide-ranging wine list of some eighty vintages. At lunchtime, tasty and substantial bar meals are available, whilst on Sundays, traditional Sunday lunch is served in the dining room. Winner for the last four consecutive years of the coveted RAC Blue Ribbon and recently gaining the ETB award "England's Warmest Hotelier" Simonstone Hall will raise the spirits of country-lovers, for it has a rural setting and superb views of the upper part of Wensleydale. Guests are welcome to bring their dogs and can spend their days exploring the delightful countryside, by car or on foot. Try one of the hotel's Anytime Breaks, and we are sure you will wish to return for a longer sojourn. Out of season, the Jeffryes are happy to accommodate conferences for up to thirty people. The comfort and tranquillity of Simonstone Hall help guests to relax and feel refreshed.

Anytime Breaks (2 or more consecutive nights half board) from £115.00 per night for two
Daily Terms from £124.00 for two
Bed and Breakfast from £100.00 for two
Lunch from £12.75 Table d'Hôte
Dinner from £22.50 and A La Carte

Gratuities at Guest's discretion
VAT inclusive
Credit Cards—Access, Visa
3 Twin, 7 Double Bedrooms (including 1 Four-poster Room)
All Rooms with Private Bathroom, TV, Tea and Coffee-making Facilities

Baby-listening, Hairdryer available on request
Open all Year. Fully Licensed
Full Central Heating. Cocktail Bar
Dogs welcome. Parking Facilities
Nearby: Golf, Fishing, Windsurfing, Hang-gliding, Birdwatching

Section 5: North Yorkshire

Helmsley—Crown Hotel
Market Square, Helmsley, York, North Yorkshire. YO6 5BJ. Tel 0439 70297

It was over thirty years ago that we tramped across Ryedale, Bilsdale and Rosedale and took refuge for the first time in the Crown at Helmsley. Exhilarated but weary, we revelled in the warmth and welcome of this country inn, where an open fire threw patterns onto the beams, the pewter and the brass. We came here again recently and, although one detects greater comfort and more modern sophistications, the character of this sixteenth-century inn remains just the same. Mr Bernard Mander has been here for over thirty years, presiding over a dining-room and bars which are snug and companionable, providing comfortable accommodation for walkers and motorists and satisfying appetites with wholesome English food. We found the menus contained a good selection of dishes—a choice of seven or eight main courses—and local beef, pork and fresh fish, including trout, appear frequently. All baking is done on the premises. Above all, however, this is an hotel of character, where a free and easy atmosphere prevails and friends are quickly made. You will find the Crown Hotel in Helmsley's market square. Before leaving the area we drove to the top of Sutton Bank, where a wide view extends across the Plain of York to the Pennines. We envied those who were staying longer at the Crown at Helmsley.

Winter Breaks available Mid October to Mid May
Weekly Terms from £310.00
Daily Terms from £44.00
Bed and Breakfast from £30.00
Bar Lunch from £1.80
Lunch from £7.00 Table d'Hôte
Afternoon Tea from £3.00
Dinner from £13.50 Table d'Hôte

Gratuities at Guest's discretion
VAT inclusive. Credit Cards—Access, Visa
4 Double, 4 Twin, 5 Single Bedrooms
1 Family Room
All Rooms with Private Bathroom, TV, Telephone, Radio, Tea and Coffee-making Facilities
1 Room with Trouser Press
Open all Year. Fully Licensed

Full Central Heating
Cocktail Bar
TV Lounge
Small Conference Facilities
Dogs allowed
Parking Facilities
Nearby: Tennis, Swimming, Golf, Fishing, Riding

Helmsley—The Feversham Arms Hotel
1 High Street, Helmsley, North Yorkshire. YO6 5AG. Tel 0439 70766. Fax 0439 70346

Helmsley, situated on the edge of the North York Moors National Park, is an attractive market town with a twelfth-century castle. Alongside the Beckdale stream on the quiet road to Rievaulx Abbey stands a small hotel of great charm and comfort. Rebuilt in 1855 by the Earl of Feversham, The Feversham Arms has been privately owned and well managed by the Aragues family since 1967. Now, although still retaining its old charm, this welcoming inn has eighteen bedrooms, all with private bathroom and every modern facility. Some bedrooms have four-poster beds and luxurious bathrooms and six of the rooms are located on the ground floor. This is definitely an hotel for gourmets, for the choice of dishes on the menu in the *Goya Restaurant* is quite remarkable, notably the fish, shellfish and game specialities. The extensive wine list includes a good selection of French *Grand Cru* and Spanish *Gran Reservas*. Richard's Bar is popular for bar snacks, whilst *Annabel's Lounge* and *Rosalind's Bar* are much enjoyed by the residents—one would need several visits to taste the forty sherries and many spirits on display. The hotel has an acre of beautiful walled gardens in which to relax, an attractive hard tennis court and a heated outdoor swimming pool, open May-October. With the exhilarating countryside featured in the James Herriot and *Brideshead Revisited* television series to explore, this is a perfect hotel in which to enjoy a 'Bonanza Break'. In addition, golf, riding, shooting and fishing can be arranged nearby.

Bonanza Break Terms on Application
Bed and Breakfast from £38.00
Bar Lunch from £2.00
Lunch from £14.00 and A La Carte
Afternoon Tea Residents only
Dinner from £20.00 and A La Carte

Gratuities at Guest's discretion
VAT inclusive. Credit Cards—Access, American Express, Diners Club, Visa
2 Family Rooms. 1 Suite
5 Four-Poster Rooms
3 Double, 7 Twin Bedrooms

All Rooms with Private Bathroom, TV, Telephone, Radio, Baby-listening, Tea and Coffee-making Facilities, Trouser Press, Hairdryer, Safe. Open all Year. Fully Licensed. Full Central Heating. 2 Cocktail Bars. Conference Facilities. Dogs allowed

Section 5: North Yorkshire

Near Helmsley, Harome—The Pheasant Hotel Harome, Helmsley, North Yorkshire. YO6 5JG. Tel 0439 71241

Harome is a truly picturesque village set on the very edge of the North Yorkshire Moors National Park. An idyllic setting for those who love the vast unspoilt tranquility of what is surely one of the most beautiful areas of Britain. The village has retained much of its character and boasts six thatched cottages. Nearby is the attractive market town of Helmsley, itself typical of this impressive area. The Pheasant Hotel is owned and run by the Binks family who created it from what, at one time, was the village smithy, two cottages and a village shop. The result is an extremely attractive hotel in perfect harmony with its surroundings. The pretty exterior is equally matched by the delightful and extremely comfortable interior. It is evident that considerable thought went into this superb conversion. All bedrooms have private bathroom, colour television, radio and direct-dial telephone plus tea and coffee-making facilities. With full central heating, comfort is ensured all year round whilst the addition of an indoor heated swimming pool is a further attraction. All rooms have a pleasant outlook, some over the village pond and mill stream. In the dining room excellent English food is served, created by Mrs Tricia Binks using fresh vegetables and fruit from the hotel garden. In addition bar lunches are served and packed lunches are available for those wishing to spend the day investigating the magic of the moors. Service at The Pheasant Hotel is efficient and friendly, and a warm welcome is assured. In all an excellent hotel for those wishing to lose themselves in the heart of this fascinating area.

Special Winter and Spring Breaks £47.00 p.p.per day. Weekly Terms from £378.00 per person. Daily Terms from £54.00
Bed and Breakfast from £35.00
Bar Lunch from £4.50. Dinner £17.50
Gratuities at Guest's discretion

VAT inclusive. 1 Suite
5 Double, 6 Twin Bedrooms
All Rooms with Private Bathroom, TV, Telephone, Radio,
Tea and Coffee-making Facilities
Hairdryer available on request

Open from March to December
Residential and Restaurant Licence
Full Central Heating. Meeting Facilities
Children over 12 years catered for
Dogs allowed by arrangement
Parking Facilities. Indoor Heated Pool

Near Helmsley, Hawnby—The Hawnby Hotel Hawnby, Helmsley, North Yorkshire, YO6 5LS. Tel 04396 202. Fax 04396 417

Right on the edge of forestland and wild moors, this nineteenth-century Drovers Inn is described by our fact-finder as 'a little gem'. Built of Yorkshire stone and with shuttered windows, it was acquired by the family of the Earl of Mexborough in the early part of the twentieth century. It is under the strict surveillance of the Countess of Mexborough, who makes regular visits of inspection. The Laura Ashley furnishings embodied in the recent total refurbishment were selected personally by the Countess. All six *en suite* bedrooms are named after the colour schemes of their elegant decor–*Rose*, *Coral*, *Jade*, *Sky*, *Primrose* and *Heather*. Their outlook beyond the garden is the charming stone-built village of Hawnby, which is peaceful and totally unspoilt. Traditional English cooking is based on fresh produce when available, from the hotel's own farm and garden, and game from the estate. It is served in a most attractive dining room with windows overlooking the lovely surroundings. To explore this area of the North York Moors National Park is to roam over gently undulating moorland, to discover secret valleys with trout streams and, in springtime, to see an abundance of wild flowers. Residents at the hotel enjoy free fishing on the nearby Rye and Seph rivers. Pony trekking, riding and tennis are all available in the vicinity. Race courses, golf courses and various abbeys add to the interest and appeal of this wide open and impressive region, as do several fascinating market towns.

Bed and Breakfast from £35.00
Bar Lunch from £1.50
Bar Supper from £2.50
Dinner from £21.00
Gratuities at Guest's Discretion
VAT inclusive

Credit Cards–Access, Visa
4 Double, 2 Twin Bedrooms
All Rooms with Private Bathroom, TV, Telephone, Radio, Tea and Coffee-making Facilities, Hairdryer, Pressing Facilities
Open from 1st March to 31st January

Fully Licensed. Full Central Heating
Dogs not allowed
Parking Facilities. Fishing
Nearby: Tennis, Outdoor Pool, Golf, Fishing, Riding, Hang-gliding, Gliding, Hill Walking

Section 5: North Yorkshire

Lastingham—Lastingham Grange Country House Hotel
Lastingham, York, North Yorkshire. YO6 6TH
Tel 07515 345

Halfway along Lastingham's little main street is a fountain which bears an inscription telling one that in 654 St Cedd founded an abbey there and called it Laestingaen. This tranquil place, in the heart of the North York Moors National Park has a recorded history stretching back over 1,300 years. Time, however, appears to have passed it by, for the sights and sounds of rural life dominate the area and visitors to Lastingham Grange Country House could hardly have chosen a more peaceful spot to spend their weekends or holidays. This old, stone-walled country house, built around an attractive courtyard, and set within delightful gardens, has all the elegance and friendliness of a small country home. We love the tastefully furnished long lounge with its carefully chosen antiques, the low welcoming entrance hall and the pretty individually styled bedrooms. There is luxurious comfort here and unrivalled hospitality. With its excellent reputation for good food to satisfy the heartiest appetite and the very personal service of Mr and Mrs Dennis Wood and their family, it has become a country house of infinite charm, to which one will long to return. The ten acres of grounds show the same care and attention which is apparent within the house. There are terraces, pergolas, rose beds, lawns and some magnificent specimen trees. This quiet slice of rural England lies off the A170 Thirsk/Scarborough road and about seven miles north west of Pickering, and, therefore, makes a perfect base for exploring the moors and dales with their wealth of ruined abbeys and castles.

Terms on Application
No Credit Cards accepted
VAT inclusive
4 Double, 6 Twin, 2 Single Bedrooms
(2 Twins can be let as Family Rooms)
All Rooms with Private Bathroom, TV,

Telephone, Radio, Baby-listening,
Tea and Coffee-making Facilities,
Trouser Press, Hairdryer
Open from March to December
Residential and Restaurant Licence

Full Central Heating
Dogs allowed by arrangement
Parking Facilities
Nearby: Tennis, Badminton, Swimming
Pool, Golf, Fishing, Riding, Sailing

Section 5: North Yorkshire

Middleham—Miller's House Hotel Middleham,
North Yorkshire. DL8 4NR. Tel 0969 22630. Fax 0969 23570

The peaceful village of Middleham is nestled in the very heart of the Yorkshire Dales and Miller's House Hotel makes a perfect base from which to explore 'Heriot country'. Step inside this elegant Georgian house and you will find attractively furnished and decorated rooms in keeping with the period of the property, with just seven *en suite* rooms (including one magnificent four poster room). The caring owners, Crossley and Judith Sunderland pay personal attention to the needs of their guests but perhaps most impressive of all is the quality of the food, for which they have recently been awarded an AA Red Rosette, and, to complement one's meal, there is a good selection of sensibly priced wines. The multi-choice menu with interesting vegetarian selections changes daily and extensive use is made of fresh local produce. Close by Miller's House is Middleham Castle, once the seat of Richard III but now the village is better known as a racehorse training centre. Guests can combine enjoyment of stunning views across Wensleydale and Coverdale with watching the racehorses exercise out on the gallops. The area is rich in opportunities for walking and touring and well stocked picnic hampers are available for guests. Miller's House offers a range of special breaks: Romantic (champagne and roses for that special occasion); Wine Tasting (two days of superb wines and gourmet meals); Racing Breaks (visit to racing stables, day at the races), Antiques; Autumn and Winter Breaks; Christmas and New Year; special rates for house parties.

Weekly Terms from £330.00
Daily Terms from £51.50
Bed and Breakfast from £33.00
Afternoon Tea from £4.00
Dinner from £19.50 Table d'Hôte
VAT inclusive. Credit Cards—Access, Visa

2 Double, 3 Twin Bedrooms
1 Four Poster Room, 1 Single Bedroom
All Rooms with Private Bathroom, TV,
Telephone, Radio, Tea and Coffee-making
Facilities, Toiletries
Hairdryer available on request

Open all Year except January
Residential and Restaurant Licence
Full Central Heating. Cocktail Bar.
Children over 10 years catered for
Dogs not allowed. Parking Facilities

Monk Fryston–Monk Fryston Hall Hotel Monk Fryston,
Leeds, West Yorkshire. LS25 5DU. Tel 0977 682369. Fax 0977 683544

'Unique' is a word that can be truly ascribed to this fascinating old manor house, which stands near the A63 road to Selby, about two miles east of the A1. Owned by the Duke of Rutland, it is, without doubt, one of England's most distinctive and best-preserved hotels. Its mellow grey stone architecture looks upon parkland and beautiful ornamental Italian gardens—one feels one could be a thousand miles from this ancient district of Elmet and the West Riding. Its foundations are rooted in the Middle Ages and, in William the Conqueror's time, it was granted to Selby Abbey. Since taking on the role of an hotel, many home and overseas visitors have decided to stay amid this antiquity and it is not difficult to appreciate their reasons for doing so. Our Sunday luncheon was really excellent, taken from a menu of ample variety, and made all the more enjoyable by the service and the views across the terrace and park. Beautiful oak panelling and huge open fires are a feature of the public rooms and, after our meal, we viewed the *Haddon Room*, which is a perfect setting for conferences and functions of all kinds. The bedrooms, some on the ground floor, successfully fuse modern-day comfort with the old and include such up-to-date etceteras as colour television, radios, telephones and tea-making facilities. Write to Mrs J M Dodd for the complete story.

Bed and Breakfast from £62.00 Single,
£92.00 Double
English Breakfast £8.20
Lunch from £12.50 Table d'Hôte
Dinner from £20.00 Table d'Hôte
VAT inclusive
Credit Cards–Access, American Express,
Visa

14 Double, 7 Twin, 5 Single Bedrooms
2 Family Rooms
All Rooms with Private Bathroom, TV,
Telephone, Radio, Trouser Press, Tea and
Coffee-making Facilities
Baby-listening and Hairdryer
available on request.
Open all Year. Fully Licensed

Full Central Heating
2 Cocktail Bars
Conference Facilities
Dogs allowed
Parking Facilities
Night Porter
Nearby: Tennis, Squash, Swimming
Solarium, Golf, Riding

Section 5: North Yorkshire

Pickering—Forest and Vale Hotel Malton Road, Pickering, North Yorkshire. YO18 7DL. Tel 0751 72722

Situated in the ancient market town of Pickering at the junction of the Malton/Whitby and Scarborough/Thirsk roads, this Georgian house of restful loveliness makes an admirable centre for sightseeing in the northern dales and moors and for visiting the coast, whilst within a thirty-mile radius the golfer or race-goer can have his fill. The hotel has a large, walled garden and a tree-shaded car park for about seventy cars. Within, you will find a welcoming and warm atmosphere. In the attractive dining-room, with views of the walled garden, the chefs present delicious and varied meals of the highest standards, including vegetarian and vegan menus. Having visited this hotel on many occasions, we think you will find it most agreeable. The bedrooms are tastefully decorated in soft traditional colours and there are three superior rooms with comfortable sitting areas. All rooms are *en suite* and have tea/coffee-making facilities, television, telephone, radio and hairdryer. From the hotel one can wander on foot into the old town, to see its castle, church, museum, antique shops and many other interesting features, and only a few minutes' walk away is the North York Moors Railway. The friendly Forest and Vale makes an excellent centre for exploring this beautiful area.

Weekly Terms from £290.00
Bed and Breakfast from £35.00
Bar Meal from £3.50
Lunch from £9.50 and A La Carte
Afternoon Tea £3.50
Dinner from £16.50 and A La Carte
Gratuities at Guest's discretion
VAT inclusive

Credit Cards—Access, American Express, Diners Club, Visa
13 Double, 3 Twin, 2 Single Bedrooms
3 Family Rooms. 12 Private Bathrooms
6 Private Shower Rooms
All Rooms with TV, Radio, Telephone, Baby-listening, Tea and Coffee-making Facilities, Hairdryer

Open all Year
Fully Licensed
Full Central Heating. Cocktail Bar
Conference Facilities
Dogs allowed
Parking Facilities
Nearby: Swimming, Golf, Fishing, Riding

Near Pickering, Middleton—Cottage Leas Country Hotel Nova Lane, Middleton, Near Pickering, North Yorkshire. YO18 8PN. Tel 0751 72129

When motoring to Middleton from Pickering and arriving at the outskirts of the village, take a right turn beside the church, follow this narrow country road for about one mile and you will discover Cottage Leas—a delightful eighteenth century farmhouse with extensive gardens and, to add to one's pleasure, two very friendly hosts in Colette and Jim Ireland. The food here is absolutely first class and the wine list is comprehensive and moderately priced. Here are *the* most comfortable and informal rooms. Beamed ceilings, an open log fire, excellent furnishings, a selection of good books and quality magazines, lamps placed right where they are needed and always a soft cushion to ensure you can relax completely. This could be your ideal home set amidst the Ryedale countryside. There is a snug bar, a restaurant with wide views of the garden and a series of *en suite* bedrooms, all with colour television and two containing four-poster beds. We loved everything about Cottage Leas and have vowed to stay there longer on our next tour of this area. A few days spent at this hotel must be a therapeutic experience, but if you wish to do more than simply 'drop out' and 'wind down', there is plenty of interest hereabouts. The North Yorkshire Moors, Castle Howard, Nunnington Hall and Yorkshire's coastal towns and villages are all within compass. Cottage Leas...the name alone is evocative of rurality and the freshest produce from the farm and countryside. And, since the owners keep it open throughout the year, it can be one's 'bolt hole' whatever one's mood.

Weekly Terms from £258.00
Bed and Breakfast from £35.00
Lunch from £11.95 and A La Carte
Dinner from £15.00 and A La Carte
Gratuities at Guest's discretion
VAT inclusive. Credit Cards—Access, Visa

2 Family Rooms. 1 Suite
1 Twin, 9 Double Bedrooms
(2 Rooms with Four-Poster Beds)
10 Private Bathrooms. 3 Private Shower Rooms. All Rooms with TV, Telephone, Radio, Tea and Coffee-making Facilities

Laundry Facilities. Hairdryer available
Open All Year. Residential and Restaurant Licence. Children catered for. Dogs allowed
Parking Facilities. Hard Tennis Court, Cycle Hire. Nearby: Squash, Badminton, Swimming, Solarium, Sauna, Golf, Fishing

Section 5: North Yorkshire

Near Ripon, Masham—Jervaulx Hall Jervaulx Abbey,
Near Masham, Ripon, North Yorkshire. HG4 4PH. Tel 0677 60235

Jervaulx Hall is in the middle of Wensleydale, which straddles the River Ure from its source on the Pennines until it meanders onto the plain of York, ten miles or so north west of Ripon. John Sharp found and bought the hall in 1979 to establish a country-house hotel. He chose well, as did the monks who founded the neighbouring abbey 800 years earlier. Turning off the A6108 road roughly midway between Masham and Middleham one is soon at the beautiful arched gatehouse. Go through and find the fountain and the lily-pond, the neat circle of gravel and the mellow front door of the house. Can this really be the hotel? Yes, in just ten minutes we were seated on basket chairs enjoying the most delightful traditional afternoon tea imaginable. It is a joy to feel at home in the low-ceilinged rooms, amid carefully chosen antiques and with fresh flowers and foliage arranged to such good advantage. Jervaulx Hall is a true country house: just large enough for one's fellow guests to comprise a house party, but not so large that a commercial feeling intrudes. All this is set in the jewel of the Dales—Wensleydale. Many may recognise it through the writings of James Herriot, but some of us have learned to treasure this dale, above all others, from our early upbringing.

All prices pertain to 1992	VAT inclusive	of 8 or more)
Weekly Terms from £365.00	5 Double, 5 Twin Bedrooms	Residential Licence
Daily Terms from £57.50	All Rooms with Private Bathroom,	Full Central Heating. TV Lounge
Bed and Breakfast from £40.00	Tea and Coffee-making Facilities, Hairdryer	Children catered for.
Afternoon Tea from £4.00	Open from Mid March to Mid November	Dogs allowed
Dinner from £17.00 Table d'Hote	(December and January parties	Parking Facilities. Croquet

Near Wensley, Askrigg—King's Arms Hotel Market Place, Askrigg,
Wensleydale, North Yorkshire. DL8 3HQ. Tel 0969 50258. Fax 0969 50635

The pastoral scenery of Wensleydale, the broadest and most fertile of the Yorkshire Dales, has a timeless beauty. Askrigg, which means 'the ash trees in the nook', is a charming village in Upper Wensleydale. The village and the King's Arms will be familiar to many from the television series of James Herriot's *All Creatures Great and Small*, the King's Arms particularly so as the *Drovers Arms* at Darowby. The King's Arms has been a welcome sight for travellers for almost two centuries. Inglenook fireplaces, saddle hooks, oak panelling, ancestral portraits and antique furniture create a mellow atmosphere. All the bedrooms have period furniture and most of them have half-tester beds or attractive brass bedsteads. However, the up-to-date comforts of central heating, direct-dial telephone, radio, tea and coffee-making facilities and *en suite* bath or shower rooms, are provided, too. The owners, Ray and Liz Hopwood, obviously take pride in running such a comfortable, historic hotel. Barrie Higginbotham is Head Chef for the hotel's new *Clubroom à la carte* restaurant and Grill Room, providing a choice of menus supplemented by tasty bar snacks in the bar or courtyard. This welcoming hotel is an excellent base for touring the Yorkshire Dales and for walking, fishing or shooting. The 'Welcome Breaks' make a short stay here a very tempting proposition.

All Prices pertain to 1992	VAT inclusive	Open all Year. Fully Licensed
Weekly Terms from £295.00	Credit Cards—Access, Visa	Full Central Heating. Conference Facilities
Daily Terms from £45.00	1 Family Room. 1 Suite	Dogs allowed at Management's discretion
Bed and Breakfast from £30.00	1 Twin, 6 Double Bedrooms	Parking Facilities
Bar Meal from £2.50	5 Private Bathrooms	Nearby: Tennis, Badminton, Fishing,
Afternoon Tea from £4.50	4 Private Shower Rooms	Riding, Sailing, Windsurfing, Shooting,
Dinner from £19.00 A La Carte	All Rooms with TV, Telephone, Radio, Tea	Hang-gliding
Gratuities at Guest's discretion	and Coffee-making Facilities, Hairdryer	

Section 5: North Yorkshire

Whitby—Saxonville Hotel Ladysmith Avenue, Whitby, North Yorkshire. YO21 3HX. Tel 0947 602631

There is much to be said in praise of Whitby with its abbey, busy harbour, fishing fleet, picturesque alleyways and Viking associations. It is surrounded on three sides by glorious countryside and there are many attractive villages nearby, such as Goathland and, in the picturesque Esk valley, Ruswarp, Sleights, Grosmont (the starting point of the North Yorkshire Moors Railway) and Lealholm, while within easy driving distance along the coast you will find Robin Hood's Bay to the south, and Sandsend, Runswick Bay and Staithes, to the north. The Saxonville Hotel is well sited, close to the sea front yet sheltered. The hotel is popular and over the years since it was founded in 1946 by the Newton family, many guests have returned to stay with the present proprietors, Roger and Peter Newton. One member of the family is always on hand to attend to your comfort. One's first impression of the hotel is good for in the bright entrance hall there is a fine beautifully polished grandfather clock and fresh flower arrangements. The cleanliness and sparkle is maintained throughout the hotel, with its well-furnished, relaxing lounges, comfortable bedrooms and spacious dining-room. The menus are attractive and reasonably priced and the ample selection on the *table d'hôte* menu can be varied by *à la carte*. There is also an interesting wine list. You will find this comfortable, friendly hotel in Ladysmith Avenue, a quiet cul-de-sac off Argyle Road on Whitby's West Cliff.

Weekly Terms from £308.00
Daily Terms from £44.00
Bed and Breakfast from £35.00
Bar Lunch from £1.10
Lunch from £7.50 and A La Carte
Dinner from £13.50 and A La Carte

Service Charge and VAT inclusive
Credit Cards—Access, Visa
2 Family Rooms
10 Double, 9 Twin, 3 Single Bedrooms
All Rooms with Private Bathroom, TV, Radio, Telephone, Tea and Coffee-making

Facilities. Hairdryer available on request
Open from Easter and mid May to mid October.. Fully Licensed
Part Central Heating
Conference Facilities
Dogs not allowed. Parking Facilities

Whitby–Seacliffe Hotel North Promenade, West Cliff, Whitby, North Yorkshire. YO21 3JX. Tel 0947 603139. Fax 0947 603139

Development of the West Cliff at Whitby occurred mainly in Edwardian and Victorian times when seaside holidays first became popular. Seacliffe presents holidaymakers with an opportunity to stay in a quiet residential area whilst being close to the beach, sports facilities, theatre and shops. Despite its prime position on the North Promenade, with sea views from many of its *en suite* rooms, accommodation is most moderately priced and the *Candlelight Restaurant* offers a vast choice of meals including a dozen vegetarian dishes. The extensive wine list would be a credit to many larger hotels. In fine weather afternoon tea is served on the lawn in the private garden. Family-run with a resident chef, and within a few minutes of Whitby town, the harbour and a golf course, this hotel enjoys a good reputation and many guests make reservations for return visits. It has a pool table, darts, video and a television lounge in addition to a colour set in every bedroom. To ensure full relaxation and freedom for parents on holiday, baby-listening is available if required. The new Spa pavilion is close to the hotel and, in the summertime, yachts and pleasure boats make a bright and colourful scene. Over to the east side of the harbour, at the top of the famous 199 steps, stands the unique church of St Mary, surrounded by the graveyard of Dracula fame, and only a short drive away are the spectacular North York Moors. Seacliffe Hotel is indeed good value all year round.

Bed and Breakfast from £26.50
Breakfast: English £5.50
Afternoon Tea from £1.50
Dinner from £10.00 A La Carte
Gratuities at Guest's discretion
VAT inclusive. Credit Cards—Access, American Express, Diners Club, Visa
4 Family Rooms. 12 Double,

1 Single, 2 Twin Bedrooms
3 Private Bathrooms. 19 Private Shower Rooms. All Rooms with TV, Telephone, Radio, Baby-listening, Tea and Coffee-making Facilities
Hairdryer available on request
Open all Year. Residential and Restaurant Licence

Full Central Heating. Cocktail Bar
TV Lounge. Children catered for
Dogs allowed. Parking Facilities
Nearby: Tennis, Putting, Squash, Badminton, Swimming, Solarium, Sauna, Golf, Fishing, Riding, Sailing, Windsurfing, Water skiing, Shooting, Hang-gliding

Section 5: North Yorkshire

York—Beechwood Close Hotel 19 Shipton Road, Clifton,
York, North Yorkshire. YO3 6RE. Tel 0904 658378. Fax 0904 647124

We added this hotel to our collection some years ago and, although it is not in the least pretentious, it has found favour with many of our readers. It is situated on the A19 just one mile north of the centre of the city and offers excellent value in this popular tourist destination. Beechwood Close is an extremely comfortable hotel in the two-star category and the owners provide a high degree of personal service and keep it spotlessly clean. All the bedrooms are tastefully decorated and have a private bath or shower. Mr and Mrs G Blythe, the proprietors, have been joined at the hotel by Mrs Blythe's parents, Mr and Mrs R A Spink, and together they have carried out many improvements to the hotel's facilities. What they have achieved makes the Beechwood Close a good choice for a stay in York. The inviting cocktail bar and the adjoining dining-room are most attractive places in which to spend an evening. The *table d'hôte* dinner menu gives a wide choice at a reasonable price. Bar meals are available both at lunchtime and during the evening and the Sunday lunch *table d'hôte* menu is a popular attraction. With its quiet location and small garden at the rear, Beechwood Close is a most convenient place to stay, particularly for families coming to explore this beautiful and historic city.

Weekly Terms from £301.00
Daily Terms from £45.00
Bed and Breakfast from £32.50
Bar Meal from £4.75
Lunch from £7.00 Table d'Hôte
Afternoon Tea
Dinner from £13.00 Table d'Hôte

Gratuities at Guest's discretion
VAT inclusive
Credit Cards—Access, American Express, Visa
5 Double, 5 Twin, 3 Single Bedrooms
1 Family Room. 8 Private Bathrooms
6 Private Shower Rooms
All Rooms with TV, Telephone, Radio, Tea

and Coffee-making Facilities, Hairdryer
Open all year except Christmas Day
Residential and Restaurant Licence
Full Central Heating
Cocktail Bar. TV Lounge
Dogs not allowed
Parking Facilities. Putting

York—Mount Royale Hotel The Mount, York,
North Yorkshire. YO2 2DA. Tel 0904 628856. Fax 0904 611171

May we introduce you to this family-owned hotel which, under the personal direction of Richard and Christine Oxtoby, ably assisted by their son Stuart and daughter Sarah, seems to go from strength to strength? You will be made most welcome by the owners, who spare no effort in making their guests feel at home and relaxed in most congenial surroundings. Two beautiful period houses have been skilfully united to produce a most comfortable hotel, where the old and the new blend harmoniously together. The dining room has lovely views over the gardens, the cocktail bar with fine oak panelling is cosy and inviting and the well furnished bedrooms are all *en suite* and offer the utmost in gracious living. A further four rooms have been added known as the *Garden Rooms*. Readers who have stayed at The Priory or Hunstrete House in Avon will know what to expect. During our visits here we have been particularly impressed with the comfortable residents' lounge, which overlooks the delightful secluded garden and the outdoor heated swimming pool, which gives delight to so many. For the energetic a trimnasium provides scope for exercise and a game of snooker can also be enjoyed. Mr Oxtoby personally carves the joints of meat and fowl at one's table at dinner-time—an almost unique service nowadays. Sunday dinner and, by prior arrangement, light lunches are available. During the day most visitors spend their time seeing York Minster, the new Railway Museum and the Yorkshire Dales. Mount Royale is a truly delightful hotel with a most convenient situation, in The Mount, for visiting York's many attractions.

Bed and Breakfast from £72.50
Dinner from £23.95
Gratuities at Guest's discretion
Credit Cards—Access, American Express, Diners Club, Visa
2 Suites. 8 Double, 12 Twin, 1 Single

Bedrooms. All Rooms with Private Bathroom, TV, Telephone, Radio,
Baby-listening, Tea and Coffee-making Facilities, Trouser Press, Hairdryer
Open from 31st Dec to 23rd Dec
Residential and Restaurant Licence

Full Central Heating. Meeting Facilities
Dogs allowed by prior arrangement
Parking Facilities
Outdoor Heated Swimming Pool
Nearby: Tennis, Putting, Golf, Fishing, Riding, Sailing

Section 5: West Yorkshire

Haworth—Old White Lion Hotel Main Street, Haworth,
Near Keighley, West Yorkshire, BD22 8DU. Tel 0535 642313

Nearly 300 years old, the Old White Lion is at the centre of Haworth, a famous village just south of Keighley itself. It is an area of such character and interest that it has been featured on television in popular serial programmes and in commercials. Although lying in West Yorkshire, on the Pennines, it is not far from the boundaries with Lancashire and North Yorkshire. Close by are the Brontë Museum, parsonage and church, with dales and moors on all sides offering numerous golf courses, pony trekking, fishing, canal cruising, rambling and rock climbing. There are the remains of once splendid castles and abbeys to be seen, and the village is the home of the Keighley and Worth Valley Railway immortalised, perhaps, in 'The Railway Children'. The Old White Lion has fourteen *en suite* bedrooms–including family rooms–and most have magnificent views. Their candlelit restaurant, which is open to non-residents, has received widespread commendation for its extensive *à la carte* and *table d'hôte* dinners, catering for all diets. Additionally, hot and cold bar snacks are provided both at lunch time and in the evenings. With a completely self-contained function room (private bar, large dance area and seating for 100), the hotel is as attractive for special social occasions as it is useful to the businessman for seminars or conferences. Residents here can relax in an oak-panelled lounge and enjoy personal service from the resident proprietors. Persons booking privately will notice that the tariff, for accommodation and in the restaurant, is extremely competitive.

Weekly Terms from £224.00
Daily Terms from £32.00
Bed and Breakfast from £23.00
Bar Meal from £2.30
Lunch from £5.60
Afternoon Tea from £3.50

Dinner from £9.00 Table d'Hote
Gratuities at Guest's discretion
VAT inclusive. Credit Cards—Access,
American Express, Diners Club, Visa
2 Family Rooms. 7 Double, 2 Twin, 3
Single Bedrooms. All Rooms with Private

Bathroom, TV, Telephone, Radio,
Baby-listening, Tea and Coffee-making
Facilities. Hairdryer available on request
Open all Year. Fully Licensed
Full Central Heating. Conference Facilities
Children catered for. Dogs not allowed

Near Otley—Chevin Lodge Yorkgate, Otley,
West Yorkshire. LS21 3NU. Tel 0943 467818. Telex 51538 CHEVLOG

To the south of Otley The Chevin rises to almost 1,000 feet, and this unique and imaginative hotel nestles amongst fifty acres of birch woods and lakes on its gentler slopes. It enjoys almost complete rural seclusion within a fifty-acre forest. Such privacy does have a price, however, for Chevin Lodge is somewhat difficult to locate and we would suggest that you send for the hotel's brochure. What this describes and illustrates is enough to whet the appetite of any country lover. A collection of solid-pine buildings, quite delightful in their layout and décor, form the centre of Chevin Lodge. Here you will find the bars, the restaurant, the function rooms and a selection of well-appointed bedrooms, each with a private bathroom and shower, colour television, a stereo cassette/radio, a direct-dial telephone and beverage-making facilities. The restaurant setting is particularly attractive and the *table d'hôte* menus for lunch and dinner are excellent value. The concept of Chevin Lodge is not a new one, but here the standards are extremely good and the project shows a great deal of flair. When one is tucked away amidst the birch trees it is sometimes difficult to remember that the whole of Yorkshire and Cumbria are within easy reach.

Terms on Application
Bar Lunch from £1.95
Lunch from £10.50 and A La Carte
Afternoon Tea from £3.75
Dinner from £16.75 and A La Carte
Gratuities at Guest's discretion
VAT inclusive
Credit Cards—Access,
American Express, Visa

5 Family Rooms. 4 Suites
24 Double, 9 Twin, 19 Single Bedrooms
All Rooms with Private Bath/Shower
Room, TV, Telephone, Radio,
Baby-listening, Tea and Coffee-making
Facilities
17 Rooms with Trouser Press and
Hairdryer
Open all Year

Residential and Restaurant Licence
Full Central Heating
Cocktail Bar. Conference Facilities
Dogs allowed. Parking Facilities
Night Porter. Tennis, Solarium, Sauna,
Fishing, Cycling. Membership of nearby
Health Club
Nearby: Squash, Badminton, Swimming,
Golf, Riding, Sailing, Windsurfing, Golf

CHANNEL ISLANDS

St Peter's Valley, Jersey

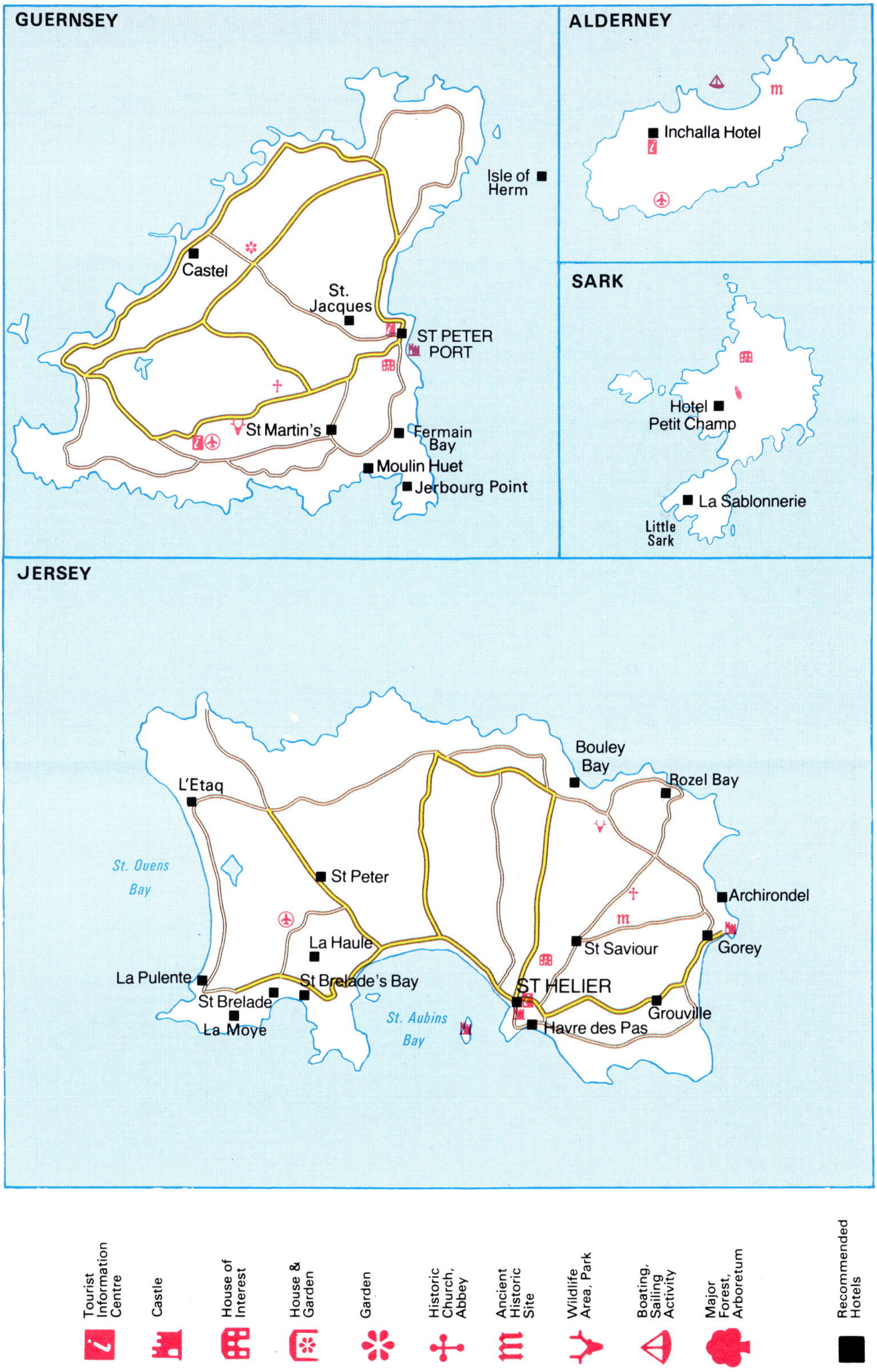

GUERNSEY

- Castel
- Isle of Herm
- St. Jacques
- ST PETER PORT
- St Martin's
- Fermain Bay
- Moulin Huet
- Jerbourg Point

ALDERNEY

- Inchalla Hotel

SARK

- Hotel Petit Champ
- La Sablonnerie
- Little Sark

JERSEY

- L'Etaq
- St. Ouens Bay
- St Peter
- Bouley Bay
- Rozel Bay
- La Haule
- Archirondel
- La Pulente
- St Brelade's Bay
- St Brelade
- La Moye
- St. Aubins Bay
- St Saviour
- Gorey
- ST HELIER
- Grouville
- Havre des Pas

Symbol	Meaning
	Tourist Information Centre
	Castle
	House of Interest
	House & Garden
	Garden
	Historic Church, Abbey
	Ancient Historic Site
	Wildlife Area, Park
	Boating, Sailing Activity
	Major Forest, Arboretum
	Recommended Hotels

Section 6 - Channel Islands

Alderney, Guernsey, Jersey, Sark

Whatever the season, the Channel Islands, appendages of the British Isles, offer some of the attractions of a Continental holiday. French is spoken (within limits) and there are good hotels to suit all purses, together with Continental cuisine, sandy beaches, rocks, magnificent scenery, green hills, friendly people and flowers in profusion.

There is, too, a reasonable certainty of sunshine, the Gulf Stream nearby adds to your swimming pleasure, and there are miles of golden sands and walks, golf, riding, cricket, tennis, yachting, bowls, dancing, international motor races and hill-climbs, or quiet spots where you just commune with nature. As a base for a holiday in any season, the Channel Islands should be in the vanguard of selection, for prices are lower than on the Continent and the temperature is often comparable.

How to get there? British Rail operates sea services from Weymouth by two modern ships with a sailing time of five and a half hours. Weekday sailings are from approximately early May until mid-October with night services on certain peak dates. Boat-trains connect with the daytime sailing and operate between London (Waterloo Station) and Weymouth Quay, but if you wish to tour around then your car can be transported on a ferry, although we should add that there is a wealth of car-hire facilities on the islands. Numerous daily air services connect the islands to the United Kingdom and France. These are operated from most main cities in Great Britain and the flight from London takes less than an hour. Full particulars can be obtained from any railway station, airline office or travel agency.

La Coupee, Sark

Section 6: Alderney and Guernsey

Alderney—Inchalla Hotel
The Val, St Anne, Alderney, Channel Islands. Tel 048 182 3220

The small, unspoilt island of Alderney has much to offer holidaymakers, including picturesque surroundings, beautiful beaches with clear waters, a golf course, sailing and excellent shore fishing. All these diversions are within easy reach of Inchalla Hotel and the warmth of the island's climate will be matched by the warmth of the welcome you will receive from the hotel's owner, Mrs V Willis. Her hotel is the most modern on the island and enjoys a superb, centrally placed position. It is situated on high ground, just outside the little town of St Anne and affords lovely views of the French coast to the east and of the Casquet rocks to the west. Within is every comfort any visitor could require. There are family, double and twin rooms, all with bathrooms *en suite*, colour television, direct-dial telephone, radio, tea and coffee-making facilities and refrigerated mini-bar. Guests may also take advantage of the hotel's sauna, jacuzzi and solarium. The restaurant is renowned for the high quality of its *cuisine* and has a deservedly enthusiastic following among local people. Whether you seek quiet relaxation in pleasant surroundings or a more energetic holiday, Alderney will meet your needs. We are confident that the staff at Inchalla Hotel will do their utmost to ensure that you have a memorable stay.

Weekly Terms from £288.75 (DB&B)
Daily Terms from £41.25 (DB&B)
Bed and Breakfast from £29.50
Bar Meal from £2.50
Sunday Lunch from £12.00 Table D'Hôte
Afternoon Tea from £2.00
Dinner from £13.00 and A La Carte
Service Charge inclusive

Credit Cards—American Express, Visa, Access
4 Double, 4 Twin, 2 Family Rooms. 8 Private Bathrooms
10 Rooms with TV, Telephone, Radio, Baby-listening, Tea and Coffee-making Facilities, Mini-bar
Hairdryer available on Request

Open all Year (excluding Christmas)
Restaurant Licence
Full Central Heating
Dogs not allowed
Parking Facilities
Solarium, Sauna, Jacuzzi
Nearby: Tennis, Squash, Golf, Fishing, Riding, Sailing, Windsurfing, Shooting

Castel—Hotel Hougue du Pommier
Castel, Guernsey, Channel Islands. Tel 0481 56531. Fax 0481 56260

'Hougue du Pommier' means 'apple-tree hill' and apples from the orchards of this fine old Guernsey farmhouse were once used to make local cider. Now the building has been transformed into a first-class hotel, offering the highest standards of modern comfort. Mercifully, much of the ambience of its past has been carefully preserved: the beautifully furnished dining room, for instance, has been designed so that six cosy eating areas represent rooms which might have been found in the old farmhouse and have been given names such as *Cider Room*, *Parlour* and *Bakery*. The *Tudor Bar* is also a most congenial spot in which to relax, with its low, beamed ceilings, inglenook fireplace and traditional furniture. Bar lunches and a carvery selection are served here every day and the dining room offers a superb *à la carte* menu and a Sunday luncheon. The bedrooms at Hougue du Pommier are fitted with every facility the modern visitor could wish for. All are most tastefully furnished and have either a bath or shower *en suite*. Ten acres of peaceful grounds surround the hotel and, set within them, you will find a beautiful tea garden, a solar heated swimming pool and a cunningly devised ten-hole pitch-and-putt course. When the friendly welcome, excellent food and comfort of this four-crown hotel have sufficiently 'unwound' you, you are sure to want to explore farther afield. The sandy beaches of Grandes Rocques and Cobo are but ten minutes' walk away and there is easy access to all parts of this lovely island.

All Terms pertaining to 1992
Weekly Terms from £196.00
Daily Terms from £28.00
Bed and Breakfast from £20.50 per person
Bar Lunch from £2.50. Lunch from £3.85
Carvery. A La Carte Dinner from £12.00
Credit Cards—Access, American Express, Switch, Visa

7 Family Rooms. 1 Single, 30 Double/Twin Bedrooms. 21 Private Bathrooms with Shower. 17 Private Shower Rooms
All Rooms with TV, Telephone, Radio, Baby-listening, Tea and Coffee-making Facilities. Hairdryer available on Request
Open all year. Fully Licensed. Full Central Heating. TV Lounge. Games Room.

Conference Facilities. Guide Dogs only allowed. Parking Facilities.
Solar Heated Swimming Pool, Sauna, Solarium, Pitch & Putt, Putting Green, Daily Courtesy Coach to St Peter Port.
Nearby: Tennis, Croquet, Squash, Badminton, Swimming, Sauna, Fishing, Riding, Sailing, Windsurfing, Water Skiing

Section 6: Guernsey

Castel, Vazon Bay–La Grande Mare Hotel, Golf & Country Club
Vazon Bay, Castel, Guernsey, Channel Islands.
Tel 0481 56576. Fax 0481 56532

The pleasure of the unexpected. The majority of Guernsey's premier hotels are in the vicinity of St. Peter Port, yet, there is a place apart where the luxury is of a five-crown standard, whose tranquility is formed by over 100 acres of private grounds, and where the pleasures of man are amply provided for by nature, outstanding recreational facilities and hotel standards of the highest order. Such is the scale of the Island, however, it is but a fifteen minutes' drive from St. Peter Port's busy winding streets to the beautiful west coast Vazon Bay and La Grande Mare Hotel. Since we are on the 'Green Isle' we shall begin with the hotel's outdoor amenities. Golf, croquet, coarse fishing in the hotel's well-stocked lakes, table tennis, basketball, the magnificent solar heated swimming pool and a hot spa bath. A stroll across the beach brings one to surfing, sailing, windsurfing, jogging, swimming and of course lazing. The hotel has appointed a golf professional, who is available to give guests general golf tuition, or improve their handicaps. Such facilities set the scene of La Grande Mare as soon as one arrives, so the quiet atmosphere within, the tasteful reception rooms, and the excellence of the bedrooms, suites, self-contained apartments and exclusive penthouse suites come as little surprise. One feels pampered, too, for regardless of the hotel's grandness, La Grande Mare is privately owned and very personally managed by the Vermeulen family. And on the principle of leaving the best until last, we come to the subject of the hotel's restaurant, which we rate as one of the finest on the Islands. The cuisine here has justly won 'excellence' and 'merit' awards from the pundits, together with Gold Awards in the Salon Culinaire and more recently the accolade 'Restaurant of the Year'. We prefer to visit the hotel in the early months, well before the holiday influx has started. Then we have the bay below much to ourselves, and can rather wallow in the fact that in London, an hour's flight away, the chances are it is overcast and possibly raining!

All terms pertain to 1992
Weekly Terms from £630.00
(2 persons sharing)
Daily Terms from £90.00
(2 persons sharing)
Bed and Breakfast from £70.00
(2 persons sharing)
Lunch from £10.50 and A La Carte
Afternoon Tea from £4.20

Dinner from £16.75 Table D'Hôte
Gratuities at Guest's Discretion.
All Major Credit Cards accepted.
11 Suites (suitable for families). 9 Double, 3 Twin Bedrooms
All Rooms with Private Bathroom, TV, Telephone, Radio, Baby-listening, Tea and Coffee-making Facilities, Trouser press, Hairdryer

Open all year. Fully Licensed.
Full Central Heating. Lift.
Cocktail Bar.
Lounge. Children catered for.
Dogs not allowed.
Parking Facilities. Night Porter.
Croquet, Putting, Outdoor Swimming, Golf, Fishing

Section 6: Guernsey

Fermain Bay, Near St Peter Port–Le Chalet Hotel Fermain Bay, Guernsey, Channel Islands. Tel 0481 35716. Fax 0481 35716

Of the many enchanting bays around the island of Guernsey, Fermain Bay is ever a favourite among amateur and professional photographers. Whether one approaches it by way of the cliff path from St Peter Port, or the narrow lane which leads one past Le Chalet Hotel, or, preferably, by motor launch from St Peter Port, the views of this sheltered bay are superb. The sands are fine, the bathing is safe and the steep cliffs are covered with vegetation which reaches almost to the water's edge. Le Chalet Hotel has an almost alpine setting and appears to float above these luxuriant natural surroundings. But the high reputation of this hotel has not been built up just on lovely views and its convienience to St Peter Port. Le Chalet, which has three star recommendation, has an excellent reputation for personal service, first class *cuisine* and a pleasing combination of modern comforts. Note, especially, the large picture windows in nearly all the rooms, which make for such a light and spacious environment. Every bedroom has *en suite* facilities, colour television, radio and beverage-making facilities. In short, Le Chalet has its own stamp of all-round excellence. It should be emphasised, too, that Le Chalet is one of three family hotels, which are owned and operated by the proprietors and their senior staff. Consequently, whilst staying there, one may take advantage of a voucher scheme allowing a certain number of guests to enjoy dinner at either Moore's Central Hotel or Hotel de Havelet, both of which are located in St Peter Port. There is a free minibus service during the day, except Sunday, which runs between the establishments.

Weekly Terms (Half Board) from £239.40	Credit Cards—Access, American Express,	Tea and Coffee-making Facilities, Hairdryer
Daily Terms (Half Board) from £35.20	Diners Club, Visa	Open from 19th April to 15th October
Bed and Breakfast from £28.20	2 Family Rooms. 15 Double, 27 Twin, 2	Fully Licensed. Cocktail Bar
Bar Lunch from £5.50	Single Bedrooms. 41 Private Bathrooms	Dogs allowed at Management's Discretion
Dinner from £13.50 and A La Carte	5 Private Shower Rooms	Parking Facilities. Nearby: Tennis,
Gratuities at Guest's Discretion	All Rooms with TV, Telephone, Radio,	Croquet, Putting, Squash, Badminton

Fermain Bay, Near St Peter Port—La Favorita Hotel. Fermain Bay, Guernsey, Channel Islands. Tel 0481 35666. Fax 0481 35413

La Favorita makes the very best use of a superb location: it is also aptly named, with a good proportion of returning guests. Comprising an old country house and a recently-added matching wing, the colourful setting is enhanced by the exotic shrubs in the picturesque hotel gardens. From its setting in a wooded valley, a five-minutes' walk brings one down to Fermain Bay, one of Guernsey's many enchanting and much-photographed beauty spots. Some of the hotel's public rooms—and many of its thirty-seven bedrooms—have impressive views over the sea towards Jersey. Rooms fronting the bay have balconies on which one may relax in the scenic tranquillity. We were given a conducted tour of La Favorita and were most impressed with the high level of the décor, the comfort and the full range of facilities available to guests. A new kitchen and restaurant are one of the most recent additions to the hotel, together with an indoor heated swimming pool, spa and sauna which guests are free to enjoy. In particular, we liked the bright, open but friendly atmosphere of the lounges and dining room, reflecting the care and pride of the resident proprietor, Simon Wood. The restaurant is reserved as a non-smoking area. St Peter Port is ten minutes away by car but, in the high season, it may be reached by ferry boats from the beach. Considering the mild climate of this area, together with the charm and interest of the surrounding bays and countryside, this is somewhere to visit at almost any time of year for a peaceful and refreshing break.

Weekly Terms from £266.00	Dinner from £10.00 Table D'Hôte	Bath/Shower Room, TV, Telephone, Radio,
Daily Terms from £38.00 (Half Board)	Service Charge inclusive. Credit	Baby-listening, Tea and Coffee-making
Bed and Breakfast from £32.00	Cards—Access, Visa	Facilities, Hairdryer. 10 Rooms with
Coffee Shop Lunch from £7.50	5 Family Rooms. 13 Double, 17 Twin, 2	Balconies. Open from 1st March to 30th
Lunch from £10.00 Table D'Hôte	Single Bedrooms (1 Room available for	Nov. Fully Licensed. Full CH. 1 Cocktail
Coffee Shop Supper from £9.00	disabled guests). All Rooms with Private	Bar. Dogs not allowed. Parking Facilities.

Section 6: Guernsey

Moulin Huet, St Martin's—Hotel Bella Luce La Fosse, St Martin's, Guernsey, Channel Islands. Tel 0481 38764. Fax 0481 39561

Up to the time of King John, Guernsey formed an integral part of Normandy. It was then spelt 'Grenezey', meaning 'green isle'–and what an apt description! This impressive granite manor house has its foundations rooted in the twelfth century and today stands alone as one of the islands' original Norman residences. A lesson in preservation, it has been carefully altered and sympathetically extended and now stands in its own wide grounds of lawns and flowerbeds. Very occasionally one finds an hotel which is an absolute gem, and, during our recent visit here, we experienced a feeling of complete satisfaction. We were greeted by Mr Richard Cann, the Managing Director, offered morning coffee in the sumptuous lounge and were immediately made to feel at home. Later, we viewed some of the bedrooms which were well appointed, with chintz curtains and pleasing colour schemes, and learnt that all the rooms provide colour television, intercom and baby-listeners and also have private bathrooms. A good selection of bar snacks is available at lunchtime. Fellow guests confirmed the reputation of Bella Luce food. At dinner the *table d'hôte* menu offers a wide variety of English and continental dishes and the *à la carte* menu comprises approximately fifty choices.

Terms on Application
Bed and Breakfast from £20.50-£38.50
Supplement for half board £8.50
Christmas programme available
Gratuities at Guest's Discretion
Credit Cards-Access, Visa
6 Family Rooms. 4 Suites
8 Double, 11 Twin, 3 Single Bedrooms

28 Private Bathrooms
4 Private Shower Rooms
All Rooms with TV, Telephone, Radio, Baby-listening, Tea and Coffee-making Facilities
Hairdryer available on Request
Open all Year. Fully Licensed
Part Central Heating. Cocktail Bar

Dogs allowed at Managements Discretion
Parking Facilities. Croquet
Outdoor Swimming Pool
Solarium. Sauna
Nearby: Tennis, Croquet, Putting, Squash, Badminton, Swimming, Solarium, Sauna, Golf, Fishing, Riding, Sailing, Windsurfing, Water Skiing

St Martin's—Les Douvres Hotel La Fosse, St Martin's, Guernsey, Channel Islands. Tel 0481 38731

Most hotels on the Island crane their necks to claim a glimpse of the sea, but here one's vista stretches to the garden gate–across delightful lawns, palm trees and colourful flowerbeds–and, in consequence, one of Les Douvres major attractions is that of quietude, even at the height of the season. Even so, Saints Bay, with its tiny fishing harbour, and St. Peter Port are within easy reach. Les Douvres Hotel is also commended for its friendly, informal atmosphere, its attractive accommodation and the high standard of its *cuisine*. The building began life in the eighteenth century as a manor house and has been most sympathetically extended, with the result that you will now find twenty bedrooms, thoughtfully equipped with colour satellite television, a radio, hairdryer, direct dial telephone, a tea and coffee tray and a private bathroom. All the rooms are tastefully decorated and furnished and many have pleasant views over the gardens. Downstairs, there are two bars, both of which have an 'old-world' décor, and delicious bar lunches are served in the *Tudor Lounge Bar*. A kidney-shaped swimming pool provides the focus of fun and relaxation outdoors and it is surrounded by a pleasant patio area, equipped with sun-loungers. Doubtless the high points of one's stay here, however, will be the excellent meals which can be enjoyed in the *Manor House Restaurant*. Both *table d'hôte* and *à la carte* menus are offered and special diets can be catered for on request. Les Douvres is a well-run and most pleasing hotel, which makes a snug retreat for off-season breaks as well as an ideal choice for a summer vacation.

Daily Terms from £31.00
Bed and Breakfast from £23.00
Bar Lunch from £3.50
Dinner from £10.00 Table D'Hôte
Gratuities at Guest's Discretion
Credit Cards—Access, Visa

3 Family Rooms. 18 Double, 15 Twin Bedrooms. 1 Single Bedroom. (1 Four Poster Room)
20 Rooms with Private Bathroom, TV plus Sky TV, Radio, Baby-listening, Tea and Coffee-making Facilities

All rooms with Hairdryer and Telephone
Full Central Heating. Cocktail Bar
TV Lounge. Dogs allowed
Parking Facilities. Outdoor Swimming Pool. Nearby: Tennis, Putting, Squash, Badminton, Solarium, Sauna, Golf

Section 6: Guernsey

St Martin's, Jerbourg Point–Idlerocks Hotel
Jerbourg Point, St Martin, Guernsey, Channel Islands. Tel 0481 37711. Fax 0481 35592

There is no disputing the fact that this hotel commands one of the finest positions in the Channel Islands, with sea views that are said to be the finest in Europe. Paul and Jan Hamill have put together an impressive team in a relatively short period of time and have gained an excellent reputation for the hotel. From many of the bedrooms, public rooms and restaurants spectacular views of the neighbouring Channel Islands and adjacent French Coast are possible. Always a reliable guide to the quality of the *cuisine* and the service is the high proportion of repeat reservations by visitors and heavy patronage of the restaurant by local residents. Our schedule gave us time for just a bar lunch, which was excellent, and the recently appointed chef has been very highly rated in the Guernsey Food Festival. Proper provision is made for children: a paddling pool, bunk beds in family rooms, baby-listening service, washing and drying facilities, the availability of cots and high-chairs, and a children's tea served in the restaurant. Conveniently alongside the paddling pool is a swimming pool for adults, both being set in attractive gardens taking full advantage of the views. From the hotel one has easy access to the start of many scenic walks along the Island's coastline to nearby beaches and coves, while the main town of St Peter Port is only a ten-minute drive. A regular bus service stops at the Idlerocks ample car park. Daily a number of boats connect Guernsey, Herm and Sark and there are day trips by air or hydrofoil to Alderney, Jersey and France.

Weekly Terms (Half Board) from £155.00 pp. Daily Terms from £25.00 pp. Bed and Breakfast from £21.00 per person. Suites from £60.00 per person per night. Bar Lunch from £5.00. Sunday Luncheon from £10.00. Dinner from £11.50 and A La Carte

Gratuities at Guest's Discretion
All major credit cards accepted
4 Family Rooms. 4 Junior Suites. 1 Suite. 4 Double, 13 Twin, 2 Single Bedrooms. Some Rooms with Balcony. All Rooms with Private Bath/Shower Room, TV,

Telephone, Radio, Baby-listening, Tea and Coffee-making Facilities, Hairdryer, Trouser Press. Open all Year. Fully Licensed. Full Central Heating. Cocktail Bar. Small Dogs allowed. Large car park. Outdoor Swimming Pool (In Season).

St Martin's—St Margaret's Lodge Hotel
Forest Road, St Martin's, Guernsey, Channel Islands. Tel 0481 35757

Guernsey has a dream-like variety of bays and coves, sandy beaches and unspoilt picnic country overlooking the blue waters of the Atlantic. To appreciate how this 'green isle' earned its name, however, one needs to travel inland. Here, amidst a surprising number of wandering roads and lanes, are green fields under cultivation, woodland and spinneys and tall hedges full of flowers. St Margaret's Lodge Hotel offers its guests a feeling of rural seclusion, but without isolation, for St Peter Port is just a short drive away and picturesque Petit Bot beach can be reached in ten minutes along leafy paths. Fully licensed and open all year, the hotel is completely modern in its appointments. All bedrooms have recently undergone major refurbishment and all offer a private bathroom, radio, colour television with satellite channel, direct dial telephone and tea and coffee-making facilities. Some rooms have a balcony overlooking the colourful gardens and the swimming pool. There are also new super *de luxe* bedrooms, family rooms and suites available. Whatever the season, there is no doubting the popularity of the *Garden Room Restaurant*, for the catering standards are very high, offering top quality local sea food produce, making the hotel one of the island's favourite rendezvous for dining out. There is even a courtesy shopping coach provided for guests. St Margaret's Lodge Hotel is under very experienced ownership (it is a sister hotel to the Hotel Hougue du Pommier in Castel). In every respect, this hotel is an inviting prospect for anyone seeking high standards and a quiet situation.

Terms on Application
Bar Lunch from £1.50
Dinner from £10.95 Table D'Hôte
No Service Charge. Credit Cards—Access, American Express, Visa
2 Family Rooms, 3 Suites. 12 Double 28

Twin, 2 Single Bedrooms
All rooms with Private Bathroom, TV, Telephone, Radio, Baby-listening, Tea and Coffee-making Facilities
Some rooms with Hairdryer, Trouser Press
Open all year. Fully Licensed. Full Central

Heating. Lift. Conference Facilities
Dogs not allowed. Parking Facilities. Night Porter. Outdoor Swimming Pool, Solarium, Sauna. Nearby: Tennis, Croquet, Putting, Squash, Badminton, Golf, Fishing, Riding, Sailing, Windsurfing, Water Skiing

Section 6: Guernsey

St Peter Port–The Duke of Richmond Hotel. Cambridge Park,
St Peter Port, Guernsey, Channel Islands. Tel 0481 726221. Fax 0481 728945

This was the first hotel to be custom-built after the Second World War and it became the first four-star establishment in Guernsey. The location could not be more ideal, for guests enjoy spectacular views over St Peter Port and the islands of Herm and Sark. Traditional standards of comfort and unobtrusive service are well observed at The Duke of Richmond–but not to the exclusion of up-to-date amenities in all bedrooms. Downstairs, hotel musicians play both background and dance music and there is a swimming pool on the south-facing sun terrace. As you would expect, the food is very good and ranges from gastronomic dishes to light meals and snacks. The wine list is carefully compiled and the wines are purchased locally by the hotel. It speaks volumes that there are still several of the staff who came to the hotel when it re-opened in 1970 running the establishment unobtrusively and at a level of efficiency which is achieved only through diligence and many years of experience. Particular mention should be made of the recreational centre which has been built in Cambridge Park. Guests at The Duke of Richmond thus have a wide range of activities available only a few minutes' walk away from the hotel, and, slightly to the north, is the island's only golf course, L'Ancresse. Top marks, then, for this first-class hotel! When requesting a brochure from the manager, Mr Nicholas Adams, you may care to enquire about the assistance offered to obtain advantageous air and sea fares.

All Terms pertaining to 1992
Weekly Terms from £350.00
Daily Terms from £50.00
Bed and Breakfast from £40.00
Bar Lunch from £5.00
Lunch from £7.50 and A La Carte
Dinner from £13.50 and A La Carte
Gratuities at Guest's Discretion

Credit Cards—Access, American Express, Diners Club, Visa. 12 Family Rooms. 1 Suite. 21 Double, 19 Twin, 21 Single Bedrooms. 70 Private Bathrooms. 5 Private Shower Rooms. All Rooms with TV, Telephone, Radio, Baby-listening, Tea and Coffee-making Facilities, Trouser Press, Hairdryer. Open all Year. Fully Licensed. Full Central Heating. 2 Lifts. 2 Bars Conference Facilities. Dogs allowed Night Porter. Outdoor Swimming Pool Nearby: Tennis, Croquet, Putting, Squash, Badminton, Swimming, Solarium, Sauna, Golf, Fishing, Riding, Sailing, Windsurfing, Water Skiing, Shooting

St Peter Port—Hotel de Havelet St Peter Port, Guernsey, Channel Islands.
Tel 0481 722199. Fax 0481 714057

This dignified Georgian house sits almost atop a steep hill on the outskirts of St Peter Port, with glorious views over the Castle Cornet and other islands of the Bailiwick. The building has enjoyed a long and colourful history, and local tradition links it both with the Duke of Wellington, and the officers of the German Army during the occupation of the island. Skilful conversions have resulted in a most pleasant and gracious hotel which retains its original charm. All the rooms are restful and well proportioned, and most attractively furnished. Every bedroom has a private bathroom, colour television, direct-dial telephone, radio, trouser press and tea and coffee facilities. In the grounds of the hotel the former coachhouse now houses the cosy *Saddle Room Bar*, the intimate *Havelet Grill* and *The Wellington Boot* restaurant. All these are extremely popular venues with visitors and locals alike, and are renowned for fine *cuisine*. If you are seeking a town house style of hotel on Guernsey, we strongly recommend the Hotel de Havelet. It has a delightfully secluded position and yet is only a short walk away from the harbour and the quaint centre of St Peter Port. This hotel now boasts an indoor heated swimming pool, sauna and jacuzzi. It is part of the Sarnia hotel Group and a limited number of guests can enjoy dinner at either Moore's Hotel or Le Chalet. A courtesy daytime mini bus service operates between the hotels daily except Sundays. The hotel is Three star and Four crown local grading recommended.

Weekly Terms (Half Board) from £294.00
Daily Terms from £43.50 (Half Board)
Bed and Breakfast from £36.50
Bar Lunch from £5.20
Lunch A La Carte
Dinner from £13.50 and A La Carte
Gratuities at Guest's Discretion
Credit Cards—Access, American Express,

Diners Club, Visa
1 Single, 35 Double and Twin Bedrooms
All Rooms with Private Bathroom, TV, Telephone, Radio, Tea and Coffee-making Facilities, Trouser Press, Hairdryer
Open all Year. Fully Licensed
Full Central Heating. Saddle Room Bar
TV Lounge. Conference Facilities

Children catered for
Dogs allowed at Management's Discretion
Parking Facilities. Indoor Swimming Pool, Sauna, Jacuzzi.
Nearby: Tennis, Croquet, Putting, Squash, Badminton, Swimming, Solarium, Sauna, Golf, Fishing, Riding, Sailing, Windsurfing, Water Skiing

Section 6: Guernsey

St Peter Port—La Frégate Hotel Les Cotils, St. Peter Port, Guernsey, Channel Islands. Tel 0481 724624. Fax 0481 720443

Nestling on a secluded hillside, this charming eighteenth-century Manor House overlooks Guernsey's capital, St Peter Port. Within the sophisticated intimacy of La Frégate lies what is certainly one of Guernsey's very best restaurants. In fact, the hotel is now managed by the man who was head chef there since 1983. The outstanding *cuisine* has won international recognition and received several awards. From the restaurant, diners have panoramic views of the harbour. The atmosphere throughout the hotel is one of relaxed dignity, with a level of service and facilities to satisfy the most critical clientele. Guernsey is renowned as an international financial centre and, for the visiting businessman, this hotel is a prestigious base. Its elegant terrace, adjacent to the bar and restaurant, is an ideal place to relax after a busy day. Of the thirteen bedrooms, all but two have spectacular southwesterly views and some have double-glazed patio doors opening on to a private balcony. A few minutes' walk from the hotel takes one to the bustling old markets, with their locally-caught seafood and traditional produce. In the near distance lie the offshore islands of Herm, Jethou and Sark. Discerning holidaymakers will appreciate the personal nature of the service, the fresh flowers gracing the public areas and the peaceful surroundings. The decor and furnishings are to the exceptionally high standards appropriate to such a superb location.

All terms pertaining to 1992
Room Rate from £50.00 Single, £95.00 Twin/Double
Breakfast: English £7.50
Breakfast: Continental £4.50
Lunch from £11.50 and A La Carte
Dinner from £18.00 and A La Carte
No Service Charge

Credit Cards—Access, American Express, Diners Club, Visa
3 Double, 6 Twin, 4 Single Bedrooms
All Rooms with Private Bathroom, TV, Telephone, Tea and Coffee-making Facilities, Trouser Press, Hairdryer
Open all Year
Residential and Restaurant Licence

Full Central Heating
Cocktail Bar
Children not catered for
Dogs not allowed
Parking Facilities
Nearby: Tennis, Squash, Badminton, Swimming, Solarium, Sauna, Golf, Fishing, Riding, Sailing, Windsurfing, Water Skiing

St Peter Port—Moore's Central Hotel Pollet, St Peter Port, Guernsey, Channel Islands. Tel 0481 724452. Fax 0481 714037

The English Town House atmosphere is something essentially individual, yet here, at Moore's, we found it transposed to the semi-continental environment of Guernsey. Moore's is, indeed, central, for it lies amidst the narrow, quiet, almost traffic-free streets which are such a feature of this old-world town. Formerly the town residence of the de Sausmarez family. Moore's is typically Georgian in appearance, although, with its flags and flower boxes for decoration, the impression is quite French. When staying at Moore's one is but a few minutes' walk away from the colourful harbour, with its two marinas, where launches and hydrofoils offer excursions to the islands of Herm and Sark. There is no reason why, of course, you should go there in the height of the season if you can get away at any other time, for there is central heating, cosiness and a warm welcome throughout the year. We found Moore's Central Hotel most agreeable and were impressed with its very reasonable tariff. The bedrooms are comfortable and equipped in the modern manner, the new Library Carvery Bar together with the Cocktail Bar have recently been added to the hotel's amenities, there is a pleasant terrace garden and the menus are varied and appetising. A great favourite with local businessmen is the *Patisserie*, where you can enjoy morning coffee, light lunches, and afternoon cream teas, with delicious gateaux and ice cream specialities. One is also able to use some of the facilities at Moore's sister hotels on Guernsey; Hotel de Havelet in St Peter Port and Le Chalet Hotel at Fermain Bay.

Weekly Terms from £213.15 (DB&B)
Daily Terms from £31.95 (DB&B)
Bed and Breakfast from £25.95
Bar Lunch from £5.50. Lunch A La Carte
Bar Supper from £6.00. Dinner from £13.50 and A La Carte. Gratuities at

Guest's Discretion. Credit Cards—Access, American Express, Diners Club, Visa. 45 Double and Twin, 3 Single Bedrooms. 48 Private Bathrooms. All Rooms with TV, Telephone, Radio, Tea and Coffee-making Facilities, Trouser Press, Hairdryer. Open

all Year. Fully Licensed. Lift from 1st to upper floors. 2 Bars. Conference Facilities. Children catered for. Dogs allowed at Management's Discretion. Night Porter. Complimentary Mini Bus Service between hotels during the day except Sundays

Section 6: Guernsey

St Peter Port–St Pierre Park Hotel
Rohais, St Peter Port, Guernsey, Channel Islands. Tel 0481 728282. Fax 0481 712041

This hotel reminds us of some of the more luxurious ocean liners in which we have sailed. The St Pierre Park Hotel, which opened in 1983, is situated within forty-seven acres of grounds and provides 134 bedrooms and suites. Prior to our arrival we felt that such a large hotel might be impersonal, but our fears proved to be quite unjustified. The reception office set the pattern: we were addressed by name and courteously shown to a bedroom which contained not only modern necessities, but niceties as well. A cheerful 'Good morning' greeted us the following day: 'We hope you slept well'. This gave us the opportunity of mentioning that we had difficulty in coming to terms with the continental duvet. 'That's easily overcome. We will instruct the chambermaid to tuck in an extra blanket', came the reply. We dined each evening in the *Victor Hugo Restaurant*, an elegant room with a Louis XV setting, and the meals we enjoyed there have earned an entry in our private notebook of memorable *cuisine*. We arrived too late for dinner one evening and were directed to the hotel's *Café Renoir* where, in a more informal atmosphere, we were equally pleased. The first-class facilities in and around the hotel tended to obscure the main purpose of our visit, which was to make St Pierre Park a base from which to continue our professional hotel-hunting. On the occasion of our next visit our distractions will be purely leisurely, with day trips to Alderney, Sark and Herm and time to enjoy the amenities of this splendid hotel.

Weekly Terms on Application
Bed and Breakfast from £85.00(Single)
Bed and Breakfast from £115.00 (Double/Twin)
Gratuities at Guest's Discretion
Credit Cards—Access, American Express, Diners Club, Visa
1 Family Room. 6 Suites

96 Double, 36 Twin, 2 Single Bedrooms
All Rooms with Private Bathroom, TV, Telephone, Radio, Baby-listening, Tea and Coffee-making Facilities, Hairdryer, Trouser Press. Open all Year. Fully Licensed. Full CH. 2 Lifts. 3 Cocktail Bars. Snooker Room. Conference Facilities
Dogs not allowed. Parking Facilities

Night Porter. 3 Tennis Courts. Croquet. Putting, Indoor Swimming Pool. 5 Solaria, 2 Steam Rooms. Trimming and Toning Table, 2 Saunas, 9-hole Golf Course, Archery. Childrens Play Area. Nearby: Squash, Badminton, Fishing, Riding, Sailing, Windsurfing, Water Skiing, Shooting

St Peter Port, St Jacques—La Collinette Hotel
St Jacques, St Peter Port, Guernsey, Channel Islands. Tel 0481 710331. Fax 0481 22585

It was over twenty-five years ago that we first enjoyed the hospitality of Squadron Leader and Mrs Peter Chambers at La Collinette Hotel. Today, as then, their hotel is one of the best on Guernsey for family holidays. Of course, much has changed there in a quarter of a century. There are now thirty bedrooms, each with *en suite* facilities, colour television, telephone and radio/intercom/baby-listening facilities. In the sheltered garden a large swimming pool, a children's pool and a poolside bar are focal points. There are a number of self-catering cottages. The décor and furnishings within the hotel are also right up to date. Because the same family still presides over La Collinette Hotel, however, the spirit of the hotel remains the same. Mr Andrew Chambers ensures that a very personal service is given to each guest—the family and their staff could hardly be more friendly and helpful. The standard of catering in the spacious, split-level restaurant also remains high, with candlelit dinners being a feature during the winter. There are two most attractive lounges and a cocktail bar with a south-facing terrace. In addition to the pools, the leisure facilities also comprise a spa, a sauna and a solarium. You will find La Collinette Hotel standing high above the town, past the colourful Candie Gardens, and within easy walking distance of the harbour. Close by is Guernsey's *Beau Sejour* centre, offering a cinema, tennis courts, bowls and an indoor swimming pool.

Weekly Terms from £192.50
Daily Terms from £22.50
Lunch from £6.00 and A La Carte
Bar Supper from £2.50
Dinner from £11.75 and A La Carte
No Service Charge
Credit Cards—Access, American Express, Diners Club, Visa

5 Suites
4 Double, 10 Twin, 3 Single Bedrooms
20 Private Bathrooms
2 Private Shower Rooms
All Rooms with TV, Telephone, Radio, Baby-listening, Tea and Coffee-making Facilities
Fully Licensed. Full Central Heating

Cocktail Bar. TV Lounge. Games Room
Conference Facilities. Children catered for
Dogs not allowed. Parking Facilities
Outdoor Swimming Pool, Solarium, Sauna
Nearby: Tennis, Croquet, Putting, Squash, Badminton, Swimming, Golf, Fishing, Riding, Sailing, Windsurfing, Water Skiing, Shooting

Section 6: Herm

Herm—The White House Hotel Herm Island, near Guernsey, Channel Islands. Tel 0481 722159. Fax 0481 710066

Peter and Jenny Wood are tenants of Herm, with a lease granted to their family in 1949 and running to the year 2050. The Island, which is only one and a half miles north-south and half a mile east-west, is off Guernsey in the Gulf of St Malo, seventy-five miles south of Weymouth and within twenty miles of the French coast. With a resident population of approximately forty people it is one of the smallest of the British Channel Islands. The Wood family refer to it as Paradise Island: it is an idyllic retreat that has changed little for centuries. For those seeking to 'get away from it all' this must be the answer. No cars. No television. No radios in public places. No Bank. No telephones in the hotel bedrooms. There are, however, electricity, gas, running water, main drainage, a Post Office, church and junior school. Visitors to Herm can reserve camping space, book into self-catering cottages or relax altogether at the White House Hotel with its old-fashioned courteous service, magnificent views, excellent cuisine and modern comforts. A private terrace overlooking green lawns runs the full length of the hotel and the entire island serves as the garden. A private outdoor swimming-pool is particularly popular with guests when the crystal-clear sea is at low tide. In the harbour village there are restaurants, a tavern, general provision shop and 'Argosy' gift shops. The nature-lover can admire the profusion of butterflies and wild flowers, go bird-watching at any time of the year or study the unique collection of sea-shells on the beaches. Sun-bathing, walking and photography are at their best in the temperate climate of Herm.

Daily Terms from £55.00 (Half Board)
Bed and Breakfast from £38.00
Bar Lunch from £4.00
Lunch from £9.00 Table d'Hôte
Dinner from £16.00 and A La Carte
Gratuities at Guest's discretion

Credit Cards—Access, Visa
13 Family Rooms
20 Double, 3 Twin, 2 Single Bedrooms
All Rooms with Private Bathroom,
Radio, Baby-listening, Tea and
Coffee-making Facilities.

Open from March to October
Fully Licensed. Full Central Heating
Cocktail Bar.
Children catered for
Dogs not allowed
Hard Tennis Court, Outdoor Swimming Pool

Infallible?
The answer is no because even as these lines are being written, hotel ownership, management and staff are changing somewhere. Invaluable? Yes, because by joining the Ashley Courtenay Circle (no extra charge) you can check up with us at any time during the current season.

A reminder.
Some of the tariffs in this book are those quoted for 1992. As prices will probably have changed for 1993, please check before booking. Please also note that the weekly and daily hotel rates shown in this book are for half board only (dinner, room and breakfast) unless otherwise stated.

Section 6: Jersey

Archirondel—Les Arches Hotel   Archirondel, Gorey, Jersey, Channel Islands
Tel 0534 53839. Fax 0534 56660

Of those who profess to know Jersey well, a fair number, we wager, will have no personal knowledge of Archirondel and, in consequence, of the many bays around the island, of which this is one of the most tranquil. There was a time when those in the know visited the bay for the view. Nowadays Les Arches Hotel is the focal point of attraction. From here you are just a few minutes' drive from the picturesque harbour of Gorey, the Royal Jersey Golf Course, and sailing and angling from St Catherines. Who would want to wander far from the hotel, when one can sun-bask around the large heated swimming pool, sip cooling drinks from the attendant refreshment bar and, about sundown, repair to the cocktail bar and the very popular night-club with its three bars? The hotel is contemporary in design and outlook and, especially for the young at heart, seems to have anticipated every holiday pleasure. The *table d'hôte* choices we have sampled here have always been nicely balanced with the popular selection of wines available and the service is both friendly and courteous. Nor has bedroom comfort been overlooked for all the rooms provide a telephone, colour/satellite television, radio, baby-listening service and a bathroom or shower *en suite*. As a holiday centre for a complete family Les Arches Hotel appears, to us, ideal. Recent winner of a coveted Hogg Robinson award.

Weekend Breaks available Christmas Programme available Weekly Terms from £196.00 Bed and Breakfast from £28.00 Bar Lunch from £4.50 Lunch from £10.50 Table D'Hôte Dinner from £12.50 Table D'Hôte Service Charge inclusive	Credit Cards—Access, Switch, Visa 29 Double, 20 Twin, 5 Single Bedrooms 34 Private Bathrooms 20 Private Shower Rooms All Rooms with TV, Telephone, Radio, Baby-listening, Tea and Coffee-making Facilities, Trouser Press, Hairdryer Open all Year. Fully Licensed	Full Central Heating. Cocktail Bar Conference Facilities. Dogs allowed Parking Facilities. Night Porter. Tennis, Outdoor Heated Swimming Pool, Sauna, Mini Gym, Golf Net. Nearby: Croquet, Squash, Badminton, Solarium, Golf, Fishing, Riding, Sailing, Windsurfing, Water Skiing, Shooting, Hang-gliding

Bouley Bay—The Water's Edge Hotel   The Slipway, Bouley Bay, Jersey, Channel Islands. Tel 0534 862777. Fax 0534 863645

It is no exaggeration to say that this is a first-class hotel, and that Bouley Bay is one of Jersey's most beautiful bays. Only the fishermen's jetty occupies the inlet with the hotel and its terraced gardens. Acquired in 1975 by Delrich Hotels, The Water's Edge has been brought up to very high standards of comfort, safety and professional management. From its commanding position, panoramic windows in nearly the whole of the public area take advantage of the vista afforded by Bouley Bay, the boats and the coast of France. The award-winning gardens offer a two-level swimming pool and an outside garden restaurant. Both garden and hotel give a sense of tranquillity which the experienced hotel visitor is quick to appreciate, although St Helier is but fifteen minutes by car. As one would expect of a good establishment, all modern facilities are provided and the public room appointments are quite exceptional. Dining in the two-level restaurant, which has a panoramic view of Bouley Bay, is a most enjoyable experience. The lounges are spacious and comfortable whilst the bar is impressively modern in its approach to providing a rendezvous. As one has come to expect from Delrich Hotels, all the bedrooms have a private bathroom, telephone, tea and coffee-making facilities, hairdryer and colour television. The Water's Edge is well recommended to discerning clientèle, and is a sister hotel to La Place Hotel at La Haule and the Duke of Richmond Hotel at St Peter Port, in Guernsey.

Terms on Application Credit Cards—Access, American Express, Diners Club, Visa 1 Penthouse Suite, 3 Family Suites, 3 Suites. 13 Double, 24 Twin Bedrooms 7 Single Bedrooms. 51 Private Bathrooms	All Rooms with TV, Telephone, Radio, Baby-listening, Tea and Coffee-making Facilities, Hairdryer Open from April to 31st October Fully Licensed. Full CH. Lift. TV Lounge. Conference Facilities. Dogs allowed by	Arrangement. Parking Facilities. Night Porter. Outdoor Heated Swimming Pool, Sauna, Sunbed, Aerobike. Nearby: Tennis, Squash, Badminton, Swimming, Solarium, Golf, Fishing, Riding, Sailing, Windsurfing, Water Skiing

Section 6: Jersey

Gorey–Dolphin Hotel and Restaurant Gorey Pier, Gorey, Jersey, Channel Islands.
Tel 0534 53370. Fax 0534 57618

International yachtsmen anchor their sleek craft just yards from this First Register hotel, which sits alongside the stone pier and in the shadow of Jersey's famous Mont Orgueil Castle. Gorey is a quaint fishing village and the views from the Dolphin are of boats bobbing at anchor and of the fifteen miles of open sea which separate Jersey from the Normandy coast. One is, therefore, not surprised to find a Fisherman's Bar in the hotel and a number of seafood specialities available in the restaurant. All this produces a very convivial atmosphere, which is appreciated by landlubbers who occupy the pleasant bedrooms and join seafarers in praising the excellent *cuisine*, the fine wines and the first-class service provided in the restaurant. We have stayed at the Dolphin, have eaten there and have brought friends to dine there, and we have never been disappointed. Close by, and reached through attractive gardens, is the wide golden expanse of Grouville Bay, which offers safe bathing and beach sports. This, in turn, is flanked by the fairways of the Royal Jersey Golf Club. St Helier, capital of Jersey, is just a short drive away, but then, everywhere is within easy reach on this delightful island. The Jersey Potteries are in the vicinity of the Dolphin. In the season there are regular boat trips to Carteret, Portbail and Granville - a perfect day excursion with plenty of time ashore. Air services operate daily to Paris and Dinard.

Weekend Breaks available
Christmas Programme available.
Weekly Terms from £196.00
Bed and Breakfast from £28.00
Bar Meal from £4.50
Lunch from £8.50 and A La Carte
Dinner from £12.50 and A La Carte
Service Charge inclusive. Credit

Cards—Access, Switch, Visa
9 Double, 5 Twin, 2 Single Bedrooms
2 Private Bathrooms.
14 Private Shower Rooms
All Rooms with TV, Telephone, Radio,
Baby-listening, Tea and Coffee-making
Facilities, Trouser Press, Hairdryer
Open all Year. Fully Licensed

Full Central Heating. Cocktail Bar
TV Lounge. Children catered for. Dogs allowed by Arrangement
Parking Facilities. Night Porter
Nearby: Tennis, Croquet, Putting, Squash, Badminton, Swimming, Golf, Fishing, Riding, Sailing, Windsurfing, Water Skiing, Shooting, Hang-gliding

Gorey–The Moorings Hotel Gorey Pier, Gorey, St Martin's,
Jersey, Channel Islands. Tel 0534 53633. Fax 0534 57618

It is said that every picture tells a tale. The quaint little town of Gorey is certainly a good illustration of pure enchantment. You will find this popular hostel nestling below the ancient Mont Orgueil Castle, with scenic views across the peaceful harbour. There is a friendly and welcoming atmosphere in this quayside haven, which has steadily built up a reputation for its seafood specialities and thoughtful wine list. It is not surprising, then, that international yachtsmen frequently drop anchor to enjoy a sumptuous lunch or dinner together with 'locals' from all parts of this historic, sun-blessed isle. If you are tempted to linger, as most are, it is advisable to book in advance, particularly during the summer months. All of the bedrooms have a private bath or shower room and colour television, and what could be more pleasing than to gaze from your window or balcony onto the blue sea and colourful yachts at their moorings in the harbour? In days gone by, this harbour was a thriving port, centre of a past oyster fishing industry. Today this sleepy haven handles sailings to the French ports of Portbail, Granville and Carteret. From Jersey airport there are daily flights to Paris and Dinard. In addition to the marine sports which abound at various places around the island, there are numerous healthy recreational pursuits on hand, including riding, badminton, tennis, croquet, shooting and golf. At sundown, a variety of entertainment opens up in many bars and discos. The Moorings is an enchanting hotel in an enchanting setting.

Weekend Breaks available
Christmas Programme available
Weekly Terms from £231.00
Bed and Breakfast from £33.00
Lunch from £10.00 and A La Carte
Dinner from £14.00 and A La Carte
Service Charge inclusive. Credit
Cards—Access, American Express,

Switch, Visa
7 Double, 4 Twin, 5 Single Bedrooms
12 Private Bathrooms.
4 Private Shower Rooms
All Rooms with TV, Telephone, Radio, Tea and Coffee-making Facilities, Trouser Press, Hairdryer
Open all Year. Fully Licensed.

Full Central Heating
Cocktail Bar. TV Lounge
Conference Facilities.
Night Porter
Nearby: Tennis, Croquet, Putting, Squash, Badminton, Swimming, Solarium, Sauna, Golf, Fishing, Riding, Sailing, Windsurfing, Water Skiing, Shooting

Section 6: Jersey

Near Gorey, Grouville—Grouville Bay Hotel Grouville, Jersey, Channel Islands.
Tel 0534 51004. Fax 0534 57416

Grouville is a pretty little holiday resort on the east coast of the island and one of its showpieces is the splendidly situated Royal Jersey Golf Course. Only 100 yards from safe, sandy beaches– reached by walking across the golf course, is the Grouville Bay Hotel—keen golfers will need no further inducement to book a holiday here. This hotel, however, has something for everyone—it is a spacious establishment which has recently been extensively refurbished. Guests can choose from fifty-four comfortable bedrooms, all have a bathroom *en suite*, and all of which are equipped with colour television, direct dial telephone, tea and coffee-making facilities, baby-listening and radio. They will, in addition, be able to relax in the very pleasant reception areas, which include a lounge bar, a residents' lounge and a cocktail bar which overlooks the golf course. We recently took lunch in the airy and newly furnished dining room and found our meal excellent, with food which was well prepared and faultlessly presented. You will not lack for entertainment at the Grouville Bay: by day, the outdoor heated swimming pool and children's splash pool set the scene for many a relaxing hour in the sunshine; by night, a discothèque (held every evening except Sunday) will keep you on your toes and, in addition, a weekly cabaret provides a glamorous finale to your evening. Water skiing, cycling, windsurfing, tennis and riding are all available nearby and a day trip to one of the sister islands is always an enjoyable diversion.

Weekly Terms from £195.00
Daily Terms from £30.00
Bed and Breakfast from £27.00
Bar Snacks from £3.00
Lunch from £6.50 and A La Carte
Bar Supper from £4.50

Dinner from £7.50 and A La Carte
Credit Cards—Access, American Express, Diners Club, Visa. 7 Family Rooms. 1 Suite. 12 Double, 31 Twin, 5 Single Bedrooms. 46 Private Bathrooms. 7 Private Shower Rooms. All Rooms with TV,

Telephone, Radio, Baby-listening, Tea and Coffee-making Facilities.
Open from 1st May to 7th October
Fully Licensed. Cocktail Bar. TV Lounge.
Games Room. Conference Facilities. Dogs not allowed. Parking Facilities. Night Porter

Rozel Bay—Le Couperon de Rozel Rozel Bay, St Martin, Jersey, Channel Islands.
Tel 0534 65522. Fax 0534 65332

Rozel Bay is one of the most picturesque bays on Jersey. Situated on the north-east corner of the island, it is small and secluded, has a fine, sandy beach and an almost Mediterranean atmosphere. It is more easily approached by sea than by road, for it has a quaint harbour below its line of attractive fishermen's cottages. Rozel Bay, however, has an even greater claim to fame: here, transformed from a Napoleonic fort and with the sea nearly lapping at its four-foot-thick defence wall, is Le Couperon de Rozel, one of the most exclusive and original hotels in the Channel Islands. If you want to eat well, you should make your way to Le Couperon de Rozel and, if you wish to eat grandly, you will choose one of its *à la carte* specialities–the lobster dishes are renowned. The imaginative rebuilding of the old wing of the hotel has included a major interior refurbishment programme adding new bedrooms, a new *à la carte* Restaurant and a new Lounge. We ourselves enjoyed this new addition to a very commendable degree of comfort. The drill square of the original barracks has become a delightfully secluded medley of flowerbeds, lush sub-tropical plants and York-stone patios and pathways. The fort itself, carefully extended and beautifully equipped, is an hotel of great charm and character. It was a delight for us to return to this very individual place where comfort, peace and good food go hand in hand.

Weekly Terms from £231.00
Bed and Breakfast from £33.00
Lunch from £8.50 and A La Carte
Bar Supper from £2.20
Dinner from £15.00 and A La Carte
Gratuities at Guest's Discretion
Credit Cards—Access, American Express, Diners Club, Visa

6 Family Rooms. 1 Suite
28 Twin/Double Bedrooms
All Rooms with Private Bath and Shower Room, TV, Telephone, Radio, Baby-listening
Some Rooms with Balcony
Open from April to October
Fully Licensed. Part Central Heating

Cocktail Bar. Lounge
Conference Facilities. Dogs not allowed
Parking Facilities. Night Porter
Outdoor heated Swimming Pool
Nearby: Tennis, Putting, Squash, Badminton, Sauna, Golf, Fishing, Riding, Sailing, Windsurfing, Water Skiing, Shooting

Section 6: Jersey

Havre des Pas, St Helier—Hotel de la Plage
Havre des Pas, St Helier, Jersey, Channel Islands.
Tel 0534 23474. Fax 0534 68642

Some hotels are remembered long after the memory of the holiday spent there has faded. The Hotel de la Plage is one such hotel. Its particular atmosphere is created from many small things which might seem insignificant, but which, taken together, make one's stay memorable–the smile from the hall porter, who remembers you from the previous visit, and the caring, personal service you receive. The Hotel de la Plage is situated at the sea's edge, close to St Helier, Jersey's sophisticated capital, and overlooks a dramatic seascape. Patrons of the Hotel de la Plage are assured of superb international cuisine, fine wines, unfailingly courteous and efficient service and comfortable, well-appointed accommodation. Each bedroom has a private bathroom, satellite television, radio, telephone and central heating. All bedrooms are served by lift. The hotel has a car park and also an exotic night-spot, the Caribbean Lounge, where entertainment is offered nightly and an added bonus to residents is that the solarium and mini-gym facilities are free of charge. Personal touches such as individual bathrobes, complimentary daily newspaper and early morning tea add to the experience. The hotel is open from April until the end of October and is under the same family ownership as the Pomme d'Or, Portelet and Merton hotels. The Aquadome and other sporting facilities at the Merton Hotel are available for use by guests of the Hotel de la Plage.

Weekly Terms (Half Board) from £315.00
Daily Terms from £45.00
Bed and Breakfast from £35.00
Bar Lunch from £5.00
Lunch from £10.00 and A La Carte
Dinner from £15.00 and A La Carte
Service Charge inclusive
Credit Cards—Access, American Express, Diners Club, Visa.

3 Family Rooms
6 Double, 59 Twin, 10 Single Bedrooms (Suites available on Request).
All Rooms with Private Bathroom, TV, Telephone, Radio, Baby-listening. Open from March to October. Fully Licensed.
Full Central Heating. 2 Lifts.
Cocktail Bar. Games Room.
Conference Facilities.

Dogs not allowed.
Parking Facilities.
Night Porter.
Solarium, Gymnasium, Sun Terrace
Nearby: Tennis, Croquet, Putting, Squash, Badminton, Swimming, Sauna, Golf, Fishing, Riding, Sailing, Windsurfing, Water Skiing, Shooting, Hang-gliding, Diving, Walking, Birdwatching, Cycling

Section 6: Jersey

St Brelade—Portelet Hotel
Portelet Bay, St Brelade, Jersey, Channel Islands.
Tel 0534 41204. Fax 0534 46625

To take an evening meal in the delightful dining-room of the Portelet Hotel, with its splendid views over St Brelade's Bay, is an unforgettable experience. Few hotels enjoy such a delightful aspect as the Portelet and, over the years, the hotel has established a reputation for offering outstanding service and a wide range of amenities. It is not surprising that so many guests return year after year. The hotel has a heated swimming pool, extensive gardens and car parking. Each bedroom has private facilities and many also have secluded sun balconies. The restaurant justifiably enjoys an excellent reputation for its international cuisine. Guests can relax with a quiet apéritif in the cocktail lounge before their meal and gently circle the ballroom to the music of the resident band afterwards. Whatever your reason for visiting Jersey, be it a honeymoon, a family holiday, a weekend break or even a business trip, the Portelet Hotel is an ideal place in which to stay. The hotel is open from the end of April to mid October and is under the same family ownership as the Merton, Hotel de la Plage and Pomme D'Or Hotels. Sporting facilities at the Merton Hotel are available to guests of the Portelet Hotel; this includes use of the new Aquadome, an all-weather complex guaranteed to give fun and relaxation to all the family.

Weekly Terms (Half Board) from £301.00
Daily Terms from £43.00
Bar Lunch from £5.00
Lunch from £10.00 Table D'Hôte
Afternoon Tea from £4.50
Dinner from £16.00 and A La Carte
Credit Cards—Access, American Express, Diners Club, Visa
10 Family Rooms. 2 Suites
68 Double/Twin, 8 Single Bedrooms

All Rooms with Private Bathroom, TV, Telephone, Radio, Baby-listening
Hairdryer available on Request
Open from 25th April to 11th October
Fully Licensed.
Full Central Heating
Cocktail Bar.
Games Room
Conference Facilities.
Dogs not allowed

Parking Facilities.
Night Porter
Outdoor Heated Swimming Pool
Nearby: Tennis, Croquet, Putting, Squash, Badminton, Swimming, Solarium, Sauna, Golf, Fishing, Riding, Sailing, Windsurfing, Water Skiing, Shooting, Hang-gliding, Sub-aqua Diving, Birdwatching, Cycling

Section 6: Jersey

St Brelade—Sea Crest Hotel and Restaurant
Petit Port, St Brelade, Jersey, JE3 8HH Channel Islands. Tel 0534 46353. Fax 0534 47316

'Just a restaurant with rooms' is the modest way in which Mr and Mrs Julian Bernstein sum up their establishment, the Sea Crest Hotel. In reality, it deserves a far more complimentary description, as we discovered when we enjoyed a few days' break at this intimate hotel recently. The restaurant with its new decor and contemporary British art on the walls, is certainly a major feature of any stay here and, with its growing reputation for the finest *cuisine*, it is fast becoming one of the most popular places at which to dine in Jersey. The *à la carte* menu will satisfy the most discerning palate and, as a trained chef, Mr Bernstein takes a very active interest in the kitchen. A meal in the Sea Crest restaurant is one to linger over and savour, whilst enjoying the spectacular views through the wide picture windows, which overlook the bay. The bedrooms deserve a mention, too, for they are very comfortable indeed and all have bathrooms *en suite*. The equipment provided includes colour television, radio, telephone, tea and coffee-making facilities and–a very thoughtful touch–a small refrigerator in which fresh milk is placed every morning. Five of the seven rooms have private balconies and all afford the same fine views as the restaurant. All the rooms were totally refurbished for the 1991 season, with hand made English furniture and beautiful French fabrics. Some of the guests we spoke to had been coming back here for the past 10 to 15 years (twice a year in some cases!) and reported that in all this time the high standard of food, accommodation and service had never varied.

Room Rate from £60.00 (Double)
Bar Lunch from £4.00
Lunch from £11.50 and A La Carte
Dinner A La Carte from £19.00 per person
Gratuities at Guest's Discretion
Credit Cards—Access, American Express,

Visa. 7 Twin Bedrooms
All Rooms with Private Bath/Shower Room, TV, Telephone, Radio, Baby-listening, Tea and Coffee-making Facilities, Hairdryer. Open all year.
Residential and Restaurant Licence.

Full Central Heating. Residents Lounge
Children catered for (over 5 years old preferred). Dogs not allowed
Parking Facilities. Outdoor Swimming Pool
Nearby: Golf, Fishing, Sailing, Windsurfing, Water Skiing, Hang-gliding

St Brelade, La Haule—La Place Hotel
Route du Coin, La Haule, St Brelade, Jersey, Channel Islands. Tel 0534 44261. Telex 4192522

Almost two decades have passed since our Circle members prompted us to visit this hotel situated in the La Haule district of St Brelade and now La Place is firmly recognised as a leading hotel of character which gives value for money. The directorate were shrewd in their appraisal of the hotel's position for it offers country-house tranquillity, away from the main tourist traffic, for those who prefer to wake to the sight of green trees and hear the birds' song, and yet easily accessible are four of the island's best bays; St Aubin, St Brelade, Beauport and St Ouen. In parts, blackened beams, low ceilings and huge open hearths reveal the hotel's 1640 origins and add a dramatic contrast to the modern décor to be found in the bar and bedroom accommodation. In the latter you will find attractive furnishings and most rooms have sunny views of the garden and attractive swimming pool. For honeymoons there is a lovely four poster bedroom which comes with a bottle of champagne. A sister hotel to the Duke of Richmond in Guernsey and The Water's Edge at Bouley Bay, in Jersey, you will find the same care and attention to detail which marks them all as top hotels of their class. This is nowhere more exemplified than in the *Cartwheel Restaurant* which is popular among local and resident visitors alike for its unique ambience. The restaurant is recommended by Egon Ronay and has won numerous gastronomic awards, including the maximum number of gold chef's hats awarded by the *Salon Culinaire*. Assistance is normally available to obtain cheaper air fares on application.

Weekly Terms on Application
Daily Terms from £35.50
Bar Lunch from £3.50
Lunch from £10.00 and A La Carte
Dinner from £18.00 and A La Carte
Credit Cards—Access, American Express,

Diners Club, Visa
3 Family Rooms. 7 Double, 29 Double/Twin Bedrooms
(1 Room with Four Poster Bed and Jacuzzi)
All Rooms with Private Bathroom,
TV, Telephone, Radio, Baby-listening,

Hairdryer. Room Service. Open from March to November
Fully Licensed. Full Central Heating
Cocktail Bar. Conference Facilities. Dogs allowed. Parking Facilities. Night Porter
Outdoor Swimming Pool. Sauna

Section 6: Jersey

St Brelade, La Moye—The Atlantic Hotel
La Moye, St Brelade, Jersey, JE3 8HE, Channel Islands.
Tel 0534 44101. Fax 0534 44102

One of Jersey's greatest charms is the feeling she imparts of being abroad and yet at home. The names of bays, rocks and old castles are French and the unusual scenery is a blend of Mediterranean-cum-Devon-cum-Cornwall. All these attractions come together perfectly at St Ouen, a most lovely bay, and the very continental Atlantic Hotel. Contemporary in every regard, the four-star Atlantic has always offered the most up-to-date facilities and, following the completion recently of a £1.25 million refurbishment programme, this has never been more true than today. Every bedroom has been completely redesigned to the highest international standards. The mahogany-finished furniture was inspired by eighteenth-century originals and the co-ordinated decor, carpets and fabrics create spaciousness and a delightful country atmosphere. New Garden Studios and two luxury suites have been added, so that guests now have the choice of fifty superior rooms. Phase One of the alterations has also bestowed a new entrance, driveway, additional parking and extensively relandscaped gardens, where some fifty new trees and 3,000 new shrubs have been introduced. But what of the inner man and cuisine francaise? When the restaurant was re-opened it heralded a new à la carte, whilst the popular Spuntino menu was extensively redesigned. If all this was not impressive enough, in addition to the heated swimming pool and all-weather tennis court, the owners commissioned a new health and leisure centre, The Palm Club, which offers a heated indoor pool, spa pool, mini gym, saunas and solarium. And if you want simply to drop out and relax, remember the hotel's position, on a headland overlooking the wide expanse of St Ouen's Bay.

Bed and Breakfast from £50.00
Lunch from £12.00 and A La Carte
Dinner from £19.50 and A La Carte
10% Service Charge
Credit Cards—Access, American Express, Diners Club, Visa
50 Twin Bedrooms and Suites

All Rooms with Private Bathroom, TV, Telephone, Radio, Hairdryer, Balcony/Terrace
Open from March to October
Fully Licensed.
Full Central Heating
Lift. Cocktail Bar.
Conference Facilities

Children catered for. Dogs not allowed.
Parking Facilities. Night Porter. Tennis Court. Outdoor and Indoor Heated Swimming Pool, Solarium, Saunas, Spa Pool, Mini Gym
Nearby: Squash, Golf, Fishing, Riding, Sailing, Windsurfing, Water Skiing

Section 6: Jersey

St Brelade's Bay—Château Valeuse Hotel St Brelade's Bay, Jersey, Channel Islands. Tel 0534 46281. Fax 0534 47110

Situated high on a hill overlooking the beautiful bay, this comfortable hotel, which is under the personal management of proprietors Tom and Mary Jordan, was once the summer residence of the famous Viscomte de St Juste. Within the very spacious and extremely well kept gardens, reclining chairs surround the open-air heated swimming-pool, with sub-tropical plants and green lawns completing the comfortable seclusion. Central to the social life of the hotel is the Tudor Bar, from which guests may take their drinks to either of the two lounges. Drinks and snacks are also served on the terrace and in the garden. *The Gallery Restaurant*, which enjoys a good reputation locally, has a *table d'hôte* menu providing a choice of Continental or English dishes, and an extensive *à la carte* menu. There are many well-equipped bright bedrooms, most of which have sunny views, many have sea-facing balconies, and all have private bathrooms. Thanks to the hotel's prime position, south-facing in the most sheltered part of St Brelade's Bay, it is ideal for early and late holidays, as well as for high-season bookings. Jersey offers a profusion of sporting activities, including golf, tennis, riding and, of course, a range of water sports. Hotel staff are always ready to assist visitors in booking excursions, seats at any of the theatres, cabarets or nightspots, and advising on hiring self-drive cars. The island is well served by direct links with UK airports and continental cities, daily car ferries from Portsmouth, Weymouth and St Malo, and hydrofoil services in the summer season.

Weekly Terms from £217.00
Bed and Breakfast from £25.00
Bar Lunch from £3.50
Lunch from £10.50 and A La Carte
Dinner from £12.00 and A La Carte
No Service Charge.

Credit Cards—Access, Visa
5 Double, 23 Twin, 5 Single Bedrooms
25 Private Bathrooms
8 Private Shower Rooms
All Rooms with TV, Telephone, Radio,
Baby-listening. Open from March to Oct

Fully Licensed. Full CH. Cocktail Bar.
Children over 5 years catered for
Dogs not allowed. Parking Facilities
Night Porter. Outdoor Heated Swimming
Pool. Nearby: Tennis, Putting, Squash,
Badminton, Golf, Fishing, Riding

St Brelade's Bay—Hotel L'Horizon St Brelade's Bay, Jersey, Channel Islands. Tel 0534 43101. Fax 0534 46269

L'Horizon is an emblem of cultured comfort and all that is best in hotel living. Internationally, she is one of the best-known hotels in Britain. The setting is there, designed by man and nature. Large picture windows ensure that there is little to obstruct the unique views of colourful gardens, fine sands and the waters of one of Jersey's most attractive bays. Stay at Hotel L'Horizon once and we wager you will think twice before you ever again seek continental sunshine! The hotel offers its guests the very best, with its beach; heated indoor swimming pool, with a wide range of water-sports instruction; sauna; spa pool; steam baths and mini gymnasium in the *Club L'Horizon* Leisure Centre, which also features an informal *Brasserie*. A pianist plays gently in the background whilst one enjoys old-fashioned afternoon teas in the main lounge. The restaurant is more than *haute cuisine* and the ambiance is perfection. *The Star Grill* offers an impressive *à la carte* menu. Another point which illustrates the sense of completeness at Hotel L'Horizon is the comfort of the bedrooms. Elegant furnishings, restful colour schemes and wonderful beds. Each room is well sound-proofed, and, consequently, the comings and goings outside are a profound secret. Our integral bathroom was beautifully equipped–singing became natural in it. Most of the bedrooms face the sea and the majority have balconies large enough for one to sunbathe or take breakfast on. Hotel L'Horizon offers the certainty of complete change at any time of the year.

Bed and Breakfast from £75.00 per person
Lunch from £15.00 and A La Carte
Dinner from £23.00 and A La Carte
Gratuities at Guest's Discretion
Credit Cards—Access, Visa
3 Suites. 4 Double, 87 Twin,
10 Single Bedrooms
All Rooms with Private Bathroom with

Shower, TV, Telephone, Radio,
Baby-listening, Trouser Press, Hairdryer
Baby-sitting available on Request
Open all Year. Fully Licensed
Full Central Heating
2 Lifts. 2 Cocktail Bars
Conference Facilities
Children catered for

Dogs not allowed. Parking Facilities
Night Porter. Indoor Swimming Pool,
Solarium, Sauna. Sub-Aqua Lessons,
Beauty and Hairdressing Salon
Nearby: Tennis, Squash, Badminton, Golf,
Fishing, Riding, Sailing, Windsurfing,
Water Skiing, Shooting, Hang-gliding,
Flying School

Section 6: Jersey

St Helier—The Apollo Hotel St Saviours Road, St Helier, Jersey, Channel Islands.
Tel 0534 25441. Fax 0534 22120

It does not enjoy a seafront location, nor does it claim a solus position, yet the Apollo is one of the few coast town hotels we recommend people to go out of their way to visit. The secret of its charms are fairly well hidden from the outside, but step off St Saviours Road into the Apollo's quiet courtyard and you will find that already St Heliers hustle and bustle begins to fade. It is inside, however, that its true character is to be seen, and if you have not stayed at the Apollo in recent years you are in for a very pleasant surprise. We will begin with the leisure facilities. A fully mosaic-tiled indoor swimming pool is the centrepiece. Adjacent to this are saunas and sunbeds, an eight-person jacuzzi spa bath, a multi-gym with all the latest apparatus, a coffee shop open from 11.00am to 10.00pm, and even an unexpected large suntrap terrace, which catches all the afternoon sun. When you want a break from invigorating activity, the Apollo's choices are equally varied. It has been renovated, extended and refurbished, so the comforts are right up to date. There is any amount of lounge space, the bars are most comfortable, and *Le Petit Jardin* restaurant has a well-earned high reputation for its *cuisine*, under the control of chef Wolfgang Bauer, and for its service. The beds are as good as any we have slept in and the bedroom facilities are extensive. *En suite* bathrooms and colour television with teletext and satellite channel are standard throughout the eighty-five rooms. Our inspectors met one guest who said that his business visits to Jersey are so regular he must have slept in every room. Our only surprise is that he ever manages to get up!

Daily Terms from £42.00	Diners Club, Visa. 4 Family Rooms	Fully Licensed. Full CH. 3 Lifts. Cocktail
Bed and Breakfast from £36.00	31 Double, 45 Twin, 5 Single Bedrooms	Bar. Games Room. Conference Facilities
Bar Lunch from £3.00	All Rooms with Private Bathroom with	Children catered for. Dogs not allowed
Lunch from £8.00 and A La Carte	Shower, TV, Direct Dial Telephone, Radio,	Parking Facilities. Night Porter
Dinner from £9.50 and A La Carte	Tea and Coffee-making Facilities,	Indoor Swimming Pool, Solarium,
Credit Cards–Access, American Express,	Trouser Press, Hairdryer. Open all year.	Sauna, Jacuzzi, Multi Gym

St Helier—Beaufort Hotel Green Street, St Helier, Jersey, Channel Islands.
Tel 0534 76500. Fax 0534 20371

Occupying a prime position only a few minutes' walk from the centre of Jersey's capital, and equally close to the sea, this exceptionally well equipped hotel is open all year, with the facilities to maintain its appeal in the less crowded months. It has a fully tiled, blue mosaic, heated indoor swimming-pool, enhanced by a small bridge, mexican wall tiles and lush greenery. This offers warm swimming throughout the year and, adjacent to it, there is a large jacuzzi spa providing bubbling water at body temperature. Colour schemes and the furnishings in the public rooms bear the stamp of a competent interior designer, establishing an ambience appropriate to the different functions of a bar, dining-room and lounge. In Brummells Bar, with its brasswork and leather seating, an exotic range of cocktails and other duty-free beverages are served to the pleasant music from the hotel's resident pianist. A wide variety of continental and English dishes are available from the *table d'hôte* and *à la carte* menus in the smart and colourful Rib Room Restaurant, prepared by award-winning chef Maurice Sones. We particularly admired the very high standard of services in all the fifty-four bedrooms. Private bathrooms with showers, remote-control colour television with satellite channels and teletext, radios, direct-dial telephones, mini bars, tea and coffee trays, trouser presses, hairdryers, writing desks and two full-size lounge armchairs. Everything for a relaxing week-end break or the fleeting business visit.

All prices pertain to 1992	Diners Club, Visa	Fully Licensed. Full Central Heating
Daily Terms from £43.00	3 Family Rooms. 1 Suite	Lift. Cocktail Bar
Bed and Breakfast from £37.00	7 Double, 43 Twin Bedrooms	Conference Facilities. Dogs not allowed
Bar Lunch from £3.50	All Rooms with Private Bathroom with	Parking Facilities. Night Porter
Lunch from £8.50 and A La Carte	Shower, TV, Telephone, Radio,	Indoor Heated Swimming Pool, Jacuzzi.
Dinner from £9.50 and A La Carte	Baby-listening, Tea and Coffee-making	Nearby: Tennis, Croquet, Putting, Squash,
Gratuities at Guest's Discretion	Facilities, Mini Bar, Trouser Press,	Swimming, Solarium, Sauna, Golf, Fishing,
Credit Cards—Access, American Express,	Hairdryer. Open all Year	Riding, Sailing, Windsurfing

Section 6: Jersey

St Helier–Pomme d'Or Hotel The Esplanade, St Helier, Jersey, Channel Islands. Tel 0534 78644. Fax 0534 37781

The Pomme d'Or Hotel, Jersey's most famous town centre Hotel, overlooks Liberation Square, the Yacht Marina and St Helier Harbour. The Hotel offers an ideal base from which to explore the Island as it is within easy access of the main shopping precincts, car parks, taxi ranks, coach and bus terminals, tourist information centre and Jersey's main sports and leisure complex, Fort Regent. The 'Pomme' has recently been refurbished to a very high standard and includes a new Reception and Lobby Bar, the impressive 'Harbour Room Carvery' and the very elegant 'La Petite Pomme' *à la carte* Restaurant and Aperitif Bar. Amongst the other amenities are the enormously popular 'Le Pommier' Coffee Shop open all day, every day, and the very friendly pub at the Pomme - 'The Wharf'. Every one of the 150 bedrooms has private facilities, trouser press, satellite television, direct dial telephone, hairdryer and tea/coffee making facilities. All bedroom floors are served by lift and the public areas are air conditioned. Renowned throughout its long and often fascinating history for its cuisine, fine wines and attentive service, the 'Pomme' has established itself as a firm favourite with visitors to Jersey. The Hotel is open throughout the year and is under the same family ownership as the Hotel de la Plage, Portelet and Merton Hotels. The Aquadome and other sporting facilities at the Merton Hotel are available for use by guests of the Pomme d'Or Hotel. Sporting activities near the hotel range from the serenity of fishing to the stimulation of squash. Jersey's coast encourages surfing, windsurfing and sailing in several bays.

Weekly Terms from £297.50. (Special Weekend Rates from £29.50, minimum 2 nights). Bed and Breakfast from £42.50
Bar Meal from £5.50
Lunch from £11.00 and A La Carte
Dinner from £15.00 and A La Carte

Service Charge Inclusive
Credit Cards—Access, American Express, Diners Club, Visa.
3 Family Rooms. 33 Double, 107 Twin, 8 Single Bedrooms. All Rooms with Private Bath/Shower Room, TV, Telephone, Radio,

Tea and Coffee-making Facilities, Trouser Press, Hairdryer. Baby-listening by Arrangement. Open all Year. Fully Licensed Full Central Heating. 2 Lifts. 2 Cocktail Bars. Conference Facilities. Dogs not allowed. Parking Facilities nearby

St Helier—The Royal Hotel David Place, St Helier, Jersey, Channel Islands
Tel 0534 26521. Fax 0534 24035

The Royal Hotel was first established in 1842 and has been flourishing ever since. A careful programme of controlled modernisation throughout its history has ensured that the hotel has kept abreast of the changing needs of its visitors. It has recently undergone a major refurbishment, with the result that it is now an immaculate establishment. We could not help being impressed with the excellent facilities now offered here and the manager, Mr J H Veloso, who is a very experienced hotelier, can justly be very proud of all that has been achieved. The bedrooms are a delight: each room has *en suite* facilities and comes fully equipped with a telephone, a radio and colour television. Some bedrooms even boast attractive Victorian-style four-poster beds! We were especially struck by the spaciousness and comfort of all the rooms, particularly of the single bedrooms, which in many hotels seem to take second place. A complete new wing has recently opened providing extra bedrooms, sun terrace, and a garden room style outdoor Brasserie. For relaxation and entertainment, there is a games room, a ballroom and two bars. In addition, guests are free to use the *Health Club* in which they can enjoy a sauna, work out on the exercise equipment, bask in the solarium or take a dip in the jacuzzi. The hotel is only a few minutes' walk from the town centre and is ideally placed for both holidaymakers and businessmen. Very competitive tour arrangements are available and further details of these can be obtained from Mr Veloso.

Weekly Terms from £267.75
Daily Terms from £48.75
Bed and Breakfast from £38.25
Lunch from £10.50 Table D'Hôte
Dinner from £15.00 Table D'Hôte
Gratuities at Guest's Discretion
Credit Cards—Access, American Express, Diners Club, Visa

4 Family Rooms. 2 Suites
14 Double, 37 Twin, 10 Single Bedrooms
61 Private Bathrooms
6 Private Shower Rooms
All Rooms with TV, Telephone, Radio, Tea and Coffee-making Facilities, Trouser Press, Hairdryer
Open all Year. Fully Licensed

Full CH. Lift. Cocktail Bar. Games Room
Conference Facilities
Dogs allowed by Arrangement
Parking Facilities. Night Porter
Solarium, Sauna, Jacuzzi
Nearby: Tennis, Squash, Badminton, Swimming, Golf, Fishing, Riding, Sailing, Windsurfing, Water Skiing, Shooting

Section 6: Jersey

St Helier—The Royal Yacht Hotel The Weighbridge, St Helier, Jersey, Channel Islands.
Tel 0534 20511. Fax 0534 67729

The name of this hotel is a reminder that the Channel Islands, those granite fragments off the Normandy coast, have been loyal to English monarchs for almost a thousand years. To the islanders, however, the sovereign is not known as the Queen of England, but simply as the Duchess of Normandy. In our experience, any visitor will be treated royally at this pleasant town-house hotel, which overlooks the harbour of St Helier and the expanse of St Aubin's Bay. It is a popular choice among Jersey folk as well as for visitors and, at regular times during the day, the bars, restaurant and grill room become centres of social activity. The hotel's white-painted and balconied exterior is typical of the nineteenth-century architecture of St Helier and, whilst the interior has been completely modernised and refurbished, this has been done in such a way as to ensure that the original elegant style is retained. We arrived by boat, stepped ashore and were soon stepping into a well-equipped bedroom which contained a private bathroom, colour/satellite television, radio and telephone. In addition to the *Victoriana Carvery Restaurant* and *The London Grill Room*, both excellent for service and value, the hotel also has an executive private dining room for small business gatherings. If you would like to stay in an hotel which is in touch with the pulse of island life and is close to the main shopping areas of St Helier and to the numerous attractions of the Fort Regent sports and leisure complex, then The Royal Yacht Hotel will suit you well.

Weekend Breaks available
Christmas Programme available
Weekly Terms from £231.00
Bed and Breakfast from £33.00
Bar Lunch from £4.25
Lunch from £6.50 and A La Carte
Bar Supper from £5.50
Dinner from £11.50 and A La Carte
No Service Charge.

Credit Cards—Access,
American Express, Switch, Visa
9 Family Rooms
22 Double, 9 Twin, 5 Single Bedrooms
18 Private Bathrooms
27 Private Shower Rooms
All Rooms with TV, Telephone, Radio, Tea and Coffee-making Facilities, Trouser Press, Hairdryer. Open all Year

Fully Licensed. Full CH.
Lift. Cocktail Bar. TV Lounge.
Conference Facilities. Dogs allowed.
Night Porter
Sauna, Sun Bed
Nearby: Tennis, Croquet, Putting, Squash, Badminton, Swimming, Solarium, Sauna, Golf, Fishing, Riding, Sailing, Windsurfing, Water Skiing, Shooting.

Have you returned your membership form?
By simply completing and returning to us the registration card inserted in this book you will automatically become a 1993 member of the Ashley Courtenay Circle, an invaluable link between author and reader. For members, we compile and revise each year special listings of hotels which offer particular amenities, such as a sauna, swimming pool, golf course (or adjacent), four-poster beds, facilities for the disabled, special Christmas programmes, vegetarian dishes, non-smoking areas and self-catering facilities. We can even direct you to hotels which are especially pleased to receive young children and dogs. These lists are free of charge. Just send a stamped addressed envelope.

Section 6: Jersey

Near St Helier–Longueville Manor Hotel
St Saviour, Jersey, Channel Islands.
Tel 0534 25501. Fax 0534 31613

We ran a poll recently among our inspectors and Longueville Manor was placed by them in the top ten of all country house hotels. It is easy to see why, for this is one of the most distinguished family-owned hotels in the whole of Britain. Mr and Mrs Simon Dufty and Mr and Mrs Malcolm Lewis, who have been here for forty-one years have impressed their personality not only into the very caring service and outstanding cuisine but also into the very fabric of this thirteenth-century manor house. They look after Longueville Manor as if it were their own home, seemingly always on duty and always on hand to assist their guests. Every room is the epitome of good taste, the bedrooms are utterly charming and fully equipped, there is a superb heated swimming pool in the grounds, and the assiduous service is an invitation to 'stay put' and be pampered. This four-star, First Register hotel, is a member of Relais et Châteaux. So, many guides and gourmets eulogise on the perfection of this place. We will turn our attention, then, to its other advantages. Less than one-and-a-half hours' flight from London, so seemingly in the depths of the country, yet only one mile from St Helier and but a few minutes from the sea—the Longueville's location is one of its strong suits. How completely satisfying is the house itself, surely one of the finest examples of Norman architecture on the island. Here you will find the gentle art of gracious living, service without any barriers, exquisite standards and such friendliness. No, we must leave others to praise. We will say simply 'if you are a seeker of the best, go there'.

Bed and Breakfast from £68.00
Bar Lunch from £8.00
Lunch from £18.00
Afternoon Tea from £2.20
Dinner from £27.50 and A la Carte
Service Charge inclusive
Credit Cards—Access, American Express, Diners Club, Visa

2 Suites. 6 Double (1 with 4-poster Bed).
24 Twin Bedrooms
All Rooms with Private Bathroom, TV with Teletext, Telephone, Radio, Hairdryer
Open all Year
Residential and Restaurant Licence
Full Central Heating. Lift
Cocktail Bar. Conference Facilities

Children over 7 years catered for
Dogs allowed
Parking Facilities
Night Porter
Outdoor Swimming Pool, Tennis
Nearby: Putting, Squash, Golf, Riding, Sailing, Windsurfing, Water Skiing

Section 6: Jersey

St Ouen—The Lobster Pot Hotel and Restaurant
L'Etacq, St Ouen, Jersey, Channel Islands.
Tel 0534 482888. Fax 0534 481574

Set in a superb position, overlooking the whole expanse of St Ouen Bay, is The Lobster Pot which, since 1951, has been recognised by international gastronomic experts, travel writers and the public as Jersey's most famous restaurant. Its history goes back to the mid-seventeenth century when it was West End Farm, owned by the Le Cornu family. Today, as a hotel and restaurant, we can summarise our opinion in one word: perfection. Some twelve years of planning and reconstruction went into the present hotel, and to give you an example, the first-floor accommodation is sound-proofed from the restaurant and bars below. Several other thoughtful features impressed us, such as a domestic-size refrigerator in each bedroom, containing two of every imaginable liquid refreshment, and in the totally refurbished kitchen area two temperature controlled wine rooms (one red, one white) plus a tank containing live lobsters. Supplementing the colour satellite television and beverage facilities in each room (all, of course, en suite) is a hairdryer, trouser press, digital clock radio/alarm and direct-dial telephone. The television sets have a satellite film channel. To everyone's benefit, there are no sales taxes or VAT charges in Jersey. St Ouen's Bay is a designated nature conservation area containing many local flora and fauna and beautiful gorse covered headlands with nature walks. The hotel enjoys the sweeping views of this magnificent expanse of golden sand and sea-scape.

Weekly Terms (Half Board) from £346.15
Daily Terms from £49.45
Bed and Breakfast from £35.50
Short breaks at inclusive prices covering flight, hire car and accommodation available
Bar Lunch from £5.00
Lunch from £9.75 and A La Carte
Bar Supper from £5.00
Dinner from £13.95 and A La Carte

Gratuities at Guest's Discretion
Credit Cards—Access, American Express, Diners Club, Visa
10 Double, 3 Twin Bedrooms
All Rooms with Private Bathroom with Shower, TV, Telephone, Radio/Alarm, Tea and Coffee-making Facilities, Trouser Press, Hairdryer, Refrigerator, Mini Bar, Sewing Kit, Toiletries
Open all Year.

Residential and Restaurant Licence (Music & Dancing)
Full Central Heating
Cocktail Bar
Dogs not allowed
Parking Facilities. Night Porter
Nearby: Putting, Swimming, Golf, Fishing, Riding, Sailing Windsurfing, Water Skiing, Shooting, Surfing, Cliff Walks

Section 6: Jersey

St Peter—Mermaid Hotel St Peter, Jersey, Channel Islands.
Tel 0534 41255. Fax 0534 45826

One of the few first-class hotels in Jersey that is not pitched along the coast, which, in itself, has many advantages during the busy high season. The Mermaid Hotel is very contemporary, yet is now long established. A contradiction it would seem, but the directorate has always kept the hotel up-to-date and the latest example of this policy is a superb indoor heated swimming pool, which is bound to be a major attraction to guests throughout the year, but more specially during the colder months. We always enjoy our visits to the Mermaid. It is luxurious and friendly, has an ideal setting in a beautiful wooded valley overlooking a small natural lake, and is within minutes of the airport. Nearly all the bedrooms have views of the lake and every room is equipped with colour television with satellite link, radio, direct dial telephone, hairdryer, trouser press, beverage trays and *en suite* facilities. The Mermaid is a great meeting place too, for the lounges are spacious and comfortable, whilst the old-world tavern offers a congenial setting in which to relax and meet friends. The *Granite Grill Room* dates from early 18th century. The restaurant is ever a favourite among Jersey folk and those appreciative of *une bonne table*. The *à la carte* and *table d' hôte* menus offer quality and variety, and the wine list is a perfect complement to the *cuisine*. At the Mermaid you will sense a feeling of snugness in the winter (there is always an open log fire burning in the tavern) and, perhaps, smugness in the summer, when you can be quiet when the island is crowded. Yet, you will not feel isolated, for island life is noted for its compactness.

Bed and Breakfast from £35.00
Bar Lunch from £3.50
Lunch from £9.50 and A La Carte
Dinner from £11.00 and A La Carte
10% Service Charge Grill Room Meals only
Credit Cards—Access, American Express,

Diners Club, Visa. 30 Double, 35 Twin, 3 Single Bedrooms. All Rooms with Private Bath/Shower Room, TV, Telephone, Radio, Baby-listening, Hairdryer, Trouser Press, Tea and Coffee-making Facilities, Toiletries
Open all Year. Fully Licensed

Full Central Heating. 2 Cocktail Bars Conference Facilities. Dogs not allowed. Parking Facilities. Night Porter. 2 All weather Tennis Courts, 9-hole Putting Green, Indoor Heated and Outdoor Swimming Pools, Solarium, Sauna, Gym

St Saviour, Belvedere—Merton Hotel Belvedere, St Saviour,
Jersey, Channel Islands. Tel 0534 24231. Fax 0534 68603

The Merton Hotel is probably the most famous in the Channel Islands. For over 70 years it has been the holiday 'home' for countless thousands of people. Situated within easy reach of the town centre and adjacent to one of Jersey's most beautiful public parks, the Merton Hotel offers the visitor to Jersey a complete holiday in the friendliest of surroundings appealing to all age groups, with its excellent facilities, smiling service and its accent firmly on value for money. Top class international entertainment at the hotel is all provided completely free of charge with dancing, cabarets and floorshows. There is a separate and fully soundproofed disco called *Bubbles* where the more energetic can dance until the early hours without disturbing anyone else. Other facilities include a bistro-style coffee shop, comfortable sun lounges and a new lounge bar, *"Kiplings"*, where you can enjoy a quiet drink. There are bar terraces for early evening cocktails and flower-filled gardens in which to relax. The hotel provides accommodation for over 650 guests and all bedrooms are furnished to a high degree of comfort. The standard of *cuisine* is excellent, and the service always pleasant and efficient. In May 1991 the latest and most exciting redevelopment, the Aquadome, opened its doors to residents. The Aquadome is an all-weather complex offering hours of fun and relaxation for all the family. Within the Aquadome there is a thrilling 80 metre waterslide, cascade pools, spas, rapids, water cannons, bubble rings, a toddlers' pool, to mention a few and is fully supervised. It also has its own restaurant which provides light refreshments. The hotel is under the same family ownership as the Hotel de la Plage, Pomme d'Or and Portelet Hotels.

Weekly Terms from £199.00. Daily Terms from £31.50. Lunch from £7.50. Dinner from £10.00. No Service Charge. Credit Cards—Access, American Express, Diners

Club, Visa. 24 Family Rooms. 35 Double, 251 Twin, 30 Single Bedrooms. 268 Private Bathrooms. All Rooms with Radio, TV, Tea and Coffee-making Facilities,

Baby-listening. Open from Feb to Dec Fully Licenced. Full CH. 5 Lifts. Cocktail Bar. Lounge Bar. 2 TV Lounges Games Room. Dogs not allowed

Section 6: Sark

Little Sark—La Sablonnerie
Sark, Via Guernsey, Channel Islands. Tel 0481 83 2061

Here is a thought for a holiday, probably different from any you have spent before. Sark is an island–three and a half by one and a half miles at its widest point, and there are no motor cars or aircraft allowed–just a vintage horse-drawn barouche to convey you and your luggage from the tiny harbour. Far away from the hustle and bustle of everyday life, it is an idyllic spot for those appreciative of Sark's peaceful charm and its opportunities for bathing, walking and climbing. La Sablonnerie is on Little Sark, an oasis of good living, with fresh butter, cream, meat and vegetables from its own farm and gardens. Excellent food and wine are served in a setting which is tranquil, relaxing and completely restorative. Once a farmhouse, now discreetly modernised, this sixteenth-century inn has much to offer. A long, low building, it flanks a sunny garden on two sides, and on ground level are the sun-trap lounge and dining-room. In the granite-walled bar, Sark-born Philip Perrée dispenses hospitality in true island fashion. His daughter, Elizabeth, manages the hotel side, and her sound training and love for *haute cuisine* together with the employment of first-class chefs, ensures that the most interesting and generous use is made of the splendid local produce available. The dining-room, scintillating by day and with fresh flowers on every table, is more so in the evening when, by candlelight, the atmosphere of La Sablonnerie, a happy blend of simplicity and sophistication, is truly felt.

Accommodation Terms on Application	2 Family Rooms. 1 Honeymoon Suite	Part Central Heating and Log Fires
Lunch from £15.00 and A La Carte	6 Double, 6 Twin, 6 Single Bedrooms	Cocktail Bar.
Afternoon Tea from £1.50	6 Private Bathrooms	Dogs allowed at Proprietor's Discretion.
Dinner from £18.00 and A La Carte	6 Private Shower Rooms	Croquet, Fishing, Riding,
10% Service Charge	Baby-listening by Arrangement	Own Horses and Carriages,
Credit Cards—Access,	Open from Easter to October	Hotel Boat Trips
American Express, Visa	Fully Licensed	

Sark—Hotel Petit Champ
Sark, Via Guernsey, Channel Islands. Tel 0481 83 2046

In your lifetime, try not to miss a visit to this magical isle. When you come, be sure to allow yourself a good two-week holiday, not only to enjoy the tranquil setting, but to explore the picturesque coastline, the scores of bays, caves and coves, and the pleasure of swimming at the numerous uncrowded beaches. All this is within easy walking or bicycling distance (no cars being allowed on the island) from the friendly atmosphere of the Hotel Petit Champ, which occupies a marvellous position on the west coast, and where you can gaze beyond to the islands of Herm, Jethou and Guernsey. Chris and Caroline Robins are the friendliest of hosts. The *cuisine* their chef prepares and serves has always been adjudged as some of the best in the islands and the menus are designed to appease discerning appetites with fresh vegetables and fish in constant supply. The accommodation has earned the praise of many guests for the thoughtful appointments. Modern in flavour and of ample proportions, they contain private bathrooms and attractive balconies which look onto the hotel's garden and the superb view of the sea beyond. Extensive refurbishing and redecorating takes place during the winter months and, in recent years, double glazing and central heating have been introduced to all bedrooms and some also now have sliding patio doors. The solar heated swimming pool is most delightfully set in an old quarry which forms a perfect sun-trap since it is sheltered from every wind. Since accommodation on Sark is limited, it is *most essential* that you book in advance.

Weekly Terms (Half Board) from £245.00	Visa. 2 Family Rooms	Full Central Heating. Cocktail Bar
Daily Terms from £35.00	3 Double, 8 Twin, 3 Single Bedrooms	TV Lounge. Children from 7 years catered
Bar Lunch from £2.50 A La Carte	9 Private Bathrooms. 7 Private Shower	for. Dogs not allowed. Horse and Carriage
Dinner from £16.00 Table D'Hôte	Rooms. 4 Rooms with Balcony, most with	Hire(Hotel's Stables), Putting, Outdoor
Service Charge inclusive	Sea Views. Open from mid April to October	Heated Swimming Pool, Fishing, Yacht
Credit Cards—Access, American Express,	Residential and Restaurant Licence	Charter available. Nearby: Tennis

WALES

Bodnant Garden, Gwynedd

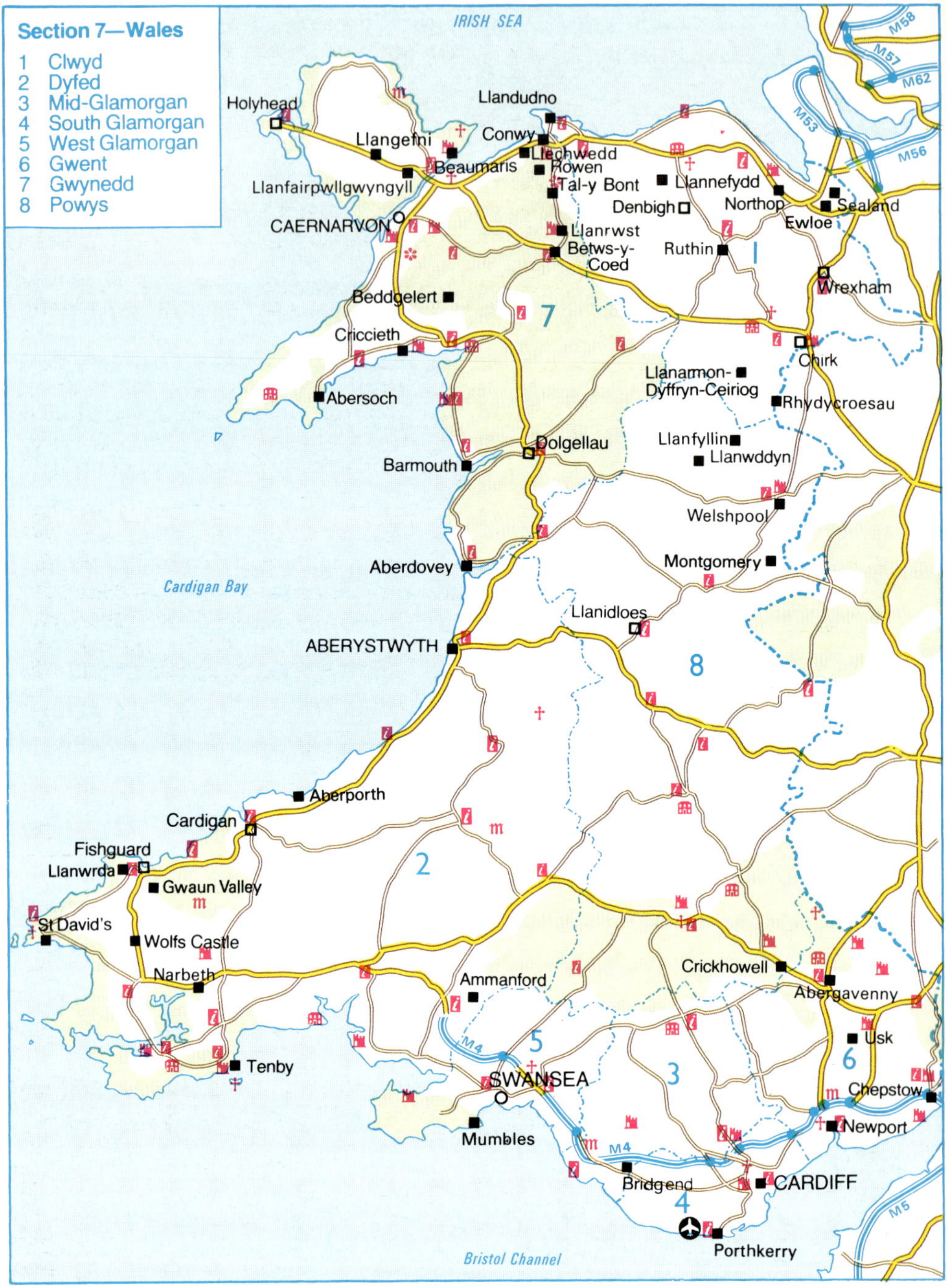
Section 7—Wales
1 Clwyd
2 Dyfed
3 Mid-Glamorgan
4 South Glamorgan
5 West Glamorgan
6 Gwent
7 Gwynedd
8 Powys
IRISH SEA
Holyhead
Llandudno
Llangefni
Conwy
Llechwedd
Beaumaris
Rowen
Tal-y Bont
Llannefydd
Llanfairpwllgwyngyll
Denbigh
Northop
Sealand
Ewloe
CAERNARVON
Llanrwst
Betws-y-Coed
Ruthin
Wrexham
Beddgelert
Criccieth
Chirk
Llanarmon-Dyffryn-Ceiriog
Abersoch
Rhydycroesau
Llanfyllin
Dolgellau
Llanwddyn
Barmouth
Welshpool
Aberdovey
Montgomery
Cardigan Bay
Llanidloes
ABERYSTWYTH
Aberporth
Cardigan
Fishguard
Llanwrda
Gwaun Valley
St David's
Wolfs Castle
Narbeth
Crickhowell
Ammanford
Abergavenny
Usk
Tenby
SWANSEA
Chepstow
Mumbles
Newport
Bridgend
CARDIFF
Porthkerry
Bristol Channel
M4
M5
M53
M56
M57
M58
M62

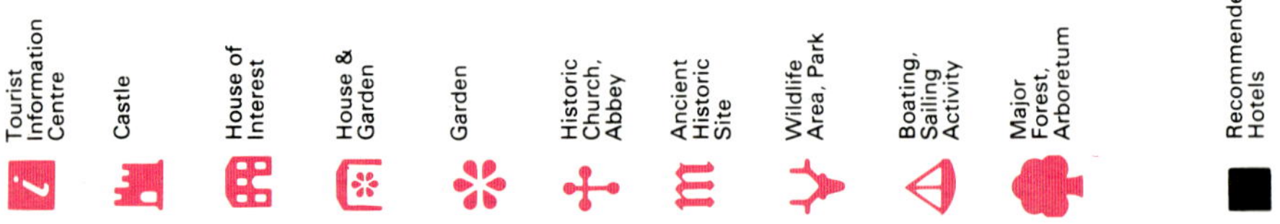
Tourist Information Centre
Castle
House of Interest
House & Garden
Garden
Historic Church, Abbey
Ancient Historic Site
Wildlife Area, Park
Boating, Sailing Activity
Major Forest, Arboretum
Recommended Hotels

Section 7 - Wales

Clwyd, Dyfed, Mid, South and West Glamorgan, Gwent, Gwynedd, Powys

Draw a straight line southwards from Chester to Chepstow and one is soon on Welsh territory. Chester, Shrewsbury, Leominster, Hereford and Chepstow are all - though not on the border - gateway towns to the eight counties which constitute a country proud of its ancestry, scenic splendour and recreational possibilities. The reason that Wales has not been overrun by tourists has had a lot to do with the fact that for many years it was difficult motoring anywhere in Wales.

This, thankfully, has changed in recent years and improved road links have reduced travel times significantly. For example, when driving between London and Tenby one now travels almost door to door on motorways and dual carriageways. The A55 'Expressway' now makes travel to the North Wales coast, including the Isle of Anglesey, fast and easy. Hoteliers on Anglesey are often asked 'how often do the ferries sail from the mainland?', when, actually, there are two bridges one can use, making access to the island trouble-free.

Of course, Snowdonia is the first objective of many visitors, but there are other areas that are worthy of exploration. Pin-point for leisure some of the tucked-away gems we have unearthed for you, such as Lake Vyrnwy for fishing; Conwy for history; the west coast and Anglesey for beautiful beaches; and numerous other tongue twisting hideaways. And as road links have improved one fact has become clear-Wales seems totally resistant to spoilation. Visit her lakes and rivers, her mountains and forests, and you will find solitude and peace like nowhere else in Britain.

Bodnant Garden, Gwynedd

Section 7: Clwyd

Sealand—The Gateway to Wales Hotel
Welsh Road, Sealand, Deeside, Clwyd. CH5 2HX
Tel 0244 830332. Fax 0244 836190

Only a five minute drive from the historic and charming city of Chester, this new and luxurious forty-bedroom hotel offers quality accommodation at a surprisingly comfortable price. Resident guests have all-day complimentary use of a superbly equipped Health and Fitness Centre, including swimming pool, therapeutic jacuzzi, sauna rooms, solarium and a gymnasium with no less than sixteen items of equipment. For social or business functions there is a large or small suite furnished and serviced to ensure that, whatever the occasion, the event runs smoothly. Their Regency Restaurant, open to non-residents, offers à la carte, flambé and table d'hôte dishes in an uncrowded and relaxing setting. Throughout the hotel, the decor, furniture and furnishings present a consistency of elegance and good taste. Whether you are touring on holiday (or a budget conscious executive visiting the nearby business and industrial park), The Gateway To Wales Hotel, with its twenty-four hour service and comprehensive range of amenities, is a most valuable centre. Located on the main A55/A550 arterial road which links Holyhead with Cheshire, Merseyside and the Midlands, Liverpool is only eighteen miles away. The heritage and culture of this area offer numerous specific places of interest, from the natural beauty of Snowdonia National Park to National Theatre productions at Theatre Clwyd Mold. Museums, zoos, castles and gardens abound in this region.

Weekly Terms (B & B) from £55.20 per day
Daily Terms (Half Board) from £68.71
Bar Meal from £3.00
Lunch from £12.50 and A La Carte
Afternoon Tea from £4.50
Dinner from £12.50 and A La Carte
Gratuities at Guest's discretion
VAT inclusive
Credit Cards—Access, American Express, Diners Club, Visa

3 Family Rooms. 2 Suites
19 Double, 17 Twin Bedrooms
1 Single Bedroom suitable
 for disabled person
All Rooms with Private Bathroom, TV, Telephone, Radio, Baby-listening, Tea and Coffee-making Facilities, Trouser Press, Hairdryer, Toiletries
Room Service. Laundry Facilities
Open All Year

Fully Licensed
Full Central Heating
Lift. Cocktail Bar
Conference Facilities
Children catered for
Guide Dogs only accepted
Parking Facilities. Night Porter
Indoor Swimming Pool, Solarium, Sauna
Nearby: Squash, Badminton, Golf, Fishing, Riding, Shooting

Section 7: Clwyd

Near Denbigh, Llannefydd—The Hawk and Buckle Inn
Llannefydd, Denbigh, Clwyd. LL16 5ED. Tel 074 579 249

This seventeenth-century coaching inn sits high in the hills overlooking the beautiful countryside of the Vale of Clwyd, and is truly off the beaten track since what was the stagecoach route to Holyhead is now a quiet country lane. Although centrally located, Llannefydd is an unspoilt village with a peaceful environment. Even the modern extension to the Hawk and Buckle is a discreet addition not intruding on the authentic frontage of the Inn. All the bedrooms are *en suite*, with modern facilities, and most have superb views over the lovely surrounding countryside. From here, guests can travel in any direction and be assured of interesting, scenic and charming places to visit. Within easy reach are Chester, Llandudno, Betws-y-Coed and Bodnant Gardens, to name only a few. There are no less than seven golf courses within thirty minutes' drive, whilst, for the angler, salmon, trout and sea fishing are all available locally. Readers' reports indicate that the restaurant meals and bar food, both of which have extensive menus, are a major attraction at the Inn, especially since both feature fresh local produce. Lamb and salmon in season are a speciality and vegetarian meals are always available. One has a wide choice of routes to reach Llannefydd which, as the crow flies, lies midway between Abergele and Denbigh. If required, Bob or Barbara Pearson will provide details.

Weekly Terms from £300.00
Bed and Breakfast from £36.00
Bar Meal from £2.95
Dinner from £12.00 and A La Carte
Gratuities at Guest's discretion
VAT inclusive
Credit Cards—Access, Visa
8 Double, 2 Twin Bedrooms

All Rooms with Private Bathroom, TV, Telephone, Tea and Coffee-making Facilities
Trouser Press, Hairdryer available on request
Open all Year
Fully Licensed
Full Central Heating

Cocktail Bar
Dogs not allowed
Parking Facilities
Solarium
Nearby: Golf, Fishing, Riding, Sailing, Windsurfing

Llanarmon-Dyffryn-Ceiriog—The Hand Hotel Llanarmon-Dyffryn-Ceiriog,
Near Llangollen, Clwyd. LL20 7LD. Tel 069 176 666

The tongue-twisting name of this tiny Welsh village means Garmon's church in the valley of the Ceiriog' and is normally abbreviated to Llanarmon DC (do add the initials for there is another Llanarmon miles away). It is a prime centre for walking, fishing and shooting and the rugged grandeur of the scenery culminates in the west at the Berwyn Mountains, which rise to almost 3,000 feet. It is beautiful unspoilt terrain in which to spend one's days, but as an antidote to its sturdiness the warmth and comfort and hospitality of The Hand Hotel could hardly be more inviting. The diversion off the A5 London/Holyhead road to visit this sixteenth-century hotel is well worthwhile. Melvin and Lilian Brunton are doing a marvellous job there. The twelve bedrooms, all with a private bathroom, are tastefully furnished and in the attractive dining-room, built from local stone, one can enjoy an extremely high standard of food and wine. Darkened beams, open fireplaces and walls irregular with age all add to the cosiness of this old farmhouse and there is, of course, full central heating. All around one can see the landscape which inspired the Welsh poet John Ceiriog Hughes, who lived nearby. Visitors to this area will appreciate the much improved road network to Chirk from Chester, Shrewsbury and the Wirral. The village is best approached from Chirk, taking the B4500 Ceiriog Valley road for about eleven miles.

Weekly Terms from £280.00
Bed and Breakfast from £29.00
Dinner £16.50
Gratuities at Guest's discretion
VAT inclusive. Credit Cards—Access, American Express, Diners Club, Visa

1 Suite. 3 Double, 9 Twin Bedrooms
(All Rooms can be let as Singles)
All Rooms with Private Bath/Shower Room
2 Rooms with TV
Baby-listening, Radio, Hairdryer available
Open from Mid March to 1st February

Fully Licensed
Full Central Heating and Open Fires
TV Lounge. Conference Facilities
Children catered for. Dogs allowed
Parking Facilities
All-weather Tennis Court, Fishing

Section 7: Clwyd

Northop Hall—The Chequers Chester Road, Northop Hall Village, Near Mold, Clwyd. CH7 6HJ. Tel 0244 816181. Fax 0244 814661

Those who 'collect' small country house places must rejoice when they discover this prime specimen. The Chequers is brimful of good points and personality and is beautifully secluded in colourful gardens and fifty acres of woodland. Once inside, good quality furniture and fabrics seem to be the order of the day. Paintwork shines; oak panelling and natural wood, such a feature of The Chequers, gleams; stained glass and interesting prints add to the mood ... and you can smell the cleanliness! There are twenty-seven bedrooms, three of which are studio suites, and all boast private bathroom, television, direct-dial telephone and lovely views over the gardens and surrounding countryside. When we can, we always find time to dine at The Chequers and our most recent visit was no exception. Our meal was reasonably priced and very well presented, and the light airy dining room was a most pleasant venue. In addition to the excellent *table d'hôte* meals, the *à la carte* menu is extensive. Fresh local fare, a Welsh dish of the day and a house speciality of Welsh lamb are all high points. And where is this rural bolt-hole in its isolated valley? Northop Hall Village is off the A55, just eight miles from Chester and only a few miles from the M56 which links with the M6 and M1. With this tremendous locational advantage it is little wonder that the hotel's elegant *Gladstone* suite and smaller syndicate rooms are in great demand for conferences and the like.

Bed and Breakfast from £49.50
Bar Snacks available
Afternoon Tea available
Sunday Lunch from £7.50
Dinner from £15.50 and A La Carte
Gratuities at Guest's discretion

VAT inclusive. Credit Cards—Access, American Express, Visa
3 Suites/Family Rooms
5 Double, 12 Twin, 7 Single Bedrooms
All Rooms with Private Bathroom, TV, Telephone, Radio, Baby-listening, Tea

and Coffee-making Facilities, Hairdryer, Trouser Press
Open all year. Fully Licensed
Full Central Heating. Cocktail Bar
Conference Facilities. Parking Facilities
Nearby: Tennis, Squash, Swimming, Golf

Ruthin—Ruthin Castle Ruthin, Clwyd. LL15 2NU. Telephone 0824 702664. Fax 0824 705978

Dating back to 1282, this once fortress had, in earlier days, a turbulent history. What a contrast it is today to stand in the sweet rose-scented Italian gardens and view the scars of battle and butchery. Beneath the castle, dungeons and secret passages still honeycomb the foundations. Above ground, today, rich relaxation and planned comfort marks every turn. If the reception hall awed us, we soon felt at home in the panelled cocktail lounge–once the library. Great taste has been exercised in carpets, curtains and furniture. Although the *Grand Salon*, restaurant and ground floor generally are showpieces, the bedrooms attracted us most. All fifty-eight rooms, served by two lifts, have bathrooms *en suite* and all are standard in respect of telephones, colour television, radio, hairdryer and central heating, but each has its own individuality, and many have countryside views overlooking the Clwyd valley. To complete this peaceful picture, all corridors are deep-carpeted, and all bedroom doors are fitted with pneumatic self-closing fitments. In the thirty-eight acres of grounds which include the ruins of the twelfth century castle with its battlements and dungeons, there are twelve and a half miles of reserved fishing on the Clwyd. Medieval banquets are held on most nights during the season and these are a great tourist draw.

Weekly Terms from £302.00
Daily Terms from £46.00 (min 2 nights)
Bar Lunch from £2.00
Lunch from £6.45
Dinner from £15.95 and A La Carte
Gratuities at Guest's discretion
VAT inclusive
Credit Cards–Access, American Express, Diners Club, Visa

12 Double (including 3 four poster rooms), 34 Twin, 6 Single Bedrooms
6 Family Rooms. 57 Private Bathrooms
1 Private Shower Room
All Rooms with TV, Telephone, Radio, Baby-listening, Tea and Coffee-making Facilities, Hairdryer.
Some Rooms with Trouser Press
Open all Year

Fully Licensed
Full Central Heating
Lift
Cocktail Bar
Games Room. Conference Facilities
Dogs not allowed. Parking Facilities
Night Porter. Fishing
Nearby: Tennis, Swimming, Golf, Riding, Shooting

Section 7: Dyfed

Aberystwyth—Belle Vue Royal Hotel Marine Terrace, Aberystwyth, Dyfed. SY23 2BA. Tel 0970 617558, 625380/1. Fax 0970 612190

Aberystwyth, which has been a popular seaside resort for almost a century, lies centrally in the long sweep of Cardigan Bay and offers safe bathing from its wide, sandy beaches. In a commanding position on the promenade is the Belle Vue Royal Hotel, an ideal location from which to observe the spectacular sunsets. The Belle Vue, which is family-owned and run by the proprietors, is a combination of Victorian architecture and modern sophistication. Both externally and internally it displays an elegant grandeur, while the friendly and efficient service make for a relaxed and comfortable stay. Catering offers a very valuable alternative between an inexpensive *table d'hôte* menu with a good choice for each course, or a more ambitious *à la carte* menu which includes several exotic dishes but is also most realistically priced. Of the thirty-eight bedrooms, thirty-two are *en suite* and all have recently been refurbished. Overlooking the town is Constitution Hill which, with its unique funicular railway and recently-installed Camera Obscura, is one of the main local attractions. Another unusual diversion is the Vale of Rheidol Narrow Gauge Railway which will take you to the waterfalls at Devil's Bridge. In addition to the normal seaside activities, Aberystwyth is an ideal centre for fishing and golf (which the hotel can offer at half green fees to residents). In the town there is also a castle, a museum, a theatre, a cinema and a concert-hall.

Terms on Application
Bed and Breakfast from £35.00
Bar Lunch from £3.50
Lunch from £8.75 and Grill Menu
Dinner from £13.50 and A La Carte
Gratuities at Guest's discretion

VAT inclusive
Credit Cards—Access, American Express, Diners Club, Visa
5 Family Rooms
9 Double, 15 Twin, 8 Single Bedrooms
24 Private Bathrooms

8 Private Shower Rooms
All Rooms with TV, Telephone, Radio, Baby-listening Tea and Coffee-making Facilities. Open all Year
Fully Licensed. Full Central Heating
Conference Facilities. Dogs not allowed

Near Aberystwyth, Chancery—Conrah Country Hotel Rhydgaled, Chancery, Near Aberystwyth, Dyfed. SY23 4DF. Tel 0970 617941. Fax 0970 624546

Three miles south of Aberystwyth on the A487 will be found the entrance to this delightful hide-away from the world at large. Drive for 100 yards and you will be quite oblivious of the sounds of traffic. Your ears will be alerted to the song of birds and your sight focused on a twenty-two-mile panoramic view across to the Plynlimmon mountain range. Substantially built in the first instance by a wealthy architect, the hotel has been completely modernised and refurnished throughout in excellent taste. The Conrah Country Hotel is now under the supervision of John and Patricia Heading, who concentrate on providing good food and fine wine both for their resident guests and for tourists in transit. Adjoining the main building is the *Magnolia Court Motel*, where each bedroom is equipped with a shower and toilet, central heating and tea-making facilities. A leisurely stay at Conrah is an absolute 'must' for, in the eighteen and a half acres of grounds, the rhododendrons and magnolias are magnificent in spring, whilst among the wild birds who make their home here is the goldcrest. Indoors you will find a heated swimming pool and a sauna. This is an hotel which, having sampled once, we can never just pass by. Indeed, when touring Wales, we always plan to stay here for at least a couple of nights.

All Prices pertain to 1992
Weekly Terms from £297.50
Daily Terms from £57.00
Bed and Breakfast from £37.50
Bar Lunch from £2.25
Lunch from £11.50 and A La Carte
Afternoon Tea from £3.00
Dinner from £19.50 and A La Carte
Gratuities at Guest's discretion

VAT inclusive
Credit Cards—Access, American Express, Diners Club, Visa
1 Family Room
11 Double, 8 Twin, 2 Single Bedrooms
15 Private Bathrooms
6 Private Shower Rooms
All Rooms with TV, Telephone, Radio, Tea and Coffee-making Facilities. Hairdryer

available on request Open from 1st January to 22nd December
Residential and Restaurant Licence
Full Central Heating. Lift. Cocktail Bar
Table-tennis Room. Conference Facilities
Children over 5 years catered for
Dogs not allowed. Parking Facilities
Croquet, Swimming, Sauna
Nearby: Tennis, Putting, Squash, Golf

Section 7: Dyfed

Near Ammanford—The Mill at Glynhir
Llandybie, Ammanford, Dyfed. SA18 2TE. Tel 0269 850672

At this quiet and secluded hotel you will find amenities to suit everyone. The whole of south Wales is spread before you, the Black Mountain and the Brecon Beacons are your backdrop and for the sporting enthusiast there is an eighteen-hole golf course next door (free to residents), pony trekking along the road at Glynhir Lodge and trout fishing in the River Loughor, which abuts onto two and a half acres of private grounds. The Mill is over 250 years old and has been handsomely transformed into a country hotel with every modern comfort. A private whirlpool bath/shower, trouser press, hairdryer, colour television, radio, telephone and tea-making facilities are standard in these luxurious rooms and all the rooms have views across the valley. The *Glynhir Suite*, which has a sitting-room, is especially attractive. Both the dining-room, which accommodates twenty guests, and the attractive lounge are within the confines of the original mill, with stone walls three feet thick. The biggest surprise in such a small hotel (eleven bedrooms) is the discovery of an indoor heated swimming pool with an underwater jet stream for exercise and massage. The staff are attentive in presenting the best home cooking, with continental specialities, and at the end of your dinner you will feel you have dined in a well-run country house. We would adjudge this family-run hotel to provide a happy and relaxed holiday at any time of the year. To find the hotel, turn right off the A483 Ammanford to Llandeilo road in Llandybie into Glynhir Road.

Weekly Terms from £252.00
Daily Terms from £38.50
Bed and Breakfast from £36.00
Lunch from £7.50 and A La Carte
Dinner from £13.50 and A La Carte
Gratuities at Guest's discretion
VAT inclusive
Credit Cards—Access, Visa

2 Family Rooms. 1 Suite
3 Double, 1 Single, 4 Twin Bedrooms
All Rooms with Private Bathroom, TV, Radio, Telephone, Tea and Coffee-making Facilities, Hairdryer, Trouser Press
Open all year except Christmas and New Year
Residential and Restaurant Licence

Full Central Heating. Cocktail Bar
Small Conference Facilities
Children over 11 years catered for
Dogs allowed
Parking Facilities
Swimming, Golf, Fishing
Nearby: Tennis, Squash, Badminton, Riding

Near Fishguard, Gwaun Valley—Tregynon Country Farmhouse Hotel
Gwaun Valley, Near Fishguard, Dyfed. SA65 9TU. Tel 0239 820531

Focal point of this delightful hotel is a stone built farmhouse dating back to 1594. This contains the restaurant, residents' lounge, a small bar, a double room and two family rooms. A further five bedrooms are located in sympathetically converted adjacent stone cottages. All rooms are furnished attractively to a very good standard, with *en suite* facilities, colour television and tea/coffee makers. The natural peace and beauty of this location is exceptional, and well worth seeking out. To this end, the hotel has produced a folder with clear instructions on how to reach it from the Carmarthen area, from Haverfordwest, from Fishguard or from Newport. An abundance of wildlife, flowers, forest walks and a sunny stretch of coastline offer interest to sightseers as well as diversions for the more active. Bathing, sailing, fishing, windsurfing, walking, bird-watching and photography are all to be enjoyed here. Also to be seen are a waterfall, caves and an Iron Age fort. Added to these features are all the charms of Tregynon itself (the name means 'a cluster of dwellings'). Within the hotel, guests can admire the massive stone inglenook, hardwood beams and, in cooler weather, welcoming log fires. Finally, and most importantly, the evening meals here are truly outstanding. In terms of choice, first quality fresh produce and presentation they are exceptional. Special breaks are available from 1st November to Easter excluding Christmas to New Year.

Weekly Terms from £230.00
Daily Terms from £35.25
Bed and Breakfast from £22.00
Lunch and Afternoon Tea by arrangement only. Dinner from £13.25 (Residents), £14.00 (Non Residents)

Gratuities at Guest's discretion
VAT inclusive. Credit Cards accepted (3% surcharge)
4 Family/Twin Rooms. 4 Double Bedrooms
5 Private Bathrooms. 3 Private Shower Rooms. All Rooms with TV, Telephone,

Baby-listening, Tea and Coffee-making Facilities, Hairdryer
Open All Year (apart from 2/3 weeks in winter). Residential and Restaurant Licence
Full Central Heating. Conference Facilities
Children catered for. Dogs not allowed

Section 7: Dyfed

Llanwrda—Glanrannell Park Country House Hotel
Crugybar, Llanwrda, Dyfed. SA19 8SA. Tel 0558 685230. Fax 0558 685784

Reaching the unspoilt areas of country necessarily involves leaving the busier roads and, in this instance, the small effort in locating your destination is amply rewarded. From Llanwrda, which is on the A40 some twenty-five miles east of Carmarthen, take the A482 northwards for five miles before taking a left turn towards Llansawel. Shortly after crossing the B4302 you will find Glanrannell Park on your left. It is a charming country house set in twenty-three acres of grounds, woodland and pastureland, bounded on one side by the Annell, a trout stream from which the hotel derives its name. There are eight bedrooms in the main house, all with private bathrooms. Within the surrounding lawns there is a delightful private lake, overlooked by the dining-room. Catering is based on fresh local produce, cooked to bring out the inherent goodness of quality meats, fish, fowl and vegetables, complemented by a good selection of wines. Resident proprietors David and Bronwen Davies set a pleasantly informal atmosphere in the hotel and their success overall was evidenced to us on meeting two sets of guests who had been regular visitors for sixteen and fourteen years, respectively. Of the two lounges, one has a library with a stock of light reading and reference books. Paddocks in the grounds are shared by a flock of black sheep and a stud of Welsh cobs. This area of the country is a naturalists' paradise, also with numerous places of interest to the historian, the sportsman and others seeking a scenic retreat.

Weekly Terms from £286.00 (Half Board)
Weekly Terms from £188.00 (B&B
Daily Terms from £46.00
Bed and Breakfast from £31.00
Bar Lunch from £3.00
Afternoon Tea from £0.70
Dinner from £15.00
Gratuities at Guest's discretion

VAT inclusive
Credit Cards—Access, Visa
2 Family Rooms
4 Double, 2 Twin Bedrooms
8 Private Bathrooms
All Rooms with Tea and Coffee-making Facilities. Open from April to October inclusive. Fully Licensed

Full Central Heating.
Cocktail Bar. TV Lounge
Children catered for
Dogs allowed
Parking Facilities
Fishing
Nearby: Fishing, Riding

Have you returned your membership form?
By simply completing and returning to us the registration card inserted in this book you will automatically become a 1993 member of the Ashley Courtenay Circle , an invaluable link between author and reader. For members, we compile and revise each year special listings of hotels which offer particular amenities, such as a sauna, swimming pool, golf course (or adjacent), four-poster beds, facilities for the disabled, special Christmas programmes, vegetarian dishes, non-smoking areas and self-catering facilities. We can even direct you to hotels which are especially pleased to receive young children and dogs. These lists are free of charge. Just send a stamped addressed envelope.

Section 7: Dyfed

Near Narberth—Robeston House Hotel & Restaurant
Robeston Wathen, Near Narberth, Dyfed. SA67 8EU
Tel 0834 860392. Fax 0834 861195

A personal welcome from Peter, Pauline or Helen Copeman awaits each visitor and is indicative of the friendly and attentive service you receive here. Situated on the A40 road from Carmarthen to Haverfordwest, Robeston House stands in six acres of grounds on a high hill overlooking the spectacular Pembrokeshire countryside. Two double en suite bedrooms, one a four-poster, have recently been added and, like the existing rooms, they are furnished in a homely, country-house style. As we reported in earlier editions of our Guide, Robeston House owes much of its popularity to the excellence of its cuisine. Their eighteenth century kitchens have been restored as a buttery and salad bar, open from 8am to 10pm, and their main restaurant serves à la carte lunches to order, as well as evening dinner. We dined from a fixed-price menu and our three course meal, with coffee, was excellent and—in value—the best we have yet encountered for such generous portions. An exceptionally fine selection of wines is stored in vaulted cellars. In the colder weather, log fires supplement the central heating to enhance the comfortable atmosphere of the public rooms. Nature-lovers, sports enthusiasts and those seeking peaceful relaxation will all find themselves well satisfied here. Historic towns, picturesque villages, a breathtaking coastline and the magnificent Preseli Hills combine to make up the charm of this county. Nearby there are the safe, sandy beaches of Tenby.

Weekly Terms (B&B) 20% discount on Daily Terms
Bed and Breakfast from £27.50
Bar Lunch from £1.40
Lunch from £4.75 and A La Carte
Afternoon Tea from £1.35
Bar Supper from £4.75
Dinner from £15.50 and A La Carte
Gratuities at Guest's discretion
VAT inclusive

Credit Cards—Access, American Express, Diners Club, Visa
1 Family Room
1 Twin, 4 Double, 2 Single Bedrooms
6 Private Bathrooms
2 Private Shower Rooms
All Rooms with TV, Telephone, Baby-listening, Tea and Coffee-making Facilities. Hairdryer available on request
Open all Year

Residential & Restaurant Licence
Full Central Heating
Cocktail Bar
Conference Facilities
Children catered for
Dogs allowed. Parking Facilities
Nearby: Tennis, Putting, Squash, Badminton, Swimming, Golf, Fishing, Riding, Sailing, Windsurfing, Water Skiing, Shooting

Section 7: Dyfed

St David's—Old Cross Hotel
The Cross Square, St David's, Dyfed. SA62 6SP. Tel 0437 720387

This charming eighteenth-century house has lost none of its charm by being completely modernised and extended. It is situated in the centre of St David's near the cathedral and the ruins of the medieval Bishop's Palace. The hotel faces the old Market Cross and has a private car park. Inside you will find a most welcoming atmosphere. The restaurant has an excellent reputation for providing the best traditional cooking and the food is enhanced by a good selection of wines. The hotel's bar snacks are also very popular. Whatever the needs of travellers, however, they will be satisfied by the warm welcome, the comfort and the *cuisine*. The bedrooms are well equipped, having private bathrooms, television, telephones and tea and coffee-making facilities. In the hotel grounds there is a bungalow with three bedrooms, one double and two twin, all equipped with wash-basins. There is also a bathroom, a toilet, a kitchenette and a small lounge with colour television. The bungalow is, therefore, ideal for use by a family or a few friends. All the hotel meals and facilities are available to those staying in the bungalow. The Old Cross is an ideal base for touring Pembrokeshire. The hotel is owned by Mr P T Lynas and managed by his son, Mr Paul Lynas.

Weekly Terms from £255.00
Daily Terms from £38.00
Bed and Breakfast from £28.00
Bar Lunch from £3.00
Afternoon Tea from £2.50
Dinner from £13.75 and A La Carte
Gratuities at Guest's discretion

VAT inclusive
5 Family Rooms
7 Double, 1 Single, 4 Twin Bedrooms
All Rooms with Private Bathroom, TV, Telephone, Radio, Baby-listening, Tea and Coffee-making Facilities, Hairdryer
Open from 1st March to 31st October

Fully Licensed
Full Central Heating
Cocktail Bar
Dogs allowed at Management's discretion
Parking Facilities
Nearby: Golf, Fishing, Riding, Sailing, Windsurfing

St David's—Warpool Court Hotel
St David's, Dyfed. SA62 6BN. Tel 0437 720300. Fax 0437 720676

This charming country-house hotel is a most comfortable base for exploring the Pembrokeshire countryside. Standing in a magnificent coastal position, it overlooks St Brides Bay and is within easy reach of St David's Cathedral to which, in earlier times, pilgrims made their way. During the summer the Pembrokeshire Coast Path, the bird sanctuaries of St David's Head and Ramsey Island and the numerous prehistoric remains attract their own 'pilgrims'. Perhaps the most fascinating feature of Warpool Court is the collection of ornamental wall tiles, which were painted by a former owner. The hotel is now owned by Peter and Julie Trier who have carried out many improvements. An all-weather tennis court is provided for guests, together with a sauna and gymnasium. However, from Easter to the end of October, the indoor swimming pool, situated in the large hotel gardens, remains one of Warpool Court's most popular facilities. Free golf on the picturesque seaside course at Whitesands has been arranged. The hotel enjoys an ever increasing reputation for the quality of its modern English *cuisine*, using only fresh local produce. Crab and seafood dishes are a speciality.

Weekly Terms from £350.00
Daily Terms from £55.00
Bed and Breakfast from £46.00
Bar Lunch from £3.00
Lunch from £13.00 and A La Carte
Afternoon Tea from £2.50
Dinner from £25.00 and A La Carte
Gratuities at Guest's discretion
VAT inclusive

Credit Cards—Access, American Express, Diners Club, Visa
8 Double, 6 Twin Bedrooms
10 Family Rooms
20 Private Bathrooms
4 Private Shower Rooms
All Rooms with TV, Telephone, Radio, Baby-listening, Tea and Coffee-making Facilities

Open February to December inclusive.
Fully Licensed. Full Central Heating
Cocktail Bar. Games Room
Conference Facilities
Dogs allowed. Parking Facilities
Tennis, Croquet, Swimming, Sauna, Gymnasium
Nearby: Solarium, Free Golf, Sea Fishing, Riding, Sailing, Windsurfing

Section 7: Dyfed

Tenby—Albany Hotel
The Norton, Tenby, Dyfed. SA70 8AB.
Tel 0834 842698

Tenby is a charming seaside resort, a joy to explore on foot. Should all the walking and the long stepway to the beach induce a healthy appetite, you will do well to be a resident at the Albany. We enjoyed quite excellent food from the reasonably priced table d'hôte menu and noted that the extensive range of hors d'oeuvres, seafoods and entrées on the à la carte menu were also good value for money. Our meal was the more pleasant because of the friendly and attentive manner of the staff on reception and in the restaurant. Originally an old coaching inn, the Albany was fully refurbished in 1989. It now embodies a heated swimming pool, a choice of bars with traditional ales and snacks available at lunchtime and in the evening. All of its twenty-four en suite bedrooms have colour television, tea and coffee facilities, and are centrally heated. As with most hotels in this quaint town, there is no private car park. However, only 250 yards away is the municipal car park (and the attractive shopping area), while the popular North Beach is just 100 yards away. Tenby enjoys a very mild climate and this, together with the safe sandy beaches, boat trips to Caldy Island and the numerous attractions of the walled town, make it suitable for long or short visits throughout the year. It is a most appealing base from which to tour the beautiful and historical South Pembrokeshire coast. Speciality weekends (Murder Mystery etc.) and late booking bargain breaks are offered throughout the year.

Special Breaks available
Weekly Terms from £220.00
Daily Terms from £36.00
Bed and Breakfast from £23.00
Bar Meals from £1.50
Lunch from £8.95 and A La Carte
Dinner from £12.95 and A La Carte
Gratuities at Guest's discretion
VAT inclusive

Credit Cards—Access, American Express, Visa
10 Double, 12 Twin, 2 Single Bedrooms
All Rooms with Private Bath/Shower Room, TV, Tea and Coffee-making Facilities
Hairdryer and Radio available
Open All Year
Fully Licensed
Full Central Heating

Cocktail Bar
Reading Room/Video Lounge
Children welcome
Dogs allowed by arrangement
Municipal Car Park
Outdoor Swimming Pool
Nearby: Tennis, Squash, Golf, Fishing, Riding, Sailing, Windsurfing, Water Skiing, Shooting, Paragliding

Section 7: Dyfed

Tenby—Waterwynch House Hotel
Narberth Road, Tenby, Dyfed
Telephone 0834 842464

Built originally as a family home in 1820 by Tenby artist Charles Norris, Waterwynch House nestles in a secluded cove on the beautiful shores of Carmarthen Bay. It is one of the very few hotels situated on the Pembrokeshire Coastal Footpath and offers a unique combination of coastal and countryside attractions. Standing in twenty-seven acres of woodland and private gardens, the hotel has seventeen en suite bedrooms, each of which has views of the sea or the gardens. We stayed overnight and found the personal service to be efficient and friendly, the comfort and facilities first-class, and the meals some of the best we have come across in a twelve-month. Add to this the fact that the tariff is most reasonable: the hotel stands highly commended and a credit to the resident proprietors, Bette and Geoff Hampton. To reach Waterwynch House, follow the A478 road from Kilgetty towards Tenby and, half a mile after the New Hedges roundabout, the private access road is signposted on your left. At the hotel, a full-size snooker table is available, the sheltered beach is immediately in front of you and there is a wide choice of scenic walks. Saundersfoot and Tenby each have their own appeal and charm, the surrounding areas including a wildlife (mammals) park, a zoo, nature trails, castles, a museum and two lighthouses, one of which is on nearby Caldey Island. Here, visitors can purchase perfumes and cosmetics made by the monks.

Weekly Terms from £195.00
Daily Terms from £29.00
Bed and Breakfast from £20.00
Lunch from £9.00 and A La Carte
Afternoon Tea from £1.75
Dinner £14.50 Table d'Hôte
Gratuities at Guest's discretion
VAT inclusive
3 Lounge Suites, 3 De Luxe Suites
4 Twin, 5 Double, 2 Single Bedrooms

14 Private Bathrooms
3 Private Shower Rooms
All Rooms with TV, Tea and
Coffee-making Facilities
Telephone, Radio and Hairdryer available on request
Open from March to November
Residential Licence
Full Central Heating
Cocktail Bar. Games Room

Conference Facilities
Dogs allowed at Management's discretion
Parking Facilities
Bowls, Croquet, Putting, Fishing,
Nature Trail
Nearby: Tennis, Squash, Badminton,
Swimming, Solarium, Sauna, Golf, Riding,
Sailing, Windsurfing, Water Skiing,
Shooting, Sea Fishing

Section 7: Dyfed & Mid Glamorgan

Wolf's Castle, Near Haverfordwest—Wolfscastle Country Hotel and Restaurant
Wolf's Castle, Near Haverfordwest, Dyfed. SA62 5LZ. Tel 043787 225/688

On our travels through Wales it seems that fishing is uppermost in the minds of many visitors. However, at Wolfscastle there is a great diversity of interests and, mercifully, no single topic dominates the evening's conversation. Here you will find a squash court and a tennis court on hand and in the vicinity are pottery and painting tuition, wind surfing, horse riding, birdwatching, walking, boating and, of course, good fishing. The hotel itself lies midway between Haverfordwest and Fishguard on the A40 road near the River Western Cleddau and overlooking the great Treffgarne Rocks. Surrounded by a barbecue and patio area and a garden, this delightful hotel has comfortable bedrooms and a restaurant which provides unusually good bar lunches and excellently prepared dinners. The latter are of exceptional quality, involving traditional as well as more adventurous dishes all using fresh commodities and home-grown vegetables. The hotel is within easy reach of many sandy coves, the Coastal Path and the beautiful Preseli Hills, and, when there is nothing more to be done, your bedroom, with its colour television and private bathroom, will provide a most agreeable pause in the daily round. It seemed to us that the hotel has many special features, but its trump card is the cheerful relaxing atmosphere generated by the ever-active resident director, Andrew Stirling.

Bed and Breakfast from £34.00
Bar Meal from £1.60
Lunch £8.50 A La Carte
Afternoon Tea from £1.50
Dinner from £16.00 A La Carte
Gratuities at Guest's discretion
VAT inclusive
Credit Cards—Access,

American Express, Visa
3 Family Rooms
13 Double, 3 Twin, 4 Single Bedrooms
All Rooms with Private Bathroom, TV,
Telephone, Radio, Tea and
Coffee-making Facilities
Open all Year
Residential and Restaurant Licence

Full Central Heating
Cocktail Bar
Conference Facilities
Dogs allowed
Parking Facilities. Tennis, Squash
Nearby: Swimming, Solarium, Sauna, Golf,
Fishing, Riding, Sailing, Windsurfing,
Water Skiing

Near Bridgend, Coychurch–Coed-y-Mwstwr
Coychurch, Near Bridgend, Vale of Glamorgan, CF35 6AF. Tel 0656 860621

The sky *is* the limit here if you book in for one of their ballooning weekends, when you can ride over the picturesque and historic Vale of Glamorgan and its Heritage Coastline. For those of us not seeking such diversions, let it be known that the Welsh name translates into 'whispering trees' and refers to the setting for this Victorian country mansion: seventeen acres of woodland gardens. Skilful restoration of the grand house to include modern facilities has retained the restful atmosphere engendered by rich panelling. The bedrooms can only be described as luxurious and, as with the rest of the hotel, possessed of a rare elegance. The *Hendre* suite provides an excellent venue for conferences or dinner/dances. Complementing this are the well-kept gardens with views over distant countryside, and embodying a heated outdoor swimming-pool. Nearby Bridgend is a market town straddling the River Ogmore, where the Ogmore, Garw and Llynfi valleys meet. Numerous castles, museums, parks and even a vineyard provide a wide variety of local interesting places to visit. Coed-y-Mwstwr is a prestigious location for small conferences and has two beautifully furnished boardrooms, with seating capacities of up to twelve and twenty persons, respectively. Discerning tourists and demanding businessmen alike will find dining here a satisfying experience, especially since the restaurant has been awarded two AA rosettes. Special 'Taste of Wales Weekends' are available.

Weekly Terms from £450.00
Bed and Breakfast from £75.00
Bar Lunch from £2.00
Lunch from £12.50 Table d'Hôte
Afternoon Tea from £1.50
Dinner from £24.00 Table d'Hôte (5 courses). Gratuities at Guest's discretion
VAT inclusive
All major Credit Cards accepted

1 Family Room, 2 Suites
14 Double, 6 Twin Bedrooms
All Rooms with Private Bathroom, TV,
Telephone, Radio, Baby-listening, Trouser Press, Hairdryer. Valet Service
Open all Year
Fully Licensed
Full Central Heating
Cocktail Bar. Lift

Conference Facilities
Children catered for
Dogs allowed. Parking Facilities
Tennis, Croquet, Swimming Pool
Nearby: Putting, Squash, Badminton,
Solarium, Sauna, Golf, Fishing, Riding,
Sailing, Windsurfing, Water Skiing,
Shooting, Hang-gliding

Section 7: Mid & South Glamorgan

Ewenny—The Heronston Hotel
Ewenny, Bridgend, Mid Glamorgan. CF35 5AW. Tel 0656 68811. Fax 0656 767391

It seems to us that the diversity and comprehensiveness of the facilities now available here completely justify the hotel's claim to be 'the most impressive business location in South Wales'. There are now eighty spacious bedrooms and executive suites, all equipped with modern amenities. Extensive and adaptable provision for conferences, receptions, banquets, presentations, dinner-dances and all similar functions is fully supported by secretarial, telex, word-processing, fax, translation, audio-visual and computer services. Despite all this, the hotel continues as a family-managed business, catering for family holidays and private parties. It has a heated indoor swimming pool, jacuzzi, steam-room, sauna and solarium. A central feature of the Heronston is the piazza-style *Ibis Court*. This is air-conditioned, can seat 250 for a formal meal, and be extended to link with the restaurant and pool area for larger exhibitions. Catering is by a team of chefs who pride themselves on the use of fresh, local produce, and have introduced a light speciality *cuisine naturelle* menu. Ewenny, easily accessible from the M4 motorway, is close to three championship golf-courses and the magnificent scenery and unspoilt beaches of the Heritage Coast. Wales' capital city Cardiff, with its ancient castle, world-renowned concert hall and superb shopping centre is less than seventeen miles away. Even closer there is tennis and sailing: the whole area is steeped in history, culture and folklore.

Bed and Breakfast from £56.00
Bar Lunch from £5.00
Lunch from £9.50 and A La Carte
Afternoon Tea from £5.00
Dinner from £12.75 and A La Carte
Gratuities at Guest's discretion. VAT inclusive. Credit Cards—Access, American Express, Diners Club, Visa

40 Double/Family Rooms
40 Executive Suites
All Rooms with Private Bath/Shower Room, TV, Telephone, Radio, Baby-listening, Tea and Coffee-making Facilities, Trouser Press, Hairdryer
Open all Year except Boxing Day
Residential and Restaurant Licence

Full Central Heating. Lift. Cocktail Bar
TV Lounge. Snooker Room
Conference Facilities. Dogs allowed by arrangement. Parking Facilities. Night Porter. Indoor and Outdoor Heated Pools, Sauna, Turkish Bath. Nearby: Tennis, Squash, Badminton, Golf, Fishing, Riding, Sailing, Clay Pigeon Shooting

Cardiff—Manor Parc Country Hotel & Restaurant
Thornhill Road, Thornhill, Cardiff. CF4 5WA. Tel 0222 693723. Fax 0222 614624

A driveway curving gracefully around a large lawn with two very beautiful mature cedar trees is a fitting foretaste of the grandeur within this superior hotel. Manor Parc has the space, facilities, decor and furniture to make it a truly exceptional venue for most types of special occasion. A purpose-built banqueting suite, catering for up to 130 people, has a panelled partition giving equally luxurious surroundings for as little as twenty guests, with a private entrance, cloakroom, bar and dance floor. This versatility provides the right atmosphere whether the event is a wedding reception, dinner dance or private party. To state that the hotel has international appeal is supported by the fact that the languages spoken here are English, French, Italian, Spanish and some German. Their spacious Cromwell Suite, suitable for executive accommodation or small private meetings, features specially imported Venetian-style walnut furniture. A similar distinctive elegance applies to the forty-cover dining room. Here, an extensive *à la carte* menu is accompanied by an eight page wine list to suit every palate and most pockets. Four of the hotel's twelve *en suite* bedrooms have south-facing balconies; the private tennis court is covered for all-weather play and there are three golf courses within a five minute drive. Manor Parc is in a quiet and peaceful setting, with several places of historical interest close by, and is only ten minutes' drive from the business areas of South and Mid Glamorgan.

Bed and Breakfast from £57.50 Single, £85 Double
Lunch A La Carte
Dinner A La Carte
VAT inclusive
Credit Cards—Access, American Express, Visa
1 Family Room. 2 Suites

1 Twin, 8 Double, 2 Single Bedrooms
All Rooms with Private Bathroom, TV, Telephone, Radio, Tea and Coffee-making Facilities, Trouser Press
Hairdryer on request
Open all Year except 24, 25, 26th December
Residential Licence
Full Central Heating

Cocktail Bar
Conference Facilities
Children catered for
Guide dogs only allowed
Parking Facilities
Night Porter. Tennis
Nearby: Squash, Badminton, Swimming, Golf, Riding

Section 7: South & West Glamorgan

Near Cardiff, Porthkerry—Egerton Grey Country House Hotel
Porthkerry, South Glamorgan. CF6 9BZ. Tel 0446 711666. Fax 0446 711690

The final approach to this nineteenth-century rectory is 'down the lane between the thatched farm cottages' and, once at the small luxurious hotel, no other habitation or road is visible. Within seven acres of lush gardens, with views down to Porthkerry Park and the sea, there are a croquet lawn and an all-weather tennis court. Inside the distinguished country house, each of the ten *en suite* bedrooms and all the public rooms have a rich and harmonious blend of superior furniture and fabrics whilst antiques, porcelain and paintings enhance every setting. One may dine by candlelight in the main dining room with its original Cuban mahogany panelling or, in the private oak-panelled dining room, enjoy sea views beyond the pretty gardens. The magnificent Edwardian drawing room, with its chandelier, figured ceiling and open fire within a splendid surround and overmantel, is an alternative retreat to the restful library. A feature of Egerton Grey is some superbly restored Edwardian bathrooms, a perfect complement to those rooms with half-tester or four-poster beds. Luncheon and dinner here are memorable experiences, with *à la carte* and *table d' hôte* menus that have received widespread praise and recognition. Everything is here for the truly exceptional conference, wedding reception or holiday break, including a warm welcome. And all around, countryside and coastline with numerous scenic and historic places of interest.

Weekly Terms on Application
Daily Terms from £47.50
Bed and Breakfast from £60.00 (2 persons)
Bar Lunch from £2.50
Lunch from £19.50 Table d'Hôte
Afternoon Tea from £2.50
Bar Supper from £7.50
Dinner from £19.50 Table d'Hôte

Gratuities at Guest's discretion
VAT inclusive. Credit Cards—Access, American Express, Visa
2 Family Rooms. 2 Suites
5 Double, 1 Single, 2 Twin Bedrooms
All Rooms with Private Bathroom, TV, Telephone, Radio, Baby-listening, Tea and

Coffee-making Facilities, Trouser Press, Hairdryer. Open all Year
Residential and Restaurant Licence
Full Central Heating. Conference Facilities
Children catered for
Dogs not allowed. Parking Facilities.
Tennis, Croquet

Near Swansea—Norton House
Norton Road, Mumbles, Swansea, West Glamorgan. SA3 5TQ. Tel 0792 404891

The Gower Peninsula has several claims to fame. It was Britain's first designated area of outstanding natural beauty (AONB), has three national nature reserves and no less than twenty-one sites of special scientific interest. On this beautiful, unspoilt peninsula, set in peaceful well-kept grounds just a few hundred yards from the seashore of Swansea Bay, is Norton House in the village of Mumbles. It is an early eighteenth century former master mariner's house whose decor and furnishings are in keeping with the elegance of the fine Georgian building. On grounds of comfort, courtesy and *cuisine* we give this hotel our highest commendation. Mumbles itself, just a short walk away, has good shopping, pubs and interesting places to visit. Gower can be enjoyed at any time of the year, with its attractive countryside, scores of coves and bays, good walks and many sporting activities. Norton House is also an ideal base from which to sample the many facets of Swansea: the Maritime Industrial Museum with its working woollen mill, an impressive leisure centre, an indoor market, the Dylan Thomas Theatre and a reconstruction of the world's first passenger tramline service that ran along the sea front from 1807 until 1960. Beside the marina development there are fine Georgian, Edwardian and Victorian homes under conservation orders. It was in Swansea that The Sunday Times Travel Supplement described a wine bar as '...the best pub found north of Salzburg'.

Bed and Breakfast from £60.00
Dinner from £15.00
Gratuities at Guest's Discretion
VAT inclusive
Credit Cards–Access, American Express, Diners Club, Visa
13 Double, 2 Twin Bedrooms
13 Private bathrooms
2 Private Shower Rooms

All Rooms with TV, Telephone, Radio, Tea and Coffee-making Facilities
7 Rooms with Trouser Press
Hairdryer available
Open all Year
Fully Licensed
Full Central Heating
Cocktail Bar
Conference Facilities

Children over 10 years catered for
Dogs not allowed.
Parking Facilities
Nearby: Tennis, Putting, Squash, Badminton, Swimming, Solarium, Sauna, Golf, Fishing, Riding, Sailing, Windsurfing, Water Skiing, Shooting, Hang-gliding

Section 7: Gwent

Abergavenny—The Llanwenarth Arms Hotel Brecon Road,
Abergavenny, Gwent. NP8 1EP. Tel 0873 810550. Fax 0873 811880

Perched on the bank of the River Usk and known formerly as Pantrhiwgoch, the restaurant and bars of this cosy hotel date back to the sixteenth century. Across a sheltered courtyard are eighteen attractively furnished bedrooms, all with *en suite* bath and shower, and amenities including telephone, trouser press and hairdryer. Every one has an open aspect over the River Usk or on to the lower slopes of Sugar Loaf mountain. There is a small residents' lounge and, adjacent to the restaurant, additional comfortable seating in a pleasant Victorian style conservatory. We were so impressed when we called in for dinner that we made a second visit very soon afterwards to sample the accommodation. Dining as non-residents we enjoyed a most excellent meal, well presented and pleasantly served and, on our return visit, a breakfast which offered plenty of choice and was accompanied by cheerful service. After settling our account, we introduced ourselves to our hosts, D'Arcy and Angela McGregor, and were given a tour round the rest of this friendly hotel. Children are made very welcome at reduced rates, and private parties, small informal conferences and wedding receptions are catered for.

Special Weekend Rates available
Bed and Breakfast from £49.00 Single, £59.00 Double
Bar Meal from £3.95
Lunch A La Carte
Dinner A La Carte
Gratuities at Guest's discretion
VAT inclusive

Credit Cards—Access, American Express, Diners Club, Visa
12 Double, 6 Twin Bedrooms
All Rooms with Private Bathroom, TV, Telephone, Radio, Tea and Coffee-making Facilities, Trouser Press, Hairdryer
Open all Year
Fully Licensed

Full Central Heating
Cocktail Bar
Small Conference Facilities
Children catered for
Dogs not allowed
Parking Facilities
Fishing

Chepstow, Tintern—The Royal George Hotel
Tintern, Chepstow, Gwent. NP6 6SF. Tel 0291 689205. Fax 0291 689448

For several miles north and south of Tintern, the Gwent/Gloucestershire boundary is defined by the River Wye, described by Wordsworth as 'The most romantic valley in Wales'. Lying in the shadow of the ruins of the famous Tintern Abbey, this seventeenth century inn was originally the Iron Master's Cottage, where it is said that he entertained lavishly. Today this practice still continues with the personal attention of the owners. The hotel is set in its own award winning gardens with large, comfortable rooms overlooking the gardens. The head chef uses the best of local produce and the menus are complemented by a fine wine list. This is a wonderfully relaxing place in which to spend a holiday or a few days break. The hotel can accommodate up to 150 people for weddings, business conferences or social occasions. Only five miles away is the quaint town of Chepstow with its medieval castle, well known race course and golf course, while in and around Monmouth and the Forest of Dean there are museums, castles, ancient iron mines and several nature trails to tempt the explorer. Although the region is so unspoilt, it is easily reached from Junction 22 of the M4 motorway.

Bed and Breakfast from £33.00
English Breakfast £6.00
Lunch from £10.95 Table d'Hôte
Afternoon Tea from £2.00
Dinner from £16.50 Table d'Hôte
Gratuities at Guest's discretion
VAT inclusive. Credit Cards—Access,

American Express, Visa
14 Family Rooms. 1 Suite
1 Single, 14 Double, 16 Twin Bedrooms
15 Private Bathrooms
8 Private Shower Rooms
17 Rooms with TV, Telephone, Radio, Baby-listening, Tea and Coffee-making

Facilities. Hairdryer available
Open all Year. Fully Licensed
Full Central Heating. Conference Facilities
Dogs allowed. Parking Facilities
Nearby: Tennis, Squash, Badminton, Swimming, Solarium, Sauna, Golf, Fishing

Section 7: Gwent

Newport—The Celtic Manor Hotel
Coldra Woods, Newport, Gwent. NP6 2YA. Tel 0633 413000. Fax 0633 412910

'What is this life if, full of care, we have no time to stand and stare?', so wrote Newport's famous son W H Davies. The tramp poet would have enjoyed the relaxed and timeless atmosphere at the impressive Celtic Manor Hotel. It is a fine nineteenth-century manor with stained-glass windows and Jacobean-style ceilings. Around it are well-kept gardens with fruit trees, vegetables and landscaped woodland with rhododendrons. To the inherent qualities of the house the management has added fabrics and furnishings in just the right styles together with modern amenities. The main staircase leads to luxurious bedrooms, each with a private bathroom, tea and coffee making facilities, colour satellite television, radio and a direct-dial telephone. Attractive four-poster beds adorn two of the rooms. There is a choice of restaurants: the elegant Flemish Renaissance-style *Hedleys Restaurant* offers a gourmet menu and outstanding specialities prepared by Trefor Jones, Welsh Chef of the Year. We were drawn, however, to the unusual *Patio Restaurant*, with its fascinating views of the surrounding countryside. The wine list, we noted, has a selection of sixty-five bins and these contain, amongst other choices, the best champagnes and the magnificent Rothschild red Bordeaux. For the energetic, the hotel has an excellent leisure complex with heated indoor swimming pool, solarium, sauna and gymnasium. In an hotel where everything is so correctly done, it is the staff who give it its personal character and there is no doubt that one of the main aims at The Celtic Manor is to provide individual attention for guests.

Terms on Application
Bed and Breakfast from £88.00 Single, £100.00 Double
Bar Lunch from £3.00
Lunch from £14.95 A La Carte
Dinner from £20.00 and A La Carte

Gratuities at Guest's discretion
VAT inclusive. Credit Cards—Access, American Express, Diners Club, Visa
4 Suites. 1 Single, 43 Double, 27 Twin Bedrooms. All Rooms with Private Bathroom, TV, Telephone, Radio, Tea and

Coffee-making Facilities, Baby-listening, Trouser Press, Hairdryer
24 hour Room Service. Open all Year
Fully Licensed. Central Heating
Conference Facilities. Dogs not allowed
Parking Facilities. Night Porter

Usk—Glen-yr-Afon House Pontypool Road, Usk, Gwent. NP5 1SY. Tel 0291 672302/673202. Fax 0291 672597

No newcomer to the Guide, this well-appointed country-house hotel has, however, a number of new features to enhance its reputation. Not only has the dining-room been doubled in size: the walls have been most attractively panelled in oak, providing a relaxing and comfortable setting for one to enjoy the genuine home cooking. The addition of twelve further bedrooms brings the total to twenty-six, all with private bath or shower, whilst a Victorian function suite, complete with lounge and bar, provides an ideal venue for parties or conferences. These changes, coupled with the personal attention of owners Jan and Peter Clarke, and a setting in spacious grounds shaded by magnificent trees, make the hotel excellent value as a centre for the numerous attractions in the area. Foremost among these are the sporting interests which include grass skiing, gliding, swimming, golf, fishing, sailing and pony trekking. Add to these the National Trust lands nearby, the lakes and reservoirs, stately homes, castles and monuments, and you have activities to suit virtually any taste. Following a day of outdoor activity, return to the hotel's most unusual library, octagonal in shape, almost thirty feet high and topped by a spire. A large, round maghogany table, seating up to twenty people, is the attractive centrepiece of the library, which serves as a conference/functions room as well as a place where guests can sit and read. Open all the year, the hotel offers special weekend and midweek breaks at reduced rates.

Bed and Breakfast from £43.50
Bar Meal from £3.50
Lunch from £9.00 and A La Carte
Afternoon Tea from £1.50
Dinner from £13.50 and A La Carte
Gratuities at Guest's discretion

Accommodation subject to VAT
Credit Cards—Access, American Express, Visa. 2 Family Rooms
1 Single, 17 Double, 6 Twin Bedrooms
All Rooms with private Bath or Shower Room, TV, Telephone, Radio, Baby-

listening, Tea and Coffee-making Facilities
Open all Year. Residential and Restaurant Licence. Full Central Heating
TV Lounge. Conference Facilities
Dogs allowed. Parking Facilities
Night Porter. Croquet

Section 7: Gwynedd

Aberdovey—Plas Penhelig Country House Hotel
Aberdovey, Gwynedd. LL35 0NA
Tel 0654 767676. Fax 0654 767783

We were lucky enough to call at the Hotel Plas Penhelig when the weather was superb and thus see it at its very best. The house, built in 1909, stands in seven acres of grounds, which include a beautiful walled kitchen garden, a nine-hole putting green and a croquet lawn, and has delightful views south over the Dovey Estuary. Indeed, one can hardly imagine a lovelier setting. The hinterland of Aberdovey is also brimful of interest, for the rugged mountains of Snowdonia are close at hand, Cader Idris lies to the north and the Talyllyn Railway is nearby. Guests at the Plas Penhelig can indulge in many activities in the area, ranging from walking, climbing, pony trekking and sailing to fishing and golf. This beautiful house, with its oak-panelled entrance hall, stained-glass windows and oak staircase, has been well developed by the proprietor, Mr David Richardson, into a beautifully appointed hotel. The furnishing of the bedrooms is particularly pleasing. The Rieben room is a delightful venue for small wedding receptions and conferences, private lunches and dinners and meetings. The food is based on fruit, vegetables and salads provided by the hotel's gardens and local meat, game and fish. Most of all David Richardson and his staff offer personal attention to their guests and they will be pleased to give you complete details of the hotel. Special Spring and Autumn breaks are available.

Weekly Terms from £270.00
Daily Terms from £49.00
Bed and Breakfast from £41.50
English Breakfast £7.00
Bar Lunch from £2.25
Lunch from £8.50 and A La Carte
Afternoon Tea from £1.75
Dinner from £14.50 and A La Carte
Gratuities at Guest's discretion. VAT inclusive

Credit Cards—Access, American Express, Diners Club, Visa
3 Family Rooms, 3 Double,
9 Twin Bedrooms
11 Private Bathrooms
1 Private Shower Room
All Rooms with TV, Telephone, Radio
Hairdryer available on request
Open from 10th March to 23rd December

Full Central Heating. Residential and Restaurant Licence
Cocktail Bar. Dogs not allowed
Conference Facilities. Parking Facilities
Tennis, Croquet, Putting
Nearby: Tennis, Squash, Swimming Pool, Golf, Fishing, Riding, Sailing, Windsurfing, Water Skiing, Walking, Climbing

Section 7: Gwynedd

Aberdovey—Maybank Hotel and Restaurant
Aberdovey, Gwynedd. LL35 0PT. Tel 0654 767500

Beauty is always in sight, or very nearly, anywhere along the Welsh coast, yet the Dovey Estuary, where it opens onto Cardigan Bay, is scenically quite exceptional. To the south the unspoilt beaches, salt marshes and dunes are enclosed in an almost mini climate, milder than most, whilst on the northern flank the pretty waterfront village of Aberdovey lies beneath a steep green hillside. Here, where the spirit of Wales is at its strongest, is an hotel with a very English name . . . The Maybank. The Maybank has only five bedrooms and its highly regarded restaurant seats just thirty people, yet, with so many of our readers having written in praise of its intimacy, comfort and good food, we needed no second bidding to sample the hotel ourselves. We can now say, with complete confidence, that Maybank will *please* you. The bedrooms are well furnished, spotlessly clean and contain modern facilities. There is also a definite personal touch, which you will appreciate the more when you have met Elizabeth and Paul Massey-Dinsdale, the owner managers. Under their influence, the hotel could hardly be more friendly and informal. Yet, the *bonne bouche* and major attraction of the Maybank is its interesting, ever-changing menu and excellent wines. The restaurant has clearly been 'discovered' by local people. So, if you do not secure a table reservation by engaging a room, you are advised to book well in advance. Fortunately, the hotel offers excellent value-for-money dinner, bed and breakfast packages to induce one to stay. We should mention finally that the nearest car park, about seventy-five yards away, is free to those staying at the hotel.

Weekly Terms from £244.65,
£139.65 (B&B). Daily Terms from £34.95
Bed and Breakfast from £19.95
Dinner from £15.95 Table d'Hôte
Gratuities at Guest's discretion
VAT inclusive

Credit Cards—Access, Visa + 3%
2 Double, 3 Twin Bedrooms
(All rooms can be let as Singles)
1 Private Bathroom. 4 Private Shower Rooms. All Rooms with TV, Tea and Coffee-making Facilities

Open all Year except 1st January to 13th February, Nov-mid Dec weekends only.
Residential and Restaurant Licence
Full Central Heating. Cocktail Bar
Dogs allowed
Free Parking nearby

Aberdovey—Penhelig Arms Hotel and Restaurant
Aberdovey, Gwynedd. LL35 0LT. Tel 0654 767215. Fax 0654 767690

Robert and Sally Hughes have made this old harbour-side inn into a quite charming and relaxing retreat. Not that it has lost any of its quaintness and character, but the comfort, especially in the guest rooms, is now of a very high order indeed, for a house with so much history behind it. The Penhelig Arms was known as Y Dafarn Fach (The Little Inn) when it was built in the 1700's, and, just as Aberdyfi has developed from a port into a rather trim and elegant little seaside resort, the inn has evolved into a mature hotel. The Penhelig Arms is, in our view, one of the best run and best positioned hotels in Wales. The views from here of the estuary and the mountains beyond are quite stunning and, on warm days, there is nothing more relaxing than sitting out beside the sea wall with a cooling drink. The general location is equally appealing, for here one is on the edge of the Snowdonia National Park and is also extremely well placed to explore the whole of mid-Wales. Yet, the attractions within the hotel are more memorable: a warm and hospitable atmosphere, furnishings and interior designs blended so carefully that there is never a jarring note, superior bedroom comfort with individual character and modern etceteras. Together with these changes, good food and fine wines have gone hand in hand. Fresh produce is always used and local fresh fish dishes are a speciality. Robert is more than an enthusiast about wine, he is committed to the subject. His cellars are extensive, show a wide depth of choice and his range of good-quality half bottles is equally impressive. He is also a fluent Welsh speaker, with an excellent knowledge of the area.

Daily Terms from £47.00
Bed and Breakfast from £33.00
Bar Lunch from £1.80
Sunday Lunch £10.50
Afternoon Tea from £1.75
Dinner £16.75

No Service Charge
VAT inclusive. Credit Cards—Access, Visa
1 Single, 7 Double, 3 Superior Twin Bedrooms. 5 Private Bathrooms
6 Private Shower Rooms
All Rooms with TV, Telephone, Radio, Tea

and Coffee-making Facilities, Hairdryer
Open All Year except Christmas Day and Boxing Day. Fully Licensed
Full Central Heating. Cocktail Bar
Children catered for. Dogs allowed
Parking Facilities

Section 7: Gwynedd

Aberdovey—Trefeddian Hotel
Aberdovey, Gwynedd. LL35 0SB
Tel 0654 767213. Fax 0654 767777

For over seventy years the Cave-Browne-Cave family has been synonymous with Aberdovey and this fine seasonal hotel, where space and elegance are the hallmark. It was in 1958 that a reader first brought the Trefeddian to our attention ('very comfortable; food and service excellent; the whole atmosphere most friendly; good golf'). Since then the hotel has gone from strength to strength and on our last visit we found a fully refurbished games room including full-size snooker table, table tennis, pool table, and a large indoor children's play area and television room, whilst the indoor heated swimming pool now has a solarium. Whatever the weather Trefeddian continues to satisfy modern expectations of comfort, *cuisine* and recreational needs. Yet, so much at the Trefeddian has remained the same. There has been no spoilage here. The air is still health laden, the well-known eighteen hole golf links is in full view of the lounges and dining room, whilst beyond it the beach has its own attractions for those not so minded. The village of Aberdovey is half a mile away from the hotel, so you will not be disturbed even in the height of the season. And, of course, at the helm are the family owners who have done so much over the years to make the Trefeddian such a lasting success. All this we were able to ponder recently over a leisurely afternoon tea in one of the attractive lounges. Here is an hotel with high standards of comfort and service, but one which has also retained an elegance which is so often lacking nowadays. This quiet corner of Wales holds many places of interest and is worth exploring either by car or on foot and the Trefeddian makes an excellent base.

Weekly Terms from £210.00
Daily Terms from £37.00
Bar Lunch from £1.30
Lunch from £7.00 Table d'Hôte
Afternoon Tea from £2.75
Dinner from £14.50 Table d'Hôte
Gratuities at Guest's discretion
VAT inclusive

Credit Cards—Access, Visa
7 Double, 30 Twin, 5 Single Bedrooms
4 Family Rooms
All Rooms with Private Bathroom, TV, Telephone, Radio, Baby-listening
Open from 20th March to 2nd January 1993
Fully Licensed. Full Central Heating
Lift. Cocktail Bar. TV Lounge

Games Room. Dogs allowed
Parking Facilities
Tennis, Putting, Swimming, Solarium, Snooker
Nearby: Golf, Fishing, Riding, Sailing, Windsurfing, Water Skiing, Shooting, Badminton, Bowling

Section 7: Gwynedd

Abersoch—Deucoch Hotel
Abersoch, Pwllheli, Gwynedd. LL53 7LD. Tel 075 881 2680

Jutting into Cardigan Bay is a strip of Wales which resembles Land's End. Towards the seaward end is Abersoch, which radiates out from the attractive harbour, petering out on a semi-circle of low hills and headlands. On this high ground, with the benefit of the whole panorama, is the Deucoch Hotel. When we first called here it was a glorious day and the situation of the hotel was shown off to its best advantage. New arrivals stand and gaze at the vista of coastline, yachts in the bay and the mountains of Merionydd stretching across the horizon. We were also much impressed with the obvious involvement of the owners, Stuart and Barbara White and their family, in the operation of the hotel, a nineteenth-century farmhouse. A good menu and a comprehensive wine list are features of the restaurant and attention is paid to the provision of locally grown fresh vegetables. In addition, an extensive bar-snack menu is available which can be served in the new conservatory overlooking the bay. Guests return often to this lovely hotel to enjoy its good food, friendly welcome and warm comfort. Those visiting Abersoch to take part in sporting activities are well served at the hotel. Ample space is available for parking both your car and your boat and arrangements are made with local golf courses for the benefit of hotel residents. Golfing breaks are available at several coastal courses including Abersoch, Pwllheli, Nefyn, Porthmadog, Royal St. David's and Caernarfon. Above all, however, one is made to feel at home here in most comfortable surroundings and in good company.

1992 Terms
Weekly Terms from £210.00
Daily Terms from £33.50
Bed and Breakfast from £22.00
English Breakfast £6.00
Bar Meal from £4.50

Dinner from £12.00 and A La Carte
Gratuities at Guest's discretion. VAT inclusive. Credit Cards—Access, Visa
1 Single, 3 Double, 4 Twin Bedrooms. 2 Family Rooms. 3 Private Bathrooms. 6 Private Shower Rooms

All Rooms with TV, Radio, Baby-listening, Tea and Coffee-making Facilities.
Hairdryer available on request
Open all Year. Fully Licensed. Full Central Heating. TV Lounge. Dogs allowed at Management's discretion. Parking Facilities

Abersoch–Neigwl Hotel
Abersoch, Gwynedd. LL53 7DX. Tel 0758 712363

Abersoch is a natural base from which to seek out the delights of the Llyn Peninsula. The objection to selecting Neigwl is that it is rather difficult to tear yourself away from an hotel which in comfort, food and personalities is practically impossible to fault. It is the highest rated hotel in its class in Abersoch, and rightly so. It had been explained to us that the Neigwl Hotel is *the* most perfect bolt-hole, a discovery of discoveries, so we doffed the mantle of the hotel inspector and took time off to stay there for a while. Now we find ourselves saying 'We can tell you of a marvellous little place, where you will get the most deliciously cooked food, and the most charming couple to wait on you. And don't forget to take your clubs, for the golf course is no more than a good chip shot away. And the beach–it's fine sand and the water is crystal clear–is no more than 250 yards away. And as for the views...' Perhaps we overlook one or two of the pleasant aspects of visiting the Neigwl, but may we be forgiven. Suffice it to say, Pat and Gerry Heptonstall, the proprietors, have created here an informal, yet comfortable atmosphere. Their bedrooms are very well equipped and everywhere is impeccably maintained. As to the cuisine? There is a saying that a menu is one thing and the fulfilment another. We commend you to the *food* at Neigwl Hotel, which is both imaginative and well presented. So, if you can drag yourself away from the splendid views or have a break from being pampered by the Heptonstall family, the Llyn Peninsula awaits your discovery.

Weekly Terms from £250.00
Daily Terms from £37.00
Bed and Breakfast from £22.50
Lunch from £9.50 Table d'Hôte
Afternoon Tea from £5.00
Dinner from £14.20 Table d'Hôte

Gratuities at Guest's discretion
VAT inclusive. Credit Cards—Access, Diners Club, Visa. 2 Family Rooms, 1 Single, 1 Twin, 5 Double Bedrooms. 3 Private Bathrooms. 4 Private Shower Rooms. All Rooms with TV, Tea and

Coffee-making Facilities. Radio, Hairdryer, Baby-listening on request. Open all Year Residential and Restaurant Licence
Full Central Heating. Cocktail Bar. TV Lounge. Children catered for. Guide Dogs only allowed. Parking Facilities

Section 7: Gwynedd

Abersoch—Riverside Hotel
Abersoch, Gwynedd. LL53 7HW. Tel 075 881 2419. Fax 075 881 2671

The Lleyn Peninsula, with a toe and a heel like Land's End in Cornwall, remains relatively unspoilt. The main north/south Welsh coast road passes it by, carrying away the tourist throng to other parts of Wales. Yet the peninsula must have the mildest climate and sunniest outlook in north Wales. A semi-circle of low hills and headlands makes the harbour town of Abersoch particularly pleasant and the palm trees which grow on the southern slopes are evidence of its equable climate. The Riverside Hotel takes advantage of another of the town's attractions, for it overlooks the picturesque harbour and has two canoes and a rowing boat which are available for the use of its guests. The hotel takes its name from the fact that the River Soch flows gently past its garden and on warm afternoons one can enjoy ample cream teas on the lawn. Inside the hotel a spiral staircase leads from the lounge, which overlooks the river, to an attractive dining-room. Another unexpected find is an indoor heated swimming pool. Stay here and you will not want for bedroom comfort, for every room has *en suite* facilities and is very well equipped. There is also a bridal suite with champagne and fresh flowers to welcome newly-weds, but to our minds the main attraction of the Riverside Hotel is the quality of the meals. John and Wendy Bakewell take great pride in producing unusual dishes such as fillets of lemon sole in saffron with mussel and chervil baked custard, as well as perennial favourites like peppered sirloin steak and fresh local plaice. Vegetarian dishes are also available on request, and a mouthwatering variety of desserts is offered on the sweets trolley.

Terms on Application
Gratuities at Guest's Discretion
VAT inclusive. Credit Cards—Access, Visa
2 Family Suites. 6 Double, 4 Twin, 2 Single Bedrooms. All Rooms with Private Bathroom, TV, Telephone, Radio,

Baby-listening, Tea and Coffee-making Facilities. Open from March to November
Residential and Restaurant Licence
Full Central Heating
Cocktail Bar
Conference Facilities

Dogs not allowed
Parking Facilities
Swimming, Sailing
Nearby: Tennis, Putting, Solarium, Sauna, Golf, Fishing, Riding, Sailing, Windsurfing, Water Skiing, Shooting

Anglesey, Beaumaris—Henllys Hall Hotel
Beaumaris, Isle of Anglesey. LL58 8HU. Tel 0248 810412. Fax 0248 811511

Henllys Hall is a country manor house built in 1852 on the site of the court of Llewelyn the Great, who was married to Princess Joan, daughter of King John. In 1294 the Welsh rebelled against the English rule and Edward I decided to build his castle at Beaumaris. His dream was never completed because he ran out of money. He gave estates to English families so they could 'police' this land he found impossible to subdue. One of these families was the Hamptons who lived on the estate until 1950. In 1852 Hansom of Hansom Cabs designed Henllys Hall as it is now. The Hamptons became a leading Anglesey family and most of them held the office of high sheriff and resided in the area until 1950 when the hall was auctioned and sold for less than £5,000 to the Franciscan Friars who set up a school for monks. It was bought in 1970 and converted into a fine hotel comprising twenty-four bedrooms all *en suite*, many with four-poster beds, a walled garden, tennis court, heated outdoor swimming pool, health place with sun beds, jacuzzi and a sauna. The food is as well prepared as the hotel—an international menu, concentrating on excellent local produce but offering a wide choice, complemented by a wine list which has been thoughtfully selected and which suits most pockets. The grounds extend to forty acres with fantastic views across the Menai Straits and Snowdonia. There is excellent sea, coarse and trout fishing. Visit Henllys Hall once and we guarantee you will go back.

Weekly Terms from £215.00
Daily Terms from £37.00
Bed and Breakfast from £31.00
Bar Meal from £3.00
Lunch from £7.50 and A La Carte
Dinner from £15.00 and A La Carte
Service Charge and VAT inclusive
Credit Cards–Access, American Express, Diners Club, Visa

8 Family Rooms. 6 Double, 6 Twin, 2 Single Bedrooms
20 Private Bathrooms
2 Private Shower Rooms
All Rooms with TV, Telephone, Radio, Baby-listening, Tea and Coffee-making Facilities. Open All Year
Fully Licensed. Full Central Heating
Lift. Cocktail Bar. TV Lounge

Games Room
Conference Facilities
Dogs Allowed. Parking Facilities
Tennis, Swimming Pool, Solarium, Sauna
Nearby: Croquet, Putting, Squash, Badminton, Golf, Fishing, Riding, Sailing, Shooting

Section 7: Gwynedd

Anglesey, Llanfairpwllgwyngyll—Carreg Bran Hotel Church Lane,
Llanfairpwllgwyngyll, Anglesey, LL61 5YH. Tel 0248 714224. Fax 0248 715983

Business and holiday travellers will find the location and the amenities of this comfortable hotel particularly valuable. It lies just across the Brittania Bridge, on the Anglesey side of the Menai Strait, offering first class road and rail access to all parts of the island with its 125 miles of unrivalled coastline. Close by, on the Welsh mainland side of the Strait, the Snowdonia National Park provides a wealth of natural beauty, with Llandudno, Bangor and Caernarfon combining historic interest with modern day activity. We have seen major improvements at Carreg Bran over several years, together with its growing popularity for many functions from wedding receptions to business conferences. Picturesque grounds and a wide choice of catering ensure that social and trade events become successful and memorable occasions. Every bedroom has an *en suite* bathroom, hairdryer, trouser press, direct dial telephone and remote control multi-channel satellite television. Within easy reach of the hotel there is golfing, sailing, windsurfing and a diversity of heritage. Guests can visit an Angora Workshop and Farm, a Butterfly Palace, Bird World, the Glanraeth Zoo or the Bodowyr Burial Chamber. The name of the village is sometimes abbreviated to Llanfair PG but it is world famous for its full length name: LLANFAIRPWLLGWYNGYLLGOGERYCHWYRNDROBWLLLLANTYSILIOGOGOGOCH.

Weekly Terms from £300.00
Daily Terms from £61.45
Bed and Breakfast from £49.95
Bar Meal from £4.75
Lunch from £9.75
Afternoon Tea from £3.75
Dinner from £11.50
Gratuities at Guest's Discretion

VAT inclusive
All Major Credit Cards accepted
4 Family Rooms. 3 Suites
1 Single, 14 Double, 10 Twin Bedrooms
All Rooms with Private Bathroom, TV, Telephone, Radio, Tea and Coffee-making Facilities, Trouser Press, Hairdryer
Open all Year. Fully Licensed.

Full Central Heating. Cocktail Bar
Games Room. Conference Facilities
Children catered for. Dogs allowed
Parking Facilities. Night Porter
Nearby: Tennis, Putting, Squash, Badminton, Swimming, Solarium, Sauna, Golf, Fishing, Riding, Sailing, Windsurfing, Water Skiing, Shooting, Mountain Walks

Anglesey, Llangefni—Nant yr Odyn Country Hotel
Llanfawr, Near Llangefni, Anglesey, Gwynedd. LL77 7YE. Tel 0248 72 3354

Take a little trouble to seek out this location and you are amply rewarded with high-standard accommodation, a licensed restaurant and art gallery. To reach this truly unique place, cross to the Isle of Anglesey by the Brittania or the Telford road bridge and follow the A5 trunk road for approximately eight miles. Just prior to reaching the Llangefni turn-off (A5114), turn left down a country lane. Nant yr Odyn is now within sight. The country hotel comprises beautifully converted farm buildings dating back to circa 1700, on the site of a dwelling recorded in the 'Chronicles of Caernarvon' as standing in 1282. From here, you can overlook the Malltraeth Marshes and the Snowdonia range, visit Anglesey's fine beaches and various National Trust properties, or take a twenty minutes' drive to the historic castles of Beaumaris and Caernarvon. At the Centre, works of prominent local artists are displayed in the Gallery and can be viewed by patrons of the adjoining restaurant, which is open to residents and non-residents. We were pleased to notice that an extensive choice of all the more popular dishes was available on both the lunchtime and the dinner menus, at most attractive prices. Our lunch was taken on the terrace outside the restaurant, where we received friendly and efficient service. The studio provides a conference facility for seminars or courses for up to forty people. Golf, tennis, fishing and windsurfing are available in the area, and there is a helicopter landing pad in the grounds of the hotel.

Weekend Breaks available
Weekly Terms Bed and Breakfast from £200.00
Daily Terms from £32.50
Bar Lunch from £3.00
Lunch from £9.00 and A La Carte
Dinner from £13.50 and A La Carte
Gratuities at Guest's discretion
VAT inclusive. Credit Cards—Access, Visa

4 Double, 7 Twin, 3 Single Bedrooms
All Rooms with Private Bath/Shower Rooms, Telephone, Radio, Tea and Coffee-making Facilities
Hairdryer available on request
Open all Year
Residential and Restaurant Licence.
Full Central Heating
Cocktail Bar. TV Lounge

Conference Facilities
Children catered for
Dogs not allowed
Parking Facilities
Nearby: Tennis, Squash, Badminton, Swimming, Golf, Fishing, Riding, Sailing, Windsurfing, Water Skiing, Shooting

Section 7: Gwynedd

Barmouth—Ty'r Graig Castle Hotel
Llanaber Road, Barmouth, Gwynedd. LL42 1YN. Tel 0341 280470

Set at the seaward end of the lovely Mawddach Estuary, the town of Barmouth has two miles of sandy beaches, safe bathing and fishing for mullet and mackerel. Half a mile from Barmouth, just off the Harlech road, is the Ty'r Graig Castle Hotel. It stands in two acres of attractively landscaped gardens overlooking Barmouth Bay. The sandy beach in front of the hotel is reached by way of a path from the hotel grounds. Built in Victorian times, the Ty'r Graig Castle has generously proportioned rooms and the stained-glass windows, wood panelling and ornate ceilings which typify that period of architecture. It is evident that the resident proprietors, Mr and Mrs David Wright, spare no effort in caring for the comfort and needs of their guests. Each day they offer four main courses, including regional specialities, and vegetarian dishes in the dining-room, which has good views of the coast. In addition, buffet meals are available in the newly completed conservatory bar, also giving superb views of the bay. There are twelve bedrooms, all with colour television and tea and coffee-making facilities. Four of the rooms have private bathrooms and eight have showers *en suite*, the four-poster room having a circular whirlpool bath. Special bargain-break terms make a stay in spring or autumn a tempting proposition. Those who are looking for a quiet informal holiday in what Ruskin described as the 'sublime Mawddach Estuary' can be sure that Ty'r Graig Castle Hotel will fulfil their requirements.

2 or 3 Day Breaks available
Weekly Terms from £270.00
Daily Terms from £44.00
Bed and Breakfast from £29.00
Bar Meal from £1.75
Sunday Lunch from £9.00 Table d'Hote
Dinner from £14.50 and A La Carte
Gratuities at Guest's discretion

VAT inclusive
Credit Cards—Access, Visa
7 Double (inc 1 Four-poster), 3 Twin,
2 Single Bedrooms. 4 Private Bathrooms
8 Private Shower Rooms
All Rooms with TV, Telephone, Radio,
Baby-listening, Tea and Coffee-making
Facilities, Hairdryer

Open from March to November.
Residential and Restaurant Licence
Dogs not allowed. Parking Facilities
Nearby: Tennis, Putting, Squash,
Swimming Pool, Golf, Fishing, Riding,
Sailing, Windsurfing, Water Skiing,
Hang-gliding, Hill Walking, Bird Watching

Beddgelert—Bryn Eglwys Country House Hotel
Beddgelert, Gwynedd. LL55 4NB. Tel 076686 210

It is likely that many people have heard of the village of Beddgelert because of the tale behind its name, which means the 'Grave of Celert'. The story is a fascinating one, but Beddgelert is worthy of your attention for other reasons, too. The village is protected by the National Trust because of its picturesque character. It stands just four miles south of Snowdon, in the shadow of Moel Hebog, at the junction of the A4085 and A498 roads, and is an excellent base for walking and climbing in Snowdonia. Beddgelert, however, is not just a good place to stay for a mountain holiday, for there are good, sandy beaches less than ten miles away, at Black Rock and Borth-y-Gest. You will find Bryn Eglwys Country House Hotel set in attractive grounds a short distance from the centre of the village. The hotel looks across the boulder-strewn River Glaslyn towards Gelert's grave and the impressive mass of Moel Hebog. The building, which was originally a farmhouse, offers comfortable accommodation. All the rooms have the benefit of central heating and all but four of the rooms have *en suite* facilities. During our visit we were impressed by the quality of the meals and the pleasantness of the service. Under the ownership of Barrie and Carolyn Barton, Bryn Eglwys is very much a family-run hotel and many guests return regularly to enjoy the personal service and warm welcome. Special weekend and midweek-break terms make a short stay here a most attractive proposition.

Weekly Terms from £255.00
Daily Terms from £43.00
Bed and Breakfast from £32.00
Bar Meal from £4.50
Lunch from £9.50 and A La Carte
Afternoon Tea from £4.50
Dinner from £13.50 and A La Carte

Gratuities at Guest's discretion
VAT inclusive. Credit Cards–Access, Visa
3 Family Rooms
2 Twin, 9 Double, 2 single Bedrooms
12 Rooms with Private Bathroom
All Rooms with TV, Telephone, Tea and
Coffee-making Facilities

Open all Year
Residential and Restaurant Licence
Full Central Heating
Cocktail Bar
Conference Facilities
Dogs allowed. Parking Facilities

Section 7: Gwynedd

Beddgelert—The Royal Goat Hotel
Beddgelert, Gwynedd. LL55 4YE. Tel 076 686 224/343. Fax 076686 422

Beddgelert, because of its situation within majestic Snowdonia, is one of the most memorable villages in Wales. The name of the village means the 'grave of Celert'—it is generally assumed that Celert was an early saint. The legend about Prince Llewelyn and his faithful dog, Gelert, only became associated with the village in the eighteenth century. David Pritchard, an enterprising landlord of the Royal Goat Hotel at that time, is said to have created the mound and erected the stone which became known as Gelert's grave. The present owners, Mr and Mrs E E Roberts, and their family have carried out an extensive programme of improvements and The Royal Goat is now a most comfortable and well-equipped three-star hotel. It has welcoming public rooms, which include two lounges, a reading room, a cocktail and lounge bar, two elegant restaurants and function and conference suites. There are thirty-two bedrooms in total, all of which have a private bath and shower, direct-dial telephone, hairdryer, trouser press, clock/radio, tea and coffee-making facilities and colour television—one can watch programmes, relayed by satellite, from all over the world! The food, whether one dines in the restaurants or takes a bar meal, is excellent and the personal attention one receives from the Roberts family and their staff makes one feel truly welcome. The proximity of the mighty Snowdon range attracts climbers, walkers and riders and, indeed, all who love awe-inspiring scenery to stay at The Royal Goat. Fishing on some of the finest waters in Wales is free to guests. Two self-catering cottages, each sleeping six persons, are also available.

Weekly Terms from £310.00
Daily Terms from £46.00
Bed and Breakfast from £33.00
Bar Meal from £5.00
Lunch from £8.75 and A La Carte
Afternoon Tea from £2.50

Dinner from £16.00 and A La Carte
Gratuities at Guest's discretion
VAT inclusive. Credit Cards—Access, American Express, Diners Club, Visa
1 Single, 14 Double, 14 Twin Bedrooms
4 Family Rooms. 1 Suite

All Rooms with Private Bathroom, TV, Telephone, Radio, Baby-listening, Tea and Coffee-making Facilities, Hairdryer, Trouser Press. Open all Year. Fully Licensed. Lift. Conference Facilities Dogs allowed. Parking Facilities

Betws-y-Coed—Craig-y-Dderwen Country House Hotel
Betws-y-Coed, Gwynedd. LL24 0AS. Tel 06902 293. Fax 06902 293

A total refurbishment and re-fitting to high standards was completed in August of 1988, recreating a true country house in period style with elegant furnishings and tasteful decor. The hotel is situated in a dramatic Alpine setting in secluded grounds, nestling on the banks of the River Conwy only minutes' walk from the tourist centre of Betws-y-Coed. Each one of the eighteen *en suite* guest rooms has an individual character and, from many, there are superb views of the river and nearby wooded slopes. This scenic outlook also characterises the *Terrace Restaurant*, which overlooks the waters edge. Here guests can select their four course dinner from the imaginative menu of the chef/proprietor. Dishes are freshly prepared, reflecting the growing interest in wholefood cuisine with the inclusion of some vegetarian dishes. This is an area abounding with nature trails and, amongst many other attractions, there are the Sygun Copper Mine, Llechwedd Slate Caverns, Ffestiniog, Conwy Valley and Bala Lake Railways, chapels and castles. The Craig-y-Dderwen Hotel arranges special leisure packages to include golf, pony trekking, skiing, fishing and shooting with useful off-season reductions. The hotel offers combined breaks with its associated hotels in Chester and Coventry (the latter being an Elizabethan manor close to the NEC).

Daily Terms from £41.00
Bed and Breakfast from £29.50
Breakfast: English £5.75
Breakfast: Continental £4.00
Bar Lunch from £4.95
Afternoon Tea from £3.00
Bar Supper from £5.95
Dinner from £15.95 and A La Carte
Gratuities at Guest's discretion

VAT inclusive. Credit Cards—Access, American Express, Visa
3 Family Rooms. 1 Suite
1 Single, 7 Double, 6 Twin Bedrooms
2 Cottages. All Rooms with Private Bathroom, TV, Telephone, Radio, Baby-listening, Tea and Coffee-making Facilities. Open All Year
Residential and Restaurant Licence

Full Central Heating
Conference Facilities
Children catered for
Dogs allowed. Parking Facilities
Croquet
Nearby: Putting, Swimming, Solarium, Sauna, Golf, Fishing, Riding, Sailing, Shooting

Section 7: Gwynedd

Betws-y-Coed—Park Hill Hotel
Llanrwst Road, Betws-y-Coed, Gwynedd. LL24 0HD.
Tel 0690 710540

Park Hill is situated in the Snowdonia National Park, in over one acre of well-kept gardens, overlooking the River Conwy, a nine-hole golf course and the village. The views are breathtakingly lovely as far as the eye can see. The hotel has eleven bedrooms (one being a four-poster room), nine with private bathrooms en suite. Each room has an early morning tea/coffee tray, remote control colour television, radio alarm and full central heating. Your hosts are James and Betty Bovaird who will be delighted to advise you on local activities, which include walking, climbing, fishing, pony trekking and golf. Our reception was warm and the only vacant room proved to be spotlessly clean and very well furnished. We enjoyed a very well presented dinner from the table d'hôte, which offered us four main dishes. Fresh produce from the hotel garden is used as often as possible. A well stocked bar will set up your appetite and is open late enough for you to enjoy a nightcap before retiring. The hotel has a magnificent indoor, heated swimming pool, with a jacuzzi type whirlpool at one end and a swim jet at the other. The pool complex is housed in a fifty foot pine log chalet, joined to the hotel by an enclosed linkway. The complex also incorporates a sauna, seating for relaxation and a verandah which opens out on to the well tended gardens.

Weekly Terms from £203.00
Daily Terms from £31.00
Bed and Breakfast from £18.50
Bar Lunch from £4.00
Afternoon Tea from £2.50
Dinner from £13.50 Table d'Hote
Gratuities at Guest's Discretion
VAT inclusive
Credit Cards—Access, American Express, Diners Club, Visa

2 Family Rooms. 3 Double, 4 Twin,
2 Single Bedrooms
7 Private Bathrooms
2 Private Shower Rooms
All Rooms with TV, Radio, Tea and Coffee-making Facilities
Open all Year
Residential and Restaurant Licence
Full Central Heating
Cocktail Bar

TV Lounge
Conference Facilities
Children over 6 catered for
Dogs not allowed
Parking Facilities
Indoor Swimming Pool, Sauna
Nearby: Golf, Fishing, Riding, Sailing, Windsurfing, Water Skiing, Shooting

Section 7: Gwynedd

Betws-y-Coed—Tan-y-Foel Country House
Capel Garmon, Betws-y-Coed, Gwynedd. LL26 0RE
Tel 0690 710507. Fax 0690 710681

'Possibly the smallest, and probably the friendliest country house in Europe'. With nine *en suite* bedrooms, most containing king-size beds, Peter and Janet Pitman's description of their transformed part-sixteenth-century manor house might be challenged on the claim to compactness, but no-one could question the hospitality. In Tan-y-Foel, 'the house under the hillside', your room will include fresh flowers, chocolates, bath robes and even tooth brushes for the forgetful. This almost traffic-free area has an air of peace and tranquillity making it a perfect place for relaxation, away from the hubbub of modern life. Beyond the mature gardens lie the magnificent Conwy Valley and the rugged peaks of Snowdonia, all the attractions of the National Park, acres of hillside farmland and gardens, and miles of public footpaths to complete the 'get away from it all' feeling. Within this little gem of a hotel, you will have plenty of superb fresh food, fish straight from the sea, local Welsh lamb, homemade bread and many more delicacies, all reserved exclusively for residents. Everything is cooked individually, to order on a daily basis, and portions are generous. Capel Garmon is where Roman legions once maintained a small lookout towards Sarn Helen, Saxon colonists worked the forested slopes, and Tudor yeoman erected the cruck timber framework of Tany-y-Foel's long barn. This whole area is rich is historic sites and structures, with mines, museums and mills adding interest. Return from these visits to convivial conversation around a log fire or, in summer, enjoy the heated swimming-pool. Tan-y-Foel is a no smoking house.

Weekly Terms from £280.00
Daily Terms from £47.00
Bed and Breakfast from £27.50
Afternoon Tea from £3.00
Dinner from £19.50
Service Charge and VAT inclusive
Credit Cards—Access, American Express, Visa
6 Double, 3 Twin Bedrooms (all doubles let as singles with supplement)

3 Private Bathrooms
6 Private Shower Rooms
All Rooms with TV, Telephone, Radio, Tea and Coffee-making Facilities, Hairdryer, Bathrobes
Open from February to December
Residential Licence
Full Central Heating
Cocktail Bar
Children over 12 years catered for

Dogs not allowed
Parking Facilities
Outdoor Heated Swimming Pool (May to Sept)
Nearby: Golf, Fishing, Riding, Sailing, Windsurfing, Water Skiing

Section 7: Gwynedd

Conwy—Castle Bank Hotel and Licensed Restaurant
Mount Pleasant, Conwy, Gwynedd. LL32 8NY. Tel 0492 593888

Visitors come in their tens of thousands from all over the world to stare at Edward I's military masterpiece, the thirteenth-century Conwy Castle. Its massive walls spread out to embrace a town of huddled houses and narrow streets. For comfort, stay at the Castle Bank Hotel, which is close to the western reaches of the town wall, has ample parking space and, surprisingly, enjoys a country-house environment. We have no hesitation in recommending the hotel whilst Sean and Marilyn Gilligan are there. They are a pleasant and enthusiastic couple who have worked hard to improve Castle Bank and to provide it with excellent facilities. Eight of their bedrooms have a private shower and toilet and all have colour television, beverage-making facilities and, a most thoughtful item, a hairdryer. The food at Castle Bank is excellent and varied and the selection includes both British and international dishes. We know a number of local people who eat there quite regularly. The Gilligans have succeeded in making Castle Bank a most hospitable establishment, for they are dedicated hoteliers who understand that hotel keeping is not just a job, but a way of life. The views from the hotel of the town and castle and across the estuary are superb. To underline the hotel's fortunate location, we should add that the Conwy Golf Club, excellent riding stables and opportunities for walking and sailing are all nearby.

Weekly Terms from £255.00
Daily Terms from £37.50
Bed and Breakfast from £26.50
Lunch from £9.00 Table d'Hôte
Dinner from £14.25 Table d'Hôte
Gratuities at Guest's discretion
VAT inclusive

Credit Cards—Access, Visa
3 Family Rooms
1 Single, 2 Double, 3 Twin Bedrooms
8 Private Shower Rooms
All Rooms with TV, Tea and Coffee-making Facilities, Hairdryer
Open from February to December

Residential and Restaurant Licence
Full Central Heating
Cocktail Bar.
Dogs not allowed. Parking Facilities
Nearby: Tennis, Solarium, Sauna, Golf, Fishing, Riding, Sailing

Near Conwy—Sychnant Pass Hotel and Four Seasons Restaurant
Sychnant Pass Road, Conwy, Gwynedd. LL32 8BJ. Tel 0492 596868. Fax 0492 870009

The peaceful setting of Sychnant Pass Hotel, just inside the Snowdonia National Park, seems far removed from the bustling streets of the walled town of Conwy. There is, however, a distance of just two miles between the town and the wooded grounds of the hotel. Brian and Jeannie Jones have created a charming hotel in this secluded spot. Elegant furniture and tasteful colour schemes please the eye, but the modern amenities which add to one's comfort have not been forgotten. Central heating maintains a pleasant temperature during the colder months and all the bedrooms have private facilities, colour television and a beverage tray. Four of the bedrooms are on the ground floor and one room has been designed with the needs of disabled guests in mind. The hotel's amenities are completed by a relaxation area, which includes a sauna, a solarium, a spa bath and massage and exercise equipment. The Four Seasons Restaurant has an excellent reputation locally for the high quality of the *cuisine* and the diversity of the dishes. Mr and Mrs Jones are happy to cater for guests who require special diets. A holiday advisory service to help guests to plan their excursions is available each evening. Whatever your choice of outings and activities, you will be made most welcome. The hotel is ideal for every member of the family, whatever the season.

Weekly Terms from £150.00 p.p.
Daily Terms from £50.00 (for two)
Bed and Breakfast from £30.00 (for two)
Bar Lunch from £4.00
Lunch from £8.00 and A La Carte
Afternoon Tea from £4.00
Dinner from £14.95 and A La Carte
Gratuities at Guest's discretion

VAT inclusive
Credit Cards—Access, American Express, Diners Club, Visa
2 Family Rooms. 1 Suite
3 Double, 1 Single, 7 Twin Bedrooms
All Rooms with Private Bathroom, TV, Telephone, Radio, Tea and Coffee-making Facilities, Baby-listening

Open all Year. Residential and Restaurant Licence
Conference Facilities
Dogs allowed. Parking Facilities
Solarium, Sauna
Nearby: Tennis, Putting, Squash, Swimming, Golf, Fishing, Riding, Sailing, Windsurfing, Water Skiing, Hang-gliding

Section 7: Gwynedd

Near Conwy, Llechwedd—Berthlwyd Hall Hotel
Llechwedd, Conwy, Gwynedd. LL32 8DQ. Tel 0492 592409

Berthlwyd Hall is a beautiful Victorian manor house surrounded by unspoilt country lanes and woodland. Amongst the many original features carefully preserved are the splendid oak panelling in the entrance hall, a magnificent galleried landing and staircase, carved fireplaces and fascinating stained glass windows. In five years, the resident proprietors Brian and Joanna Griffin, have achieved an excellent reputation for their *Truffles* restaurant and obtained high praise for the refinement in an increased number of spacious and luxurious bedrooms. The Griffins have a perfect pedigree as hoteliers. Joanna has attended courses on Institutional and Hotel Management, accounting and advanced cookery, putting these skills to use in her own catering business, followed by a period as a Conference Manager for Trust House Forte. Brian expanded his knowledge of good food and wine when the couple spent five years living in the gastronomic Perigord region of France. Today he imports his own wines direct from the vineyards and, as centrepiece in the restaurant, there stands a 140-year-old wine press which the couple brought back from Bordeaux. Berthlwyd Hall is an appropriately elegant base from which to discover the majestic peaks of Snowdonia, Bodnant Gardens, historic Chester, the dramatic coastline of the Lleyn peninsula and many famous historic houses and castles. Golf, riding, sailing, fishing, clay pieon shooting and a large artificial ski run are all within easy reach. A Welsh Tourist Board highly commended hotel.

Weekly Terms from £200.00
Daily Terms from £40.00
Bed and Breakfast from £25.00
Bar Meal from £3.50
Lunch from £15.50 and A La Carte
Afternoon Tea from £2.50

Dinner from £15.50 and A La Carte
Service and VAT inclusive
Credit Cards—Access, Visa
1 Family Room, 1 Four-poster Room,
1 Twin, 4 Double Bedrooms,
All Rooms with Private Bathroom, TV,

Radio, Tea and Coffee-making Facilities,
Hairdryer. Open All Year
Fully Licensed. Full Central Heating
Cocktail Bar. Games Room
Conference Facilities. Children catered for
Dogs allowed. Parking Facilities

Near Conwy, Rowen—Tir-y-Coed Country House Hotel
Rowen, Conwy, Gwynedd. LL32 8TP. Tel 0492 650219

Tir-y-Coed Country House Hotel is situated four miles inland from Conwy, off the B5106 road in the beautiful Conwy valley. It stands in an acre of leafy, landscaped gardens in a south-facing position. The owners, Ken and Gwyneth Kirkham, work hard to ensure that their guests enjoy a relaxing stay with consistently good meals. Their caring attention makes you feel welcome as a family guest. All the rooms are immaculately appointed and equipped with a private bath or shower room, colour television and tea and coffee-making trays. Most of the rooms have superb views of the garden and of the green hills and oak trees on the eastern edge of the Snowdonia National Park. Here you can take life at an easy pace, gazing at the breathtaking views and watching buzzards soaring on the air currents. Just a few miles away is one of the finest gardens in Britain, namely, Bodnant Garden, which is particularly beautiful when the rhododendrons are in bloom. What can you do in the evening at the Tir-y-Coed? Enjoy a good meal and, then, in a peaceful and tranquil setting, read about Welsh castles and history and the birds of Snowdonia. By day you can visit many interesting places in the area–castles, woollen mills, an operational seventeenth-century flour mill and narrow-gauge railways. Those who enjoy country pursuits will be spoilt for choice, for Snowdonia offers superb climbing, walking, pony trekking and fishing.

Weekly Terms from £205.50 (sharing Twin/Double)
Daily Terms from £30.95 (sharing Twin/Double)
Bed and Breakfast from £20.50 (sharing Twin/Double)
Bar Lunch from £3.00
Dinner from £10.45 Table d'Hôte
Gratuities at Guest's discretion

VAT inclusive
1 Single, 2 Double, 3 Twin Bedrooms
1 Family Room. 5 Private Bathrooms
2 Private Shower Rooms
All Rooms with TV, Tea and Coffee-making Facilities. Baby-listening
Trouser Press, Radio and Hairdryer available on request
Open from March to November

Residential and Restaurant Licence
Part Central Heating, part Electric Heaters
Dogs allowed by arrangement
Parking Facilities
Nearby: Tennis, Putting, Badminton, Swimming, Golf, Fishing, Riding, Sailing, Windsurfing, Water Skiing, Dry Ski Slope

Section 7: Gwynedd

Near Conwy, Tal-y-Bont—The Lodge
Tal-y-Bont, Conwy, Gwynedd. LL32 8YX. Tel 0492 660766

Situated on the B5106, five miles from the historic town of Conwy, this versatile small hotel, nestling in the tranquil Conwy valley, is a most convenient base for those wishing to explore the heritage of North Wales or discover the spectacular beauty of Snowdonia National Park. Bodnant Gardens is just across the valley, so there is much to do whilst staying here. Barbara and Simon Baldon have created a lovely welcoming atmosphere of comfort and caring at The Lodge. The decor is very tasteful and the *en suite* bedrooms have all been refurbished to a high standard with all the extras one would expect—central heating, television, radio and tea and coffee-making facilities; plus all the little unexpected touches which make a stay at The Lodge so special. The restaurant has a strong local reputation and the excellent standard of catering and presentation shows why. Much of the soft fruit, herbs and vegetables served at The Lodge are grown in its own garden and Mr Baldon makes good use of the high quality produce available locally including Conwy salmon, Welsh lamb, local trout. The menus are extensive and the wine selection most comprehensive. Wining and dining in the elegant and attractive dining room is, therefore, a most enjoyable experience, especially as the staff are so attentive and pleasant. The warmth and friendliness of all at The Lodge coupled with skilled service and attention to every aspect of hospitality, show why so many people return again and again.

Weekly Terms from £235.00
Bed and Breakfast from £20.00
Lunch from £5.50 and A La Carte
Afternoon Tea from £2.50
Dinner from £14.50 and A La Carte
Gratuities at Guest's discretion

VAT inclusive
Credit Cards—Access, Visa
4 Double, 6 Twin Bedrooms
All Rooms with Private Bathroom, TV, Telephone, Radio,
Tea and Coffee-making Facilities

Hairdryer available on request
Open all Year. Fully Licensed
Full Central Heating. Conference Facilities
Dogs allowed . Parking Facilities
Nearby: Tennis, Croquet, Putting, Squash, Badminton, Swimming Pool, Solarium

Criccieth—Plas Isa Hotel
Porthmadog Road, Criccieth. Gwynedd, LL52 0HP. Tel 0766 522443

Set in the centre of Criccieth, the Plas Isa faces south, overlooking the bay and the castle. It is an ideal base from which to tour Snowdonia and explore the numerous harbours and beaches of the Lleyn Peninsula. A reputation for providing comfort, good fare and a friendly welcome is most ably maintained by Pam and Joe Mayo. All the twelve bedrooms have a bath and shower room *en suite*, central heating and the usual facilities. Throughout the hotel there is an impressive quality about the furnishings and the décor. A testimony to the high standards of the catering, the attractive dishes and the courteous service, is the number of local residents who patronise the Plas Isa restaurant. There is a good wine list to complement the food menus. Places of interest within easy reach include the Lloyd George Museum, the renowned Festiniog Railway, St Cybi's Well and the distinctive house of Penarth Fawr. Driving due north, mostly on the A487, will take you to Caernarfon with its Castle and the Roman Fort (Segontium). Your return journey could take the famous Pass of Llanberis, below Snowdon. A very good selection of sporting activities is available in the Criccieth region, mostly outdoor, all of them certain to make you value to the full the wholesome meals and the warm welcome provided at Plas Isa.

Bed and Breakfast from £23.50
Bar Supper from £3.50
Dinner from £10.00 A La Carte
Gratuities at Guest's discretion
VAT inclusive
Credit Cards—Access, Diners Club, Visa
2 Family Rooms
5 Double, 6 Twin Bedrooms, 1 Suite

All Rooms with Private Bath/Shower Rooms, TV, Telephone, Radio, Baby-listening, Tea and Coffee-making Facilities
Closed 25/27 December 1992
Residential and Restaurant Licence
Full Central Heating. Cocktail Bar
Conference Facilities

Children catered for
Dogs allowed by arrangement
Parking Facilities
Nearby: Tennis, Putting, Squash, Swimming, Solarium, Golf, Fishing, Riding, Sailing, Windsurfing, Water Skiing, Shooting

Section 7: Gwynedd

Criccieth—Bron Eifion Country House Hotel
Criccieth, Gwynedd. LL52 0SA
Tel 0766 522385

These are sweet-sounding names to holidaymakers, for they conjure up pictures of a tranquil country house set near a pleasant seaside resort. Close by is the Lloyd George Museum, Festiniogg Railway and other scenic attractions of the Lleyn peninsula. Here the sportsman and the less strenuously inclined can be content. There are rich pleasures for the angler in local lakes and rivers and the ardent golfer need not travel far to reach some very good courses. Bron Eifion itself is one of the most civilised country houses we know. Its quiet mood and many lovely features seem to intimate that here will be found gracious living and Mr Bob Lilley, who is continually upgrading the hotel in period style, is on hand to ensure that this is exactly what his guests will discover. The house stands at the brow of a wooded estate just to the west of the town, off the A497 road to Pwllheli, and enjoys extensive views over Cardigan Bay. We dine at the hotel regularly throughout the year and the meals and service are excellent, with vegetarian dishes always available. Those who stay here talk of complete comfort. Those who live in this northernmost corner of Cardigan Bay also know that because the mountains of Snowdonia rise behind the town and since it has a sheltered south-facing position, Criccieth can be as mild in winter as south Devon. It is really unnecessary to add that you will be well looked after at the Bron Eifion, for in this long-established family-run hotel such things have always been the owners' first concern.

Weekly Terms from £266.00
Daily Terms from £40.00
Bed and Breakfast from £34.00
Lunch from £8.95 and A La Carte
Dinner from £17.00 and A La Carte
Gratuities at Guest's discretion
VAT inclusive
Credit Cards—Access, Visa
3 Family Rooms. 7 Double
(inc 5 four-poster rooms),

12 Twin Bedrooms
(de luxe bedrooms available)
All Rooms with Private Bathroom, TV,
Telephone, Radio, Tea and Coffee-making
Facilities, Hairdryer
Trouser Press available
Open all Year
Residential and Restaurant Licence
Full Central Heating
Cocktail Bar. TV Lounge

Conference Facilities
Dogs allowed
Parking Facilities
Helipad
Croquet, Putting
Nearby: Tennis, Squash, Golf, Fishing, Riding, Sailing, Windsurfing, Water Skiing, Clay Pigeon Shooting, Driven shoots,
Lloyd George Museum

Section 7: Gwynedd

Dolgellau, Ganllwyd—Dolmelynllyn Hall
Ganllwyd, Dolgellau, Gwynedd. LL40 2HP
Tel 034140 273

This country house hotel is as romantic as its name, 'meadow of the yellow lake', and the oldest part, *The Old Hall*, now used as the winter bar and private dining room, dates from the fifteenth century. Set in the Ganllwyd valley where the River Mawddach flows through on its way to its magnificent estuary and surrounded by formal gardens, there is an air of peace and tranquility here, a feeling of having stepped into another, more peaceful world. The hotel is run in a very personal way by the Barkwith family, whose home it is, and retains the warm friendly atmosphere of an Edwardian country house. Recently redecorated and refurnished in period style, all eleven bedrooms and bathrooms are individually designed to a very high standard. The *Conservatory Bar*, overlooking the gardens and mountains, provides the perfect venue for a pre-dinner drink before enjoying the superbly prepared and beautifully presented dinner served by friendly and attentive staff. The menu changes daily and provides interesting dishes using a wide selection of local produce. Dolmelynllyn is ideally suited as a centre for visiting the numerous places of interest, or for relaxing and allowing the 'overworked brain' to unwind. Walks abound–the Rhaiadr Ddu (Black Falls) are close by, plus several castles, slate mines, woollen mills and, of course, the 'great little trains'. For the fisherman there are now some ten miles of river and lake fishing free to guests. Total peace is assured since the hotel does not cater for functions of any kind: we were very impressed when we last visited and urge you to experience for yourself the warm and friendly welcome given by the Barkwith family.

2 Day Break from £110.00 (Low Season), £120.00 (High Season) Extra days pro rata
Weekly Terms from £367.50 (Low Season), £402.50 (High Season)
Bed and Breakfast from £40.00 (Low Season), £42.50 (High Season)
Afternoon Tea from £3.75
Dinner from £21.00 Table d'Hôte
VAT inclusive

Credit Cards—Access, American Express, Diners Club, Visa
1 Suite. 3 Double, 4 Twin,
3 Single Bedrooms
10 Private Bathrooms.
1 Private Shower Room
All Rooms with TV, Telephone, Radio, Tea and Coffee-making Facilities, Hairdryer, Bathrobes, Newspaper
Some Rooms with Trouser Press

Open from March to November
Residential and Restaurant Licence
Full Central Heating. Cocktail Bar
Children over 8 years by arrangement
Dogs allowed
Parking Facilities. Fishing
Nearby: Golf, Fishing, Riding, Sailing, Windsurfing, Water Skiing, Shooting, Hang-gliding

Section 7: Gwynedd

Dolgellau—Dolserau Hall Hotel
Dolgellau, Gwynedd. LL40 2AG. Tel 0341 422522

Situated amidst some of the most spectacular countryside, with superb views from every window, Dolserau Hall and its owners, Marion and Peter Kaye will offer you a very warm welcome. Built in 1863 to replace the original house, a famous Quaker meeting place, Dolserau Hall was a family home for over 100 years before being opened as an hotel. There are comfortable lounges to relax in and the spacious, airy bedrooms, all with private facilities, have recently been refurbished and equipped to a high standard. The *Winter Garden* restaurant, originally the Victorian conservatory with its lovely views of the Wnion valley provides an ideal setting in which to enjoy the *cuisine* of Dolserau Hall. The four course *table d'hôte* menu changes daily, offering home-made dishes carefully prepared by the Head Chef, Huw Roberts, using local fresh produce whenever possible. The menu is supplemented by selected *à la carte* dishes and there is always a vegetarian choice available. We were impressed to see that the hotel has written its own 'Out and About' leaflet giving ideas of things to do whilst in the area. There are beautiful walks, spectacular drives, railways, castles, gardens, mines, craft centres and many other interesting attractions. Detailed leaflets are also available to guests and Marion and Peter are always on hand to help you plan your days. If you are looking for peace and tranquillity in a setting which must surely be one of the most impressive in the whole of Wales, you need search no further Dolserau Hall should be your choice.

Weekly Terms from £295.00
Daily Terms from £42.50
Bed and Breakfast from £36.00
Bar Supper from £6.50
Dinner from £17.00 Table d'Hôte
VAT inclusive. Credit Cards—Access, Visa
3 Family Rooms. 4 Double, 4 Twin,
3 Single Bedrooms

14 Private Bathrooms
All Rooms with TV, Telephone, Radio,
Tea and Coffee-making Facilities
Baby-listening, Hairdryer available
Open All Year. Fully Licensed
Full Central Heating
Lift. Cocktail Bar
Conference Facilities

Children catered for
Dogs allowed
Parking Facilities
Nearby: Tennis, Putting, Squash, Golf,
Fishing, Riding, Sailing, Windsurfing,
Water Skiing, Shooting, Climbing

Near Dolgellau, Bontddu—Borthwnog Hall Country House Hotel
Bontddu, Dolgellau, Gwynedd. LL40 2TT. Tel 034149 271

If you have decided to explore Snowdonia, or just want to be as spoiled and pampered as one can be, stay in this superb country house and allow yourself to be looked after by Derek and Vicki Hawes and family. The hall is set in two and a half acres of garden, with fifteen acres of saltings, leading down to the river Mawddach, and an RSPB reserve adjoining. Derek and Vicki have created an atmosphere in which you can relax in traditional comfort and hospitality of a country house and you can be sure of their individual attention because there are only three letting bedrooms, each double, centrally heated, and furnished in keeping with the elegance of the house. Their restaurant is known for miles around. Enjoy pre-dinner drinks in the cosy bar, or on the terrace lawn overlooking the beautiful Mawddach estuary. Choose from *table d'hôte* or *à la carte* menus and complement the dishes of your choice with fine wines selected from the extensive wine list recognised by the Ashley Courtenay Cellar Search. After dinner, take a stroll through the grounds, or, for a wider view of Welsh scenery, visit the art gallery to look at the moodiness and the brilliance of the wild landscape, captured in watercolours, oils and prints. Take time to enjoy the gallery, you might find a treasured gift for a special occasion, or a lasting souvenir to remind you to return to this enchanting hotel, where you will always be sure of a welcome. Whilst you are at the hotel enquire about the Welsh Arts Council 'Collectorplan' service, which will enable you to buy works of art on a yearly interest-free loan.

All Prices pertain to 1991
Bargain Breaks rates on application
Weekly Terms from £295.00
Daily Terms from £50.00
Bed and Breakfast from £40.00
Lunch from £8.00 Table d'Hôte

Dinner from £14.50 and A La Carte
Gratuities at Guest's discretion
VAT inclusive. Credit Cards—Access, Visa
1 Double, 2 Twin Bedrooms
All Rooms with Private Bath/Shower
Room, Radio, Tea and Coffee-making

Facilities. TV and Telephone on request
Open all year except 23rd to 27th
December. Restaurant Licence.
Non-smoking Bar/Restaurant
Dogs not allowed. Parking Facilities
Fishing

Section 7: Gwynedd

Llandudno—Belle Vue Hotel
26 North Parade, Llandudno, Gwynedd. LL30 2LP. Tel 0492 879547

'Personally and professionally managed by the owners' wrote our inspector, which is high praise for a seventeen-bedroom seaside hotel in a prime position with lovely sea views. One need only study the *table d'hôte* and *à la carte* menus and, in particular, the wine lists with their Gourmet Bin page, to realise that here is something well out of the ordinary. Credit for this goes to Alex and Penny Gamez, whose hard work in making their guests feel welcome is rewarded by many of them booking regular return visits. A fully qualified chef produces the excellent meals, served in the attractive restaurant which has splendid views of the bay. We appreciated the jug of iced water brought, unrequested, to our table, and noted the happy atmosphere amongst the resident diners. Both menus offer a wide choice of appetising dishes. For overnight accommodation there are single, double, twin and family rooms, all of which have colourful soft furnishings, *en suite* bath or shower, direct-dial telephone, hairdryer and a video player to supplement the television. There is ample car parking behind the annexe, where table tennis and snooker are available. Nearby attractions include a dry ski slope and a variety of water sports can be enjoyed in the area. To the north, one can drive out on a toll road to a country park whilst inland there is the Welsh Mountain Zoo to be visited. Prominent amongst the scenic attractions along the Vale of Conwy are Bodnant Gardens and Felin Isaf Mill, whilst to the west lies all the beauty of the Snowdonia National Park.

Weekly Terms from £142.00 Bed and Breakfast, £199.00 Half Board
Daily Terms from £31.50
Bed and Breakfast from £22.50
Lunch from £4.00
Dinner from £9.00 and A La Carte
Gratuities at Guest's discretion
VAT inclusive

Credit Cards—Access, American Express, Diners Club, Visa
2 Family Rooms. 8 Double, 5 Twin, 2 Single Bedrooms. 7 Private Bathrooms. 10 Private Shower Rooms. All Rooms with TV, Video, Telephone, Radio, Tea and Coffee-making Facilities, Hairdryer
Open from March to November

Residential and Restaurant Licence
Lift. Games Room. Children catered for
Dogs allowed. Parking Facilities
Nearby: Tennis, Putting, Squash, Badminton, Swimming, Solarium, Sauna, Golf, Fishing, Sailing, Windsurfing, Water Skiing, Dry Ski Slope, Toboggan Run

Llandudno—Cornerways Hotel
2 St David's Place, Llandudno, Gwynedd, LL30 2UG. Tel 0492 877334/876207

For a small hotel, Cornerways is quite impressive. Quietly situated, it is only a short level walk from Llandudno's principal shopping area. All of the seven bedrooms have the benefit of *en suite* facilities. The rooms are decorated in a pretty and refreshing garden theme and are extremely comfortable. Each bedroom has colour television, clock radio, hairdryer and trouser press as well as tea/coffee-making facilities and complimentary toiletries. Also impressive is the standard of catering; the menu is both varied and well prepared, complemented by a nicely balanced wine list. Service in the restaurant could not be faulted and, indeed, this is a prominent feature of the hotel from the moment of arrival when you are welcomed by your charming hosts Sheila and Jeff Rumbold. Nearby lies some of Wales' most outstanding scenery and this popular resort is an excellent base from which to visit the coastal regions and Snowdonia. For the active there is golf, swimming, sea fishing and even dry slope skiing. For anyone seeking a country house style hotel close to the sea where a policy of personal attention is actively pursued and to whom good food and good value are important then Cornerways can be highly recommended. However, being both small and successful, it follows that accommodation should be booked well in advance.

Weekly Terms from £175.00
Daily Terms from £25.00
Bed and Breakfast £20.00
Gratuitites at Guest's discretion
Credit Cards not accepted
1 Twin, 1 Single, 5 Double Bedrooms

All Rooms with Private Bath/Shower Room, TV, Radio, Tea and Coffee-making Facilities, Hairdryer, Trouser Press
Open from Easter to 1st November
Residential Licence

Full Central Heating
Dogs not allowed
Parking Facilities
Nearby: Swimming, Golf, Sea Fishing, Dry Ski Slope, Victorian Tram Cars

Section 7: Gwynedd

Llandudno—The Empire Hotel
Church Walks, Llandudno, Gwynedd. LL30 2HE. Tel 0492 860555. Fax 0492 860791

We have a number of recommendations in Llandudno, Wales' largest resort, yet our list would be incomplete if The Empire did not stand prominently among them. We have visited it in every season, experienced weather conditions at their best and worst, yet our impressions remain constant. The hotel is grandly designed for holiday pleasure and when mentioning the array of facilities here we could, perhaps, be forgiven for overlooking one or two. An outdoor swimming pool with heated whirlpool; an indoor pool with attendant sauna, Turkish steam room, heated whirlpool and water-jet massage; a beauty therapist; and a video library are all at one's disposal. Yet the personal touch is paramount at The Empire. One recognizes it in the welcome, the very helpful service and in the quality and presentation of the food, which is far from the ordinary. And in the fitments and fittings, too, for the hotel has, for a number of years, been the personal crusade of the owners, Mr and Mrs L Maddocks. They have raised the standard of comfort all round. Many of the bedrooms boast marble-floored bathrooms and jacuzzi baths, Victorian cast-iron beds with pocket-sprung mattresses, and silk drapes and antique furniture. Adjacent to the hotel is 'No 72'. This Victorian town house has been lavishly restored to provide eight distinctive bedrooms of the highest quality. Needless to say, guests staying at 'No. 72' have the full use of all the hotel's facilities, including the three excellent restaurants, the bars, weekly dinner dances, et cetera. No hotel can supply *everything*, but The Empire certainly provides more than most.

Weekly Terms from £225.00
Bed and Breakfast from £35.00
Bar Lunch from £3.50
Lunch from £10.50 Table d'Hôte
Bar Supper from £8.75
Dinner from £16.50 and A La Carte

Service and VAT inclusive
Credit Cards—Access, American Express, Diners Club, Visa
4 Family Rooms, 7 Suites, 35 Double, 12 Twin Bedrooms All Rooms with Private Bathroom, TV, Video, Telephone, Radio,

Baby-listening, Tea and Coffee-making Facilities, Trouser Press, Hairdryer, Safe
Open from 1st Jan to 19th Dec 1993
Fully Licensed. Full Central Heating
Lift. Conference Facilities. Children catered for. Dogs allowed in certain rooms only

Llandudno—Gogarth Abbey Hotel West Shore,
Llandudno, Gwynedd. LL30 2QY. Tel 0492 876211/2. Fax 0492 879881

A house once renowned mainly for its literary associations, but now better known for its warmth of welcome and hospitality. A little girl on holiday in Llandudno in 1862 was the inspiration for the children's classic, Alice in Wonderland. Her name was Alice Liddle and she spent long vacations at Gogarth Abbey, then her family's summer residence. Indeed, Lewis Carroll wrote a large part of his celebrated novel whilst staying in the house. The near perfect location, which attracted the Reverend Liddle to this spot originally, remains totally unspoilt. Gogarth Abbey lies in spacious grounds on the quieter, select West Shore of Llandudno, and the views it commands over the Snowdonia mountain range, the Conwy Estuary and the Isle of Anglesey are spectacular in every way. Now a well appointed hotel, with every bedroom equipped with *en suite* facilities and all the usual modern sophistications, guests will find space, comfort and a wide range of leisure activities. There is an indoor heated swimming pool, sauna, solarium, games room, putting, golf driving range and French boules. Golfers may not realise that there are no less than six eighteen-hole courses within easy reach of the town. The Irving family, who are very well known in Llandudno hotel circles, have embarked on a major refurbishment programme of the hotel, which will ensure that Gogarth Abbey retains its position as one of the resort's premier hotels. And there are none in the town with a better or more quiet situation.

Weekly Terms from £288.00
Daily Terms from £37.00
Bed and Breakfast from £37.00
Bar Lunch from £5.00
Lunch from £9.00 and A La Carte
Dinner from £17.50 and A La Carte
Service and VAT inclusive
Credit Cards—Access, American Express,

Diners Club, Visa
2 Family Rooms. 2 Suites. 13 Double, 13 Twin, 10 Single Bedrooms. All Rooms with Private Bathroom, TV, Telephone, Radio, Baby-listening, Tea and Coffee-making Facilities, Trouser Press, Hairdryer, Mini-Bar. Open All Year. Fully Licensed
Full Central Heating. Cocktail Bar

Games Room. Conference Facilities
Children catered for. Parking Facilities
Night Porter. Tennis, Croquet, Putting, Squash, Indoor Swimming Pool, Solarium, Sauna, Windsurfing, Water Skiing, Shooting
Nearby: Tennis, Badminton, Golf, Fishing, Riding, Sailing, Hang-gliding

Section 7: Gwynedd

Llandudno—Headlands Hotel
Hill Terrace, Llandudno, Gwynedd. LL30 2LS. Tel 0492 877485

The Headlands Hotel has a superb location adjoining the country park at the foot of the 679-foot-high Great Orme's Head and just a few minutes' walk from the delightful rock garden known as Happy Valley. It has a marvellous view of the magnificent crescent-shaped bay of Llandudno and, beyond, of the scenic splendour of Snowdonia. In the evening, with lights glittering in the town, the panorama has a fairy-tale quality. The resident proprietors of the Headlands, Brenda and George Woods, devote themselves wholeheartedly to giving their guests personal attention and the warmest hospitality at reasonable prices. Guests return time and again to savour the views from the delightful conservatory upstairs, to sample the *apéritifs* in the lounge bar and to share the convivial atmosphere of the lounge. Of the seventeen comfortable bedrooms, twelve have private bathrooms and three have showers *en suite*. Beverage-making facilities, colour television, radio and direct-dial telephones complete the amenities in the rooms, some of which have four-poster beds. Fresh produce is cooked with care, so that the meals which are served in the bright and cheerful dining-room are full of flavour. There is hotel parking for six cars and, since the Headlands is at the head of a quiet cul-de-sac, guests can also park their cars in the road. The hotel is conveniently near the promenade, the shopping centre and theatres, as well as a host of leisure activities such as swimming, squash, golf, riding and windsurfing.

Weekly Terms from £190.00
Daily Terms from £30.00
Bed and Breakfast from £26.00
Bar Lunch from £1.50
Dinner from £15.00 Table d'Hôte
Gratuities at Guest's Discretion
VAT inclusive

Credit Cards—Access, American Express, Diners Club, Visa
6 Double, 3 Twin, 4 Single Bedrooms
4 Family Rooms. 15 Private Bathrooms
All Rooms with TV, Telephone, Radio, Tea and Coffee-making Facilities
Open from March to December
Residential and Restaurant Licence

Full Central Heating
Cocktail Bar
TV Lounge
Dogs allowed
Limited Parking Facilities
Nearby: Tennis, Putting, Squash, Swimming, Solarium, Sauna, Golf, Fishing, Riding, Sailing, Windsurfing, Water Skiing

Llandudno—The Ormescliffe Hotel
Promenade, Llandudno, Gwynedd. LL30 1BE. Tel 0492 877191

We like what we have seen and heard about this friendly hotel, which has been run on popular and proficient lines for a number of years. Many of its rooms provide dress-circle views of Llandudno's arc of well-washed sands, which are hemmed in by the limestone headlands of the Great and Little Ormes. One of Llandudno's long established hotels, The Ormescliffe has, in the course of years, expanded to take in adjoining houses and now claims an extensive frontage on the Promenade. Modernly equipped, yet retaining much of its Victorian character, a sense of solidity prevails as one passes from room to room, although no one could accuse The Ormescliffe Hotel of being dull. For those who seek it, dancing and entertainment during the season can be found in the recently extended and refurbished ballroom, there is a playroom where youngsters can let off steam and also a well-equipped games room. Because of its reputation for sound catering (the *table d'hôte* menus with good choices at each course are changed daily) the hotel's dining room is open to non-residents. Conference and meetings are also accommodated in the ballroom and in smaller meeting rooms. It is, however, as a family holiday hotel for which this two-star hotel is best known, and its tariffs represent excellent value for money whatever the season. Being Wales' largest resort, Llandudno offers a host of attractions to suit all visitors.

All Prices pertain to 1992
Weekly Terms from £235.00
Daily Terms from £35.50
Bed and Breakfast from £25.50
Bar Lunch from £2.50
Dinner from £10.00 Table d'Hôte
Gratuities at Guest's discretion
VAT inclusive
Credit Cards–Access, Visa

7 Family Rooms. 12 Double, 30 Twin, 11 Single Bedrooms
41 Private Bathrooms
19 Private Shower Rooms
All Rooms with TV, Radio, Baby-listening, Tea and Coffee-making Facilities. Trouser Press and Hairdryer available on request
Open from 6th February to 1st January
Fully licensed. Central Heating and
Bedroom Heaters
Lift. Cocktail Bar. TV Lounge
Games Room. Conference Facilities
Dogs allowed but not in public rooms
Parking Facilities
Nearby: Tennis, Putting, Squash, Badminton, Swimming, Solarium, Sauna, Golf, Fishing, Riding, Sailing

Section 7: Gwynedd

Near Llanrwst, Maenan—Maenan Abbey Hotel
Maenan, Near Llanrwst, Gwynedd. LL26 0UL. Tel 049 269 247/230

Maenan Abbey Hotel is a magnificent Victorian country house, which is set in spacious grounds and woodlands in the heart of the Conwy Valley. Situated adjacent to the A470 on the edge of the Gwydyr Forest in the Snowdonia National Park, it has a favourable position only ten minutes away from the famous Bodnant Gardens. There are picturesque walks to the rocky heights called Cadair Ifan Goch (the chair of the legendary Red Giant). Whilst nature has provided the ultimate in beautiful surroundings, the hotel has a praiseworthy reputation amongst those who visit the Vale of Conwy. It is renowned amongst local people for the quality of its food and its excellent value for money. Every Saturday night the locals' bar rings to the beautiful sound of Welsh voices singing in harmony. Although the hotel is equipped with modern amenities (all the bedrooms have either a bath or a shower room *en suite*), the original charm and character and the inherent qualities of the building have been retained. During the winter welcoming log fires blaze in the two bars and in the magnificent entrance hall. Throughout the hotel the décor and furnishings seem to be just right for the environment. It is good to see that great care has been taken both in improving the facilities of the hotel and in retaining the old country-house character. We strongly recommend Maenan Abbey, not only for its warmth and charm, but also for its excellent *cuisine*.

All Terms pertaining to 1992
Weekly Terms from £195.00
Bed and Breakfast from £42.50
Bar Meal from £1.50
Lunch from £7.85 and A La Carte
Afternoon Tea from £1.75
Dinner from £14.95 and A La Carte
Gratuities at Guest's discretion

VAT inclusive
Credit Cards—Access, American Express, Diners Club, Visa
2 Family Rooms
1 Single, 2 Double, 5 Twin,
2 4-poster Bedrooms
10 Private Bathrooms
3 Private Shower Rooms.

All Rooms with TV, Telephone, Radio, Baby-listening, Tea and Coffee-making Facilities, Trouser Press, Hairdryer
Open all year. Fully Licensed
Full Central Heating and Log Fires
2 Cocktail Bars. Conference Facilities
Dogs allowed. Parking Facilities
Fishing, Shooting

Infallible?
The answer is no because even as these lines are being written, hotel ownership, management and staff are changing somewhere. Invaluable? Yes, because by joining the Ashley Courtenay Circle (no extra charge) you can check up with us at any time during the current season.

A reminder.
Some of the tariffs in this book are those quoted for 1992. As prices will probably have changed for 1993 please check before booking. Please also note that the weekly and daily hotel rates shown in this book are for half board only (dinner, room and breakfast) unless otherwise stated.

Section 7: Powys

Crickhowell–Gliffaes Country House Hotel
Crickhowell, Powys. NP8 1RH
Tel 0874 730371. Fax 0874 730463

One hundred and fifty feet above a beautiful stretch of the River Usk, midway between the Brecon Beacons and the Black Mountains, Gliffaes stands distinctively, south-facing within twenty-nine acres of outstandingly picturesque gardens. The mature grandeur of the lawns and pond, the flower-beds, shrubs and trees, is reflected in the dignified but welcoming furnishings and decor within the hotel. It is family-owned by the Brabners, whose presence there since 1948 accounts for the consistent standards of elegance and comfort throughout Gliffaes. A comprehensive tariff offers a wide choice of accommodation and catering, including packed lunches for guests wishing to explore the numerous scenic attractions of this unspoilt and historic area. Salmon and trout fishing are foremost among the sport available to anglers, arranged by the hotel. Other activities in the vicinity include putting, croquet, bowls, tennis and a golf practice net. Approach to the hotel is by a quarter-mile drive, flanked by rhododendrons, a foretaste of the relaxing and impressive life-style to be enjoyed here. Atmosphere within Gliffaes is in the country house tradition, spacious rooms combining restful settings with memorable outlooks. Recently, a substantial outlay on re-fitting of the kitchens has ensured the continued provision of the very best standards of English country house cooking at realistic prices, presented with a friendly informality. The dining room and bar open on to a terrace, also reached via a sun-room adjoining the Regency style drawing room. Additional seating in the billiard room, with a full size table, provides something of a club atmosphere. All very tranquil.

Weekly Terms from £345.00
Daily Terms from £56.00
Bed and Breakfast from £32.00
Bar Lunch from £3.50
Lunch from £10.50
Afternoon Tea from £5.75
Dinner from £17.50 and A La Carte
Service Charge and VAT inclusive
Credit Cards —Access, American Express, Diners Club, Visa

3 Family Rooms. 19 Double Bedrooms (3 in converted lodge)
17 Private Bathrooms. 5 Private Shower Rooms. All Rooms with Telephone, Radio, Baby-listening, Tea and Coffee-making Facilities. Hairdryer available on request
Open from 26th February to 31st December 1993
Fully Licensed. Part Central Heating and Electric Heaters

Cocktail Bar. TV Lounge. Games Room
Conference Facilities
Dogs allowed in kennels and lodge
Parking Facilities. Tennis, Croquet, Putting, Fishing, Birdwatching
Nearby: Squash, Badminton, Swimming, Golf, Riding, Sailing, Windsurfing, Water Skiing, Clay Pigeon Shooting, Hang-gliding

Section 7: Powys

Llanwddyn—Lake Vyrnwy Hotel
Lake Vyrnwy, Llanwddyn, Powys, SY10 0LY. Tel 069 173 692. Fax 069 173 259

Lake Vyrnwy is the source of much of Liverpool's water supply... but what a source! This must be one of *the* most beautiful spots in Wales. Cradled in the Berwyn Mountains, the lake lies between Dyfnant Forest and the Snowdonian National Park. At any time of the year the colouring is magnificent, the atmosphere is one of infinite peace and the view from Lake Vyrnwy Hotel is one of the finest imaginable. Perched on the hillside, the hotel commands the length and breadth of the lake. It has attracted the tourist and the country lover from all over the world, but has never allowed this beautiful place to be exploited or spoilt. Every bedroom has *en suite* facilities and is very individual in terms of furnishings and decor. The atmosphere is one of a traditional country lodge, yet quality and comfort are never overlooked. Due to be completed at the end of 1992 is a new conference centre with a capacity for 120 people. The hotel has its own extensive market garden, from where daily the chefs select fruit, vegetables and herbs as these come into season. The varying menus are in a 'Grand Country Style', to fulfil healthy appetites and elegant tastes. For example, *Panache* of seafood with home-made salmon sausage may sit alongside Welsh lamb casserole with honey roast onions and wild mushrooms, both complemented by an extensive wine list. Then there are the daily pursuits: sole shooting rights over 24,000 acres, sole fishing rights on the 1,100 acre lake, walking trails, cycling, birdwatching, tennis and sailing, or one may merely sit back and contemplate the tranquillity and beauty of the lake and its surroundings.

Two Day Breaks and Special Honeymoon Package available
Bed and Breakfast from £69.50 (Double/Twin)
Bar Meal from £2.50
Dinner £21.50

Gratuities at Guest's discretion
VAT inclusive
Credit Cards—Access, American Express, Diners Club, Visa
35 Double/Twin, 3 Single Bedrooms
All Rooms with Private Bath/Shower

Rooms, TV, Telephone, Radio, Baby-listening, Hairdryer.
Open all Year. Fully Licensed
Full Central Heating and log fires
Conference Facilities. Children catered for
Dogs allowed but not in Public Rooms

Llanfyllin—Bodfach Hall
Llanfyllin, Powys. SY22 5HS. Telephone 069184 272

'*Multum in parvo*' ('so much in so little'), aptly describes this lovely country-house hotel which is set in four acres of magnificent grounds. Go to Bodfach Hall at any time between March and mid-November—if possible, go when the rhododendrons and azaleas are in full bloom—and you are likely to conclude that this is one of the most beautiful and tranquil spots in Wales. Beyond the perfectly tended gardens is meadowland, through which runs a trout stream. The house itself is over 300 years old and, thanks to the owners, Mr and Mrs Ian Gray, it still retains the charm of a bygone age. Oak panelling, ornamental ceilings and gleaming copper and brass contribute greatly to its restful dignity. The hotel is not lacking in modern comforts, however. There are nine charming bedrooms, most of which command striking views, and they all have a bath or shower room *en suite*, colour television and beverage-making equipment. Bodfach has a reputation for well cooked homely food. The four course *table d'hôte* dinner menu is augmented by a small choice *à la carte* and dishes for vegetarians. Snacks and meals in the *Powys Bar* are available at lunch time. There is a putting green within the grounds and in the unspoilt countryside of Montgomeryshire and Shropshire there is so much to see and do. For many people, however, the hospitable atmosphere of the house and gardens is sufficient attraction to bring them back time and again.

Weekly Terms from £240.00
Daily Terms from £44.50
Bed and Breakfast from £30.00
Bar Meals available
Sunday Lunch from £9.95 Table d'Hôte
Dinner from £14.50 and A La Carte
Gratuities at Guest's discretion
VAT inclusive. Credit Cards—Access, American Express, Diners Club, Visa

2 Family Rooms
2 Double, 3 Twin, 2 Single Bedrooms
7 Private Bathrooms
2 Private Shower Rooms
All Rooms with TV, Radio, Tea and Coffee-making Facilities, Hairdryer
Open from 1st March to 18th December
Fully Licensed

Part Central Heating
Conference Facilities
Dogs allowed
Parking Facilities
Putting, Fishing
Nearby: Tennis, Squash, Swimming, Golf, Fishing

Section 7: Powys

Montgomery—The Dragon Hotel
Montgomery, Powys. SY15 6AA. Tel and Fax 0686 668359/287

Overlooked by castle ruins, Montgomery is a town of established character and charm. It lies close to the Powys/Shropshire boundary, with Town Hill vantage point to one side and the Offa's Dyke Path to the other. A short drive away there is Powys Castle at Welshpool and the eastern end of the Welshpool and Llanfair Light Railway. Two museums, two golf courses, and fishing on the Wye or the Severn all add to the attractions in this area for the tourist. The Dragon is an old hotel, parts of it dating back to the mid 1600's, when it was a coaching inn. Although it has fifteen bedrooms, all with *en suite* bath or shower rooms, Mark and Sue Michaels promote their hotel as their home. They have implemented a programme of modernisation, including an indoor heated swimming pool in a separate chalet, to enhance levels of comfort whilst retaining much of the original character. A friendly atmosphere and attentive service were in evidence, and made lunch here an enjoyable break. Their menu and their wine list display a variety to delight the connoisseur and everything is realistically priced. This attention to quality applies equally to the pasta bar as it does to the main dining room. A unique feature of The Dragon is an enclosed patio, created from the former coaching entrance way, but the hotel also has a large private car park. Altogether an ideal centre for the touring motorist or cyclist, a relaxing base for the serious walker and a refreshing retreat for ramblers. Full central heating ensures a warm welcome for off-season visitors.

Weekly Terms from £206.00 (B & B)
Bed and Breakfast from £33.50
Bar Lunch from £1.75
Lunch from £9.75 and A La Carte
Bar Supper from £5.25
Dinner from £14.50 and A La Carte
Gratuities at Guest's discretion

VAT inclusive. Credit Cards—Access, American Express, Visa
9 Double, 4 Twin, 2 Single Bedrooms
13 Private Bathrooms
2 Private Shower Rooms
All Rooms with TV, Radio, Tea and Coffee-making Facilities, Telephone

Hairdryer, Ironing Facilities, Shoe Cleaning available on request
Open All Year
Fully Licensed. Children catered for
Dogs allowed by arrangement
Parking Facilities
Nearby: Tennis, Golf, Fishing, Riding, Shooting, Hang-gliding

Welshpool–Golfa Hall Hotel
Welshpool, Powys. SY21 9AF. Tel 0938 553399. Fax 0938 554777

Up until a short while ago it was simply a Listed farmhouse building on the Powis Castle Estate, but you will have no trouble finding the Golfa Hall Hotel. Quit Welshpool by the A458 Dolgellau/Machynlleth road, which runs parallel with the Llanfair narrow gauge steam railway, and after one-and-a-half miles you will arrive in picturesque territory—open countryside, wooded hills, a golf course and the hotel's eight acres of gardens and grounds. If you can drag yourself away from the view you should step inside and appreciate this lovely old house to the full. It is one of those small and satisfying places, blended so cleverly for hotel purposes that its ambience quickly makes one feel completely at home. There are just ten bedrooms; singles, doubles and twins, with some large enough to be easily adapted for families. We settled into a room whose frills and fancies made it both restful and most comfortable. A private bathroom and all the usual modern etceteras were at hand, plus some personal touches which made us feel especially welcome. The resident managers, are, indeed, very caring hosts. They describe their food as 'imaginative country cooking in plentiful supply'. They also clearly choose only the best cuts and the freshest produce, and augment these with appetising sweets, a wide range of Welsh cheeses, limitless after-dinner coffee, and some excellent wines, many available in half bottles. A fellow diner, a non-resident, asked us if we were enjoying our stay at Golfa Hall. We replied, 'the hotel and area are like an oasis in a desert'. On reflection that just about sums it all up perfectly!

Weekly Terms from £220.00 Single, £175.00 p.p. Twin. Bed and Breakfast from £37.00 Single, £27.50 p.p. Twin
Bar Lunch from £1.75
Lunch from £9.95 Table d'Hôte
Afternoon Tea from £3.50

Dinner from £18.00 and A La Carte
Gratuities at Guest's discretion
VAT inclusive. Credit Cards—Access, American Express, Diners Club, Visa
7 Double, 4 Twin Bedrooms (3 Rooms can be used as Family Rooms)

All Rooms with Private Bathroom, TV, Telephone, Radio, Baby-listening, Tea and Coffee-making Facilities, Trouser Press, Hairdryer. Open all Year. Fully Licensed Full Central Heating. Conference Facilities Children catered for. Dogs allowed

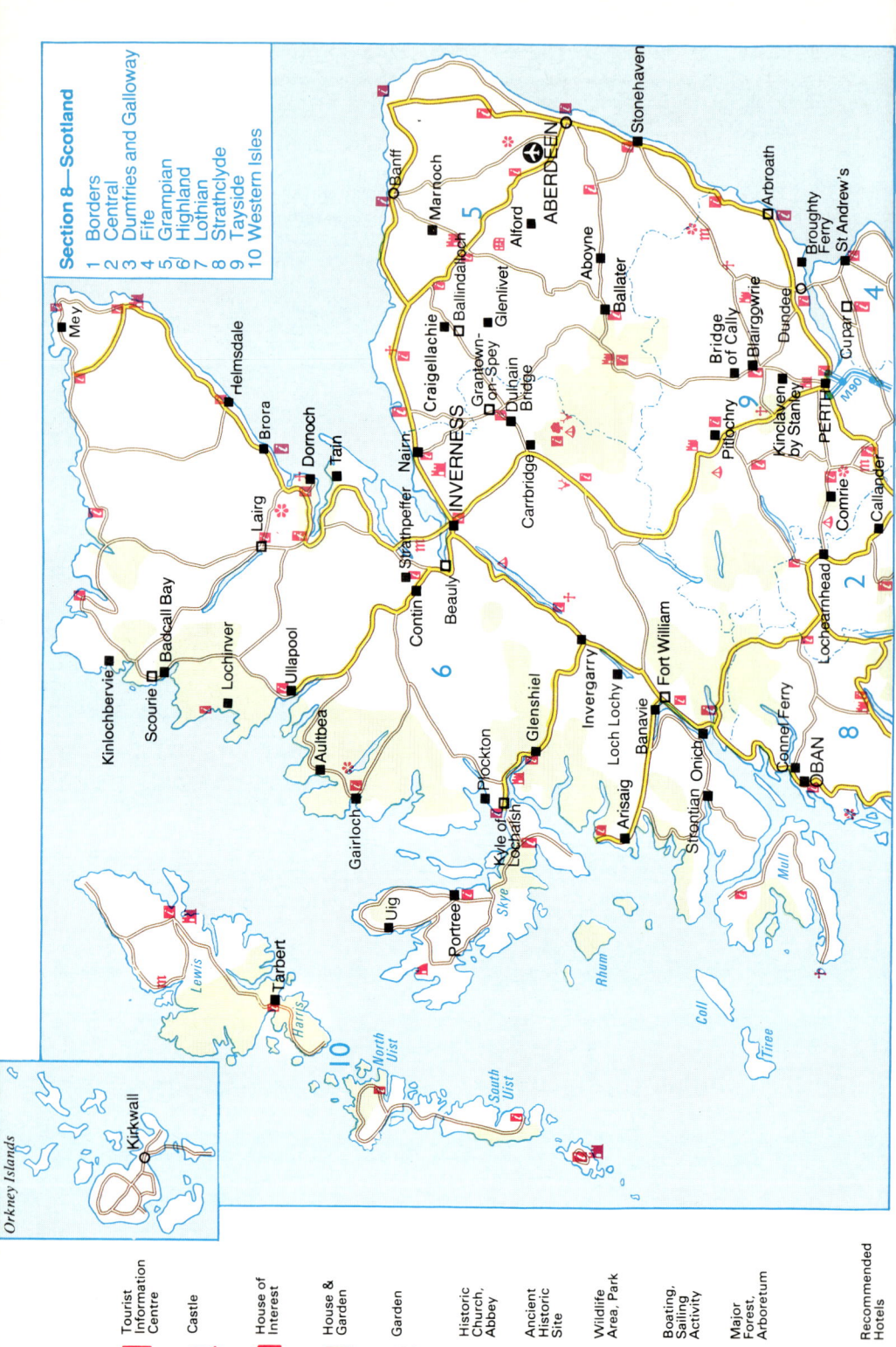

SCOTLAND

Urquhart Castle overlooking Loch Ness

Section 8 - Scotland

Borders, Central, Dumfries and Galloway, Fife, Grampian, Highland, Lothian, Strathclyde, Tayside, Western Isles

> 'Amange the bonie winding banks,
> Where Doon rins, wimplin, clear;
> Where Bruce ance ruled the martial ranks,
> An' shook his Carrick spear...'

Within these lines by Robert Burns is the very essence of Scotland. Whereas England is pastoral and cosmopolitan, Scotland is rugged with a fierce national pride. As a choice for a holiday it can offer a great deal more than most of its competitors. Tourists flock to the Trossachs, visit the mountains, moors and forests around Balmoral and Braemar, see the lochs and islands of the West Coast and trek across the green fields and rolling hills of the Lowlands and the mountains of Galloway.

If you are planning a first visit to Scotland our advice is to tour, but do not attempt to cover the whole country in one visit - one of the many surprises that visitors encounter is its size. Should you be travelling up from the south of England you can save time by making use of the extensive car/train services which are organised by British Rail. Although we prefer to visit Scotland for its winter sports and in early spring, most people time their vacations during the summer months and it is, therefore, a sound policy to plan your touring holiday in advance and secure, where possible, your hotel accommodation beforehand.

Golf is Scotland's national game and here you will find some of the most challenging courses in the world. Bring also your fishing tackle and your gun for you can enjoy water sport and game in plentiful supply. Finally, do also come forearmed with some knowledge of Scotland's fascinating and turbulent history. Any time spent in preparation will be repaid many times through the enrichment of your holiday.

Highlands Scene

Section 8: Borders

Dolphinton, Near West Linton—Dolphinton House Hotel
Dolphinton, Near West Linton, Peebles-shire. EH46 7AB. Tel 0968 82286

For more than 400 years the 186 acres surrounding Dolphinton House have belonged to the Mackenzie family. The present red sandstone house was started in 1801, on the site of an older manor, facing the dramatic rhododendron covered South Hill across the valley. The hotel, opened in 1987, is operated by Arthur and Susan Bell, owners of the *Scottish Gourmet*. Keir Hill, in the grounds, contains the unexcavated remains of an Iron Age fort. Guests are welcome to climb to its top through the beech woods and look down the valleys of both the Tweed and Clyde rivers. The Master Chef and his team preside over the hotel kitchen using only the finest of Scotland's great raw materials. Menus are changed daily to suit the seasons. Detailed research from leading wine experts has gone into the creation of a keenly priced, comprehensive wine list. Arthur Bell's philosophy is that fine wines are the essential complement to gourmet cooking. His view is that it is better to serve a guest with a top quality wine at a reasonable price than to ruin a superb meal with an indifferent plonk! All the bedrooms have *en suite* bathrooms or showers. Some have their own lounges and all are furnished carefully with antique prints, delicate Victorian Ayrshire lace, Laura Ashley wallpapers and the little touches that help to re-create the atmosphere of a Victorian country house. Tea and coffee-making facilities and colour television in each room are provided and there is an extensive library of interesting books. If you stay at the Dolphinton once, you will return again and again to this relaxing haven from the pace of modern life.

Daily Terms from £59.50
Bed and Breakfast from £48.25
Bar Lunch from £5.00
Lunch from £8.95 Table D'Hôte
Afternoon Tea from £1.25
Dinner from £19.50 Table D'Hôte

No Service Charge. VAT inclusive
Credit Cards—Access, American Express, Diners Club, Visa
2 Suites. 8 Double, 2 Twin Bedrooms
All Rooms with Private Bath/Shower room, TV, Telephone, Radio, Tea and

Coffee-making Facilities, Hairdryer
8 Rooms with Trouser Press
Open all Year. Fully Licensed. Full C H.
Cocktail Bar. Conference Facilities.
Children catered for. Dogs allowed in Bedrooms only. Parking Facilities

Hawick—Kirklands Hotel
West Stewart Place, Hawick, Roxburghshire. TD9 8BH. Tel 0450 72263

It is appropriate that Hawick should appear at the beginning of our Scottish chapter, because for many Sassenachs this Borders town is their first halting place in Scotland. It is pleasantly poised at the confluence of Slitrig Water and the River Teviot, about halfway between Carlisle and Edinburgh on the main A7 road. The Kirklands Hotel is also a great attraction. It has the immense advantage of being just a few minutes' walk from the centre of Hawick, although from the quiet of the hotel garden there is a pleasant outlook across the town and surrounding hills. Barrie Newland has made this charming Victorian house into an immaculate and hospitable hotel, which he has extensively refurbished in the style of the period. Centrally heated thoughout, the hotel has spacious bedrooms, which are well equipped with colour television, radio, telephone and beverage-making facilities. We enjoyed the friendly atmosphere at the Kirklands when we called. The hotel is warm and comfortable and the food is first class. The owner has built up an excellent reputation for his interesting and ambitious *à la carte* menus, which he complements with a sensible and well-balanced wine list. Whatever brings you to this famous wool and knitting town, do seek out the Kirklands Hotels in West Stewart Place. Families and businessmen will enjoy true Scottish hospitality from Mr Newland and his staff.

Weekly Terms from £250.00
Daily Terms from £70.00 Double, £52.00 Single
Bed and Breakfast from £50.00
Bar Meal from £4.95.
Lunch from £9.50 and A La Carte
Dinner from £15.00 and A La Carte
Gratuities at Guest's Discretion
VAT inclusive

Credit Cards—Access, American Express, Diners Club, Visa
7 Double, 5 Twin Bedrooms
(Family Rooms available)
10 Private Bathrooms
2 Private Shower Room
All Rooms with TV, Telephone, Radio, Tea and Coffee-making Facilities, Baby-listening,

Hairdryer, Trouser Press
Open all Year. Fully Licensed
Full Central Heating
Cocktail Bar. Games Room
Dogs allowed
Parking Facilities. Croquet
Nearby: Tennis, Putting, Squash, Swimming Pool, Solarium, Sauna, Golf, Fishing, Riding, Shooting

Section 8: Borders

Jedburgh—The Glenfriars Hotel
The Friars, Jedburgh, Borders. TD8 6BN. Tel 0835 62000

Despite the turbulent history of the area, recalled by the presence of several castles, battlefields, historic ruins and monuments, one's overall impression of the Borders is of soft green rolling hills and lush valleys. Sir Walter Scott and John Buchan are just two of the many famous authors who have used this area as a romantic setting to some of their novels. Such famous salmon rivers as the Tweed and Teviot meander across the country to the high cliffs, secluded harbours and beaches of the Berwick coastline. In addition to the historic landmarks referred to above, there are many other places of interest in the locality for the discerning traveller. And where better to stay than Glenfriars Hotel standing in its own grounds, overlooking Jedburgh, yet just a short walk from the town centre. Only recently opened but already gaining quite a reputation in the area, this hotel imparts the friendly atmosphere of a well run comfortable establishment. All the *en suite* bedrooms are tastefully furnished with modern comforts, including electric blankets. The cooking is done by Mrs Bywater and is of the highest standard, with an emphasis on local prime beef and lamb and special diets are willingly catered for. The hotel has a pick-up service for guests arriving by coach or bus in the Borders, just another instance of the caring attitude of the owners.

Prices pertain to 1992
Weekly Terms from £295.00
Daily Terms from £46.50
Bed and Breakfast from £32.00
Lunch from £6.00 Table d'Hôte
Dinner from £14.50 Table d'Hôte
Gratuities at Guest's discretion
VAT inclusive

Credit Cards—Access, American Express, Visa
2 Double, 2 Twin, 2 Single Bedrooms
3 Private Bathrooms. 3 Private Shower Rooms. All Rooms with TV, Radio, Tea and Coffee-making Facilities, Hairdryer, Electric Blanket

Open All Year except Christmas and New Year. Residential Licence
Full Central Heating
Children catered for. Dogs allowed
Parking Facilities. Nearby: Tennis, Squash, Badminton, Swimming, Solarium, Sauna, Golf, Fishing, Riding, Shooting

Kelso—Sunlaws House Hotel
Sunlaws by Kelso, Roxburghshire. TD5 8JZ. Tel 05735 331. Fax 05735 611

The number of people who have said that this is one of the most elegant small hotels in Scotland increases. Its owner, the Duke of Roxburghe, has adapted the stately house near Kelso into an hotel of great charm, having purposely retained much of the atmosphere of a Scottish family house. Thus guests come to shoot and fish (there is a rod and gun room for equipment, a drying room for clothes and freezers to store game and fish), play golf on local courses and go pony trekking and riding from various stables. If you simply want to take life easily for a while, then the hotel's 200 acres of gardens and parkland, which stretch along the banks of the Teviot, offer rest and seclusion. The house itself is beautifully preserved. There is a delightful conservatory, club-like library bar, comfortable drawing room and most pleasant dining room. The twenty-two bedrooms, all furnished to his Grace's own taste, culminate in the splendid *Bowmont Suite*. The *cuisine* is in character with the rest of the house. In their respective seasons there are grouse, venison and pheasant from the Duke's estate, and salmon and trout from the Tweed—all cooked with great flair by chef David Bates. To complement your meal you may even select a wine from the Duke's personal cellars at nearby Floors Castle–open to the public on most days in the summer and housing wonderful collections of tapestries, porcelain and paintings. Kelso, straddling the Tweed river, is a handsome town of cobbled streets and tall town houses. This is the area that inspired Sir Walter Scott to write his novels, incorporating many local legends. Sunlaws House in the Tweed Valley ... an outstanding hotel attraction in one of Scotland's chief glories.

Weekly Terms on Application
Bed and Breakfast from £82.00
Bar Lunch from £6.50
Lunch from £14.50 Table D'Hôte
Afternoon Tea from £4.75. Dinner £25.00
Gratuities at Guest's Discretion. VAT

inclusive. Credit Cards—Access, American Express, Diners Club, Visa
3 Family Rooms. 1 Suite. 10 Double, 1 Single, 10 Twin Bedrooms
22 Rooms with Private Bathroom, TV, Telephone, Radio, Tea and Coffee-making

Facilities, Hairdryer. 10 Rooms with Trouser Press. Baby-listening available
Open All Year. Fully Licensed. Full Central Heating. Cocktail Bar. Conference Facilities. Children catered for. Dogs allowed. Parking Facilities. Night Porter

Section 8: Borders

Peebles—Cringletie House Hotel
Peebles, Borders. EH45 8PL. Tel 072 13 233. Fax 07213 244

We have been happy to recommend this mansion house of character and charm for twenty years, for, under the personal direction of Mr and Mrs Stanley Maguire, high standards are maintained. The hotel stands well back from the main Edinburgh/Peebles road (A703) and is surrounded by over twenty-eight acres of beautiful gardens and woodland. During the time we have known Cringletie House it has built up an enviable reputation for its outstanding *cuisine*, and lovers of good food come from far and wide for the enticing delicacies and the wines which await them. On the accommodation side, Cringletie House is not lacking either—the well equipped, spacious bedrooms are attractively decorated, all have have their own bathrooms, colour television, telephone, trouser press and hairdryer. Other amenities include an attractive cocktail bar, which was formerly the library, a non-smoking lounge, a lift and central heating. Outside there are facilities for croquet, tennis and putting within the extensive grounds, with a first-class golf course at Peebles just two miles away. Trout and salmon fishing on the nearby River Tweed can also be arranged. Finally, with Edinburgh a mere twenty miles away, Cringletie House makes an excellent centre from which to see the many beauty spots and such local places of historic interest as Traquair House and the Border abbeys.

Bed and Breakfast from £43.00 (sharing Twin/Double)
Lunch from £5.50 Table D'Hôte
Sunday Lunch £14.00 Table D'Hôte
Dinner £23.50 Table D'Hôte
Gratuities at Guest's Discretion
VAT inclusive
Credit Cards—Access, Visa

4 Double, 8 Twin, 1 Single Bedroom (2 Rooms can be let as Family Rooms)
All Rooms with Private Bathroom, TV, Telephone, Baby-listening, Trouser Press, Hairdryer, Books, Magazines
Open from early March to 2nd January
Fully Licensed
Full Central Heating

Lift
Cocktail Bar
Children catered for
Dogs allowed
Parking Facilities
Hard Tennis Court, Croquet, Putting
Nearby: Fishing, Riding

Selkirk—Heatherlie House
Heatherlie Park, Selkirk, Borders. TD7 5AL. Tel 0750 21200

Most visitors to Scotland from across the Border tend to travel northwards in stages and many see the Borders town of Selkirk as a useful first stepping-stone on their tours. Yet, stay in this famous touring and fishing centre for a day or two and we wager you will wish to stop and put down roots for a while. The Ettrick Forest rises behind, the River Ettrick (excellent salmon and trout) flows past, and the town and surrounds abound with literary and historic interest. And then there is Heatherlie House Hotel. It is quiet and well situated in wooded grounds, is privately owned and personally run by the proprietors, Mr and Mrs S Fleming, and, of course, Mrs Fleming, a Bavarian by birth, has made quite a mark locally and beyond with her food. She avoids the modish; her menus include dishes from Scotland, the continent and the Middle East, personally prepared and attractively presented. There is also an excellent and very reasonably priced wine selection. Nor will you want for comfort if you stay at Heatherlie House. The hotel is spotlessly clean, nicely decorated and every bedroom boasts a private bathroom, television and beverage-making facilities. In the vicinity the opportunities for sport and relaxation seem limitless: rambling; riding; golf; fishing; country mansions; gardens; Sir Walter Scott memorabilia; Edinburgh just an hour's drive away. So, by and large, whether it be to wine and dine, or spend days and nights, this elegant Victorian mansion is more than ever a must for those seeking high standards and excellent value in Scotland.

All Prices pertain to 1992
Daily Terms from £28.00
Bed and Breakfast from £19.00
Bar Meal from £3.50
Dinner from £9.50 and A La Carte
Gratuities at Guest's discretion

VAT inclusive. Credit Cards—Access, Visa
2 Family Rooms
1 Single, 2 Double, 2 Twin Rooms
6 Private Shower Rooms
All Rooms with TV, Tea and Coffee-making Facilities. Hairdryer available on request

Open All Year except Christmas Day and New Year. Fully Licensed. Full Central Heating. Cocktail Bar. Children catered for Dogs not allowed. Parking Facilities
Nearby: Swimming, Golf, Windsurfing Fishing, Riding by arrangement

Section 8: Borders

Peebles—Venlaw Castle
Edinburgh Road, Peebles, Borders. EH45 8QG
Tel 0721 20384

Surrounded by lush green slopes populated by colourful shrubs, this fine building, with its round tower and craw stepped gables in the old baronial style, stands in an impressively commanding position. Hosts here for some forty years are the Cumming family, who run the hotel with quiet efficiency, assisted by their hand-picked staff. Tasteful decor and comfortable furnishings add to the relaxed mood of the public rooms and the roomy nature of the bedrooms, of which nine have en suite bathrooms. We enjoyed an excellent meal in the sparkling clean dining room where much of the food is freshly grown locally in some of the richest farmland in Britain. To complement your meal there is an excellent wine list. As an example of the ways in which modern amenities have skilfully been introduced into the mature building, the cocktail bar has been fashioned from the original library, retaining shelves of valued volumes and a welcoming log fire. From the secluded gardens of Venlaw Castle you can walk directly on to the hills surrounding Peebles, or take a short drive to the many galleries and gardens, museums and castles that lie gathered around Biggar to the west, near Peebles itself and on the road eastwards to Walkerburn. Your hosts will acquaint you with details of the many local places of interest and of such leisure amenities as golf, tennis, bowling, trail riding and 'the best' salmon fishing in Britain. Nearby Traquair House dates from the tenth century and has been visited by no less than twenty-seven kings.

Weekly Terms from £240.00	5 Family Rooms. 1 Single, 3 Double,	Fully Licensed
Daily Terms from £40.00	3 Twin Bedrooms	Full Central Heating
Bed and Breakfast from £30.00	5 Private Bathrooms	Cocktail Bar. Conference Facilities
English Breakfast £7.00	4 Private Shower Rooms	Children catered for. Dogs allowed
Dinner from £9.50 and A La Carte	All Rooms with TV, Telephone,	Parking Facilities
Gratuities at Guest's discretion	Baby-listening, Tea and Coffee-making	Nearby: Tennis, Putting, Squash,
VAT inclusive	Hairdryer available on request	Swimming, Golf, Fishing, Riding, Sailing,
Credit Cards—Access, American Express, Diners Club, Visa	Open from end March to beginning November	Shooting, Hot Air Ballooning

Section 8: Central

Polmont, Falkirk—Inchyra Grange Hotel
Grange Road, Polmont, Falkirk, Stirlingshire. FK2 0YB. Tel 0324 711911. Fax 0324 716134

Conveniently situated half a mile from Grangemouth and four miles from Falkirk, close to the M9 Edinburgh to Glasgow motorway, this is a most pleasant hotel offering the best of both worlds. From outside one gets the impression of an imposing country house, while within one finds every modern amenity. The spacious dining room is particularly impressive, with its floor-to-ceiling windows on two sides, looking out over the pleasant grounds. The food which we sampled from both *table d'hôte* and *à la carte* menus, was prepared with care and well presented. The meal was complemented by an extensive wine list and could not have been more enjoyable. The public rooms, including the welcoming cocktail bar, are furnished to the highest standards. This is also true of the attractive and well-equipped bedrooms. All have their own bathroom and feature colour television, radio and telephone as well as other modern amenities. Conference secretaries should note that this country hotel also has excellent facilities for small and large business gatherings, private functions and wedding receptions. The *Pelican Leisure Club* within the hotel offers leisure facilities to appeal to all ages, including a swimming pool, spa, saunas, steam room, gymnasium and beauty room. There is also an attractive licensed restaurant overlooking the pool. In conclusion, it should be noted that weekend breaks are available at reduced terms.

Bed and Breakfast from £76.00 Single mid week, £50.00 per room weekend
Bar Meal from £3.50
Lunch from £8.50 and A La Carte
Dinner from £15.50 and A La Carte
Gratuities at Guest's Discretion
VAT inclusive. Credit Cards—Access, American Express, Diners Club, Visa

3 Suites. 4 De Luxe Rooms
10 Double, 18 Twin, 8 Single Bedrooms
All Rooms with Private Bathroom, TV, Telephone, Radio, Tea and Coffee-making Facilities, Hairdryer, Mini Bar
Trouser Press available on Request
Open All Year. Fully Licensed
Full Central Heating

Cocktail Bar. Children catered for
Conference Facilities. Dogs allowed
Parking Facilities. Night Porter
Swimming Pool, Solarium, Sauna, Jacuzzi, Steam Room, Gymnasium, Snooker Room
Nearby: Golf

Port of Menteith—The Lake Hotel
Port of Menteith, Perthshire. FK8 3RA. Tel 08775 258. Fax 08775 671

In the superb scenery of the Trossachs, just two miles east of Aberfoyle, the Lake of Menteith is noted for a small island on which Inchmahome Priory still stands, once a haven for both Mary Queen of Scots and Robert the Bruce. The Lake Hotel, with its conservatory restaurant separated from the water's edge by a lush green lawn, provides spectacular views over the lake onto the hills of the Trossachs–Rob Roy MacGregor country. It is difficult to imagine a more picturesque setting. The hotel belongs to the Leroy family, and enjoys the highest commendations and exceptional standards of comfort and *cuisine*. In their *Bistro*, starters, main courses and sweets are all prepared on the premises by their chef, with special provision for vegetarians and for children. There are *table d'hôte* and *à la carte* menus in the restaurant where, to order, special dishes can be cooked. We wished our stay could have been extended to enable us to sample more of the superb meals listed. The Lake Hotel offers substantial reductions for out-of-season bookings, with further discounts for 'Minibreaks' of two nights or more. In such fairy-tale surroundings, the natural beauty of the area provides a change of scene with each season and has a special spring and autumn appeal. Within the hotel there are all the facilities for luxurious relaxation, opportunities to discuss the next tour of the lochs, forests and mountains and a tempting choice of refreshments.

All Prices pertain to 1992
Weekly Terms from £231.00
Daily Terms from £39.00
Bed and Breakfast from £25.00
Bar Meal from £5.00
Lunch from £7.00 and A La Carte
Dinner from £19.50 and A La Carte

Gratuities at Guest's Discretion
VAT inclusive. Credit Cards–Access, Visa
5 Double, 7 Twin Bedrooms
All Rooms with Private Bathroom, TV, Telephone, Radio, Baby-listening, Tea and Coffee-making Facilities, Hairdryer, Laundry Facilities. Open all Year. Fully

Licensed. Full Central Heating
Conference Facilities
Children catered for by arrangement
Dogs allowed at Management's Discretion
Parking Facilities. Nearby: Tennis, Putting, Squash, Badminton, Golf, Fishing, Riding, Sailing, Water Skiing

Section 8: Dumfries & Galloway

Near Castle Douglas, Auchencairn—Balcary Bay Hotel Auchencairn,
Near Castle Douglas, Kirkcudbrightshire. DG7 1QZ. Tel 055664 217/311

This lovely country-house hotel has a secluded setting on the edge of Balcary Bay, facing Heston Isle (infamous as a smugglers' haunt), the Solway coast and, beyond, the Cumbrian hills. The unspoiled countryside of Galloway has a rich variety of walks along the coast, over hills and through forests. There is plenty of choice, too, for golfers, anglers and those who enjoy riding. Standing in three acres of gardens, a few minutes' drive from Auchencairn and only ten miles from Castle Douglas, Balcary Bay Hotel has a fascinating history—the house was purchased by a firm of shippers in 1645, who used it as a headquarters for smuggling and storing their goods. Today it retains much of its old character and atmosphere, but modern amenities are provided. There are seventeen bedrooms, all with en suite bathroom except one which has a shower room and all equipped with colour television, radio, telephone, beverage facilities and hairdryer. There is a cocktail bar and two comfortable lounges, one with log fire. The *cuisine* in the dining-room is first class, based on local delicacies such as Galloway beef, Heston Isle lobsters and Balcary Bay salmon, and the wine list is equally impressive. Balcary Bay Hotel offers excellent hospitality in a superb setting, making it an ideal holiday hotel.

Special Breaks on application
Bed and Breakfast from £30.00
Bar Meal from £3.00
Lunch from £10.00 and A La Carte
Afternoon Tea from £3.00
Dinner from £17.00 and A La Carte
Gratuities at Guest's Discretion. VAT inclusive
Credit Cards—Access, Visa

1 Family Rooms. 3 Single, 6 Double, 7 Twin Bedrooms
16 Private Bathrooms
1 Private Shower Room. All Rooms with TV, Telephone, Radio, Tea and Coffee-making Facilities, Hairdryer
Trouser Press available on Request
Open from March to November inclusive
Fully Licensed

Full Central Heating
Cocktail Bar. Snooker Room
Children catered for. Dogs allowed
Small Conference Facilities
Parking Facilities
Croquet, Fishing, Sailing, Windsurfing, Water Skiing
Nearby: Golf, Fishing, Riding

Near Dalbeattie, Colvend—Clonyard House Hotel
Colvend, Dalbeattie, Kirkcudbrightshire. DG5 4QW. Tel 055 663 372

Dalbeattie, on the Urr water, was built in 1780 and owes its existence to the impressive granite quarries. Two and a half miles away is the well known Mote of Urr, an eighty foot mound surrounded by a fosse, while one mile to the west is the ruined castle of Botel, once the home of John de Baliol, founder of Baliol College, Oxford in the thirteenth-century. Clonyard House is situated in seven acres of secluded woodland on the Solway coast between Rockcliffe and Kippford. The drive leads under a canopy of mature trees and rhododendrons to the place of welcome. Children can play safely in the grounds and dogs are allowed. The Thompson family are your hosts and ensure that everything runs smoothly. There are fifteen bedrooms, all *en suite*. The hotel is popular and we were lucky to get one of the twelve ground floor rooms, complete with colour television and tea and coffee making facilities. These ground floor bedrooms have modern furnishings and fittings, carefully chosen, and a private patio overlooking the garden. The menu is varied and the food very well prepared and served. The sweet trolley with home-made, but very professionally finished gâteaux, was a delight. Clonyard House is always busy and seems a great favourite with yachtsmen from the nearby sailing centres. The residents' lounge is located on the first floor, providing a quiet haven for those who wish to read or snooze.

All Prices pertain to 1992
Weekly Terms Bed and Breakfast from £173.25
Bed and Breakfast from £27.50
Bar Meal from £4.00
Dinner from £12.00 and A La Carte
Gratuities at Guest's Discretion
VAT inclusive
Credit Cards—Access, Visa

2 Family Rooms. 1 Suite
3 Double, 9 Twin Bedrooms
(Double Rooms can be let as Singles)
All Rooms with Private Bath/Shower Room, TV, Telephone, Radio, Baby-listening, Tea and Coffee-making Facilities
Hairdryer available on Request
Open all Year

Fully Licensed
Full Central Heating
Cocktail Bar. TV Lounge
Small Meeting Facilities
Dogs allowed
Parking Facilities
Nearby: Tennis, Golf, Riding, Sailing, Windsurfing, Shooting, Gliding

Section 8: Dumfries & Galloway

Dumfries—Cairndale Hotel
English Street, Dumfries. DG1 2DF
Tel 0387 54111. Fax 0387 50555

If you are contemplating exploring southern Scotland, and we strongly advise that you do–it is generally unspoilt, uncrowded and very accessible–there is no better place to start than Scotland's fair 'Queen of the South', Dumfries. So, the Cairndale Hotel comes immediately to mind. The story of this well established hotel has, in recent years, been the story of the Wallace family, who have made it one of the region's leading hotels. Outwardly, it fits into the pattern of Dumfries, for almost every corner of the town shows facades of rust-red sandstone, which matches the soil hereabouts. Inside, however, the hotel's individualism is plain to see. Seventy-six bedrooms, all with *en suite* bathroom and modern facilities, while the *Executive Rooms* include queen size double bed, mini-bar, trouser press and jacuzzi spa baths! As a further indication that only the best is good enough for the Wallaces, the food is excellent and is shown to advantage against table appointments of the highest quality. Prime Galloway beef arrives from the family's own butchers business and all the *à la carte* dishes and tempting specialities are prepared by David Williams. Excellent fare is also served in the new *Sawney Beans Bar and Grill*. There are dinner dances on Saturdays, and every Sunday evening throughout the summer months you may experience Scotland's culture as well enjoying the taste of Scotland, for The Cairndale Ceilidh is a very popular and professional entertainment. For the energetic, a new leisure centre, the *Barracuda Club*, has just opened. So, there is much to impress one here, and a great deal to keep you happily occupied.

Weekly Terms on Application
Bed and Breakfast from £30.00
Lunch from £4.95 Carvery and A la Carte
Dinner from £15.00 and A La Carte
Service Charge and VAT inclusive
Credit Cards—Access, American Express, Diners Club, Visa
3 Suites. 7 Executive Rooms. 2 Family Rooms. 12 Double, 32 Twin, 20 Single Bedrooms. 68 Private Bathrooms

8 Private Shower Rooms
All Rooms with TV, Telephone, Radio, Tea and Coffee-making Facilities, Hairdryer.
Suites and Executive Rooms with Trouser Press, Mini Bar, Jacuzzi Bath
Open all Year
Fully Licensed
Lift. Conference Facilities
Children catered for.
Dogs allowed by Arrangement

Parking Facilities. Night Porter
Barracuda Club-Indoor Heated Pool, Sauna, Steam Room, Spa Bath, Solarium, Gymnasium, Health/Beauty Salon, Toning Tables
Nearby: Tennis, Putting, Squash, Golf, Fishing, Riding, Sailing, Windsurfing, Water Skiing, Shooting

Section 8: Dumfries & Galloway

Dumfries, Carrutherstown—Hetland Hall Hotel
Carrutherstown, Dumfries. DG1 4JX. Tel 0387 84201. Fax 0387 84211

Surrounded by forty five acres of beautiful parkland, this hotel lies mid-way between the charming towns of Dumfries and Annan, on the A75 Euro Route to Ireland. Accommodation is shared between an elegant country house and, in contrasting architectural style, a more recent wing which has been converted to provide a number of well furnished *en suite* bedrooms with modern facilities. Distributed in the older part of the hotel are the lounge, cocktail bar, residents' lounge and dining room, all having views over the extensive grounds. We selected our dinner from a menu of familiar dishes: it was served with a smile and, as with breakfast the next morning, helpings were generous. Polished hardwood floors with attractive occasional rugs are a feature of the lounge and the entrance hall. This latter area is graced by a sweeping Italian walnut staircase and well placed floral decorations. Hetland Hall has excellent conference facilities in their recently refurbished *Executive Room* and *Otter Suite*, with modern visual aids, for the use of up to 200 day delegates or forty-four residential delegates. The larger of these rooms is equally suitable for wedding receptions, dinner dances, exhibitions and clan gatherings. Guests have a wide variety of interesting local places to visit, including Threave Gardens and Horticultural School, Caerlaverock Castle, Arbigland Gardens, Ruthwell Cross and Museum, the Robert Burns Centre in Dumfries and, of course, Hadrian's Wall. Alternatively, within the hotel, the energetic can enjoy snooker, indoor badminton, table tennis, a fitness centre, sauna and solarium.

Weekly Terms from £270.00
Daily Terms from £55.00 Single
Bed and Breakfast from £55.00 Single
Bar Meal from £4.00
Lunch from £10.00 and A La Carte
Afternoon Tea from £5.00

Dinner from £16.50 and A La Carte
Gratuities at Guest's Discretion. VAT inclusive. Credit Cards—Access, American Express, Diners club, Visa
2 Family Rooms. 1 Suite
8 Double, 12 Twin, 6 Single Bedrooms

24 Private Bathrooms. 5 Private Shower Rooms. All Rooms with TV, Telephone, Radio, Tea and Coffee-making Facilities, Trouser Press, Hairdryer. Open all Year.
Fully Licensed. Games Room
Conference Facilities. Children catered for

Gatehouse-of-Fleet—The Murray Arms
Gatehouse-of-Fleet, Kirkcudbrightshire. DG7 2HY. Tel 0557 814207. Fax 0557 814370

When travelling from the south one's introduction to Scotland will probably be the Dumfries and Galloway region. Gatehouse-of-Fleet is a small country town of character in an outstanding conservation area. Many acres of land are under the National Trust Conservation agreements and many thousands of acres are Forestry Commission woodlands. Gatehouse lies within one of Scotland's Scenic Heritage Areas, rich in history and archaeological interest, with a great variety of plant and bird life. Good hotels are few, but this former posting inn, where Robert Burns wrote *Scots Wha Hae*, conveys more of the atmosphere of a country house than of a busy wayside inn. Apart from modern comforts, the passing traveller will experience a restfulness and a standard of catering which is well above the average. The *Lunky Hole Lounge and Snack Bar* offers hot and cold buffet meals and snacks. Unless one has a fixed timetable or is contemplating a crossing to Ireland from Stranraer, the shortest sea route, the temptation to linger at The Murray Arms can become too great to resist. The countryside is unspoilt and comparatively unknown, there are lochs and the River Fleet to fish and rough shooting, stalking, and sea bathing are all nearby. The hotel's amenities include the *Garden Cottage Suite* consisting of a twin bedroom, a sitting-room and a bathroom.

Weekly Terms on application
Bed and Breakfast from £38.00
Bar Meal from £3.50
Afternoon Tea from £3.00
Dinner from £15.50 Table d'Hôte
Gratuities at Guest's discretion
VAT inclusive
Credit Cards—Access, American Express, Diners Club, Visa

2 Family Rooms. 1 Suite
4 Double, 5 Twin, 1 Single Bedrooms
All Rooms with Private Bathroom, TV, Telephone, Radio, Baby-listening, Tea and Coffee-making Facilities, Hairdryer
Open all Year
Fully Licensed
Full Central Heating
Cocktail Bar. TV Lounge

Conference Facilities
Dogs allowed but not in Public Rooms
Parking Facilities. Night Porter
Croquet, Putting
Nearby: Tennis, Squash, Badminton, Swimming, Golf Fishing, Riding, Sailing, Windsurfing, Water Skiing

Section 8: Dumfries & Galloway

Gretna Green—The Gretna Chase Hotel
Gretna, Carlisle. CA6 5JB. Tel 0461 37517

Gretna Green became famous for providing couples with the opportunity of a speedy marriage under eighteenth century Scots law. Marriages were performed at various establishments including Allisons's Bank Toll Bar—the first house in Scotland. John Murray, the tenant, was a very successful businessman who could outwit most of the other marriage house proprietors, but he could not provide stabling for his clients' horses. He therefore built The Gretna Chase Hotel on the English side of the border, opposite the toll bar, in 1856. John Hall is the present owner of this small but extremely comfortable hotel, which still offers honeymooners the romance of a magnificent four-poster bed in the bridal suite. The bar meals are appetising and ideal for the traveller in a hurry or for a midday snack. The cold buffet offers generous ploughman's and squire's lunches, roast meats and salads, with sandwiches cut to order. The dining room is very popular, catering for seventy with an *à la carte* menu offering thick juicy steaks and several dishes made from locally caught salmon. The large oak refectory table displays a grand selection of mouthwatering sweets. Many of the bedrooms overlook the beautiful award winning gardens which provide a superb display of colour throughout the year as well as a romantic background for wedding photographs. Next time you are crossing the border stop at this charming hotel to refresh yourself for the rest of the journey.

Bed and Breakfast from £24.00
Bar Meal from £6.00
Lunch from £11.00 A La Carte
Dinner from £12.50 A La Carte
Gratuities at Guest's Discretion
VAT inclusive

Credit Cards—Access, American Express, Diners Club, Visa
2 Single, 5 Double, 2 Twin Bedrooms
All Rooms with Private Bath/Shower Rooms, TV, Tea and Coffee-making Facilities. Hairdryer available on Request

Open from 1st February to 31st December
Fully Licensed. Full Central Heating
Small Conference Facilities
Children catered for
Dogs not allowed
Parking Facilities

Lockerbie—The Dryfesdale Hotel
Lockerbie, Dumfries-shire. DG11 2SF. Tel 05762 2427/2121

When travelling northwards on the A74, Lockerbie is the first major town one encounters after crossing the border from England. The countryside here is gentle and sloping, although the hills, moors and forests of Galloway lie just beyond. Continue north on the A74 road past the town and this former manse, dating from the eighteenth century, can just be seen to the left behind a tree-lined ridge, nestling in five acres of grounds. The hotel is now in the ownership of the Smith family who have added six ground floor bedrooms, all en suite, with full facilities for the disabled. Colour television, telephone and tea and coffee-making facilities are standard in all bedrooms. The public rooms are similarly attractive and full central heating and log fires emphasise the hotel's year-round appeal to the passing motorist. Also we consider that The Dryfesdale Hotel is an excellent base for a complete Lowlands holiday. This is the land of Robert Burns and Robert the Bruce and in nearby Dumfries the house where Burns spent his last years is now preserved as a museum. Now that the cost of travelling has become a major part of one's holiday budget, this part of Scotland has an obvious advantage for those coming from the south. This area provides most things that sportsmen, artists, antiquarians and sightseers would wish to find.

Bed and Breakfast from £46.00
Bar Meal from £4.50
Lunch from £10.00 and A La Carte
Afternoon Tea from £2.95
Dinner from £15.75 and A La Carte
Service Charge and VAT inclusive
Credit Cards—Access, American Express,

Visa. 1 Family Room
10 Double/Twin, 4 Single Bedrooms
14 Private Bathrooms
1 Private Shower Room
All Rooms with TV, Telephone, Tea and Coffee-making Facilities, Baby-listening
Open all Year. Fully Licensed

Cocktail Bar. TV Lounge
Conference Facilities
Dogs allowed. Parking Facilities
Nearby: Tennis, Squash, Golf, Fishing, Riding, Sailing, Windsurfing, Water Skiing, Shooting, Curling

Section 8: Dumfries & Galloway

Lockerbie—Somerton House Hotel
Carlisle Road, Lockerbie, Dumfries-shire. DG11 2DR. Tel 05762 2583. Fax 05762 2384

The Burgh of Lockerbie is the last major town before crossing the Scottish Border. Somerton House Hotel is within an hour's drive of Glasgow and Edinburgh and only twenty-five miles from Carlisle, making it the ideal stopover for travellers both north and south. It is an attractive late Victorian mansion, converted to a small hotel many years ago, offering single, double and family rooms, most of them with pleasant views over the well-kept gardens and surrounding countryside. Within a few miles there are many places of historical interest, including Lochmaben Castle, famous for its connections with Bruce, Repentance Tower renowned for its associated romantic tragedy, and Ecclefechan, the birthplace of Thomas Carlyle. During their first few years at Somerton House, Sam and Patricia Ferguson have made many improvements. Most commendably, they have resisted the temptation to create *en suite* facilities by reducing room sizes. They have achieved the same results by changing door positions of existing bathrooms and by using small rooms to make large bathrooms. One very large bathroom we saw had the Victorian suite in excellent condition together with the most enormous polished brass heated towel rail. Another distinguishing feature of the house's design by Alexander (Greek) Thomson is the now almost extinct Kauri timber panelling and fine fireplaces. A great setting in which to enjoy Galloway pork, beef and lamb, also an incomparable selection of Scottish Malts and cask-conditioned Real Ale.

All Prices pertain to 1991
Weekly Terms on request
Bed and Breakfast from £28.25
Bar Meal from £4.95
Afternoon Tea from £4.50
Dinner A La Carte
VAT inclusive

Credit Cards–Access, American Express, Visa
2 Family Rooms
1 Single, 2 Double, 2 Twin Bedrooms
6 Private Bathrooms, 1 Private Shower Room. All Rooms with TV, Telephone, Radio, Baby-listening, Tea and Coffee-making Facilities, Hairdryer

Open all Year except Christmas Day and New Years Day
Fully Licensed
Children catered for
Dogs allowed by arrangement
Parking Facilities

Moffat—Beechwood Country House Hotel
Moffat, Dumfriesshire. DG10 9RS. Tel 0683 20210. Fax 0683 20889

Twelve acres of beech woods surround this attractive country house overlooking the gentle Annan valley and the little town of Moffat tucked away in this peaceful south-west corner of Scotland. The house is Victorian, built in the middle of the last century, originally as Miss Thomson's private adventure boarding establishment and school for young ladies! Times have changed and your hosts today are Jeff and Lynda Rogers who offer a welcome as warm as their log fires. Imaginative dishes with style and flair are created, using the best available local produce. Every dish can be complemented by one of the fine wines on the excellent wine list. But take your time, there is more to come—an excellent cheese-board and fresh fruit complete your meal. Take your coffee to the lounge with a brandy and some home-made petits fours. The bedrooms are beautifully furnished. Tea, coffee, Horlicks and Ovaltine are provided and a small jug of fresh milk is yours for the asking. Afternoon tea can be served either in the lounge or in your bedroom. Gourmet' packed lunches are available if requested and can include individual bottles of French red or white wine, champagne or fruit juices as required. An extensive library offers books for all tastes and there is also a wide selection of board games. For the more energetic there are many fine walks to enjoy and a challenging 18-hole golf course nearby. Fishing, riding and tennis are available.

Weekly Terms from £320.00
Daily Terms from £51.50
Bed and Breakfast from £34.90
Sunday Lunch £11.50
Dinner from £18.25 Table D'Hôte
Gratuities at Guest's Discretion
VAT inclusive. Credit Cards—Access, American Express, Visa

1 Family Room. 3 Double, 3 Twin Bedrooms. (Doubles/Twins let as Singles)
6 Private Bathrooms
1 Private Shower Room
All Rooms with TV, Telephone, Radio, Baby-listening, Tea and Coffee-making Facilities, Hairdryer
Open all Year

Residential and Restaurant Licence
Full Central Heating. Cocktail Bar.
Small Conference Facilities
Dogs allowed
Parking Facilities
Nearby: Tennis, Squash, Badminton, Golf, Fishing, Riding, Shooting

Section 8: Dumfries & Galloway

Moffat—Moffat House Hotel
High Street, Moffat, Dumfriesshire. DG10 9HL. Tel 0683 20039. Fax 0683 21288

Another hotel which we really took to during our Scottish tours this year was Moffat House. There are a variety of reasons why this long-established hotel should be included in one's itinerary. It is in the historic burgh of Moffat and lies on the main Carlisle/Edinburgh road, so is a convenient halfway house between central England and central Scotland. Then there are the attractions which would induce one to stay here: golf, fishing, trekking, hill walking and the Lowlands scenery, including a famous view of Devil's Beef Tub. Finally, and perhaps this should come first, there is much to admire about Moffat House Hotel itself, an imposing Adam style mansion with a large forecourt, lawns and flower beds. There is also a large, pleasant garden at the rear with a quite magnificent oak tree as a centre piece. Inside, the house still bears the elegance of the eighteenth century, especially the spiral staircase and the other examples of Adam craftsmanship. Our bedroom was impressive in itself, being located in one of the round towers. It contained everything we needed for comfort, including an *en suite* bathroom well supplied with soft towels and toiletries. The *cuisine* at Moffat House is all *à la carte* and we found it to be delicious. Our Solway salmon was outstanding. So, do try to stay at Moffat House if you can. It is friendly and very relaxing, and the Reid family are happy if you succumb to the atmosphere they have created.

Weekly Terms from £330.00
Daily Terms from £53.00
Bed and Breakfast from £38.00
Bar Meal from £4.00
Dinner from £17.00 and A La Carte
Gratuities at Guest's Discretion

VAT inclusive. Credit Cards—Access, American Express, Visa
3 Family Rooms
7 Double, 7 Twin, 3 Single Bedrooms
All Rooms with Private Bath/Shower Room, TV, Telephone, Radio,

Baby-listening, Tea and Coffee-making Facilities, Hairdryer.. Open all Year. Fully Licensed. Full Central Heating. Cocktail Bar. Small Conference Facilities
Children catered for. Dogs allowed
Parking Facilities

Newton Stewart—Kirroughtree Hotel
Newton Stewart, Galloway. DG8 6AN. Tel 0671 2141. Fax 0671 2425

In a world of declining standards it is refreshing to come across an hotel where the entire accent is on quality and giving satisfaction to its guests. This fine old mansion house, which dates back to 1719, has been completely refurbished and is now one of the most luxurious country-house hotels in Britain. All the bedrooms are beautifully furnished and there are four honeymoon or wedding anniversary suites, which are an absolute dream. The bedrooms have different colour bathroom suites and are equipped with colour television, radio and telephone. Seven of the rooms are on the ground floor. However, it is the food which is getting the most praise, which is not surprising as it is acknowledged as some of the finest in Scotland. There is also an outstanding wine list. The hotel is set in eight acres of elevated grounds, with beautiful views, and its neat lawns, rhododendrons and colourful flowerbeds add to the scenic charm of Kirroughtree as a whole. One's first impression is that a more restful and secluded spot could not be found. However, for the more active resident, free golf is available at five local courses and there is free use of the leisure facilities at the sister hotels of the North West Castle, Stranraer and Cally Palace, Gatehouse-of-Fleet. Salmon and trout fishing, horse riding, beautiful walks and safe sandy beaches are close at hand. The McMillan family won the 1990 RAC Credit to Industry award and the hotel has been given four stars by the RAC and five crowns by the Scottish Tourist Board.

All Terms include free Golf at 5 Courses
Weekly Terms from £385.00
Daily Terms from £58.00
Bed and Breakfast from £50.00
Lunch from £10.00 A La Carte
Afternoon Tea from £1.50
Dinner £20.00 Table D'Hôte. VAT inclusive
Credit Cards—Access, Visa

3 Family Rooms. 4 Suites. 3 Single, 6 Double, 6 Twin Bedrooms
All Rooms with Private Bathroom, TV, Telephone, Radio, Hairdryer, Bathrobes, Fruit
Open from early February to 3rd January
Fully Licensed. Full Central Heating
Cocktail Bar. Conference Facilities

Children over 10 years catered for
Dogs allowed by Arrangement
Parking Facilities. Night Porter
Tennis, Croquet, Pitch and Putt, Bowls
Nearby: Tennis, Swimming, Free Golf, Fishing, Riding, Sailing, Windsurfing, Water Skiing, Shooting

Section 8: Dumfries & Galloway

Newton Stewart—Corsemalzie House Hotel Port William,
Newton Stewart, Wigtownshire. DG8 9RL. Tel 098 886 254. Fax 098 886 213

This would be an excellent choice for those seeking an hotel away from it all, for, although the postal address is Port William, Corsemalzie House lies six miles away from the village. The hotel is set out on the moors (Machars) of Wigtownshire in lovely wooded grounds. This country mansion was built in the nineteenth century so that its owners could enjoy the country pleasures of the area. The property was bought by the McDougall family thirty years ago and much time and effort have been devoted to restoring the house and gardens to their former glory. The house has been rebuilt on the upper floors to provide fifteen bedrooms, all with private bath or shower rooms, remote-controlled colour television, direct-dial telephone, radio and tea and coffee-making facilities. We very much appreciated the comfort of our room and awoke, refreshed, to a chorus of bird song. The beautiful dining-room is the setting for excellent meals and many dishes are offered as part of the 'Taste of Scotland' and 'Taste of Galloway' schemes. A good variety of bar lunches and suppers is also available. Mr and Mrs Peter McDougall take a personal interest in the welfare of their guests. They can give you plenty of suggestions for interesting tours and walks during your stay. There are, of course, many outdoor activities to keep you occupied. The hotel has extensive fishing rights for trout and salmon, and has golfing arrangements with two local courses. Other recreations in the area include rough shooting, driven pheasant shooting, riding and pony-trekking. Within the hotel's garden is putting and croquet.

Weekly Terms from £273.00
Daily Terms from £39.50
Bed and Breakfast from £31.50
Bar Meal from £3.75
Lunch from £10.75 Table D'Hôte
Afternoon Tea from £2.00

Dinner from £16.75 Table D'Hôte
Gratuities at Guest's Discretion
VAT inclusive. Credit Cards—Access, Visa
1 Family Room. 7 Double, 7 Twin Bedroom
All Rooms with Private Bath/Shower
Rooms, TV, Telephone, Radio,

Baby-listening, Tea and Coffee-making Facilities. Open from 7th March to 20th January. Fully Licensed
Full Central Heating. Conference Facilities
Dogs allowed. Parking Facilities
Croquet, Putting, Fishing, Shooting

Portpatrick—Fernhill Hotel Heugh Road, Portpatrick,
Near Stranraer, Wigtownshire. DG9 8TD. Tel 077681 220

A variant of the name often used is Fernhill Golf Hotel which, in one extra word, identifies the main appeal of this dignified and comfortable building. Before describing any of the hotel's attractions however, it must be emphasised that the location, accommodation and excellent catering must commend the hotel to all seeking a peaceful and picturesque retreat, regardless of their interest in sport. A Victorian conservatory adds to the charm of the original building and affords guests a superb view over the village and the Irish Sea. A new extension containing six beautifully furnished bedrooms (three on the ground floor) all with superb views and spacious reception area, blends well with the original building. The first tee of the cliff-top Dunskey Course, well respected by the golfing press, is literally only a five-minute stroll from Fernhill. Fishing, and particularly shooting in the winter season bookable through an agent, are available. Other sporting activities in the area are listed in the summary alongside. Hugh and Anne Harvie, the resident proprietors, employ a superb chef and the *cuisine* here is widely regarded as the best in the area. All the staff, operating in such a well-appointed environment, make the visitor immediately appreciative of the service he receives. Portpatrick itself has attracted many visitors over the centuries, with its seacoast ranging from rugged cliffs and unfrequented coves to family-safe beaches. It offers superb walks and there are castles, keeps and sub-tropical gardens to visit.

Terms on Application
Gratuities at Guest's Discretion
VAT inclusive
Credit Cards—Access, American Express, Diners Club, Visa
2 Family Rooms
1 Single, 3 Double, 16 Twin Bedrooms

19 Private Bathrooms
1 Private Shower Room
All Rooms with TV, Telephone, Radio, Baby-listening, Tea and Coffee-making Facilities, Hairdryer
Open all Year. Fully Licensed
Full Central Heating

Limited Conference Facilities
Dogs allowed. Parking Facilities
Golf, Fishing, Riding, Sailing
Water Skiing and Shooting by arrangement with agent
Nearby: Tennis, Putting, Squash

Section 8: Fife

St Andrews—Rufflets Country House & Garden Restaurant
Strathkinness Low Road, St Andrews, Fife. KY16 9TX
Tel 0334 72594. Fax 0334 78703

Over forty years ownership and management by the same family is a rare achievement and, during this period, Rufflets has undergone numerous changes, with its complement of *en suite* bedrooms increasing from seven to twenty-seven. The original house, designed by Dundee architect Donald Mills, was built in 1924, and, together with Rose Cottage, stands in ten acres of exceptionally beautiful gardens: twice recently they have won an award for garden of the year. Although only one-and-a-half miles from the world famous 'Home of Golf', the surroundings are tranquil and the location convenient for sightseeing and other leisure pursuits. In the immediate vicinity there are art galleries, British Golf Museum, Fife Folk Museum, Sealife Centre, several castles and gardens, the colleges of St Andrews University (the oldest in Scotland) and wide beaches. On your return to the dignified comfort and friendly service which are evident in all parts of the hotel, you will want to relax with an aperitif in their spacious cocktail bar or elegant drawing room before taking dinner in their *Garden Restaurant*. Menus here change daily, reflecting the availability of fresh local produce and the widespread use of vegetables, fruits and herbs from Rufflets' own kitchen garden. The fine quality of the catering, particularly the Scottish dishes, is one of the main reasons that the hotel has long enjoyed both national and international recognition. All the public rooms, and many of the bedrooms, overlook the colourful formal gardens. In winter, the warm decor of the drawing room, with its sparkling chandelier, and welcoming open fire is particularly inviting.

Weekly Terms (B&B) from £248.50	10 Family Rooms	Children catered for
Bed and Breakfast from £35.50	3 Double, 8 Twin, 6 Single Bedrooms	Dogs not allowed
Bar Lunch from £5.00	All Rooms with Private Bathroom, TV,	Parking Facilities
Lunch from £12.50 and A La Carte	Telephone, Radio, Baby-listening, Tea and	Night Porter. Putting
Afternoon Tea from £3.75	Coffee-making Facilities, Trouser Press,	Nearby: Tennis, Croquet, Squash,
Bar Supper from £10.00	Hairdryer	Badminton, Swimming, Solarium, Sauna,
Dinner from £22.50 and A La Carte	Open from February to December	Golf, Fishing, Riding, Sailing, Clay Shooting
Service Charge and VAT inclusive	Fully Licensed	
Credit Cards—Access, American Express,	Full Central Heating	
Diners Club, Switch, Visa	Cocktail Bar	

Section 8: Fife and Grampian

St Andrews—St Andrews Golf Hotel 40 The Scores, St Andrews, Fife. KY16 9AS. Tel 0334 72611. Fax 0334 72188

No hotel in St Andrews can totally disassociate itself from golf, not even this popular place, which prefers to view the sea rather than the golfers and their caddies who converge on the famous links. The sport, however, does not dominate here and guests are not inclined to forget that St Andrews has other attractions—a sandy coastline, a twelfth-century castle, the oldest university in Scotland and a location which is ideal for touring the central Highlands. The St Andrews Golf Hotel also benefits enormously from the progressive policy pursued by Brian and Maureen Hughes. Indeed, as we are writing these lines, their hotel is undergoing major interior refurbishment which is raising the standards of comfort and of the facilities to a very high level. Excellent *à la carte* and *table d'hôte* menus, featuring the best of local produce, are served in the restaurant, complemented by one of the finest wine lists in this part of the country. Every bedroom contains a private bathroom, colour television, a radio and beverage-making facilities and, in addition, such thoughtful items as a hairdryer, trouser press with iron, dressing gown, fresh fruit and flowers. The public areas are all tastefully and comfortably furnished with a cocktail bar opening on to a patio and garden, lounge with magnificent sea views and the basement bar/restaurant, *'Ma Bell's*–a favourite meeting place for town and gown.

Weekly Terms from £465.50
Daily Terms from £66.50
Bed and Breakfast from £52.50
Bar Lunch from £6.00
Lunch from £12.50 and A La Carte
Dinner from £21.50 and A La Carte
Gratuities at Guest's Discretion
VAT inclusive

Credit Cards—Access, Visa
5 Double, 6 Twin, 2 Single Bedrooms
10 Family Rooms. 20 Private Bathrooms
3 Private Shower Rooms
All Rooms with TV, Telephone, Radio, Baby-listening, Tea and Coffee-making Facilities, Hairdryer, Trouser Press
Open all Year

Fully Licensed. Full Central Heating
Lift. Cocktail Bar. Conference Facilities
Dogs allowed. Parking Facilities
Night Porter
Solarium, Sauna
Nearby: Tennis, Putting, Golf, Fishing, Riding

Aboyne—The Balnacoil Hotel Rhu-na-Haven Road, Aboyne, Aberdeenshire. AB3 5JD. Tel 03398 86806. Fax 03398 87050

Situated just off the A93 road, mid-way between Ballater and Banchory, Balnacoil has the triple benefits of easy accessibility, the appeal of a wooded country setting and, despite this, scenic open views—from its bedrooms and from some of the public rooms—of a large part of the Dee valley. In the nineteenth century, Queen Victoria drew attention to the great natural beauty of this valley and its surroundings. A fine example of Edwardian architecture, the hotel is set on the river bank, tranquil and yet with many sporting pastimes near at hand. Internally, each room has received individual treatment, with quality fabrics and tasteful use of colour. In addition to the excellent *en suite* facilities in every bedroom, there are nice touches such as the presence of a pot pourri and a selection of books. One area that we must single out for special mention is the bar. It adjoins the hotel but is entered separately and, without doubt, is one of the most attractive bars we have seen in Scotland, with a wide choice of bar food available. In the main dining-room, the cheerful and attentive service was enhanced by the waiter's good knowledge of the extensive wine list. The appeal of this list made us wish that more labels were stocked in half bottles. We applaud the provision of two *table d'hôte* menus, at differing prices, with a broad selection of alternative dishes on both. Their *Hunters Restaurant*, with its pitch-pine panelling, has the right ambience in which to enjoy a memorable meal. Business visitors to Deeside are catered for at The Balnacoil with private meeting rooms and full back-up services.

Weekly Terms from £285.00
Daily Terms from £47.00
Bed and Breakfast from £51.00
Bar Lunch from £3.95
Lunch from £11.00 Table D'Hôte
Afternoon Tea from £5.00

Bar Supper from £6.95
Dinner from £18.00 Table d'Hôte
Gratuities at Guest's Discretion
VAT inclusive. Credit Cards—Access, American Express, Diners Club, Switch, Visa. 6 Double, 3 Twin, 3 Single Bedrooms

All Rooms with Private Bathroom, TV, Telephone, Radio, Baby-listening, Tea and Coffee-making Facilities, Trouser Press, Hairdryer, Bathrobes, Mineral Water
Open all Year. Fully Licensed. Full CH
Conference Facilities. Children catered for.

Section 8: Grampian

Aboyne—Birse Lodge Hotel
Aboyne, Aberdeenshire. AB3 5EL. Tel 03398 86253

Many of our friends stay at Birse Lodge when their holidays include fishing the Dee and we continue to hear nothing but praise of the standards to be found here. From personal experience we would emphasise the warm welcome from the resident manageress, the excellent food with a different dining room menu every evening, the extensive bar meals served in the sun lounge and the personal comfort. Just as important, of course, is location. Here one is in the heart of Royal Deeside, positioned equidistant from Aberdeen and Braemar, surrounded by four acres of policies and with the river flowing nearby. Birse Lodge is run on country-house lines. Once the dower house for the Huntly Estates, Lord Huntly being the Chief of the Gordon Clan, it has been improved and extended so that all the newly refurbished bedrooms have private facilities, there is full central heating and plenty of comfort including colour television, telephone and beverage-making facilities in all bedrooms. It is, therefore, an excellent hotel for tourists and sportsmen, or those wishing to dine out on some of the best food which is served in the area. We have recommended Birse Lodge for many years and always enjoy returning to this hotel of character, where one receives a full measure of Scottish hospitality. The grounds are a delight, ideal for respite or a game of putting and nearby there is a multitude of sporting opportunities, including water skiing, golf and gliding.

Bed and Breakfast from £39.00
Bar Meal from £4.25
Afternoon Tea from £1.75
Dinner from £16.00 Table D'Hôte
Gratuities at Guest's Discretion
VAT inclusive. Credit Cards—Access, American Express, Visa

3 Double, 6 Twin, 3 Single Bedrooms
11 Private Bathrooms
1 Private Shower Room
All Rooms with TV, Telephone, Tea and Coffee-making Facilities
Hairdryer available on Request
Open all Year

Fully Licensed
Full Central Heating
Dogs allowed but not in Public Rooms
Parking Facilities. Putting
Nearby: Tennis, Squash, Badminton, Swimming, Golf, Riding, Water Skiing, Hang-gliding, Hill Walking

Near Alford, Kildrummy—Kildrummy Castle Hotel Kildrummy,
By Alford, Aberdeenshire. AB33 8RA. Tel 09755 71288. Fax 09755 71345

Donside is noted for its beauty and here, just off the A97 Ballater to Huntly road, you will find Kildrummy Castle Hotel. It overlooks the ruins of the thirteenth-century castle from which it takes its name and is set within Kildrummy Castle Gardens, which offer a varied and beautiful spectacle throughout the seasons. Each time we return to this handsome hotel, we are impressed by the graceful staircase, the attractive flower arrangements and the original tapestry wall hangings. The furnishings throughout are in keeping with the elegance of the building. There is a large, comfortable lounge bar, a library with book-lined walls and a beautifully furnished drawing-room. Skilfully co-ordinated curtains, carpets, wallpapers and bed covers, together with wardrobes, chests and dressing-tables shining from careful polishing, make the bedrooms most attractive. The handsome dining room is warmed by a welcoming open fire. The hotel has an excellent reputation for the quality of its food and the menus have been created to make the most of Aberdeenshire's prime meat, fish and game. Guests here can enjoy salmon and trout fishing on a three-and-a-half-mile private stretch of the River Don, play golf on a wide range of courses or simply stroll through the delightful gardens. Kildrummy Castle Hotel is a convenient base for exploring Deeside, Donside and the Spey Valley. Mr T Hanna, the proprietor, and his friendly staff will make you most welcome.

Weekly Terms from £385.00
Daily Terms from £55.00
Bed and Breakfast from £48.00
Lunch from £13.00 and A La Carte
Dinner from £25.00 and A La Carte
Gratuities at Guest's Discretion
VAT inclusive
Credit Cards—Access, American Express, Visa

1 Single, 4 Double, 8 Twin Bedrooms
3 Family Rooms
15 Private Bathrooms
1 Private Shower Room
All Rooms with TV, Telephone, Radio, Tea and Coffee-making Facilities, Trouser Press, Hairdryer
Open from 1st February to end December
Fully Licensed

Games Room
Conference Facilities
Children catered for
Dogs allowed
Parking Facilities
Fishing
Nearby: Golf, Riding, Shooting

Section 8: Grampian

Ballater—Darroch Learg Hotel
Braemar Road, Ballater, Grampian. AB35 5UX. Tel and Fax 03397 55443

The Darroch Learg was built in 1888 when Deeside was becoming increasingly popular following Queen Victoria's discovery of the area. Formerly a country house, it is now an hotel of twenty bedrooms, fifteen in the main house and a further five in Oakhall, a turreted mansion built in the Scottish baronial style. Both houses stand in five acres of well tended grounds above Ballater with the golf course and River Dee below and the peaks of the Grampian Mountains along the sky line. Ownership has remained in the Franks family since 1961, control now having passed to the younger generation. Recent years have seen much refurbishment and the addition of a conservatory to the dining room has been particularly successful. Good quality furnishings enhance each room and a number of antique pieces have been collected over the years, helping to retain the relaxing country house atmosphere. The drawing room and separate smoke room offer a peaceful haven throughout the day. Pre-dinner drinks are served here and guests may choose from a varied, daily changing menu. Dinner is served in the conservatory with its light and airy atmosphere and wonderful outlook to the hills. Lovers of the countryside will take delight in the area, which has many places of interest. Outdoor sports include golf, fishing, gliding, mounbtain biking, riding, shooting and skiing. Sightseers will enjoy the National Trust properties, whisky distilleries and fine scenery.

Weekly Terms from £308.00
Daily Terms from £50.50
Bed and Breakfast from £32.00
Lunch from £9.00 Table D'Hôte
Dinner from £18.50 Table D'Hôte
Service and VAT inclusive

Credit Cards—Access, Visa
8 Double, 10 Twin, 2 Single Bedrooms
(1 Room with Four Poster Bed)
16 Private Bathrooms
4 Private Shower Rooms
All Rooms with TV, Telephone, Radio,

Baby-listening, Tea and Coffee-making Facilities, Trouser Press, Hairdryer
Open from 1st February to 30th November
Residential and Restaurant Licence
Children catered for. Dogs allowed
Parking Facilities

Ballater–Pannanich Wells Hotel
South Deeside Road, Ballater, Aberdeenshire. AB35 5SJ. Tel 03397 55018. Fax 03397 55038

A mile from the nearest building, this historic hotel occupies a commanding position high on the side of Pannanich Hill. Noted since 1760 for its healing waters, and frequented by Lord Byron as a boy and student, it stands among pine and larch trees, with incomparable views over the Dee Valley. Only eight miles to the west is Balmoral Castle, summer residence of the Royal Family. Examining a map of the area will reveal vast open spaces south of Ballater, with only one small road intruding, terminating at Spittal of Glenmuick just above Loch Muick. Upper Deeside is noted internationally for its walking and hill climbing, and the famous Glenshee ski playground is only half an hour's drive from the hotel. Notable among the many other outdoor sports are fishing, riding, golf and gliding. For the motorist, roads over the Grampian Mountains or east to Aberdeen provide a wide variety of scenery and numerous places of historic or natural interest. There are just five *en suite* rooms at the hotel, where every comfort and caring personal attention is accorded to visitors. The *table d'hôte* menus, changed daily, offer a fine choice of wholesome food including a vegetarian dish, complemented by a list of French and German wines with a most helpful tasting guide. Greeting guests, on arrival in their rooms, are fresh flowers, a basket of fruit, a selection of toiletries and-of course-a jug of Pannanich water.

Weekly Terms from £300.30
Daily Terms from £45.00
Bed and Breakfast from £33.75
Special Rates available
Business Package £57.00
Bar Lunch from £2.50
Lunch from £7.50 Table d'Hôte

Dinner from £19.00 and A La Carte
VAT inclusive. Credit Cards–Access, Visa
1 Single, 2 Double, 2 Twin Bedrooms
All Rooms with Private Bathroom, TV,
Telephone, Radio, Tea and Coffee-making Facilities, Trouser Press, Hairdryer,
Refrigerator. Open all Year

Fully Licensed
Full Central Heating
Children not catered for
Dogs allowed
Nearby: Tennis, Putting, Swimming, Golf, Riding, Water Skiing, Shooting, Hang-gliding, Gliding, Skiing

Section 8: Grampian

Craigellachie—Craigellachie Hotel
Craigellachie, Aberlour, Banffshire. AB38 9SR
Tel 0340 881 204. Fax 0340 881 253

Craigellachie is not just a pretty name. We think it is one of the loveliest villages in Moray. The rivers Spey and Fiddich blend just here and Thomas Telford's slender iron bridge is a striking landmark. A centuries-old coaching inn, later rebuilt as a Victorian hotel of elegance and spaciousness, has served those who have come to enjoy the picturesqueness of the area. Recently, this hotel has undergone another renaissance, for the owner, Tomas Gronager, has lavished a great deal of time and money, and no small amount of flair, in transforming this former sporting hotel into a place of charm and comfort. The requirements of sportsmen (rod-rooms, gun lockers, etc.) are still met, but, in addition, there is now a great deal more to admire. We dined here recently and it is clear that local produce is used to the full. Nothing comes from the freezer! The wine list is impressive and the Quaich Bar carries a connoisseur's stock of single malt whiskies. Move from room to room ... the lounges; dining room; games room; gentlemen's room, with its leather chairs, books and cigar boxes; and the bedrooms, furnished with a mixture of antiques and quality reproductions ... and you will agree that everywhere is in perfect taste. There is a multi-gym, a sauna and a sunbed, and as for fishing, shooting or stalking, everything is laid on for your needs. Salmon on the Spey from March to September; roe stalking from May onwards; autumn salmon and brown trout on the Fiddich.

Weekly Terms from £395.00
Daily Terms from £68.25
Bed and Breakfast from £43.50
Bar Meal from £4.00
Buffet Lunch from £9.75 incl.Sunday Lunch
Dinner from £24.75 Table D'Hôte
Gratuities at Guest's Discretion
VAT inclusive

Credit Cards—Access, American Express, Diners Club, Visa
3 Family Rooms
12 Double, 10 Twin, 5 Single Bedrooms
All Rooms with Private Bathroom, TV, Telephone, Radio, Tea and Coffee-making Facilities, Hairdryer
Baby-sitter available on Request

Open all Year. Fully Licensed
Full Central Heating
Cocktail Bar. Rod Room
Games Room. Conference Facilities
Dogs allowed. Parking Facilities
Sauna, Solarium, Exercise Room, Fishing, Shooting

Section 8: Grampian

Glenlivet—Minmore House Glenlivet, Ballindalloch,
Banffshire. AB3 9DB. Tel 08073 378. Fax 08073 472.

The full significance of 'individual attention' is realised here: afternoon teas, picnic hampers for day or night excursions, assistance with arrangements for numerous sporting activities, fresh fruit and flowers in your bedroom, together with home-made biscuits—the welcome is warm and genuine. Belinda Luxmoore has spent the last fifteen years owning and running hotels in Wales and Devon so the care, catering and comfort are all founded on experience. Also, in this land of distilleries, there are literally scores of different malt whiskies available at the bar. Minmore House, once the home of the owner of the nearby Glenlivet Distillery, is set in four acres of attractive gardens, in which there is an outside swimming pool, hard tennis court and croquet lawn. In and around the famous Speyside Valley, a myriad of outdoor activities and interests await the fisherman and photographer, the artist and the ornithologist, the marksman and the climber, the equestrian and historian, while the golfer has at least ten courses within an easy drive of the hotel. Add to this the craft workshops, country parks, nature and wildlife reserves, farm museums and the newly developed Lecht ski area, and it is clear that here the visitor has a quite exceptional range of healthy, educational and absorbing diversions available. Your hostess will be only too pleased to advise and assist you in selecting those most suited to your taste—and you will appreciate the wholesome and appetising five-course dinner on your return.

Weekly Terms from £290.00	1 Family Room. 1 Four Poster Room	Fully Licensed. Full Central Heating
Daily Terms from £45.00	5 Double, 3 Twin, 2 Single Bedrooms	Conference Facilities. Children catered for
Bed and Breakfast from £29.50	10 Private Bathrooms. 1 Private Shower	Dogs allowed. Parking Facilities
Dinner from £16.50	Room. 10 Rooms with Tea and	Hard Tennis Court, Croquet, Swimming,
Service Charge and VAT inclusive	Coffee-making Facilities	Fishing. Nearby: Squash, Swimming, Golf,
Credit Cards—Access, Visa	Open from May to October	Fishing, Riding, Windsurfing, Shooting

Near Huntly, Marnoch–The Old Manse of Marnoch
Bridge of Marnoch, Huntly, Grampian. AB54 5RS. Tel 0466 780873

A peaceful atmosphere, both within the hotel and in the surroundings of the Deveron Valley, set the mood for one to take a leisurely delight in the truly outstanding *cuisine*, an intriguingly different wine list and a selection of almost thirty different teas. This is somewhere for the discerning and sociable person. Accommodation is for just ten guests, who meet for pre-dinner drinks and dine on a four-course set meal. With a little prior notice, vegetarian and other special diets are imaginatively catered for. In addition to conventional wines from the traditional vineyards of the world, and some delicious highland wines, a fine range of organic wines is offered, originating from grapes produced using the minimum of chemicals and no additives. Also listed are six non-alcoholic drinks. In a recent competition for the best British breakfast menu, the Old Manse of Marnoch was a runner-up (second only to a major London hotel) with a vast choice of fruit and fruit juices, porridges, cereals, fish, meats, eggs and prepared dishes, complemented by a choice of many beverages. We must repeat: the *cuisine* here is quite exceptional. Everything is prepared in their own kitchen, including the breakfast baking and even the after-dinner mints. Books and paintings provide interesting relaxation in the comfortable lounges. Helpful guides to the sporting and scenic attractions of the area are provided in the well-appointed bedrooms.

All Prices pertain to 1992	VAT not applicable	Toiletries. Open all Year
Daily Terms from £50.00 p.p. 2 nights or	No Credit Cards accepted	Restricted Licence. Full Central Heating
more. Bed and Breakfast £35.00 p.p. 2	3 Double, 2 Twin Bedrooms	TV Lounge. Library. Children over 12 years
nights or more. Packed Lunch £6.00	4 Private Bathrooms, 1 Private Shower	catered for. Dogs allowed. Parking Facilities
Dinner £20.00 Table d'Hôte	Room. All Rooms with Radio, Tea and	Nearby: Swimming, Golf, Fishing, Riding,
Gratuities at Guest's Discretion	Coffee-making Facilities, Hairdryer,	Sailing, Windsurfing, Water Skiing,

Section 8: Grampian

Stonehaven—The Heugh Hotel Westfield Road, Stonehaven, Grampian. AB3 2EE. Tel 0569 62379. Fax 0569 66637

The distinctive silver-gray granite is used most effectively in this late-Victorian baronial mansion. There is, indeed, no mistaking this attractive hotel, for it is elaborately turreted and crenellated, as befits the building which occupies the heugh, or height, of this interesting coastal resort. We like the genuine welcome one receives here and the friendliness of the Hermanns family and their staff. The Heugh Hotel is very much a family endeavour: Wilhelm personally supervises the kitchen; his wife, Joy, welcomes guests at the reception; their son Kevin and his wife Jean, assist in reception and in the dining room. And how successful they have been. For whenever visitors stay in this area, whether in Aberdeen or along Deeside, for many, dinner at the Heugh appears to be part of their holiday. The heavy demand for meals in the lounge bar attests to the local popularity of the hotel's *cuisine*, which is evident, too, in the dining room, although here Wilhelm insists that a leisurely atmosphere prevails. There is an inglenook fireplace in the dining room, attractive wood panelling in many of the rooms, and the Bavarian-style tapestries one sees are the work of Mrs Hermanns, senior. There are five bedrooms upstairs so, advance booking is desirable, and each is equipped with a private bathroom, colour television and beverage-making facilities. The fishing port of Stonehaven, with its sea-girt castle, has become a most favoured resort. Castles line the Dee valley, including Balmoral, and the Highland scenery hereabouts is breathtaking.

Weekly Terms (B&B) from £240.00 sharing Twin/Double
Bed and Breakfast from £37.00
Bar Meal from £5.50
Lunch A La Carte
Afternoon Tea from £3.50
Dinner from £16.50 A La Carte

Gratuities at Guest's Discretion
VAT inclusive. Credit Cards—Access, American Express, Visa
2 Double, 3 Single Bedrooms
All Rooms with Private Bathroom, TV, Radio, Telephone, Tea and Coffee-making Facilities, Hairdryer, Trouser Press

Open all Year. Fully Licensed. Full Central Heating. Conference Facilities. Children catered for. Dogs allowed. Parking Facilities Nearby: Tennis, Putting, Squash, Badminton, Swimming, Solarium, Sauna Golf, Fishing, Riding, Windsurfing, Water Skiing

Infallible?

The answer is no because even as these lines are being written, hotel ownership, management and staff are changing somewhere. Invaluable? Yes, because by joining the Ashley Courtenay Circle (no extra charge) you can check up with us at any time during the current season.

A reminder.

Some of the tariffs in this book are those quoted for 1992. As prices will probably have changed for 1993 please check before booking. Please also note that the weekly and daily hotel rates shown in this book are for half board only (dinner, room and breakfast) unless otherwise stated.

Section 8: Highland

Arisaig, Beasdale—Arisaig House
Beasdale, By Arisaig, Inverness-shire. PH39 4NR
Tel 068 75 622. Fax 068 75 626

Truly exceptional amongst the finest: in every respect Arisaig House sets standards that few can even approach. An impressive grey-stone building, superbly restored after a fire in 1937, it stands serene in twenty-one acres of gardens skilfully laid out to include walled rose gardens, vegetable gardens, manicured lawns stretching down to the sea, rhododendrons and azaleas shaded by giant sequoia and wellingtonia and, nearby, a croquet lawn. Take tea on the terrace overlooking these lovely gardens, with a backdrop of seemingly endless mountain ranges and the ever-present murmur of the sea. Your family hosts, Ruth, John and Andrew Smither, maintain the splendid interior of the house with impeccably good taste and furnishings to please the most discerning guest. Their chef's epicurean offerings present a delightful choice of freshly prepared wholesome dishes complemented by a lineage of fine chateau bottlings to suit the palate of every connoisseur. Everywhere the decor is conducive to a mood of luxurious relaxation, whether one is enjoying a game in the billiards room, fresh coffee in the morning room, a good book in the drawing room or the scenic views framed by every window in the house. In this unspoilt area there are drives and walks aplenty, ferry-boats to Skye and the Outer Hebrides, boats to Eigg, Muck, Rhum and Canna, names which tempt the traveller to explore. All this excellence is most aptly reflected in the splendid Arisaig House brochure.

Bed and Breakfast from £49.50 per person
Bar Lunch from £10.00
Afternoon Tea from £8.50
Dinner £29.50 and A La Carte
No Service Charge
VAT inclusive
Credit Cards—Access, Visa
6 Double, 7 Twin, 2 Single Bedrooms

All Rooms with Private Bathroom, TV, Telephone, Trouser Press, Hairdryer, Toiletries, Bathrobes
Open from late March to end October
Residential Licence
Full Central Heating and Log Fires
Cocktail Bar. Billiard Room

Meeting Room for up to 12 persons
Children over 10 years catered for
Dogs not allowed
Parking Facilities
Croquet
Nearby: Sea or Loch Fishing by arrangement

Section 8: Highland

Aultbea–Aultbea Hotel
Aultbea, Ross-shire. IV22 2HX
Tel 0445 731201. Fax 0445 731214

In our opinion, the coastal road of Wester Ross, from Loch Torridon to Ullapool, offers some of the world's most attractive scenery. Aultbea lies half-way along this road, on the shores of Loch Ewe. On a dark winter's evening we could swear that we saw the ghosts of the merchant ships assembling in the loch for a wartime transatlantic convoy, but these ghosts are dispelled in the mediterranean blue of the loch in summer. Only the seals assemble to watch us as we walk along the shore. The Aultbea is a typical highland village hotel, skilfully brought up to date by Peter and Avril Nieto. Residents and visitors have a splendidly wide choice of food and refreshments, ranging from sandwiches on home-baked bread, through freshly brewed speciality teas and childrens snacks, an excellent selection of grills and salads on the *Waterside Bistro and Bar* menu, to dinners from *table d'hôte* or *à la carte* menus served in the ambience of the *Zetland Restaurant*. We met chef Alan Morrison, whose talents are many and who inclines towards French specialities. The *table d' hôte* dinner menu offers a fresh choice each day and includes such delicacies as prime Torridon venison steak marinated in red wine, Loch Broom Lobster Thermidor and duckling in cherry brandy sauce. Peter Nieto's liqueur trolley carries excellent vintage port and rare cognacs: his carefully selected wine list has over fifty labels and, in the bar, there are more than forty single malt and de luxe whiskies. A wonderful evening's relaxation to round off a day of walking, fishing or touring the impressive lochs, forests, mountains and streams of this unspoilt area. There is also available a luxury self-catering lodge.

Weekly Terms from £300.00
Daily Terms from £48.00
Bed and Breakfast from £28.50
Bar Meal from £3.00
Afternoon Tea from £4.00
Dinner from £19.00 and A La CArte
Gratuities at Guest's Discretion

VAT inclusive
Credit Cards–Access, Visa
1 Family Room
1 Single, 4 Double, 2 Twin Bedrooms
5 Private Bathrooms. 3 Private Shower Rooms. All Rooms with TV, Telephone, Radio, Baby-listening, Tea and

Coffee-making Facilities, Trouser Press, Hairdryer. Open all Year
Fully Licensed
Full Central Heating. Cocktail Bar
Children catered for. Dogs allowed
Parking Facilities
Nearby: Fishing, Sailing, Windsurfing

Section 8: Highland

Brora—Royal Marine Hotel Golf Road, Brora,
Sutherland, Highland. KW9 6QS. Tel 0408 21252. Telex 76165

The renowned Scottish architect, Sir Robert Lorimer, originally designed this as a private Country House in the 1930's. A recent change of ownership has brought extensive restoration and modernisation—especially in the rebuilt kitchen and the facilities in every spacious bedroom—but the rich character remains. One feature in particular caught our eye: the original carved wood fireplace surrounds. Of the eleven *en suite* bedrooms, one has a four-poster suite, another a jacuzzi suite and there is a large Marine family room. Since Brora is a thriving golf and fishing resort, the hotel is obviously especially attractive to sportsmen. In addition to the four championship courses in this locality, and the hotel's own boat on Loch Brora for fishermen, the Royal Marine has a heated indoor swimming pool and sauna, a full size snooker table and access to the four-lane curling rink during the winter months. Other attractions in the area include Dunrobin Castle, Clynelish Distillery, a wool mill and an award winning Heritage Centre, open from May to October. The region abounds with wildlife which can be seen in its natural habitat, and the rock formations in Sutherland—the least densely populated area in Europe—are of outstanding interest to geologists. Climbers, walkers or bird-watchers can return to this hotel assured of meals to satisfy the heartiest of appetites. In the dining room, *table d'hôte* and *à la carte* menus are based on the best of fresh local produce, with bar lunches or evening 'Fireside' suppers also available.

Weekly Terms from £350.00
Daily Terms from £55.00
Bed and Breakfast from £40.00
Lunch from £10.00 Table D'Hôte
Dinner from £17.50 Table D'Hôte
Gratuities at Guest's Discretion

VAT inclusive. Credit Cards— Access, American Express, Diners Club, Visa
1 Family Room. 2 Suites
2 Double, 6 Twin Bedrooms
All Rooms with Private Bathroom, TV, Telephone, Radio, Baby-listening, Tea

and Coffee-making Facilities
Hairdryer available on Request
Open all Year. Fully Licensed. Full Central Heating. Cocktail Bar. TV Lounge
Games Room. Conference Facilities
Dogs Allowed. Parking Facilities

Carrbridge—Dalrachney Lodge Hotel Carrbridge,
Inverness-shire. PH23 3AT. Tel 047984 252. Fax 047984 382

Situated in fourteen acres of colourful grounds, this imposing building was acquired by Helen and Grant Swanney in 1988. It had been the principal hunting lodge of the Countess of Seafield and, in the conversion to a spacious and comfortable hotel, the atmosphere of its Victorian background has been re-created. A wealth of activities await sportsmen and outdoor enthusiasts booking in at Dalrachney Lodge. The hotel has its own stretch of the River Dulnain and those with an interest in fishing can try out their skills on the local salmon and trout. Stags' heads and sporting rifles, oil paintings of the Highland scene, mingled with ceramics from older cultures, adorn the walls. The graceful staircase is enlivened by an imposing stained glass window. An excellent selection of books and magazines adds warmth to the comfortable lounge, with its views southwards over the Cairngorm Mountains. This is an area for many sports other than the seasonal shooting: fishing, sailing, canoeing, swimming, skating, riding, birdwatching, walking and pony trekking. In the hotel dining room, guests have a choice of *table d'hôte* and *à la carte* menus, both offering a selection of dishes based on wholesome fresh produce, cooked to order. The Scottish Tourist Board has awarded four crowns commended, RAC three stars. For holidaymakers and business people, a most accommodating hotel.

Weekly Terms from £290.00
Daily Terms from £47.00
Bed and Breakfast from £29.50
Bar Meal from £2.45
Lunch from £5.70
Dinner from £16.50 and A La Carte
Gratuities at Guest's discretion
VAT inclusive. Credit Cards—Access, American Express, Visa

3 Family, 4 Double, 1 Single, 3 Twin Bedrooms. 10 private Bathrooms
1 Private Shower Room
All Rooms with TV, Telephone, Radio, Tea and Coffee-making Facilities, Hairdryer
Open all Year
Fully Licensed
Full Central Heating
Cocktail Bar.

Conference Facilities
Children catered for
Dogs allowed. Parking Facilities
Fishing
Nearby: Tennis, Putting, squash, Badminton, Swimming, Sauna, Golf, Fishing, Riding, Sailing, Windsurfing, Water Skiing, Shooting

Section 8: Highland

Mey—Castle Arms Hotel
Mey, Caithness, Highland. KW14 8XH. Tel 0847 85244

With its double glazing and central heating, this north-facing hotel offers a cosy haven with breathtaking views of the Orkneys across the often stormy waters of the Pentland Firth. Situated on the John o'Groats peninsula, and formerly a nineteenth-century Coaching Inn, it is adjacent to the Castle of Mey, the Queen Mother's Highland home. Commended to us by a friend, our visit to this warm and friendly hotel was something of a revelation. A recently completed programme of modernisation has skilfully enhanced the comfort and decor in the restaurant, the lounges and in the three bars. Every bedroom has television and provision for making tea and coffee: the bathrooms have facilities for disabled people. Our dinner of local fish and fresh vegetables was cooked to perfection and served in the attractive restaurant which overlooks a small landscaped garden. Everything in the hotel is under the direct supervision of the proprietor, Ms Morrison, who appears to be in several places at once without becoming in the least flustered. A particularly interesting feature is the gallery of unique photographs of the Queen Mother: selected prints of these, and local crafts, are available for purchase at the Castle Arms. Accommodation, food and wine are all on a most moderate tariff.

Bed and Breakfast from £22.00
Weekly Terms (B&B) as above less 10%
Bar Meal from £3.20
Afternoon Tea from £1.95
Dinner from £8.20 A La Carte
Gratuities at Guest's discretion
VAT inclusive

Credit Cards—Access, Visa
1 Family Room
4 Double, 3 Twin Bedrooms
2 Private Bathrooms
6 Private Shower Rooms
All Rooms with TV, Telephone, Tea and Coffee-making Facilities

Hairdryer available
Open all Year
Fully Licensed
Full Central Heating. Cocktail Bar
Children catered for. Dogs allowed
Parking Facilities
Nearby: Fishing, Riding, Shooting

Dornoch—The Burghfield House Hotel
Dornoch, Sutherland. IV25 3HN. Tel 0862 810212.

In these days when hotels are so often changing hands, it is always pleasing to learn of one which has been run by the same family since 1946. This is the case with Burghfield House, where the Currie family do such a fine job in looking after their guests. Standing in over five acres of gardens and overlooking the thirteenth-century cathedral and Dornoch, it is an ideal place for a family holiday. Only a few minutes away is the famous Royal Dornoch Links, one of the oldest and most renowned courses in the United Kingdom, where golf has been played since 1616 and golf can be arranged on six nearby courses. The Curries specialise in catering for golf parties and offer reduced rates early and late in the season. Golf, however, is not the only sporting amenity available as there are miles of safe and sandy beaches nearby which are suitable for swimming, sunning and sailing, whilst fishing is available on several lochs. Active people also need rest and good food and the Currie family know just what to provide. Most of the bedrooms and public rooms have been refurbished over the past year. For further unwinding, we noted two lounges, two cocktail bars and a television and games room. The food is first class: the extensive *table d'hôte* and *à la carte* menus range from classical to Highland fare and the best of local produce is always used. Burghfield House is well worth your patronage for a first-class holiday.

Bed and Breakfast from £27.50
Bar Meal from £4.50
Lunch from £5.50 and A La Carte
Dinner from £12.50 and A La Carte
Gratuities at Guest's Discretion
VAT inclusive
Credit Cards—Access, American Express, Diners Club, Visa

10 Family Rooms. 22 Double/Twin,
4 Single Bedrooms
30 Rooms with TV, Telephone, Hairdryer
All Rooms with Private Bathroom, Radio, Baby-listening, Tea and Coffee-making Facilities
Open from 1st April to 31st October
Fully Licensed

Full Central Heating
2 Cocktail Bars. TV Lounge
Games Room. Conference Facilities
Dogs allowed
Parking Facilities
Night Porter. Putting
Nearby: Tennis, Squash, Swimming, Golf, Fishing, Riding, Shooting

Section 8: Highland

Onich, by Fort William—Allt-nan-Ros Hotel
Onich, by Fort William, Highland. PH33 6RY
Tel 08553 210/250.Fax 08553 462

Every bedroom in this exceptional hotel has a breathtaking view of the wider, southern part of Loch Linnhe. In all respects, the setting and the service here are second to none. A gracefully curving drive, lined by colourful flowering shrubs, sweeps up to the stately house, fronted by lush lawns and backed by mature trees. In our conducted tour of the sumptuously furnished hotel, we were particularly impressed by the modernity and cleanliness of the kitchens. Clearly they provide all the facilities to support the imaginative menus of which the partners are justifiably so proud. One often reads of wines 'complementing' superb dishes: here they positively challenge the cuisine. Some 150 bins, listed over twelve pages, cover the world's major vineyards, most bottles with an informed summary of their characteristics and many available—most commendably—also in half bottles. Helpful general descriptions precede the listings for each wine-producing area. Allt-nan-Ros most certainly provides a superb opportunity for connoisseurs of good food and fine wine to indulge themselves and, equally, a splendid chance for the uninitiated to become acquainted with the best. A great many natural features in this area provide objectives for walkers to work off any excesses in dining: the West Highland Way, running south from Fort William towards Glasgow, passes the eastern end of nearby Loch Leven, while for the less energetic, motoring is a pleasure on the quiet scenic roads amidst stunning scenery.

Weekly Terms from £280.00
Daily Terms from £50.00
Bed and Breakfast from £35.00
Bar Lunch from £7.50
Lunch from £7.50 and A La Carte
Afternoon Tea from £3.50
Dinner from £17.50 Table d'Hôte
Gratuities at Guest's discretion
VAT inclusive

Credit Cards—Access, American Express, Diners Club, Switch, Visa
2 Family Rooms
9 Double, 7 Twin, 3 Single Bedrooms
18 Private Bathrooms
3 Private Shower Rooms
All Rooms with TV, Telephone, Radio, Baby-listening, Tea and Coffee-making Facilities, Hairdryer, Electric Blankets
7 Rooms with Trouser Press

Open from 1st April to early November
Fully Licensed
Full Central Heating
Cocktail Bar. Conference Facilities
Children catered for
Dogs allowed
Parking Facilities
Fishing, Windsurfing, Walking, Birdwatching

Section 8: Highland

Near Fort William—The Moorings Hotel & Restaurant Banavie, Fort William, Inverness-shire. PH33 7LY. Tel 0397 772 797. Fax 0397 772 441

The excellent location of this hotel is surely one of its most attractive features. Set in the very heart of the Scottish Highlands it overlooks Neptune's Staircase, the series of locks built to form the Caledonian Canal affording passage to vessels from one side of Scotland to the other to avoid the hazardous and lengthy voyage around the notorious Cape Wrath. Beyond rises Ben Nevis, the highest point in the United Kingdom, surrounded by the dramatic and imposing peaks of the majestic Mamores. The Moorings Hotel is a modern, purpose built hotel with a strong nautical theme. All bedrooms have private bath/shower rooms, television, telephone, tea and coffee facilities plus baby-listening devices. The lounge bar has a layout reminiscent of a ship's deck with a wealth of nautical features and brass fittings. The rosette winning restaurant is furnished in Jacobean style and offers a superb menu based on Taste of Scotland featuring wholesome and fresh local dishes such as Angus beef, Speyside pheasant, Lochy trout and, of course, the incomparable Scottish salmon. The cellars offer a wide range of wines selected to complement the menu. Also there is a bistro, again decorated in nautical style with oak beams and panelling whilst an open fireplace gives a cheerful and warming reception in colder weather. The service is both efficient and friendly with much attention to detail, all of which ensures that a stay, long or short term, whether for business or relaxation, is an unqualified success.

Weekly Terms from £364.00
Daily Terms from £58.00
Bed and Breakfast from £35.00
Bar Meal from £5.50
Afternoon Tea from £5.00
Dinner from £23.00 and A La Carte
Gratuities at Guest's Discretion
VAT inclusive

Credit Cards—Access, American Express, Diners Club, Visa
1 Family Room, 1 Four-Poster Room
3 Single, 19 Double/Twin Bedrooms
All Rooms with Private Bath/Shower Room, TV, Telephone, Radio, Baby-listening, Tea and Coffee-making Facilities. Open all Year. Fully Licensed

Full Central Heating
2 Cocktail Bars
Conference Facilities
Dogs not allowed
Parking Facilities
Nearby: Tennis, Putting Squash, Swimming, Solarium, Sauna, Golf, Fishing, Riding

Near Fort William, Onich—The Lodge On The Loch Creag Dhu, Onich, Near Fort William, Inverness-shire. PH33 6RY. Tel 08553 237/238. Fax 08552 463

We always return to this delightful hotel, familiar to many of our readers as The Creag Dhu, because of its panoramic setting and the warmth of its welcome. The hosts, Norman, Jessie and Laurence Young, are genuinely concerned to help their guests make the most of a Highland holiday—they offer talks and slide shows on the area and plenty of suggestions for local walks, tours and boat trips. The dining-room, with its spectacular view southwards of Loch Linnhe, offers excellent Highland fare, and 'Taste of Scotland' delicacies and vegetarian dishes are always featured on the menus. Each of the bedrooms at the front of the hotel has a bay-windowed sitting area from which to appreciate the panorama of mountains and sea. The hotel also has one ground floor room suitable for the disabled. The hotel's beautiful setting, in five acres of grounds, and its co-ordinated natural furnishings combine to produce a remarkably relaxing atmosphere. The Lodge On The Loch, one mile north of Ballachulish Bridge, is strategically placed for touring the western Highlands, an area of outstanding natural beauty and grandeur while the presence of the Gulf Stream ensures a temperate climate in which palm trees, azaleas and rhododendrons flourish. The hotel is open over Christmas and New Year for festive breaks in the appropriate style. Hotel guests have exclusive use of the hotel's leisure club in Ballachulish, just three miles away. This is a truly splendid spot in which to stay.

Weekly Terms from £339.00
Daily Terms from £52.00
Bed and Breakfast from £35.00
Lunch from £3.50 and A La Carte
Dinner from £22.00 and A La Carte
Gratuities at Guest's Discretion

VAT inclusive. Credit Cards—Access, Visa
1 Family Room. 2 Single Bedrooms
7 Double, 8 Twin Bedrooms
12 Private Bathrooms
6 Private Shower Rooms
All Rooms with TV, Telephone, Radio,

Baby-listening, Tea and Coffee-making Facilities, Toiletries, Trouser Press, Hairdryer. Open from 1st February to 4th November, Christmas and New Year
Fully Licensed. Full Central Heating
Dogs allowed. Parking Facilities

Section 8: Highland

Gairloch—Creag Mor Hotel and Restaurant
Charleston, Gairloch, Ross-shire, IV21 2AH
Tel 0445 2068. Fax 0445 2044

Only rarely do our inspectors eulogise about a hotel on all counts—but this is one such occasion. In their opinion, the service here could be a lesson to any hotelier on how an hotel should be run. Readers may not be surprised, therefore, to learn that many of the staff here, at the time of our visit, were on the final year of the catering and hospitality honours degree course. They are a great credit to resident proprietors Larry and Betty Nieto. Tasteful and luxurious bedrooms have every amenity including trouser press and hairdryer, with en suite facilities in every one comprising bath and shower. All rooms look over the hotel's extensive landscaped grounds or the spectacular scenery of Wester Ross. Leading off from the sumptuous reception area is the split-level *Gallery Lounge*, which enjoys superb views of Skye and the Outer Isles. Here too, as in other parts of the hotel, the charming water-colour original paintings adorning the walls are for sale. In the *Buttery* and in the *Mackenzie Room* Restaurant, the choice of food and wine must meet the requirements of every palate and every pocket. The selection is wide, the basic ingredients fresh and wholesome and the presentation absolutely superb. Their *Bothan Bar*, in common with the cocktail bar, offers over 100 different brands of malt and blended whiskies. The Creag Mor is a perfect base from which to explore the many interesting and scenic places in the Gairloch area, and to enjoy golf, pony-trekking, fishing, sailing, water-skiing or walking. This exceptional setting and the warm highland hospitality (including twenty-four hour room service) is, here, on an exceedingly moderate tariff.

Weekly Terms from £301.00
Daily Terms from £38.00
Bed and Breakfast from £22.00
Bar Meal from £4.50
Afternoon Tea from £3.00
Dinner from £18.50 and A La Carte
Gratuities at Guest's Discretion
VAT inclusive
Credit Cards—Access, Visa

2 Family Rooms. 1 Suite
8 Double, 1 Single, 7 Twin Bedrooms
All Rooms with Private Bathroom, TV, Telephone, Radio, Baby-listening, Tea and Coffee-making Facilities, Trouser Press, Hairdryer, Room Service
Open all Year
Fully Licensed
Full Central Heating

Cocktail Bar. Games Room
Conference Facilities
Children catered for
Dogs allowed
Parking Facilities
Night Porter
Nearby: Tennis, Swimming, Golf, Fishing, Riding, Sailing, Windsurfing, 4-wheel Bike Safari

Section 8: Highland

Glenshiel—Kintail Lodge Hotel Glenshiel, Kyle of Lochalsh, Ross-shire. IV40 8HL. Tel 059981 275

When travelling along Glen Shiel from the south the peaks of the Five Sisters range are signposts that the very best of the Highlands is about to begin. Lochs, glens and hills, a hop across to Skye, streams and cascades are all here to savour. At the foot of the highest peaks, and with views along the whole length of Loch Duich, is the former shooting lodge which has become Kintail Lodge. Margaret and Stuart Henderson spent many annual holidays in the area and, when the opportunity of buying this lovely hotel arose, they needed no second bidding to give up successful careers in the south and to take over their 'dream come true'. They offer twelve attractive bedrooms, ten *en suite* and with the usual modern comforts. Downstairs are a small residents' lounge, with a pleasant fire and a good selection of reading matter; a lounge bar for the exclusive use of diners and residents; a sun lounge with beautiful loch views; and a well appointed dining room. The *cuisine* is the province of Margaret Henderson and her dishes are a splendid attraction, particularly her imaginative local fish specialities, which are also available at breakfast. The wine list is a fine complement to the menus and is reasonably priced. You will find Kintail Lodge in a setting of some grandeur with its four acres of walled garden stretching down to the loch. Kintail is for climbers, walkers, bird-watchers and anglers. Naturalists will enjoy watching the seals and otters and, perhaps a school of dolphin which occasionally frequent the area.

Prices pertain to 1992
Daily Terms from £49.50 (June-Sept)
Special 2 days Break (Nov-April), £74.00 p.p. £35.00 p.p. thereafter
Afternoon Tea from £2.00
Dinner from £17.00 Table D'Hôte

Gratuities at Guest's Discretion
VAT inclusive. Credit Cards—Access, Visa
5 Double, 4 Twin, 3 Single Bedrooms
7 Private Bathrooms
3 Private Shower Rooms
All Rooms with TV, Tea and Coffee-making

Facilities. Open from 2nd January to 23rd December. Fully Licensed
Part Central Heating. Cocktail Bar
Children catered for. Dogs allowed
Parking Facilities
Nearby: Fishing, Riding

Near Grantown-on-Spey, Dulnain Bridge—Skye of Curr Hotel Tigh-na-Sgiadh, Dulnain Bridge, Near Grantown-on-Spey, Inverness-shire. PH26 3PA. Tel 047985 345

The Skye of Curr hotel is a small baronial mansion set in the heart of the Spey valley. It was built as a private residence for a distinguished family and tastefully converted into an hotel without losing any of the charm of an elegant and hospitable country house. Situated in approximately three acres of well-wooded grounds, there are superb views of the Cairngorms and the Cromdale Hills. The reception rooms are beautifully appointed and extremely comfortable. A welcoming log fire and a profusion of flowers add to the attractiveness of the sitting-room. One can relax and enjoy excellent food, for which the Skye of Curr Hotel is well known, in the candlelit dining-room. The bedrooms are spacious and comfortable and offer beautiful views. The fertile Spey valley is in sharp contrast to the rolling moorlands which lie south of Grantown-on-Spey but there is much to reward the traveller. Skiing, fishing, pony trekking and golf are just a few of the many activities which can be arranged and the Aviemore Centre, Scotland's major skiing resort, is only ten miles distant. The area is excellent for touring, climbing, hill walking or gentle walks in spectacular scenery.

Daily Terms from £39.50
Bed and Breakfast from £24.00
Bar Meal from £3.50
Dinner from £15.50 Table D'Hôte
Gratuities at Guest's Discretion
VAT inclusive. Credit Cards—Access, Visa
3 Family Rooms
1 Single, 2 Double, 3 Twin Bedrooms

7 Private Bathrooms
All Rooms with TV, Tea and Coffee-making Facilities, Hairdryer
Open all Year
Fully Licensed
Full Central Heating
Cocktail Bar
TV Lounge

Children catered for
Dogs allowed
Parking Facilities
Nearby: Tennis, Putting, Badminton, Swimming, Solarium, Sauna, Golf, Fishing, Riding, Shooting

Section 8: Highland

Helmsdale—Navidale House Hotel Navidale, Helmsdale,
Sutherland. KW8 6JS. Tel 04312 258

A number of our readers have written to us in praise of Navidale House. One of these correspondents wrote of the '. . . high standards of service, friendly but professional . . . Excellent food. . . and splendid house wines.' Another said, 'I cannot speak too highly of the efforts being made by the present owners to achieve the highest standards in all aspects of hotel management. The atmosphere/ambience is friendly, willing and nothing is too much trouble.' A third reader ended her report by saying, 'I do not hesitate to recommend this hotel to you.' Thus nominated, proposed and seconded, Navidale House became one of the prime objectives of our recent Scottish tour. Having stayed there ourselves, we are happy to endorse all these comments. Mr and Mrs Marcus and Colleen Blackwell, the resident proprietors, are indeed enthusiastic and caring hosts. The amenities within are in the best traditions of a country-house hotel, with log fires, homely comforts and attractive accommodation. In addition to the bedrooms in the main hotel and annexe, there are two chalets in the grounds which are suitable for families of 4 to 6 people. Marcus Blackwell is responsible for the menus, which offer an excellent and exciting choice and he makes good use of the very best Scottish produce, including venison, lamb, beef and seafood. The Navidale House is a welcome addition to the list of good hotels in East Sutherland. Its glorious setting, the excellent fishing hereabouts and the Blackwells' warm welcome should not be missed.

Weekly Terms from £350.00
Daily Terms from £47.00
Bed and Breakfast from £35.00
Bar Lunch from £4.50
Afternoon Tea from £2.50
Dinner from £19.95 Table D'Hôte

Gratuities at Guest's Discretion
VAT inclusive. Credit Cards—Access, Visa
6 Double, 6 Twin Bedrooms
All Rooms with Private Bathroom, TV, Tea and Coffee-making Facilities. Trouser Press and Hairdryer available on Request

Open from February to November
Fully Licensed. Full Central Heating.
Cocktail Bar. Children catered for
Dogs allowed. Parking Facilities. Shooting Nearby: Tennis, Squash, Golf, Fishing

Invergarry—Glengarry Castle Invergarry, Inverness-shire.
PH35 4HW. Tel 08093 254. Fax 08093 207

This impressive mansion was built by the Victorian architect, David Bryce, for the Ellice family, founders of the Hudson Bay Company. This is Clan Donald country and the ruins of Invergarry Castle bear witness to the work of Butcher Cumberland after the Battle of Culloden in 1746. The hotel lies in sixty acres of woodland, with pathways and walks, and is reached from the Inverness/Fort William road near the junction with the road to Skye. From the hotel a path leads to a jetty on Loch Oich, which is used by yachtsmen making the Inverness and Fort William journey by water. Glengarry Castle Hotel could not be better placed for touring the Highlands, whilst the fisherman can enjoy excellent trout fishing on the loch. Mr and Mrs D M MacCallum, with their sons, Robert and Donald, have created an almost perfect rural retreat in Glengarry Castle. This restful ambience is apparent immediately upon arrival. The entrance to the hotel is impressive, with high ceilings, natural woodwork, stags' heads, oil paintings, open fireplaces and a showcase of birds which were caught in the vicinity. In true country-house style there is no bar, but drinks are readily available by ordering at the reception, and the dining room offers a good selection of wines to accompany one's meals. We found the food to be home cooking at its best, with full use of local produce, including trout from Loch Lochy. Above stairs the bedrooms are spacious and comfortable. Finally, Glengarry Castle offers, in our opinion, excellent value for money.

Weekly Terms from £283.50
Daily Terms from £45.00
Bed and Breakfast from £29.50
Bar Lunch from £2.75
Lunch from £8.50 Table D'Hôte
Afternoon Tea from £3.20

Dinner from £15.50 Table D'Hôte
Service and VAT inclusive
Credit Cards—Access, Visa
4 Family Rooms
5 Single, 7 Double, 10 Twin Bedrooms
25 Private Bathrooms

All Rooms with TV, Telephone, Radio, Baby-listening, Tea and Coffee-making Facilities. Open from 6th April to 19th October. Residential Licence
Full Central Heating. Dogs allowed
Parking Facilities

Section 8: Highland

Inverness—Lochardil House Hotel Stratherrick Road, Inverness, Highland. IV2 4LF. Tel 0463 235995. Fax 0463 713394

Within five acres of fine lawns, banks of shrubs and mature trees, stands a handsome castellated structure dating from 1878. Open country is only a short walk away, although the hotel is a mere one and a half miles from the centre of Inverness,—the expanding business centre of the north. In the restaurant of Lochardil House, adorning the walls, are priceless Gobelin tapestries, portraying the story of Esther. Also noteworthy here is the generosity of helpings from the range of excellent menus, frequently reviewed by the *Chef de Cuisine*. Complementing the healthy and appetising dishes is a three page wine list with helpful descriptions. We were particularly impressed by the range of lunches and suppers available in both of the bars: starters, main courses (many in full and half portions) to suit every appetite and pocket, several alternative vegetarian dishes, a children's menu and slimmer's dishes. A wide choice of sweets including one or two traditional hot puddings, and everything here at most competitive prices. For social and business functions there is the Victoria Suite, a bright and colourful area with its own bar, facilities for the disabled and seating for up to 140 people. With nearby roads radiating in every direction, and a spacious car park, the hotel must be as convenient for conferences as it is hospitable for the holidaymaker.

Weekly Terms from (B&B) £300.00 Single, £420.00 Double
Bed and Breakfast from £50.00 Single, £70.00 Double
Bar Meal from £6.00
Lunch from £9.50 and A La Carte
Afternoon Tea from £3.50
Dinner from £15.0-0 and A La Carte

Gratuities at Guest's discretion
VAT inclusive. Credit Cards —Access, American Express, Diners Club, Visa
1 Family Room. 6 Double, 2 Twin, 3 Single Bedrooms. 7 Private Bathrooms
5 Private Shower Rooms
All Rooms with TV, Telephone, Radio, Tea and Coffee-making Facilities,

Trouser Press, Hairdryer
Open all Year. Fully Licensed
Full Central Heating. Cocktail Bar, Games Room. Conference Facilities. Children catered for. Dogs not allowed. Parking Facilities. Nearby: Tennis, Putting, Squash, Badminton, Swimming, Solarium, Sauna, Golf, Fishing, Riding, Sailing

Isle of Skye, Portree—Rosedale Hotel Portree, Isle of Skye. IV51 9DB. Tel 0478 3131. Fax 0478 2531

Since the Rosedale Hotel is the only one on the Portree waterfront, most of its public rooms and bedrooms have a unique prospect across the sheltered harbour of Portree to the Isle of Raasay. Several fishermen's houses were cleverly adapted to produce a bright, airy, modern hotel without losing the original character. The dining-room offers a high standard of *cuisine*, utilising as much fresh local produce as possible. There are two very comfortable lounges for the use of residents and a good selection of Highland malt whiskies, including the local Talisker, is to be found in the bar. Portree, as the capital of Skye, is the natural focal point for activity on the island and it is ideally placed as a touring centre. The scenery is spectacular, particularly in the Cuillin Hills where walkers and climbers are rewarded by the sight of dramatic skylines and impressive views. The hotel offers several holiday packages for stays of more than two days. All the packages include accommodation, breakfast, five-course dinner and admission to three places of interest. Stay longer and car-ferry charges are included, too. In addition, a seven-day, two-island holiday is available in conjunction with the Isle of Raasay Hotel, Raasay. Full details are available from the Rosedale Hotel. We have always found the hotel a particularly pleasing one—the Andrew family, who run it with the help of very efficient staff, are always ready to help their guests to enjoy their holiday.

Weekly Terms from £339.00
Daily Terms from £50.50
Bed and Breakfast from £33.00
Dinner from £17.50
Gratuities at Guest's Discretion
VAT inclusive

5 Double, 13 Twin, 5 Single Bedrooms
16 Private Bathrooms
7 Private Shower Rooms
All Rooms with TV, Telephone, Radio, Tea and Coffee-making Facilities
Open from mid May to end of September

Fully Licensed. Full Central Heating
Cocktail Bar. Dogs allowed by Arrangement
Parking Facilities
Nearby: Tennis, Squash, Badminton, Swimming, Golf, Fishing, Riding, Sailing, Windsurfing

Section 8: Highland

Isle of Skye, Uig—Uig Hotel Uig, Portree, Isle of Skye.
IV51 9YE. Tel 047042 205. Fax 047042 308

Halfway up the Trotternish peninsula on the western side, this whitewashed landmark beckons invitingly to travellers using the drive-on/off MacBrayne steamers to the Outer Hebrides as well as to motorists from the mainland. We took to this hotel instinctively and Grace Graham and her son, David Taylor, proved delightful hosts. After a mini lunch, delightfully served in the sun lounge, consisting of soup, sandwiches, cheese oatcakes and good coffee, we felt that here was an hotel which we would like to make our base for a few days.

A feature of this hotel, apart from good fare, all-round comfort and warmth (there is central heating throughout) is the artistic ability of Grace Graham. The whole décor and furnishing of the hotel is, thanks to her, most pleasing. Apart from the twelve bedrooms in the hotel, equally inviting quarters are available in *Sobhraig House*, winner of a Civic Trust accommodation award. All bedrooms have private bathrooms or showers and provide a very good standard of accommodation. The coastal roads on this wild and beautiful island lead to small fishing and crofting villages and many scenic splendours can be seen from the route. For the adventurous the hotel has a stable of eight horses for pony trekking and packed lunches can be provided. Advance bookings are most advisable for meals and rooms.

Weekly Terms on Application
Daily Terms from £45.00
Bed and Breakfast from £30.00
Bar Lunch from £3.50
Afternoon Tea from £2.50
Dinner from £17.00
Gratuities at Guest's Discretion
VAT inclusive

Credit Cards—Access, American Express, Diners Club, Visa
2 Double, 11 Twin, 5 Single Bedrooms
9 Private Bathrooms
11 Private Shower Rooms
All Rooms with TV, Telephone, Radio, Tea and Coffee-making Facilities, Hairdryer
Open from mid April to early October

Fully Licensed. Full Central Heating
Cocktail Bar
Meeting Facilities
Children over 12 years catered for
Dogs allowed by Arrangement
Parking Facilities. Pony Trekking
Nearby: Tennis, Squash, Swimming, Fishing, Walking, Climbing

By Lairg—The Kinlochbervie Hotel
By Lairg, Sutherland. IV27 4RP. Tel 097182 275. Fax 097182 438

Settlements and negotiable roads in Sutherland are few and the distances from one inhabited place to another are often lengthy. Hence, the postal address of Kinlochbervie is Lairg, some forty-seven miles away, so do not be caught out! For here we are in one of the most magnificent and unspoilt outposts of Scotland. The genteel tourist may think it a good place to leave, but for others, including ourselves, it is heaven sent. Discover primitive Cape Wrath; Sandwood Bay, the most beautiful bay on Scotland's west coast; and the warm and hospitable Kinlochbervie Hotel, whose reputation has not been fostered by publicity, but by the enthusiasm of those who go there. Rex Neame enjoyed a long career in the brewing and wine trade before he and his wife grasped eagerly the opportunity of owning this hotel. They take a pride in the excellence of the *cuisine*. The chef, Mark Sayers, who smokes his own fish (the smoked haddock we had for breakfast was outstanding), maintains *Cordon Bleu* standards and uses local produce to the full. After all, the Kinlochbervie fleet ties up daily in the harbour below. Our bedroom was comfortable and provided all modern day courtesies. Downstairs there is a comfortable residents' lounge for those moments when one seeks rest and quiet and, perhaps, a good read. We enjoyed it all; the comfort, good food, banter, and sporting opportunities. A guide for walkers is available. Guests are offered sea and loch fishing for brown trout. Stalking can be arranged, and diving, whilst birdwatchers can visit Handa by boat.

All Prices pertain to 1992
Weekly Terms from £399.00
Daily Terms from £66.00
Bed and Breakfast from £40.00
Bar Meal from £1.90. Lunch from £1.90
Dinner from £27.50 Table d'Hôte

Service and VAT inclusive
Credit Cards—Access, American Express, Diners Club, Visa. 5 Family Rooms
4 Double, 5 Twin Bedrooms
All Rooms with Private Bathroom, TV, Telephone, Radio, Tea and Coffee-making

Facilities, Trouser Press, Hairdryer
Closed November to March. Fully Licensed. Full Central Heating. Children catered for. Dogs allowed. Parking Facilities. Nearby: Golf, Fishing, Riding, Sailing, Shooting, Boat Trips

Section 8: Highland

Loch Lochy—Corriegour Lodge Hotel
Loch Lochy, by Spean bridge, Inverness-shire. PH34 4EB
Tel 039781 685. Fax 039781 685

Standing in six acres of mature woodland and garden, this former Victorian hunting lodge not only has outstanding views over Loch Lochy: its contrasting grounds include a small lochside beach area and jetty. Whether you are sampling the local venison, salmon or Highland lamb in the *Loch View Restaurant and Conservatory*, relaxing beside a log fire in the lounge or rising in one of the comfortable *en suite* bedrooms, there is a compelling sense of well-being from the warm, rich decor and the picture-book scenery framed by every window. Your friendly and attentive hosts, Rod and Lorna Bunney, see to it that you receive a sincere welcome and quite exceptional service, ensuring a relaxed and memorable stay in this superb retreat. With a *cuisine* comprising many imaginative dishes plus a wide choice on their lunch menu and a most interesting wine list, visitors are delightfully refreshed between excursions into the surrounding dramatic terrain of lochs, waterfalls, forests, mountains and rivers. A profusion of outdoor sports, historic castles, museums and scenic drives adds to the diverse charm and interest of this unspoilt area. Enjoy a ride on the steam train of the West Highland line or take the Whisky Trail to many of the distilleries in this region. Rates at Corriegour Lodge, which is STB Highly Commended and also a member of *The Taste of Scotland*, are most reasonable and even more attractive for special three-day half-board breaks. No matter how extended your visit, there will always be more to be seen, new culinary delights to be sampled and renewed pleasure in the hospitality. Quality Scottish gifts and crafts are on sale here.

Weekly Terms from £269.50
Daily Terms from £44.00
Bed and Breakfast from £28.00
Bar Meal from £4.25
Dinner from £17.50 Table d'Hote
Gratuities at Guest's discretion
VAT inclusive
Credit Cards—Access, Visa
1 Family Room. 3 Double, 3 Twin,

2 Single Bedrooms
6 Private Bathrooms
3 Private Shower Rooms
All Rooms with TV, Tea and Coffee-making Facilities
Hairdryer available
Open from March to October inclusive
Fully Licensed

Full Central Heating and Log Fire
Cocktail Bar
Children over 8 years catered for
Dogs not allowed
Parking Facilities
Nearby: Swimming, Solarium, Sauna, Golf, Fishing, Riding, Sailing, Windsurfing, Water Skiing, Shooting

Section 8: Highland

Lochinver—The Inver Lodge Hotel
Lochinver, Sutherland. IV27 4LU. Tel 0571 844496. Fax 0571 844395

Tucked away on the north-west corner of Scotland, looking across the North Minch to the Isle of Lewis, the village is a curving half-mile of cottages lining a single street, facing the loch from which it draws its name. There is an island at the mouth of the loch, protecting the fishing fleet from sudden storms and creating a natural harbour for the boats. But, for those who love untamed places it is the wildness of the land behind the village which pulls like a magnet—and against this compelling landscape is set the Inver Lodge Hotel. The spacious bedrooms have private bathrooms, colour television, radio, telephone and panoramic views from every window. Each has also a trouser press and hairdryer as well as tea and coffee-making facilities. There is a sauna, solarium and billiards room. A drying room is provided and a daily laundry service. The whole hotel is luxuriously appointed. Stags' heads and salmon adorn the walls of the public rooms, there being a magnificent twelve pointer in the lounge bar with an enormous forty-four pound salmon landed in 1907. Free trout fishing is offered to guests and there are facilities for salmon on the Kirkaig, Oykel and Upper Inver. The Inver Lodge makes an ideal base for those touring the north-west. Leisurely drives along the coast road north, over the Kylesku Bridge to Cape Wrath, pass through some of Scotland's most beautiful scenery, while the southern route takes you towards Inverpolly nature reserve and the beautiful Summer Isles.

Terms on Application	7 Double, 7 Twin Bedrooms	Fully Licensed. Full Central Heating
VAT inclusive	All Rooms with Private Bathroom, TV,	Cocktail Bar. Billiard Room
Credit Cards—Access,	Telephone, Radio, Baby-listening, Tea and	Dogs allowed. Parking Facilities
American Express, Diners Club, JCB, Visa	Coffee-making Facilities, Trouser Press,	Solarium, Sauna, Fishing,
Suilven and Canisp Rooms	Hairdryer, Mini-bar	Motor Launch for Hire
4 Superior Rooms	Open from 1st May to 20th October	Nearby: Riding

Nairn—Carnach House Hotel
Delnies, Nairn, Highland. IV12 5NT. Tel 0667 52094

Situated amidst eight acres of gardens and woodlands is Carnach House Hotel. It is owned and run on a very personal basis by Graham and Andrea Stubbs and evidence of their care can be found throughout the hotel. The spaciousness of the house is immediately apparent on entering the hall and it continues in the comfortable lounge and bar where a large selection of malt whiskies adorns the wall. There are twelve bedrooms at Carnach House and all are comfortably furnished and harmoniously decorated. They all have private facilities, colour television, telephone and tea and coffee-making facilities. Although the hotel is centrally heated throughout, an open fire is kept in both the lounge and the bar–and what better way of starting a relaxing evening than by savouring an eighteen-year old Macallan before tasting the delights of the local produce, beautifully cooked and presented in the cosy restaurant? We cannot think of anything. The restaurant has a good reputation locally, something we always regard highly. The surrounding area is full of interest: within reach are Speyside, the beaches of the Moray Firth, Nairn with its golf courses and plenty of fishing. Historical appetites are catered for with great castles such as Cawdor and Brodie within easy reach as well as Culloden Battlefield and Fort George Military Museum. And who knows...'Nessie' might just pop up as you are driving past on the beautiful routes on either side of the loch!

Weekly Terms from £381.50	6 Double, 1 Single, 5 Twin Bedrooms	Children catered for
Daily Terms from £57.50	8 Private Bathrooms. 4 Private Shower	Dogs allowed
Bed and Breakfast from £40.00	Rooms. All Rooms with TV, Telephone,	Parking Facilities
Bar Meal from £1.80	Radio, Tea and Coffee-making Facilities,	Riding. Croquet
Sunday Lunch from £9.50 Table D'Hôte	Trouser Press	Nearby: Tennis, Putting, Squash,
Dinner from £17.50 Table D'Hôte	Hairdryer available on Request	Badminton, Swimming, Golf, Fishing,
Gratuities at Guest's Discretion	Open all Year. Fully Licensed	Sailing, Windsurfing, Water Skiing,
VAT inclusive. Credit Cards—Access,	Full Central Heating. Cocktail Bar	Shooting, Hang-gliding
American Express, Visa	Conference Facilities	

Section 8: Highland

Plockton—The Haven Hotel
Plockton, Ross-shire. IV52 8TW. Tel 059 984 223/334

Established at the end of the eighteenth century as a fishing community, the village of Plockton is now a conservation area. This peaceful and beautiful village, situated on the lochside and surrounded by hills, has long been a favourite of ours. It is, therefore, a special pleasure to be able to recommend an hotel here. Built more than 100 years ago as a merchant's residence and recently carefully converted and extended, The Haven is now a comfortable and well-appointed hotel. Centrally heated throughout, the hotel includes two pleasant lounges (one with an open log fire), a conservatory, well-equipped bedrooms and a spacious dining-room, where one may dine by candlelight. The specialities of the house include salmon and prawns from the local lochs, Highland venison and the best Scottish beef, lamb and pork. A well-chosen wine list complements the excellent quality of the *cuisine*. Packed lunches are available on request for those who wish to spend their days hill walking, climbing, boating, fishing, pony trekking or simply touring. In our opinion, Wester Ross, with its mountains and glens, waterfalls and sea lochs, is one of the most beautiful areas of Scotland. Marjorie Nichols and John Graham, the resident proprietors, will be happy to advise you about places of interest near at hand and farther afield. They have created a warm and friendly atmosphere in their delightful hotel and they ensure that all their guests have a happy and memorable stay.

Weekly Terms from £335.00
Daily Terms from £44.00
Bed and Breakfast from £31.50
Bar Lunch from £2.00
Lunch from £2.00 and A La Carte
(Feb/March & Nov/Dec Lunch for
 Residents only). Dinner from £18.50
Gratuities at Guest's Discretion

VAT inclusive. Credit Cards—Access, Visa
6 Double, 5 Twin, 2 Single Bedrooms
All Rooms with Private Bathroom, TV,
Radio, Telephone, Tea and Coffee-making
Facilities, Trouser Press, Hairdryer
Open from February to 20th December
Residential and Restaurant Licence
Full Central Heating

Children over 7 years catered for
Dogs allowed but not in Public Rooms
Parking Facilities
Non-smoking Lounge, Dining Room
Nearby: Golf, Fishing, Sailing, Windsurfing,
Boat Hire

Near Scourie, Badcall Bay—The Eddrachilles Hotel
Badcall Bay, Scourie, Sutherland. IV27 4TH. Tel 0971 502080/502211. Fax 0971 502477

Our first impression of The Eddrachilles Hotel was of its truly superb position. It overlooks the island-studded Badcall Bay, which is surrounded by rocky hills and, in our view, is one of the finest of a series of thirty or forty rocky bays in the area. How delighted we were to arrive at this 200-year-old house, to find that it had been refurbished and extended to provide modern amenities. The proprietors, Mr and Mrs Wood, take pride in personally running the hotel. Guests are assured of excellent homely meals and a good selection of wines in the stone-walled and flag-stoned dining-room. Bedroom comfort has not been overlooked either, for all the rooms have private bath or shower rooms and there is heating throughout the hotel. The Eddrachilles is an excellent base for a tranquil or an active holiday. There are many beautiful walks, either in the mountains inland or amongst the hills and the numerous small lochs strewn with water lilies. Naturalists and ornithologists will find the area fascinating—Handa Island, famous as a bird sanctuary, is only a few miles to the north and can be reached by boat from Tarbet. A boat can be hired from the hotel for a day's fishing or for exploring the seclusion of the small islands of Eddrachilles Bay. The hotel has some brown-trout fishing and arrangements can be made with the local angling club for fishing in some of the well-stocked lochs. We are happy to recommend a stay in this beautiful, remote area of Scotland.

Weekly Terms from £280.00
Daily Terms from £41.00
Bed and Breakfast from £30.60
Bar Lunch from £2.50
Dinner from £10.50 and A La Carte
Gratuities at Guest's Discretion
VAT inclusive
1 Family Room

3 Double, 7 Twin Bedrooms
4 Private Bathrooms
7 Private Shower Rooms
All Rooms with TV, Telephone, Radio, Tea
and Coffee-making Facilities, Trouser
Press, Hairdryer, Ironing Facilities
Open from 1st March to 30th October
Fully Licensed

Full Central Heating
Cocktail Bar
Children over 3 years catered for
Dogs not allowed
Parking Facilities
Loch Fishing, Boats for hire
Nearby: Fishing

Section 8: Highland

Strathpeffer—Brunstane Lodge Hotel
Golf Road, Strathpeffer, Highland. IV14 9AT. Tel 0997 421261

Discerning locals regularly patronise this hotel for the quality and size of the food helpings. This attractive, family run hotel was described by our inspectors as 'one of the best smaller hotels we have seen anywhere'. They were impressed also when they found some rare vintages in addition to those on the wine list. A fine choice of malt whiskies, usually about forty, is available as well. Built in 1895, the hotel has a decor very much in the Victorian style: all the woodwork is natural pitch-pine, beautifully hand carved, and there are some colourful stained glass windows. Each of the seven bedrooms is individually decorated, furnished to the highest standards and all have superb views over the valley of the Peffery to the Cromarty Firth, or to the mountains of Wester Ross. Strathpeffer itself, once popular as a health resort with sulphur springs, now houses a doll museum with nursery memorabilia, in the remains of the baths complex. The area around the village offers numerous enjoyable walks and views, and abounds in trout lochs. Sea and river fishing are available locally, as are golf and climbing. In fact, this is altogether a most attractive centre for touring the Highlands and Islands. And what could be nicer after a comfortably tiring day out than the warm welcome awaiting you on your return, from resident proprietors Alistair and Mary Anne McKay, who take a justifiable pride in creating a warm friendly atmosphere in which to relax and enjoy the splendid home cooking.

Weekly Terms from £220.00
Daily Terms from £38.00
Bed and Breakfast from £25.00
Bar Lunch from £3.50
Bar Supper from £4.00
Dinner from £13.00 Table d'Hôte

Gratuities at Guest's discretion
VAT inclusive. Credit Cards—Access, Visa
1 Family Room. 1 Suite
1 Single, 2 Double, 2 Twin Bedrooms
4 Private Bathrooms, 3 Private Shower Rooms. All Rooms with TV, Radio,

Baby-listening, Tea and Coffee-making Facilities, Hairdryer, Ironing Facilities
Pay Telephone at Reception
Open all Year. Fully Licensed. Full Central Heating. Cocktail Bar. Conference Facilities
Children catered for. Dogs not allowed

Near Strathpeffer, Contin—Coul House Hotel
Contin, Ross-shire. IV14 9EY. Tel 0997 421487. Fax 0997 421945

A half-mile driveway leads you to this secluded country-house hotel which stands in seven and a half acres of grounds. The one-time stately home and seat of the Mackenzies of Coul still retains, as an hotel, the atmosphere of the 'more leisurely days of carriages and gentlefolk'. The proprietors do their utmost to maintain this feeling and most certainly succeed in the beautifully proportioned *Octagonal Lounge*, the comfortable and spacious cocktail lounge, the elegant dining-room and the entrance lounge, with its massive carved fire mantel and log fire. Nearly all the rooms have beautiful, peaceful views and all of the bedrooms have private bathrooms, television, radio and telephone. The cooking is of a high standard and offers a choice between traditional Scottish fare (the hotel is recommended in the 'Taste of Scotland' scheme) and more adventurous continental *cuisine*. A kilted bag-piper plays in the garden at Friday dinnertime in the summer. The hotel has its own trout and salmon fishing and also arranges fully inclusive golfing, rambling, sight-seeing and pony-trekking holidays. Additionally, the surrounding area has much to offer the sportsman (sailing, climbing, good walking, shooting, deer stalking and various indoor sports are available locally), the historian and those who wish to explore. On occasion entertainment and dancing are provided in the unusual and characterful *Kitchen Bar*, where guests have a good chance to meet the locals.

Weekly Terms (Half Board) from £248.50
Daily Terms from £48.00
Bed and Breakfast from £31.00
Bar Meal from £3.50
Dinner from £21.50 and A La Carte
No Service Charge. VAT inclusive
Credit Cards—American Express, Diners Club. 3 Family Rooms

4 Single, 7 Double, 7 Twin Bedrooms
20 Private Bathrooms
1 Private Shower Room
All Rooms with TV, Telephone, Radio, Baby-listening, Tea and Coffee-making Facilities, Trouser Press, Hairdryer
Open all Year. Fully Licensed
Full Central Heating. Cocktail Bar

TV Lounge. Games Room
Conference Facilities
Dogs allowed. Parking Facilities
Nearby: Tennis, Putting, Squash, Badminton, Swimming, Sauna, Golf, Fishing, Riding, Sailing, Windsurfing, Shooting

Section 8: Highland

Tain—Morangie House Hotel
Morangie Road, Tain, Ross-Shire. IV19 1PY.
Tel 0862 892281

The small Ross-shire town of Tain, close by the shores of the lovely Dornoch Firth is a former royal burgh, deriving its name from the Norse 'Thino' meaning an assembly and was originally granted its charter in 1066. The hotel is a former Victorian mansion on the northern outskirts of the town, built in 1903 by a noted local architect, whose grand design provides the spacious and elegant rooms. The house has been extensively modernised and tastefully decorated to maintain the character of the building, which has a particularly fine collection of stained glass windows lighting the hallway and many of the public rooms. There are eleven bedrooms, individually decorated and furnished to the highest standards. All have *en suite* bathrooms, telephone, colour television, tea and coffee-making facilities, hairdryer and trouser press. The master bedroom has a large four-poster bed, while the bathroom boasts a whirlpool corner bath. Complementing the comfort and elegance of the bedrooms, the bar and dining room offer the best of Highland food and drink with salmon, venison and game in season beautifully prepared and attentively presented. Dornoch Firth has much to interest the visitor, with beach, bowling green, tennis courts and public gardens. There is a fascinating museum and visitors are welcome at the famous Glenmorangie distillery. If you are an outdoor enthusiast, take your pick of fishing, shooting, hill-walking or just exploring the wonderful northern Highlands. Tain has a first class golf course–only one of several in the area, with the world-famous championship course at Dornoch, half-an-hour's drive away. Residents at Morangie House qualify for a reduction on golf fees at Tain Golf Club.

All Prices pertain to 1992
Weekly Terms from £210.00
Bed and Breakfast from £30.00
Bar Meal from £3.50
Lunch from £6.00 and A La Carte
Afternoon Tea from £3.00
Dinner from £15.50 and A La Carte
Gratuities at Guest's Discretion
VAT inclusive

Credit Cards—Access, American Express, Diners Club, Visa
1 Family Room
6 Double, 2 Twin, 2 Single Bedrooms
9 Private Bathrooms
2 Private Shower Rooms
11 Rooms with TV, Telephone, Radio, Tea and Coffee-making Facilities, Trouser Press, Hairdryer

Open all Year. Fully Licensed
Full Central Heating. Cocktail Bar
Dogs not allowed. Parking Facilities
Nearby: Tennis, Putting, Squash, Badminton, Swimming, Solarium, Sauna, Golf, Fishing, Riding, Sailing, Windsurfing, Water Skiing, Shooting, Hang Gliding

Section 8: Highland

Strontian—Kilcamb Lodge Hotel
Strontian, Argyll. PH36 4HY. Tel 0967 2257

Ardnamurchan is a particularly beautiful and unspoilt peninsula which offers peace and tranquillity to its visitors, as well as a very wide choice of holiday activities. Kilcamb Lodge Hotel stands at the head of Loch Sunart and is strategically situated to explore this lovely area. The hotel is an eighteenth century hunting lodge, lovingly restored, standing in thirty acres of grounds with natural lawns leading down to half a mile of shoreline on Loch Sunart. It is a haven for wildlife with wild cats, pine martens, red and roe deer, otters, buzzards, eagles and many sea and shore birds seen within the grounds. The hotel has mountain bikes and boats with outboards for hire, or if you prefer to explore Loch Sunart aboard the hotel's luxury 37ft yacht this can be arranged. The food is of a high standard taking full advantage of fresh local food and vegetables. Special diets can be catered for. Open log fires, warm and comfortable rooms and a warm and most friendly welcome from your hosts, Ann and Gordon Blakeway, together with son Peter and his fiancée Bernice, will make your holiday in this lovely area memorable.

Weekly Terms from £365.00
Daily Terms from £58.00 (1/2 nights)
Bed and Breakfast from £37.50
Dinner from £22.00
Gratuities at Guest's Discretion
VAT inclusive

2 Singles, 4 Double, 4 Twin Bedrooms
5 Private Bathrooms
5 Private Shower Rooms
All Rooms with Tea and Coffee-making Facilities
Hairdryer and Baby-listening available on Request. Open from April to October.
Fully Licensed. Full Central Heating.
Cocktail Bar
Parking Facilities. Fishing. Shooting
Nearby: Golf, Fishing, Riding, Sailing, Windsurfing, Shooting

Ullapool—The Harbour Lights Hotel
Garve Road, Ullapool, Ross-shire. IV26 2SX. Tel 0854 612222

We stayed at The Harbour Lights very early in the year, before the weather in Wester Ross begins to welcome the visitor. So, our preferences were taken up with short expeditions, the hotel's welcoming log fires, a connoisseur's selection of malts, the excellent menus, and Scottish hospitality at its most caring, so gladly given by the owners, Marilyn and Danny Gordon. It was good to experience a 'different' Ullapool on this visit—warm, cosy and utterly relaxing—for, as the year progresses, motoring, exploring, hill-walking, pony trekking and bird-watching all contribute to the region's popular appeal. Whilst at The Harbour Lights, the lovely gardens which border on Loch Broom, and afternoon teas on the terrace become important parts of the guests' daily round. At all times of the year, however, everything is just as it should be here. The hotel is comfortable and well appointed, and the bedrooms are all modernly equipped. Roberto, the chef, takes the best of the catch from the harbour and prepares mouth-watering seafood to complement his Scotch beef and venison specialities, and will delight in meeting a request for Italian or vegetarian dishes. The wine list and the whisky collection reflect Danny's keen interest in these subjects. The comfort of guests is paramount with Marilyn, who also ensures that flowers add colour to all the public rooms. Ullapool simply must be included in the itineraries of those in search of the best of northern Scotland, and The Harbour Lights is easily the best of hotels there.

All Prices pertain to 1992
Weekly Terms from £298.00
Daily terms from £45.00
Bed and Breakfast from £30.00
Room Rate from £24.00
Bar Meal from £4.95
Afternoon Tea from £1.75
Dinner from £19.00 and A La Carte

Gratuities at Guest's discretion
VAT inclusive. Credit Cards—Access, Visa
1 Family Room. 9 Double, 9 Twin, 3 Single Bedrooms. 10 Private Bathrooms
12 Private Shower Rooms
All Rooms with TV, Radio, Baby-listening, Tea and Coffee-making Facilities, Hairdryer
21 Rooms with Telephone

Open all Year. Fully Licensed
Central Heating.
Children catered for
Dogs allowed
Parking Facilities.
Nearby: Tennis, Putting, Squash, Badminton, Fishing, Riding, Sailing, Mountaineering, Hill Walking

Section 8: Lothian and Strathclyde

East Linton—Harvesters Hotel
Station Road, East Linton, Lothian. EH40 3DP. Tel 0620 860395

Located amidst the golfing mecca of East Lothian, we have often felt that this attractive village should be called Tinton or Tyneton, for it sits beside the River Tyne, which scurries along a rock-filled course towards the sea at Dunbar. The village is in the north-eastern extremity of Lothian and contains a notable church and bridge, a famous mill and a good hotel . . . the Harvesters. A substantial eighteenth-century country house and its adjacent coach house beside the river were converted into this comfortable hotel of great character, which has been developed to a high standard. We have never been better received here, nor have the hotel and its attractive grounds looked in better heart. Nearby is the striking coastline of Lothian with its dramatic seascapes (at Tantallon Castle it is breathtaking); at one's door are the beautiful Lammermuir moorlands where many hidden villages reward the exploring motorist or walker; and just thirty minutes' drive away is the centre of Edinburgh, a city of history and culture. It is little wonder that visitors to the city of Edinburgh see the Harvesters as a pleasant rural alternative to city hotels and that those living in Edinburgh are attracted to the Harvesters' food. The varied dishes and wines, served with true Scottish hospitality, are much praised by residents and diners. We also found the hotel's prices, in particular the *demi pension* package rates, offered really good value.

Terms on Application
Bed and Breakfast from £28.00
Bar Meal from £4.75
Afternoon Tea from £4.75
Dinner from £8.95 and A La Carte
Gratuities at Guest's Discretion
VAT inclusive. Credit Cards—Access, American Express, Diners Club, Visa

3 Family Rooms. 4 Double, 3 Twin Bedrooms. 2 Single Bedrooms
8 Private Bathrooms
2 Private Shower Rooms. All Rooms with TV, Radio, Telephone, Tea and Coffee-making Facilities, Baby-listening
Hairdryer available on Request
Open all Year

Fully Licensed
Full Central Heating
Conference Facilities
Dogs allowed
Parking Facilities. Fishing
Nearby: Tennis, Putting, Squash, Badminton, Swimming, Golf, Fishing, Riding, Sailing

Dunoon, Hunter's Quay—The Royal Marine Hotel
Marine Parade, Hunter's Quay, Dunoon, Argyll. PA23 8HJ. Tel 0369 5810. Telex 779873

Here is one of Scotland's best, so plan your itinerary to stay at The Royal Marine, Hunter's Quay or, at any rate, make it a halting place for a meal. Eastward it looks over the shimmering waters of the Firth of Clyde; below lies the steamer pier, where ferries ply to and fro from McInroy's Point; whilst behind, the rounded hills of the Cowal peninsula make this a peaceful and sheltered setting. The Royal Marine Hotel was built in 1889 as the club house of the Royal Clyde Yacht Club. As such, it provides dress circle seats of life and scenery on the Clyde. King George V often used the hotel as a base when racing his yacht. The Royal Marine is not famed merely for its history and location, however, for there is great comfort here, a convivial atmosphere and one of the highest standards of *cuisine* on the peninsula. It is also a popular headquarters for business, pleasure and social occasions. If you can divert your gaze from the marvellous views, you will note that the public rooms have been restored with infinite care. All the bedrooms have been refurbished and *en suite* facilities added. The working heads of the past few years are four partners, Mr and Mrs Peter Arnold and Mr and Mrs Martin Greig and, if the truth were known, we suspect that their warm hospitality is a dominating factor at The Royal Marine. Do go there: Glasgow is no more than twenty-six miles away and Edinburgh seventy-five.

Weekly Terms from £210.00
Bed and Breakfast from £36.00
Bar Meal from £2.50
Dinner from £11.50 Table D'Hôte
Gratuities at Guest's Discretion
VAT inclusive. Credit Cards—Access, Visa
3 Family Rooms. 11 Double, 12 Twin, 9 Single Bedrooms. 9 Private Bathrooms

25 Private Shower Rooms
All Rooms with TV, Telephone, Baby-listening
Open all Year
Fully Licensed
Full Central Heating
Cocktail Bar

Games Room
Conference Facilities
Dogs not allowed
Parking Facilities
Nearby: Tennis, Putting, Squash, Swimming, Sauna, Golf Fishing; Riding, Sailing, Windsurfing, Shooting

Section 8: Strathclyde

Isle of Islay—Port Askaig Hotel
Port Askaig, Isle of Islay, Argyll. PA46 7RD. Tel 049 684 245. Fax 049 684 295

We are delighted to continue our recommendation of this excellent two-star hotel. It sits appealingly above the small hamlet of Port Askaig, with its pier, and is in constant touch with the ebb and flow of activity when the car ferries arrive daily from the mainland and the Isle of Jura. For 400 years an inn has stood here and the present eighteenth-century building now offers all modern comforts (including some private bathrooms) with good Scottish fare and varied menus. Mr and Mrs F T Spears, the resident owners, have been purveyors of friendly hospitality here since 1958 and ensure that their hotel provides all the virtues of island living. Islay itself, some twenty-five miles long and twenty miles wide, is the most southerly of the Hebridean islands and offers a great variety of attractions to the holidaymaker. The natural beauty of the landscape, with its mountains, lochs, woods and fields, offers an endless panorama to the walker or motorist. The Gulf Stream warms the waters which lap the many sandy bays and magnificent caves and also provides excellent sea fishing all round the coast. Inland, there are a number of well-stocked lochs and rivers where trout and salmon fishing is available, either from boat or bank. It is, however, the unforced pace of the island which is its chief attraction. To the ornithologist, the naturalist, the photographer and the artist Islay is an endless joy. Last, but not least, the island is justly famous for its fine malt whisky.

Weekly Terms from £330.00 incl.car ferry
Daily Terms from £46.00
Bed and Breakfast from £27.00
Bar Meal from £2.50
Lunch from £7.50 Table D'Hôte
Afternoon Tea from £0.80

Dinner from £15.00 Table D'Hôte
VAT inclusive. 1 Family Room
2 Double, 5 Twin, 2 Single Bedrooms
2 Private Bathrooms
2 Private Shower Rooms
All Rooms with TV, Radio, Tea and

Coffee-making Facilities,
Laundry and Drying Facilities
Hairdryer available on Request
Open all Year. Fully Licensed
Full Central Heating. Dogs allowed
Parking Facilities

Largs, Skelmorlie—Manor Park Hotel Skelmorlie,
Near Largs, Ayrshire. PA17 5HE. Tel 0475 520832. Fax 0475 520832

There are times when we are sorely tempted, in our wanderings, to stray from the main purpose of this guide and lure you to this place or that, largely because of our love of the old—fine masonry, elegant ornamentation and so on. This alone is sufficent reason for visiting Manor Park Hotel, a beautifully preserved early Victorian building erected upon the site of a seventeenth-century dower house. Its fifteen acres of lawns, shrubberies, water gardens and woodland ensure its seclusion. However, the hotel's success is based not only on its site and scenic advantages, but also on its excellent gastronomic reputation. The interior has been completely modernised, but without detracting from the country-house atmosphere. One is therefore able to appreciate the magnificent Adam-style entrance hall and the superb oak staircase, with an ornate well and a cupola above. The bedrooms are spacious and furnished to a very high standard, with telephone, television, tea-making facilities, a hairdryer and a private bath or shower room as standard amenities. Many bedrooms and all the public rooms have spectacular views across the Firth of Clyde towards the islands and mountains of Argyll. We urge you to experience all the hotel has to offer, namely, the food and wine, the furnishings and the superb gardens. Write to the Manager, allowing some elasticity of dates and arrange your itinerary accordingly.

Bed and Breakfast from £35.00
Bar Lunch from £2.15
Lunch from £10.00 and A La Carte
Afternoon Tea from £1.65
Dinner from £19.50 and A La Carte
Gratuities at Guest's Discretion
VAT inclusive. 2 Family Rooms. 1 Suite

12 Double, 7 Twin, 4 Single Bedrooms
All Rooms with Private Bath/Shower Room, TV, Telephone, Radio, Tea and
Coffee-making Facilities, Hairdryer
Open all Year. Fully Licensed
Full Central Heating
Cocktail Bar

Conference Facilities
Dogs not allowed
Parking Facilities
Indoor Heated Swimming Pool
Putting Green
Nearby: Tennis, Golf, Fishing, Riding, Sailing, Windsurfing, Water Skiing

Section 8: Strathclyde

Kilwinning—Montgreenan Mansion House Hotel
Montgreenan Estate, Near Kilwinning, Ayrshire. KA13 7QZ
Tel 0294 57733. Fax 0294 85397

Many visitors to Scotland have their sights set on the Highlands and very little else. They may, however, be interested to learn that Ayrshire is one of the principal destinations for Scottish holidaymakers. It is a land of forests, good beaches, championship golf courses, splendid castles, country parks and Burns' memorabilia (the great poet was born in the village of Alloway). Scottish friends of ours have found another reason for returning there as often as possible, since they discovered this elegant country mansion. It really is a superb place, set in forty-five acres of grounds—it is very exclusive, but pleasantly informal. There are only twenty-one bedrooms, but they are the last word in luxury. Some have jacuzzi baths, others have magnificent circular beds and the Bridal Suite would appeal to any newly-weds. The history of the Montgreenan Estate stretches back to 1310, but the present country mansion was built during the early part of the nineteenth century. The hotel contains many lovely features and has been furnished to the highest standards. The food and service are more than a match for the surroundings and the table d'hôte and à la carte menus feature French and Scottish dishes–flambé dishes are a speciality. You will find the Montgreenan Estate in the attractive countryside just inland from Irvine. There are no less than thirty golf courses within forty-five minutes' drive of the hotel! If you have other interests, however, Mr and Mrs Dobson, the owners, and their staff will gladly advise on suitable itineraries.

Weekly Terms on application
Daily Terms from £56.00
Bed and Breakfast from £66.00
Lunch from £13.75 and A La Carte
Dinner from £23.00 and A La Carte
Gratuities at Guest's Discretion
VAT inclusive.
Credit Cards—Access, American Express, Diners Club, Visa
3 Suites. 10 Double, 8 Twin Bedrooms

All Rooms with Private Bathroom with Shower, TV, Telephone, Radio, Tea and Coffee-making Facilities, Trouser Press, Hairdryer, Mini Bar
Open all Year
Fully Licensed
Full Central Heating
Lift. Conference Facilities.
Children catered for by Arrangement
Dogs allowed by arrangement

Parking Facilities
Night Porter.
Hard Tennis Court, Croquet,
Golf (5 holes), Putting.
Nearby: Squash, Badminton, Swimming, Solarium, Sauna, Golf, Fishing, Riding, Sailing, Windsurfing, Water Skiing, Shooting

Section 8: Strathclyde

By Lochgilphead, Lochgair—Lochgair Hotel
Lochgair, Near Lochgilphead, Strathclyde. PA31 8SA. Tel 0546 86333

The scenery in this part of Argyll is breathtaking—with hill, tree and loch combining to give the visitor a glimpse of Scotland which they will surely never forget. Azaleas and rhododendrons grow wild and the many different varieties add a splash of colour to a canvas already painted with stunning views of misty islands scattered in the shimmering sea. Lochgair Hotel is here, situated some seven miles north of Lochgilphead and seventeen miles south of Inverary on the A83 Glasgow–Campbeltown road. It lies approximately two hundred yards from lovely Lochgair, which offers safe anchorage for yachts sailing on Loch Fyne. This family run hotel offers a warm welcome to all discerning travellers who enjoy good food in friendly, comfortable surroundings. All bedrooms have private bathrooms and each has its own tea and coffee making facilities. Colour television is available in the bedrooms by request, but the cosy cocktail bar with its log fire, the beautifully furnished lounge and attractive dining room entice the visitor downstairs to join an international guest list, who have come to fish, shoot, visit the nearby Crarae Gardens or merely to tour the islands of this beautiful part of Scotland. We were made to feel very welcome by all members of staff and we certainly hope to return.

Weekly Terms from £275.00	Credit Cards—Access, Visa	Part Central Heating
Daily Terms from £42.00	1 Family Room	Cocktail Bar
Bed and Breakfast from £29.50	2 Single, 6 Double, 4 Twin Bedrooms	Small Conference Facilities
Bar Meal from £3.50	All Rooms with Private Bathroom, Tea and Coffee-making Facilities	Children catered for
Afternoon Tea from £2.50		Dogs not allowed
Dinner A La Carte	TV and Hairdryer available on Request	Parking Facilities
Gratuities at Guest's Discretion	Open all Year	Nearby: Fishing, Riding, Sailing, Shooting
VAT inclusive	Fully Licensed	

By Maybole—Ladyburn
By Maybole, Ayrshire. KA19 7SG. Tel 06554 585. Fax 06554 580

To seek out this family home is to discover the traditions and the gracious life-style of past generations in the remote and beautiful areas of Scotland. Ladyburn, which stands on the edge of the magnificent estate of Kilkerran, was acquired in the late seventeenth century by the Fergussons of Kilkerran and remained in their hands until the death of Frances, widow of Sir James Fergusson. Today it is the home of David and Jane Hepburn and their family. Guests in their home are invited by the present owner of Kilkerran, Sir Charles Fergusson, to walk and enjoy the estate and its policies, perhaps chancing upon the last of a group of Silver Firs planted by Lord Kilkerran in 1707 to mark the Treaty of Union between Scotland and England. Within Ladyburn, antique furnishings inherited by the Hepburns grace the public rooms while, in the elegant bedrooms, modern and traditional facilities are carefully combined to provide maximum comfort and convenience. In the heart of Ayrshire's Burns country, this is an ideal base from which to explore. Ladyburn is some five miles from Maybole, which is on the A77 Stranraer to Ayr road. From the centre of Maybole turn onto the B7023 signposted Crosshill & Girvan. On reaching Crosshill, turn right at the War Memorial, signposted Girvan B7023 (B741)—you will also see a signpost to Kilkerran. After two miles turn left again, following the sign to Kilkerran and Ladyburn. Go over the bridge, bear left, and after about three-quarters of a mile cross another bridge. Ladyburn is on your right.

Weekly and Daily Terms on application	Dinner from £21.95	3 Private Bathrooms, 4 Shower Rooms
Bed and Breakfast from £130.00 (Double)	Gratuities at Guest's discretion	All Rooms with TV, Telephone, Radio, Tea and Coffee-making Facilities, Hairdryer
Room Rate from £120.00	VAT inclusive. Credit Cards—Access, American Express, Visa	Residential Licence. Children over 16 by arrangement. Dogs by arrangement only
Breakfast: English £10.00, Continental £7.50. Lunch from £12.50	7 Double Bedrooms	Parking Facilities. Croquet
Afternoon Tea from £4.50	1 Self-contained Flat	

Section 8: Strathclyde

Oban—The Manor House
Gallanach Road, Oban, Argyll. PA34 4LS. Tel 0631 62087. Fax 0631 63053

Oban is deservedly a very popular tourist centre in its own right. It is also the starting point for ferry services to the islands of Lismore, Mull, Coll, Tiree, South Uist, Barra and Colonsay. To the north and to the south, good coastal roads provide a continuously changing panorama of dramatic scenery, whilst inland there is the diversity of all the lochs, glens, mountains and forests of Strathclyde. The Manor House is in a quiet location, a short walk away from the ferry terminal, right on the shores of Oban Bay. Most of the accommodation, and the public areas, have magnificent views over the bay to the adjacent islands and to the mountains of Morvern and Mull. Of late Georgian architecture, it was built in 1780 as the principal residence of the Duke of Argyll's Oban Estate, in those times accompanied by coach house, stables, coachman's cottage, walled garden and an oyster-bed on the sea shore. For a period from 1845 onwards, Admiral Otter used the Manor as his home and base whilst carrying out the Hebridean survey of dangerous waters on the west coast. In the recent refurbishment by the Leroy family, great care has been taken to preserve the elegance of those bygone days. This is particularly evident in the dining room, where guests may select from an interesting blend of Scottish and French dishes in an atmosphere of dignified charm. Complementing the *cuisine* with its emphasis on fresh local sea produce and game in season—there is a cellar of fine wines and a range of after-dinner malt whiskies.

All Prices pertain to 1992
Weekly Terms from £231.00
Daily Terms from £39.00
Bar Lunch from £5.00
Dinner from £19.50 and A La Carte
Gratuities at Guest's Discretion
VAT inclusive
Credit Cards—Access, Visa

6 Double, 5 Twin Bedrooms
All Rooms with Private Bathroom, TV, Telephone, Radio, Baby-listening, Tea and Coffee-making Facilities, Hairdryer
Open from 1st February to 25th December
Fully Licensed
Full Central Heating
Cocktail Bar

Children catered for by arrangement
Dogs allowed at Management's Discretion
Parking Facilities
Nearby: Tennis, Squash, Badminton
Swimming, Solarium, Sauna, Golf, Fishing, Riding, Sailing, Windsurfing, Water Skiing, Shooting

Near Oban, Connel Ferry—Falls of Lora Hotel
Connel Ferry, By Oban, Argyll. PA37 1PB. Tel 063171 483. Fax 063171 694

The famous Falls of Lora are, in fact, extremely impressive rapids, which are most spectacular at ebb-tide, when the waters leaving Loch Etive are forced through the Connel narrows over a rocky bed and ledge. Life at the Falls of Lora Hotel, farther up the loch by the A85 road, flows much more smoothly. Warm and spacious rooms, comfortable furniture and most helpful service all contribute to a slow tempo and an unhurried existence for guests. Although we had known about the hotel for some time, a letter from one of our readers spurred us to action. It read '... the bedrooms and public rooms have all been refurbished to a high standard and the service is friendly and efficient—the food well prepared, presented and of a good standard...' We arrived at the hotel on a Sunday, when the chef prepares a superb presentation buffet. On another night of the week he prepares a seven-course 'Taste of Scotland' dinner. The original part of the house, built in 1886, might well have been designed as an elegant country hotel. The lounge, the attractive cocktail bar, with its selection of over 100 whiskies, and the restaurant are very inviting. A modern, centrally heated wing has been added to the hotel and this has greatly extended the range of accommodation. There are inexpensive family rooms, comfortable twins and doubles and a number of most luxurious rooms which feature half-tester, king-size four-poster and circular beds and delightful bathrooms, one with a jacuzzi.

Daily Terms from £29.50
Bed and Breakfast from £17.50
Bar Meal from £1.75
Afternoon Tea from £1.50
Dinner from £17.50 Table D'Hôte
Gratuities at Guest's Discretion

VAT inclusive. Credit Cards—Access, American Express, Diners Club, Visa
4 Family Rooms. 3 Luxury Double, 6 Double, 11 Twin, 6 Single Bedrooms
All Rooms with Private Bathroom, TV, Telephone, Radio, Baby-listening

5 Rooms with Hairdryer
3 Rooms with Trouser Press. Open all Year except Christmas and New Year.
Fully Licensed. Full Central Heating
Conference Facilities. Dogs allowed
Parking Facilities

Section 8: Strathclyde and Tayside

Turnberry—Malin Court Hotel
Maidens, Near Turnberry, Ayrshire. KA26 9PB. Tel 0655 31457. Fax 0655 31072

Between a golfing mecca and one of the most magnificent private estates in Scotland (Culzean Country Park) lies Maidens, a small seaside village on the Ayrshire coast, alongside Turnberry. It has glorious seascapes and views of Ailsa Craig but it also has a very fine and unusual hotel, which we dicovered on a recent visit. Malin Court stands on a slight rise just south of the village of Maidens, in grounds which are being developed with walkways and seating to take full advantage of the lovely views. It is set around a very pleasant courtyard garden, but it is unorthodox in that it is in part hotel and in part residential accommodation. This combination, however, should not deter one from calling here and enjoying the facilities and ambiance of Malin Court. The bedrooms have been refurbished in the most attractive manner and they contain all modern creature comforts. Additional bedrooms, a function suite and lounges have recently been added. The restaurant and cocktail bar, too, have been completely restyled and the whole effect is most pleasing and relaxing. The catering is based on huge breakfasts, extensive bar meals, home-baked Scottish teas, and *table d'hôte* and *à la carte* dinner specialities. Whether you follow golf, Burns or beautiful gardens we recommend Turnberry, the adjoining seaside village and this friendly hotel unreservedly. And do visit the 'Electric Brae', a natural phenomenon, which defies one's senses.

Weekly Terms from £275.00
Bed and Breakfast from £49.00
Bar Lunch from £5.50
Lunch from £9.50 Table D'Hôte
Afternoon Tea from £2.50
Bar Supper from £4.95
Dinner from £17.50 Table D'Hôte
Gratuities at Guest's Discretion

VAT inclusive.. Credit Cards—Access, American Express, Diners Club, Visa
5 Double, 12 Twin Bedrooms
All Rooms with Private Bathroom, TV, Telephone, Radio, Baby-listening, Tea and Coffee-making Facilities, Hairdryer, Trouser Press. Open all Year. Fully Licensed. Full Central Heating. Lift.

Cocktail Bar. TV Lounge. Conference Facilities. Children catered for
Dogs allowed by Arrangement
Parking Facilities. Night Porter
Nearby: Tennis, Putting, Squash, Swimming, Golf, Fishing, Riding, Sailing, Windsurfing, Water Skiing, Shooting

Near Blairgowrie, Bridge of Cally—Bridge of Cally Hotel
By Blairgowrie, Perthshire. PH10 7JJ. Tel 025 086 231

The hotel is situated in the unspoiled village of Bridge of Cally, six miles north of Blairgowrie on the A93, overlooking the River Ardle on which it owns fishing rights for salmon and brown trout. There are nine bedrooms, six with bathrooms and showers *en suite*. The comfortable residents' lounge has a colour television and relaxing refreshment can be taken in the welcoming cocktail bar. Shooting on nearby moors can be arranged through the hotel and the walking is first class. Pony trekking is also available. There are many fine golf courses, the nearest being Rosemount, at Blairgowrie. The hotel is ideally suited for motoring expeditions to Braemar, perhaps for the gathering on the first Saturday in September, to Glamis, childhood home of the Queen Mother and the wild life park at Blair Drummond. During the winter skiing is normally available fifteen miles away at Glenshee. Ski tows and a chair lift operate when conditions permit and the chair lift also operates during the summer. The dining room is comfortably appointed. Begin the day with a traditional Scots breakfast, setting you up for six hours' hard walking perhaps. End with a magnificent dinner, complemented by a small, but carefully selected cellar. Your hosts are Mr and Mrs Tolland and family who quite clearly enjoy helping to create happy holidays for their guests.

Terms on Application
Gratuities at Guest's Discretion
VAT inclusive
Credit Cards—Access, Diners Club, Visa
4 Double, 1 Single, 4 Twin Bedrooms
3 Private Bathrooms

3 Private Shower Rooms
Open from mid-December to October
Fully Licensed
Full Central Heating
Cocktail Bar
TV Lounge

Children catered for
Dogs allowed by arrangement
Parking Facilities. Fishing
Nearby: Golf, Riding, Shooting, Skiing, Hill Walking, Climbing

Section 8: Tayside

Broughty Ferry, Dundee—Tayview Private Hotel
71-73 St Vincent Street, Broughty Ferry, Dundee. DD5 2EZ. Tel 0382 79438

This small, comfortable and spotlessly clean private hotel can be found on St Vincent Street in Broughty Ferry, close to the castle which stands on a rocky spur towering over the tiny harbour, and near the Royal Tay yachting harbour, shops and transport. For those coming on business or pleasure to the Dundee area it is ideally situated being only fifteen minutes from the city centre. Creeper-clad and unpretentious from the outside, the Tayview is immaculate within and one is impressed immediately by the superior quality of the furnishings and fittings. All of the bedrooms have been fitted with a radio/intercom, vanity unit and have electric blankets and fires to ensure even temperatures during inclement weather, whilst television is available on request. The two *en suite* twin bedrooms are furnished in town house style whilst all the rooms have thoughtful extras such as fruit, biscuits, truffles, magazines. Peaceful nights are the rule rather than the exception as the hotel is in a quiet area away from the noise of traffic and there is ample street parking for one's car. Breakfasts are silver service and Danish style open sandwiches are available all day. Visitors will find much of interest in this area, including Glamis Castle home of the Queen Mother, a country park at Monikie and relics of ancient history scattered across the countryside. To those of our readers who enjoy a round of golf we suggest that you bring along your clubs as there are excellent links not far away at Monifieth and Carnoustie.

Bed and Breakfast from £25.00	3 Double, 6 Twin, 2 Single Bedrooms	Residential Licence. Part Central Heating
Breakfast: English £5.00	2 Private Bathrooms	Children not catered for
Breakfast: Continental £3.50	TV and Hairdryer available on Request	Dogs not allowed
Gratuities at Guest's Discretion	All Rooms with Radio, Baby-listening,	Parking Facilities
VAT inclusive	Trouser Press	Nearby: Tennis, Putting, Golf, Fishing,
Credit Cards—Access, Visa	Open all Year	Riding, Sailing, Water Skiing

Cleish—Nivingston House
Cleish, Kinross-shire. KY13 7LS. Tel 0577 850216. Fax 0577 850238

Turn off the M90 at Junction 5 and continue for approximately two miles and you will soon find yourself at the welcoming entrance of Nivingston House. It is, however, easy to forget the proximity of the motorway, for the hotel has a peaceful setting at the foot of the Cleish Hills and is surrounded by twelve acres of landscaped gardens. Scotland's tradition for hospitality is upheld to the full here and you will enjoy a warm welcome; the aim is to make your stay comfortable in every way and competent and attentive staff will take good care of you. All the public rooms are most attractive and are furnished in a style which emphasises the relaxing atmosphere of the hotel. After enjoying a perfectly cooked meal in the pretty restaurant, we withdrew contentedly for coffee and liqueurs to the cosy lounge bar, where a log fire blazes cheerfully during the winter months. The hotel offers excellent accommodation—each bedroom has a different colour scheme and character and has a name rather than a number. A high standard of comfort is common to all the rooms and luxurious bathrooms, remote-control television and telephones are standard features. Nivingston House can be recommended for a truly restful stay amidst beautiful countryside. Trout fishing can be enjoyed at nearby Loch Leven and one can play golf at St Andrews and many local courses. The hotel is also an ideal base for a touring holiday and offers easy access to Edinburgh, Perth and Stirling.

Weekly Terms on Application	VAT inclusive. Credit Cards—Access,	Fully Licensed
Daily Terms from £72.00	American Express, Visa	Full Central Heating. Conference Facilities
Bed and Breakfast from £45.00	2 Family Rooms. 1 Suite	Dogs allowed. Parking Facilities
Bar Lunch from £5.00	2 Single, 10 Double, 5 Twin Bedrooms	Croquet. Putting
Lunch from £16.50 Table D'Hôte	All Rooms with Private Bathroom, TV,	Nearby: Tennis, Squash, Badminton,
Afternoon Tea from £4.50	Telephone, Radio, Baby-listening, Tea and	Swimming, Solarium, Sauna, Golf, Fishing,
Dinner from £27.50 Table D'Hôte	Coffee-making Facilities, Hairdryer	Riding, Sailing, Windsurfing, Water Skiing,
Gratuities at Guest's Discretion	Open all Year	Shooting, Hang-gliding

Section 8: Tayside

Comrie—The Royal Hotel
Melville Square, Comrie, Perthshire. PH6 2DN. Tel 0764 70200. Telex 76277 KILKIE

Listed as a building of historic interest, this establishment has been offering hospitality and comfort, together with good food and wine, to travellers such as ourselves since 1765. Like many others before us, we have been most impressed by the hospitality offered. *Table d'hôte* and *à la carte* menus featuring a number of Scottish dishes are offered in the dining-room, which is tastefully decorated. Mr and Mrs I Gordon, the proprietors, are now pleased to offer silver service at dinnertime. The walls of the cocktail bar are attractively decorated in the Gordon tartan—bar suppers are served until 9pm and a selection of no less than fifty malt whiskies is available. The Royal Hotel provides most comfortable accommodation, too. All the attractively furnished bedrooms have a private bath or shower, television, telephone, radio and tea and coffee-making facilities. If you wish to sleep in style, we suggest that you choose the splendid four-poster room. The Royal Hotel is, indeed, an ideal place to stay for a night when touring Scotland, but, with glorious scenery all around, it should also be considered for a leisurely holiday. Golfers, in particular, are well catered for, as a number of excellent courses are within easy reach. In addition, sailing, water skiing, boating and fishing, in both river (private stretch) and loch, are at hand.

Weekly Terms (Half Board) from £259.00
Daily Terms from £40.00
Bed and Breakfast from £25.00
Bar Meal from £4.00
Lunch from £4.00 and A La Carte
Dinner from £17.50 and A La Carte
Gratuities at Guest's discretion

VAT inclusive. Credit Cards—Access, American Express, Visa
1 Single, 5 Double, 3 Twin Bedrooms
All Rooms with Private Bathroom, TV, Telephone, Radio, Tea and Coffee-making Facilities. Baby-listening, Trouser Press, Hairdryer available on Request
Open all Year

Fully Licensed
Full Central Heating. Cocktail Bar
Snooker Room. Conference Facilities
Dogs allowed by Arrangement
Parking Facilities
Nearby: Golf, Fishing, Riding, Sailing, Windsurfing, Water Skiing, Shooting

---

Have you returned your membership form?
By simply completing and returning to us the registration card inserted in this book you will automatically become a 1993 member of the Ashley Courtenay Circle, an invaluable link between author and reader. For members, we compile and revise each year special listings of hotels which offer particular amenities, such as a sauna, swimming pool, golf course (or adjacent), four-poster beds, facilities for the disabled, special Christmas programmes, vegetarian dishes, non-smoking areas and self-catering facilities. We can even direct you to hotels which are especially pleased to receive young children and dogs. These lists are free of charge. Just send a stamped addressed envelope.

Section 8: Tayside

Kinclaven by Stanley—Ballathie House Hotel
Kinclaven by Stanley, Perthshire. PH1 4QN.
Tel 0250 883268. Fax 0250 883396

The Ballathie House Hotel offers its guests a taste of the 'charm and tranquility of a more gracious age'. The building itself has a splendid French baronial facade and the public rooms are spacious and elegant. The drawing room overlooks the extensive lawns which slope to the riverside, while the morning room is an airy retreat with a view of the fine gardens and croquet lawn. Most of the twenty four bedrooms have expansive views of the estate's spacious lawns and every one has a private bath or shower room. Everywhere the thoughtful good taste is in evidence: walls hung with framed mirrors and fine paintings, plants and fresh flowers adorning period tables, furnishings and light fittings of distinction, superior carpets and drapes. A suite and two bedrooms are on the ground floor and suitable for guests with disabilities. The award winning *cuisine* (AA 2 rosettes) is imaginative and varied using the best of fresh local produce; Tay salmon and local game are seasonal delicacies. Ballathie House is ideally placed for nearby Perth, Blairgowrie or Scone Palace, and Edinburgh is only an hour's drive away. A variety of activities is available on the estate including trout and salmon fishing and clay pigeon shooting, or guests can choose from numerous renowned golf courses. Despite the almost stately surroundings, the house has an informal atmosphere, with a friendly and attentive staff and has a four crown de luxe rating from the Scottish Tourist Board. This is somewhere to delight all discerning visitors and a perfect base for the keen fisherman or golfer. Directions: from A93 at The Beech Hedges signposted for Kinclaven and Ballathie, or off the A9, two miles north of Perth through Stanley.

Weekly Terms from £400.00
Bed and Breakfast from £48.00
Bar Lunch from £5.50
Lunch from £14.50 Table D'Hôte
Dinner from £24.00 Table D'Hôte
Gratuities at Guest's Discretion
VAT inclusive. Credit Cards—Access, American Express, Diners Club, Visa

1 Suite
7 Double, 11 Twin, 5 Single Bedrooms (incl. 2 Rooms and Suite on Ground Floor)
All Rooms with Private Bath or Shower Room, TV, Telephone, Baby-listening, Tea and Coffee-making Facilities, Trouser Press, Hairdryer
Open from 1st March to 15th February

Fully Licensed. Full Central Heating.
Cocktail Bar. Meeting Facilities (2-25 persons)
Dogs allowed by Arrangement
Parking Facilities
Tennis, Croquet, Putting, Fishing, Shooting
Nearby: Squash, Badminton, Swimming, Solarium, Sauna, Golf, Riding

Section 8: Tayside

Kinross–Windlestrae Hotel and Restaurant
Kinross, Tayside. KY13 7AS. Tel 0577 863217. Fax 0577 864733

Kinross lies directly to the west of Loch Leven and, in the centre of this charming Scottish town, amidst acres of beautiful gardens, is this extensively refurbished hotel and restaurant. Windlestrae is an enchanting name which means 'the wind grasses' and, in the hands of the experienced resident hoteliers Terry and Jean Doyle, an exclusive atmosphere has been blended with welcoming modern comfort. An unusual feature is their most attractive two-level *Pampas* cocktail lounge. This overlooks the patio and garden and is a popular meeting-place for taking an aperitif with friends whilst browsing over the restaurant menu. Our initial visit was for a bar lunch but we understand that for many guests the name Windlestrae has become synonymous with *haute cuisine*. In addition to nineteen *en suite* bedrooms and the spacious public rooms, the hotel has a fully fitted conference room for private seminars and a second, larger room for bigger meetings. There are two suites complete with sitting-rooms and jacuzzi and, for all guests, there is an in-house sauna available. Kinross is a golfer's delight with two fine courses adjacent to the hotel and several notable others within driving distance. Tourists have a wealth of scenic and historic sites in the vicinity, with the Ochil Hills and the Firth of Tay nearby. The Doyles will not be resting on their laurels and we expect to be reporting on yet more bedrooms and facilities to meet the growing demand for accommodation here.

Weekly Terms from £345.00
Weekly Terms (B & B) from £240.00
Bed and Breakfast from £37.50
Bar Lunch from £3.95
Lunch from £10.50 and A La Carte
Afternoon Tea from £1.50
Bar Supper from £8.50
Dinner from £14.00 and A La Carte

Gratuities at Guest's Discretion
VAT inclusive. Credit Cards–Access, American Express, Diners Club, Visa
3 Family Rooms. 2 Suites
1 Single, 4 Double, 14 Twin Bedrooms
All Rooms with Private Bathroom, TV, Telephone, Radio, Baby-listening, Tea and Coffee-making Facilities, Trouser Press,

Hairdryer. Open all Year. Fully Licensed
Full Central Heating. Conference Facilities
Children catered for. Dogs allowed
Parking Facilities. Sauna
Nearby: Tennis, Croquet, Putting, Squash, Badminton, Swimming, Solarium, Sauna, Golf, Fishing, Riding, Sailing, Windsurfing, Water Skiing, Shooting, Hang-gliding

Perth–Parklands Hotel and Restaurant
St. Leonards Bank, Perth, Tayside. PH2 8EB. Tel 0738 22451. Fax 0738 22046

'A classical town house in a parkland setting' is how proprietors Pat and Allan Deeson describe their meticulously refurbished hotel, originally the home of a Lord Provost of Perth. Most of the superbly equipped *en suite* bedrooms overlook the open green space of Perth's famous South Inch Park, with its additional attractions of bowling, putting and boating. Nearby, the ancient city of Perth-best seen on foot-has excellent shops, a museum and art galleries. Within Perthshire there are several great castles and houses to be visited, a Whisky Trail including stops at several famous distilleries, many golf courses and such sports as fishing, skiing, horse-riding and hang-gliding. Perth Theatre and Pitlochry's Festival Theatre provide excellent evening entertainment. The Deesons, who also own Nivingston Country Hotel and Restaurant in Cleish, have details of these attractions to guide visitors. Both hotels are noted for their exceptional *cuisine*: at Perth for Scottish fare of the highest quality, partnered by a selection of international dishes. Space precludes even a summary of the dinner menus but, as an illustration of the standard set, how about a breakfast including fruit juices, porridge, cereals, kedgeree, Loch Fyne kippers, devilled kidneys, scrambled free-range eggs with smoked salmon, accompanied by home-baked bread and rolls.

Weekly Terms on Application
Bed and Breakfast from £70.00
Seafood Buffet from £7.50
Lunch from £10.50 and A La Carte
Dinner from £20.00 and A La Carte
VAT inclusive. Credit Cards–Access,

American Express, Visa
7 Double, 7 Twin Bedrooms
All Rooms with Private Bathroom, TV, Telephone, Radio, Tea and Coffee-making Facilities, Hairdryer. Open all Year
Residential Licence. Full Central Heating

Conference Facilities. Children catered for
Dogs allowed. Parking Facilities
Nearby: Tennis, Putting, Squash, Badminton, Swimming, Solarium, Sauna, Golf, Fishing, Riding, Sailing, Windsurfing, Water Skiing, Shooting, Hang-gliding

Section 8: Tayside and Western Isles

Pitlochry—Birchwood Hotel
2 East Moulin Road, Pitlochry, Perthshire. PH16 5DW. Tel 0796 2477

Our recommendations in this popular town would not be complete without a mention of Birchwood Hotel. It is particularly welcoming, being family owned and managed, and guests will immediately be aware of the personal service given by the Harmon family. All those who tour the central Highlands will eventually arrive at Pitlochry, bounded on three sides by massive peaks and watered by Loch Tummel, which sends its river tumbling through the town. Few places in Britain are set in such magnificent scenery or provide such sporting amusement. After a day of recreation or exploration, or an evening spent at the celebrated Pitlochry Festival Theatre, guests of the Birchwood will find the hotel a very happy and relaxing place to which to return. It stands in four acres of grounds in East Moulin Road and provides lovely views. We spent a restful night here, enjoyed the delicious, freshly prepared food and felt the pampered guests of Brian and Ovidia Harmon. All the bedrooms have private facilities and are equipped with colour television, a tea and coffee tray and telephone. Fresh fruit is provided daily. The restaurant is open to non-residents and offers both *table d' hôte* and *à la carte* menus. Although Pitlochry has a convenient location on the main A9 road, we would not note the Birchwood down as purely a transient call. The welcome is so genuine and the area so full of beauty that it deserves a reasonable slice of holiday time.

Weekly Terms from £275.00
Daily Terms from £45.00
English Breakfast £7.50
Lunch from £7.00 and A la Carte
Afternoon Tea from £5.00
Dinner from £17.00 and A La Carte
VAT inclusive. Credit Cards—Access, Visa

1 Single, 6 Double, 6 Twin Bedrooms
3 Family Rooms
7 Private Bathrooms
9 Private Shower Rooms
All Rooms with TV, Telephone, Radio
Tea and Coffee-making Facilities, Fruit
Open from March to November

Residential Licence
Full Central Heating
Dogs allowed by Arrangement
Parking Facilities
Nearby: Putting, Golf, Fishing, Riding, Sailing, Shooting, Bowling, Curling

Isle of Harris, Tarbert—The Harris Hotel
Tarbert, Isle of Harris, Western Isles. PA85 3DL. Tel 0859 2154

If we were asked to name the most unspoilt region of Britain, we would have to nominate the Outer Hebrides. Lewis and Harris form a single island which, although well populated, contains wide empty tracts. It is an ideal location in which to relax, breathe exhilarating fresh air and forget for a while the everyday cares of the world. We recommend The Harris Hotel, which lies virtually adjacent to the car-ferry terminal, with its services to Skye and North Uist. Although the hotel is an ideal place to stop over whilst island hopping, we do suggest that you stay for several days, for short car journeys from here bring one to spectacular rock and water scenery, interesting antiquities and some of the finest beaches in Europe. The hotel itself could not be more warm and welcoming. There is comfort in every room and interest at every turn—in the dining room one can see where J M Barrie scratched his initials in the window casement. The intimate residents' bar must surely have one of the largest selections of malt whiskies in the north. During our stay we enjoyed home-cooked food of the highest quality and occupied a most comfortable bedroom. This is, indeed, a place to linger. There is much on the island to interest the ornithologist, archaeologist and botanist. The walker, climber and fisherman will also enjoy a stay here. A visit, too, to the homes of the Harris tweed weavers, possibly to buy a length of their famous fabric at source, is also well worthwhile.

All Terms pertaining to 1992
Weekly Terms from £247.80
Daily Terms from £35.40
Bed and Breakfast from £26.25
Bar Meal from £3.00
Lunch from £6.95 and A La Carte
Afternoon Tea from £3.00

Dinner from £13.00 and A La Carte
Gratuities at Guest's discretion
VAT inclusive. Credit Cards—Access, Visa
2 Family Rooms. 7 Double, 12 Twin, 4
Single Bedrooms. 14 Private Bathrooms
2 Private Shower Rooms
Baby-listening, Hairdryer available

Open all year. Fully Licensed
Part Central Heating. Cocktail Bar
TV Lounge. Conference Facilities
Children catered for. Dogs allowed
Parking Facilities
Nearby: Fishing, Hill Walking

STOP PRESS. *The following places have been suggested to us, although our inspectors have not had the opportunity of seeing them before this edition closed for press. They are, therefore, not recommended, but may be worthy of your patronage. Reader reports on any of these establishments would be very welcome.*

The Royal Chase Hotel, Enfield, Middlesex EN2 8AR.
It is but a stepping stone from the centre of London, the M25 (hence Heathrow Airport) and the principal routes to the North. So, location is a big bonus when staying there. The hotel's facilities impress, too: 100 bedrooms, a grill bar, a medley of function suites, outdoor swimming pool, bars and 300 parking places. You may choose to reside in London's fumes if you wish, but the attractions of the Royal Chase Hotel's six acres in the green belt are undeniable. *Tel: 081 366 6500.*

The Royal Oak, Yattendon, Newbury, Berkshire, RG16 0UF.
Yattendon lies to the north of the M4 and is one of the few privately-owned villages in England. The Royal Oak may sound like a pub, but this is actually a country hotel of the highest standards. Its chefs produce mouth-watering Anglo-French choices, which are changed daily. The bar, with an atmosphere which has changed little in three centuries, also tempts one with unusual food at reasonable prices. *Tel: 0635 201325. Fax: 0635 201926.*

The Nurse's Cottage, Sway, New Forest, Hampshire SO41 6BA.
It is tiny, but according to reports it also has a big heart. Tony Barnfield established his Licensed Guest House only recently and it already has a faithful following. Good value, informality, simple but fresh home-cooking and good all-round comfort seems to be the watch-word here. The village of Sway is ideally placed, too, if you like the uncluttered life. *Tel/Fax: 0590 683402.*

The Studland Dene Hotel, 2 Studland Road, Alum Chine, Bournemouth.
Alum Chine is worth visiting for its own beauty. But here, too, is an hotel with plenty to interest the holiday-maker. There is ample comfort behind its appeal, a carvery, a bar with live entertainment, nice looking bedrooms, and the personal touch of the proprietor, Bob Malin. Hotels in Bournemouth are legion, but this one comes with numerous commendations. *Tel: 0202 765445 Fax: 0202 765745.*

The Kingstown Hotel, Hull Road, Hedon, North Humberside HU12 8DJ
It displays the rather modest motto, 'A nice place to stay'. The Kingstown, however, has gained a plethora of accolades, one being ETB 4-Crowns Highly Commended. We have seen only copies of the hotel's menu and wine list, but both are wide-ranging in their appeal, and very well priced. The whole approach excites us and we shall stay there next season. *Tel: 0482 890461 Fax: 0482 890713.*

Hayton Hall, Near Wetheral, Carlisle, Cumbria, CA4 8QD.
The owners clearly aim for the highest standards and offer guests a very personal service. All this befits the hotel's situation, of course, where 'acres of grounds include delightful park and woodland, ornamental lakes and formal rose gardens ... watch the deer grazing gently on the lawn, and the snow-white Peking ducks drifting on the tranquil lily-covered lakes'. *Tel: 0228 70651. Fax: 0228 70010.*

4 South Parade, York, YO2 2BA.
A welcoming card reads: *'We have tried to create a warm and friendly atmosphere, where you will feel at home and be able to relax in comfort, whilst enjoying your visit to York. Robin and I are here to look after you.' 'Dial 2 on your telephone to reach us at any time, day or night. We will bring you a tray of tea or coffee or anything else that you would like. You only have to ask'.* Temptation enough! *Tel: 0904 628229*

The Ashley Courtenay Circle

By the time any guide book has been printed the information it contains has become out of date. As in other spheres of life, the hotel world is constantly changing and for this reason, many years ago, we set up the ASHLEY COURTENAY CIRCLE. The 'Circle' is well named, for it is based on the simple premise that if the members were to write and tell us their personal impressions of the hotels they had visited, be they favourable or otherwise, we should be in a much stronger position to answer the enquiries of other members.

We now receive hundreds of letters every year from home and overseas readers requesting every type of information regarding their holidays and business requirements. With the wealth of information we have at our disposal we are able to give each enquiry our personal attention. Although an hotel may appear in our guide, our up-to-date records may show that it has changed hands or even that it has closed down. We will almost certainly have additional reports from our inspectors and, probably from Circle members, which may either uphold the hotel's Ashley Courtenay recommendation or, alternatively, raise doubts about its standards. By contacting us before booking your holiday you could avoid disappointment and a great deal of unnecessary expense.

We compile and revise special listings of hotels offering particular amenities, such as a swimming pool, a golf course, a sauna, four poster beds, special Christmas programmes, vegetarian dishes, self-catering facilities, non-smoking areas and facilities for the disabled. We can even direct you to hotels which are especially pleased to receive young children and dogs!

Joining the ASHLEY COURTENAY CIRCLE is absolutely free and any of the above lists are obtainable for the price of a stamped addressed envelope. To register as a member simply complete (block capitals please) and return the registration card which you will find bound into this book. We look forward to hearing from you.

Special Discount Offer to all Circle Members

Every year we set aside a quantity of the new edition of our guide especially for members of the Ashley Courtenay Circle. When each new edition of the guide becomes available, you, as a member will be sent details entitling you to purchase the book at a saving of thirty percent on the usual retail price.

Please send us your observations on any of our recommended hotels by using the following report forms. In this way, you can strengthen the Ashley Courtenay Circle . . . an invaluable link between publisher and reader.

My Name and Address is:

Name _____

Address _____

_____

Details of Hotel

Name _____

Address _____

_____

Telephone number _____

Owner/Manager _____

Details of my visit

I stayed _____ day/s at this hotel

Dates: From _____ to _____

I lunched/Dined on _____

General Assessment of Hotel

I found the following services:	Excellent	Good	Average	Poor
Cleanliness	☐	☐	☐	☐
Comfort	☐	☐	☐	☐
Catering	☐	☐	☐	☐
Service	☐	☐	☐	☐
Amenities	☐	☐	☐	☐

REPORT

_____

_____

PLEASE CONTINUE OVERLEAF

Report continued

Please send this form to:

ASHLEY COURTENAY LIMITED,
16 Little London, Chichester, West Sussex, PO19 1PA (Telephone no. 0243 775521)

I have no connection in any way with the owners or management of this hotel.
Any adverse comments in this report should be treated with confidentiality.

SIGNED _____ Date _____

My Name and Address is:

Name _____

Address _____

_____

Details of Hotel

Name _____

Address _____

_____

Telephone number _____

Owner/Manager _____

Details of my visit

I stayed _____ day/s at this hotel

Dates: From _____ to _____

I lunched/Dined on _____

General Assessment of Hotel

I found the following services: Excellent   Good   Average   Poor

Cleanliness   ☐   ☐   ☐   ☐
Comfort   ☐   ☐   ☐   ☐
Catering   ☐   ☐   ☐   ☐
Service   ☐   ☐   ☐   ☐
Amenities   ☐   ☐   ☐   ☐

REPORT

_____

_____

PLEASE CONTINUE OVERLEAF

Report continued

Please send this form to:

ASHLEY COURTENAY LIMITED,
16 Little London, Chichester, West Sussex, P019 1PA (Telephone no. 0243 775521)

*I have no connection in any way with the owners or management of this hotel.
Any adverse comments in this report should be treated with confidentiality.*

SIGNED _____ Date _____

My Name and Address is:

Name _____

Address _____

_____

Details of Hotel

Name _____

Address _____

_____

Telephone number _____

Owner/Manager _____

Details of my visit

I stayed _____ day/s at this hotel

Dates: From _____ to _____

I lunched/Dined on _____

General Assessment of Hotel

I found the following services:

	Excellent	Good	Average	Poor
Cleanliness	☐	☐	☐	☐
Comfort	☐	☐	☐	☐
Catering	☐	☐	☐	☐
Service	☐	☐	☐	☐
Amenities	☐	☐	☐	☐

REPORT

_____

_____

PLEASE CONTINUE OVERLEAF

Report continued

Please send this form to:

ASHLEY COURTENAY LIMITED,
16 Little London, Chichester, West Sussex, PO19 1PA (Telephone no. 0243 775521)

I have no connection in any way with the owners or management of this hotel. Any adverse comments in this report should be treated with confidentiality.

SIGNED _____ Date _____

My Name and Address is:

Name _____

Address _____

_____

Details of Hotel

Name _____

Address _____

_____

Telephone number _____

Owner/Manager _____

Details of my visit

I stayed _____ day/s at this hotel

Dates: From _____ to _____

I lunched/Dined on _____

General Assessment of Hotel

I found the following services:	Excellent	Good	Average	Poor
Cleanliness	☐	☐	☐	☐
Comfort	☐	☐	☐	☐
Catering	☐	☐	☐	☐
Service	☐	☐	☐	☐
Amenities	☐	☐	☐	☐

REPORT

_____

_____

PLEASE CONTINUE OVERLEAF

Report continued

Please send this form to:

ASHLEY COURTENAY LIMITED,
16 Little London, Chichester, West Sussex, PO19 1PA (Telephone no. 0243 775521)

*I have no connection in any way with the owners or management of this hotel.
Any adverse comments in this report should be treated with confidentiality.*

SIGNED _____ Date _____

My Name and Address is:

Name _____

Address _____

_____

Details of Hotel

Name _____

Address _____

_____

Telephone number _____

Owner/Manager _____

Details of my visit

I stayed _____ day/s at this hotel

Dates: From _____ to _____

I lunched/Dined on _____

General Assessment of Hotel

I found the following services:	Excellent	Good	Average	Poor
Cleanliness	☐	☐	☐	☐
Comfort	☐	☐	☐	☐
Catering	☐	☐	☐	☐
Service	☐	☐	☐	☐
Amenities	☐	☐	☐	☐

REPORT

_____

_____

PLEASE CONTINUE OVERLEAF

Report continued

Please send this form to:

ASHLEY COURTENAY LIMITED,
16 Little London, Chichester, West Sussex, PO19 1PA (Telephone no. 0243 775521)

I have no connection in any way with the owners or management of this hotel.
Any adverse comments in this report should be treated with confidentiality.

SIGNED _____ *Date* _____

ENGLAND

Alcester	246	Blanchland	294
Alcombe	108	Blandford Forum	92
Aldbury	222	Blockley	210
Aldeburgh	242	Blunsdon	128
Aldridge	247	Bodinnick-by-Fowey	20
Aldwick	172	Bognor Regis	172
Allendale	296	Bolt Head	75
Alnwick	298	Bonchurch	151
Alston	256-257	Boreham Street	169
Amberley	213	Borrowdale	266-267
Ambleside	257-263	Bournemouth	92-98
Ampney Crucis	205	Bourton-on-the-Water	205, 207
Appleby-in-Westmorland	264	Bovey Tracey	43
Appleton-le-Moors	299	Bowness-on-Windermere	267-268
Arundel	172	Brackenthwaite	269
Ashburton	39	Bradford-on-Avon	124
Ashford	158	Brancaster	226
Ashford-in-the-Water	199	Brands Hatch	159
Ashton-under-Lyne	285	Branston, Lincs	223
Askrigg	308	Branston, Staffs	241
Astley Abbots	236	Bratton Fleming	44
Avon	142	Braunton	51
Axminster	40	Bray-on-Thames	135
Bagshot	162	Bridgnorth	236-237
Bainbridge	300	Bridgwater	108
Bakewell	200-201	Bridport	98-99
Bare Village	292	Brighton	165-166
Barnard Castle	284	Bristol	7
Barngates	260	Brockenhurst	140-141
Barnstaple	40	Broxton	196
Barrow-in-Furness	265	Bryher	38
Bassenthwaite	265	Bude	12-13
Bath	6-9	Budleigh Salterton	44, 82
Battle	164-165	Burford	233
Beaulieu Road	146	Burley	141
Beer	41	Burpham	172
Belford	294	Burton-upon-Trent	241
Bellingham	296	Bury	285
Berkswell	245	Buttermere Valley	269
Bibury	206	Buxton	201
Bideford	41-42, 47	Cadnam	142
Billesley	247	Calbourne	151
Birmingham	248	Cambridge	195
Bishops Tawton	42	Carbis Bay	13
Blackpool	289	Carlisle	265, 269-270
Blakeney	225	Carlyon Bay	33-34

Castle Combe	124	Driffield	287
Castle Donington	202	Dulverton	110
Catterall	289	Dunster	111
Chaddesley Corbett	214	Easington	256
Chagford	45-46	East Grinstead	174
Chale	152	Eastbourne	167-168
Chardstock	40	Easton Grey	127
Charlton	173	Eastwell Park	158
Charmouth	99	Ebford	55
Cheddar	109	Ecclerigg	283
Chelston	85	Elterwater	263
Cheltenham	207-208	Emsworth	143
Chelwood	9	Evesham	214
Chester	196-198	Ewloe	198
Chichester	173	Exebridge	111
Chillington	63-64	Exeter	54-55
Chipping Campden	209	Exford	112
Christchurch	100, 142	Exmoor National Park	123
Churchill	10	Exmouth	56-57
Cirencester	205, 209	Falmouth	14-18
Clappersgate	262	Farrington Gurney	8
Clare	242	Faugh	270
Cleobury Mortimer	237	Felixstowe	243
Climping	174	Finedon	232
Clitheroe	290	Formby	293
Clovelly	47	Fowey	19-20
Coleford	210	Freshwater Bay	152
Coleford	48	Frome	112
Colestocks	60	Fullers Moor	196
Colyford	48	Garstang	289
Constantine Bay	28	Golant by Fowey	20
Corfe	101	Goosnargh	291
Corsham	125	Gorleston-on-Sea	226
Coventry	249	Grange-in-Borrowdale	271
Crantock	14	Grange-over-Sands	271-274
Crediton	48-49	Grasmere	273
Cricklade	129	Gravesend	159
Crosby-on-Eden	270	Great Longstone	200
Croyde	50	Great Yarmouth	226
Croyde Bay	51	Greta Bridge	284
Croydon	163	Grimston	227
Crudwell	126	Halland	169
Dartford	159	Harnham	125
Dartmouth	51-53	Harome	304
Dawlish Warren	54	Harrogate	301
Deddington	234	Harwich	203
Dittisham	51	Haslemere	164
Dorchester	101-102	Hassop	201
Dovercourt	203	Hatherleigh	58

awes	302	Little Stretton	238
awkchurch	58	Littlebourne	160
awkhurst	160	Lizard, The	21
awnby	304	London, Greater	185
aworth	311	London, SW1	183-184
ayling Island	143-144	London, SW5	182
aywards Heath	175	London, SW7	183
eads Nook	270	London, W1	184
easley Mill	84	London, W2	181
elmsley	303-304	London, WC1	182
ereford	215	Longhorsley	297
erstmonceux	169	Looe	21-22
exham	295-296	Lostwithiel	23
illsford Bridges	69	Ludlow	239
itchin	220	Lydford	65
olford	113	Lyme Regis	103-104
olsworthy	59	Lymington	144-145
oniton	60	Lympsham	123
ook	149	Lyndhurst	145-146
ope Cove	60-61	Lynmouth	65-66
ousel Bay	21	Lynton	66-69
ove	166	Lytham St Anne's	292
unstanton	226	Maidencombe	86
unstrete	9	Maidenhead	135
fracombe	62	Malmesbury	126-127
minster	115	Manchester Airport	286
nstow	62	Marlow	195
reby	265	Masham	308
endal	275	Matlock	202
eswick	267, 271, 276-278	Mawnan Smith	17-18
ewstoke	11	Medmenham	195
idderminster	214, 237	Melksham	128
ilve	114	Membury	69
ing's Lynn	226-227	Mevagissey	23-24
ing's Norton	248	Middleham	306
ings Coughton	246	Middleton	307
ingsbridge	63-64	Midhurst	176
ingsteignton	63	Milford-on-Sea	146-147
irkby Stephen	279	Milton Common	234
nutsford	197	Minehead	108, 115-117, 119
Langho	291	Mithian	33
Langrish	148	Monk Fryston	306
Lanreath	22	Montacute	118
Lastingham	305	Moonfleet	107
Ledbury	216	Morchard Bishop	49
Lewes	169	Morecambe	292
Lichfield	241	Moreton-in-Marsh	210
Lincoln	223	Morpeth	297
Little Langdale	263	Much Birch	215

Mullion Cove	24	Ripon	30
Nafferton	287	Rokeby	28
New Milton	147	Romaldkirk	28
Newbury	136-137	Ross-on-Wye	216-21
Newby Bridge	279	Rosthwaite	26
Newquay	25-27	Rothay Bridge	259, 26
Newton Abbot	63	Rotherwick	14
Newton Poppleford	70	Rowton	19
North Bovey	70	Royal Forest of Dean	210-21
North Petherton	108	Ruan High Lanes	3
North Walsham	228	Ryde	15
Northam	41	Rye	170-17
Northampton	232	Saffron Walden	20
Norwich	228-229	Salcombe	72-75, 8
Nunney	112	Saltburn-by-the-Sea	25
Nyetimber	173	Saltford	
Okehampton	71	Sandbanks	10
Old Harlow	203	Sanderstead	16
Old Hunstanton	230	Sandown	15
Oswestry	240	Saunton Sands	7
Otley	311	Seahouses	29
Otterburn	297	Sedlescombe	16
Padstow	28	Shaldon	7
Paignton	71-72	Shanklin	154-15
Parkham	42	Shap	280
Peasmarsh	170	Shaw	128
Penjerrick	18	Shepton Mallet	12
Penrith	280-281	Sherborne	105
Penzance	29	Sheringham	229, 23
Petersfield	148	Shipbourne	16
Pickering	307	Shipton-under-Wychwood	235
Pinhoe	55	Sidmouth	70, 77-8
Poole	104	Silchester	138
Porlock	119	Simonstone	302
Porlock Weir	120	Singlewell	159
Port Isaac	30	Slaidburn	290
Portloe	31	Slaugham	175
Portscatho	31-32	Soar Mill Cove	81
Portsmouth	148	South Molton	82-84
Powburn	298	South Wootton	227
Preston	291	South Zeal	71
Pulborough	176	Southerton	82
Ramsbottom	285	Southport	293
Ramsey	288	Southsea	148
Rangeworthy	10	St Agnes	33
Ravenstonedale	279	St Albans	220-221
Reading	138	St Austell	33-34
Redcoats Green	220	St Ives, Cambs	196
Rhydycroesau	240	St Ives	34

Just-in-Roseland	35	Warminster	129
Kew Highway	37	Wasdale	280
Lawrence	153	Washingborough	224
Mary's	38-39	Wellingborough	232
Mawes	35-36	Wells	122
amford	224	Wensley	308
oke Fleming	53	Weston Favell	232
onehouse	212	Weston-super-Mare	11, 123
ow-on-the-Wold	212	Westonbirt	213
ratford-upon-Avon	245-247	Weymouth	107
reatley-on-Thames	139	Whitby	309
roud	213	Willingdon	168
udland Bay	106	Willington	199
udbury	242-243	Wilton	218
utton Coldfield	249	Winchester	150
windon	128-129	Windermere	282-283
ymonds Yat	217	Windsor	139
alland Bay	22	Winsford	123
arporley	199	Witherslack	274
aunton	121-122	Woodbridge	244
etbury	213	Woolacombe	89-91
hame	235	Woolton Hill	137
hatcham	136	Worcester	219
hornthwaite	277-278	Worfield	237
horpe Bay	204	Worthing	177
hurlestone	74	York	310
intagel	37		
iverton	85		
onbridge	161	**CHANNEL ISLANDS**	
orquay	85-87		
orrs Park	62	Alderney	315
otland Bay	156	Archirondel (J)	324
otnes	88	Belvedere (J)	337
refonen	240	Bouley Bay (J)	324
revone Bay	28	Castel (G)	315-316
ring	222	Fermain Bay (G)	317
rotton	176	Gorey (J)	325-326
unbridge Wells	161-162	Grouville (J)	326
wo Bridges	88	Havre des Pas (J)	327
wyford	138	Herm	323
Jllingswick	215	Jerbourg Point (G)	319
Jllswater	281	La Haule (J)	329
Jlverston	279	La Moye (J)	330
Jnderskiddaw	277	Little Sark	338
Jpton-upon-Severn	218	Moulin Huet (G)	318
entnor	153, 157-158	Rozel Bay (J)	326
owchurch	219	Sark	338
Wadebridge	37	St Brelade (J)	328-330
Wareham	107	St Brelade's Bay (J)	331

St Helier (J)	327, 332-335
St Jacques (G)	322
St Martin's (G)	318-319
St Ouen (J)	336
St Peter (J)	337
St Peter Port (G)	317, 320-322
St Saviour (J)	337
Vazon Bay (G)	316

WALES

Aberdovey	357-359
Abergavenny	355
Abersoch	360-361
Aberystwyth	345
Ammanford	346
Anglesey	361-362
Barmouth	363
Beaumaris	361
Beddgelert	363-364
Betws-y-Coed	364-366
Bontddu	372
Bridgend	352-353
Cardiff	353-354
Chancery	345
Chepstow	355
Conwy	367-369
Coychurch	352
Criccieth	369-370
Crickhowell	377
Crugybar	347
Denbigh	343
Dolgellau	371-372
Ewenny	353
Fishguard	346
Ganllwyd	371
Gwaun Valley	346
Haverfordwest	352
Llanarmon-Dyffryn-Ceiriog	343
Llandudno	373-375
Llandybie	346
Llanfairpwllgwyngyll	362
Llanfyllin	378
Llangefni	362
Llangollen	343
Llannefydd	343
Llanrwst	376

Llanwddyn	3
Llanwrda	3
Llechwedd	3
Maenan	3
Mold	3
Montgomery	3
Mumbles	3
Narberth	3
Newport	3
Northop Hall	3
Porthkerry	3
Robeston Wathen	3
Rowen	3
Ruthin	3
Sealand	3
St David's	3
Swansea	3
Tal-y-Bont	3
Tenby	350-3
Tintern	3
Usk	3
Welshpool	3
Wolf's Castle	3

SCOTLAND

Aberlour	40
Aboyne	397-39
Alford	39
Arisaig	40
Auchencairn	38
Aultbea	40
Badcall Bay	41
Ballater	39
Ballindalloch	40
Banavie	40
Beasdale	40
Blairgowrie	42
Bridge of Cally	42
Brora	40
Broughty Ferry	42
Carrbridge	40
Carrutherstown	39
Castle Douglas	38
Cleish	42
Colvend	38
Comrie	42

nnel Ferry	424	Loch Lochy	414
ntin	417	Lochgair	423
aigellachie	400	Lochgilphead	423
lbeattie	389	Lochinver	415
Inies	415	Lockerbie	392-393
lphinton	384	Maidens	425
rnoch	406	Marnoch	401
lnain Bridge	410	Maybole	423
mfries	390-391	Mey	406
ndee	426	Moffat	393-394
noon	420	Nairn	415
st Linton	420	Navidale	411
lkirk	388	Newton Stewart	394-395
rt William	407-408	Oban	424
airloch	409	Onich	407-408
atehouse-of-Fleet	391	Peebles	386-387
enlivet	401	Perth	429
enshiel	410	Pitlochry	430
antown-on-Spey	410	Plockton	416
etna Green	392	Polmont	388
awick	384	Port Askaig	421
elmsdale	411	Port of Menteith	388
unter's Quay	420	Portpatrick	395
untly	401	Portree	412
vergarry	411	Scourie	416
verness	412	Selkirk	386
le of Harris	430	Skelmorlie	421
le of Islay	421	Spean Bridge	414
le of Skye	412-413	St Andrews	396-397
edburgh	385	Stonehaven	402
elso	385	Strathpeffer	417
ldrummy	398	Strontian	419
lwinning	422	Tain	418
nclaven by Stanley	428	Tarbert	430
nross	429	Turnberry	425
yle of Lochalsh	410	Uig	413
airg	413	Ullapool	419
args	421	West Linton	384

ISBN 0 905881 23 0

© Ashley Courtenay Limited, 1993
No part of this book may be published in any
form (except reviews) without permission

Distributed by
D Services, 6 Euston Street, Freemens Common,
Aylestone Road, Leicester, LE2 7SS

Typesetting by
Ashley Courtenay Limited, 16 Little London,
Chichester, West Sussex, PO19 1PA

Cartography by
Estate Publications, Bridewell House,
Tenterden, Kent

Printed and bound in Great Britain by
The St Ives Group, St Ives House, Lavington
Street, London, SE1 0NX

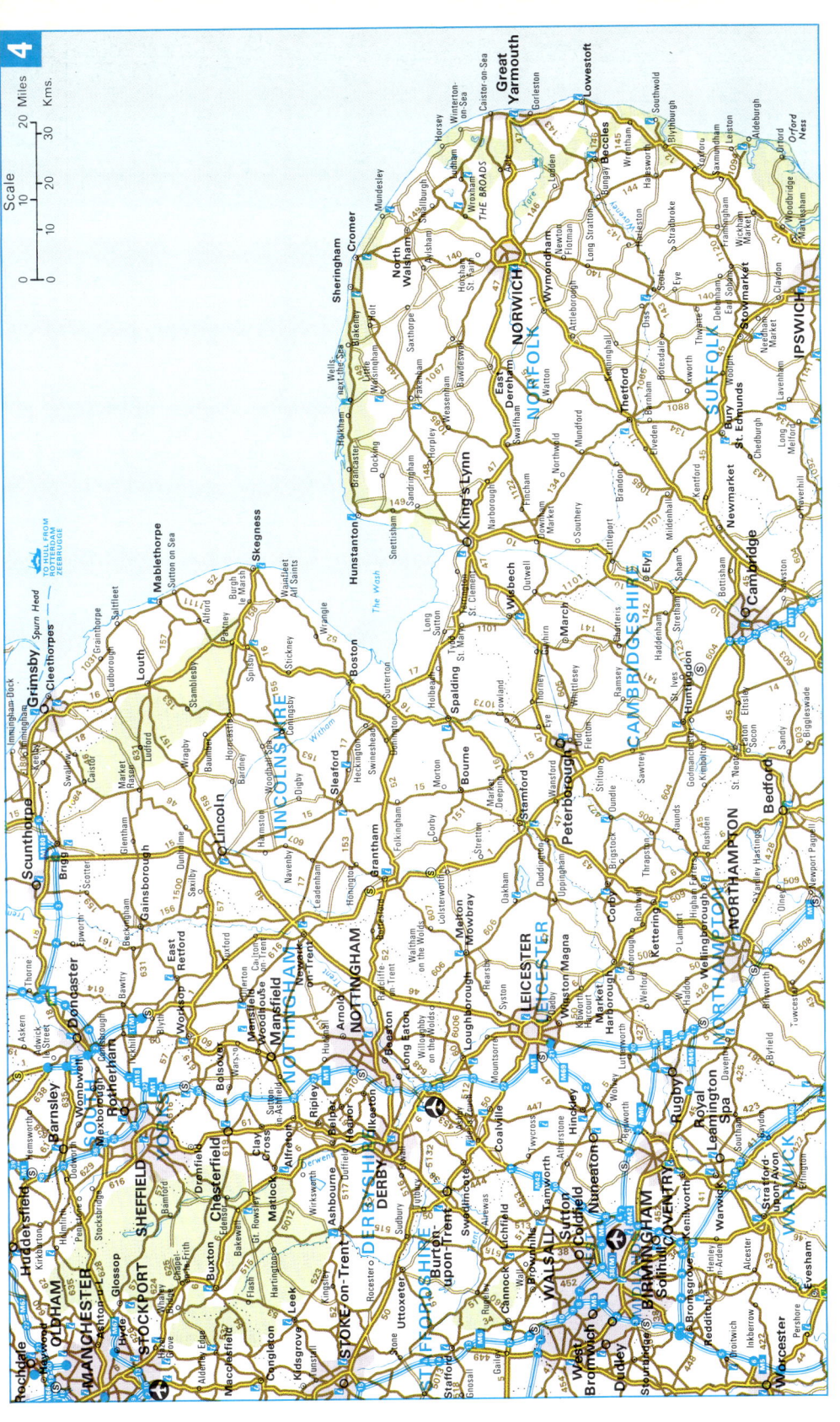

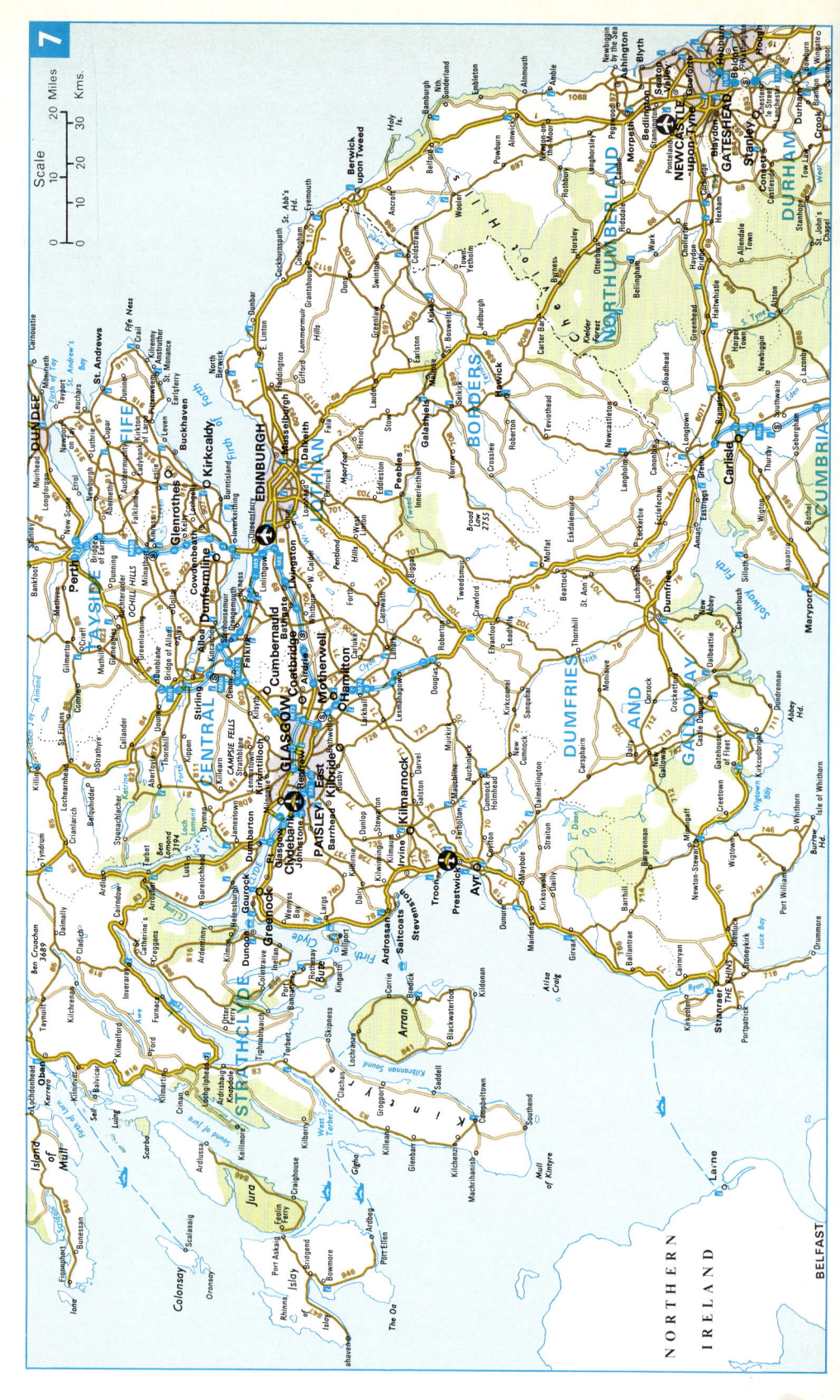

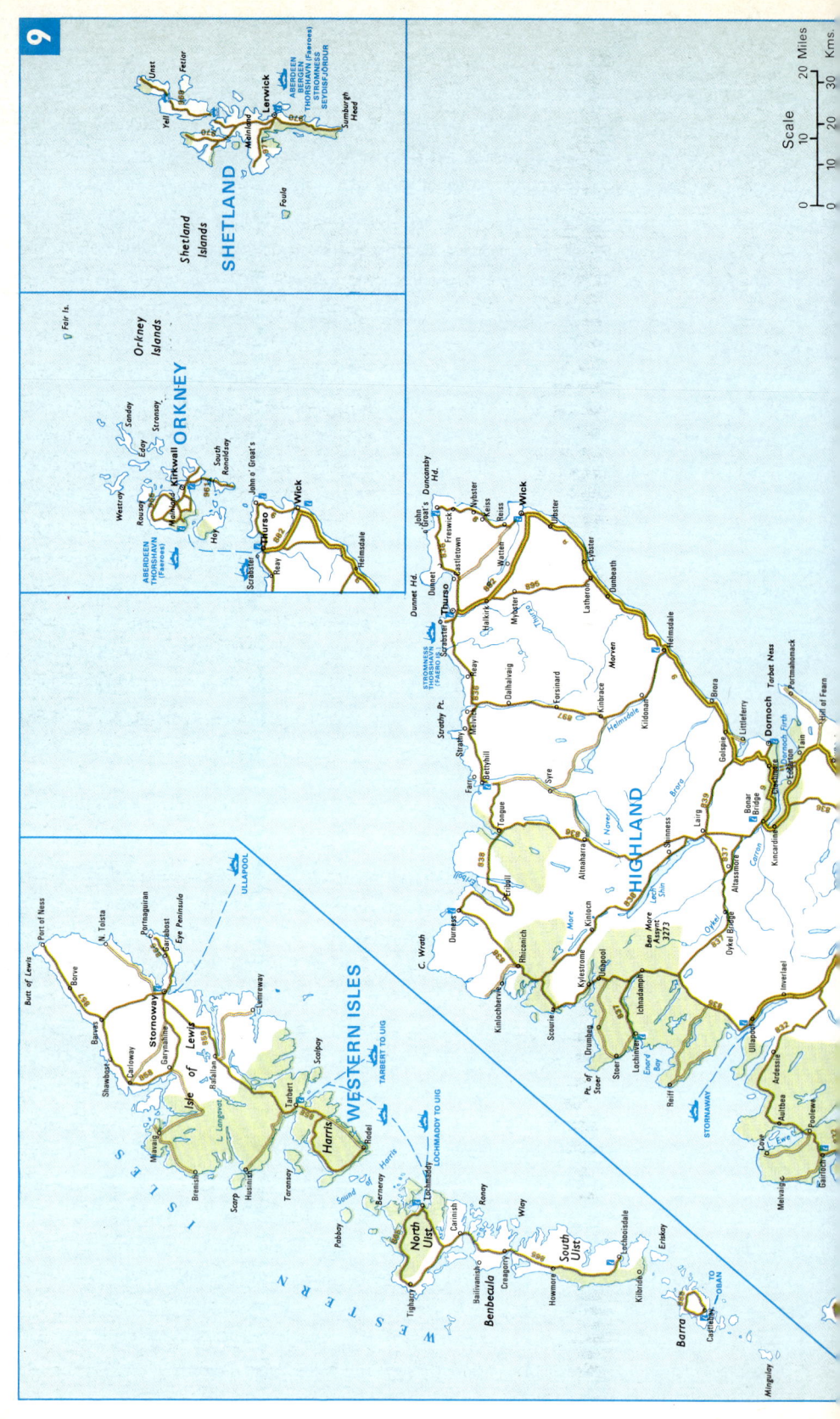

ASHLEY COURTENAY CIRCLE

Your Personal Introduction to Ashley Courtenay Recommended Hotels

1993

PLEASE RETAIN THIS PORTION AS YOUR PERSONAL

Bookmark

Please affix stamp

ASHLEY COURTENAY
16 LITTLE LONDON
CHICHESTER
WEST SUSSEX
PO19 1PA
ENGLAND

We compile and revise special listings of hotels offering, particular amenities, such as a sauna, swimming pool, golf course (or adjacent), four-poster beds, facilities for the disabled, special Christmas programmes, vegetarian dishes, non-smoking areas and self-catering facilities. We can even direct you to hotels which are especially pleased to receive young children and dogs!

Joining the Ashley Courtenay Circle is absolutely free and any of the above lists are obtainable for the price of a stamped addressed envelope. Also, every year we set aside a quantity of the new edition of the guide especially for members. When each new edition of the guide becomes available, you, as a member, will be sent details entitling you to purchase the book at a saving of approximately 30 per cent on the usual retail price.

The Ashley Courtenay Circle – an invaluable link between publishers and reader.

NAME

ADDRESS

MEMBERSHIP NUMBER
D3 01692

--- CUT HERE ---
Detach the card and keep it safe in your credit card wallet.
It is your introduction to over 1500 Ashley Courtenay recommended hotels.

The Ashley Courtenay circle was set up in 1946 and for the past 46 years has been an invaluable link between its members. For the cost of a telephone call, or a stamp, we will give you the latest information we have on hotels in this guide. This is an entirely FREE service to members, which can save time, money and disappointment. Our recommendations are based on our last visit, but if every member were to write and tell us of their personal impressions – favourable or otherwise – we should be in a much stronger position to answer the queries of other members.
Return this card today and become a registered member of the ASHLEY COURTENAY CIRCLE and you can also receive a **30% discount** on the price of your next edition of 'The Ashley Courtenay and Daily Telegraph Guide to Recommended Hotels'. This offer is restricted to the U.K. only.

I purchased the 1993 edition from _____

Name (Mr, Mrs, Miss) _____ Membership Number (see opposite) _____

Address _____
(BLOCK CAPITALS PLEASE)
_____
_____
_____

PLEASE FILL IN AND POST TODAY!